CODENAME
INTELLIGENTSIA

CODENAME INTELLIGENTSIA

THE LIFE AND TIMES OF
THE HONOURABLE
IVOR MONTAGU
FILMMAKER,
COMMUNIST,
SPY

RUSSELL CAMPBELL

The
History
Press

Cover Illustrations
Front: Ivor Montagu at the time of his wedding, 1927, photograph by
Sasha. (Getty Images/Hulton Archive)
Back: *Left:* With George Bernard Shaw in *Melodie der Welt*, 1929
(frame): Montagu seated on a handy pile of bricks, concealing the fact
that 'my old grey flannel trousers had a big hole in the seat through
which my shirt projected'. (Private collection)
Centre: Montagu's *Daily Worker* press pass, 1939: when the Soviet
Union invaded Finland the paper asked him to go to Russia as a war
correspondent, but he was refused an exit permit. (By permission of the
Labour History Archive, Manchester)
Right: Montagu in a lighter moment: he had a 'warm and certainly
idiosyncratic charisma'. (By permission of the People's History Museum)

First published 2018

The History Press
The Mill, Brimscombe Port
Stroud, Gloucestershire, GL5 2QG
www.thehistorypress.co.uk

British Library Cataloguing in Publication Data.
A catalogue record for this book is available from the British Library.

ISBN 978 0 7509 8705 9

Typesetting and origination by The History Press
Printed and bound in Great Britain by TJ International Ltd

CONTENTS

ACKNOWLEDGEMENTS

Codename Intelligentsia required a great deal of research. I am first of all deeply indebted to the archivists who eased my way and made much of the work a joy. I would like to thank especially Darren Treadwell at the Labour History Archive, Jonny Davies of BFI Special Collections, and Kathleen Dickson and Steve Tollervey at the BFI National Archive. I would also like to acknowledge the help of Anja Göbel at the Stiftung Deutsche Kinemathek. Susan Halpert at Harvard University's Houghton Library was of great assistance, as were the interloan staff at the Victoria University of Wellington Library.

With respect to film history, Charles Barr has been a constant source of suggestions and information. Others who have generously contributed their knowledge are Jo Botting, Bert Hogenkamp, Richard Taylor, David Bordwell, Terence Dobson, John Sedgwick, Hiroshi Komatsu and Paul Hammond.

In the fields of political and intelligence history I am most grateful for the advice and collaboration of David Burke, Emily Lygo, Timothy Shenk, Bill Logan and Barry Pateman.

For help with translation I would like to warmly thank Galya Brockie, Steve Marder, Jeremy Macey, Gerd Pohlmann and Bert Hogenkamp.

For his knowledge of the cinema, assistance with illustrations, and expert advice regarding publication I am particularly grateful to Patrick McGilligan, author of *Alfred Hitchcock: A Life in Darkness and Light*.

I am highly appreciative of the commitment of Mark Beynon at The History Press, who enthusiastically took on a project at which many other publishers had baulked.

Finally, for their hospitality and ongoing support and encouragement, I am very grateful to Win Campbell (who put me up in London), Bob Tristram (who dutifully read the manuscript chapter by chapter as it emerged), Andrea Bosshard, Gerd Pohlmann, Svenda Ström, Rachel Juniot, and my daughter Camille Wrightson.

Russell Campbell
Wellington, September 2017

GLOSSARY

AP	Associate Producer
BBFC	British Board of Film Censors
BSP	British Socialist Party
BUF	British Union of Fascists
CC	Central Committee (CPGB)
CI	Communist International
CNT	Confederación Nacional del Trabajo, Spanish confederation of anarcho-syndicalist trade unions
Comintern	Communist International
CP or CPGB	Communist Party of Great Britain
CPSU	Communist Party of the Soviet Union
CPUSA	Communist Party of the United States of America
ECCI	Executive Committee of the Communist International
FBO	Film Booking Offices
FSU	Friends of the Soviet Union
FWFS	Federation of Workers' Film Societies
G–B	Gaumont-British Picture Corporation
GPU	*Gosudarstvennoye politicheskoye upravlenie* (State Political Directorate), Russian/Soviet security intelligence service and secret police, 1922–23
GRU	*Glavnoye razvedyvatel'noye upravleniye* (Main Intelligence Directorate), Soviet military intelligence agency
IAH	*Internationale Arbeiterhilfe*, International Workers' Aid or Workers' International Relief

ILD	International Labour Defence
ILP	Independent Labour Party
KPD	*Kommunistische Partei Deutschlands* (Communist Party of Germany)
LBC	Left Book Club
LCC	London County Council
LP	Labour Party
LWFS	London Workers' Film Society
MI5	Military Intelligence, Section 5, common name for the UK Security Service
MI6	Military Intelligence, Section 6, common name for the UK Secret Intelligence Service
NCLC	National Council of Labour Colleges
NMM	National Minority Movement
OGPU	*Obyedinyonnoye gosudarstvennoye politicheskoye upravleniye* (All-Union State Political Directorate), Soviet security intelligence service and secret police, 1923–34
OMS	Organisation for the Maintenance of Supplies
NKVD	*Narodnyy komissariat vnutrennikh del* (People's Commissariat for Internal Affairs), Soviet law enforcement agency incorporating security intelligence service and secret police, 1934–43
NUSW	National Union of Scientific Workers
PCF	*Parti communiste français* (French Communist Party)
PFI	Progressive Film Institute
SA	*Sturmabteilung*, paramilitary wing of the Nazi Party
SB	Special Branch of the London Metropolitan Police
SCR	Society for Cultural Relations between the Peoples of the British Commonwealth and the Union of Socialist Soviet Republics
TUC	Trades Union Congress
VOKS	*Vsesoiuznoe obshchestvo kul'turnoi sviazi s zagranitsei* (All-Union Society for Cultural Relations with Foreign Countries)
WEB	West European Bureau of the Comintern, based in Berlin until March 1933
WIR	Workers' International Relief, name in English for the IAH
WPC	World Peace Congress/Council

1

PROLOGUE

intelligentsia, n. The part of a nation (orig. in 19th-cent. Russia) that aspires to intellectual activity and political initiative; a section of society regarded as educated and possessing culture and political influence.

Oxford English Dictionary

'IN EVERY society,' as the German sociologist Karl Mannheim observed, 'there are social groups whose special task it is to provide an interpretation of the world for that society. We call these the "intelligentsia".' This is the case history of a member of the British intelligentsia in the twentieth century. It focuses particularly on the interwar years, a period that extended, in the case of someone like Ivor Montagu who identified closely with the Soviet Union, to the entry of that country into the war against Hitler in June 1941. As biography, it is deliberately partial. It deals very little with Montagu's personal life. It focuses on two of his existential passions, film and left-wing politics, and all but ignores two others: zoology and table tennis. It pays scant attention to his work as a translator and literary agent. Apart from a skimpy epilogue, it halts abruptly at a point when he still had more than half his life to live. But within the delimited time span, it seeks to explore in depth his role as an active participant in the cultural and political ferment of the era.[1]

'The fact of belonging to the same class, and that of belonging to the same generation or age group, have this in common,' Mannheim wrote, 'that both endow the individuals sharing in them with a common location in the social and historical process, and thereby limit them to a specific range of potential experience, predisposing them for a certain characteristic mode of thought and experience, and a characteristic type of historically relevant action.' Montagu's class was that of the liberal, progressive wing of the bourgeoisie, with a newly acquired aristocratic tinge; his generation that which grew up with the art form of the twentieth century, the cinema, and which in their youth experienced, if from afar, both the horror of the Great War and the exhilaration of the Russian Revolution. As this book will reveal, Montagu would, like others of his time, become (semi-) detached from his class through a conscious act of rebellion and throw in his lot, as a freelance intellectual, with the proletariat.[2]

The intelligentsia, Arthur Koestler was to write, are 'the liaison agents between the way we live and the way we *could* live according to the contemporary level of objective knowledge.' Those who were 'snugly tucked into the social hierarchy' obviously had 'no strong impulse towards independent thought', while 'the great majority of the oppressed, the underdogs, lack the opportunity or the objectivity or both, for the pursuit of independent thought.' And thus it is that 'the function of independent thinking falls to those sandwiched in between two social layers, and exposed to the pressure of both.'[3]

Codename Intelligentsia is a study of Ivor Montagu as such a 'liaison agent', a go-between. It is the story of a young man from a privileged background who set out on his journey through life possessed of a desire both to immerse himself in the cultural life of modernity and to rectify social injustice. The following pages will disclose where the journey took him. It is a tale of the times.

★

'Of what use is Siberia to Russia?' is question III of the 7-year-old schoolboy's Geography examination. His answer follows: 'Russia sends her prisoners to Siberia, where they work, and there is hardly any colder and more horrible place than Siberia.'[4]

It is 1911, and the young Hon. Ivor Montagu is doing well in his first year at Mr Gibbs's preparatory school in Sloane Street, central London. When the results come out, he tops the class in Geography, as well as in Bible

Lessons, Arithmetic, Reading, and Grammar. Backing this up with second place in Tales, English History, and Recitation, and third in Natural History and Dictation, he comes first overall. Only a sixth in Picture Study, and a lamentable ninth in Writing and French, blot his copybook.[5]

It is a promising start for the man who was to be called (by Michael Balcon, the renowned film producer) 'one of the first real intellectual artists of the cinema', and (by Rachael Low, doyenne of British film historians) 'an exceptional man in many ways and a brilliant film maker'. He was, wrote the critic Geoff Brown, 'the period's most dynamic, visible, and well-connected fighter for art cinema'. If he was not to receive honours for his work in film, by the end of his life Montagu had been awarded the Order of Liberation, 1st Class (Bulgaria), the Order of the Pole Star (Mongolia), and the Lenin Peace Prize, and inducted into the International Jewish Sports Hall of Fame. He had a 'warm and certainly idiosyncratic charisma', declared the Communist footballer Jim Riordan, and Balcon, with whom he worked for a number of years, responded to his 'warm and generous nature'. 'Ivor Montagu was an idealist,' concedes journalist Ben Macintyre in a recent book, 'but his actions were treasonable.'[6]

Ivor Goldsmid Samuel Montagu was born in London on 23 April 1904 to a banker, Louis Samuel Montagu, and his wife Gladys Helen Rachel, *née* Goldsmid. He was the third son: Stuart had been born in 1899, and Ewen in 1901. A daughter, Joyce, was to follow in 1909. Montagu was the family name, but hadn't been so for long. Ivor's paternal grandfather had been born (in 1832) Montagu Samuel, but he was enrolled at school by mistake as Samuel Montagu, and it was decided to keep the change. The boy, son of the Liverpool watchmaker/pawnbroker Louis Samuel, became a budding young financier and founded the merchant bank of Samuel & Montagu, later Samuel Montagu & Co., in 1853. In 1894, the year he was created a baronet, the switch was formalised, and he was granted a Royal licence to assume Montagu as a surname.[7]

Set up as a bullion broking business at the time of the Australian gold rush, the bank did well, and Samuel Montagu prospered. He became Liberal Member of Parliament for Whitechapel from 1885 to 1900, espousing causes of social justice including aid for the poor and the small farmer and the municipalisation of public utilities. He was also active in facilitating the emigration of Jews persecuted in Eastern Europe, and in the provision of working-class housing. In 1907, despite his belief that the hereditary peerage was an obstacle to social reform (he was treasurer of the National League for the Abolition of the House of Lords), he was made a baron, the second Jewish peer in Britain after Rothschild. There were claims, of course, that he had bought his titles. In his autobiography, Ivor simply notes that his grandfather 'was widely celebrated for philanthropic exercises, no doubt there were the usual contributions to the party funds.'[8]

The newly minted aristocrat thought of calling himself Lord Montagu, and made enquiries with the existing Lord Montagu of Beaulieu, who replied, 'I have no objection to sharing my name with you, if you will share your money with me.' So instead he became the first Baron Swaythling, named after the village and railway station adjacent to his country seat at South Stoneham, near Southampton. This name-switching was observed with acerbic wit, possibly tinged with anti-Semitism, by Hilaire Belloc, who composed a ditty on the subject:

> Montagu, first Baron Swaythling he,
> Thus is known to you & me.
> But the Devil down in hell
> Knows the man as Samuel.
> And though it may not sound the same
> It is the blighter's proper name.[9]

Ivor's father, Louis Montagu, inherited the title on Samuel's death in 1911. The 2nd Baron Swaythling, who carried on in the banking business, was a less public figure than the 1st. He did not run for office, but was a Liberal in the family tradition and took his seat in the House of Lords (while expressing his belief in a unicameral legislature). Active in Jewish causes, he was a leading figure in the League of British Jews and served as President of the Federation of Synagogues. In religion Louis was staunchly orthodox (although he disobeyed the injunction not to mix dairy products and meat, claiming to have found a passage in the Bible which vindicated his position). A man of solid build, 'opinionated' and 'stubborn' according to Ivor, he was a keen shot and excellent golfer, loved fishing, and was President for a time of the Hampshire County Cricket Club. At home he entertained frequently, played bridge, enjoyed jigsaws, and collected japonaiserie.[10]

Lady Swaythling, Ivor's mother, was ten years younger than her husband, having married at 19. Gladys Montagu was the daughter of the prominent Zionist Albert Goldsmid, the first Jewish colonel in the British Army and the founder of the Jewish Lads' Brigade. Ivor describes her as 'very pretty, gay, charming, vivacious … constantly ready to laugh and pleased by jokes.' She managed the large household, being 'perpetually, visibly, busy'; she was a popular Society hostess, took singing lessons, was an enthusiastic fencer, and worked for charity. Amongst her close friends was Princess Victoria Mary ('May'), who became Queen Mary when her husband acceded to the throne as George V in 1910. Both Ivor's parents were accomplished linguists: Gladys knew French and German, with 'smatterings of Hebrew, Spanish and Italian', while Louis spoke fluent Japanese. They were a happy couple.[11]

The Montagus and their Samuel relatives were part of a 'West End Cousinhood' of leading Jewish families who had made their fortunes during the expansionary imperial era of Victorian commerce. Others included the Rothschilds, the Goldsmids, the Montefiores, the Cohens, the Waleys, and the Solomons. Many had played prominent parts in the movement for Jewish emancipation.[12]

Politics was in the air in the Montagu household, Ivor relates. The boy rubbed shoulders with 'the potentates and ministers who needed entertaining as part of my father's financial routine.' Uncle Edwin and Cousin Herbert were 'rising meteors of the Liberal Party': Edwin Montagu, Louis's brother, was MP for Chesterton (West Cambridgeshire), private secretary to (and personal friend of) Prime Minister Herbert Asquith, and subsequently Under-Secretary of State for India; Herbert Samuel, Louis's cousin, was MP for Cleveland and a member of Asquith's Cabinet as Chancellor of the Duchy of Lancaster and later Postmaster-General (in 1909, as Assistant Home Secretary, he piloted the Cinematograph Films Act through Parliament). Ivor's Aunt Lily (Lilian Montagu, Louis's sister) was a campaigner for women's welfare and a founder of liberal Judaism – much to her father's dismay.[13]

The Montagu family home was 28 Kensington Court, in the West End. In his memoirs, Ivor describes in loving detail the ornate carved furniture, the lacquered cabinets, the marquetry, the chairs upholstered in scarlet silk and chestnut-coloured leather, the decorative tiles, the wooden panelling, the art nouveau fireplaces, the candelabras, the parquet floors. One feature

particularly fascinated the young boy, a pokey servants' lift, whose function
was 'to carry trays or washing baskets or themselves invisibly past the gentle-
manly regions when untimely menial presence might offend convention'.[14]

Surpassing the London home in grandeur, however, was the 2nd Baron's
country estate, Townhill Park House. Adjoining Samuel Montagu's South
Stoneham property and bought by him towards the end of the century
for Louis's use, it comprised a villa dating from the 1790s and extensive
grounds. The building was decaying; under Swaythling ownership, it was
restored and enlarged in Italianate style by the architect Leonard Rome
Guthrie in 1911–12, and after the war a music room and boudoir were
added for Lady Swaythling. Most impressive of the renovated spaces was the
elegant music room, in which works by Gainsborough, Turner and other
artists were displayed, 'perfectly illuminated' against polished walnut panels
of exquisite craftsmanship. The gardens, noted for their rhododendrons and
camellias, were laid out by the leading designer Gertrude Jekyll.[15]

Townhill Park was a veritable fiefdom replete with cowhouse, dairy, sta-
bles, poultry houses, pigsties, potting sheds, barns and tool rooms. There
were kitchen gardens, hothouses and orchards, and a retinue of menser-
vants, gardeners, chauffeurs, maids, cooks, and nannies, as well as secretaries,
accompanists, and tutors. Here, Ivor was to spend the weekends and holidays of his childhood and youth.[16]

Formalities were observed. Evening dress for dinner was *de rigueur* (Ivor
was forever untidy and perpetually embarrassed by his mother smarten-
ing him up in public). There were annual rituals, like the cricket match in
summer between the houses of Townhill and South Stoneham (Ivor loved
cricket but was handicapped through lack of skill in batting, bowling, and
throwing), the shooting parties in autumn (Ivor says he never shot for entertainment), and the New Year's Eve balls (Ivor hated dancing, and disliked all
physical contact). The young master was waited on hand and foot. 'I was a
spoiled brat,' he admits. 'I never cooked, washed up, made the beds, mended
or tidied my clothes, cleaned my shoes.'[17]

Young Ivor's interest in the cinema was sparked by the family's ownership
of a praxinoscope – an optical toy that, when rotated, gave an illusion of
movement to its drawn figures of, for example, a horse and rider jumping. At
the age of 4 or 5 he was taken by his nursemaid to Hale's Tours, a simulated
railway journey in which views filmed from a train were projected inside an

imitation carriage. Later he saw pictures (in a 'fleapit' in High Street) star-ring John Bunny, 'Pimple' (the popular comedian Fred Evans), and Mr and Mrs Sidney Drew, while at the Scala off Tottenham Court Road, with his mother, he saw early colour films – novelties such as *The Opening of a Rose* (in red and yellow slow motion) and spectacles like the imperial pageant *The Delhi Durbar* (1912).[18]

Another film he saw was of Robert Falcon Scott's ill-fated Antarctic expedition, a disaster that made a strong impact on the Montagu children because of family connections. He also saw the Herbert Ponting photo-graphic exhibition, and was allowed to select a print for himself – his brothers chose shots of the ship *Discovery*, while Ivor opted for killer whales.[19]

Ivor was a voracious reader and graduated from boys' adventure stories to Conan Doyle, H.G. Wells and ultimately Darwin. He enjoyed exploring the natural world, particularly around Townhill (the zoological rather than the botanical – 'plants were dull compared with things that moved'). He made friends at school and one, Anthony Asquith, was the son of the Prime Minister. He once spent an afternoon with Anthony launching a model aeroplane over the garden wall at No. 10 Downing Street and getting a policeman to fetch it.[20]

After Mr Gibbs's school Ivor was sent, at the age of 9, to Mr Barton's. Here he was to board, but this experiment came to an abrupt end when Ivor reported to his parents that after lights out the younger boys had been 'bidden to tickle one of our older companions in strange places, to our no small resentment'. Ivor was also a day boy at Westminster, the prestigious public school where he was sent later, properly attired in Eton suit and top hat, from the ages of 13 to 15. He did not, he claims, 'enjoy any part of it.' There was some superb teaching in French and German, and he was per-mitted to his relief to draw rats rather than cylinders and pyramids in the art class. But he rebelled sharply against the school's authoritarianism: 'The ultimate evil and oppression to me was being expected to accept standards ready made, without right of challenge to them.' He rejected the whole public school system, designed, as he was later to argue, 'to separate out and train an elite class, destined to form part of a ruling apparatus as principals or subordinates, to have charge, at home and in the Empire.' Sneaking out of compulsory games and military cadet parades, he began to pursue his zoo-logical interests off his own bat at the British Museum (Natural History).[21]

Meanwhile, the Great War was raging. Ivor's father served for a time in Alexandria, responsible for keeping records of Gallipoli casualties; later, both parents were heavily involved in the work of the Wounded Allies' Relief Committee, receiving decorations from Belgium, Serbia, Romania and Japan for their efforts. Brother Stuart was in the trenches in France, a Lieutenant in the Grenadier Guards. Ivor made his contribution by knitting for the troops. And then in 1917, when he was playing with model ships, he invented a naval war game involving the movement of the opposing fleets by mathematical calculation of speeds and distances (visibility conditions to be decided by the umpire). Admiral Jellicoe himself came to Kensington Court and played, resulting in an invitation to the 13-year-old schoolboy to lecture on his brainchild to the Naval Staff College. However, the offer was not finally taken up, since in the interim, Ivor reports, 'I had become a socialist and decided I was against war.'[22]

When questioned later in life by the cinematographer Freddie Young as to why he had become politically radical, Montagu recalled a childhood incident:

> When I was a small boy, my father, Lord Swaythling, had a big house in the country. I was quite lonely and I made friends with the gardener's son and we used to play together. One day we went into the peach house and we both took a peach off the tree. We were in the middle of eating our peaches when in came the head gardener, and he slapped his son for stealing fruit and he sent him off crying. Then he turned to me and said, 'I think you should go back to the house, sir.' At that moment, Freddie, I was struck by the unfairness of things, and I've been a communist ever since.[23]

Whatever the origins of his anti-establishment views, they were nourished at a tender age by such tracts as Karl Liebknecht's *Militarism and Anti-Militarism* (1907) and *This Misery of Boots* (1908) by H.G. Wells, which Montagu considered 'the best socialist propaganda pamphlet I have ever read'. Liebknecht argued that possession of arms was one of the means by which the ruling class sustained its domination over the majority of the population, and that in militarism, reaction and capitalism were 'defending their most important position of power against democracy and the working class.' Wells, taking footwear as his starting point, refused to accept the proposition that 'a large majority of people can never hope for more than to be shod in a manner that is frequently painful, uncomfortable, unhealthy, or unsightly.' The reason for the current unsatisfactory state of affairs was private property and profit-taking: 'Is there no other way of managing things,' he asked, 'than to let these property-owners exact their claims, and squeeze comfort, pride, happiness, out of the lives of the common run of people?' He concluded by calling for socialist revolution: 'The whole system has to be changed, if we are to get rid of the masses of dull poverty that render our present state detestable to any sensitive man or woman.'[24]

Ivor also read two pamphlets by George Bernard Shaw, a friend of the family, whom he would lunch with from time to time. These were *Socialism for Millionaires* and *Socialism and Superior Brains* – titles which Ivor ('I blush to admit it') thought appropriate to him. He confesses, however, that 'they did not mean much to me when I tried to understand them.'[25]

Wells proclaimed, 'Everywhere we must make or join a Socialist organisation,' and Ivor complied, becoming (in 1918) a member of the Central London branch of the Marxist-oriented British Socialist Party. The BSP had been bitterly divided on its attitude towards the war. The internationalists, led by the Jewish East End organiser Joe Fineberg, opposed the war as reactionary and imperialist. They had gained a majority in 1916, and since then the Party had conducted a strenuous anti-war struggle. Among its prominent leaders when Ivor joined were the general secretary Albert Inkpin and the Clydeside militant John MacLean, while Russian émigré Theodore Rothstein exerted a powerful influence behind the scenes. The Central London branch met every two weeks at a café run by female anarchists in High Holborn.[26]

The BSP distributed socialist pamphlets, defying police bans on seditious literature. Ivor assisted by temporarily storing a consignment of Lenin's *State and Revolution* on the upstairs landing at Kensington Court ('No one would look for them there, I averred'). This essay, with its confident prediction that the 'proletarian state will begin to wither away immediately after its victory, because the state is unnecessary and cannot exist in a society in which there are no class antagonisms,' was to prove highly influential on the British left, especially in making the concept of the dictatorship of the proletariat acceptable 'to many who initially found the doctrine uncongenial'.[27]

Lord and Lady Swaythling were unaware that they were harbouring a teenage radical. When they found out – discovering Ivor's speech notes for a debate on 'Revolutionary Action versus Parliamentary Action' – there was trouble. His mother asked him to leave the BSP, while his father ordered him 'to desist from politics'. Montagu may have been thinking of this occasion when he later recalled that his generation was reacting against 'the Victorian horror – morally fortified by Biblical injunction and precedent – whereby the paterfamilias considered it not only his right but his duty to expect absolute obedience from his children, and unlimited gratitude.' Now, amidst 'tears and anger', he rejected his parents' demands. Finally, Montagu recounts, 'a minimum compromise was reached. I was to promise faithfully that, whatever I did politically in the future, I should not, until I was 21, spend more of my allowance upon politics than I was spending now.' An armistice was declared, and 'amiable coexistence outwardly resumed' on the understanding that Ivor would keep his promise for the next six years. 'More or less,' he says, 'I did.'[28]

Ivor also joined the Labour Party (to which the BSP was affiliated), and in December 1918 took part in the general election campaign in support of his uncle Leslie Haden Guest, who was standing in Southwark for Labour. 'Each day after school,' Ivor recalls, 'I put my top hat and white tie in the underground luggage office, took out a cap and a red tie and went off to Southwark.' He did clerical work and tried canvassing, though found he was too shy for it. It was the first British election with universal male suffrage from age 21, and the first to permit female voting, from age 30. Haden Guest, who had converted to Judaism prior to his marriage to Lady Swaythling's sister Carmel in 1910, was the first Jew to stand for Parliament as a Labour candidate. He was unsuccessful, but the Labour Party made strong gains against the Conservatives and Liberals. Lloyd George, who had supplanted Asquith as PM in 1916, won a landslide victory on his coalition ticket; Lord Swaythling, an Asquith supporter, was decidedly angry.[29]

Tensions accompanied demobilisation following the end of the war in 1918. Ivor, top hat and all, found himself caught up in a police attack on a protest march of discharged soldiers. He joined the fray, bringing down a policeman by striking him on the ankle with his silver-headed ebony cane. Less dramatic was his participation in the socialist think-tank organisation the Fabian Society, among whose leading lights were Shaw and Wells, and of which he was elected a member in 1919. He also joined the League of Free Nations Association, 'a British organisation to promote an active Propaganda for the formation of a World League of Free Nations as the Necessary Basis of Permanent Peace in the future'. (Simultaneously Ivor's father was at the Paris Peace Conference as a member of a delegation of British Jews seeking to incorporate religious freedom and non-discrimination in any treaty creating new states or enlarging old ones.)[30]

The Russian Revolution of 1917 and the subsequent civil war had made a profound impact on the Jewish establishment in Britain. Delight at the overthrow of the Tsar in March and legal enactment of Jewish Emancipation in April had been followed by dismay at the Bolshevik seizure of power in November. The attractions of communism as a doctrine to significant sections of the Jewish population in Britain and abroad was of deep concern to the moneyed elite, as was the potential to arouse anti-Semitism of an association of Jews with revolutionary activity. On 23 April 1919, the *Morning Post* published a letter to the editor signed by ten leading members of the English Jewish community, including Lord Swaythling. Attacking sympathy towards Bolshevism that had been expressed, albeit ambiguously, in recent articles in the Jewish press, the signatories expressed their desire 'to disassociate ourselves absolutely and unreservedly from the mischievous and misleading doctrine which these articles are calculated to disseminate.'[31]

The 'Letter of the Ten', as it came to be called, was widely noticed. It would undoubtedly have exacerbated tensions between Louis and his son, who turned 15 on the day it was published. A comrade in the BSP (J. T. Lyne, on behalf of the branch secretary T.E. Quelch) was certainly alert to this possibility: writing to Ivor in November, he said, 'My eyes being open, I saw the letter to the *Morning Post* under the signature of Lord Swaythling and others and wonder if your position is made difficult for you. Please do not consider it patronage if I tender my sympathy to you on this account.'[32]

In point of fact, the BSP was undergoing a crisis. The Party had adopted a strong pro-Soviet line, and was a leading player in the Hands Off Russia campaign launched in January 1919 to oppose Allied intervention on the side of the Whites. However, when delegates to the annual conference carried a resolution announcing their objective to 'SEIZE THE REINS OF POWER, OVERTHROW THE RULE OF THE LANDLORD AND CAPITALIST CLASS, ESTABLISH THE DIRECT RULE OF THE WORKERS AND PEASANTS BY MEANS OF SOVIETS, AND

WIND UP THE CAPITALIST ORDER OF SOCIETY', the ultra-left enthusiasm was too much for some. The National Treasurer, H. Alexander (a prominent businessman who was also a leading figure in the Central London branch) and the Editor of the Party paper *The Call*, E.C. Fairchild, addressed a letter to members on 9 June resigning their positions, explaining that in their view the Party's aim should be to strive for the social revolution by appealing to organised labour 'in its millions', co-operating with other socialist organisations, and adopting 'a policy not so far away from the everyday thought of the working class, so that all possibility of its acceptance by them is destroyed.'[33]

Ivor was apparently sympathetic to this point of view, as were others. He stopped paying Party dues in June, ceased attending meetings, and let it be known that he intended to resign. When Lyne wrote, he explained to Ivor that 'a few members of the Branch are endeavouring to "pull" it together again,' that both Quelch and the chairman, Revington, were 'moderates', and that Montagu's active support would strengthen the moderate position. There is no evidence that Ivor responded favourably to this appeal; he seems instead to have quietly dropped out of active politicking.[34]

By this time the BSP had voted by an overwhelming majority to affiliate to the Third (Communist) International – commonly abbreviated to Comintern – which had been founded in March. In 1920, assisted by a flow of funds from Moscow facilitated by Theodore Rothstein, it was a prime mover in the merger of socialist organisations that resulted in the formation of the Communist Party of Great Britain. T.E. (Tom) Quelch became a founding member of the CPGB, as did Albert Inkpin, who was to be the new Party's first secretary. Ivor did not, at this stage, join. In his autobiography he contends that this was 'for domestic reasons, rather than considered political choice' – which suggests that his main concern was not to further antagonise his parents.[35]

It was also probable that he was concentrating on his studies. In his final year at Westminster in 1919, he qualified for admission to Cambridge University. However, Trinity College, where his brothers Stuart and Ewen were enrolled, would not accept him until he turned 17. Angry, he rejected Trinity and took exams for King's instead. He passed, but King's was also reluctant to take a 16-year-old.[36]

To fill in the waiting time, in 1920 Ivor enrolled in Zoology and Botany courses at the Royal College of Science in London, one of the constituent colleges of the Imperial College of Science and Technology. Here he was taught by the socialist Lancelot Hogben, who became a major influence on his thinking: it was he, Montagu explained, who 'completed my conversion to a Marxian interpretation of history.' It was at this time also that Ivor institutionalised his fervour for Southampton Football Club (cherry-stripe scarf and rosette, rattle and megaphone) by becoming the first president of its Supporters' Club; Ewen was vice-president. The young radical was in a state of restless anticipation.[37]

2

CAMBRIDGE

FINALLY, IN 1921, Ivor went up to Cambridge. 'This was the soil,' he says, 'in which I expanded like a flower.' He was not one of the favoured students who lived in at King's College. His lodgings in his first year were 'rather distant in the suburbs', then he moved to the more convenient St Edward's Passage, opposite the college gates. Here, with a young couple and their baby, he found himself 'extremely comfortable'.[1]

Cambridge in the early 1920s reflected the fading glories of imperial Britain. Formal education was not then, Montagu was to argue, its function: rather 'it was mainly a sort of adjunct to, or cheap substitute for, the European Grand Tour,' aimed at turning boys into gentlemen. Racism and anti-Semitism lurked beneath the polite surfaces of daily discourse. Female students were relegated to the outskirts, not permitted to graduate, and excluded from the Union and the dramatic societies. Intellectually the university lagged: 'Of Marx and Freud, for example, hardly more than a soupçon had as yet trickled through into our fool's paradise,' wrote Basil Willey, who was a young English lecturer at the time. There were, of course, exceptions: King's, for example, was strong in economics and classics.[2]

Despite its shortcomings, it was a vibrant environment for the rebellious third son of the 2nd Baron Swaythling, who could now escape the chafing constraints of his parents' tutelage. If he paid little attention to his studies at Cambridge, he was nevertheless able to undertake scientific expeditions in the summer breaks, while indulging to the full his expanding interests in sport, debating, theatre, journalism, film and politics.

'Academically I did nothing, learned nothing, achieved nothing, during my three years at Cambridge,' writes Montagu, with perhaps a little exaggeration. He could not stay awake during lectures, and seldom attended classes, considering that he had learnt it all before at the Royal College of Science. Enrolled in Zoology, he failed the Tripos examination, yet managed 'by a fluke' to achieve an ordinary pass, graduating with a BA in 1924. This was followed in due course by an MA – which was awarded, he explains, 'simply by one's father keeping up periodic payments for a given time'.[3]

In zoology what absorbed him were his field trips, arranged under the auspices of the British Museum (Natural History). He focused on small burrowing mammals. In the summer of 1922, as one of a group of undergraduates, he hunted mice and voles on the Scottish islands of Islay and Jura; among their finds was a remarkable elderly shrew whose characteristics he described in his first scientific paper, *On a Further Collection of Mammals from the Inner Hebrides*, published as a pamphlet by the Zoological Society of London in December. The specimens the young researchers collected were deposited with the museum.[4]

The 1923 expedition took him further afield, to Yugoslavia. This time Ivor was in charge, and he took along a fellow undergraduate from Cambridge named Cotton. After some hair-raising adventures in the mountains of Slovenia and Croatia (which he described in articles for the *Cambridge Mercury*), they brought back on the train, to the bemusement of customs officials, a diverse collection of specimens including cave-dwelling grasshoppers, live scorpions, twenty-six *Proteus* (a red-gilled amphibian), two examples of *Pisidium sp.* (a pea clam), and a baby wolf cub.[5]

The summer of 1924, university studies completed, saw Montagu and his Cambridge friend Bancroft Clark (a Quaker shoemaker from the West of England) traipsing across the hot Hungarian plains in quest of the rodent *Spalax*, a blind mole-rat that spends its entire life underground. The creatures were plentiful but elusive, and despite digging up hundreds of yards of burrows the researchers were unable to lay their hands on a single specimen. Undaunted, Montagu was able to deduce from close study of the pockmarked clay the fact that the *Spalax* uses its nose to dig with, a 'fascinating discovery' that he duly wrote up in a scientific paper published in January 1925.[6]

While at Cambridge, Ivor maintained his keen interest in sport. He played tennis, and in April 1922 wrote a letter to *Lawn Tennis and Badminton* complaining that the authorities' juggling up and down of the age limit for junior players had deprived him of a chance of competing in a championship matched with players of his own age. At university he played regularly in the College second team. Ivor also had a brief, unsuccessful foray playing football.[7]

However, it was table tennis, a favourite recreation at Townhill, that principally preoccupied him. According to his own account, Montagu was the initiator of the Cambridge University Ping-Pong Club, founded in Lent Term (January–March) 1921. Immediately popular, the club (which changed its name to the CU Table Tennis Club in October 1922) organised championships, inter-college tournaments and team contests against out-of-town opponents. Ivor was in the top echelon of players but never a champion, and his form was unreliable. In the first fully representative clash with Oxford University, in March 1923, he was the only player in the team to lose a match. 'Montagu was a great disappointment,' the Cambridge magazine *The Granta* lamented, 'exhibiting form very much worse than that which he had displayed in previous games.'[8]

Beyond Cambridge, Montagu was instrumental in reviving a sport that had not been played competitively on a national scale for almost twenty years. Making contact with a Manchester businessman, A.F. Carris, who had similar ideas, and in collaboration with other enthusiasts including veterans Percival Bromfield and J.J. Payne, he helped establish what became the English Table Tennis Association (they discovered Ping-Pong was a registered trade name), and was elected its president – all 'before my eighteenth birthday,' he boasts.[9]

Undoubtedly, he had a personal love of playing, but there was also a political motivation behind the evangelical zeal with which the young student promoted the sport. Table tennis, he pointed out, with its cheap equipment and without any requirement for expensive grounds or premises, was 'a sport particularly suited to the lower paid ... its low cost meant that it could give pleasure and exercise indoors to youth of a class that, in towns and in those days of low wages and small public subsidy for sport, enjoyed little enough outdoors of either.'[10]

In 1924 Ivor published *Table Tennis To-Day* (Heffer, 56 pages, 1s 6d), one of the first manuals of the sport. It was warmly welcomed by the *Daily Mirror*, which called it 'one of the best and most informative books ever published on the popular game.' The reviewer T.L.-E. (undoubtedly Theyre Lee-Elliott) in *The Granta* called it 'an invaluable book,' lauding its inclusion of the (recently revised) rules and information on the history of the game, choice of implements, and playing technique. Lee-Elliott, however, noted that table tennis was 'played by the vast majority as an innocent amusement, and to such players the serious, analytical spirit in which they are here urged to approach the game may be distasteful.' Another, anonymous, reviewer was not so convinced of the seriousness of tone. 'There are so many Mr Montagu's [*sic*] in this book,' he or she wrote:

> Sometimes, pleasantly informative, he instructs; sometimes he poses abstrusely behind a welter of pseudo-mechanical phrases. For a few pages he seems wrapt in crusading vigour and shamelessly defends and propagates his subject; and then, here and there, an irritating twist persuades us he is treating the whole affair fantastically, as an obscure, unnecessary joke.

The appearance of the book was certainly noticed by the Cambridge undergraduates; a student publication on 17 May complained that, 'Ivor Montagu has done nothing during the past week except produce his book on Table Tennis and ride a horse down King's Parade. Surely from Ping Pong to equestrianism is a far cry.'[11]

The Cambridge Union debates in the interwar years constituted, according to T.E.B. Howarth, 'a very erratic barometer of political and social opinion amongst undergraduates.' Frequently featuring distinguished visitors, they were heavily attended. Ivor's uncle Edwin Montagu, a former President of the Union and prominent debater in his time at Cambridge, had spoken on one such occasion. This was shortly after his forced resignation as Secretary of State for India in March 1922, following what Ivor describes as a virulent Tory attack.[12]

Ivor's debate, however, was an in-house affair. On 29 April 1924, at the invitation of the newly elected President of the Cambridge Union Society, R.A. Butler (Pembroke), Ivor led the negative team on the motion 'That Legislation should be enacted to deal with Strikes.' The affirmative was headed by F.G.G. Carr, of Trinity Hall. According to *The Gownsman*, Ivor did not make an impressive debut:

We have had to wait so long for a maiden speech from the Hon. I. Montagu
... that we may be pardoned for being disappointed. He will never set the
Thames, probably not even the Cam, on fire. Both his manner and his
tone are irritating, and the faultless English of his sentences becomes so
involved as to make a fog through which his meaning only glimmers. He
pretended to have been irritated by Mr Carr, and expressed a fear that
laws against strikes would be as ineffective as Prohibition.[13]

Ivor was a keen theatregoer, and amongst the memorable productions he
attended during his final year as a student were Shakespeare's *Hamlet* (New
Theatre, Oxford), Aristophanes' *The Birds* (New Theatre, Cambridge), and,
in London, Ernst Toller's *Man and the Masses* (New Theatre), Shaw's *Saint
Joan* (New Theatre), Congreve's *The Old Batchelour* (Regent) and Beatrice
Mayor's *The Pleasure Garden* (Regent). At Cambridge, Montagu tells us, 'a
family touring company had settled in a small hall in the railway district ...
The lines were given every ounce of dramatic ham, the audience hissed and
cheered ....' The company performed four or five plays a week and Ivor
claimed to have seen nearly every show. He was curious how the audience
would respond to Shaw, and for this purpose secured from the playwright
himself the rights to *The Shewing-up of Blanco Posnet*, a 'sermon in crude
melodrama' that the Lord Chamberlain had banned in 1909, no doubt
because of its explicit (and favourable) portrayal of a prostitute. The play
was duly performed at the People's Theatre on 24 and 25 April 1924; it went
down well, Montagu reports, but its performance disclosed an extraordinary
fact – 'None of the cast could remember lines ... they were perfectly ready
to gag and made up most of the text freely as they went along.' Ivor was able
to remit the sum of eight shillings and three pence to GBS as royalties.[14]

Another of Ivor's pursuits at Cambridge was publishing and editing.
In 1923 he corresponded with a fellow undergraduate, William A. Harris,
who because of ill health was disposing of two journals of which he was
proprietor, *Youth* and *The Old Cambridge*. Nothing seems to have come
of these negotiations, but soon after Ivor started up his own publication,
Cambridge University Times, which was in newspaper format and unillus-
trated. T.S. Eliot praised an article Ivor wrote for it entitled 'A Communist
Approves of Compulsory Military Service' ('I think the argument was
only the obvious one that it must be useful to a revolutionary to know

how to operate a machine-gun'). Dissatisfied, however, Montagu bought
The Cambridge Mercury – possibly in partnership with his 'closest companion in a number of the classical dissipations of University youth,' Angus
MacPhail – from its student founder, Cedric Belfrage. His first issue as
editor (No. 13, 30 April 1924) contained his statement of satisfaction
('With this present number we are content, we indicate to the intelligentsia the weight of our metal') and his promise of more to come ('And
at May Week, about the 8th June, we shall publish a double number, fat,
excellent, copiously illustrated, and packed with advertisements'). No. 14
did indeed appear, on 2 June. Montagu derived much pleasure from mas-
terminding the mix of poems, articles, short stories, and graphics in the
two numbers he edited. Harold Acton offered a translation of Mallarmé's
poem 'Saint', table tennis star Lee-Elliott contributed woodcuts, and the
Communist Barnet 'Woggy' Woolf was responsible for both verse and caricatures. An admiring reader wrote after Ivor's first effort that 'everything
was worthy of Cambridge' and that 'Mr MacPhail's article was as brilliant
as his famous jumpers.' Yet financially, Ivor confesses, he 'made a mess of
trying to run it.' It cost him all his spare cash.[15]

The other aspect of his journalistic activity was writing. For the *Cambridge
Mercury* he began with art criticism, observing of Augustus John's *Madame
Suggia* that 'he has left the 'cellist's lower limbs like match-sticks beneath
her skirt, and … the lower part of her 'cello is so utterly without support
that its fall to the ground seems inevitable.' After his account of travels in
Yugoslavia, he then moved into reviewing the theatre, contributing notices
on *A Midsummer Night's Dream* (produced by Donald Calthrop), Gordon
Bottomley's verse drama *Gruach*, *Phoenix* by Lascelles Abercrombie, *Progress*
by C.K. Munro, and the Oxford University Dramatic Society production of
Hamlet (which offered 'a smooth spontaneity and balance' but was marred
by the fact that Mr Gyles Isham, as the protagonist, 'did not understand that
he was in love with his mother … I must point out that the realisation of
Hamlet as an incest play, yet more significant than *Oedipus* itself, is essential
to its plausibility'). All these efforts were unmarked by any particular political perspective, but his Communist leanings came to the fore in his critique
of Toller's *Man and the Masses* and the misreadings, through doctrinal ignorance, it had received: 'Read Kautsky's attack on Bolshevik policy. Read
Trotsky's reply, published in English, with the title *The Defence of Terrorism*.

Learn the meaning of the following terms: Materialist Conception of History, Class-consciousness ...' (Here the terminology closely approaches that of an outspoken manifesto he published around this time under the title 'Prophecies', which will be examined in Chapter 4.)[16]

One piece he wrote for the *Mercury* contains possibly his first published film criticism. This was 'How Many Times' (30 April 1924), an essay reflecting on what kinds of plays and films could bear being seen more than once. In the course of his argument he discusses *A Woman of Paris* (Charles Chaplin, USA, 1923) ('The story, like the ideology and sub-titles of Mr Chaplin, is not very sophisticated; but the characterisation of the two principal protagonists, played by Miss Purviance and M. Menjou, is not anywhere excelled ... there is no foot of film non-essential, no moment that does not advance the action ...'); *Das Cabinet des Dr Caligari/ The Cabinet of Dr Caligari* (Robert Wiene, Germany, 1920) ('The madness in the film is purely subjective; the objective nature of the film is, on analysis, found only to consist in the exaggerated, furtive, terror-struck, terror-striking attitudes of the actors, and the overwhelming, distorted architectural shapes'); and *Die Strasse/ The Street* (Karl Grune, Germany, 1923) ('Certainly the most important film yet produced ... an expressionistic treatment of sexual repression ... passionately exciting and absorbingly instructive').[17]

For *The Granta* Ivor wrote book reviews. In some thirty pieces contributed between May 1923 and June 1924 he passed judgement on fiction and nonfiction alike, on literary novels and short stories, science fiction and detective fiction, adventure stories and ghost stories; on poetry, plays, translations of the classics, and autobiography; on books of natural history and polar exploration (Herbert Ponting's *The Great White South*), biographical portraits and scientific prognostication (J.B.S. Haldane's *Daedalus, or Science and the Future*), political theory and travel, the playing of auction bridge and the history of racing. Little unifies this eclectic outpouring, except perhaps the frequently jocular tone (befitting *The Granta*'s immersion in undergraduate humour) and a characteristic mannerism Montagu developed in which he slates the work under review, before discovering nonetheless some beauties in it and commending it to his readership. He is liberal in dispensing both accolades (T.S. Stribling's *Fombombo* is 'the most excellent novel of action of the century') and brickbats ('I have never before met with such ill-constructed nonsense,' he writes of H.E. Scarborough's *The Immortals*:

'Its being written was preposterous, its publication was inexcusable'). It is noteworthy that Montagu deploys a personal voice and is not shy to sing his own praises, however tongue-in-cheek he may be: he references 'players of skill and determination like myself' when discussing bridge, for example, while he declares that Eugene O'Neill was 'in those days ... properly appreciated on this side of the Atlantic only by Mr. MacDermott, Mr. Ervine and myself; we three, I fear, are the only persons in England with a proper sense of modern dramatic values.'

Cinema, perhaps because he was over-extended in other directions, does not figure largely in Montagu's memoir of his Cambridge years. There was the time he saw Cecil B. De Mille's *The Ten Commandments*, and a student wag called out from the audience, 'Only six need be attempted.' More significantly, he remembers organising a special screening of *The Cabinet of Dr Caligari*, negotiating the censorship hurdle. (At a party in his rooms after the show, the biologist J.B.S. Haldane seated himself in a revolving chair, stuck a 'floppity chiffon hat on his head, took my terrestrial globe in one hand as a sort of combined orb and sceptre, twirled himself round, and announced that he was descended from Hwulfdun and rightful King of Scotland.') But Ivor does not seem to have played an active role in the Cambridge University Kinema Club, set up by Peter Le Neve Foster in November 1923. The club hosted a variety of lecturers, including prominent director George Pearson (whom members later observed shooting *Reveille* at the Famous Players-Lasky studio at Islington), and also undertook its own amateur production.[18]

Writers Julian Bell and Christopher Isherwood maintained that politics was 'seldom considered or discussed' at Cambridge University in the 1920s. The general tenor was certainly apolitical or Conservative, yet there were a bevy of energetic socialists who opened fire at the status quo whenever the occasion arose. For some, Kingsley Martin recalls, 'Socialism was the fashion ... it was just so much intellectual wild oats'; for others, Montagu among them, it was the early phase of a lifelong commitment.[19]

Ivor's chief field of activity was the Labour Club, which met in rooms at Magdalene College, had between 100 and 150 members, and whose president for a time was his brother Ewen. He became a member of the Executive. Apart from taking part in debates himself (including one at Oxford), Ivor helped organise meetings, recruit debaters, and invite visiting speakers. One time an invitation went out, after a fierce fight won by the right wing in the club, to J.H. Thomas, general secretary of the National Union of Railwaymen. To the leftists, Thomas was anathema for his perceived role in betraying inter-union solidarity, and Montagu devised a scheme whereby posters announcing the meeting carried the words 'ALL MEMBERS ARE REQUESTED TO BE ON THEIR BEST BEHAVIOUR'. The hint was enough, he relates; the visit was called off.[20]

The Labour Club had six seats on the Cambridge Trades Council, and Montagu was, according to his own account, one of only two regular attenders; the other was Barnet Woolf, who was a working-class Jew from the East End of London. Here, outside a university environment, Ivor 'spoke less and learned more.' He was later to explain to Trotsky that 'it became very noticeable to me that whenever myself or Woolf attempted to secure the consideration of problems in the light of Marxian principles, though we might secure momentary victory or majority, the fact that the principles were enunciated only by University delegates, had the effect invariably of causing the Trade Union delegates to feel that Communism or Marxism was academic, doctrinaire, not properly in working-class interest.'[21]

In May 1924 (with an eye, he confesses, to the zoological trip he hoped soon to make to the Soviet Union) he invited members of a Soviet trade union delegation currently in London to visit Cambridge; among the four who came were Mikhail Tomsky, the leader of the All-Russian Central Council of Trade Unions, and Vasiliev Yarotsky, a functionary in the Soviet trade union foreign department, who spoke excellent English. The visitors were especially keen to have the lodgings of John Maynard Keynes at King's pointed out to them, since they were impressed by his contributions as an economist to post-war debates on international relations.[22]

Within the Labour Club, Montagu and 'a caucus of like-minded radicals' set up a ginger group called the Spillikins, to provide, he says, a 'backbone' to the club (Ivor designed the tie for this 'juvenile cabal' – black with large red spots). Referred to as 'a Communist enclave', it is probably the group described elsewhere as 'a very small, though active and vocal, Communist society with perhaps thirty members' which Howarth mentions in his history of Cambridge between the wars. In Montagu's autobiography he downplays such explicit identification: 'I cannot truthfully call us Communists, even though I should like thus to be able to claim early membership,' he writes, 'because we did not discuss Communism or, most of us, knew then properly what it was.' Nevertheless, there were certainly Party members in the circle, including the biochemist Barnet Woolf, the mathematics student Philip Spratt, the crystallographer J.D. (Desmond) Bernal, and the journalist Allen Hutt, while others if not already members were moving towards it, like the historian A.L. Morton and Montagu himself. There was also a certain Michael Roberts, who was suspected of being a fascist spy. In a 1929 letter to Trotsky, Montagu stated straightforwardly that he was a member at Cambridge of the Young Communist League, but in later years he was less definite. In *The Youngest Son* he says that Woolf distributed postcards that 'had something to do with the Young Communist League, but, if they constituted us formally members and our ensemble a branch, it was the last we heard of it, for we never had any formal business to transact, communications to report, or dues to pay.' The first official Communist Party branch was not set up at Cambridge University until 1931.[23]

Undoubtedly a strong influence on these left-wing undergraduates was the economist Maurice Dobb, in whose rooms the Spillikins came into being and usually met. Dobb studied history and economics at Pembroke College between 1919 and 1922, did research at the London School of Economics for the next two years, completing his PhD, and returned to Cambridge as a lecturer in 1924. A man of strong Marxist convictions, he had more than once, as a student, been dunked fully-clothed in the Cam for openly espousing them. Dobb joined the Communist Party of Great Britain in 1922, and was the only academic known to have been a Party member in Britain in the 1920s.[24]

Montagu struck up a warm personal relationship with Dobb, whom he describes as 'a slim, extremely elegant young man with fair hair and perfect pink complexion, of modest, almost diffident manners … he was so neat, in contrast to the rather scruffy appearance of most of us, that the saying was that if we ever wanted to print underground leaflets we should be able to do so in Dobb's trouser-press.' The Marxist economist treated his protégés well: his 'bourgeois upbringing ensured that he furnished his guests with a steady stream of tea and éclairs.' Dobb's Communist affiliations were well-known and he would frequently take part in debates promoting a left-wing or pro-Soviet point of view, but he had to tread carefully so as not to unduly alarm the university authorities.[25]

Dobb is reported to have been a member of a Communist nucleus in the National Union of Scientific Workers, along with Arthur Serner, Clemens Palme Dutt and Alfred Bacharach, after economists were admitted to the union in January 1924. According to Richard Deacon (Donald McCormick), the NUSW helped secure an industrial research scholarship to Cambridge for the brilliant young Russian physicist Peter Kapitza, whom Montagu got to know and like when he arrived in Cambridge later that year.[26]

As a zoologist Montagu, of course, needed no special dispensation to join NUSW, and he duly became a member. In July 1924 he was engaged in correspondence with leading figures of the union regarding an upcoming visit of British scientists to Moscow. Ivor had apparently raised the matter with his old teacher Dr Lancelot Hogben, of the Society for Experimental Biology. Hogben told Montagu to 'get in touch with Bacharach 4 Gerrard St to see NUSW is represented.' Hogben also apparently contacted Bacharach himself, since the latter wrote to Ivor saying:

Dear Montagu, I have a peremptory and uninforming letter from Lance, ordering to get in touch with you about an alleged 'mission' of British & other scientists to Moscow this summer. He says he wants the NUSW to be represented, which is a good idea. But I know nothing of the whole business, so I should be grateful if you would send me a few details.[27]

Meanwhile, working within the Labour Party as the Communist Spillikins were doing was fully in line with CPGB strategy at this time. The policy had been urged on his British comrades by Lenin, against stiff opposition, in his influential 1920 pamphlet *'Left-Wing' Communism, an Infantile Disorder*, and it was by now mandated by the Communist International. The CPGB had, in fact, repeatedly applied for affiliation to the Labour Party, but each time had been rebuffed. Nonetheless, it was the expectation that at election time Communists would support the Labour candidate in those electorates (the vast majority) in which no CPGB candidate was standing.[28]

In accordance with this policy, Ivor – who happily identified himself as a Communist at this time, although he was not a Party member – energetically campaigned for Labour Party candidates in elections, as he had done for Leslie Haden Guest in London. At the November 1922 general election he supported the Labour candidate for the Cambridgeshire constituency, Albert Stubbs, an organiser for the Workers' Union, against the sitting member – who happened to be his uncle, Edwin Montagu. The 18-year-old student found himself trying to hold audiences of agricultural workers till the candidate arrived; he discovered that his speeches failed to carry conviction since the argument came from an outsider and did not spring from direct knowledge and personal experience.[29]

For Edwin, it was a 'nasty and brutal campaign'. With coalition governments in power, he had enjoyed bilateral support from Liberals and Conservatives in the past, but this time the Tories ran their own candidate. Blaming Edwin for his promotion of moves towards self-government in India, the Tories attacked him with a vengeance 'in what was perhaps the most sordid contest in the election. Hooligans filled his halls with noise. He was heckled and barracked.' Meanwhile, Stubbs was receiving enthusiastic support, and in line with growing Labour strength around the country he came in a close second to the Tory; Edwin was several thousand votes behind in third place. It was the end of his political career, but Ivor believed his uncle did not bear him a grudge, 'taking it for granted that I should support my own principles.'[30]

Ivor again campaigned for Stubbs, once more without success, in the general election of December 1923; the seat was held by the Conservatives. This was the election in which his student friend Aubrey Clark, campaigning for Labour in the Northampton electorate, wrote to Ivor saying, 'I think I like electioneering more than any other amusement – it is a pity that parliamentary politics is not likely to last long enough to have a really good fling at it.' In the event the election resulted in the first Labour-led government in British history. A further campaign Ivor attached himself to was that of Fenner Brockway, the Independent Labour Party secretary, standing for Labour in the March 1924 Westminster Abbey by-election. The seat had been held by the Conservatives and Brockway was up against a Tory, a Liberal, and Winston Churchill, standing as an independent 'Constitutionalist'. Ivor volunteered to work for Brockway, 'detesting Churchill and all that he stood for.' Churchill lost to the Tory by forty-three votes. At the announcement of the result he 'wept unashamedly'; Ivor had 'never before seen a grown man weep in public and this made me think quite differently of him.'[31]

At Cambridge the forum for extra-curricular discussion was a club
known as the Heretics, 'conspicuous in its heyday in the twenties for
total freedom of thought, the sort of emancipated irreverence which one
associates with the eighteenth-century *philosophes*, and general moral free-
wheeling'. Montagu called it the 'intellectual snob society'; he, of course,
joined. The Heretics, he says, 'managed to induce on to its lecture list an
astonishing series of the intellectual lions of the day, who, after performance,
would proceed to someone's rooms in college where we could interrogate
them far into the night.' Here he came in contact with J.B.S. Haldane ('perhaps the greatest Heretic of all' in the view of university historian Howarth);
with the philosopher R.B. Braithwaite and the educationalist A.S. Neill,
the gynaecologist Norman Haire and the art critic Roger Fry, the economist Joan Robinson and the history student, at that time, Alexander Tudor
Hart. He 'did not take at all' to Bertrand Russell, but struck up important
'pupil–teacher relationships' with the Marxist theorists Rajani Palme Dutt
and Robin Page Arnot.[32]

On top of all this, Ivor found time for billiards, chess, and bridge, and
he would occasionally attend a race meet. He ventured into gastronomy
by founding a Cheese-Eaters' League, whose members wore a miniature
yellow rosette in their buttonhole. Among the exotic samples they procured
were a hard camel's-milk cylinder from Egypt and a 'delicate white soft
thing' from the Arabian desert. They were particularly keen to try whale's-
milk cheese, but despite overtures to the British Museum (Natural History),
this was not to be had.[33]

Meanwhile, Ivor chased girls. There was a woman he met while debating at Oxford whom he took to dinner and the theatre. Her elfin face and
hair of deep red mahogany kept him 'desperately awake at night'. Alas, she
did not think of him 'in that way', and married a Unitarian minister. In
Cambridge he frequented a salon run by the remarkable Lella Secor, an
American journalist, anti-war campaigner and birth control activist, who
had married Philip Sargant Florence, an economics don who became president of the Heretics in 1924. 'Dear Lella!' exults Ivor. Her salon 'attracted
young people of both sexes by her political glamour and held them by
her effervescence and charm.' Here he met several young women whom
he found attractive, but his, in retrospect, clumsy mode of courtship precluded the development of any close attachment. 'I think now,' he was later

to write, 'that the reason for my lack of success in romance at this time was the fact that I had no social graces whatever.'[34]

While somewhat bored with the proceedings of the Biological Tea Club on the afternoon of 22 March 1924, Ivor found himself jotting down a poem, stimulated by the memory of seeing a fire-bellied toad in Kupjak, Croatia, the previous June. As subsequently amended later in the day, the verse read:

Trees without memory
ascending like a scene
on floor packed with
ochre leaves ~~round green~~ merging moss

Standing large footed in
shallow fawn mud spreading
I pierce serene
surface opaque to frog

Reflecting on it, Ivor determined that psychoanalysis was in order. 'The phallicism of the ascending tree should be noted,' he wrote. 'Ochre connected with colour of character of loved object. Scene, floor, packed, refer to another loved object (one only desired erotically even consciously); round green probably refers also to her, noting the colour of her made up eyes … serene surface probably refers to a belief in the loved object's virginity, opaque to frog a desire (unconscious) for conviction that she was not inevitably attached to her fiancé …'. Sex was on his mind.[35]

Poetry writing was one activity Montagu would not pursue further.

He fell in love, 'head over heels'. She was from Newnham, the women's college. 'Among the intellectuals and would-be intellectuals of the day, in numerous coteries of art and science,' she exerted a 'bewitching and all-conquering attraction'. Like the woman from Oxford, his new inamorata accepted him as a companion but no more. Still, Ivor 'stuck like a burr' and tried desperately to woo her. Boasting of his swimming prowess, he accepted her dare to dive off the Poole Harbour ferry in Dorset, and had to be rescued. Another time, clambering round cliffs on the North Devon coast, he became paralysed by fear, which he overcame only after her repeated entreaties. Fortunately they saw the funny side. The unrequited love was to yield one bitter-sweet moment on his last evening at Cambridge, the summer night 'languid and refreshing', punting on the Cam with the lady, two dear male friends, and several bottles of wine. With one of the friends, Bancroft Clark, he then headed off for the plains of Hungary.[36]

On return from the zoological mission, Ivor began to write up the results, and resumed his London divertissements. He joined the South Kensington branch of the Labour Party. He remained active in the Fabian Society. He had also been elected a member of the 1917 Club, whose object was 'to provide a meeting place for the interchange of opinion and information relating to Democracy and Internationalism.' Its president was none other than the Prime Minister himself, J. Ramsay MacDonald. Here he played table tennis, against Kingsley Martin, whom he knew from Magdalene College, and Francis Meynell, the poet (and Comintern smuggler); other members included Maurice Dobb and Desmond Bernal. To prepare for his longed-for trip to the Soviet Union, which could not be undertaken, because of his father's opposition, until he turned 21, he enrolled in evening classes in Russian at the Marylebone Institute; the instructor was 'a little old émigré lady who used Berlitz methods'.[37]

Questions of a future career were pressing. The allowance from his father was about to expire. But meantime there was just enough left in the kitty to go travelling again. Since he was thinking of perhaps making a living from translation, Montagu headed off to the Continent in November 1924, rucksack on his back, to track down two playwrights. In Paris, he found Fernand Crommelynck, and secured from him an option on *Le Cocu magnifique*. Ernst Toller, who had recently been released from prison after serving five years for revolutionary political activity, was more elusive. The trail led from Lugano in Switzerland, to Vienna, and eventually to Berlin. Tracked down, Toller received Montagu warmly, and they talked far into the night. English-language options on his plays were already committed, but the two became friends and the way was left open for future business collaboration.[38]

It was a good trip, overall. Ivor saw the Fratellini at the Cirque d'Hiver in Paris, Goldoni's *The Servant of Two Masters* in Vienna, and Shaw's *Der heilige Johanna*, directed by Max Reinhardt and starring Elisabeth Bergner, in Berlin. (He made the acquaintance of Bergner and was 'totally bowled over' by her.) In Swiss TB sanatoria he visited his teenage cousin David Guest

– Leslie Haden Guest's son – and his Cambridge acquaintance Alexander Tudor Hart, feared to be near death. He went walking in the mountains, wrote his translation of *Le Cocu* in the Austrian village of Sonntagsberg (his French having no doubt improved since his days in Mr Gibbs's prep school), created a minor disturbance by sleeping overnight in what was – unbeknownst to him – a brothel in Vienna, turned down a sexual proposition from a woman about to be married in Prague, and got back to Townhill just in time for Christmas.[39]

What for the new year? Montagu was intent on pursuing zoology as his profession, but jobs only came up sporadically, and to pursue research he needed funding. His father was amenable, but wanted proof of Ivor's capacity by his being awarded a grant. Ivor was informed, however, that he was highly unlikely to receive a research grant because, as was well-known, his family were well-endowed. 'Impasse. Dead end.'[40]

The alternative was for his father to continue paying Ivor an allowance while he explored other options. Lord Swaythling was reluctant. He wanted to know what his son would be doing before he parted with his money. Ivor was stubborn. 'I on the contrary considered that he owed me at any rate *some* moral obligation – magnitude subject to argument – in that the upbringing for which he had been responsible had accustomed me to a certain kind of life that it would be tyranny arbitrarily to end.' Ivor wanted certainty, 'a frank relationship untinged with self-suspicion of sycophancy'. He demanded to know where he stood. Lord Swaythling, on the other hand, felt, as Ivor was later to acknowledge, that to accede to his son's demand 'would have seemed to him abandonment of the responsibility that love bade him retain.' And since he was a man who 'would declare right and wrong so rigidly as to brook no discussion,' there matters stood.[41]

Lady Swaythling intervened. At her urging his father consented to continue the allowance he had been paying for one more year. 'If he by the financial year's end approved of what I was then doing, he might continue it. If not, not.' For Ivor the crisis was 'shelved only, not resolved.' But at least he would continue to receive an unearned income of £500, twice the average wage. He could look ahead to 1925, the year in which he would reach his majority, with some degree of confidence.[42]

3

FILM CULTURE

IVOR DECIDED TO try film journalism. He had met Canadian-born Beverley Baxter, editor of the *Daily Express*, when the protégé of magnate Lord Beaverbrook came and stayed for a weekend at Townhill. In London, Baxter received him and gave him tips on the newspaper business. But film reviewing was no job for a young man, Baxter decreed. Critics were recruited from the ranks of reporters too old to go chasing news stories. 'You need something more active,' he told the flummoxed Montagu.[1]

Lord and Lady Swaythling invited John Walter, proprietor of *The Times*, to dinner. This procured an interview for their son, as a result of which he was offered a tasty proposition. For £25 advanced in expenses, he would go to Berlin and write a report on the German film industry. Ivor accepted, hooked up with his Cambridge pal Angus MacPhail, and set off. (Ivor booked third class on the train, but Angus preferred first, and offered to pay Ivor's supplement if he would play chess with him for half a crown a game all the way to Berlin. 'I am ashamed to say,' Ivor says, 'I lost on the deal.') It was probably late January 1925.[2]

Ivor had prepared well, and had introductions. The most valuable was to the foreign editor of the German film trade paper, the *Lichtbildbuehne*. Heinrich Fraenkel was 'a small pleasant man, with nutcracker face' who spoke perfect English as a result of being isolated in Britain as a teenager during the war. Fraenkel 'could give introductions to everyone in Berlin.' Hence he and Angus met, says Montagu in his sweeping fashion, 'all the stars, all the directors', though he singles out only Emil Jannings. Jannings had recently starred in Paul Czinner's *Nju – Eine unverstandene Frau/Husbands or Lovers*, a triangle drama, which they saw and which 'struck us as a revelation of the possibilities of commenting profoundly on human relationships by cinema.' They saw films 'medieval, rococo, contemporary, expressionist and futurist'; they saw, too, the sets at Ufa, the major German studio – houses 'so stupidly solid and naturalistically (but totally unnecessarily) real that they must have cost as much or more than if they had been built to live in.'[3]

The journalistic mission was a failure. Montagu returned Walter's advance, regretting that he felt unable to write anything on German cinema – 'I had now learnt enough to know I did not know enough.' Blaming his overcaution on his scientific education, Ivor concluded that he was not 'properly cut out for journalism'. Yet in another respect the trip had a fruitful outcome.[4]

On the train home, Montagu got talking to Hugh Miller, a handsome 35-year-old actor who was returning to England after working alongside Olga Chekhova on the Anglo-German co-production *The City of Temptation/Die Stadt der Versuchung*. They bemoaned the state of film culture in Britain compared with that of Germany, 'lamenting the unadventurousness of the British cinema, the fact that a combination of boorish censor, American film domination and a timid film industry had effectively put a stranglehold on all experimentation.' Theatre had its Stage Society, which mounted for its subscription audience the exciting and challenging new works of Shaw, Ibsen, Strindberg, Pirandello, Gorky, Cocteau. Why could not London have a Film Society?[5]

The idea was not new. Miller is reported to have discussed such an initiative with the drama critic Alexander Bakshy as far back as before the war. The Stoll Picture Theatre Club had assembled intellectuals to discuss film in 1919, and young director Adrian Brunel had tried to get a Cinemagoers' League off the ground in 1920. Very recently, in November and December 1924, film critic Walter Mycroft had proposed in his column in the *Evening Standard* a film society that could screen pictures that were commercially unavailable (he was particularly frustrated by the inability of London audiences to see Murnau's *Phantom*).[6]

And France had proved it could be done. Ciné-clubs, founded by cinéastes like Ricciotto Canudo, Louis Delluc, Germaine Dulac and Léon Moussinac, were flourishing, while the Théâtre du Vieux Colombier in Paris (which Montagu was familiar with) had been converted in 1924 by

Jean Tedesco into a specialist cinema for film as art. In England the time was ripe, and Montagu, still not 21, was the man with the time, energy, connections and chutzpah to make it happen.[7]

The first thing was to recruit allies. Adrian Brunel, a filmmaker with artistic aspirations and a friend of Miller's, was an obvious choice. The conspirators collared him in the dress-circle of the London Pavilion, at the premiere of Ernst Lubitsch's *Forbidden Paradise* (10 February 1925). Brunel recounts that 'my friend, Hugh Miller, approached me with a tall and dark stranger who smiled at me friendlily and waved his hand in greeting.' Brunel had at this time a number of shorts and two features – *The Man Without Desire* with Ivor Novello and *Lovers in Araby* with Miles Mander – to his credit. His heartfelt endorsement of the project was secured. Meanwhile, in Berlin, Fraenkel received news of the venture with enthusiasm, telling Ivor: 'I am sure you will get all the German pictures you want for your purpose and under the conditions outlined in your letter.'[8]

Next in line was the film critic Iris Barry, then of the *Spectator* and *Vogue*. In her columns she had championed film as an art form worthy of serious critical attention and celebrated avant-garde innovation as an avenue for cinema to develop. Ivor attributes Barry's enlistment to Miller, but she herself credits Montagu:

> It began with a telephone call from an unknown person – a man who said that his name was Ivor Montagu, that he had been lunching with Hugh Miller the actor and they both wanted to come and talk to me ... About something to do with the cinema. And as the cinema was one of the things that interested me most at the time, to a degree which most of my friends regarded as eccentricity or mania, I said that they had both better come round at once and have tea with me so that we could talk.

After the men had outlined the scheme, 'My agreement was immediate and enthusiastic and we got out pencils and paper at once to sketch a programme of action.'[9]

Walter Mycroft certainly had to be included, especially because Montagu had liked his review of Arthur Robison's boldly expressionist *Schatten – eine nächtliche Halluzination/Warning Shadows*, shown in London the previous November. 'Tiny and hunchbacked,' according to Montagu, he 'was invaluable because he knew the minds and ways of his fellow film critics, and what had to be done to get newspaper space.' Mycroft was happy to lend his support. 'When I first met Ivor Montagu all but twenty years ago,' he recalls in his memoirs, 'he was slim, arresting and a wholly captivating young man just down from Cambridge, who looked like a youthful Trotsky, which resemblance I think he liked to encourage.' Mycroft embraced the film society idea because it gelled with his own conception of cinema:

> There was already an avant-garde which believed in the film of the future and was interested in certain, but few, films of the present, because they pointed the way to that future. These films were non-commercial and were, in fact, despised by the 'trade' as it did not mind calling itself. They were the kind of films I had been writing about for years.

If all went to plan, it would become possible to 'track down all such films, secure them and ensure for them an audience that wanted to see them.'[10]

To advance the cause Iris Barry threw a party at her house in Guilford Street, as she liked to do. (Montagu describes her as 'dark, slender, capable and calm with extremely well-shaped features and a crop as tight as Beatrice Lillie's or a Dutch doll's.') She invited Montagu and Miller, Brunel and Mycroft – and two others who were successfully swept up into the project, her friend Sidney Bernstein, a film exhibitor, and the sculptor Frank Dobson, whom Bernstein apparently brought along. 'It was a stroke of luck that Sidney's imagination was struck that night,' Montagu wrote. 'He was the only one of us on the real inside of films, as well as, probably, the only person in the industry of those days who shared our enthusiasm for "the arts".' Bernstein was, according to Ivor, a 'slim, tall, elegant handsome creature, with humorous eyes and a boxer's nose, liberal and enterprising in his ideas, catholic, comfortable and choosy in his surroundings, generous and loyal to friends and family, an unpredictable and nerve-wracking adventure to work for or – I should guess – to live with'. His participation in the film society undertaking was crucial because he had clout with the big industry players. Discussions went on late that night; Bernstein and Montagu left together in the early hours of the morning, in the pouring rain.[11]

On 23 April, Ivor celebrated his 21st birthday. And then, since he was now at liberty to travel to the Soviet Union and planned to depart very soon, the conspirators decided it was time for a launch. Ivor knew just the person to call on for this ceremonial purpose – his mother. She agreed to host a luncheon. Ivor drafted the invitation: 'My mother Lady Swaythling will be very pleased if you will come to lunch here at 1 o'c on Wednesday next the 6th [May]. This lunch is to inaugurate the Film Society ...'[12]

The chosen guests were heavily representative of the media, and after being regaled, no doubt, with a fine sample of Kensington Court hospitality, they were ushered into the library for a press conference. Here Ivor and Iris Barry proclaimed the aims of the Film Society, which were expressed as follows in a promotional leaflet issued around this time:

> The Film Society has been founded in the belief that there are in this country a large number of people who regard the cinema with the liveliest interest, and who would welcome an opportunity seldom afforded the general public of witnessing films of intrinsic merit, whether new or old.

> At the moment, although it is possible in the course of a year, for a member of the ordinary cinema-going public to see such remarkable films as: *Warning Shadows*, *Greed*, *The Last Laugh* and *The Marriage Circle*, at long intervals and often after considerable difficulty in discovering where and when they may be found, it is not possible for such a person to go during any week in the year into any picture house in England and be sure of finding one of abiding merit.

> The Film Society proposes to remedy this condition by showing films which reach a certain aesthetic standard, to a limited membership on Sundays, in the same way that plays are shown by the Phoenix and Stage Societies. A certain number of these films are made every year, and as they appeal to a minority, they are frequently denied to those who would most enjoy them; on the rare occasions when they have been publicly exhibited, they have been carelessly cut and edited as in the case of *Caligari*, and so titled as to be incoherent. It is the intention of the Society to provide a programme of the most lively and varied interest with an appropriate and well-played musical setting.

It is felt to be of the utmost importance that films of the type proposed should be available to the Press, and to the Film trade itself, including present and (what is far more important) future British film-producers, editors, cameramen, titling experts and actors. For, although such intelligent films as *Nju* or *The Last Laugh* may not be what is desired by the greatest number of people, yet there can be no question but that they embody certain improvements in technique that are as essential to commercial as they are to experimental cinematography.[13]

Montagu and Barry announced that the society would begin its activities in October, and confidently predicted that the performances would be 'unhampered by the censor'. One of Ivor's ambitions confided to the journalists was to show Erich von Stroheim's celebrated *Greed* in its original, uncut version. 'This took eight hours when it was first shown in America. In England they cut it to two hours. If necessary we will give it in two instalments of four hours each, and perhaps serve dinner or tea in the interval.'[14]

Press reaction was generally favourable, though the trade papers were cautious. Montagu later commented that 'they seemed to regard our exploration of any other criterion of film judgement than box-office as an intrusion not only dangerous to their readers' interests but even immoral.' Of the mainstream film reviewers, Caroline A. Lejeune of the *Manchester Guardian* proved a disappointment. She had written to Ivor saying, 'I'm ready to be most enthusiastic over any scheme that will start a Vieux Colombier, or anything like it, in London. I should be glad to do what I could to help at any time, both on paper and with any suggestions that might be of use.' And she had accepted Lady Swaythling's invitation to lunch. But when the Film Society plan was revealed, she felt it smacked of exclusivity: 'The doors will be shut against all but the fully subscribed.' According to Ivor, she called the promoters 'bloated plutocrats', and proclaimed 'with red-hot obstinacy that nothing could be of any use that was not open to the public.' He conceded that 'in a sense she was not wrong' – but a subscription society was necessary at this stage, in his view, to pave the way for the arthouse cinemas to come.[15]

It was determined that there would be a Council, comprising Montagu, Brunel, Miller, Barry, Bernstein, Dobson and Mycroft, with Montagu as chairman. As secretary, they appointed the highly efficient Miss J.M. (Josephine) Harvey, who ran a concert agency, and her office at

56 Manchester Street, Marylebone, became the Society's address. But it
was necessary to canvass support further afield. Ivor was advised that the
legal structure for the society would need to be a not-for-profit limited
liability company. Shareholders in the company, at £1 a share, would act
as 'guarantors' – and could hopefully provide a veneer of respectability to
what could otherwise seem (in its quest to avoid censorship, for example) a somewhat dodgy undertaking. By the time of the press conference,
a number of high-profile backers had already been procured, including
Ivor's acquaintances George Bernard Shaw and Roger Fry, and biologist Julian Huxley. As Ivor left for the first of his two jaunts to the Soviet
Union that year (to be recounted in Chapter 4), the quest went on; and in
the end an impressive array of names adorned the Society's roster of shareholders. Among others there were Lord Ashfield ('a most useful name as
at that time he ran the Underground'), Lord Swaythling, Ivor's father,
who brought Ashfield in, and Lord David Cecil, the historian. There were
the renowned actress Dame Ellen Terry and her daughter Edith Craig,
theatre director; the painters Clare Atwood and Augustus John; Professor
(of English) Jack Isaacs, and J. St Loe Strachey of the *Spectator*; the actor
Ben Webster; John Maynard Keynes and J.B.S. Haldane from Cambridge;
Heinrich Fraenkel, who lent his support from afar; Angus MacPhail and
Anthony Asquith, setting their sights on a film industry career; George
Co-oper, screenwriter and director; Edward McKnight Kauffer, graphic
artist, whom Ivor induced to design the Society's logo; and George A.
Atkinson, film critic of the *Daily Express*. And there was H.G. Wells,
whom Iris Barry chased up, as Ivor was in Russia and he had 'charmingly
promised' to be a member; Wells did not demur, but 'wanted the draft of
our articles altered where we had him down as "writer"; he said he should
be listed as "man of letters".'[16]

Much of the donkey-work, after Ivor's departure, fell to Iris Barry. Her
connections as a film journalist both at home and abroad were invaluable,
but persistence was required. In a somewhat despairing letter to Montagu
written probably towards the end of May, she confesses:

> I shudder at the idea of meeting you again, for you are bound to be dis-
> mayed at the very small progress that seems to have been made. I can only
> swear I have done everything possible – have written letters till my arm

ached, telephoned until I dread next quarter's bill & called on people (to little purpose) as assiduously as a dun.

People had not responded, no films had yet arrived, she had not been to Paris as planned because she had no money, and Miss Harvey was being expected to provide for 'notepaper printing postage telephones & her own salary' out of the £5 Bernstein had advanced. Still – 'I'm sure you will soothe me nicely when you come & make me feel all is well & that I've not really got anything to grumble about. Please try!' No doubt Ivor did, since Iris remained an energetic and enthusiastic supporter of the cause.[17]

Doing the legal work was Walter D'Arcy Hart, Ivor's cousin and the family solicitor. It was under his guidance that the articles of association for the society itself and for its parent company were drawn up. Hart's reply to a letter Ivor sent him in connection with the costs for this work hints at something of the conflicts the young socialist aristocrat must have been experiencing at this time. Hart wrote:

When I sent you the two bills I asked you to pay the disbursements and invited you to pay such of the costs as you thought fit. I do not think you could have expected more. All that you had to do was to accept my invitation and name the figure, and I am sorry that you have thought it desirable to make entirely unnecessary and inaccurate remarks. Perhaps, however, you were only trying to be humourous [sic]. We are quite ready to accept £50 in settlement, but I should like you to realise that this sum is considerably less than what the work involved has actually cost my firm, without allowing for any payment for my services. Yours ever, Walter Hart. P.S. I reciprocate your love and kisses and that sort of thing.

It can be conjectured that Ivor's letter, in gauchely trying to make a joke of the affair, betrayed his sense of bad faith in accepting favours from the family law firm.[18]

The Film Society needed a venue. Veteran director George Pearson recollected that Miller, whom he knew as an actor in his film *Reveille*, introduced him to Montagu in the Islington Studio canteen. 'I was instantly impressed by Montagu's strong personality,' Pearson says. 'He was thick set and sturdy; a tousled head of black hair fell over deep-set eyes that held me as I listened.'

Ivor explained the Film Society project; he wanted advice on finding a large, centrally located cinema that would be amenable to periodic private shows. Pearson was strongly supportive but unable to help. Fortunately, one of the Society's shareholders stepped in. Lord Ashfield was able to secure the use, free of charge, of the comfortable, 1,400-seat New Gallery Kinema in Regent Street for Sunday afternoon screenings once a month.[19]

There were three classes of subscription to the Society: three guineas, two guineas and one guinea (£3.3.0, £2.2.0 and £1.1.0). Each entitled the member to one seat at eight performances, it having been determined that the Society would close down over the summer months. Perhaps vindicating Lejeune's reservations, the venture was clearly aimed at an affluent middle-class membership; even the cheapest rate was two to three times what ordinary cinemagoers would pay for eight film screenings. Publicity proved effective, and by the time of the first scheduled performance some 900 members had paid their dues.[20]

The subscription revenue was certainly required, since though the Society planned, for the most part, to borrow films without paying rental, and had acquired the New Gallery at no charge, Montagu's team 'meant to show the films in no hole and corner fashion.' They wanted, in this era of silent pictures, 'the best orchestra and the best music' – which meant scores being prepared and musicians hired. There were costs, too, for freight and customs duties, for entertainment tax, and for titling, since a foreign film needed to have translated intertitles shot and inserted (a function which Brunel's small editing company performed for a fee 'so ridiculously nominal it was daylight robbery of himself').[21]

The programmes for the first season were selected on the basis of all the intelligence the group could gather about adventurous and esoteric cinema internationally: films Montagu and Miller had seen or heard about in Germany, gossip acquired in their role as critics by Mycroft and Atkinson, reports of experimental work showcased at Le Vieux Colombier. Then expeditions to the Continent would be needed for negotiations and, sometimes, physical collection of prints. But it was not only features and avant-garde shorts that the young *cinéastes* were after: 'Our policy,' Montagu explains, 'was to concern ourselves not only with "art" but with every use of film that did not reach the commercial screen in Britain at that time.' Hence they acquired for screening old short films (to be shown in the 'Resurrection' series), scientific films (the 'Bionomics' series), short comedies (Brunel's burlesques were especially valued), technical films (particularly those showing developments in cinematography), animated films, and documentaries.[22]

Montagu was keen to counteract the impression that the Film Society would be catering to 'snobs' and 'intellectuals', simply providing erudite entertainment for an educated elite. Hence he emphasised his hope that the screenings would contribute to the technical advance of British cinematography, and at the beginning it was proposed that all cameramen attached to British studios be admitted free of charge. When *The Kinematograph Weekly* accused the Society of being 'highbrows', Ivor leapt to its defence. 'All that we urge is this,' he wrote. 'The factors that make a picture interesting and important in the development of the kinematograph (that is to say, ingenious technique of acting, of production, of lighting, of design, and so forth) are often quite independent of the factors that make for popular success. Now, it often happens that a picture important from this point of view is quite rightly, in most instances, judged unsuitable for public exhibition by the Trade, owing to its morbidity, or that obscurity which we agree in labelling highbrow, or some similar cause. It is obvious that we can be chiefly useful, both to the Trade and to the intelligent public interested in the kinema, by showing this sort of picture.' He concluded by expressing the hope that 'the Trade will begin to look on us and use us as a sort of research station for trying out the experimental and studying the past.'[23]

It was something of a forlorn hope. With the prominent exceptions of a few individuals such as Bernstein and Pearson, the Trade proved reluctant to respond to the Society's overtures. Antagonism to the venture from within the film industry was such that before long Brunel was forced to sever his ties, as his employers (Gainsborough Pictures) 'insisted that my association with the Society would damage the prestige of the films I made for them!'[24]

Two weeks before the scheduled opening performance there was a curious turn of events. Atkinson, having clearly changed his mind about the support he had offered the Society, published an article deriding it in the *Sunday Express*. 'The sponsors of this society,' he declared, 'are a number of earnest young men of the type that uses well-formed phrases to express half-formed ideas, and a number of equally earnest young women of the type that exchanges femininity for a political point of view.' He attacked the Society for selecting only Russian and German films (in fact, there were no Russian pictures on the play list, since none were to be had), and pontificated:

> The only essential difference between Russian and German art and art elsewhere is that the proportion of lunatics in Russian and German artistic circles is demonstrably much higher than in other countries, and I strongly recommend the Film Society to include in its critical forces a number of competent alienists able to detect mental aberration masquerading as aesthetic value.

But the most damaging claim followed. There was a 'rumour current in Filmland,' he asserted, 'that the Film Society is not wholly free from political bias of an obnoxious colour. The society's links to Moscow seem to be friendlier than is relevant for an organisation formed to establish "good taste" in Great Britain.'[25]

What ensued next is not entirely clear. In an inaccurate and highly coloured account of the incident in *The Youngest Son*, Montagu asserts that members of the Society Council issued a writ against the paper, but he, although 'the most seriously libelled', refused to join in (since he saw nothing wrong in sympathising with Soviet Communism). However, he intervened with Lord Beaverbrook, the proprietor of the *Sunday Express*, and negotiated a settlement including costs and a withdrawal. Whatever the truth of this may be – and the grounds for a libel action appear very slim – a retraction, was in, fact published two weeks after the initial column. Atkinson wrote:

> Our attention has been called, on behalf of Miss Iris Barry, Mr Sidney L. Bernstein and Mr Adrian Brunel, and the other members of the Film Society, to an article which appeared in our issue of the 11th October 1925 … We are happy to say at once that we had not the slightest intention of imputing any political motives or bias to the Society or to the members of the Committee, nor do we in any way suggest that they are in any way connected with the Bolshevist movement … We are pleased to express our apologies to the Society and its executive and regret if we have given any cause for offence.[26]

Then, at the last minute, another crisis. Montagu had wrongly assumed that just as the Stage Society, being a private club, could avert the censorious gaze of the Lord Chamberlain, so the Film Society could escape the purview of J. Brooke Wilkinson, pettifogging Secretary of the British Board of Film Censors. Not so: the Cinematograph Films Act of 1909, though it did not mention censorship, had been held to allow local authorities the power, for the protection of the public, to stipulate all the conditions under which films could and could not be screened. And generally speaking, local authorities required that screening venues under their jurisdiction only show films that were certificated by the BBFC, which was an industry body set up to smooth the way for commercial distributors and exhibitors; private societies were only exempt if they held their film shows in private houses. What is more, what was proposed would contravene an established ban on Sunday performances before 6.30 p.m. The Film Society was forced to make a desperate appeal to the London County Council, and it was successful, but only just. 'We pulled out every establishment stop we had,' Ivor admits. The Society received an emergency dispensation for their first show, and then, by a narrow majority vote, a censorship and Sunday screening waiver for the whole of the 1925–26 season.[27]

The way having been cleared, the first performance, on the afternoon of Sunday, 25 October 1925, was quite an occasion. 'A procession of Daimlers, Bentleys and Rolls' stopped outside the cinema. 'Half the snobs in London, intellectual and social, were at the opening,' Ivor relates. 'Iris, who had flung herself into the thick of the battle, more than held her own in a tall black super-poke hat and wide scarlet ribbon, like a witch.' The *beau monde* of Bohemia turned out, Brunel recalls. 'Chelseaites and Bloomsburians were in evidence – young men with beards and young women in homespun cloaks.' Mycroft concedes that 'certainly we were arty and odd, and ran to beards and floppy black hats and novel ties that were sometimes, but by no means always, flamboyantly non-old-school'; but Bernstein 'never wore anything but suits,' and it is doubtful if the habitually untidy (but clean-shaven) Montagu was ostentatiously attired.[28]

The crowd that afternoon were treated to a full two and a half hours of entertainment. Walter Ruttmann's 'absolute films' *Opus 2*, *Opus 3* and *Opus 4* – studies in abstract imagery in motion, never before seen in Britain – opened the show (with a drum accompaniment). Then came

How Broncho Billy Left Bear County (1912), inaugurating the Resurrection series, and the premiere of Brunel's new burlesque short, *Typical Budget* (a take-off of the newsreel *Topical Budget*). The feature presentation was Paul Leni's *Das Wachsfigurenkabinett/ Waxworks* (1924), an Expressionist horror-tinged fantasy starring the great actors of German silent film, Emil Jannings, Conrad Veidt and Werner Krauss. Montagu admitted in his programme notes that 'from the dramatic point of view, *Waxworks* is not exception-ally good,' but argued that the set design and composition were 'of great pictorial beauty', the stylised acting of the Wax Figures was of interest, and that the ending of the film, a dream of the Jack the Ripper character, was 'as brilliant and successful as anything that has been attempted in the cin-ematograph'. The performance was rounded out with a comedy, Chaplin's *Champion Charlie* (or *The Champion*, 1915).[29]

The remaining seven programmes in the first season followed this pattern. Features from Germany were strongly favoured: the Film Society premiered Ludwig Berger's *Der verlorene Schuh/ Cinderella* (1923), Robert Wiene's *Raskolnikov* (1923), and Czinner's *Nju* (1924), as well as showcasing Wiene's *Das Cabinet des Dr Caligari/ The Cabinet of Dr Caligari* (1920) in unmuti-lated format. From France came Marcel L'Herbier's *Feu Mathias Pascal/ The Late Matthew Pascal* (1926), from the United States, as a revival, Ernst Lubitsch's *The Marriage Circle* (1924), and from Japan – the first Japanese fea-ture to screen in England – Minoru Murata's *Machi no Tejinashi/ The Street Juggler* (1925). The impressive range of avant-garde shorts included Henri Chomette's *À quoi rêvent les jeunes films*, René Clair's *Entr'acte*, and *Ballet mécanique* by Fernand Léger and Dudley Murphy, while there were scien-tific documentaries on the Dysticus beetle, the circulation of the blood, and X-ray cinematography. Amongst other offerings were a D.W. Griffith short (*The Sheriff's Baby*, 1913), a Mack Sennett slapstick comedy (*The Fatal Mallet*, 1914, with Chaplin), and another of Brunel's burlesques (*So This is Jollygood*). The eighth and last performance of the season was on 30 May 1926.[30]

'There were fights and quarrels a-plenty,' Montagu related, and a 'riot' erupted over *Entr'acte* – or possibly *Ballet mécanique*. 'Strange what pas-sions can be roused, far more savage than politics, by the pros and cons of challenges to logic. We had just thought the picture delightful, a witty cod. But cries and catcalls rang out, pundits within the audience came within an ace of punching each other.' Frank Dobson was sitting near the Bloomsbury art critic Clive Bell, 'whose excitement was fever pitch in defence of what he regarded as an unjustly denigrated opus of genius.' On the same programme as *Entr'acte*, the scientific short *Dysticus* also aroused the audience. When close-ups of the exceptionally voracious water beetle attacking tadpoles and a fully-grown newt were projected, there was 'violent hissing' – 'How horrible the passionate implacable fury of the cannibalistic struggle followed by the surrender and stricken resignation to the fate of the loser,' Mycroft observed. 'The Film Society audience, morbidly interested though it was in the inner mechanism, could not stomach this.'[31]

Keeping up the supply of films necessitated ongoing trips abroad for Ivor and his associates. He negotiated with Elisabeth Bergner in Berlin for *Nju*, and with the Count Étienne de Beaumont in Paris for *À quoi rêvent les jeunes films* ('he had to be approached directly in a huge and elegant Paris mansion standing in its own grounds, via an introduction from a Marquise friend of my mother's whose mansion was even bigger and slightly decayed'). Montagu also negotiated in Paris for Charles Delacommune to present his experimental abstract short *The Valse Mephistophilis of Liszt* with his patented synchronising apparatus (shown at the fourth performance in January 1926). On one expedition he was accompanied by Mycroft. They slept on wooden seats in the French train ('Ivor's principles … involved travelling third class'), and shared a room in a cheap hotel that had a bath, 'not attached to it, but in it … it stood in the middle of the floor at the bottom of the bed, gaunt and grim with all its shuddering pipes exposed like entrails.' On the way home they struck a gale in the English Channel and were violently ill.[32]

It was on one of his Paris jaunts that Ivor encountered, in a boulevard dance hall, 'a young girl, brunette, dark-eyed, round-faced'. He found her attractive, and took her, no doubt a little clumsily, on to the dance floor. On his return to London, friends asked why he hadn't slept with her: 'Are you a eunuch?' Finding no good answer he went back to Paris, and to his delight she accomplished his sexual initiation with professional finesse. They struck up a friendship, corresponded, and he saw her once again. Then, 'she wrote me that she had a young man soldiering in North Africa and sent me a photograph of herself and their son.' This young woman is very likely the Mado who wrote from Paris to '*mon cher petit* Ivor' on 11 May 1926, upset that he had not replied to her previous letter, asking that he send her what she had asked for – it will not be a present because she will reimburse him

– hoping that he will help her furnish her apartment for her '*petite famille*', desiring that the General Strike come to an end and England get back to normal, so that Ivor will be '*sans soucis*' as before, and begging him to write soon. Sending him her '*plus gros baisers*', Mado signed off as '*votre petite amie qui vous aime bien bien fort*'. The appeal was unavailing; the friendship lapsed. 'Altogether an adventure unoriginal, even banal,' Montagu concludes, 'but a step in life that autobiography should not omit.'[33]

In the meantime he had met Hell. Eileen Hellstern was a typist, the daughter of a skilled South London bootmaker who had died some years earlier. She was the same age as Ivor; at the time he met her, in autumn or winter 1925, she had a 3-year-old daughter, Rowna Ely, from an earlier relationship.[34]

Ivor was smitten. The woman he encountered at the Celtic Typewriting Bureau and who refused to lend him a pound from the petty cash was 'peaches and cream with a round, marshmallow beauty, deceptively soft but concealing an occasional and devastating frankness of speech and honesty of judgement'. Others, too, were impressed: Mycroft describes Hell as 'good-looking self-reliant efficient and decisively spoken'; to Brunel, she was 'magnificent and incomparable'. Little by little, Ivor and Hell began seeing more of each other, going about together, quarrelling, making up, separating again.[35]

By now Ivor had left Kensington Court and had settled into a small furnished flat at No. 19, Old Buildings, Lincoln's Inn. It was up 'an extremely narrow, winding staircase' and had poky, low-ceilinged rooms. There was a charlady, Mrs Henry, who 'did' for him, and cooked a little as well. Mrs Henry, 'thin, acidulous-looking, mournful, fond of drink, her softened complexion beset by lines of red and blue capillaries, with pointed nose' was 'exceedingly kind, industrious, patient with quirks, totally uninterfering, a faithful friend'. Here the aspiring *cinéaste* unsuccessfully courted young ladies and sallied out into the volatile, slowly stirring London of the mid 1920s.[36]

He kept up his theatre-going. Apart from the classics – Shakespeare at The Old Vic, Dryden at The Aldwych, Beaumont & Fletcher at The Scala, Marlowe at The New Oxford – there were the contemporaries: Arnold Bennett, Richard Hughes, Stark Young, Sean O'Casey. Ivor also attended ballet, and was particularly enamoured of music hall, in pursuit of which he and Hell made up a foursome with MacPhail and his partner Marjorie

Russell. For a year or more, Ivor recounts, they devotedly attended every engagement of their idols, the sisters Renee and Billie Houston, who had a surreal comedy act.[37]

The diminutive Elsa Lanchester, actress and singer, was also a favourite. Known for her Victorian music-hall laments such as 'The Ratcatcher's Daughter' and bawdy Cockney ballads, Lanchester was on the bill of the variety show Ivor attended at the Royal Court Theatre in January 1925. He was also enrolled for the Select Evenings that she and her partner Harold Scott held on Sunday nights at their bohemian nightclub, the Cave of Harmony. Here works by the more experimental contemporary writers (Pirandello, Schnitzler, Strindberg, Synge) were performed, and the cultural intelligentsia (in evening dress or not, as they preferred) hobnobbed.[38]

Montagu fleetingly joined the theatre's creative coterie when, in its 1925/26 season, the Stage Society performed Crommelynck's saucy *Le Cocu magnifique* in his translation. (Hoping to achieve a seduction, Ivor read the play to the actress Gwen Ffrangcon-Davies, whom he thought suitable for the leading role, in his cosy Lincoln's Inn flat; alas, his guest departed 'with no contacts more intimate than the tips of the fingers'.) Directed by Theodore Komisarjevsky and with Peggy Ashcroft in the starring role of the devoted wife driven towards infidelity by her husband's pathological jealousy, it failed to create much of a stir. George Bernard Shaw read Ivor's text and pronounced it 'a remarkable job', but commented: 'The extravagance of the Cocu is a quality of the play – indeed it is its subject – but the conduct of the woman is a difficulty; the author has not succeeded in making it either natural or credible.' A failure to connect with English sensibilities, as well as anticipated difficulties with the Lord Chamberlain should public production be contemplated, probably account for this staging of Ivor's 'juvenile labour of love' going unremarked. To his disappointment, Montagu was unable to find a publisher for his translation before his option expired.[39]

To add another string to his bow, Montagu arranged with Ernst Toller, with whom he remained on friendly terms, to act as his English-language literary agent. A letter from the playwright penned while he was in London in December 1925 appointed Ivor 'to deal with all matters respecting my writings in English, either for publication or theatrical & other production. No agreement is valid unless confirmed by you for me, & you are entirely authorised to approve all arrangements on my behalf.' The agreement catapulted Montagu into an involved series of negotiations with Toller's German agents, theatrical agents in the UK and USA, translators, publishers, and theatres, without, one suspects, much financial reward.[40]

But he had also found a more reliable source of income. Buoyed by the success of the Film Society and defying Beverley Baxter's admonitions, he had persuaded the Sunday newspaper *The Observer* to take him on, in November 1925, as film reviewer. (His later claim that he was 'the first film critic *The Observer* ever had' is not strictly accurate; the paper's theatre critic, 'H.H.', had been writing film reviews as well on a fairly regular basis since September 1924.) 'Authorised to write weekly short notices that, it was agreed, should be paid for at space rates if printed or at a minimum if crowded out,' he embarked on a project that would absorb him for the next six months.[41]

Given a chance to address an audience of filmgoers outside the Film Society's cultured coterie, 'I.M.' came out swinging, launching a ferocious assault on the middle-brow pictures beloved (he no doubt imagined) of his middle-class readership. In his first column he assailed the Rudolph Valentino vehicle *The Eagle* (Clarence Brown, 1925):

> The picture has no merit of any kind whatsoever. A fast, exciting, if hackneyed story is made dull, slow, inconsequent, and every dramatic situation is bungled, set out without being led up to climactically ... Everyone's acting was preposterous. Mr Brown must have found directing Mr Valentino rather like directing a sack of potatoes.

Then, after Christmas, he let fly at the rereleased *Peter Pan* (Herbert Brenon, 1924). H.H. had liked it when it first came out: 'There is nothing in it to dismay, but everything to delight. Peter himself has crossed the Atlantic and returned to us without a trace of a twang and with his native charm enhanced.' Montagu's take on the Barrie adaptation was diametrically opposed. 'A lamentable picture,' he declared, 'this is everything that the film should not be. The technique is astonishingly bad for a modern America picture ... the photography is curiously flat throughout ... No one connected with the picture seems to feel the slightest sincere emotion. The actors have the air of performing a rite, a charade ...' (At the time of this review Ivor was advised by his editor that 'The Chief suggests that the notices should be as short, quick and bright as possible, and that we should be careful to judge the films rather from the point of view of the educated reader than of that of the expert: i.e., we must avoid technicalities and too professional a point of view.')[42]

Montagu's critical orientation was by no means a blanket preference for the European over the Hollywood product, as these reviews and Film Society programming might suggest; indeed, in his first column he counted himself among 'those of us who believe that American films are the finest in the world – that they possess a cinematic sense of pace and space that is in contrast with the often deliberateness of German and Swedish and the staginess of Russian films'. This was illustrated in the Douglas Fairbanks swashbuckler *The Black Pirate* (Albert Parker, 1926), over which Montagu enthused:

> Mr Fairbanks's imaginative breadth and courage has made something which, though in later years it may seem but a primitive beginning, can today arouse in us only clamorous admiration. Never has his pictorial imagination shown such audacity ... His whole picture is so compact, the story so exciting, the atmosphere so fixed and gripping.[43]

It was in grasping the dynamic quality of cinematic space that American directors were superior to the British, exemplified by Herbert Wilcox of *The Only Way*. In that film, Ivor wrote:

> All that happens, from beginning to near the end, appears stale and dead. Looking at it is like being surrounded by framed pictures on a boarding-house wall ... His picture is made up of a series of sets and groups, each one of which he seems to feel quite statically and separately, like a theatre scene between the rising and falling of the curtain.[44]

Anticipating by nearly thirty years the auteurist position of the French *Cahiers du cinéma* critics, I.M. championed his favourite directors – Chaplin, Wiene, Lubitsch, Von Stroheim – praised emerging talents such as Alfred Hitchcock ('he has made some of it [*The Pleasure Garden*] so interesting as to make one eager and optimistic for his future'), and stressed again and again the good director's ability to triumph over inferior material. The story of Lubitsch's *Kiss Me Again*, for example, was 'hackneyed', but 'the way in which the whole is told is exquisite.' Cecil B. DeMille was an ultimate case in point: his films were 'hokum' – 'his pictures are always nonsense about people who do not exist, who would be in an asylum or a magazine if they did, and who, in any case, are a nuisance and uninteresting' – and yet DeMille was 'an amazing and interesting director with a feeling for the cinema in his finger tips' whose 'natural instinct for telling a story' and 'bewildering directing skill' resulted in his films, in this case *The Road to Yesterday*, being 'extremely exciting'. In a related aesthetic move, Montagu lambasted faithful cinematic adaptations of material from other media, regarding them as laborious (this was one of his complaints about *Peter Pan*), and praised filmmakers who created 'something quite new' out of what they were given to work with. Thus 'Mr Von Stroheim's *Merry Widow* is Stroheim, not Lehar or George Graves. This means that it is a delightful and vigorous film.'[45]

Montagu's immersion in film history and passionate commitment to the future of cinema were evident also in his acute comments on genre (especially comedy), on performance, on scripting and editing (he was frequently critical of lack of plausible motivation, poor pacing and lack of dramatic structuring), on production design, and on cinematography. He was always alert to audience response, and would admit to the guilty pleasure of enjoying a film that violated his aesthetic tenets: of *Partners Again* (Henry King, 1926), a lightweight comedy, he wrote: 'One feels a little ashamed at liking so thoroughly verbose a picture.'[46]

Thoroughly appreciative of the cinema as an artform generating collective emotion, Ivor was nonetheless uncomfortable with the 'physiological orgy' he anticipated King's *Stella Dallas* (1925) would provoke. He predicted:

> Two thousand sobs will be swallowed in two thousand throats. Two thousand noses will dip, snivelling, into a nearly equal number of pocket-handkerchiefs (tie-up with the great white sale next door). And, after the performance, the air will be heavy with the powdery evidence of recent facial repairs.

Montagu has since been rightly taken to task for this gendered response to a women's genre: quoting the passage, Laura Marcus observes that he 'deplored the sentimental response of the (female) audience.' Yet it is worth

noting that far from writing the picture off, as many male critics of melodrama were wont to do, Montagu praised *Stella Dallas* highly:

> The film is entirely true to itself, and, in its convention, makes no error
> of exaggeration, strikes no false note of character … Miss Belle Bennett
> sweeps in the grand manner into the portrayal of an engrossing and
> moving character. The internal coherence of the picture, which makes
> her performance possible, is to be attributed to the care and sincerity of
> the director … [47]

Seldom did ideology enter into Montagu's *Observer* critical practice, focused
as it was so strongly on style over content. And yet there is one tantalising
analysis, a strikingly proto-Brechtian discussion of Chaplin's *The Kid* (1921).
'The tragedy is impersonal,' I.M. writes, 'it lies in the helplessness of poor
people in the face of that undiscriminating benevolence or that Law against
which they can struggle but cannot appeal … And the tragedy is worked
to its climax without the pressure of a single wicked character … The two
seizures and separations of Mr Coogan from Mr Chaplin come not from
malice, but from the duties and positions of the protagonists engaged. It
is exactly the Marxist Interpretation of History: the method of Mr Shaw
in *Saint Joan*. The spectator feels a sort of Weltschmerz rather than an
individual sympathy.'[48]

On the few occasions when he did feel compelled to make overt political
judgement, Ivor ran into difficulties. The first crunch came with DeMille's
The Volga Boatman (1926), a cross-class romance set at the time of the
Russian Revolution. It was not that the picture was anti-Bolshevik; it was
simply that DeMille's version of the historical events was preposterous –
Ivor's corrected proof reads:

> First he re-wrote the Bible … Today he shows one way in which the
> Russian revolution might have happened if it had not happened the way
> it did. The result is something like the dream one can imagine a prosper-
> ous American business man with the mind of a child of two – an Elk or
> Kiwanis or something – to experience the night after paying one hun-
> dred dollars for a seat at the Chaliapin concert in the Metropolitan Opera
> House, New York.

But of course the film was by DeMille, whose directing skill Ivor so admired. 'His extraordinary showmanship and graphic clearness prevent this farrago of disagreeable nonsense from ever becoming wearisome …' The review never made it into print. 'The Editor has decided,' Ivor was told, 'that it will be better for *The Observer* to make no reference to the Volga Boatman Film, on account of its evidently undesirable qualities.'[49]

The second contretemps arose over the Great War film *The Big Parade* (King Vidor, 1925). After a complimentary review of standard length, Ivor proposed to append 'a word of politics'. This covered two matters. Firstly, he repudiated the campaign conducted by his fellow critics against the film on the grounds that it focused only on American troops in the war, 'And the sooner the film world realises that its dislike of this film is founded on the jealous knowledge that it is itself too tasteless, ignorant of its own craft to represent the British warrior … the more hopeful will be the outlook for British pictures.' Secondly, he rejected Shaw's view of *The Big Parade* as 'pacifist in effect'. On the contrary, Ivor argued that 'the film rouses the audience first to patriotic bellicosity, then to sheer bloodthirstiness, and it would have to be a very thorough tragedy at the end which would make that rousing salutary rather than pernicious.' *The Observer* printed the main review (at first even that was to be cut down), but could find no room for the political appendix, even after Ivor had personally pleaded his case. The writer took umbrage, despite his editor reasonably pointing out that 'There is no contributor to *The Observer* who does not submit cheerfully to the cutting of his copy. Copy is not cut, as they well realise, to slight the contributor, but to fit the page. No newspaper could go to press if it were not free to compress its matter.' Montagu, though, 'would not continue a job which the paper so determinedly regarded as insignificant.' He returned his press passes for the picture theatres.[50]

It was June 1926. He was out of work. But since his father had renewed his allowance at the beginning of the year, this was of no severe consequence. What was probably more on his mind, the General Strike having just been defeated, was politics.

4

THE PROLETARIAN CAUSE

BACK IN 1924, while still at Cambridge, Montagu's developing political ideas were being shaped in the context of a dispiriting Britain in which, as his fellow Spillikin Philip Spratt later observed, 'A million unemployed had already become a permanent thing. Baldwin looked like perpetuating stagnation for twenty years, and when MacDonald replaced him he did nothing to change the prospect. Ambitious young men were feeling stifled.' The consequence, Spratt maintained, was that 'complete ethical nihilism ... prevailed – in theory – among the more intellectually fashionable under-graduates. I accepted this doctrine for some time, as did all the communist intellectuals I knew.'[1]

In Montagu's case, 'nihilism' could perhaps be more accurately character-ised as a radical rejection, on moral grounds, of the values of his society, along with a flailing search for an acceptable alternative. The debating topic from his BSP years, revolutionary action versus parliamentary action, returned to absorb him. At the Swaythling dinner table, Ivor had plenty of opportunity to observe at close quarters, and talk to, the politicians who were his father's guests. He had no great respect for them. He found them ignorant, self-serv-ing, and without interest in the long-term amelioration of society:

They were indifferent to the question whether misery and exploitation might not be inherent in the current form of society; its moral aspects were equally irrelevant. Either they were totally sceptical about the pos-sibilities of social analysis, or clearly content with any solution that would 'last their time' – that is, preserve the structure of privilege for the length of their life span and active enjoyment.[2]

In exploring the revolutionary model for change, Montagu read Trotsky. He found the implacable *Communism and Terrorism*, written while the author was commanding the Red Army in the heat of the Civil War, to hold an unimpeachable logic. In answer to Karl Kautsky's rejection of revolutionary violence, Trotsky pours scorn on the notion of a peaceful, parliamentary road to socialism: it is 'one of the most puerile illusions possible'. It is folly to believe a ruling class will relinquish power without a brutal struggle: 'In vain would we … begin to seek in our time, anywhere in the world, a regime which, to preserve itself, did not have recourse to measures of stern mass repression.' Violence is necessary both to overthrow the bourgeoisie and then to secure the position of the proletariat in power: 'The man who repudiates terrorism in principle – i.e., repudiates measures of suppression and intimidation towards determined and armed counter-revolution, must reject all idea of the political supremacy of the working class and its revolutionary dictatorship.'[3]

Ivor was convinced. 'What a brilliant and sound and undeniable theory,' he declared, in his article 'Prophecies', to be found among his papers in the Labour History Archive. It is in the form of pages torn from an unidentified journal, and though undated, internal evidence points to publication in mid-1924. Here Montagu the self-proclaimed revolutionist makes a wordy and repetitious pronouncement that the world of 'occidental industrial civilisation' is coming to an end, and that it will 'reorganise itself in a manner in which its structure will be suited to the needs of the people living in it.' This will not be achieved 'one step at a time' by Mr MacDonald and his Labour government; moreover, it is clear that 'democracy is politically a tyranny differing, as far as political freedom is concerned, only from dictatorship in its untidiness and inefficiency.' To ensure that the birth of the new world order is no miscarriage, the undergraduate *enfant terrible* continues, 'we must be violently and inflexibly tyrannical and disciplined, as in Italy and Russia.' The Italian example is compromised by its over-reliance on an individual, but Russia enjoys 'a disciplined party inspired by political theory …'[4]

Ivor was thus favourably predisposed towards the dictatorship of the proletariat when he set out to see it at first hand. He prepared methodically, securing a visa for the USSR through the good offices of Mikhail Tomsky, the Soviet trade union head. Tomsky was also President of the Hunters' Union, and since Montagu would be hunting voles, this was entirely appropriate. Ivor forewarned Yarotsky, the other trade union official he had met in Cambridge, of his visit, and received the blessings of Peter Kapitza, whose mother and brother were in Leningrad – Kapitza wrote to them 'asking them to help you find rooms, and be helpful in every way possible'. These communications did not go unnoticed by the British Security Service (MI5), which at this time opened a file on the Honourable Ivor:

> Tomsky. (T.U.D.) / Safe. /P. 142 / 9.4.25 / Information was sent to S.I.S. that Ivor MONTAGU, born in 1904, was writing to Comrade Yarotski, of the Trade Delegation here, calling him 'Tovarish'. From the letter it would appear that MONTAGU had already asked Tomsky to get him a visa to enter Russia for which he apparently had applied a month before. If he could get a visa by the beginning of May it would suit him quite well.

The entry then adds mysteriously: 'It was believed that the proposed visit to Russia might be connected with Platinum.'[5]

He received friendly advice from an acquaintance, Princess Alexandra ('Sasha') Kropotkin, daughter of the famed anarchist Prince Peter Kropotkin. Born and raised in Britain, Sasha lived in Russia from 1915 until after her father's death in February 1921 and was now, in her late thirties, working as a reporter on the *Daily Express*. She did not share her father's anarchist views, being more of a moderate social democrat; after the February Revolution she had been close to the provisional government, and on friendly terms with Kerensky. (Kerensky offered Kropotkin a post in his government as Minister of Education, which he brusquely declined.) When attempting to return to England to raise humanitarian funds in 1918, Sasha was apparently arrested and briefly imprisoned by the Bolsheviks; she was nevertheless sympathetic towards certain aspects of the Soviet regime.[6]

'Dear Ivor,' she wrote, 'I hope this is alright addressing you thus, & it isn't necessarily kept for the garden & games only?' Entrusting him with a letter for Lunacharsky (Commissar of Education), who had given her a play to translate, she promised that her mother would put him in touch with theatrical people, hopefully including Stanislavsky, and wished him an interesting time. She then went on:

> I want you to remember that Russia has many conflicting traditions. That every Russian has the East in his heart & the West in his head. That the Russian people have been arrested in their development, & that the fact that Alexander II only carried out the liberation of the serfs by half – that is to say he gave them freedom & nowhere to be free, – is the fundamental reason why a) the revolution in Russia has been successful, & b) why it has taken and is taking the course it is. It is also why no government in Russia will be successful (materially & basically) which does not consist in the majority of peasants or their real representatives. I do not look forward to this phase of my country's development, but I know it to be inevitable. And it is better to meet it than to fight it. It is for this reason as much as for vaguer ethical reasons that the dictatorship of the Communist party is doomed to failure in the long run.
>
> Whether the glamour of the wordy idealism of those in power will dazzle you or not I do not know. Discrepancies between ideals & facts are always to be found. There is this in Russia, & there is also much dishonest love of power – as elsewhere. These things are deplorable but not the real root of that unsatisfactory state which even the most ardent Communists do not deny.
>
> … I trust that notwithstanding those profound disillusions, which if you think deeply & honestly enough, await you, you will come out of my country with this belief & with the desire, which you already have I believe, to assist in every way in your power, a people which deserves far more respect than is given us today.
>
> One word of advice – <u>never</u> express <u>any</u> opinion while you are in Russia.
>
> Bon voyage
>
> Sasha Kropotkin

In a postscript, she gave Ivor the address of the Kropotkin Museum (her father's birthplace in Moscow), and added: 'Please tell Mother that [I] have [been] advised by responsible Soviet people not to go to Moscow, as I will never get out again & as there are too many people anxious to be nasty to me there!'[7]

Ivor's father remained opposed to the trip and made a last-minute attempt to dissuade him. Treating his son to a juicy roast beef lunch at the bank, Lord Swaythling told his son that information from a network of informants in Russia led him to believe that 'as soon as I crossed the frontier, I should be seized and held to bring pressure on him to withdraw his signature to the recent "bankers" manifesto' in which he and others had joined to urge the British government not to extend any trading credits to USSR until the Tsarist debts were recognised. Besides, plague was widespread and a foreign visitor was certain to catch it.[8]

Ivor was undeterred. In mid-May 1925 he travelled on a Soviet steamship through the Kiel Canal to Leningrad, spending several weeks there and in Moscow. His object was to set in place arrangements for the expedition he would make with Bancroft Clark in the summer, tracking down the rare vole *Prometheomys* in the Caucasus mountains. In addition, he hoped to secure a supply of Soviet pictures for the Film Society. In the first aim he was successful; in the second he was to be frustrated.

Kapitza's mother and brother, an ethnologist, were his hosts in Leningrad. A retired teacher, 'a rubicund woman of infinite motherly energy' whose husband had been a Kadet Party member of the Duma and subsequently executed during the Civil War, Madame Kapitza surprised Montagu with her attitude towards the revolutionary regime. 'You do not understand,' she told him. 'Here there is something new being built by our people. It is for everybody and by everybody. How can one not take part?'[9]

In the former capital he did zoological study and made contacts at the Academy of Sciences, visited the Hermitage, and went to the theatre and cinema. Of the films he saw, he mentions only *Stepan Khalturin* (Alexander Ivanovsky, 1925), about the would-be assassin of Tsar Alexander II: a film he describes as 'remarkable for its bad lighting, rotten photography, poor continuity, and childish ideology', but which gripped the attention of the spectators at the workers' club where he watched it. One Sunday morning Montagu bemused a crowd of several hundred locals by insisting on swimming in the frigid, fast-flowing waters of the River Neva, dodging ice floes and seals.[10]

Moving on to Moscow, he stayed uncomfortably at the 'dingy and fantastically expensive' Savoy Hotel (where he was plagued by throaty female voices on the phone saying '*Ya vas lyublyu*' – 'I love you'), until rescued by Yarotsky, who put him up in his own two-room flat; Ivor slept on the floor. Yarotsky introduced him to 'interesting people'. There was the 'mighty-bearded' Solomon Lozovsky, a prominent Bolshevik revolutionary who was general secretary of the Red International of Labour Unions (RILU or Profintern) and who 'looked like a ginger Viking'. There was also Yakov Peters, 'a quizzical quiet man' encountered when out for a walk one day. Peters, a Latvian revolutionary, had lived some years in London and had belonged, like Ivor, to the British Socialist Party. After the October Revolution he was one of the founders of the Soviet state security police, the Cheka, and was heavily involved in implementing the Red Terror following the attempt on Lenin's life in August 1918. He had continued as a senior official of the Cheka's successor organisations, the GPU (1922–23) and OGPU (from 1923).[11]

Ivor continued to pursue his theatrical interests, though he does not mention if he caught up with Madame Kropotkin or had a chance to encounter Stanislavsky. The director Vsevelod Meyerhold, whom he was keen to meet, was out of town, so he had to make do with seeing photographs of his famed 1922 constructivist production of *Le Cocu magnifique* and attending a performance of Nikolai Erdman's *The Mandate* at the Meyerhold Theatre. He was successful in following up an introduction to the other renowned theatre experimentalist, Alexander Tairov. At the Bolshoi he saw productions of Aristophanes' *Lysistrata* ('superb'), the operas *La Périchole*, *Prince Igor* (boring except for the Polovtsian dances) and *Boris Godunov*, at which he was 'struck all of a heap and overwhelmed by the opulence and magnificence', and the ballets *Petrushka*, *Les Sylphides*, and *Don Quixote*.[12]

As an eager cultural tourist, Montagu viewed canvases by Matisse and Picasso at the Shchukin Museum, and by the Russians Valentin Serov and Ilya Repin at the Tretyakov Gallery. He saw over the Kremlin, and joined the queue to gaze on the waxen features of Lenin, his beard unexpectedly red, laid out in his temporary wooden mausoleum in Red Square ('a moving experience'). Yarotsky took him to observe a law court in action, and to a conference of the Art Workers' Union at the Bolshoi, followed by a gala performance featuring brachydactyl dwarf tumblers from England. And he had time to play tennis (in bedroom slippers) on the hard clay courts of the British Embassy. (He had a letter of introduction from Foreign Secretary Austen Chamberlain, and was entertained to lunch by the Chargé d'Affaires, Robert Hodgson, with whom he raised the vexed question of the twenty-six Baku Commissars.)[13]

There remained his filmic mission. Ivor was prepared, on behalf of the Film Society, to 'bear the entire expense of import, duty, preparation of English titles, presentation in the West End at a single performance' of selected Soviet pictures that had not found a commercial distributor. This would serve as both cultural and business promotion. He outlined the idea to Yarotsky, who sent him, with a letter, to Proletkino, the trade union sponsored studio that made films principally to supply workers' clubs. Proletkino liked Montagu's scheme but explained that only Sovkino, the body charged with administering the film industry in the USSR, had the right of export of Soviet productions. So he was sent along to Sovkino, again with an introductory letter.[14]

Muscling his way on the overcrowded trams, Montagu made his way to the studio. Armed, additionally, with a recommendation from Tomsky, he was able to go right to the top. Konstantin Shvedchikov, who had once hidden Lenin in his home before the Revolution, was the Party functionary who headed Sovkino. Ivor was kept waiting. Finally, struggling to make himself understood through an interpreter who knew no English or French and 'spoke rather less German than I do', he put his case to this 'ancient warrior with shaggy grey hair, abundant grey moustache and sidewhiskers and shaggy pointed beard' – in vain. The complicated non-commercial position the Film Society would be in, with its hoped-for avoidance of censorship, was 'quite untranslatable into terms credible to Soviet understanding. Shvedchikov was polite enough, but a brick wall. "We are here only to buy or sell," was his refrain.' Montagu complained to Yarotsky, who referred him to Comrade Meshcheryakov of Narkompros, the People's Commissariat for Education. Ivor followed this up, but his overtures again came to naught.[15]

Rebuffed, Ivor returned to Leningrad, where his spirits were raised by a delightful acquisition: a bear cub named Masha. Masha accompanied him on his voyage home on the steamer, sharing his cabin (disconcertingly climbing onto the top bunk with him) or howling when confined to her cage on deck. When the ferocious weather permitted it, passengers spoiled Masha with biscuits and milk; exasperated with her noise, crew members (Ivor later discovered) kept her quiet with brandy. At the London docks, zoo staff took her in for quarantine.[16]

A live cub was not the only zoological item Ivor brought back from Russia. On 23 June Peter Kapitza wrote to him from Cambridge, thanking him for being so kind 'as to bring me the bear skin and all the rest'. Finding Iris Barry and Sidney Bernstein had been ably advancing the cause of the Film Society in his absence, Ivor turned his attention to his forthcoming return to the Soviet Union and the British Museum scientific expedition, for which the arrangements were now in place.[17]

Here a sliver of evidence suggests that there was more to his travel to the socialist fatherland than films and voles. In early July, shortly before his departure, Montagu received a somewhat guarded communication from Maurice Dobb:

> My dear Ivor,
>
> Herewith Millar's letter. Millar says that he knows Y., so you might mention that to Y. & tell him to communicate direct to Millar about anything further that may arise out of the matter. Craik may try to make out that he is the victim of victimisation by the 'right', so you can tell Y. privately the true facts, and tell him the letter is being sent with the knowledge of the Party here.

This intriguing snippet evidently refers to a dispute within the working-class education organisations affiliated to the Plebs League, comprising the residential Central Labour College in London and the non-residential labour colleges around the country, whose co-ordinating body was the National Council of Labour Colleges (NCLC). J.P.M. Millar, a former student of the Central College, was the energetic General Secretary of the NCLC, whereas William W. Craik, translator of the Marxist theorist Joseph Dietzgen and author of *Outlines of the History of the Modern British Working-Class Movement* (1917), was until February 1925 Principal of the Central College; Dobb was a member of the Plebs League Executive. Millar was resistant to CPGB influence over the Labour College movement, fearing that it would imperil financial support from the unions, but the fact of the matter in this case was that Craik had been dismissed for embezzling College funds. Dobb's letter carries the clear implication that Craik had appealed to Yarotsky for support, but that the CPGB was supporting Millar – and that Montagu was a trusted Party courier in the affair.[18]

He went this time by train, accompanied by Bancroft Clark and two hunting dogs – the Hunters' Union was keen to obtain male setters from Britain for breeding purposes. Heinrich Fraenkel arranged to meet them en route in Berlin, appropriately enough at the Zoologischen Garten station. The trip was uneventful apart from a stifling hours-long stop at a Baltic state frontier, when Ivor eventually defied the closed-windows edict and the armed guard outside enforced it by smashing the glass with a steel-studded mountain boot. They were unpunished – Britishers in those days carried clout, Montagu speculates.

From Moscow, they took the train south to Vladikavkaz, a five-day trip enlivened by discussions with an economist about the Moscow Soviet budget, and with two brothers, Nepmen, about the curiously flexible system of taxation imposed under the New Economic Policy. From Vladikavkaz, having added a zoology professor, Sergei Turov, and his lab assistant to their little team, they went by lorry up to their destination, Krestovy Pereval. This halt was situated at an altitude of 8,000ft in the Caucasus mountains, at the top of the pass on the military road from Ossetia to Georgia. Here the only known *Prometheomys* in the world had been found.[19]

Several days digging, with the assistance of four local peasants, proved fruitless. The voles were not to be outwitted. Ivor conceived a plan of using poison gas to smoke them out, and cadged a ride down to Tiflis (Tbilisi) to try and procure the necessary chemicals. A posse of cavalry escorted the truck on the final part of the journey into town – Georgia had been invaded by the Red Army and annexed to Soviet Russia in 1921, there had been a ruthlessly suppressed nationalist uprising the previous year, and now there was renewed talk of 'bandits'. Montagu reached the scorching capital unscathed and, bearing credentials from Tomsky, was led into the presence, at Party headquarters, of the General Secretary of the Transcaucasian Federation.[20]

This 'elegant and extraordinarily handsome dark young man' was helpful. Montagu was to return to Krestovy Pereval while inquiries were made. On his arrival back he discovered his team were overrun with diminutive quadrupeds, alive and dead, which had been brought in by the local peasants when they heard the crazy foreigners would pay for them. Many mice – but also *Prometheomys*. No need for poison gas.[21]

Getting the specimens back to Britain in good condition, however, proved a challenge, especially as Ivor and Bancroft had much more travelling to do. They did another stint of trapping, for variant species, on the plains north of the Caucasus, repaired to Tiflis (where they witnessed a procession welcoming a German trade union delegation), and then made the long train journey back to Moscow via Baku, on the Caspian Sea. Meanwhile the *Prometheomys* fought and killed one another, escaped from their cages in the goods van, had to be recaptured with the assistance of a squad of Red Army men, got infested with parasites (as did their handlers), and began to die of disease. Ivor hastened the process with one creature by coating it in alcohol to kill the bugs; it was mortally chilled and died within ten seconds. None of the menagerie remained alive by the time Ivor and Bancroft set sail from Leningrad; post-mortems indicated lung infection.

Before that, however, they were stuck in Moscow waiting for exit permits. In the hotel dining room they encountered the just-married John Maynard Keynes and Lydia Lopokova, Keynes waxing lyrical about the smooth ride the slow Soviet trains afforded. (Apropos his Russian experience, Keynes would write: 'It is hard for an educated, decent, intelligent son of Western Europe to find his ideals here, unless he has suffered some strange and horrid process of conversion which has changed all his values … in Western industrial conditions the tactics of Red revolution would throw the whole population into a pit of poverty and death.') Bancroft, in accordance with his business interests, visited shoe factories, 'then pretty rough'. Ivor, no doubt, delivered his letter to Yarotsky, though he makes no mention of it in his autobiography.

In the 'Ethnographical Shop', he purchased skull-caps and 'a wondrous robe in broad stripe upon stripe of brilliantly blended hues and softly watered silks' as a parting gift for his former girlfriend, and seized the opportunity to see more theatre, this time the Glinka opera *Ruslan and Ludmila*, based on a poem by Pushkin.[22]

More significantly, Montagu had time to visit another film studio – again with an introductory letter from Yarotsky. Mezhrabpom-Russ had an intriguing history. Russ was the only production company to survive from before the Revolution; its owner had fled but much of the equipment was left behind, and the production chief Moisei Aleinikov organised the remaining actors and technicians into a collective. Under extraordinary conditions during the Civil War, with all involved freezing and on the verge of starvation, they had succeeded in shooting a feature, *Polikushka*, from

Tolstoy's story. Directed by Alexander Sanin, the film was widely appreciated for its artistic qualities when eventually released in 1922. By 1924 the
situation for filmmaking in the Soviet Union had greatly improved, and in
that year the Russ collective received an influx of capital from a Comintern
organisation with an interest in the cinema's propaganda potential.[23]

'Mezhrabpom' was the Russian acronym for the *Internationale Arbeiterhilfe*
(IAH), which had been founded at Lenin's instigation in Berlin in 1921 as
a disaster relief agency. Its head was the remarkable working-class entre-
preneur Willi Münzenberg. Once the Volga famine was over, Münzenberg
expanded the IAH's sphere of activities to encompass a broad range of
mass-media and cultural initiatives aimed at promoting the Communist
cause internationally. To complement the IAH's growing publishing empire
in Germany, Münzenberg moved the organisation decisively into film production in the Soviet Union with the formation of Mezhrabpom-Russ.[24]

Montagu was able to view all the studio's productions, and was impressed.
He was particularly struck by the futuristic costumes of the recently produced science fiction movie *Aelita* (Yakov Protazanov, 1924). When writing
about Soviet cinema later in the year, he would praise the high technical quality of this studio's output: 'To this day only the productions of
Mezhrabpom persistently maintain a level high enough to bear comparison
in this respect with the average technique of American films ... [they are]
invariably excellently photographed, and are generally admitted in Russia
to be better than those of the other producing groups.'[25]

What was more, Mezhrabpom's status as a Comintern organisation
meant that there was a possibility of bypassing Sovkino's monopoly on film
exports. Montagu offered to include three of the studio's productions in the
Film Society's first-year programme: *Aelita*, *Kollezhski registrator/The Station
Master* (Yuri Zheliabuzhsky, 1925) – a period drama based on a Pushkin
story – and the overtly political *Yevo prizyv/His Call* (Protazanov, 1925),
which featured Lenin's appeal for workers to show greater commitment to
the Communist Party being brought to a village after his death in January
1924. Mezhrabpom-Russ manager Francesco Misiano accepted the proposition, but stipulated that everything had to be done through the Berlin
office of the IAH. Montagu accordingly wrote out his scheme in tripli-
cate, with copies for Berlin, Moscow, and the Workers' International Relief
(WIR) office in London.[26]

While awaiting departure Montagu also penned short articles for publication in Britain, vanquishing the inhibitions he had experienced in Berlin earlier in the year. In 'Lawn Tennis in Soviet Russia', the budding young journalist reported that the sport was becoming more popular, having overcome 'the odium of being considered a bourgeois game' from which it suffered in the early years after the Revolution; now however, with younger workers 'so thoroughly taking up sports and athletics of all kinds, lawn tennis has become a proletarian game as respectable and orthodox as football, basketball and rowing …' Football was an undeveloped, amateur game in the Soviet Union at this time; Ivor had brought along training manuals with rules of the game, refereeing charts, and a leather-bound FA handbook tooled in gold as gifts from the English Football Association. In 'Football in Soviet Russia' Montagu stressed the sport's popularity with workers, noted that the huge distances effectively ruled out contests between centres apart from the annual Moscow–Leningrad matches, and observed with some bemusement that charging another player for the ball was not permitted. Contact, it was thought, could result in injuries: young Communists told Ivor that 'we play to get fit, and make ourselves healthy; not to injure ourselves. What would be the use of doing that?'[27]

'Present Day Russia and the Film' was published in three instalments in *The Kinematograph Weekly*. Here Ivor outlined the structure of the Soviet industry – which of course differed substantially from the British free-market model, especially in eliminating the profit-oriented film renter and exhibitor. He informed the film trade readers that imported pictures were popular, except for high-society comedies and romances, which Russians could not relate to; in Soviet productions, 'the evening-necked heroine and the white-waistcoated, plaster-haired villain of American melodrama give place to the beautiful female commissar, with sheep-skin hat and goat-skin coat and bomb in either hand, pursued by lustful White generals, shaggy and horrible.' A vast number of Soviet features were in fact 'propaganda of varying directness', but 'this does not mean that they are not often excellent pictures', the recent history of the country providing much good material for working up into 'fast, exciting films'. In particular, Montagu praised *His Call* ('an excellent melodrama in which pace and continuity are never sacrificed'), *Krasnye partizany/Red Partisans* (Vyacheslav Viskovsky, 1924), *Krasnye diavolyata/The Red Devils* (Ivan

Perestiani, 1923) about the struggle against the anarchist Makhno in the Ukraine, and *Musulmanka/The Mussulman Girl* (Dmitrii Bassalygo, 1925), centring on the revolution in Bokhara. Montagu regretted that 'in other similar films of this group abominable photography and triteness make them very bad indeed.'[28]

The Soviet Union in 1925 was experiencing a period of relative calm after the tumultuous years of Civil War and famine. The Bolshevik revolutionaries had achieved their major goals: the capitalist class had been defeated, landowners expropriated and major industries nationalised. All opposition had been successfully repressed: anarchists imprisoned or deported, independent workers' organisations crushed, Mensheviks and Socialist-Revolutionaries consigned, as Trotsky reported with relish, to 'the dustbin of history'. Religion was suppressed (though Muslims fared better than Christians and Jews), and Bolsheviks controlled the trade unions, the universities, and the media. Within the Communist Party, factions had been outlawed; and the struggle for power in the Politburo following Lenin's death was being carried on out of the public gaze.[29]

Given his socialist beliefs, it is curious that Montagu seems to have made very little attempt to assess these developments. In his writing at the time and in his later memoirs, there are none of the encomiums on the Soviet experiment that fellow political pilgrims from the West were wont to pronounce. But if he experienced any of the disillusionment that Sasha Kropotkin predicted he would, he did not let on. He was, he says, 'deeply impressed, above all, by the sense of comradeship there and, in the current cant phrase, the evidence of the wind of change.' One instance of this was the informal procedure adopted in the courtroom he visited, where he watched two factory workers ('an elderly grizzled woodworker and a motherly female') adjudicate, along with a trained lawyer, in civil cases of child maintenance and assault. Another was an incident he witnessed when he was leaving the Bolshoi one night. Observing the head of state, Mikhail Kalinin, giving a lift to a pair of soldiers who were going his way, Ivor was struck by his 'utterly benign and unaffected' manner.[30]

He was interested in the status of ethnic minorities, particularly Jews, in the new society. In an unpublished manuscript, Montagu writes of a Jewish tailor he met who worked in a clothing factory:

Not so long ago I was working at my bench. A man left his place & sat beside me. He drew out an enormous knife & started sharpening it. 'What are you doing that for?' I asked. 'To cut your throat, & those of all the other dogs of Jews.' I knocked him down & a scuffle followed. The affair was reported to the workmen's disciplinary committee & I was named as the aggressor. I gave my account & they exonerated me, & offered to move me to another floor. They did not, however, punish the man.

Montagu observes that Lenin's speech 'On Pogroms against the Jews', made soon after he assumed power, had been widely disseminated, and comments: 'Anyone who has cognisance of the pitiful state of Russian Jews in former times will realise the progress towards tolerance implicit in the background of this story. If these are the worst complaints which a Jew can raise, what a vast stride has been made!'[31]

While still in Moscow, Montagu, as a member of the National Union of Scientific Workers, wrote to London enquiring about joining the National Minority Movement (NMM). This Communist-led organisation, formally launched in August 1924, aimed to co-ordinate left-wing activity in the trade unions. On 16 September 1925 its general secretary, Harry Pollitt, replied to Ivor, now back in England, enclosing an associate membership form and requesting him to 'indicate at the same time any special work that you feel you could carry out for us in the localities where you reside.' A few days later Pollitt wrote again, saying, 'I have pleasure in enclosing you our associate membership card, for which I have paid a donation of 1/-, and if you will immediately refund that amount to me I will wish you God's Speed in all your further studies in zoology.'[32]

Montagu had returned to Britain at a time of great optimism on the left wing of the labour movement. On 'Red Friday', 31 July, the Miners Federation of Great Britain, with the support of railwaymen, had defeated a savage wage cut threatened by the employers, with Stanley Baldwin's Conservative government agreeing to a temporary (nine-month) subsidy to maintain miners' wages. Pollitt recounts that this victory gave 'a feeling of strength and elation to all the delegates' at the Trades Union Congress annual conference held at Scarborough in September. TUC President Alonzo Swales of the engineers' union, in his address from the chair, declared: 'All around are signs of an awakening consciousness in the peoples of all countries that the present system of society is condemned.' Amid 'rousing denunciations of the Conservative government's hostility toward Russia', an Anglo-Russian Trade Union Committee, which had been launched in May after negotiations between Soviet trade unionists (led by Tomsky) and the TUC General Council, was warmly endorsed. Tomsky attended the conference as a fraternal delegate – but if the capitalist press is to be believed, aroused the wrath of the British unionists for staying at a luxurious seaside hotel and being unapproachable.[33]

Despite his favourable impressions of the Soviet Union, Ivor did not yet join the Communist Party. 'I still did not know enough about Communism or Marxism,' he avers. 'I admired both Lenin and Trotsky, and could not understand the issues between the Soviet Party and Trotsky which were then reaching the surface.' But he consorted with Communists and 'found among them the only political friends of like approach.' And when twelve leaders of the Party were put on trial in November for sedition and incitement to mutiny, he attended the court hearings in support. The guilty verdicts handed down to all the defendants, leading to terms of imprisonment of six or twelve months, reinforced Montagu's view, shared by many, that the charges had been trumped up: the aim was clearly to secure a 'beheading of the left' in the run-up to the coming showdown over the miners' dispute, settlement of which had only been postponed.[34]

At the Depositions hearing in the case, one of the Communist publication excerpts read into the record contained the suggestion that a workers' defence organisation was needed: 'Councils of Action in the Localities must prepare to defend the Working Class Movement against the unwarranted attacks of the Police and their Fascist satellites by forming Workers' Defence Corps.' There had been considerable discussion of this issue in the labour press, and the revelation in September that the government had created a corps of strike-breakers, the Organisation for the Maintenance of Supplies (OMS), for use in the event of labour unrest, made the perceived need more urgent. A Communist Party statement published in October read: 'Meet the threat of organised strike-breaking and capitalist violence by insisting on the right to tell your brothers in the Army and Navy that they must not scab on the workers, and by forming your own Defence Corps against the OMS and the Fascisti!'.[35]

But it was unclear how such groups would be organised. Montagu now took it upon himself to advance the proposal. In December he transferred to the Holborn Labour Party – a very active left-wing electorate branch, whose members included Desmond Bernal – and prepared a motion on workers' defence patrols to be presented at a Party meeting. His Cambridge friend Kingsley Martin, now teaching at the London School of Economics, initially agreed to propose it. However, Martin had second thoughts, and wrote to Ivor withdrawing his offer and apologising for letting him down. 'I want the Government to put themselves much more in the wrong than they have so far before such an organisation is created,' he declared. He felt that it would 'immediately strengthen the Fascists & the Government supporters of the OMS for such an organisation to exist &, as a pacifist, I want to ensure that any violence comes from that side & not from ours.'[36]

Undeterred, Ivor sent a lengthy draft memo on his plan for a 'working class police body' to Maurice Dobb for his comments. The functions of this defence force would be to preserve order at meetings and rallies, to picket peacefully, to protect 'labour property and persons', and in the event of a large-scale strike, to assist in the distribution of supplies and to prevent workers assembling (so that they would not become targets for police or 'armed opposing force'). The members of this 'rigorously disciplined' organisation would be 'badged, or better still, equipped with a red armlet with a large black "D"'. The body would be under the control of the Trades Councils, and the idea should be sounded out with the councils along with Labour Party branches, left-wing groups, and the TUC General Council.[37]

A curious aspect of the proposal was Ivor's idea that the defence corps would bring a 'Spartan, Puritan element' to the labour movement. 'Members of the Force,' he argued, 'should be prevented from drinking, gambling, dancing and so forth exactly like Party members in Russia.' He gave himself as an example:

> The author of this memorandum ... likes the theatre and cinema, he used to play cards, one day he may dance. He wastes a great deal of time and energy and does not feel inclined to do anything else. But if he were a member of some self-denying body, if he wore a badge and were under the illusion that he must abandon his simple pleasures as a duty because his spare time was usefully organised, he would cheerfully do so.[38]

Unsurprisingly perhaps, Dobb skips over this section in his otherwise extensive notes on the memorandum. Writing to Ivor on 28 December, he was
generally supportive ('I think the scheme does very well & puts all the main
points well'). But he firmly rejected Montagu's suggestion that, for fear of
alienating moderate opinion, Communists should be publicly dissociated
from the scheme. There was a danger, which Ivor underestimated, of the
body coming under the control of 'Rights'. Dobb was equally dismissive of
the idea that if the TUC declined to endorse the proposal, the Independent
Labour Party might act as sponsor ('ILP is merely a MacDonald organ, &
to bring body under its control would castrate it at birth'). But he was
keen for the project to advance, urged Ivor to arrange for it to be discussed
and adopted at Trades Council meetings ('Woolf [presumably Barnet] says
he cd. get Hackney'), and offered to come to London if he could be of
any help. Writing again on 12 January 1926, Dobb was pleased to hear that
Alf Purcell and George Hicks, members of the TUC General Council, were
arranging for Trades Councils to take up the proposal. But he was cautious:
'Is this being definitely arranged, or should something be organised to this
end?' Dobb also suggested pursuing publication possibilities: 'Do you think
it would be any good publishing it in *T.U. Unity*. Hutt I believe still has
charge of that … .' He agreed with Montagu's view that it was 'essentially a
thing for organising from the centre, & for official adoption & initiative.'[39]

To what extent Trades Councils did in fact consider the proposal at this
stage is not clear, but momentum was certainly building. At the National
Minority Movement Conference of Action on 21 March, attended by
delegates from 547 organisations including fifty-two Trades Councils, a
resolution was passed 'To form (through and under the supervision of the
Trades Councils) Workers' Defence Corps, in order to protect working-
class speakers from bourgeois terrorism, to protect trade union headquarters
from Fascist incendiarism, to defend strike pickets against police interference, and, finally, build up a powerful working-class force, capable of
defending the political and industrial rights and liberties of the workers.'[40]

Montagu kept up the pressure, writing on 7 May to Walter Citrine, Acting
Secretary of the TUC General Council, with a revised and shortened version of his memorandum. Ivor now proposed that the General Council
of the Trade Union Congress 'take the initiative in organising in each
locality under the control of the local Trades Council a volunteer patrol

body of Trade Unionists'. But by now, as he admitted ('Please find time to look at this memorandum. Not urgent – but if and when you have an odd moment'), it was effectively too late. The General Strike had broken out.[41]

Ivor's cousin Sir Herbert Samuel had, at the government's request, chaired a Royal Commission (without worker representation) inquiring into the mining industry. Its report, published in March, recommended measures of improvement including nationalisation of royalties (but not of the mining companies), amalgamation of pits, and better working conditions; immediately, however, there would need to be a reduction in wages. 'That Baldwin was merely using the Commission as a mask to gain a breathing-space for his strike-breaking preparations would never have mattered to Herbert, a man of perfect integrity and uprightness,' Montagu remarked; he was 'one of those aggravating creatures in whose character you can find no fault but who are themselves so certain they can do no wrong that often they serve blindly as a means of wrongdoing in others.' As it turned out, both the employers and the union rejected the report, a stalemate was reached, the miners refused to accept reductions in wages and conditions when their contract expired at the end of April, and on 1 May they were locked out. Emergency negotiations with the government failed, and on 3 May the TUC called a general strike in support of the miners.[42]

The response was overwhelming. More than 1.5 million transport workers, railwaymen, dockers, printers and iron and steel workers heeded the call and joined the 800,000 locked-out miners. Sidney Bernstein immediately threw open his theatres for the use of unionists (whereupon local authorities threatened to withdraw his licence). Councils of Action sprang up around the country, and – no doubt much to Montagu's satisfaction – workers' defence corps were in fact set up in a number of localities. At Methil, in the Fife coalfield, a defence corps strengthened after police charges on mass pickets 'marched in military formation through the town to protect the pickets. The police did not interfere again.'[43]

Ivor was a Labour Party representative on the Holborn Trades Council. Along with the electorate LP executive, it was transformed into a Council of Action. Delegates from affiliated unions 'sat in almost permanent session in a small local hall,' maintaining communications with strikers around the country. Ivor's comrade Desmond Bernal 'took on the role of street-corner orator, giving speeches each day from 6 to 11 May at Leather Lane and

New North Street.' Ivor became a cycling courier, detailed in particular to deliver the TUC bulletin, the *British Worker*. He pedalled through the strike-bound streets dodging armoured cars, overturned vehicles and blackleg buses driven erratically by Cambridge undergraduates, with bundles of the paper perched precariously on the handlebars. (It was even more precarious on one run when he was half-blinded, his glasses having been smashed in a scuffle with newsboys.)[44]

The *British Worker* was matched by the government's *British Gazette*, edited with bloodcurdling relish by Chancellor of the Exchequer Winston Churchill. No regular papers could appear because of strike action, a policy to which Montagu was vehemently opposed. 'For God's sake release the Press' he implored Citrine, when sending him his defence patrol memorandum. For affecting public opinion, which was sympathetic towards the miners, 'the Press is far more useful to us than our opponents' – particularly as the population was getting BBC radio news that favoured the government/employer position. Ivor even drafted an announcement that could be made when sending the printers back to work. Citrine was unmoved. He replied: 'On these matters of policy it is very difficult to explain in a letter just the reasons actuating decisions; our Committee feel that they have taken the right course.'[45]

The Holborn Council of Action executive worked from a Bloomsbury flat. They were under constant surveillance by police spies; to show their contempt, Montagu says, they 'sent out hot cups of tea to cheer them in the drizzle,' and played goodnatured pranks on them. The police reports no doubt found their way to MI5; a note on Montagu's file from this time in fact records that he 'has for some time been known to associate with the inner ring of the Communist Party' and that on 6 May he 'was observed to be in the company of several communists at 38, Great Ormond Street' (the NMM office). On 10 May a Home Office Warrant was taken out by Scotland Yard on 'The Hon. Ivor MONTAGUE [*sic*]', enabling his correspondence to be intercepted.[46]

The strike was solid, and substantial international financial support, organised through the IAH in Berlin by Willi Münzenberg, was forthcoming. But essential services were maintained through the administration's use of the OMS and the armed forces. When Samuel, with the government's blessing, unofficially approached the TUC General Council offering to help work out a settlement formula, the union leaders leapt at the opportunity. Negotiating behind the back of the miners, the Council agreed on a series of points based on the Commission report, and without securing any commitment from the government ordered a return to work on 12 May. Montagu comments that the agreement with 'Slippery Sam', as he came to be called, 'in no way bound the government, which ignored it, and no doubt always intended to, though in the first hours of confusion after the calling-off this was not apparent to the rank and file.' The Council had, however, 'attained their object, which was: to get the monkey of responsibility for a semi-revolutionary situation off their own backs at any cost, even though that meant the desertion of the miners and their abandonment to a grim war of attrition that they were bound to lose.'[47]

It was a total surrender, and activists in the unions were infuriated and dismayed at the perceived betrayal by their leaders. Criticism of the General Council from the CPGB was, however, muted; the Comintern had sent a delegation comprising Tomsky, David Alexandrovich ('Max') Petrovsky and Arthur Ewert to convince the Communist leadership to accept the TUC handling of the dispute. Improvements in relations between Great Britain and the Soviet Union achieved through the Anglo-Russian Trade Union Committee (which numbered among its members men who had ordered the return to work) were not to be jeopardised.[48]

During the strike, Communists bore the brunt of government repression. Of the total of approximately 2,500 arrests, more than 1,000 were of Party members. Typically, activists were imprisoned for two–six months for making speeches or distributing literature (such as strike bulletins) 'calculated to cause disaffection'. Bob Stewart, CPGB Acting General Secretary, was fined £100 and costs, while Marjorie Pollitt, wife of Harry Pollitt (still in prison), was charged as publisher of the *Workers' Bulletin* and given the alternative of a fine of £50 with costs or three months' jail. Ivor's cousin Olive Franklin (daughter of Louis's sister Henrietta) wrote to him asking if he could collect some money for the Party fines, mentioning these two cases in particular. £170 was wanted in all. 'I am sure you have heaps of wealthy friends so you can't be let off for being poor yourself!' Olive wrote. Ivor's response is not known, but on 22 June the Holborn Labour Party and Trades Council acknowledged his donation of £5 5s 0d to the Miners' Women & Children Fund (with the comment 'Note yr remarks re Anon').[49]

Ivor remained active in the left-wing group of the Holborn Labour Party, but demoralisation was setting in. In July the group suffered a set-back, and it came close to being dissolved. Desmond Bernal, in his diary, began to use terms such as 'plot' and 'conspiracy'. Then came a sledgehammer blow. At its 1924 conference the Labour Party had determined that Communists would be ineligible for membership, and it had now begun to enforce the ruling. With the CPGB leaders being released from prison, the Labour Party executive were determined, according to Montagu, 'that as soon as possible their flock must be decontaminated from any inter-course with them.' Constituency parties that refused to expel Communists would be cut asunder. 'Although no CP member, I was of course against this,' he says. Holborn voted not to implement the directive and was accordingly disaffiliated; in a letter to members of the left-wing group, Bernal and others claimed that the real reason for disaffiliation was 'our attempts to formulate a policy consistent with socialism' and 'our uncom-promising hostility to co-operating with the Lloyd Georgian liberals, and the consequent necessity on the part of the National E.C. to water down the Party's policy …' Other local parties in London suffering the same fate by September 1926 included Battersea, Bethnal Green, Chelsea, East Lewisham, West Ham and Westminster.[50]

Ivor's participation in the General Strike exacerbated the already tense relations that prevailed with his parents. His mother was so angry, he recounts, that 'she forbade me ever to return should I now cross the threshold to rejoin my comrades.' His father, though equally upset, took a different line: expostulating with Lady Swaythling, he declared: 'If he has assumed obligations to his friends, which he should not have done, of course, then he will have to carry them out.' Ivor credits the appeal of 'no victimisation' made by Stanley Baldwin after the strike was over for his mother finally relenting.[51]

With the defeat of the strike, the Labour onslaught on Communists, and conflicts with his parents, one can imagine that it was with a feeling of relief that Montagu turned his attention at this time from politics to film.

5

THE FILM INDUSTRY

IN THE MID-1920s the production sector of the British film industry was in a sorry state. The number of features produced had fallen steadily from 145 in 1920 to 45 in 1925; it was to drop further to 37 in 1926. Fewer than 5 per cent of films reaching the public were British made. The pioneering producer Cecil Hepworth had gone bankrupt, and even the Stoll company, which was in a strong position since it had its own cinema chain, was forced to drastically curtail its output. Production finance was difficult to obtain, and there was a lack of investment in infrastructure.[1]

The reason for the decline was claimed to be the stranglehold Hollywood firms exerted over distribution and exhibition through practices of 'blind' and 'block' booking, as well as the fact that American films could undercut the local product in price since their costs had already been recouped in the domestic market. Film audiences were said by newspaper commentators to be 'under a foreign yoke', being forced to endure 'the hopeless vulgarity and triviality of most American pictures', but this would not long continue: 'The British public has long ago revolted against the excruciating pictures dumped upon it by the Americans.' Legislation to free up the market for the British production industry was urgently needed, as a generation was growing up 'whose notions of life and morality as inculcated by the films are almost wholly derived from foreign sources and set to foreign standards'. Inquiries were held and reports issued calling for action, but by the end of 1925 the government had yet to move.[2]

On 24 January 1926 Ivor Montagu gave a Sunday afternoon talk, as one of a series of lectures on 'Some Suggested Reforms' held at the Guildhouse in Eccleston Square, London SW1, on 'The Reform of the Cinema'. Acknowledging that films, to be profitable, had to satisfy the 'gross feeders', Montagu contended that 'it was possible to produce interesting pictures if the persons who were engaged in the making of the films were really interested in them.' This was not the case: there was an absence of 'craft spirit', and 'those who were making money out of the industry never had a sufficient interest in it to spend money upon it.' Turning to the schemes being advanced for reforming the industry, as by the introduction of a quota, he said: 'The idea seemed to be that all those people who by their incompetence, lack of taste, lack of intelligence, and lack of sense of what the public wanted had brought the British industry to its bankrupt and inanimate condition should be safeguarded by legislation in future from the consequences of their own stupidity.' A much more suitable suggestion, he went on, would be 'to remove from the film-producing industry all the persons at present engaged in it, because the presumption was that they had had their chance. He did not mean that they had had an equal chance with foreign producers – undoubtedly they had not – but it was necessary to have in the film industry people who took pleasure in it for its own sake.' He proposed the creation of a national studio, which would 'promote the introduction of new blood and intelligence', as well as reducing the cost of production and allowing for the possibility of 'a certain amount of experiment'. Repertory groups should be established 'owning their own pictures and extending their range', while films could be of enormous use in higher education, 'for example, in biological science'.[3]

Ivor no doubt exempted from the category of those that 'had had their chance' his friend Adrian Brunel, and he would certainly have made an exception also for the up-and-coming producer Michael Balcon. The son of Jewish immigrants from eastern Europe, Balcon began in the film business in 1920 as a provincial renter based in Birmingham. He and his partner Victor Saville then moved to London, made advertising films, and in 1923 produced their first feature, the high-budget *Woman to Woman*. Daring for its time, this melodrama, directed by Graham Cutts and starring Betty Compson (imported from the USA at enormous cost) was a great success.

Balcon went on to found, with Cutts, the Gainsborough company, based at studios in Islington. He had an international perspective and lambasted fellow British producers for their insularity; he was committed to achieving high technical quality, and made a co-production agreement with the German company Emelka to this end. He was also an avid member of the Film Society, that 'Mecca of all cineastes' as he later called it.[4]

Balcon chose his collaborators carefully, avoiding 'almost entirely the floaters, old reliables and professional hacks who were so numerous'. Cutts remained his director of choice, but there was also the young Alfred Hitchcock, who was shooting films under the Emelka deal in Munich.

And in 1925 Brunel, while maintaining his editing company, took up a contract at Gainsborough, continuing to make his short burlesques while awaiting the opportunity to return to features. It was Brunel, most likely, who introduced Montagu to Balcon, and the producer was happy to make use of the Cambridge intellectual's analytical talents. In February 1926 Balcon invited Ivor to take a look at one of his new films; it was probably Hitchcock's *The Pleasure Garden*, with Virginia Valli. Balcon was encouraged by Montagu's response. 'We are pleased you liked the picture,' he wrote. 'Your suggestions are most useful. You are perfectly right and we shall alter the titles before release.'[5]

Montagu had become interested in the aesthetics of intertitles – a vexed question in the silent cinema – through his work with Brunel in preparing foreign productions for Film Society screening. Brunel's operation ('a sort of film knacker's business – repair and rebeautification of ravaged pictures') was conducted in cramped rooms above a film laboratory at 6 Dansey Yard in Soho. There was 'a tiny office, small enough to be crowded by one desk ... an equally claustrophobic projection theatre seating some four or five', and up a winding staircase, minuscule cutting rooms. Youthful aspirants to the shrinking film industry would hang about trying to make themselves useful in the hope that eventually they would be placed on the payroll. In Montagu's case, as with others such as Angus MacPhail, Brunel finally took pity and put the supplicant on staff, though this 'was, of course, not quite the same as finding us a regular salary'. The money probably didn't worry Ivor too much; he still had his stipend from his father. And now he had his foot in the door: he had embarked on a career in film production.[6]

Though Brunel was eleven years older and Montagu looked on him as a mentor as well as boss ('He seemed to me awfully old and wise'), the two cemented a friendship. With Ivor's collaboration, Brunel extended his series of satiric productions by setting his sights (gently) on the plutocracy. *Life, Love and Laughter at Swaythling Court* was filmed one weekend at Townhill: 'We used the garden, innocent guests and often unwilling family,' Montagu tells us, adding that the film had never been shown to trade or public. (The title was a play on the Betty Balfour film *Love, Life and Laughter*.) This home movie, historian Rachael Low records, cost £20; it was recently rediscovered and found to be much in the vein of Brunel's professional burlesques with their comic intercuts of found footage and excruciating puns in the intertitles – here Townhill is described as 'a fine orifice in the European style'.[7]

Ever one for socialising, Montagu met with the Dansey Yard crew and other friends at 'a sort of lunch club' in a small local restaurant, the Alexis in Lisle Street; the regulars included theatre personalities John Gielgud, Harold Warrender, Charles Laughton, Elsa Lanchester, Kate Cutler and Edith Craig, along with journalists Iris Barry and Yvonne Kapp. He was also a member of the 'Pack' of filmmakers that gathered daily at the Legrain coffee shop in Brewer Street, Soho, particularly when times were slack. This group included the producer Mick Balcon, directors Adrian Brunel, Graham Cutts, Alfred Hitchcock, and Victor Saville, writer/director Edwin Greenwood, writer Eliot Stannard and cinematographer Henry Harris. Here, Balcon recalled nostalgically, amid 'the smell of roasting coffee beans' they would 'discuss the prospects of work and the films we hoped to make one day.'[8]

Montagu was also a very keen attender at the 'hate parties' held by Brunel and his 'dark, petite, good-looking' wife Babs. The participants were in films or on the fringes, and would gather after a premiere or a Film Society screening to 'discourse in turn on everything in cinema we most hated: renters or Wurlitzer organs or mottled title backgrounds'. Here Ivor and his girlfriend Hell would bemoan the state of the industry (though in 'jovial and constructive' manner) with Mick and Aileen Balcon; with Miles Mander, the actor and director; with the theatre manager Vivian Van Damm; with Alex Stewart ('Sasha'), the photographer, and his wife Leila, a publicity manager; with Sidney Bernstein and Iris Barry; and occasionally, too, with

the directors Herbert Wilcox and Victor Saville. (Graham Cutts, whom
Montagu suspected of blocking Brunel's advancement at Gainsborough in
order to protect his own career, was unlikely to have been on the guest list.)
It was probably inspired by these parties that Montagu jotted down at this
time a list of his hates, which included 'all vocal singing anytime during any
picture', 'all scenarists except Jock Orton' (who also worked for Balcon),
'mostly – the members of the Film Society', and 'Hitchcock because he
ought to catch fish and lay down wine in a monastery & anyway he is
only a clever twister with a facile smile, Brunel because he is a sentimental
impostor with no sense of humour, all other British directors for various
reasons (N.B., this is jealousy)'.[9]

Ivor's parents were clearly happier with his filmmaking than with his
political activities. In June 1926, not long after the near rupture caused by
the General Strike, Lady Swaythling dropped him a note telling him of an
upcoming camp of the Jewish Lads' Brigade at Birchington on Sea: 'Please do
your utmost to try & get somebody to take some cinema films of the work in
progress,' she wrote, 'as we want to show this so very badly at the great J.L.B.
concert in October.' Whether Ivor responded to this plea is not known.[10]

In August Balcon, at Brunel's suggestion, again called upon Montagu.
A crisis had arisen: Hitchcock's latest film, *The Lodger*, shot at the Islington
studios, had been completed but Gainsborough's distributor C.M. Woolf of
W. & F. Film Service was dissatisfied with it; moreover, one of Hitchcock's
two German pictures, *The Mountain Eagle*, had also been shelved. Over a
restaurant lunch of mashed potatoes and fried onions Balcon commissioned
Montagu to see what he could do with *The Lodger*, an Ivor Novello thriller
based on a popular novel by Marie Belloc Lowndes, which in turn had
been inspired by the Jack the Ripper murders. If *The Lodger* were to be successful, perhaps *The Mountain Eagle* could be released in its wake.[11]

Montagu did not think there was anything much wrong with *The Lodger*.
Perhaps it was just too highbrow for Woolf's taste – Hitchcock had been
influenced by the expressionist lighting and camerawork he had seen in
Germany. The remedy was not to lower the tone – certainly not: 'It was
at once obvious that what the film needed was editing *toward*, not *away
from*, its exceptional qualities.' The changes proposed by Montagu and readily accepted by Hitchcock and Balcon were relatively minor: the number
of intertitles was reduced (Ivor was inspired by *Warning Shadows*, which

had none); the name of the potential victim, Daisy, was repeated on screen, to ominous effect; the graphic artist McKnight Kauffer was brought in to design the opening titles and intertitles in modernist style; and additional long shots of the climactic lynching chase were filmed.[12]

Hitchcock, looking at this time like 'a somewhat enlarged edition of Harry Langdon' had, says Montagu, 'an absolutely warranted confidence in his own taste and judgement as far as technical matters of filmmaking were concerned', but he was gracious in accepting the imposition of a 'spoiled young outsider' on his project. He and Ivor became friends, talking the problems over together. 'He accepted my ideas without demur, I his with pleasure.' The alterations proved sufficient to sway W. & F., and *The Lodger* when released early in 1927 proved a critical and commercial success. *The Mountain Eagle* was also taken off the shelf, and Hitchcock became a welcome addition to Brunel's hate party coterie.[13]

Meanwhile Ivor, after a sojourn in Berlin with a scratch table tennis team, attended the Congrès International du Cinématographe in Paris from 27 September to 3 October 1926. He was a Film Society delegate, along with Adrian Brunel, Iris Barry, Walter Mycroft and Angus MacPhail. The congress, the first of its kind, was organised by the French National Committee of Intellectual Co-operation under the auspices of the League of Nations, and aimed 'to formulate the problems of international organisation which present themselves in regard to the motion picture and to study them scientifically with a view to future solutions'. The wide range of topics dealt with included production and distribution, education by means of the film, legal and trade problems, and the relation between the motion picture and the other arts. Discussion evidently focused in the end on the educational as opposed to the commercial aspects of the industry, and the conference led to the formation two years later of the International Educational Cinematographic Institute (IECI).[14]

Back in London, Montagu became involved once again in the business of the Film Society, of which he remained chairman, as it prepared to launch its second season. A crisis was looming. The British Board of Film Censors, concerned at the Society's screenings of uncensored films, was pressuring the London County Council over its indulgence of the practice. The Society was compelled to undertake a defence of its activity. In a memorandum to the LCC, it stated:

The Society maintains that certain pictures and parts of pictures may possibly be unsuited to indiscriminate public exhibition (being, if passed,
liable to uncontrolled salacious or political advertisement), and yet not
unsuited to sober consideration by an unimpassioned sober audience ...
[some scenes] unsuitable for public show, may, by virtue of beautiful photography or ingenious lighting, be proper food for study by those more
concerned with technique than with subject.

As Jamie Sexton has commented, 'The Film Society thus used its intellectual and respectable status as a cultural weapon, drawing a qualitative
difference between its members and the audience that attended commercial
cinemas.' The special pleading proved effective, and the LCC renewed the
Society's censorship waiver for a further year. On 24 October, the season
opened with a programme including Robert Wiene's stylish thriller *Orlacs
Hände/The Hands of Orlac* (Germany, 1924).[15]

Nothing more having as yet eventuated from his film doctoring,
Montagu now toyed again with the idea of making a living as a journalist. He approached Lord Beaverbrook, who offered him a chance: 'Would
you like to try writing some *Evening Standard* notes, and sending them to
me direct? If they are no good I will destroy them, if well done I will send
them on to the Editor.' The magnate, who had a high opinion of Montagu,
believed that he would have 'an understanding of news values'. Nothing
eventuated from this, however, very likely because writing of another kind
was now absorbing Ivor's interest.[16]

Balcon had decided to assign Brunel a feature to direct. It was to be a
Great War film, since these were in vogue – Hollywood's *The Big Parade*
had been a sensation, and it was shortly to be followed by *What Price Glory*;
British producers had made battle re-enactments such as *Zeebrugge*, *Ypres* and
Mons and wartime romances including *Woman to Woman* and *Mademoiselle
from Armentieres*. Brunel was uneasy with the assignment ('nearly every war
film was based upon the chivalry, bravery and sacrifice of men in the fighting forces, and inevitably was pro-war propaganda'), but he and Ivor came
up with a compromise, a '*non-battle* picture' set away from the front lines in
the milieu of an aristocratic family. Montagu's original idea (or unoriginal,
as he self-deprecatingly describes it), jotted down with Hell's input as she

lay ill, was elaborated into a treatment under the title *Après la guerre*, and accepted for production by Gainsborough.[17]

With some further contributions from Brunel and Montagu, the treatment was developed into a screenplay by studio regular Eliot Stannard, retitled *Blighty*, and promptly put into production. For the key role of the French wartime sweetheart, already an iconic figure, Brunel and Montagu were determined to secure the services of the young actress Nadia Sibirskaia because of her 'deeply moving performance' in *Ménilmontant*, which had shown at the Film Society. ('I am not quite sure, however,' Montagu comments, 'whether the tremendous effect of that film owed more to the fine acting and direction or to the appearance, in scarcely lit double or triple photography, of a momentary vision then unique to all of us, the actress's nude back view.') According to Montagu, she was reluctant to come to England, and had an unhappy time during the shoot; Brunel found her highly temperamental. Her performance, however, was superlative: 'In the role of a French single mother bringing her baby to meet the English upper-middle-class parents of its now dead father,' Christine Gledhill comments, 'Sibirskaia offers up her face and being to the camera with a stillness and transparency quite unlike anything produced by British performers.'[18]

Blighty was released in March 1927 to a strongly favourable critical reception and good box office. Brunel claimed that it 'was, quietly, an anti-war picture rather than a pro-war picture', pointing to its lack of blatant jingoism and hate-the-Hun sentiment. But evoking sadness rather than anger, it was bereft of the outrage at the horrors of war that permeated such productions as the French *J'accuse!* (1919) and the later *Journey's End* and *All Quiet on the Western Front* (both 1930). It certainly bore no trace of the socialist war-resister perspective that had motivated the teenage Ivor Montagu to withdraw from lecturing to the Naval Staff College in 1917. Brunel acknowledged the constraints he and Montagu were working under in noting that 'it fulfilled the requirements of a popular patriotic picture, in that it showed a decent English family behaving decently.' As the critic Roy Armes was later to comment:

Blighty offers a view of war that omits the dirt and squalor and uses the love affairs of the younger generation not to probe the problems posed by class and nationality but to celebrate the myths of the British aristocracy: gallantry in action and tolerance in behaviour, patriotism and self-sacrifice but always tempered with resolute self-control.[19]

One area in which the film did, perhaps, offer a new outlook was in its depiction of loosening in the British class structure. The French peasant girl, having borne a grandson for Sir Francis Villiers, is accepted into the family, while the Villiers' chauffeur, having risen through the officer ranks during the war and been awarded a permanent commission, becomes an acceptable partner for Sir Francis's daughter. Other films such as *Comradeship* (Maurice Elvey, 1919), *General Post* (Thomas Bentley, 1920), as well as *Woman to Woman* had portrayed transgressive wartime romances and the suggested refiguring of class relations brought about by the conflict, but *Blighty* was very likely one of the first British films to endorse, through its happy ending, the marital coupling of persons of such widely disparate social backgrounds. It was, of course, a theme that was personally dear to the Honourable Ivor's heart.

By this time Montagu had secured a permanent position at Gainsborough. He had been called in by Balcon to do a repair job on Cutts's South Sea shipwreck epic *The Rolling Road*, since 'some of the action was insufficiently clear and the big scenes did not come off effectively.' Montagu asked for retakes to be shot, but Cutts, in a bad mood, bungled the job and Ivor had to do them himself. It was his first experience of directing. His other contribution was to insist on the shortening of scenes in which the semi-naked middle-aged protagonist (Carlyle Blackwell) chased an equally *déshabillée* ingénue (Flora Le Breton) along the sandy shores of their desert island. The images, Montagu insisted, were not erotic but repellent. There was resistance, but Balcon stood by him and Ivor got his way. Thereupon, in November 1926 and still only 22 years of age, he found himself employed to supervise both scripting and editing at Gainsborough, and he transferred from Dansey Yard to the company's studios at Islington. (This was despite the fact that when working on *The Lodger* he had complained to Balcon about both the office and the studio.) With this ascent into respectable paid employment, MI5 evidently decided that Montagu was no longer a security threat; on 26 November his Home Office Warrant was cancelled.[20]

Balcon respected Montagu's intelligence and generosity, and found him an invaluable right-hand man. On 2 December he wrote to Ivor concerned about the censorship angle on *The Vortex*, the adaptation of Noël Coward's play that Brunel was slated to direct. The concern was justified. As Montagu explains, 'the censor was certain to eviscerate any guts it might have possessed at birth, and Noël Coward's plot: "Mother, will you give up lovers if I give up drugs?" necessarily became: "Mummy, will you give up going to teas and dances if I give up cigarettes and aspirins?" not the most compelling of dramatic issues.' On 8 December Balcon wrote asking Ivor's opinion on whether the enclosed synopsis for a third 'Rat' story held promise (*The Rat*, starring Ivor Novello and based on a play he had co-authored, had been a big success in 1925, and this had been followed up by *The Triumph of the Rat* in 1926.) On 7 January 1927 the studio head informed Montagu that negative cutting on *The Rolling Road* had been suspended in view of criticism, and a decision was required on whether Miss Le Breton was required to do further scenes, while on 16 February Balcon requested a fairly comprehensive synopsis of *One of the Best* (about the disgrace of a young military officer in the Regency period) for submission to the War Department.[21]

Much of Montagu's attention at this time was given to *Downhill*, an Ivor Novello vehicle based on a play the actor had co-authored, which Hitchcock was to direct. The tale of a public schoolboy's disgrace as the result of a false accusation, degradation as a young man in France, and eventual redemption, struck Montagu as implausible, and he was concerned about the dearth of physical action. A treatment he prepared radically altered the story, presenting the protagonist as 'a race-car driver, given to piano playing and drugs, eventually brought to his senses by a suitable love interest in the person of the headmaster's daughter.' He also made an ambitious proposal to utilise the Phonofilm process to record 'a flowing melody, in a minor key', which would be provided by Novello and played in theatres during scenes in which his character was at the piano. Possibly as a result of time constraints, the changes were not accepted, and Eliot Stannard's subsequent screenplay returned to the storyline of the play. The sonorisation idea was also not taken up.[22]

Spending the day on scripts and half the night editing, Montagu found it an exhausting schedule. 'I was working harder than I ever had before,' he recalls.:

There were no unions in the film industry in those days and I worked nearly right round the clock. During daytime I had to be in conference

with Mick or the film directors, arguing about scenarios, or sometimes
keeping actual or prospective cast sweet; nights – when I could be quiet
and undisturbed, either alone or with an assistant – I worked at cutting,
over at Islington, perpetually on the treadmill to maintain the schedules.

He became '(not unnaturally) tired, irritable and ready to pick a quarrel with
anybody and march out at the drop of a pin'. On 24 February, after some
disagreement, he wrote offering his resignation. Balcon replied: 'I quite
agree that your resignation is available when I require it – I do not happen
to require it, Ivor.' (In a tribute after Balcon's death in 1977, Montagu wrote:
'Working for Mick Balcon was a very personal affair. It was like a rather odd
sort of marriage. You could quarrel and break away, but neither side lost a
friend. The tie was an elastic one – it could stretch but not snap.')[23]

Montagu was not too busy to keep up his role as a public intellectual. On 5 January he addressed the Parents' National Educational Union
at University College, London, giving one of a number of talks on
'Modern Educational Agencies', his subject being the cinema. Lauding
the 'subtleties of expression and delineation of character' now possible in
film, he regretted that more of the 'discriminating public' did not attend
screenings; the great bulk of the audience 'went once or twice a week
without being particularly interested in the film, but for the experience of
a comfortable seat at a reasonable price, warmth, music, and rest, and for
the spectacle of light and colour to a greater degree than existed in their
own lives'. As he had done previously, he emphasised the importance of
film in education.[24]

His major extracurricular pursuit at this time was, however, table tennis.
The organisation Montagu had founded was restructured as a nation-
ally representative body under the energetic leadership of a former trade
union official, W.J. Pope, and became the English Table Tennis Association
in 1927; Ivor, despite his initial resistance to the plan, remained chairman. Meanwhile, following on discussions in Germany over summer
1926, Montagu staged European Championships at the Memorial Hall in
Farringdon Street, London, in December (he was the non-playing English
captain), and an International Table Tennis Federation (ITTF) was formed.
Ivor was elected chairman, later renamed president, a position he would
continue to hold for the next forty years. (A recent publication suggests that

this was a dastardly ingenious scheme of Montagu's with political motivation: 'Convinced that the sport could spread Communism throughout the world,' Nicholas Griffin writes, 'he founded the International Table Tennis Federation, eventually engineering its path to Mao's China.')[25]

On 10 January 1927, Ivor Goldsmid Samuel Montagu of 20 Old Buildings, Lincoln's Inn, and Eileen Mansfield Hellstern of 3 Mostyn Road, Brixton, were married at the Bloomsbury register office. The witnesses were Angus MacPhail and Marjorie Russell. There was a hitch, since Ivor, standing on principle, did not have a ring: he believed bestowing a ring on the bride to be an 'odious ritual' signifying that henceforth she would become the husband's property, and he had no intention of subjecting Hell to such humiliation. To his surprise and discomfiture, he was informed by the registrar in the midst of the ceremony that it was a legal requirement. Marjorie came to the rescue, offering up her own ring for the purpose. The formalities duly completed, Ivor went off to chat up an actress Mick Balcon wanted in a forthcoming picture, leaving, he says, Angus and Marjorie to lunch the bride. 'That Hell neither wept nor swore never to see me more is due perhaps less to a forgiving nature than to the fact that she already knew what she was taking on,' he wryly observes.[26]

The intention was to keep the wedding a secret. Neither Ivor nor Hell wished to inform their family. And for some weeks the secret was kept; Hell continued living in Brixton and commuting to her work at a dressmaker's in the city, while Ivor remained at Lincoln's Inn and toiled away in his Gainsborough job. But one night, on a visit to Kensington Court, Ivor was 'inexpressibly moved' by a rare moment of intimacy with his father – 'the first time in my life he had ever made a gesture towards even an appearance of respect for any of my ideas' – and in gratitude let on about the marriage.

The shock, that his son should wed someone so beneath himself in social status, was for Lord Swaythling immense: he was 'struck down by what he clearly regarded as an irremediable calamity', and only slightly appeased by learning that Hell, though she had not been brought up in the faith, was Jewish. 'Yes, but why did you have to marry her?' he kept muttering, to which the shaken young man could only reply, 'I do not know.' For Ivor, as an intellectual protégé of Shaw and Wells, this meant an acknowledgment of the need to re-examine Victorian assumptions about marriage; for Lord Swaythling, though, 'all he understood, and I did not in my naîveté realise this until long afterwards, thinking it over, was simply that I already regretted what I had done.'[27]

In contrast to the parental reaction on learning of his General Strike activities, on this occasion it was his mother who was the less intransigent. 'She did not reproach,' Ivor explains, 'so much as seek details. I remember her saying, "But I thought you were fond of one of the Houston sisters, the younger one with the short hair."' He replied, if he recalls right: 'Yes, but Hell has just the same haircut.' His impression was that Lady Swaythling was distressed more for her husband's sake than for the deed itself, and 'sought chiefly to mollify and console him'. Montagu left them to sort out their feelings.[28]

It was not long after this that the press learnt of the affair. London was placarded with posters announcing 'PEER'S SON MARRIES TYPIST' (or was it 'BARON'S SON WEDS SECRETARY'?). The sensational news was flashed across the Atlantic: in New York, it was 'HON. IVOR MONTAGU MARRIES A TYPIST'; in Washington, 'TITLED BANKER'S SON TAKES TYPIST BRIDE'; in Chicago, 'SON OF ENGLAND'S RICHEST MAN WEDS STENOGRAPHER'. Ivor and Hell were besieged, the papers desperate for a photograph of the bride. The groom was raging, obstinate: 'Her face should NOT become public property.' The newlyweds resorted to wig and mask, and to escaping from the Old Buildings through the window and across the roof. It could not continue. Ivor's journalist friend Walter Mycroft, under fire for not giving his *Evening Standard* editors the scoop, persuaded the couple to have Alex Stewart do the job professionally. Ivor was not entirely won over by the results, but 'at least he managed to give her a satisfying languishing and romantic look.' The picture was published, and the furore died down. In Brixton, William Ernest Ely, Rowna's father, turned up, after many years, and enquired after his daughter's welfare. He was not admitted, and did not return.[29]

The hectic pace at Gainsborough slackened enough, by March, for Ivor to be able to take a break. The young couple's choice of a honeymoon destination was determined by the rodent specialist at the British Museum who, on being consulted, advised Ivor that the BM was very desirous of acquiring porcupines from Sicily. (Ivor had by this time renounced all ambition to become a professional zoologist – at the end of 1925 he had 'thrown away' an opportunity to undertake completion of the standard *History of British Mammals* – but he retained a keen amateur interest.) Ivor and Hell thus formally celebrated the commencement of a life of connubial bliss trekking along the dusty roads of Castelbuono under a parching sun, and skinning trapped mice (since porcupines were not to be found) in a flea-ridden room at the village inn. (Curiously the American press was reporting at this time that the Hon. Ivor collected fleas dead or alive and 'chloroforms the live ones himself'.) Other irritants included a student assistant who kept trying to inveigle his way into Hell's bed, the Fascist local chief of police who took to lounging in their room, and, in Palermo, laughing crowds who had never till then beheld the spectacle of a young woman with short-cropped hair and a knee-length skirt. The prize catch of the expedition was a live marten, which accompanied them, not without tribulations, to Paris, where it devoured its own feet and had to be destroyed.[30]

Having dinner at Kensington Court on their return, the couple discovered they were both ill. Ivor was packed off to a nursing home with jaundice, while Hell, who had contracted an obscure strain of typhoid, was put to bed in the home of in-laws who scarcely knew her. It is likely that her weakened condition softened the attitude of Ivor's parents towards her; besides, they had likely received a favourable report on Eileen Hellstern from Louis's younger brother Lionel, who had been deputed (Ivor surmises) to check her out. Lady Swaythling had received many letters of sympathy when the marriage was made public, including one from Queen Mary; Ivor maintains that it read simply, 'Dear Gladys, I feel for you, May,' but according to the *Berkeley Daily Gazette* there was more to it than that. 'Lady Swaythling did not take kindly to the news of her son's marriage,' the American paper reported. 'Neither did Mayfair. No one suggested that the bride should be received in society, least of all the new in-laws. This version reached Queen Mary. She immediately sat down and wrote Lady Swaythling a warm letter congratulating her on her son's marriage and evincing the keenest delight in the romance of it.' That letter, the *Gazette* claimed, 'was tantamount to a command that Lady Swaythling should follow the traditional custom and present her new daughter at court which she is now dutifully expected to do.' To cap this possibly apocryphal version of events, it was said that 'the Queen's democratic gesture is being enthusiastically applauded by young Montagu's radical friends.'[31]

When fit enough, Montagu resumed work at Gainsborough. Buoyed by the 'colossal success' *Blighty* enjoyed at a preview screening in Birmingham, he returned to editing on *Downhill* and another Hitchcock film, *Easy*

Virtue, adapted from a Noël Coward play. *Downhill* featured a remarkable subjective sequence showing the viewpoint of the protagonist, suffering from delirium, as he returns to London from abroad. Wavy handheld shots of busy city streets are overlapped in a series of dissolves and superimpositions, in a highly effective collaboration between cameraman and editor. 'I have never met anyone in British pictures,' Ivor was to write of Hitchcock in his memoirs, 'with whom I found creative work more agreeable and more congenial … no one else I met in British films shared the analytical approach that I had learned from science, or could be articulate about it.' But a disagreement arose.[32]

There was a scene in *Downhill* in which an amorous game between an actress and her two lovers was played out in a taxi, with one of the men facing the couple on the back seat from the tip-up seat opposite. 'The director's ingenious idea,' Montagu explains, in one of his many accounts of this episode:

> … was to show, from a view directly above, the six knees of the three people and reveal the personal relationships by the contacts and avoidances of the knees. Excellent and, because connected by logic, not vitiated by the unusualness of the viewpoint. But unfortunately the wrong lens had been used, and the apparent distance of the knees from the spectator was so great as to jolt the spectator out of engrossment, for he could not but realise that he could not have seen what he saw unless the roof of the taxi had been removed. The ideal spectator must be an ideally placed *possible* spectator; the impossible jars.[33]

Since Ivor could not bring himself to cut Hitchcock's shot in, and because, he says, 'I hate to quarrel with people I like about matters only of taste,' he used his 'precious independence' – he was still in receipt of his father's allowance – to give notice. In a letter dated 14 April to Michael Balcon, he explained: 'I have discussed the picture *Downhill* with Mr Hitchcock. Mr Hitchcock's views on the powers and duties of a film editor differ from my own. In these circumstances it is clearly undesirable that I should edit *Downhill*, a view shared, I believe, by Mr Hitchcock.' He went on: 'Unless, therefore, I be required to edit the picture by my contractual obligations I shall certainly not undertake the work.' It was a stand on principle: 'I wish also to be released from further regular employment by the company. I am not satisfied that I can work to the best advantage while my powers and duties are insufficiently clearly defined.' Nonetheless, he wanted to keep open the possibility of freelance work: 'I shall however be happy to undertake any specific separate task if on any future occasion my service should be helpful either to you or to the company.'[34]

The following week, the resignation having been effected, Balcon wrote to say that Iris Barry had been in touch and 'seemed anxious to make a story of this.' Balcon was of the view that neither he nor Montagu wanted any publicity over the matter, 'and I told her that there was really nothing to talk about but that you had merely resigned from a regular occupation to devote your time to other important matters, also that you prefer to do freelance work. I do hope that I was expressing your viewpoint on this matter.' The following month *Downhill* was trade shown. The knee shot in the taxi was from head height; it had clearly been retaken.[35]

To suit his new marital status Montagu now moved to slightly more commodious lodgings, along with Hell, at 43 Leicester Square. Situated at the exact south-west corner of the square, the flat had a poky staircase and small, but light, rooms, except those that gave on an inner well. Downstairs there was an expensive restaurant 'where we could not afford to eat for pleasure but often did for business entertainment.' The young couple furnished it with leftovers from Cambridge and the fruits of a spending spree in Tottenham Court Road, including a double bed made of timbers from the Watford Old Church. Hell was a firm believer in the merits of double beds for the married. 'She says that if you have a sense of humour,' Ivor was to relate, 'you can hardly go to bed with your bottoms bumping up against each other when you are not on speaking terms, so you have to make up your quarrels before bedtime.' The Soviet film director Sergei Eisenstein, visiting in 1929, described it as 'an astonishing narrow little house (with three windows)', next door, he observed, to the Studio publishing company.[36]

Ivor enjoyed being at the centre of the metropolis, despite the ceaseless din outside; it suited his new freelance lifestyle. 'Theatres and cinemas, galleries and exhibitions, all the places where you must eat, study or negotiate with colleagues or with rivals a few paces away,' and being able to settle down over work 'till it was finished, maybe in the small hours, and then stroll back an easy distance through pale dawn streets deserted except for an occasional dustman'. He also discovered a new pastime at the next-door billiard saloon. Meanwhile, Hell had given up the rag trade to take a job at Gainsborough, becoming continuity girl for Brunel on his production of *The Vortex*.[37]

At this time Montagu took part in an ambitious audience-research survey undertaken by Angus MacPhail on behalf of Sidney Bernstein and his chain of cinemas. Typically combative, Montagu is reported to have been one of only two respondents, of several hundred thousand, to denounce British films. The most newsworthy aspect of the results was what they revealed of the predominant attitude of the upper classes towards this new form of mass entertainment. Five bishops replied that they were not in the habit of frequenting cinemas ('Never go, as it strains my eyes,' said the Bishop of Chichester); thirteen peers said they never went at all. As for Lord Swaythling, 'all he required was a comfortable seat in which to smoke and as good air as possible.'[38]

A few days before this story was published, Ivor and Hell accepted an invitation to spend a weekend at Townhill. Ivor's father, having come to know Hell, wished his son to understand that his doubts were at an end. 'He accepted the marriage and wished me to regard ourselves as reconciled.' The weekend went well, but Lord Swaythling caught a chill from which, compounded with acute gout, he never recovered. Returned to Kensington Court, he slipped into a coma and died at 57 in the early hours of Saturday 11 June. Ivor with his brothers Stuart and Ewen stood by the body, wearing prayer shawls and reciting the Kaddish. 'We all realised,' Montagu writes, 'that our lives would henceforth fall into a new pattern.'[39]

Following a funeral at the Willesden Jewish Cemetery and a memorial service at the New West End Synagogue in Bayswater, the brothers gathered at Kensington Court for a reading of the will. The 2nd Baron Swaythling may have been one of the richest men in Britain, but the bulk of the inheritance went to his widow and his eldest son. Ivor discovered that a codicil dated 8 February 1927 – that is, after his father had learnt of the marriage – deprived him of three-fifths of what was to have been his portion. The resultant sum, £20,000, was not to be his outright, but to be placed in a trust fund from which he would draw interest, to protect him 'from the danger incurred by people who are not engaged in any active business life'.[40]

It is clear from Ivor's unpublished autobiographical manuscript, written forty odd years later, that the partial disinheritance rankled, even while he acknowledged the privileged position a private income afforded him. 'Two-fifths of a loaf is very much more comfortable than no bread,' he observes philosophically. 'I could be a rebel with comparative impunity.' And he quotes William Morris, who 'puts it rather caustically':

When the poor man thinks – and rebels, the whip lies ready anear;
But he who is a rebel and rich may live soft for many a year,
While he warms his heart with pictures of all the glory to come.

The interest income turned out to be roughly equivalent to the allowance he had been receiving; and while he could not touch the capital, he could raise credit on it.[41]

Montagu's working life was at this time mainly centred on Brunel's editing company in Dansey Yard. 'The variety of the work,' Brunel was to write, 'was one of its many attractive qualities. We never knew from week to week what would be coming in. Next week's film might be American, Burmese, or Japanese; it might be a spy drama, a village comedy or a medical instructional film. Again, anything might happen in connection with the work; one of us might have to go to Berlin, Rome or Paris; or F. J. Perry, the [future] tennis champion, might call in for a game of table tennis with Ivor, his coach; or we might have a sudden trade-show job, requiring three or four of us to go down to a film studio and work on the editing of a film for forty-eight hours without going to bed ...' Montagu confirms that 'people would call us in to remedy a catastrophe, or when they were unexpectedly short-handed, or if an unscheduled problem cropped up.' The bread and butter, however, remained the preparation of English versions of foreign productions.[42]

In August 1927, Montagu graduated from employee to partner, and the company Brunel & Montagu Ltd was formed. The directors comprised the two principals along with Frank Wells, the son of H.G., who was intent on making a career in the industry. Ivor had now to smarten up, at least when he was required to negotiate with industry executives. 'When it was decided that Ivor should call on a certain firm, the staff was called in to edit his untidy appearance,' Brunel explains. 'One of us would brush and comb his hair, another would clean his shoes; a third would brush his suit, and a fourth would be called upon to lend Ivor a tie, because his was too shabby or else he had forgotten to put one on that day.' (Inspired by the colour of the *pissoir* outside the front door in Dansey Yard, Montagu in fact designed a staff tie for the firm, 'green with thin diagonal strips of gold'.)[43]

Brunel & Montagu Ltd provided Ivor with a happy environment in which he was able 'to work with others who were so like-minded that all contributed their experience and particular angles to the consensus without rivalry.' His editing workmates, along with his partners Brunel and Wells, included from the start T. Lionel ('Tod') Rich, 'an upright lugubrious type of man with a strong sense of humour that he would die rather than allow to appear in his demeanour', and J.O.C. ('Jock') Orton, 'shorter and heavier, with a rosy complexion and hair receding from the forehead, ex-Captain R.F.C.'. Angus MacPhail had by this time left to become scenario editor at Gainsborough, but the crew were joined by Ian Dalrymple, another former editor of *The Granta* at Cambridge. A recruit who was to become a particular friend and collaborator of Ivor's was a Russian refugee, Sergei Nalbandov (later Nolbandov), 'a peculiar man with a fund of peculiarly amusing stories' who had worked for the Moscow Narodny Bank and subsequently in diverse enterprises like 'inducing all of us to invest in hundredweights of Soviet honey that had got over-ripe in the docks'.[44]

The work of the company's crew of editors was generally not credited ('But for this fact,' Brunel comments, 'ours would have become a household name in all cinemas, for not only was the volume of our business considerable, but we dealt with many of the most famous films of those days.') It is not easy, therefore, to identify specific creative contributions of Montagu and his fellow editors at this time. According to Rachael Low, however, one film that Ivor was responsible for editing was *The Fake*, which was trade shown in September 1927. This adaptation of a play by Frederick Lonsdale was directed by Georg Jacoby and featured Elga Brink as a young woman forced to marry a degenerate drug-addicted aristocrat to satisfy the ambition of her politician father.[45]

Another production the company worked on at this time was *Taras Bulba*, a sixteenth-century Cossack epic based on Gogol's story. The film had been produced in Germany in 1923 by the expatriate Russian

Joseph Ermolieff, formerly a studio head in Yalta. Montagu recounts that Ermolieff 'wandered about Europe setting up vast super-spectacles without knowing how to dispose of them to the markets when they were finished.' Despite its lavish appearance, *Taras Bulba* had in fact been shot cheaply and hastily. On letting the Film Society have it for their October performance, Ermolieff asked that it be re-edited, and the job fell naturally to Brunel & Montagu; the English version ended up considerably shorter than the original. 'The child of these talkie times has little conception of the freedom of action a skilful adapter had in the elastic silent days,' Montagu writes, 'when with a few conscienceless cuts – "loose-wristed" Frank used to call them – a whole character or episode could be eliminated, tempo accelerated, a theme transformed.'[46]

Among other pictures the firm prepared for Film Society screening were *Hagidera Shinju/ The Tragedy of Temple Hagi* (Hotei Nomura, Japan, 1923), an innovative classical adaptation that required titles to be written to compensate for the absence of a live narrator (shown 8 January 1928); *Ingmarsarvet/Jerusalem* (Gustaf Molander, Sweden, 1925); from a novel by Selma Lagerlöf (5 February 1928); and F.W. Murnau's version of Molière, *Tartuffe* (Germany, 1925) (1 April 1928). Major editing jobs for Montagu and for Adrian Brunel (when he was able to tear himself away from his directing at Gainsborough) were Alexander Macdonald's *The Unsleeping Eye*, a New Guinea jungle adventure featuring a drunken gold miner fighting natives, released in May 1928, and Walter Summers' *The Marquis of Bolibar*, a costume drama set in 1808 during the Peninsular War in Spain. The latter was trade shown in July 1928 and achieved a West End booking, which, however, was cancelled owing to the popularity of newly intro-duced talking pictures at the theatre.[47]

Ivor gained a reputation among his fellow workers as an eagle-eyed editor. Recalling his time with the company more than forty years later, Ian Dalrymple wrote:

My happiest memory of the preparation of a Film Society programme was when Frank Wells, in Ivor's absence in Moscow at a scientific (? or Table Tennis) Happening, prepared Pudovkin's *The Mother*. Having gone sedulously through & through the film, Frank decided that it would be improved if he took out from one of the most impressionistic passages a

flash of a piece of ladder about this size [sketch of film strip with 7 frames].
When Ivor ran the film on his return he at once detected its absence &
demanded its replacement: and all hell broke loose as we searched the bins
for the [sketch of film strip with 7 frames].[48]

Simultaneously with his editing practice, Montagu was refining his
theoretical approach to film. 'Social Ideology in the Cinema', published
in *The Plebs* in August 1927, is significant for its early fusion of applied
Marxist and Freudian concepts in its analysis of the movie industry and its
popular appeal (while betraying the same streak of cultural elitism as that
on which the Film Society based its claim to exemption from censorship).
Arguing that, because of their cost structure, films under capitalism can
only be made to satisfy a nondiscriminating mass audience, Montagu contends that the entertainment they provide 'is in the nature of a release of
repression, repression relating usually to the sexual or economic life of the
individual'. The viewing situation aids this process: 'A cinematographic
performance takes place in conditions of relative comfort … relative
darkness … and in the presence of warmth and music. These conditions
are peculiarly favourable to the construction of fantasies.' Films help fulfil
these fantasies:

> In a capitalist civilisation in which the mating of the common citizen is so
> hampered and indissoluble, and in which the worker's life, from the small-
> ness of his purse, is so constantly sordid and disappointing, the films always
> assume the character of histories of sexual relations beween attractive pro-
> tagonists, long delayed and frustrated but reaching eventual consummation.'

And likewise:

> In a system in which the common citizen is engaged in an occupation
> from which he derives little satisfaction, and which he endures only as
> an earning chore or task, in which, moreover, the worker is a wage-slave
> or subordinate, his fantasies always deal with heroes who act throughout
> only of their own free will, who begin despised, climb the social ladder
> and end triumphant and honoured.

Hence the absence of tragedy: ' ... the very prevalence of the happy or triumphant ending is an indication of the repressed and unsatisfactory life of the
common member of society.' Of course, things were different in Russia ... [49]

Meanwhile, lobbying by the Film Producers' Group of the Federation of
British Industries was finally bearing fruit. The Cinematograph Films Act,
after a laborious passage through Parliament for most of the year, was passed
into law in December 1927. Soon known as the Quota Act, it restricted
blind and block booking and introduced quotas for British films – to start
with, 7.5 per cent for renters and 5 per cent for exhibitors, both to rise by
stages to 20 per cent by 1936. Perhaps from now on, as Montagu had predicted, the bulk of British producers would be 'safeguarded by legislation ...
from the consequences of their own stupidity'. But for the time being, he
had other things on his mind.

6

CULTURAL RELATIONS

If the muses may be suspected of political tendencies, the deity that presides over the cinema is certainly Socialist. – Eric Walter White[1]

IMMEDIATELY ON HIS return from the Soviet Union in September 1925 Montagu received a letter from Catherine Rabinovitch, honorary secretary of the Society for Cultural Relations between the Peoples of the British Commonwealth and the Union of Socialist Soviet Republics [sic], known for short as the SCR. She had heard of his 'very interesting trip to Russia' from Mr Ashley Dukes, a member of her Committee. Mr Dukes (a playwright and theatre critic) thought that Ivor might care to join the SCR, and they would be very glad to have him as a member. Moreover, his name had been suggested as a guest and speaker at one of their next functions. Enclosing a copy of the society's annual report, Mrs Rabinovitch invited him to call and make an appointment to talk with her.[2]

The SCR was the British affiliate of VOKS, the All-Union Society for Cultural Relations with Foreign Countries. The need for the young revolutionary state to cultivate contacts with the Western intelligentsia had been recognised by Theodore Rothstein, who in the early 1920s, after his expulsion from Britain, headed the Press Section of the Commissariat of Foreign Affairs. It was apparently at his instigation that the Commissariat set up, in December 1923, a United Information Bureau (OBI) as a section of the Committee on Foreign Aid (KZP). The tasks of the OBI were defined as 'propaganda among the foreign intelligentsia through acquainting them with the cultural gains and work of the Soviet Republic'. Driving the new organisation was the head of the KZP, Olga Kameneva, a leading Bolshevik, wife of Politburo member Lev Kamenev and sister of Leon Trotsky. In April 1925 the OBI was transformed into VOKS, ostensibly independent of the government, with Kameneva still at the helm.[3]

In sponsoring the formation of cultural friendship societies internationally Kameneva collaborated with Willi Münzenberg and his Berlin-based IAH, although at times there were clashes because of differing priorities.

In London Dr Varvara Polovtsev, head of the IAH-affiliated (Soviet) Russian Red Cross, was charged with organising British intellectuals. As a result of her efforts the SCR was established in July 1924, with Margaret Llewelyn Davies as Chairman, Mrs Rabinovitch as Hon. Secretary, Prof. L.T. Hobhouse as President, and a raft of vice-presidential luminaries – including E.M. Forster, Julian Huxley, John Maynard Keynes, H.G. Wells and Virginia Woolf – to add lustre to the enterprise.[4]

According to a 1929 Special Branch report on the activities of Soviet organisations in Britain, the functions of the SCR were 'completely in the hands of' the UK Cell of the Russian Communist Party, through its control of appointments – 'the secretary is appointed by the Cell and the candidates for the Executive Committee are nominated by the Cell' – and through the positions held by Cell members in the various sections. At the time Montagu was approached, making sure the organisation adhered to Soviet objectives would undoubtedly have been the responsibility of Executive Committee members Polovstev, Andrew Rothstein, and L.F. Gueruss. Rothstein, the son of Theodore, was a member of the Communist underground coordinating clandestine intelligence operations in Britain; Gueruss was an employee of the Soviet Embassy. The principal objective of the SCR as announced in its first annual report was 'to collect and diffuse information in both countries on developments in Science, Education, Philosophy, Art, Literature, and Social and Economic Life' to be achieved by means including lectures, conferences, exhibitions, publication and translation.[5]

Montagu must have responded favourably to Mrs Rabinovitch's overtures. On 5 February 1926 in Cambridge he gave a lecture for the SCR, accompanied by lantern slides, on 'The Russian Theatre and Cinema of Today'. The talk was in conjunction with an SCR exhibition of Russian Posters, Books & Peasant Handicraft, and was organised by Maurice Dobb.

Ivor also reviewed the exhibition – which offered examples of fine art publications alongside the 'Popular Peasants Library' and illustrated children's books, as well as posters on education, agriculture and health – in the *Sunday Worker* of 7 February. Though the content of Ivor's talk was not recorded in the SCR's annual report, it may be surmised it was somewhat more favourable to new developments in Russian theatre than Basil Dean's lecture for the SCR, likewise given after a trip to the Soviet Union, later in the year. Dean was scathing about the 'Extreme Left' theatre of Meyerhold, denouncing his production of Tretyakov's *Roar, China!* as 'a vicious piece of propaganda against England and America' and describing Meyerhold as 'a fanatical politician prostituting his art to a political cause.'[6]

Meanwhile, Montagu persevered in his self-appointed mission to bring Soviet motion pictures to the United Kingdom. By the beginning of 1926 the only post-Revolution features to have been screened in Britain were *Morosko* (Yuri Zheliabuzhsky, 1924) – a folk tale acted by members of the Moscow Art Theatre, which was released in October 1925 – and the Tolstoy adaptation *Polikushka*, which had been distributed noncommercially by the WIR (including one week at a cinema 'ignorantly, without submission to the censor' which, as Montagu reported, 'nearly led to serious trouble'). In addition, there had been *Red Russia* – 'old news reels, severely censored and given counter-revolutionary subtitles by the censor', while the WIR made available an assortment of fictional and nonfictional shorts depicting aspects of life in the Soviet Union to workingmen's clubs, miners' lodges, Labour Parties, Co-operative Societies, etc.[7]

Ivor's immediate plans for remedying this lamentable situation were to secure the three Mezhrabpom-Russ features he had selected, during his visit to Russia the previous year, for screening at the Film Society. Willi Münzenberg's assistant in Berlin, Louis Gibarti (a Hungarian Communist whose real name was Laszlo Dobos) had discussed the idea with Montagu in London. On 9 January Gibarti wrote to him saying, 'We are fully agreeing with your plan concerning the film *His Call* and will not fail to let you know when the picture will be sent across.' The following week Montagu was in Berlin and presented himself at IAH headquarters with introductions to Münzenberg from Comrades D. Bogomolov, First Secretary at the Soviet Embassy in Britain, and R. Bailey of the WIR. He was told: 'We had just decided to accept your scheme when there came from Russia, Comrade

Aleinikov. Nothing can be done without his permission and he is inclined to oppose it.' Moisei Aleinikov, the production chief at Mezhrabpom-Russ, met with Montagu and explained that he did not approve of the plan since he intended to go to England and try to sell the pictures himself. In the event Aleinikov does not appear to have come personally to London, but in March a company representative, Herman Basler, arrived on a mission 'to obtain a satisfactory arrangement' for *The Station Master*. In the same letter in which he introduced Basler to Montagu, Gibarti promised again to dispatch *His Call*, but it never arrived.[8]

Still hopeful, Ivor kept up a correspondence with Mezhrabpom-Russ manager Francesco Misiano in Moscow. Following Ernst Toller's interceding on Montagu's behalf, Misiano wrote on 23 March saying the company was happy to deliver films to England, but only by way of purchase. The 'glowing acclaim' [*glänzende Erfolge*] their films had achieved abroad – he enclosed a German review of *The Station Master* – seemed a guarantee that Montagu's organisation would easily find a way of solving the financial problem.[9]

Montagu's frustration boiled over. 'Dear Comrade Messiano [*sic*],' he wrote:

You must allow me to speak frankly. Your business methods are those of an idiot or a child. How many times have I told you that I have not got any money, that I do not and cannot buy films? Don't you realise I am just as anxious to help Russian film productions in England as you are, probably more anxious judging from the ridiculous way in which your organisation has wasted the last ten months? Don't you understand that no matter what good reports I, or Mr Bernstein, or your newspaper clippings give by hearsay of Russian films, NO BUSINESS MAN in England will pay a penny piece for them until he has seen them in this country for himself? Why then don't you send copies over here for an agent to hawk round trying to sell? The answer is (1) Because your agent at W.I.R. in London is a poor over-worked comrade with no knowledge of the film trade and no time to do anything anyway, and (2) Because to import them costs money in duty etc. Very well then, why haven't you taken advantage of my offer, made to you last August, and repeated by letters and telegrams (unanswered by you) about twice a month, to place at your disposal the services of myself and my organisation in defraying the cost of import and helping to sell any copies you send?

You do nothing but talk rubbish about the successes of your films in Germany. Have you never been outside Russia? Don't you know that German culture, German politics, German artistic tastes, above all the German film world are different from those in England? Your films are good enough, certainly, but exploitation methods that succeed with them in Germany will have to be very different before they succeed with them in England.

Producers from all Europe jump to avail themselves of the aid we can give to so-called artistic films, and yet you, owing to your stupidity, think that because we offer to give Russian producers the same aid free and without profit we must necessarily be trying to deceive you.

Yours,[10]

The letter may never have been sent; there is, in any event, no reply from Misiano in the files. Montagu now changed tack and attempted to revive negotiations with Sovkino, which had been unavailing the previous year. In July, Ivor was informed by Kniga (England) Ltd, a sales and translation agency for Russian books, that the company had been appointed the agent for Sovkino in Britain. Kniga were happy to deal with Montagu, who had helped them in arranging a preview screening of *Vsem na radost* ('All for Joy', Alexander Anoshchenko, 1924). But Kniga's lack of experience in film distribution would clearly prove a handicap. Montagu attempted to push things along by contacting directly the Soviet trade mission (*Torgpredstvo/ Handelsvertretung*) in Berlin, the body responsible for handling Soviet films in Western Europe. Bogomolov at the Embassy came to Ivor's assistance by sending a letter to Sovkino explaining his intentions and begging them 'to note this and to instruct the Berlin representation to assist Ayvar Montague [*sic*] in his work.'[11]

The *Photokino Abteilung* of the Berlin *Handelsvertretung* wrote to Montagu in January 1927 approving his proposal with regard to the films *Aelita* and *His Call*. But months went by and still nothing concrete eventuated. Montagu had to be content with trotting out the battered WIR print of *Polikushka* at the Film Society on 10 April, explaining that the copy of the film had been 're-edited throughout to reduce the "jumps" due to wear and tear'. The Society had finally succeeded in bringing a Russian film to its members, but the adaptation shot in 1919 of a tale of serfdom dating back to 1863 was a far cry from something like the pulsating *Bronenosets 'Potyomkin'/Battleship Potemkin* (Sergei Eisenstein, 1925) which had been thrilling German audiences for the past year with its revolutionary politics and aesthetics, and which was banned in Britain. The following month the Arcos raid and subsequent events were to make any form of business or cultural relationship with the Soviet Union even more difficult.[12]

Relations between Baldwin's government and the USSR had been uneasy from the start, when the Conservatives had come into power on the back of the infamous Zinoviev letter of October 1924. Though many in politics correctly assumed the letter to have been forged, the administration had other more reliable information of what they regarded as Comintern meddling in British affairs, which continued to accumulate in the years that followed. Tensions were heightened during the General Strike, when Soviet trade unions attempted to give financial support to the strikers, and in 1927 hardline Cabinet members and Conservative backbenchers became alarmed at secret service reports of hostile propaganda and espionage directed at Britain from the USSR. When MI5 advised that a confidential army training manual had been photocopied by an employee of Arcos – the All-Russian Co-operative Society, established following the 1921 Anglo-Soviet trade agreement – the government took the opportunity to pounce. On 12 May police raided Soviet House, home to Arcos and the USSR trade delegation, and for three days searched and seized documents, using pneumatic drills and acetylene torches to force their way into strong rooms. Eventually some 3 tons of paper were hauled away, but the crucial incriminating document was not among them, and no telling evidence of Soviet espionage was uncovered. The government found itself forced to use material garnered from signals intelligence (thereby revealing that it had cracked Soviet codes used for encrypting telegrams) in order to justify the breaking off of diplomatic and trade relations, which occurred two weeks later. The Soviet Union responded with vehement denunciation of alleged British plotting to overthrow the Bolshevik regime and summary executions of former aristocrats claimed to have links with British intelligence.

The rupture had a severe impact on the SCR, as many of its Russian members – including Dr Polovtsev – belonged to Soviet organisations in

London and were expelled. Finances were badly affected. The committee
debated whether or not to continue, with Catherine Rabinovitch arguing
that the society should cease operations. She was outvoted, however; a call
for emergency financial support went out to members, and the SCR strug-
gled on, albeit with little contact with VOKS.[13]

Montagu was preoccupied with other matters. Between 14 and 17 May
he attended the Middlesex vs Hampshire cricket match at Lord's, in the
same week he took in performances of *Convicts* by Norman Lee at the
Holborn Empire and a variety show (including Harry Lauder) at the
Victoria Palace, and on 1 June he went to the second day of the Epsom
Races (he picked the winners in the first and third races, but was out of luck
in the others). Then, on 11 June, his father died.[14]

In July Montagu was jerked back to the consideration of Soviet films
and how to get them to Britain with a letter from Rose Cohen in Moscow.
Cohen, an East End girl of Polish Jewish parentage, was a founder member
of the CPGB. In 1921, as an employee of the Labour Research Department,
she met Comintern representative Max Petrovsky, who had come to
Britain to facilitate financial support for the LRD. Cohen was enlisted into
Comintern work, and in 1922–23 she is believed to have travelled widely in
Europe carrying large sums of money to Communist parties, before taking
up employment in Moscow for the English section of the Comintern's
press department. Back in London from the end of 1924, with her 'black
hair, red cheeks, flashing eyes, a provocative smile and a quick wit' Rose
was popular in Communist circles and caught the eye of Harry Pollitt, who
on many occasions (fourteen, he claims) proposed to her and was turned
down. Ivor met her at a party given in 1925 for Willie Gallacher and others
of the twelve CPGB leaders when they were briefly out on bail prior to
their imprisonment. In 1927 Cohen moved to Moscow and worked with
Petrovsky (British Comintern representative since 1924), as his secretary; at
some point they were married.[15]

Cohen now asked Ivor if he was still interested in Russian films, and if so,
she could make arrangements to let him have some of the 'really interesting'
pictures that were being made in connection with the tenth anniversary of
the Russian Revolution, which was to be a very big affair. She asked for a
quick response, 'because you know from somewhat bitter experience that
things tend to move rather slowly here.'[16]

Ivor responded positively, but without much hope. 'I can handle any Russian film material to the best advantage,' he wrote. Pictures that were suitable for public exhibition he could import and sell; others he could distribute to working class district cinemas. If a film was likely to raise political difficulties, he could 'handle it in a tactful manner, getting government permission, showing it to the press and critics, etc.' As for expenses, he was 'very keen to pay ... within the limits of my pocket, and give all services free as agent for Russian stuff of any kind ... but they persist in expecting me to pay for the films into the bargain and as I have no money, we get no forrader.' Any proceeds would be returned – 'of course there won't be much because of the closed nature of the market here, but at least the stuff will be seen, and sold as well as it can be.' However – 'I despair of them ever seeing the light.' He concluded by saying he longed to come out again for a visit ('nowhere else is as invigorating as Russia'), and sending his love to Yarotsky and Tomsky.[17]

Montagu's next move was to get back in contact with the *Photokino Abteilung* of the Soviet *Handelsvertretung* in Berlin. He reminded the agency of their previous correspondence, including the trade mission's agreement to the Film Society's offer to import titles such as *Aelita* and *His Call* 'entirely at our own expense, title them in English at our own expense, and at the conclusion of our single performance return them immediately to you at our expense either with English titles or exactly as we receive them'. Restraining the impatience he had expressed to Misiano of Mezhrabpom-Russ, he added tactfully, 'Owing we presume to some misunderstanding, you took no further action and we have never received any of the films then agreed upon ...' However, he and Walter Mycroft of the Film Society Council would shortly be visiting Berlin and they looked forward to reopening the matter.[18]

The *Photokino Abteilung* replied saying they were greatly interested in Montagu's proposal. A useful conversation and some film previewing seems to have taken place during his visit, which was probably around 13–20 September. It was on this trip that Ivor was able to see, in addition to a variety performance at the Vornehme Cabaret in Munich, the groundbreaking production of Ernst Toller's *Hoppla, wir leben!* (with interspersed film montages) at the Piscatorbühne in Berlin. He may also have made further contacts in the film industry, as he carried an introduction from Sidney Bernstein to First National Pictures.[19]

Back in London, Montagu recapitulated the position regarding Soviet film distribution in England in a letter to the trade mission, explaining that Mr Enders (of the company Film Booking Offices) had the first option of selecting Russian films for exhibition in England, but that he could take only pictures that would be acceptable to the censor and which were of sufficient commercial appeal; there were thus many Russian films, 'often of high technical merit', which he did not select.[20]

Intriguingly, this revived initiative reawakened MI5's interest in Montagu. A Home Office Warrant was issued on both him and Mycroft at 6 Dansey Yard on 30 September, the reason given being, 'These people ... are in touch with Tomski and Yarotski of the U.S.S.R. C.C.T.U. with a view to the importation of Russian Films, including propaganda films into this country.' On 24 October, a request was made to extend the warrant to cover telegrams sent to the cable address of Brunel & Montagu Ltd.[21]

Meanwhile, preparations were under way in the Soviet Union for a massive international propaganda exercise. VOKS, in co-ordination with the Comintern's agitprop department, the foreign commission of the trade unions, and Münzenberg's IAH, planned to invite a thousand foreign delegates for a 'Congress of Friends' to be held in conjunction with the celebrations for the tenth anniversary of the Revolution. Cohen realised that this would provide an excellent opportunity for Montagu to visit and again plead his case. On 10 October she wrote to Ivor proposing that he come to the USSR as a delegate ('you can regard this letter as an official invitation'), arriving as soon as possible, and assuring him that the film authorities were 'very keen' on his idea.[22]

Although she was not specific, Cohen was undoubtedly acting on behalf of the Comintern; Petrovsky was a high-ranked official in the Anglo-American section and very likely had connections with the agitprop department. On receiving the letter Montagu cabled Yarotsky on 19 October: 'ROSE ASKS ME COME MOSCOW AS DELEGATE IS THIS OFFICIAL READY START BY AIR INSTANTLY AND WHERE DO I GET VISA'. On the same day he successfully negotiated an advance of £20 from the *Evening Standard*, in consideration of which the paper would receive first rights on any articles or interviews of his resulting from the trip.[23]

Hence the summons Montagu received to CPGB headquarters in King Street from Bob Stewart of the Party's central committee did not exactly come out of the blue, as he makes it sound in his memoirs. At this time Ivor did not know him well. The rugged-face Scot, he recounts, was grim and abrupt. 'We have had a request from the Communist International for you to go at once to Moscow,' he said. 'How soon can you leave?'[24]

Stewart was head of the CPGB's clandestine organisation. In the Party's early days he travelled to Moscow and returned 'with wads of banknotes hidden in a belt round his ample waist'. In 1923 he began working at Comintern headquarters as a CPGB representative, and on Lenin's death he had been part of an international delegation charged with bringing the body back from Nizhny Novgorod to lie in state in the capital. Back in Britain he was involved in Soviet-subsidised agitprop work among the armed forces and in passing military information to the Russians. Now, he appeared distinctly conspiratorial in issuing his young client with a yellow document on Party notepaper calling for every assistance to be given to Comrade Ivor Montagu, 'travelling to Moscow on business for the Communist International' – and warning, 'Don't show it to anyone.'[25]

According to Montagu's account, he was on the train to Berlin – where he would have to get his visa for the Soviet Union – that same afternoon. Onward progress from Germany was not so expeditious. His CPGB credentials availed for naught with the Soviet Ambassador, whom Ivor dragged out of bed in the dead of night. The impatient traveller was forced to wait some days for his visa to arrive, holed up in an apartment with a landlady who provided accommodation to comrades in transit, with his small stack of ready cash steadily diminishing. 'Nothing to spare for theatre, cinema, even reading matter,' he laments; still, he managed to get to a performance of Gerhart Hauptmann's *Dorothea Angermann* at the Deutsches Theater, directed by Max Reinhardt, with Werner Krauss and Oskar Homolka. It was probably at this time that he drew up an ambitious list of places and people he would like to see on this Russian visit, including the expected Palace of Labour (Yarotsky, Tomsky ...), VOKS (Kameneva ...), film studios, Bolshoi, Meyerhold Theatre, Academy of Sciences, and Zoological Museum, but also a ballet school, police court, clinics and hospitals, Kremlin buildings, ethnographical and modern art museums, and workers' clubs. His *Evening Standard* agenda read: '1. Stalin, 2. English spies, 3. Minority [perhaps a reference to the Opposition led by Trotsky]'.[26]

The alleged spies were certainly in the news. On 21 October the trial of 'the latest batch' opened at the Supreme Military Tribunal in Moscow. Five Russians were accused of selling Soviet secrets to a member of the British Mission. *The Times* reported that, 'As is usual at Soviet trials of this kind, certain of the prisoners show a surprising eagerness to assist the prosecution with "spontaneous disclosures".'[27]

Finally, Party officials in London cabled the Comintern in Moscow explaining that Ivor was stranded in Berlin awaiting instructions, and shortly thereafter the visa arrived. Another train journey and he belatedly reached the Soviet Union. It was probably 26 October.[28]

No one was there to meet him at the Moscow station, as far as he could see. Penniless and hungry, rucksack on his back, he 'stumbled off over the cobbles' to Comintern HQ. 'Here,' he recounts, 'within dirty double doors, was an ill-lit stone-paved ante-room and behind a long grille a bespectacled *dvornik*, or guardian, reigned in all his glory. Supplicants, after approaching him, waited in corners for the wheels to grind.' Montagu's English credentials failed to impress this doughty official, who demanded a proper *propusk*, and let fly an angry torrent of Russian when Ivor tried to insist. Rebuffed, the traveller trudged on to the trade union building, where, luckily, he found Yarotsky. 'Where *have* you been?' his friend demanded. 'The militia have been looking for you all over Moscow. The Comintern have been phoning everyone. They had a delegation at the station to meet you, but you weren't there.' It turned out that they had waited where the first-class carriages pulled up; Ivor had travelled 'hard'.[29]

The situation resolved, Montagu settled in to Room 201 at the Bolshaya Moskovskaya Hotel and set about his business. It would seem that he did not join up with the large British delegation for the anniversary celebrations, but was given special treatment. As was customary with foreign intellectuals, he was issued with a minder, a 'guide interpreter' who it turned out was an American with a Bowery accent deported for 'criminal anarchy', a man who 'spoke Russian worse, and knew his way around Moscow far less, than I did.' Very likely the OGPU, to whom such minders reported, was overstretched. As the disenchanted CPUSA leader Benjamin Gitlow later recounted:

Behind the greatest show ever put on display, an army of communists were busy at work, watching the delegates, steering them, moulding their opinions, getting them into the predestined grooves from which they were to carry on their work in their respective countries on behalf of the Soviet government and the communist world superstructure.

Ivor probably needed little steering from his Bowery companion: he was impressed by the 'bright and apparent confidence of all the working people' and the improvement in living standards since his last visit – 'material prosperity increases, clothes are cheaper, boots cheaper, etc.'[30]

To judge by the sketchy day-by-day summary of his activities Montagu jotted down, he wasn't able to achieve many of the goals he had set himself for this visit. He was, nevertheless, able to pack a lot in. He saw quite a bit of Rose Cohen, and something of Petrovsky and Yarotsky. He met up with the zoologist Sergei Ognev, and visited the zoo. On the 29th he went shopping – it was the day that three of the five 'British spies', having been condemned to death, were shot. He saw Mussorgsky's opera *Boris Godunov*, and went with Cohen to Tretyakov's *Roar, China!* at the Meyerhold (or such at least was the plan). He also caught Offenbach's *La Périchole* and Aristophanes' *Lysistrata* at the Moscow Art Theatre, and a concert to celebrate the tenth anniversary of the Revolution at the Bolshoi. As chairman of the International Table Tennis Federation he met with the heads of the Table Tennis section of Sport Kult, and competed with 'what seemed to be all the keenest players in Moscow' at the Comintern. (He tells an amusing story about how the rubber-covered racquet he wired Hell to send express from London – so that he could show off his 'cherished spins' – failed to arrive, turned back at the border labelled 'Rubber goods, not permitted to be imported into USSR'). And with his minder at his side he witnessed, from the gallery of the Bolshoi, Molotov make 'an endless detailed economic report – Stalin sitting tactfully and inconspicuously on the platform in the third row'.[31]

The *Evening Standard* published little on the Soviet Union in this period. A 5 November story from Moscow headed 'SOVIET FREES 20,000 CONVICTS', by-lined 'Our Own Correspondent', was perhaps from Montagu's pen; it detailed the amnesty declared by the government to mark the tenth anniversary, describing it as 'one of the most sweeping in the history of Russia and a most daring experiment'. Another story, again by 'Our Own Correspondent', appeared on 18 November and reported the suicide (two days earlier) of former Bolshevik diplomat Adolf Abramovich Joffe, although by this time Ivor had returned to England.[32]

But Montagu's principal mission was seeing Soviet films and achieving agreement, if he could, on his plans for their importation to Britain, and in this he was assiduous. No doubt at Petrovsky's instigation, he enlisted the support of Alfred Kurella, who headed, along with Béla Kun, the Comintern's agitprop department. After the arrangements twice fell through, the pair were finally able to meet with Sovkino head Shvedchikov on 1 November. They discussed Montagu's scheme, which Shvedchikov promised to consider and respond to. Over the following days Ivor was able to appraise the latest offerings from the studios. The films he previewed were a mixture of the contemporary and the historical: *Zhena/ The Wife* (Mikhail Doronin, 1927), a drama of marital infidelity in the NEP years; *Poet i tsar/ Poet and Tsar* (Vladimir Gardin and Yevgeni Chervyakov, 1927), a period drama about the relationship between Pushkin and Nicholas I; *Dekabristi/ Decembrists* (Alexander Ivanovsky, 1927), which dramatised the 1825 St Petersburg revolt; *Devyatoye yanvarya/ Ninth of January/ Bloody Sunday* (Vyacheslav Viskovsky, 1925), about the shooting of demonstrators outside the Winter Palace in January 1905; *Papirosnitsa ot Mosselproma/ The Cigarette Girl from Mosselprom* (Yuri Zhelyabuzhsky, 1924), a contemporary romantic comedy; and *Protsess o tryokh millyonakh/ Three Thieves* (Yakov Protazanov, 1926), a satirical comedy matching crime and big business. Meanwhile, Montagu's patience (buttressed by heavyweight Comintern backing) was being rewarded: his proposal – 'seed cast on soil less stony than had been the case two years before' – was given Shvedchikov's approval.[33]

The greatest excitement of his film viewing was the gala premiere at the Bolshoi of Vsevolod Pudovkin's epic spectacle for the tenth anniversary, *Konyets Sankt-Peterburga/ The End of St Petersburg*. This political narrative, with its dynamic re-enactment of the October Revolution, 'seemed to me,' Montagu was to write, 'the most wonderful picture I had seen up to that time'. Less impressive was the curtain-raiser, Boris Barnet's rushed *Moskva v Oktyabre/ Moscow in October*. The film was thrilling and featured an 'admirable' performance from Arkady Rosengolts, the Soviet *chargé d'affaires* recently expelled from Britain. Stalin, however, did not fare so well on screen. Playing himself, he was 'so shy that he looks constantly at camera and grins self-consciously.' (But then, 'Stalin, whether shy by purpose or second nature, carries self-consciousness to a fault whenever he appears in public.') And there was another problem. 'In desperation to finish,' Ivor explains, 'Barnet, who needed battle scenes for the capture of the Kremlin by workers' militia from its garrison of officer detachments, and could find no other explosion shot in the library but one of the demolition of a church, printed and cut it in a dozen times. When taken, his library item had been a most harmless and respectable scene of town-planning; as it appeared that gala night, alas, every time the Red Guard fired a church (the same church) came down with a loud orchestral bang.' Results were uproarious. (Sergei Eisenstein's anniversary film *Oktyabr/October* was not finished in time for the celebrations; he was engaged in a massive re-edit, ordered by Stalin, to expunge Trotsky from the events depicted.)[34]

At this time, in fact, the challenge of the Opposition, led by Trotsky with Zinoviev and Kamenev, to the control wielded by Stalin and his associates was reaching a climax. In 1926 all three dissidents had been expelled from the Politburo, and Zinoviev removed from his position at the head of the Comintern. As the power struggle continued in 1927, the Opposition strove, under the considerable handicap of the ban on factions, to rally popular support. Trotsky took to addressing secret meetings of workers in their homes and factory cellars. Publication of the Opposition's *Platform* having been forbidden, it was duplicated in an underground printing press and distributed clandestinely. Stalin struck back. The print shop was raided by the OGPU, and three prominent leaders of the Opposition who took responsibility for it summarily dismissed from the Party. On 28 September, Trotsky was forced off the executive committee of the Comintern, the motion of expulsion being moved by the British representative, J.T. Murphy. On 23 October, while Montagu was awaiting his visa in Berlin, Trotsky made a last, defiant speech at the Party's central committee plenum, warning that Stalin aimed to exterminate all opposition and forecasting bloody purges to come. He was interrupted by 'threats, gibes, and curses', and inkpots, heavy books, and a glass were flung at him from the chairman's table. Stalin had his way, and Trotsky and Zinoviev were expelled from the central committee.[35]

Montagu was only vaguely aware of these developments. The move against the Opposition was important news, and Ivor did manage to 'puzzle out a few sentences of the big discussions about it reported in the press'.

But he was 'quite unconscious' of the demonstrations staged by Trotsky and his supporters on 7 November, the day of the tenth anniversary parade in Red Square. In his VIP stand with his minder at his elbow, he had no inkling that out of his line of sight, and in Leningrad, the Opposition was making its 'appeal to the masses'. The dissentient cohorts, mostly students and office workers, were determined to march with slogans challenging the official line. But the government was well prepared; militiamen and vigilante groups were on standby. The demonstrators were pelted with missiles; they had their banners and posters yanked from their hands and torn to shreds. Many were beaten up. Photographs of Lenin, Trotsky and Zinoviev displayed from hotel balconies were ripped down by the OGPU; Trotsky's car was shot at, and his windscreen smashed. In Red Square, on the tribune above Lenin's mausoleum, British Communist Willie Gallacher gave a short speech, telling the assembled troops that they 'must all the time be on guard ... to protect the Party and country from corrupt traitors within.' Congratulated by his 'good comrade Joseph Stalin', he was then dispatched, he says, to speak against Trotsky, but when he got to the destination his services were not required: 'A group of Red Army men was at the hotel door, keeping back a crowd of angry workers who were trying to get at Trotsky. It would have been a bleak day for him if those workers had got at him.'[36]

The masses, Babette Gross reports, failed to be roused: 'They felt the party should resolve its problems in private not in front of the entire nation'; while foreign delegates observing or learning of the outbursts were bemused, 'at a loss to understand what was behind all this'. One such was Margaret McCarthy from the UK Young Communist League. 'It was with utter amazement and dismay ... while still exhilarated by the extraordinary pageant of mass fervour we had witnessed through the hours' that she heard that evening of the demonstrations: 'I could not understand ... I felt only that, in the face of such great spirit and such mass belief and hope as we had shared that day, it seemed mean and petty and perverse to counter-demonstrate.'[37]

Oblivious to the drama, Montagu carried on watching films and playing table tennis. On 9 November he had another session with Shvedchikov, and it may have been on this occasion that he was prompted to reflect on the organisation of the Soviet film industry. In a typescript from this time, he observes:

Many Soviet friends put to me what is evidently a burning question: should the Soviet Union have a centralised film city, a Hollywood, possibly in the Crimea? I am an outsider and not deeply informed of your problems but I should like to contribute a few observations on this question from the experience of the Western world.

There were certainly organisational advantages to the idea, but these were possibly outweighed by the 'psychological' disadvantages. 'I do earnestly believe that segregation of the film colony in Hollywood runs the serious danger of uprooting the artist, denationalising him and making him forget the cultural traditions and life interests of the people around him,' he wrote. He finally came to the conclusion that there should be a production centre in the south, with all-year sunshine, offering business and production training for technicians, but producing only comedies and adventure movies, 'the less realistic type of film', while the existing studios should be retained for the important films and creative film workers, 'in touch closely with the life of the great centres'.[38]

On 10 November Ivor was one of 947 delegates to attend the Congress of Friends, the international gathering to which the multitude of Soviet sympathisers had been invited. In her welcome, Lenin's widow Nadya Krupskaya described the guests as the 'best flower of everything progressive, everything revolutionary ... the best flower of future civilisation'. Then Soviet Premier Alexei Rykov got down to brass tacks. The delegates were to take away a correct impression of his country, which had emerged with unprecedented speed from one of the most backward states in Europe. The current standard of living should be compared not, for example, with that of America, but with that of Russia under tsarism. Most significantly, he broached the touchy issue of political violence. 'We are forced to employ repression for the defence of the dictatorship of the working class,' he declared – a sentiment with which Montagu, if he held true to the opinions expressed in his student article 'Prophecies', could only concur.[39]

In his book *Operation Mincemeat* about Ivor's brother Ewen, Ben Macintyre strongly implies that this 1927 mission of Montagu's to Moscow was a stage in his recruitment as a secret agent. 'Someone in the upper reaches of the Soviet state was taking good care of Ivor Montagu,' he darkly observes. Unless and until the Soviet intelligence archives are opened or other evidence comes to light, the question cannot be settled. But he was not an obvious candidate for espionage. He was not in government service; he did not have access to confidential military or industrial information; and his pro-Communist leanings had been openly proclaimed. He was a 23-year-old film editor. A more likely scenario, perhaps, is that his favoured treatment was simply as a result of the Comintern agitprop department becoming convinced of the merits of his scheme for getting Soviet pictures shown in Britain.[40]

As Ivor departed Moscow, fearful (he confessed to Ernst Toller) of 'what the fruits of this opposition quarrel will be', the ruling clique in government moved to consolidate its position. On 14 November, Trotsky and Zinoviev were expelled from the Party, and Kamenev from the central committee. Then at the 15th Congress of the Party in December, Stalin intensified the pressure. Zinoviev and Kamenev wilted: publicly recanting, they were readmitted into the Party's good graces, while 2,500 Oppositionists also withdrew their support for Trotsky. The 1,500 who remained loyal to the Opposition were expelled. Trotsky, who refused to recant, was condemned to exile, and in January 1928 he was put aboard a train for the Kazakh city of Alma-Ata (Almaty).[41]

Back in London in November, Montagu received an invitation from Willi Münzenberg to attend a conference in Berlin to organise the production and distribution of proletarian films, but it is unclear whether he attended, and indeed whether the conference actually took place. Scientific work was still on his mind, and he corresponded with his colleague in Vladikavkaz, Professor Turov, who wished to add rodent furs to the exchange of books they were carrying out.[42]

With a view to repaying some of the hospitality he had received in Russia, he wrote to the Home Secretary (Joynson-Hicks) enquiring whether there would be any objection to Yarotsky's wife Eve coming to England for a short holiday. He gave his 'personal guarantee that, during the whole of that time, she would neither transgress the labour regulations by taking employment nor hold any kind of political communication with persons in this country', but this proved unavailing: some weeks later he was informed that the Secretary of State 'regrets he is not prepared to authorise the grant of facilities to enable Mrs Yarotski to come to the United Kingdom.' Ivor was not inclined to let the matter drop. In the New Year he attempted to enlist the intervention of his brother Stuart, now the 3rd Baron Swaythling and a member of the House of Lords. Enclosing the correspondence, Ivor wrote that he could multiply the instances of 'politically harmless' Russian citizens being refused admission to the UK. He felt that in this case 'my very comprehensive guarantee should have set them at rest'; the fact that his guarantee – 'obviously a pledge of my honesty and reputation' – was disregarded was not a matter he could afford to ignore. He asked Stuart to see if he could secure him an appointment with the Home Secretary. Stuart did not oblige. He did not think he could ask the minister 'to waste his time to send me what I am sure would be a stereotyped reply as the regulations are regulations' and 'the question of your "honesty and reputation"' did not come into it. Ivor was not satisfied. There were no regulations excluding nationalities:

> There is only a legal power to the Home Secretary to admit or reject individuals as he may think fit. He uses this to admit only Russians about whom influential people make a fuss. In this case I am the influential person making a fuss, and ask you to be the channel used in fussing him because I have kept free from politics so far in my dealings with Russian matters, and do not wish to go to him through a Labour member.

Stuart, it would seem, either did not care to do any fussing, or did not fuss persuasively enough. Eve did not get her visa.[43]

Ivor was invited to the AGM of the SCR on 21 November. The society had weathered the storm of the breaking off of diplomatic relations well, although the membership, previously a quarter Russian, was now almost exclusively English, and it was necessary to issue another appeal to members to help out financially. It was able to mount an 'At Home' in December, at which recent visitors to the USSR shared their impressions. Mr Charles Roden Buxton reported on the 'decided improvement in the industrial, social and labour conditions of the country' and remarked on the 'cheerfulness, bustle and activity of life in Moscow, as contrasted with that of Leningrad', while Mrs F. Ranson, a member of the VOKS-sponsored delegation, spoke of factory housing estates and 'the cultural side of the Soviet co-operative movement which includes creches, workers' clubs, libraries, playgrounds for the children, meeting places, concert halls and day and evening schools for adults'.[44]

Belonging to the organisation was now proving indispensable to Ivor. He had decided again to pursue prospects as a translator, and wrote to Catherine Rabinovitch on 8 December stating that he was 'engaging in a series of Russian translations from such authors as Leonov, Ehrenburg, Kataev, Brissov [Bryusov] and Romanov.' He wished to have these author-ised ('if there is any means of so doing'), and asked for information on existing translations in order to avoid overlapping. Rabinovitch was able to inform him that for much of what he proposed, others had got there before him. In response, Montagu narrowed his field, saying that he was particularly interested in Bryusov's *Fiery Angel* – a suggestion that did not impress Rabinovitch. Bryusov's novel of sixteenth-century Germany was published in 1908; Rabinovitch felt that the young translator should tackle something more modern. 'But surely we are interested in Russian art and literature not only of today but also in its growth and past,' Montagu retorted. While admitting that 'for me too the modern work makes a stronger appeal,' he argued that 'the book in question seemed to a glance to be one of an interest and merit making it deserve [*sic*] of an audience among English speaking peoples.' The rights, it seemed, were available; this was a project he could go on with.[45]

Translating from German was also something he considered. Having attended an At Home given by Mrs Victor Gollancz on 15 December (at which Miles Malleson read his new play *Ladies and Gentlemen*), Ivor wrote to her husband asking if he would be interested in a translation of Feuchtwanger's enormously successful 1925 novel *Jud Süss*. No, was Gollancz's response.[46]

The performing arts continued to attract Montagu's interest. In December he saw Shaw's *The Admirable Bashville* and Aldous Huxley's *Happy Families* at the Chelsea Palace, and a variety show at the Alhambra. But the most intriguing event of the month would undoubtedly have been a concert demonstration at the Royal Albert Hall of electronic 'Music from the Ether' performed on the 'Theremin Apparatus' by its Russian inven-tor. Undoubtedly unbeknownst to those in the audience was the fact that Professor Leo Theremin, who was a Bolshevik supporter and had per-formed for Lenin, had been recruited by Soviet military intelligence (GRU) in 1925, and was en route to the USA on a spying mission.[47]

It was not that films had disappeared off Montagu's radar. He was excited by stills he had seen from Carl Dreyer's *La Passion de Jeanne d'Arc/ The Passion of Joan of Arc*, explaining to Bernard Shaw that 'the film consists mainly of the faces of peasants, soldiers and monks and Joan reflecting their emotion as the six hours [the last six hours of her life] proceed. These faces are quite without makeup and are impressive to a rare degree.' (Shaw replied: 'What on earth is a still?') Ivor contributed an amusingly curmudgeonly piece to the January issue of *Close Up*, commenting on the items shown at the seventeenth performance of the Film Society (16 October 1927) in ways that contrasted strongly with the studied neutrality of the programme notes he wrote for the society. Hans Richter's avant-garde *Rhythmus* (*Rhythmus 21*, 1922), he wrote, is 'one of his least attractive works. Rhythm is essentially the quality which, as a whole, the film lacks.' *The Face on the Bar Room Floor* (1914) is 'a really bad Chaplin' ('The essence of his art is the subduing and hiding of himself ... Therefore, when he presents a burlesque ... we are instantly aware of the emptiness.') From the technical point of view, the most interesting comments were on colour, occasioned by the screening of clips illustrating the British Polychromide colour process. 'The writer,' he averred, 'abhors colour. He is an apostle of the black and white league.' Still – among the selections shown, 'in several places we are pleasurably astonished. One of Betty Faire's hats, the silver fish, the white and red Japanese Goldfish, and one amazing shot of shadows and lights on ice with a pink skater give a hint of a quality that might convert us if it could be reached more often than very rarely.' *Close Up* could have provided an outlet for more of Montagu's criticism, but he disliked the ethos of the magazine: on 7 February he wrote to the editor, Kenneth Macpherson, saying, 'I find myself in such profound disagreement with most of the criticism published in *Close Up* that it is not likely I shall send you any further material for publication' – although he offered to help in other ways.[48]

Meanwhile, he had had what proved to be a short-lived tryout as film reviewer on the *Sunday Graphic*. 'This was right up my alley,' Ivor recalls, 'for I should be paid £20 a week and had only to write a few hundred words surrounded by cheesecake pictures and spend a few hours viewing, free, films, that I should no doubt have had to see somehow, paying, anyway.'

He reviewed Hitchcock's *Easy Virtue*, complaining that the director had rendered Noël Coward's complex characters as 'dragons of convention, stock gargoyles of Puritan ill-will' and the heroine 'a poor bruised swan'; he felt that Hitchcock 'did not try' since the story was uncongenial to him, but nevertheless 'the eye is constantly delighted by scenery and composition, the head satisfied by a reasonable story told at times, as in the court-room scene, with eloquence.' The Scottish costume drama *Annie Laurie* (directed by John S. Robertson) was 'instinct with every badness to which a film is heir, not an aspect but is faked and wrong. Each character is taken from its place in a filing system …', but again there were mitigating factors: 'in spite of all this the picture moves and grips' because, Montagu contended, 'it was a masquerade enjoyed in the making.' Harry d'Abbadie d'Arrast's *A Gentleman of Paris* was distinguished by the presence of Adolphe Menjou – 'his sympathy, his suavity, his sybaritic delicacy', while Murnau's Hollywood debut *Sunrise* shone 'with all the polish that perfection of technique can give' but was sometimes 'too well-made'.[49]

Alas, it would seem that he could not achieve the required popular touch. Editor W. Thompson Hill wrote to Montagu on 21 January regretting that 'our experiment will have to end at the experimental stage. The plain truth is that your stuff is rather too good for the average reader of a paper of my type.' Montagu took his release before the agreed two months were up, being reluctant 'to add to my arduous duties as captain of the English Table Tennis team' when 'no permanently continuous series was to be gained by it.'[50]

His table tennis duties in fact took him in the last week of January to Stockholm, where the world championships were being staged. The young squad of fifteen led by Montagu as non-playing captain was unable to wrest the team title from Hungary – although the men's pair including 18-year-old Fred Perry won a silver in the doubles, and the team performed creditably overall, coming in third. A character sketch published at this time by the *Daily Express's* gossip columnist 'The Dragoman' described Ivor as 'a curious and sympathetic figure such as Disraeli would have loved. He is extremely dark, clean-shaven, and be-spectacled, and talks in a very soft voice with great precision of language.'[51]

Meanwhile, under the Sovkino agreement, fitful progress was being made in regard to Ivor's agency for Soviet films. For some time the *Handelsvertretung* did not reply to his letters, and in December he sent a colleague, Mr P. Simunek, to Berlin as a Brunel & Montagu 'sales agent' to try to speed up negotiations, part of which involved making available suitable British films in exchange. This apparently proved fruitful, as on 22 December Montagu wrote to Comrade Zehrer saying, 'Your letter of the 14th received with pleasure,' and agreeing to the scheme proposed, with several caveats. He argued that Zehrer's plan to offer the films on the market before submission to the censor would reduce the possible price they could fetch. And he felt that the first batch of films Zehrer intended to send would pose acute censorship problems. These were: *Mat/Mother* (Vsevolod Pudovkin, 1926), about a young worker and his family during the 1905 revolution; *Krylia Kholopa/Ivan the Terrible/Wings of a Serf* (Yuri Taritch, 1926), a historical melodrama concerning an inventive serf at the court of the brutal tsar; and *Tretya meshchanskaya/Triangle Love/Bed and Sofa* (Abram Room, 1927), a contemporary comedy-drama that raised issues of sexual mores and abortion. Ivor considered that *Bed and Sofa* might be all right, but suggested that the other two be replaced by the less potentially controversial *Chelovek iz restorana/The Man from the Restaurant* (Yakov Protazanov, 1927), a melodrama exposing exploitative class relationships prior to the Revolution, and *S.V.D. – Soyuz velikogo dela/The Club of the Great Deed* (Grigori Kozintsev and Leonid Trauberg, 1927), a historical drama of underground conspiracy at the time of the Decembrist uprising. A second batch, once the groundwork had been laid, could include Pudovkin's *The End of St Petersburg* as well as *Mother*, together with the contemporary comedy *Chashka chaia/A Glass of Tea* (Nikolai Shpikovsky, 1927). *Ivan the Terrible*, he hastened to add, would be 'welcomed at any time by the Film Society'.[52]

A compromise agreement seemed to be reached, since on 31 December Montagu wrote again to Zehrer saying, 'we will be glad to receive the films named sent immediately to our address and then to proceed with them as outlined by you and agreed by us.' But there was some hitch. In a long letter dated 18 January to Petrovsky, Ivor expressed his frustration with the stipulations Berlin was making. 'I am almost inclined to say,' he wrote, 'that they appear to have agreed to the scheme only under compulsion from Shvedchikov and the Moscow Sovkino, and are trying to sabotage it by making a nuisance of themselves over details.' The problem – which had clearly not been overcome – was that he was not being permitted to select for himself the films he would deal with as a trial, but instead was being asked to accept 'the three which I would pick out as most difficult for this market.' Moreover, *His Call* – which he had striven to obtain for two years now – and *A Glass of Tea* were refused to him 'on the grounds that they are old!'[53]

With his importing plans temporarily stalled, Montagu was at least able to facilitate the exhibition of a Soviet feature for SCR members. This was – again – the worn print of *Polikushka*. It was screened twice in the one evening on 8 February at the premises of a distributor in Wardour Street, preceded by a talk by Ivor on Russian cinema. Some indication of the interest was that 'there was such an overwhelming demand from members for seats for their friends that the small hall could have been filled ten times over.' Despite its age, the film reportedly 'aroused a deep interest owing to the wonderful emotional acting of Moskvin, one of the finest actors of the Moscow Art Theatre, and by the dramatic power of Tolstoy's story.' In thanking him for his kind help, Catherine Rabinovitch expressed the hope that 'this is only the beginning of a series of more up to date Russian films.' No doubt the beleaguered Montagu wearily felt the same way.[54]

7

SUBVERSIVE CINEMA

Sir F. HALL asked the Home Secretary whether he has received any Report from the police authorities as to certain films containing subversive propaganda which have been brought into this country from Russia; what steps are taken to prevent aliens or others suspected of revolutionary tendencies from bringing propaganda films or literature into this country; and whether he will consider taking further powers to enable this to be done effectively?

Sir W. JOYNSON HICKS I receive reports as occasion arises in regard to the importation or proposed importation of films of this character, and appropriate steps are taken. As at present advised I do not think any further powers are required in this connection.[1]

IF MONTAGU WAS determined to get Soviet films into Britain, the government was just as determined to keep them out — ensuring in particular that those of a revolutionary character would be barred from general release. As Nicholas Pronay has convincingly argued, the Home Office 'never wavered in its belief that censorship of the cinema was necessary; that it should be concerned with other matters as well as morality and that it should be ultimately under Home Office control.'[2]

The mechanisms by which this was achieved were to some extent hidden from public view, given that the British Board of Film Censors was nominally independent of government. Care was taken, for a start, to ensure that the staff of the BBFC were entirely reliable. The president was appointed after consultation with the Home Secretary; during the 1920s this was an elderly MP, T.P. O'Connor, who stated that he 'thought it was necessary to keep, not only in touch with, but in the friendliest relations with the Home Office.' The long-serving secretary, J. Brooke Wilkinson, was intimately involved with serving state ideological objectives, to the extent that during the war he had been in charge of British film propaganda to neutral nations, and in his BBFC capacity was a member of a secret Subcommittee on Censorship chaired by a Minister and with representatives from police, secret services and the Press Proprietors Association. Montagu would have had no way of knowing that Brooke Wilkinson was in close contact with MI5, with whom he would 'routinely swap information about undesirable films and industry developments' – including news of Montagu's activities garnered through mail intercepts.[3]

The system had been put to the test with the importation by the distributor Film Booking Offices (FBO) of *Battleship Potemkin* in 1926. Alarmed by a published statement of Trotsky that the film should be shown to British sailors for revolutionary purposes, the Director of Naval Intelligence requested the Home Secretary do everything he could to prevent its exhibition. A special screening was arranged at the BBFC involving representatives from the Home Office, Admiralty, Special Branch and MI5; O'Connor did not attend. It was then determined that 'the BBFC would refuse a certificate on its own responsibility and that no mention would be made in the records concerning the presence of civil servants, police and intelligence officers.' With local authorities falling in line with the BBFC, the film was subjected to a total ban for years to come.[4]

In the early months of 1928, however, the machinations of the government were not Montagu's immediate concern. He had a business to run. And if Soviet pictures were not allowed, perhaps a little homegrown subversion, in the form of satirical comedy, would not go amiss.

He had secured a patron, in the person of the American film importer Arthur Levey. Resident in England for the last eight years, Levey had had business dealings with Montagu and they had struck up a friendship. Levey now offered to back the production of short comedies – three to start with – to be directed by Ivor, provided the original stories were supplied by H.G. Wells. No doubt partly because his son Frank was to be included in the package, H.G. was agreeable, stipulating only that the films star Elsa Lanchester

– a condition Ivor was only too happy to comply with. Levey's colleague Simon Rowson of Ideal Films (a long-established production and distribution firm) and Mick Balcon of Gainsborough were drawn in as partners, and Angle Pictures Inc. was launched in May 1928.[5]

The company had a capital of £2,500, the major shareholders being Arthur Levey, Ideal Films, and Gainsborough, with Frank Wells and Ivor Montagu contributing smaller amounts. Montagu was to be managing director, the other directors being Rowson, Balcon, Levey and Wells. Ivor extracted the money he needed for his share of the capital, not without difficulty, from his brother Stuart, who was a principal in the family bank and managed the trust fund left him by his father. Stuart wished to know more details of the prospectus and contractual arrangements; Ivor replied: 'I am not in a position to give you all the details you speak of, and I do not think (as you have little knowledge of the film business) that they would convey much to you.' Eventually he supplied more information, and the tiff was resolved; on 20 May he was able to report to Rowson, then in New York, 'the Company has been registered and all proceeds smoothly.'[6]

The choice of H.G. Wells was a canny one, as his prestige ensured that a distribution contract (with Ideal) could be secured in advance. But it proved problematic. Although several of his novels had been successfully adapted for the cinema, he had no experience of screenwriting (and when he tried it, for a project of his own, the resulting script proved impossibly overburdened with titles and other written inserts). As Montagu tells the story, the author was elusive. 'But at last I ran him to earth in a flat in Paris … I came straight from the overnight train and roused him out of bed. He gave me breakfast while, in his dressing gown, he wrote down *Blue Bottles*. The other two *Day-Dreams* and *The Tonic* were more difficult but I dug my heels in. Finally they emerged as about a paragraph each and I flew back triumphant to London on the afternoon plane.'[7]

H.G.'s 'scraps of paper' were elaborated into scripts by Ivor and Frank Wells, the pair straining desperately to invent visual gags. A floor in the Gainsborough studio at Islington was secured, and a 'happy ship' assembled. Lanchester's partner Charles Laughton was recruited to play a villain in each of the films, while others roped in included Harold Warrender, 'one of our dearest cronies at the Soho restaurant where we always lunched', the boxer Joe Beckett and the sexologist Norman Haire. On camera was

Freddie Young, Frank Wells was art director, Tod Rich served as production manager, while continuity was handled by Hell. Shooting took place in August-September, and whether in the studio or out on location, as on the beach at Rye for *Day-Dreams*, the creative collaboration was shot through with an infectious sense of fun; the films were to be prize exemplars of 'the aesthetics of play' Christine Gledhill identifies in the more experimental British cinema of the 1920s.[8]

Something of the spirit with which the young crew tackled the production is suggested in this account by Freddie Young of a pickup shot for *Day-Dreams* filmed in 'icy January water':

> The real fun was doing the location off Southend, where for the shark's fin we used a piece of three-ply on a submerged float pulled along by a concealed line. Then it came to the drowning. Charles [Laughton] wasn't there, so Ivor Montague [*sic*], who was roughly the same build, dressed up in the rajah's costume and jumped into the water.
>
> 'All right, Ivor,' I called out, 'the camera's turning.'
>
> Ivor exhaled bravely and plunged his head under the water. However, we had reckoned without his natural buoyancy: his back disappeared but his large bottom remained afloat. After several seconds he came up spluttering, 'How was that?'
>
> From the way we were falling about laughing he needn't have asked.
>
> 'You didn't sink, Ivor.'
>
> 'Oh. OK, let's try it again.'
>
> The same thing happened again.

Young eventually became the successful stuntman himself. Ivor recounts: 'I burned my overcoat on a stove trying to stop shivering in the cafe where we all tried to roast ourselves to normal blood temperature afterward.'[9]

Elsa Lanchester had had limited film experience up to this point. Back in 1925 she had starred in an elaborate home movie spoof as a cabaret girl in *The Scarlet Woman: An Ecclesiastical Melodrama* written by Evelyn Waugh and directed by Terence Greenidge, and she had had small roles in *One of the Best* (T. Hayes Hunter, 1927) and *The Constant Nymph* (Adrian Brunel, 1928) (Brunel commented: 'Anyone who knows this brilliant woman will appreciate her influence on the gaiety of our community. What a glorious sense of humour!'). But the starring role in these three shorts would be an opportunity to showcase her comic talents and really launch her cinema career.[10]

Undoubtedly Lanchester was the inspiration for the Cockney skivvy character she plays in each of the films, and the irreverent burlesque that is their mode. In having Elsa tangle with a scurrying battalion of police (*Blue Bottles*), fantasise about a life of sensuous luxury in Paris (*Day-Dreams*), and hamfistedly thwart a plot to hasten an elderly relative's death (*The Tonic*), the filmmakers manoeuvred to fire satirical jabs at capitalist society's law enforcement (the police escalate to infantry, planes, tanks and warships), top-hatted elite, and avaricious petty bourgeoisie.

Editing was completed by the end of the year, apart from the shark's fin pickup. But release of the shorts was held up because of Quota Act complications. (The 1927 legislation had had a variety of unforeseen consequences, impacting particularly on non-mainstream productions.) In the event it was not until September 1929 that the films were trade-shown. Press reaction was strikingly split. The *Manchester Guardian* found the plots slight, the tempo slow, and the jokes at times tedious. On the other hand, *The Times* declared:

> Mr Wells supplies a plot which lends itself admirably to cinema fantasy, and at the same time burlesques with great good humour the cruder manners of the screen. Mr Wells could not have been better served in the direction of his stories than by Mr Ivor Montagu, whose satire, though keen, is never malicious. In his employment of trick photography, unusual camera angles and symbolism, we observe a criticism of contemporary technique which blends very happily with its subject. Mr Montagu has evidently enjoyed himself directing these films, and his enjoyment is infectious.[11]

Regrettably, not many spectators would have the chance to decide for themselves. The delay in release meant that silent pictures were by now virtually obsolete. Bookings were few and far between, and Angle Pictures, failing to recover its costs, was wound up. In retrospect, Montagu was philosophical. 'The pictures were not good but they were not *all* that bad either,' he comments. The brute fact was that 'conception occurred in a world of silent films. Parturition in a world already invaded by sound …'[12]

Montagu made another film in 1928 – an instructional short, *Table Tennis To-day*. Produced for Brunel & Montagu and shot mid-year at the Islington studios, this silent two-reeler featured world champion Zoltán Mechlovits and other leading players. Surveying the equipment of the game and demonstrating strokes by means of slow-motion analysis, the film perhaps did not benefit from the fact that its director was the world's leading authority on table tennis; it has a very pedantic feel, with a pace that at times is deadly slow. Released early in 1929, it secured few bookings, though prints were also sold (at £10 each) for private exhibition. Ever optimistic, Ivor sounded out the chances of the film in America with his old Cambridge acquaintance Cedric Belfrage, now a film critic and press agent in Hollywood. The response was not encouraging. 'As to table tennis,' Belfrage wrote, 'the only times I have ever heard it referred to here, frankly, have been in the spirit of ribaldry and banter. As for instance: "Is Charley much of a lay?" "No, darling, he's lousy – no technique, no versatility, and worst of all, no anything." "Oh well, I expect he's just marvellous at ping-pong" (sniggers) … . I should say … that your only chance of selling the picture in this neck o' the woods is to put comic sub-titles in it, synchronise the bouncing of the ball with the sound of falling pig-iron, and put it out as a mirth-quake.'[13]

At this time Montagu made a curious appearance in front of the camera. In September 1928 the German experimentalist Walter Ruttmann came to London to shoot scenes for his montage sound film *Melodie der Welt*, a kind of global expansion of his *Berlin: Die Sinfonie der Grosstadt* of the previous year. Ruttmann wanted George Bernard Shaw to say a few words, and asked Ivor to arrange it. Shaw refused to appear unless Montagu did also. Hence the pair took up station on the backlot of the Elstree studio, Montagu sitting on a 'handy pile of bricks' to conceal the fact that 'my old grey flannel trousers had a big hole in the seat through which my shirt projected'. In the clip subsequently incorporated in the film, they proceed to run through an unlikely spiel, Shaw enquiring the way to St Albans, and then asking, 'By the way, have I the pleasure of speaking to Mr Ivor Montagu?' Montagu assents. 'Well, my name is Bernard Shaw,' his interlocutor continues. 'I had the pleasure I think of meeting you at your mother's, and at Cambridge.' 'That's right, yes,' says Ivor, before agreeing to Bernard Shaw's suggestion of tea. Shaw's voice recorded harmoniously; Montagu was put off by the sound of his own, finding the tone 'disconcerting, affected and unexpectedly Cambridge'.[14]

A few months earlier Ivor had been offered the chance to direct an adaptation of *Arms and the Man* provided he could induce Shaw to part with the rights; the playwright, however, remained staunchly opposed to cinematic versions of his work. Still, on one occasion he did make an exception and, out of friendship, offered Ivor a short story, 'Aerial Football'. Ivor thought it would make 'a very bad, if not impossible, film' and regretfully declined. Undeterred, the would-be writer/producer/director began concocting other ideas. One was for a murder story in which the murderer fixes the crime on an innocent man. Suspense would be built up with 'the paraphernalia of justice gripping the man in error' and the film would end with 'a wrongful execution and a melodramatic too late exposure of the real criminal'. Montagu thought the story very attractive and told Rowson he would probably script it even if it was not to go ahead immediately. Cost: at least £8,000. A second idea was much cheaper, at less than £4,000. This was 'a domestic story about a woman married for ten years who decides to leave her husband, and doesn't. Naturally little action, but I believe I know an actress of such talent that she could hold sympathy throughout 5,000 feet ...'[15]

A third project was brought to Montagu by his uncle, Leslie Haden Guest. The former MP had been touring the Dominions for the Empire Marketing Board and while in Canada received an offer of support from the Alberta government for a film to be shot at the Peace River Settlement in the northwest of the province. Conferring, Haden Guest and Montagu had decided that neither a travelogue nor a dramatic film with professional cast would find support; a dramatic story depending on the natural surroundings, along the lines of *Chang* (shot in the wilderness of northern Thailand) might however have strong prospects. This film, for which Ivor wrote a treatment, would work up human interest 'as the family is isolated among bears and beasts in the snow and with springtide floods as climax'. Montagu worked assiduously at raising finance for the venture, including approaching Lord Beaverbrook and pitching it to Rowson at Ideal Films and Gaumont-British, Walter Mycroft at British International Pictures, Herbert Wilcox at British & Dominions, Balcon at Gainsborough, and others at British Instructional and Paramount. He also independently received a promise of £4,000 as a guarantee and £1,000 as capital. Though he aroused a great deal of interest in the project, no firm arrangement could be reached. Typical of the log-jams frustrating Montagu was that involving Gainsborough, which would put up £5,000 if their American allies Tiffany would match that figure. Tiffany, however, rejected the proposition after hearing from Canadian exhibitors that 'they were not interested in showing films of Canadian life.'[16]

Montagu was all the more eager to get projects off the ground as the coming of sound film was threatening the viability of Brunel & Montagu Ltd. 'It was impossible then,' Brunel explains, 'to persuade film people that talkies needed any kind of constructive and creative editing or even that editors could do anything to adjust defects in synchronised films – editors were relegated to the position of film joiners, defeatists who accepted what they got and just assembled it.' The company's staff dramatised their plight in a playful silent skit, a minute in length, *Brunel & Montagu* (1928). Ian Dalrymple, Montagu, Brunel and Tod Rich, in a collective suicide pact, make their farewells and leap from a rooftop. But fortune steps in: a news flash announces 'Brunel Flotation Enormous Success' and the four conspirators re-emerge unscathed, with broad grins.[17]

As a countermeasure against technological redundancy Montagu dreamt up a plan for a proposed private company, Film Portraits Ltd ('Think how many mothers are sufficiently interested in their children to keep life-albums, full of recorded doings and portraits. It is certain that, if one judiciously chose rich addresses, a large number of clients could be obtained.') The outline included proposed charges and financial costings, but nothing seems to have eventuated from the idea. Another product of Montagu's fertile imagination was a proposed scheme whereby a newspaper would finance the production of a film serial in six to ten episodes, which would contain deliberate continuity errors; a prize competition would be run for patrons to spot them. The budding entrepreneurs of Brunel & Montagu were confident that 'there is no reason why this should not be taken by every cinema-house in the country, and substantial profit accrue to the newspaper undertaking the venture.' However, this, too, failed to materialise, very likely a casualty of uncertainty in the industry as the new technology was fitfully introduced.[18]

While these plans were brewing Ivor kept busy in other spheres. In April 1928, as President of the Southampton FC Supporters Club, he proposed the toast, at its Second Annual Dinner, to the Southampton Football Club (he was no doubt relieved that toasting His Majesty the King was the duty of the Chairman). In June he debated on the topic of Film with Ashley Dukes, the playwright, at the 1917 Club. Considering that at this time

Mr Dukes had seen not a single moving picture, this must have been a curious contest. In October Montagu responded to a query from Victor Gollancz
about the feasibility of a 'biggish book on the history of the Cinema' with an
ambitious outline for such a volume, saying that the research would take 'a lot
of time and something in expenses' and 'with that absence of mock modesty
which characterises me, I can say that I don't think you could find anyone
better suited to the job than myself.' For whatever reason, the project failed to
materialise, but later in the month Ivor lectured in London on Education and
the Cinema, as part of a series of lectures on education, and at Southend-on-
Sea on the film industry for the Southend Branch of the National Council of
Labour Colleges. Also in October, he was elected to the executive committee
of the Society for Cultural Relations.[19]

As Toller's representative, Montagu was heavily involved from late 1927
onwards in projects to get *Hoppla, wir leben!* translated and staged in an
English-language version. It was a frustrating process. He was convinced
that for full impact any production should incorporate the film montages
that had been a striking feature of the play's presentation in Berlin. Piscator,
after much delay, agreed to send the film, but asked a price that no theatre
in Britain could afford. Hopeful that Piscator would see reason (Montagu
put Toller's German representative, Oesterheld, and later Toller himself,
on the case), Ivor proceeded in promoting what was to be a 'lavish' production jointly mounted by the Stage Society and the Film Society. This,
however, fell through when the Stage Society suffered some heavy financial
losses. Eventually Montagu approved a Gate Theatre, Dublin, production in
February 1929. Piscator was talked down to a reasonable figure, and the film
arrived – but too late to be used.[20]

Meanwhile, Montagu was finally making progress in importing Soviet
films. 'At last,' he writes, 'the constipated pipeline began to flow, and there
started to arrive, for the first time in Britain, and for the Film Society to
show, the sequence of the classic Soviet silent masterpieces.' The films were
acquired by Brunel & Montagu through the Soviet *Handelsvertretung* in
Berlin, and then prepared for screening, with translated titles, by Montagu.
The Film Society was able to exhibit features irrespective of the censorship
position, while for general release Brunel & Montagu negotiated with FBO
and subsequently Pro Patria Films Ltd, which took over from FBO the
British distribution rights to Soviet films in early 1929.[21]

The first of the new batch to be shown was Pudovkin's *Mother*, on 21 October 1928. This powerful distillation of the Gorky novel set during the 1905 Revolution 'set London agog for a week' – though it failed to impress Ashley Dukes, who declared, at the tea-room discussion following the screening, that it was Bolshevik propaganda and that 'the stage had been trying the same methods thirty years ago'. This 'grossly heretical' view was not shared by others taking part, who included Anthony Asquith, artist Edmund Dulac, aspiring cineaste Herbert Marshall, and the German cinematographer and director Karl Freund, with Montagu acting as chairman and interpreter. Some of the press was sympathetic – the *Daily Express* columnist, for example, declared *Mother* to be 'almost overwhelmingly poignant ... stark and magnificent', allowing that 'the film is, of course, implicitly revolutionary, but the propaganda is only incidental, and subsidiary to the main theme.' But the alarm raised in conservative circles can be gauged by the reaction of the *Sunday Times* critic who, while calling it 'the most astounding picture I have yet seen' denounced it as an 'untruthful, one-sided, unfair', accusing Pudovkin of 'weighting his scales and offering to us under the guise of art an intolerable and agonising tissue of lies callously calculated to waken our sympathies without just cause, and misdirect them for political or national objects. It is not good propaganda. For it is sheer, patent, unadulterated mendacity ...'[22]

Montagu had to withstand a minor backlash from certain Film Society members, one of whom, noting the chairman's 'Communistic' sympathies, protested that the Society appeared to be embarking on a course of screening films 'which I, and many other people who are not completely unintelligent, consider a prostitution of art, a perversion of the truth, and a menace to our country's well-being'.[23]

Mother was shown without any cuts to the Film Society membership. But when submitting the film on behalf of Brunel & Montagu to the BBFC in the hope of obtaining a certificate for general release, Ivor had stripped it of much of its inflammatory content, and amended the titles 'in an attempt to emphasise that discouragement of hatred and conflict which is implicit in the film.' The picture was nevertheless banned, on the grounds that it showed strike scenes and the cavalry firing upon workers. Objecting that other films incorporating equivalent material had been passed, Montagu succeeded in persuading the BBFC president, T.P. O'Connor, to view it on appeal. This required special arrangements. The elderly MP had not, according to Montagu, seen a film for many years – 'he was partly paralysed and could not ascend the stairs to the office and projection theatre.' *Mother* was accordingly screened on 5 December at O'Connor's flat, where 'nearly his whole time was spent squinting backwards over his shoulder in case the then-dangerous nitrate stock caught fire.' The appeal was unavailing. O'Connor was apologetic. In a letter to Ivor, he wrote: 'I had no choice of course, but if good will could have influenced me, the film would have been passed.' Government control over the supposedly independent BBFC could not have been more evident.[24]

Montagu was resilient. He now pulled off a coup by securing a visit by Pudovkin himself at the time of the Film Society screening of his *The End of St Petersburg* on 3 February 1929. This was a stirring occasion. As Paul Rotha reported: 'At one portion of the film, the action was worked to a crescendo by gradual short-cutting, with the title "All power to the Soviets!" at the peak of emotion. The audience was observed to start gradually stirring, then muttering, until eventually many persons rose to their feet, cheering and clapping.' When this 'riot' was reported in the press by a 'naughty journalist, writing over three different names in about twenty different papers', according to Montagu, a hue and cry arose. There were questions in the Commons about this 'Russian picture commissioned for propaganda purposes in connection with the tenth anniversary of the Russian Revolution'; but Joynson-Hicks was keen to dampen down controversy, and asserted that 'such incidents as occurred have been exaggerated, and I do not contemplate any further action in the matter.' Pressure was, however, put on the London County Council, which accordingly impressed upon the Film Society 'the need for co-operating with the licencees in securing the strict observance of the conditions subject to which permission is granted to exhibit uncensored films.' The LCC continued: 'I am to add that the Council deprecates the exhibition by the Society of any film which is likely to lead to disorder or unseemly incidents of any kind, and in this connection I am to remind you that Rule 8 (a) forbids the exhibition of any film which is likely to lead to disorder.'[25]

Another sequel to the *End of St Petersburg* screening was a lawsuit. The *Sunday Pictorial* published an article by Walter Mutch under the heading, 'What We are Tolerating – Propaganda Efforts behind Latest Russian Importation'. Mutch declared:

The picture is so subversive in character that, last Sunday, the repressed emotions of the Film Society audience flamed into roars of revolutionary cheering at the title 'All Power to the Soviets', and into yells of derisive delight at the spectacle of a portrait of the Tsar being carried on a pole by a half-witted, bow-legged convict . . . . We were told it was based on history. It is history debased. It is a tale told with fanatical Bolshevist bias ...

Unwilling to let this pass unchallenged, Council members of the Film Society including Montagu issued a writ of defamation against Sunday Pictorial Newspapers (1920) Ltd and Mutch, claiming:

The said words meant and were understood to mean that the Plaintiffs and each of them in exhibiting or causing to be exhibited as aforesaid the said film *The End of St Petersburg* had knowingly done so in order to spread Bolshevist principles and political propaganda in Great Britain; and that they had intentionally given an exhibition as aforesaid which they knew or ought to have known was subversive of law and order and of constitutional government ... [and, as a result of the publication, the plaintiffs had been] greatly injured in their character reputation and credit [and] brought into public hatred ridicule and contempt.

The *Sunday Pictorial* settled out of court and printed an apology.[26]

Immediately after the screening, Pudovkin had given a talk for Society members at Stewart's Restaurant in Regent Street. He spoke English, Montagu records, 'not fluently, but well enough – a little stiffly, as though he had a plum in his mouth – for he had learned it from English officers, fellow prisoners-of-war during the war of 1914–18.' Montagu and Sergei Nalbandov helped in preparing his address, carefully marking the accentuation. Entitled 'Types Instead of Actors', it gave expression to Pudovkin's belief that 'to show, alongside real water and real trees and grass, a property beard pasted on the actor's face, wrinkles traced by means of paint, or stagey acting is impossible.' Pudovkin linked the use of non-actors to Kuleshov's experiment with montage, and explained how he had obtained a look of rapture on the faces of a crowd of Mongols in *Potomok Chingis-Khana/The Heir to Genghis Khan/Storm Over Asia* (1928) by engaging a Chinese conjuror. But his listeners were most struck by his comments on sound film. 'I visualise a film,' he said, 'in which sounds and human speech are wedded to the visual images on the screen in the same way as that in which two or more melodies can be combined by an orchestra.' Rejecting synchronous dialogue altogether as 'an ingenious trick that is useless to anyone', he proposed instead an expressionist aesthetic that, by incorporating 'all the sounds of the whole world, beginning with the whisper of a man or the cry of a child and rising to the roar of an explosion' would reach 'unthought-of heights'.[27]

Pudovkin was, according to Montagu, 'a genial, rugged, simple man, the most direct and plain in human sympathy of the great Soviet directors'. He enjoyed his stay in Britain. 'He had not been more than a few hours in London,' Ivor recalls, 'when he threw himself down in our armchair at Leicester Square and exclaimed: "Oh why, oh why, did I make *Storm Over Asia* – I like the English so much."' (The film was an attack on British imperialism.) Montagu was struck by the director's 'intense and vigilant observation', citing the occasion when they saw a 'boots' in a hotel corridor knock on a door, who then 'stooped his body almost in a loop and cupped his ear with his hand almost in contact with the door. Pudovkin pointed out that if one made an actor in a film perform so exaggerated a movement everyone would say it was unnatural.' Ivor threw a party for him the night before he left. After he had gone the Film Society received a bill for seven shillings; in referring it to Montagu, Miss Harvey appended a note: 'What about this? I don't feel the F.S. ought to pay for having Pudovkin's suits pressed!!'[28]

Montagu was in an upbeat mood. On 7 February he wrote to Petrovsky in Moscow saying that his film work was going well and that he was to start on another production (it is not clear what project he was referring to). When that was finished, 'I should dearly like to come to Moscow and work in conjunction on a Russian film, possibly with Pudovkin … I should propose to come, not as a student but with a definite assistant's job, expenses and all duly paid. In return I could probably arrange an advance guarantee for the distribution of the picture in England, possibly in France.'[29]

By April he was not so sanguine. No reply having been received from Petrovsky, he wrote again, explaining that though his drive to import Soviet films had finally been crowned with success, he had not made money out of it. 'Unfortunately, there is one thing I am bad at – extremely bad – and that is my own business. I haven't managed to get any commission out of this work, and, in fact, it has cost so much time and made me so neglect my own film production work that I am heavily in debt!' The reason was that distribution rights were being handed to an established company:

> Do you remember how you and Kurella were indignant, that in Germany Sovkino let the small proletarian-minded businesses popularise Russian films, and then, when all the hard pioneer work had been done, gave all the good money-making films to the ordinary big commercial firms. So Sovkino does always, but I have no regrets, for I went into it with my eyes open and indeed I think the English firm that now has the contract is highly reliable.

But he was out of pocket, and still angling for film work in the Soviet Union, asking Petrovsky to put in a good word for him with Sovkino and Mezhrabpom.[30]

There was again no reply, and by the following month Montagu's financial situation had deteriorated further. The film industry's changeover to sound was badly affecting the viability of Brunel & Montagu Ltd, and Ivor was discharging staff and contemplating closing down. On 14 May he received a letter from the bank telling him he was £117 7s 1d overdrawn, and requesting him to fulfil his promise to keep the account in credit 'at the earliest possible moment'. He had reached an agreement through the Berlin *Handelsvertretung* to edit Pudovkin's Soviet-German co-production *Zhivoy trup/Die lebende Leichnam/The Living Corpse* (1929) for the British market, but as he explained in a letter to the director, this had fallen through. Ivor did not improve his position by turning down offers from the financiers who backed the Wells comedies for him to direct filmed stage plays, countering with 'schemes for synchronisation in counterpoint', which were labelled 'experimental' and rejected. (He had proposed a two-reel adaptation of Poe's *The Black Cat* and *The Tell-Tale Heart* using 'indirect sound-image association' to create 'the highest possible pitch of terror'.) Hence his alternatives were: 'to wait in England without work (or resume zoological work) until, in perhaps a year's time, the English production revives and accepts rational sound techniques from other countries; or to go abroad.' He was thinking of trying his luck in America, he told Pudovkin.[31]

His life had almost taken a different turn. On 10 April he was approached to stand for the Labour Party against Home Secretary Joynson-Hicks ('Jix') in the Twickenham electorate in the forthcoming general election. Ivor's response was cautious. 'My position is as follows. In spite of twelve years uninterrupted association with the Labour Party, I have had little active political experience or ambition, for I have been engaged during that time principally on work on which I fancied myself more directly useful.' He did not wish to spoil any other potential candidate's chances, but 'if there were any unanimous opinion that I could be of service in the division, the pleasure of giving Jix a good run would be quite enough to persuade me to try and justify it.' The offer was evidently well received, for on 17 April he declared that he was 'game to go ahead', but with a proviso: 'I must remind you that I cannot and will not spend money on the campaign. I can find a small car, and the deposit; but, apart from my present financial position, I do not think it proper, that in the case of a proposed eleventh-hour candidature of this kind, its acceptance should be influenced by the possible expectation of finance.' This may have proved a sticking point. As it turned out the Labour candidate in the 30 May election was T.J. Mason, who polled 15,121 votes to Joynson-Hicks's 21,087, giving the sitting MP, despite a nationwide swing to Labour, a comfortable election-night majority. The election was the first with full female suffrage, and resulted – no doubt to Montagu's satisfaction – in Baldwin's Conservative administration being replaced by a minority Labour government led by Ramsay MacDonald, with the support of the Liberals.[32]

Montagu's willingness to stand for Labour in this election indicates a certain distance from the Communist Party. The CPGB had adopted the 'Class Against Class' line mandated by the Comintern, and its election programme declared, 'The Labour Party has chosen the capitalist class. The Communist Party is the party of the working class – the Labour Party is the third capitalist party.' But Ivor's stance did not indicate a loss of interest in revolutionary politics. On 1 July he wrote to Trotsky, now in exile in Turkey, offering 'to be of assistance in any way possible.'[33]

Meanwhile, he continued his ventures in translation. Several essays on film technique by Pudovkin had been published in Russian in 1926, and in a German version in 1928. Working from both texts, and incorporating in addition Pudovkin's February talk to the Film Society, Montagu prepared an English translation that was published as *On Film Technique: Three*

Essays and an Address by Gollancz in October. In Montagu's hands the prose style, appropriate to the technical subject matter, was bare and unadorned. With the same cavalier conviction with which he cut foreign films shorter for the British market, he did not hesitate to edit the text where he felt the original would mislead an English-speaking readership – thus in rejecting Pudovkin's advocacy of writing a script such that each reel of the film will be self-contained, he made a self-confessed 'wide textual alteration'. He also took advantage of the footnotes to advance pet theories of his own, for example on intertitling. The resultant publication, as one of the first books of film theory to appear in English, proved to be widely influential. Boldly advancing the manifesto of the Soviet montage school that 'the foundation of film art is *editing*' and that 'every object, taken from a given viewpoint and shown on the screen to spectators, is a *dead object*, even though it has moved before the camera … it is no more than raw material for the future build-ing-up, by editing, of the movement that is conveyed by the assemblage of the various strips of film,' Pudovkin 'placed cinema's workings under a scientific microscope to a degree never previously attempted by filmmakers in the West or in serious film literature.'[34]

Bryusov's *The Fiery Angel* was very different. An adventure novel laced with the occult, magic, demonic possession and satanic ritual, it was rendered in translation in a slightly antiquated tone that does not jar but suits its historical subject. In composing his version Montagu worked harmoniously with his friend Sergei Nalbandov. 'Our method was admirable,' he explains. 'He, who is bilingual, would submit himself to rigid cross-examination while I scribbled down a literal version of the text, even to the Russian word-order – then I would throw the original away and write the product in fresh English from my literal notes.' Completing the translation in September, Montagu wrote to the novelist Arnold Bennett asking if he would read the 130,000-word manuscript and give advice. Bennett, saying he was extremely busy, declined. Montagu was nonetheless able to find a publisher in Humphrey Toulmin, who issued the book in 1930. As Catherine Rabinovitch had feared, it did not set the world on fire. 'In books my taste was too idiosyncratic,' Montagu later lamented. 'I rejected Sergei's suggestion of Sholokov's *Quiet Don*, which could have made me a fortune in royalties (I always insisted on retaining an interest in my translations and never accepted the more usual outright fee), and preferred Bryusov's *Fiery Angel*, the novel on which the Prokofiev opera is founded, which must have sold at most a hundred copies before it was remaindered.'[35]

From 2–7 September Ivor attended the first International Congress of Independent Cinema at the chateau of La Sarraz, Switzerland, as a delegate of the Film Society. He was accompanied by Jack Isaacs, a lecturer in English literature at King's College, London, and a stalwart of the society. The congress was the initiative of the French writers Robert Aron and Janine Bouissonouse, and was held under the benign sponsorship of the progressive chatelaine, Mme Hélène de Mandrot. The objective was to gather the forces of those committed to film as art – represented here by avant-garde filmmakers and enthusiasts from film societies and film journals – and to lay the groundwork for an international federation and a production base.[36]

Films were shown on a screen 'spread between the ancient arches'. Montagu presented, incomplete, the New Zealand filmmaker Len Lye's animated *Tusalava*, made with assistance from the Film Society; according to Ivor, Lye was one of only two experimental filmmakers in Britain at the time. Delegates gave reports on the situation of independent filmmaking in various countries of Europe, the United States, and Japan. Montagu spoke for Britain, outlining the structure and operations of the Film Society. These 'rather staid' proceedings, Montagu relates, were disrupted by the delayed arrival of 'three strange figures dressed from head to foot in blue zipper boiler suits': these were Sergei Eisenstein and his collaborators, Eduard Tisse and Grigori Alexandrov, just embarking on an exploratory venture into the capitalist West. Eisenstein was a captivating presence: 'of medium height, plump, with fine hands and a big head, the tallest brow you ever saw, a big fluffy quiff on top of that, small mischievous sparkling eyes, and a mouth that could be very determined indeed'.[37]

Before long the ebullient Soviet director cajoled the delegates into improvising a film on the spot. Independent Cinema, impersonated by the languishing Bouissonouse with film reels as breastplates, was chained in the turret of the castle under the guard of the forces of Commercial Cinema, among whom were lance-wielding film theorist Béla Balázs and the sweating, armour-clad Isaacs. To the rescue came a medieval army of independents, including critics Léon Moussinac as d'Artagnan and Jean-Georges Auriol, who joined in the fray with a typewriter turned machine gun. Disaster on the rooftop was narrowly averted when the tiles began to slip, almost catapulting Moussinac and Tisse, camera in hand, to the ground. Nominally directing this farrago was German filmmaker Hans Richter, with Ivor as his assistant. *Storm über La Sarraz/ Tempête sur La Sarraz/ The Storming of La Sarraz* is sadly lost.[38]

When congress deliberations resumed, politics intruded. According to Eisenstein's account, the Soviet delegates called for the West's creative intelligentsia to establish 'an ideological rapprochement with the radical-revolutionary movement in Western countries'. He notes that 'aesthetes and paladins of pure art begin to bristle, but it is fairly easy to rout them.' However, there is a Fascist group around the Italian Futurist Enrico Prampolini. This is less easily countered, but 'by a 'united front' of revolutionary and even of radically inclined groupings we were able to switch the totally apolitical character of the congress's 'conclusions' and, more than that, to eradicate completely the anti-Soviet tinge of several proposals that the lame Prampolini and someone from the group of French organisers of the congress tried to impart.' And Eisenstein continues: 'Here for the first time we meet up with that potential of the intelligentsia which would in time put on the lackey's livery of Fascism and assist it in its vile and bloody work. We stand shoulder to shoulder against them in real action with two friends who are very dear to me; Ivor Montagu, from England, and Léon Moussinac, from France.'[39]

On his return from Switzerland, Montagu took part in the 3rd International Congress of the World League for Sexual Reform, held in the Wigmore Hall, London, from 8 to 14 September 1929. The aims of the League, adopted after the 2nd Congress in Copenhagen, were 'to help to create a new legal and social attitude (based on the knowledge which has been acquired from scientific research in sexual biology, psychology and sociology) towards the sexual life of men and women.' Sessions, accordingly, were devoted to such topics as Marriage and Divorce, Venereal Disease and Prostitution, and Birth Control, Sterilisation, and Abortion.[40]

Ivor's topic was 'The Censorship of Sex in Films'. In his paper, subsequently published with the proceedings of the conference, he reverted to themes he had explored in his 1927 article 'Social Ideology and the Cinema'. Repression and lack of fulfilment, he argued, 'both in the sexual sphere and in the domain of the ego, is characteristic of the life of the ordinary man and woman, perhaps particularly so today.' The cinema was particularly fitted to providing release and sublimation in day-dreaming, and the censor abetted this 'by allowing a maximum of erotic stimulation, so long as only parts of the body are employed which fall within a certain geographic pattern ... and by allowing a maximum of promiscuity so long as its precise extent remains clouded ...' As a result: 'Accepted moral standards and repression are unshaken, an effective sexual day dream provided, and the whole of life enveloped in a romantic, rosy cloud, in which nothing suffers except truth, reality and the art of the film ...'[41]

In going on to ridicule the BBFC provisions regarding display of the human body and sexual activity (the Board had banned a shot of copulating snails), noting that topics such as marital infidelity and the lives of prostitutes were forbidden, and pointing out that 'any serious un-selfconscious treatment of the human form is impossible' and that 'any kind of serious representation of sexual problems, any portrayal of the inevitably sordid and unhappy consequences of many sexual laws and customs, is quite out of the question,' Montagu was, it seemed, presenting a damning indictment of film censorship as practised in Britain. But in a surprising twist he then went on to call, not for its abolition, nor even for its relaxation – 'rather do I demand a strengthening.' The reasoning was that loosening the censor's grip for ordinary commercial exhibition would open the floodgates to pornography; but the authority should have the power, as with the theatre, to license the private exhibition of material 'not suitable for the whole indiscriminate public'. The paper thus reiterated arguments made by the Film Society in its special pleading to the LCC in 1927; in doing so, it betrayed the paternalistic assumptions of the cultural elite of the time, and it is possibly in recognition of this that Montagu in retrospect characterised his contribution to the congress as 'particularly unmemorable'.[42]

Ivor extended his examination of the subject in his pamphlet *The Political Censorship of Films*, published the same month. Here there were new considerations. 'If, in the moral sphere, the unofficial position of the Board introduces an obstructionist degree of conservatism and orthodoxy,' he wrote, 'in the political field it introduces a more sinister element.' A stringent ban on politically controversial films was being implemented without any democratic accountability, since the BBFC, although purportedly an independent industry body, was in fact responsive to government wishes.[43]

This had come about because of the indirect, non-legislated, manner in which film censorship had been introduced, and much of Montagu's pamphlet was devoted to disentangling the labyrinthine constraints then

besetting the exhibition of films in the UK, examining the implications of
the 1909 and 1927 Acts, explaining the powers of the BBFC and of local
authorities, and delving into the definition of private performance and the
distinction between inflammable (35mm) and non-inflammable (16mm)
film stock (relevant because the 1909 Act under which censorship was exercised applied only to inflammable film). What had emerged was 'the growth
of a network of regulations entirely binding anyone who desires to use the
film as a means of controversial expression'.[44]

Montagu's voice was not the only one being raised at this time against political censorship, the topic being a lively one because of the high-profile banning
both of Soviet features such as *Battleship Potemkin* and *Mother*, and of Herbert
Wilcox's Edith Cavell film *Dawn* (1928). George Bernard Shaw contended:

> All the censorships, including film censorship, are merely pretexts for
> retaining a legal or quasi-legal power to suppress works which the
> authorities dislike. ... The screen may wallow in every extremity of vul-
> garity and villainy provided it whitewashes authority. But let it shew a
> single fleck on the whitewash, and no excellence, moral, pictorial, or
> histrionic, can save it from prompt suppression and defamation. That is
> what censorship means.

And in her idiosyncratic polemic *Film Problems of Soviet Russia* (1929),
Bryher (Annie Winifred Ellerman) delivered a robust broadside against
the system: 'We are rapidly arriving at the point,' she wrote, 'when a small
minority, utterly out of touch with conditions of today, control what we
shall read, see, say and do.'[45]

Montagu was thus not out on his own in calling for action. But the remedy
he proposed was perhaps unexpected. As with sexual representation, there
was no question of the abolition of censorship – certainly not for the '*ordinary
commercial screen*'. What was required, he suggested, was for the BBFC to be
replaced by 'an official censorship, responsible and answerable for its acts in
the Houses of Parliament.' It was with this in mind that he circulated copies of
his pamphlet to a number of MPs, suggesting the formation of a small parliamentary group to discuss strategies for change. An informal meeting was held
on 26 September, and Ivor's brother Ewen enlisted to provide legal advice.
Among those involved were Fenner Brockway, of the ILP, and Labour MPs

Ellen Wilkinson and John Strachey. At this stage, ambitiously, Montagu hoped to show six Soviet features, banned or about to be banned, to a parliamentary committee, to the Home Office, and then to all members of parliament, in a bid to get the censorship decisions reversed.[46]

Meanwhile, Montagu lent his support to an initiative that might enable workers' film groups to circumvent political censorship. His pamphlet had included, as an appendix, a 'Basis for a Model Organisation to Distribute Vetoed Films', and it was with this possibility in mind that the London Workers' Film Society (LWFS) and a national Federation of Workers' Film Societies (FWFS) were founded in autumn 1929. Although not announced as such, the project was a Communist one: it was in line with the policy of the Red International of Labour Unions (to which the National Minority Movement was affiliated) to co-ordinate industrial and cultural activities, and the organisations' executive committees were dominated by Party members. In addition, a distribution and production company, Atlas Films, was set up under Communist auspices in order to supply films to the newly-formed workers' film societies.[47]

FWFS, the organisation to which Montagu was most closely connected, had as its objective 'to bring the Cinema to the service of the working class, and by the special distribution, and ultimately the special production of propaganda films to further the political and social aims of the working class.' The idea was to combat the efforts of capitalist cinema to 'dope the workers', and to use film as a weapon in the class struggle. By no means were the workers' societies to be low-cost replicas of the Film Society: 'It is not intended that Societies should become social centres for dilettantes or that their film work should give effect to bourgeois ideals of "Art in the Cinema", etc.' Principally, their function was to exhibit Soviet and other proletarian films, and to support by cultural means the political and industrial programme of the CPGB.[48]

The principal mover and shaker in these developments was Ralph Bond, who until recently had been secretary of the CPGB-led National Left Wing Movement (by now liquidated as being incompatible with the 'Class Against Class' Comintern line). In addition to assuming prominent roles in LWFS and Atlas Films, he became secretary of FWFS, while a lower-profile activist, R. Plummer, became chairman, and Emile Burns treasurer. Montagu was elected vice-chairman; thereupon he submitted his resignation as chairman of the Film Society, stating that, having 'recently become vice-chairman of a Workers Film Federation the object of which is avowedly political', it was 'possible that my position as Chairman, or even member, of the Council may lead to misunderstanding prejudiced [*sic*] to the Society's interest.'[49]

FWFS was an immediate success. The London society, despite difficulties negotiating the censorship obstacles, attracted large audiences to its screenings; affiliated societies sprang up in other large cities including Birmingham, Liverpool, Manchester, Cardiff, Glasgow and Edinburgh; and within a few months local production of workers' newsreels under the aegis of Atlas Films commenced. Unsurprisingly, given the Class Against Class line, however, the workers' film movement led by FWFS did not gain the backing of the Labour Party or its affiliates. In January 1930 Montagu wrote to Monica Ewer of the *Daily Herald* (the Labour paper) – who was herself listed as a FWFS Council member – seeking her publication's support and denying that the organisation was Communist ('We only have a few C's on the council faute de mieux, you know, people rushing in where angels fear to tread'), but whether disingenuous or simply naive, he was not believed and Labour kept aloof.[50]

Nonetheless, Montagu must have experienced great satisfaction that reinforcements had now arrived in his long battle to get Soviet pictures seen in Britain, despite the tactics of the authorities (which included ongoing surveillance by MI5). He could now personally move out of the front line. His name features very little in the minutes of FWFS executive committee meetings in the early months of the organisation's existence. And although several sources list Ivor as a member, as well, of the executive of LWFS, his papers do not include records of LWFS meetings and it is likely he participated only peripherally, if at all.[51]

Meanwhile, Montagu had kept up the pressure on the censorship front. His old adversary Joynson-Hicks, now Viscount Brentford, joined in the debate, publishing a pamphlet, *Do We Need a Censor?* The former Home Secretary's position was clear. 'Although I am not what I believe is called a "cinema fan",' he wrote, 'having very rarely time to visit these places of amusement and instruction, I am told that there are still a good many films exhibited which the country could do better without.' His chief worry appeared to be pictures 'exhibited in India and in the East, showing the white woman as an object of degradation': it was 'undoubtedly essential that all nations which rule in Eastern countries should see to it that the pride and character of their womanhood is maintained unimpaired.'

Closer to home, he believed the trend of public opinion was 'towards a more stern enforcement of the law'. Significantly, in a move that placed him in the same camp as Montagu, Brentford declared that the present system of unofficial censorship was 'not very satisfactory in theory' – and indeed he doubted very much whether it would last beyond Mr O'Connor's life. (He did not, of course, acknowledge any Home Office involvement in the banning of Soviet films such as *Battleship Potemkin*.)[52]

Whether Brentford's implicit support, from a conservative perspective, for a more direct state censorship of films rang any alarm bells with Montagu is difficult to say. It is telling nonetheless that the focus of the parliamentary committee at this stage was not to call for outright change but to find an assured way, under current legislation, 'to exhibit specialised films to learned societies, schools and study groups of all kinds.' However, legal advice that the parliamentarians received from the Attorney General, Sir William Jowitt, was that an Act of Parliament would be needed to change the present position. The group of MPs whom Montagu had assembled met again on 17 December, and on 24 February 1930, at an all-party meeting in the Commons that he organised with Ellen Wilkinson, the Parliamentary Films Committee was inaugurated. By this time inconsistent rulings by the London County Council in respect to workers' film society screenings were drawing attention to flaws in the system, and Montagu urged the committee to press the LCC for reform. Thereafter, given his imminent departure for the United States, he left the initiative in the hands of film critic Robert Herring, 'as it would be a tragedy after the preparatory ground has been broken, if the enlisted members were allowed to slip away.'[53]

While all this was going on there had been other things absorbing Montagu's attention. He had written a screenplay from T.S. Stribling's South American adventure novel *Fombombo*, and it was being considered at British International Pictures. His wife Hell, in addition to managing a pioneering birth-control clinic in King's Cross for Harley Street gynaecologist Dr Norman Haire, was reorganising a dirt-track syndicate. The couple were looking for more spacious accommodation, so that Hell's mother Kate and daughter, Rowna, could comfortably live with them. Most pressingly, there was for Ivor the difficult task of trying to keep work flowing through Brunel & Montagu Ltd, and more generally the question of how to orient himself professionally in an industry undergoing radical transformation.[54]

8

HOLLYWOOD

IN 1929 THE British film industry was in the midst of the upheaval caused by the advent of sound. Montagu, like many who had grown to love silent cinema, was apprehensive, fearing that dynamic visual language and montage would give way to static canned theatre. This, he observed, was already happening. Heavily influenced by Pudovkin, he rejected the whole concept of synchronous sound. It was not just sync dialogue that was redundant: 'To show a door slamming, and make the noise of its slam; to show a vase shatter on the floor, and render the sound of its breaking is to use two impulses to communicate to the listening spectator a concept that might equally well be conveyed by one.' His position made it difficult for him as the studios converted to the new audiovisual medium. He refused to direct straight adaptations of plays, while the producers could not see the commercial potential in the experimental use of sound that he proposed.[1]

In the right hands, Montagu granted, the new technology could be deployed creatively: Hitchcock's *Blackmail* (released in June 1929), one of the first British talkies, was, he wrote admiringly, 'more than first-rate'. And in August he and a 'strong contingent' of Film Society members gathered to witness the latest work of the Austrian composer Edmund Meisel, whose electrifying score for *Battleship Potemkin* had done much for the success of that film in Germany. Meisel had undertaken to create a soundtrack for *The Crimson Circle/Der rote Kreis*, an Edgar Wallace mystery thriller directed as a British-German co-production by Friedrich Zelnik. The film had dialogue; what Meisel did – as he explained to the audience 'with a wealth of expressive gestures and flashing smiles' – was compose music, devise sound effects and oversee the recording and synchronisation. His listeners, as reported by the *Daily Express*, were 'duly impressed – for Herr Meisel's "effects" are, indeed, revolutionary ... So complicated, indeed, was the jigsaw formed by the interweaving of Herr Meisel's themes, each of which was allotted to one of the characters, that I was not surprised to hear that he had spent many months completing them at Wembley – with four different bands ...'[2]

Meisel was said to be experimenting with placing loudspeakers at different spots around the auditorium 'to enhance the verisimilitude of the sound film', and the new potentialities opened up by audio technology also excited Montagu's imagination. In an undated memo apparently intended for the Western Electric company, he elaborated on such questions as the wiring of a small sound studio for Independents, apparatus for exterior sound recording ('How far is it possible to eliminate undesired noises by selection in the recording apparatus? ... Is there any extra-light and handy apparatus?'), and the development of small studios specifically for post-shooting synchronisation. The following year Western Electric was claimed to be 'pursuing certain methods of research recommended by Mr Montagu towards solving the multi-lingual problem economically'.[3]

It was precisely because of American superiority in sound technology that Montagu had set his mind on trying his luck in Hollywood. 'Some of us cocky Europeans might think we had, and we did [have], a few better and more original ideas for application of the available machinery than had yet been tried,' he recalled, 'but Hollywood was the place where it was available, and the greater experience of its employment on the studio floor.' When Ivor learnt, probably at La Sarraz, that Eisenstein and his colleagues had similar intentions, he decided to join forces with them. 'We laid our plans together,' he records, 'and I was to go on ahead.' But first of all, the Russians were to come to London. Eisenstein accepted a Film Society invitation to be present at the first British screening of *Battleship Potemkin* on 10 November, to be followed by a series of lectures.[4]

The *Potemkin* premiere, held at the large-capacity Tivoli Palace in the Strand, to which the Film Society had now moved, was a triumph for Montagu. As he explained in the programme notes: 'The negative has so often been cut and matched to meet the requirements of various countries that it is now difficult to draw a perfect positive,' but though the print he had obtained from the trade delegation in Berlin was 'not entirely satisfactory', it was, 'unlike any other copy previously shown outside Russia … complete; following, in arrangement and colour, the original nearly exactly'. ('Colour' perhaps refers to the famous hand-painting of the warship's red flag.) The film was accompanied by an orchestra playing Meisel's original score, conducted by the composer himself.[5]

It is significant that Montagu, perhaps with an eye on the censorship authorities, was at pains to point out in the programme notes that 'the story shown in the film differs very materially from the historical incident.' In particular, the massacre of civilians, which appears in the film as 'entirely wanton', in fact followed rioting and arson, while the incident of the mutineers' ship sailing unmolested through the Admiral's fleet was 'probably to be ascribed less to fraternity than to timidity'.[6]

The impact of the film on the audience, which included many aspiring young filmmakers as well as London's progressive intelligentsia, was undoubtedly considerable; as Michael Balcon later wrote: 'One can remember, if not quite recapture, the excitement of seeing for the first time the work of the great Russian masters, Eisenstein and Pudovkin – *Battleship Potemkin*, *End of St Petersburg*, *Mother* and others.' But the director himself was grumpy. *Potemkin* had been preceded by the premiere of John Grierson's fishing trawler documentary *Drifters*, whose montage had been heavily influenced by Eisenstein's work; Eisenstein complained that it 'had given away all the best parts' of his own film. And he was unhappy with the Meisel music, complaining that it turned his picture into an 'opera', and that Meisel had ruined the showing by 'having the film projected slightly slower than normal, without my agreement, for the sake of the music. This destroyed all the dynamics of the rhythmic relationships …'[7]

If this contretemps caused a rift in the Eisenstein–Montagu relationship, it was not a lasting one – although possibly the Soviet director exacted his revenge by the 'cruel fun' he indulged in at the Brunel & Montagu offices, where he made a toll call to Japan costing the firm a punishing £10. Nonetheless, Ivor was an eager member of the small selected group who attended Eisenstein's course of lectures at Foyle's bookshop over the period 19–28 November, along with the lecturer Jack Isaacs, the critic Robert Herring, the budding acolyte Herbert Marshall, and, among others, the up-and-coming filmmakers Anthony Asquith, Basil Wright, Arthur Elton, Ian Dalrymple, Thorold Dickinson and, 'darting in and out', John Grierson. Eisenstein bemused and provoked his students by talking, at first, of everything *but* film: of Kabuki plays and James Joyce, Webster and Coleridge, Toulouse-Lautrec and Daumier, Charles Darwin and Zola. Underpinning it all, however, was the concept of montage and the idea that 'film montage was the *cinematic* aspect of a particular form of expression used by artists in other media'. Eisenstein went into considerable detail in defining types of filmic montage, and declared that in the new cinema sound would play a big role 'as one of the elements of the new montage system'. For Montagu (who did not attend every lecture), the key thing was that Eisenstein obliged the participants 'to think for ourselves and give our filmic solutions of real events and literary passages.' At the same time, a workshop in experimental filmmaking organised by Montagu was held in a small studio upstairs at Foyle's under the direction of Hans Richter. This resulted in the production of a satirical short, *Everyday*, in which Eisenstein plays an English bobby.[8]

Intensely curious, Eisenstein took the opportunity to poke into many odd corners of London and further afield, accompanied usually by Jack Isaacs or another member of the film-loving fraternity. (Isaacs 'was able to escort him round the byways frequented by Ben Jonson, whom Eisenstein revered far more than Shakespeare.') Sidney Bernstein threw a party for him, along with Alexandrov and Tisse, who were then also in England; Montagu was probably among the 'Film Society grandees' who were regaled with a feast of Russian food. Eisenstein, 'wearied by the atmosphere of the smart, sophisticated crowd', did not, according to his biographer, have the happiest of evenings.[9]

On 7–9 December Montagu took Eisenstein to Cambridge, where they stayed with Maurice Dobb (who also held a party for his distinguished guest), breakfasted with the philosopher Richard Braithwaite, and lunched at High Table in Trinity at the invitation of Peter Kapitza (it was on this occasion, as Montagu gleefully recounts, that the renowned physicist Sir J.J. Thomson confided to Eisenstein that he had 'witnessed a Kye-nimatograph performance once'). Eisenstein lectured on Russian films, according to one account, or 'the general problems of the theory of cinema' according to another. A highlight of the visit was the performance at King's of the masque of *Comus* directed by Lydia Lopokova: the girls' parts were, as convention decreed, taken by young men, and afterwards, Montagu relates, 'the undergraduates sat around with drinks, sometimes on each others' laps.' The Russian's 'eyes goggled and he whispered to me: "The authentic atmosphere of Oscar Wilde".' Eisenstein was much taken with the university environment, 'the high arches soaring into the gloom of Gothic naves … the Latin grace read antiphonal … all the other quaint and charming details …' He seriously considered abandoning cinema for an academic career, something that Montagu subsequently did his best to abet as a backstop should a Hollywood contract not eventuate. Back in London, Ivor took Eisenstein to visit Shaw at Whitehall Court; the playwright 'was, as ever, gentle and extremely hospitable.' Eisenstein rounded out his UK visit with a talk on 'Film Production in Soviet Russia' given to SCR members on 13 December.[10]

Shortly before the New Year Eisenstein returned to Paris, and it was possibly in January 1930 that Ivor and Hell joined him there on a visit to a certain establishment in the rue Blondel, 'where the hostesses, all middle-aged and plain but with a special talent, sat beside us on the red plush sofas but without clothes, chatting calmly of their husbands and children and kitchens and how much they earned in the working day, until the time came to display this talent which was an ability to pick up coins from the edge of the table with an organ not usually so employed.' Eisenstein's 'appetite for experience was insatiable'; a little later, in Berlin, Ivor accompanied him on a visit to Magnus Hirschfeld's museum of *Sexualwissenschaft*.[11]

Montagu now focused his attention on his foray to the United States. The venture was made possible by a £500 loan from his uncle Lionel, race-horse owner, gambler, and partner in the family bank Samuel Montagu & Co. 'It appears,' says Ivor, 'that he had met Adolph Zukor, Paramount chieftain, over the gaming tables at Monte Carlo and, as was natural, received a wide-open invitation to visit which he now converted into an introduction for me.' Montagu assiduously went about procuring further entrées to the American motion-picture business; by the time he set sail, on 5 March, he was equipped with letters of introduction to David Sarnoff of RCA, Douglas Fairbanks and Mary Pickford, Charles Chaplin, William Fox, Winfield Sheehan (vice-president of Fox Films), and B.P. Schulberg and Walter Wanger of Paramount. With a view to assisting Eisenstein find a project to direct, Shaw gave Ivor an option on *The Devil's Disciple*, and Wells the rights, as he thought, to *The War of the Worlds* (he had forgotten that he had long ago sold the rights in perpetuity to Paramount). Montagu's distributor friend Arthur Levey was a most enthusiastic backer of the venture; mistaking the Shaw property that was available, he wrote:

> You should ... confide to Mr Zukor and such others of the American leaders of the industry that one of the primary factors of your visit is to obtain a Contract for the American distribution of productions to be made by the 'IVOR MONTAGU UNIT' the first of which will be BERNARD SHAW'S 'ARMS AND THE MAN' directed by EISENSTEIN under your personal supervision.'

He offered to come to New York to advise on the signing of the contract. Ivor himself was not as upbeat as his supporters. 'I am feeling miserable about the idea of America,' he wrote to Iris Barry, 'and am only sustained by my general principle that a move in any direction is always a move in the right direction.'[12]

Montagu sailed from Southampton on the SS *Majestic*, his fastidious travel agent having reserved for him a table in the dining saloon and a deckchair. Levey cabled him best wishes for a very pleasant crossing, 'CERTAIN YOU WILL HAVE GREAT SUCCESS WITH MONTAGU PRODUCTION UNIT AS THE COMBINATION OF MONTAGU SHAW AND EISENSTEIN ARE UNSURPASSED AND WILL CREATE A FURORE IN THE TRADE'. That the Honourable Ivor was at least a minor celebrity on board is indicated by the fact that the *New York Times* reported his arrival when the ship berthed in Manhattan on 11 March.[13]

Montagu's hostess in New York was Mrs Henry Moskowitz, whose daughter Miriam was married to Ivor's cousin Cyril. A former social worker, the formidable Mrs Moskowitz had become campaign manager and adviser to New York governor Al Smith, and in that capacity, it was said, 'wielded more political power than any other woman in the United States'. (Montagu was introduced to Smith, whom he found 'a slight man of enormous dignity and charm'; in the presidential campaign of 1928 he had been beaten, so his supporters thought, by his Catholicism – 'all the bright people around', Ivor found, were depressed by the victory of the 'incompetent and overrated Hoover'.) Henry Moskowitz was self-effacing; he was a civil rights campaigner and co-founder of the National Association for the Advancement of Colored People (NAACP), but Ivor mentions only his mixing the salad at mealtimes 'like a true paterfamilias'.[14]

Through his hosts' connections Montagu met Walter White, NAACP secretary (who told him a hair-raising story of racial prejudice in the South), and partook of a literary lunch at the Algonquin. He got to see Mei Lan-Fang ('China's Greatest Actor') and his company of actors, dancers and musicians; a performance by Artef (Workers Theatrical Alliance) of *Aristocrats* by H. Arones; Marc Connelly's all-black *The Green Pastures*; and an African-American drag show in Harlem. He inspected Western Electric research labs, and talked to the 'highfalutin' Sarnoff at rival RCA. Observing filming at Paramount's East Coast studios, he was astonished that the director could give his instructions to a huge array of assistants and technicians without addressing any of them directly: 'He just went on speaking in a low voice, indicating his wishes, and the following flock was so perfectly organised that each knew and noted down what would affect himself.'[15]

Pursuing his literary interests, Montagu secured commissions for an article, from the *Saturday Evening Post*, and a book, from Simon & Schuster, both on table tennis. (The article was duly written and the book begun, and Ivor generously recompensed for his efforts; but no publication ensued because of threats of legal action by Parker Brothers, the owners of the 'Ping-Pong' trade name.) He hawked his English version of *Le Cocu magnifique* around the theatrical agencies, arousing interest but no takers. He succeeded in tracking down the nefarious individual who had published a pirated edition of his translation of Pudovkin's *On Film Technique*, but not in extracting any money from him.[16]

During the war Ivor's mother had promoted an entertainment club for US Navy personnel in Hampshire. Franklin D. Roosevelt had then been Assistant Secretary of the Navy and had met her; now, as successor to Smith as New York state governor, he and his wife Eleanor showed their appreciation for Lady Swaythling's work by inviting her son to the executive mansion at Albany. He was received very hospitably. Roosevelt, already, according to Montagu, 'a wounded lion of a man', entertained his guests with his 'splendid torso resting regally in a lounge chair in the middle of the drawing room'; his 'schoolboyish tales' embodying a romantic view of the Great War were spellbinding. But Ivor was also struck by the politician's tough pragmatic cunning in the tactics of government.[17]

Montagu's major challenge at this time was to try to secure a Hollywood contract for Eisenstein and his team – which was to include Ivor and Hell. Negotiations were complicated by the fact that Eisenstein was in Paris (where he was encountering visa difficulties), and that any arrangement had to be approved by Sovkino through its American agency Amkino in New York. The two most hopeful prospects appeared to be Douglas Fairbanks of United Artists, who had been enthusiastic about *Potemkin* in Moscow and had already made overtures to Eisenstein, and Paramount Pictures, which had built a reputation for sophistication based on imported European talent. Fairbanks was in Hollywood, but Montagu succeeded in interesting Paramount's vice-president, Jesse L. Lasky, in the scheme, particularly recommending *The War of the Worlds*. Lasky sailed for Paris promising to see Eisenstein there, and Montagu set his sights westward.[18]

Around the middle of April, Ivor travelled to Los Angeles on the inaugural flight of a new Lindbergh airline that, for the first time, flew coast-to-coast in thirty-six hours (with an overnight stop in Kansas City). He made his way to Hollywood, where he took a small room in the Roosevelt hotel. What struck his eye in the unfamiliar California environment was the 'wilderness of white villas, the square patches of grass in front of them lining the streets kept green by revolving sprays of water-drops, and at each corner a more garishly coloured and inventive course for miniature golf'.[19]

Before long, he was fond of recounting, he was immersed fully nude in Fairbanks's Turkish bath, in the company of others similarly stripped down, including the host himself ('superb and brown') and 'a number of the great moguls who shall be nameless because they were unbeautiful' – they included producers Samuel Goldwyn and Joseph Schenck. 'The array of bodies recalled a medieval Last Judgment or a Cézanne bathing composition,' as Montagu later described it.[20]

Fairbanks immediately came up with a proposition. As Montagu explained it in a cable to Eisenstein in Paris, 'DOUGLAS INTERESTED IDEA ALL OF US SPEND YEAR HERE WORKING OUT AND MAKING BEST CONCEIVABLE SOUND AND TALKING VEHICLE FOR HIM INCLUDING ALL EXPERIMENTS MEISELESZQUE SOUND ETC TURNING D INTO MICKEY MOUSE STOP COULD YOU SUCCEED OR IS IT NOT YOUR STUFF.' No response was forthcoming; not surprisingly perhaps, given that Eisenstein was about to enter delicate negotiations with Jesse Lasky for a more open-ended project than the tightly constrained – if highly original – one envisaged by the swashbuckling star striving to make the transition to talkies. In the event Fairbanks headed to Europe, where the expectation was he would discuss story ideas with Eisenstein directly.[21]

Universal also expressed an interest in procuring Eisenstein's services. Studio head Carl Laemmle Sr, 'an elderly gnome-like man, bald, round-shouldered and very kindly', sent for Montagu and discussed projects and prospects. He was eager, Ivor thought, to conclude a deal. But Carl Laemmle Jr, the 'total opposite' of his father, came in and scuppered all such thoughts. 'Smart, dapper, handsome, black-haired, clad in a white silk shirt and white kid riding breeches with gaiters, he sat on the edge of his father's enormous desk with one foot on the ground, switching his riding crop while his father pleaded with him.' It was clear that the son would veto any proposal. Montagu minced no words in his report to Eisenstein: 'Old father Laemmle was very anxious' to engage him, 'but he is decrepit, & pathetically under the thumb of his shit of a son – an odious conceited creature, who forbade his father from proceeding.'[22]

Meanwhile the Soviet director talked, commencing 21 April, with Lasky and his offsiders Albert Kaufman and Richard Blumenthal at the George V hotel in Paris. Paramount offered Eisenstein a six-month contract to make a film in the USA, for which he would be paid $500 a week while the subject was agreed on and scripted, and $3,000 a week once filming commenced. Eisenstein was adamant, however, that the contract had to include Alexandrov and Tisse. Finally, it was agreed that there would be total remuneration of $900 a week, $500 for Mr Eisenstein and $100 each for Mr Tisse, Mr Alexandrov, Mr Montagu, and Mrs Montagu. The contract was signed on 3 May; Montagu was not privy to the detail of the negotiations. Eisenstein immediately set about securing a visa and obtaining passage to the United States with Tisse; Alexandrov, who was completing work on *Romance sentimentale*, a short film the trio had shot on commission, would follow.[23]

These developments were much hyped in the press by Montagu's friend Cedric Belfrage. As Hollywood Correspondent of the London *Film Weekly*, Belfrage extolled his colleague's exploits under the heading 'Crashing Hollywood's Gates – Young Englishman Does It in Exactly One Week – Ivor Montagu's Amazing Success'. Describing Ivor as 'fantastically attired, as ever, in sombre and amorphous clothing, with hair ever so slightly tamed from its pristine uncouthness', Belfrage credited Montagu with 'selling' Eisenstein as a director to Paramount 'with a salary of £10,000 per production – the contract to include an excellent job for Ivor himself as a kind of supervisor.' Flippant in tone ('I doubt if there are as many roubles in all Russia as Eisenstein will receive from the beneficent Jesse L. Lasky'), the article had a political edge. Montagu himself, 'with about half the wealth of Britain in his family's coffers,' Belfrage claimed, 'turned around and became a Communist, just to be different.' Eisenstein would gain the opportunity to pick up Hollywood tricks of the trade, and so 'for the first time Russian film makers will learn how to sugar the pill they want the world to swallow. Thus America is innocently helping her arch-enemy to propagandise for Communism.' Tongue-in-cheek, certainly; but Belfrage might have been a little more circumspect if he had realised redbaiters were waiting in the wings.[24]

Montagu had none of the dazzling riches alluded to in the papers; in fact, his funds were running low. Presenting his letters of introduction to the Paramount executive B.P. Schulberg, he explained that he wanted 'to be in some story from its inception, while the story treatment was worked out, to see how they adapted it, and what processes it went through and suffered before it was finally completed.' He secured a three-week contract at $200 a week and was assigned as story consultant to a writing team adapting a minor Hungarian play, Lajos Zilahy's *The General*, to the screen as a vehicle for Paramount stars Kay Francis and Walter Huston. The associate producer in charge of the project was the Russian-born J.G. Bachmann, whom Ivor warmed to; the writer whom he collaborated with was the Hollywood veteran Albert S. Le Vino, for whom he developed considerable respect. The story was a triangle drama set in Russia ('Who in America has heard of Hungary?' explained Schulberg) during the war. In *With Eisenstein in Hollywood*, Montagu amusingly details the vicissitudes the project underwent: how he and Le Vino, with a little help from Shakespeare, completed their treatment; how the assigned director, Rowland V. Lee, declared at the production conference that the script was impossible, admittedly privately that it was not bad, and then demanded major changes to suit the young actress whom he favoured to take the place of Kay Francis; and how in short order Lee, his latest film meeting a poor reception at a sneak preview, was taken off the project and Francis reconfirmed. Montagu, in any event, had had his (uncredited) input. *The Virtuous Sin*, directed by George Cukor and Louis J. Gasnier, was released on 1 November; Ivor did not see it.[25]

Much as he liked and admired the people he was working with, Montagu quickly developed a contempt for the system. 'In making pictures,' he wrote

to Eisenstein, 'they are incredibly stupid. Like children. Or rather, quite
unlike children because with no vestige of imagination.' He particularly
noted that: 'I have seen many scenarios & in none of them is there even any
idea of scenarising the sound.' Ivor elaborated on this analysis in a letter to
Leon Trotsky, with whom he was now corresponding.

> The minds of this large community, now increased to fifth city in the
> United States seem vaporised by their concentration (what a contradictory
> metaphor!) upon the provision of entertainment. It is a condition of that
> entertainment that, in order that the audience may be released from the
> cinema after the performance perfectly satisfied, with a feeling that all is
> right with the world, it shall never concern itself with real forces, or even
> with real characters motivated by real motives.

As a result a sort of 'willed superficiality' was bred in the minds of those
engaged in the industry, 'a reluctance to allow their minds to consider life,
even their own experience, except through an artificial and roseate formula.
Their minds shrink from logical exercise as a severed worm shrinks from the
spade.' No doubt, he told Trotsky, any picture Eisenstein made in Hollywood
would not, in itself, be of value, but 'the experience should be of inestimable
importance to his colleagues on his return.'[26]
   To his uncle Lionel, he complained that he was bored – 'and know
I shall go on being bored, drearily. Well, this cannot be helped.' He promised that he was 'certainly not going to give up the game, and I shall stick
to it as long as I can see any chance at all still remaining, either of direct
profit or of reaching such a position as could be capitalised on returning to England.' To his New York friend Lewis Galantière, he expressed
confidence that his Paramount job could be his entrée to the business:
'No doubt, if I were industrious, hard working, and polite, instead of
being bored, rather short, and homesick, [it] would land me within twelve
months in a very elevated position indeed.' In fact, the studio was urging
him to stay on and work permanently for them. But he doubted if he had
the patience for it.[27]
   Part of the reason for his discontent, as he saw it, was Hollywood's geo-
graphical location. 'This place is so remote from the rest of the world,' he
lamented to his uncle, 'from the interests one has elsewhere, and the work

in itself is not of a character to compensate for the loss of the intellectual activities of civilisation.' In his letter to Eisenstein, he spelled it out:

> This place is incredibly & infernally dull as a place to live in. One has continually the feeling of being in a remote backwater, far distant from any living current of civilisation. After all, it is 3000m. from New York, & N.Y. is far enough away from civilisation. It is a sort of holiday or artificial city, with little sense or smell of America in it.[28]

Eisenstein at this time was en route from Cherbourg on the SS *Europa*; he was to disembark in New York on 12 May. Montagu would have liked to meet him there, so that they could 'absorb national consciousness' together, but his employment at Paramount ruled that out. Instead, as he explained to his future partner, he was taking the opportunity to become familiar with the studio's personalities and methods so that they could 'avoid tactical errors' when they started work there as a team. He was taking care not to breathe a word of their plans for sound montage: 'It is better to leave this until we are all together & can mutually discuss psychology & tactics of getting one's own way.' Ivor was soon able to report that he was 'building up, as hard as I can, links of goodwill with the studio staff'.[29]

While Eisenstein created a stir with movie industry publicists and Ivy League academics alike on the East Coast, and proceeded westwards via Detroit and Chicago (meat works and gangsters were top of his to-see list), Montagu settled in. Discovering it was impossible to get around Los Angeles without a car, he hired one, and wrecked it the same evening. He went swimming with Belfrage at Malibu. He had lunch with Mary Pickford, who wanted him to use his influence with Shaw to release *Caesar and Cleopatra* so she could play the empress. He played poker with studio confederates, accepting invitations so as not to offend, and steadily accrued losses – 'the trouble was the divergence between the salary scales of those sitting round the table.'[30]

At this time Montagu received, unexpectedly, a letter from Herbert Ponting, whose photograph of Antarctic killer whales he had acquired as a schoolboy, and whose book *The Great White South* he had reviewed while at Cambridge. Ponting declared himself an admirer of Ivor's film *Blue Bottles*, and went on to seek his advice about the commercial exploitation in

Hollywood of his new invention, the 'Distortagraph', an optical process for producing moving caricatures on film. Montagu replied courteously, drawing attention to the gulf in the film industry between the perfection of a device and its marketing.[31]

In June Hell flew in to join him, and Ivor's letter of introduction to Chaplin, which had sat unanswered for six weeks, finally bore fruit: they were invited to the comedian's Beverly Hills residence for an informal tea party. The tennis court was of 'clinging asphalt that took spin beautifully' and perfectly suited Montagu's game; he was in devastating form, and only Chaplin himself, 'superbly fit', could score against him. It was a wonderful day, and 'the foundation of a beautiful friendship'.[32]

Eisenstein arrived on 16 June, and before long he and his offsiders Alexandrov and Tisse were ensconced along with Ivor and Hell in a rented hill-top house in Coldwater Canyon, Beverly Hills. It was Spanish-style, 'a snow-white block up on the side of the mountain' in a then remote and unfrequented area. The group hired a black couple, Rose and Lester, as cook and butler, and acquired an old De Soto, described by Marie Seton as 'the most rattle-trap car in which a "great" director ever rode about in the annals of Hollywood history' (on one occasion Montagu forgot to put the handbrake on and 'it ran straight down the hill and across the road below into someone else's field, nearer half than a quarter mile'). Hell ruled the household 'with a rod of iron' and outlawed liquor, mindful of Prohibition and aware that the team were vulnerable to attacks motivated politically or through professional jealousy. (The Russians were upset: although none of them drank, they felt they would be lacking in hospitality to guests.) For a short time the group were joined by Ivor's young sister Joyce, travelling on holiday with her childhood nursemaid Mabel.[33]

It was in Hollywood that Ivor at last gave up the Jewish observances that he had kept since childhood. 'Long after I had ceased to believe in any reason for this,' he recounts, 'right into adulthood, I continued to practice the dietary laws, sporadic synagogue attendance, the fasts and so forth. I told myself that I wanted to be quite sure my disbelief was not a rationalisation to fit my convenience.' But on being asked by Eisenstein 'why on the Day of Atonement I proposed to fast for the twenty-five hours, and, on explaining, being faced by a second question: "Wasn't I quite sure?" that I at last realised I was being a fool and packed it up.'[34]

The studio encouraged the newcomers to take their time getting their bearings. In a two-car convoy, they went on exploratory excursions. One visit was to a show ranch owned by razor-blade millionaire William King Gillette. On another occasion they drove through a forest of redwoods whose majestic scale excited Eisenstein's visual imagination – and served as an inspiration for his 'dynamic square' lecture to the Academy of Motion Picture Arts and Sciences, in which he called for a screen that could change shape to incorporate 'the male, the strong, the virile, active, *vertical* composition'. Their most ambitious journey, Ivor recounts, was into the desert, skirting Death Valley, and on to Yosemite National Park.[35]

There was also the social round. Eisenstein hit it off with Chaplin, and the Russians joined the Montagus on frequent visits to the comedian's estate, one of whose outstanding features was a swimming pool exactly replicating the contours of his famous bowler hat. Charlie took them to the funfair at Venice on Independence Day, and sailing on his yacht for a three-day trip, amidst sea lions and flying fish, to Catalina Island. Eisenstein taught Chaplin obscene Russian oaths which the comic would yell out to the emigré doorman at Romanov's restaurant (run by exile Grand Dukes and Duchesses) as they drove past.[36]

Heinrich Fraenkel, Montagu's friend from Berlin, was now in Hollywood and introduced the group to Berthold Viertel, the director, and his wife Salka, a screenwriter. Through the Viertels they met Greta Garbo, who 'radiated warmth, serenity, good sense.' Lasky arrived on the West Coast and invited Eisenstein, Montagu and Hell to dinner with the Schulbergs. After the meal, the menfolk retreated to 'impossibly padded, doze-inducing, deep armchairs'. The Paramount chieftain was looking his recruits from abroad over. Montagu relates that when Lasky asked them 'what *do* you think of our pictures?', they hesitated a fraction of a second too long.[37]

Getting down to work at the studio, the filmmakers began to discuss potential projects. Many ideas were tossed around. Eisenstein tactfully kept quiet about his ambition to film Karl Marx's *Capital*. *The War of the Worlds* was soon dropped by tacit consent. *The Devil's Disciple*, Montagu says, was 'never a starter', and *Arms and the Man* was also rejected. Eisenstein 'laughingly dismissed' two of Paramount's suggestions, *The Martyrdom of the Jesuit Missionaries in North America* and Eugene O'Neill's *The Hairy Ape*. Surprisingly, Lasky proposed Ferdinand Bruckner's explosive *Die Verbrecher* (*The Criminals*), a plea for the decriminalisation of homosexuality that had caused a scandal when staged in Hamburg in 1928. Bachmann suggested Rudyard Kipling's *Kim* and a work by the investigative journalist Albert Londres (whose exposé of the white slave trade, *The Road to Buenos Aires*, Eisenstein had attempted to set up as a project in France). Leon Monosson, head of Amkino in New York, had hopefully put forward Alexander Serafimovich's *The Iron Flood*, a novel about a Red Army unit escaping encirclement during the Civil War. James Joyce had offered *Ulysses*, but Eisenstein was not enthusiastic about its potential as a movie; nor did he fancy Vicki Baum's *Menschen im Hotel* (soon after to be filmed as *Grand Hotel*). Instead, he toyed with the idea of a film on the life of the notorious armaments tycoon Basil Zaharoff, but this too did not advance beyond preliminary discussions.[38]

The project the team settled on was one dear to Eisenstein's heart. *The Glass House* originated in an idea he had had visiting Berlin in 1926 and observing the extensive use of glass in modern architecture. It may also have been inspired by Yevgeny Zamyatin's dystopian novel *We*, in which the population lives almost entirely within glass walls, although Montagu asserts that Eisenstein never made reference to it. In Eisenstein's vision, the characters of his film (who included lovers, bootleggers, a policeman, a poet, a laundress, a nudist, and a shoestore clerk) would live in a tall glass building, able to observe one another, but not doing so until something occurs to make them 'furtive, suspicious, inquisitive, terrified'. Eisenstein was insistent that it was not a fantasy, but an ordinary, down-to-earth story, and the writers the studio brought in to develop a script from the outline he sketched out were hard-bitten plotters of gangster movies. Nothing gelled. Montagu could not see the merit of the concept and chafed at Eisenstein's obstinate attachment to it; years later, in retrospect, he was ready to grant that the Russian may have seen 'more deeply than any of us supposed' into the impact urban conglomeration was having on the human condition. But in July 1930, as Eisenstein's biographer Ronald Bergan comments, 'From the incoherent, fragmentary, plotless, episodic synopsis, it would be difficult to blame Paramount for rejecting it.'[39]

Attention switched to another idea Eisenstein was enthusiastic about, an adaptation of Blaise Cendrars' *L'Or*, which he had secured the rights to in Paris. *Sutter's Gold*, as it was known in English, was a biographical novel published in 1925 tracing the extraordinary life of the Swiss adventurer and

pioneering US settler John Augustus Sutter (1803–1880). Sutter's flourishing agricultural community in California was, paradoxically, laid waste
when gold was discovered on his property, the aspect of the story that particularly appealed to Eisenstein: 'I wanted to express the disastrous role of
the gold strike on Sutter's California lands, the destruction and ruin of his
fertile estates and of him, through the vivid impression made on me by the
California gold dredgers still at work today.'[40]

Eisenstein had his heavily annotated copy of the novel, and immersed
himself in all the historical literature he could lay his hands on. Montagu
supplied him with a précis and notes on characters and incidents, and wrote
out their agreed broad division of the action into (initially nine) reels.
Together with Alexandrov they made a research trip to the Sacramento
Valley where the gold rush had taken place, and to the San Francisco water-
front. They soaked up atmosphere, visited Fort Sutter, found relics like the
saw from Sutter's sawmill, talked to elderly women who as little girls had
been bounced on Sutter's knees. Eisenstein sketched, Alexandrov took
photos, and Montagu made notes and recorded reminiscences. Then it was
back to Coldwater Canyon, and they were ready to write.[41]

'We worked like a conveyor belt, round the clock,' Montagu explains.
'Eisenstein would be closeted with Grisha [Alexandrov], narrating verbally
the treatment he had planned. Grisha would go off and write it.' As soon
as it was written it would be typed up and translated by staff provided by
Paramount. Montagu would then read the English text and go over it with
Eisenstein, discussing and revising.

> Then I would go off and rewrite it. Hell would receive my manuscript –
> my handwriting is so erratic that few, if any, can cope with it but she, and
> I have never learned to master a typewriter, so she would have to type fair
> copies. The Paramount staff would then make more copies of this final state.

Eisenstein, dealing with different stages of the narrative at the one time,
'would have to keep the whole thing in his head and switch from one to
the other, like a chessmaster giving a simultaneous display.' In three days, the
team working almost without pause, the script was finished.[42]

Montagu was pleased with it. 'The most marvellous story I've ever run
into,' he wrote to Robert Herring. He and Alexandrov shared credit, and

indeed, as he stated, contributed to its authorship, but fundamentally it was 'a true Eisenstein creation'. He was especially gratified that they had remained staunchly committed to their vision for the future of sound film, rejecting the dialogue-based model of the talkies of the time, 'the exact correspondence of image and its natural causally associated sound'. The script is rich with detailed indications of individual sounds and particularly their combinations, arranged as montages or 'symphonies'. Thus, for example, 'The sounds of the blacksmith's instruments, the girl's giggles, the neighing of the horse, the screams of the man losing his teeth, the flute, the choppings are all arranged in this rhythm although they retain their natural and recognisable sound.' A sonic climax is reached when gold is discovered and the heavy thuds of picks and the 'hoarse grate' of shovels 'pervade the whole land. And beneath this tearing sound the dominion of Sutter falls to waste and destruction ...'[43]

While Eisenstein worked on design sketches, Paramount executives scrutinised the script. Word came back that it was a splendid piece of work, but unacceptable. Perhaps, as Eisenstein and his biographer Marie Seton suspected, there was an ideological veto: 'Paramount didn't like the moral imbedded in *Sutter's Gold* – that gold is the source of destruction to man and nature.' This accords with the view of Schulberg's son Budd, then working in the Paramount publicity office, who writes: ' ... their story of how the gold discovered at Sutter's ranch destroyed a legitimate pioneer was too radical for the money men in New York who had the final say on studio decisions.' Possibly, as Montagu was inclined to believe, the project fell victim to studio factional infighting. Very likely, in any case, what clinched the negative decision was what was officially given as the reason – the high cost of a project that had doubtful box-office prospects. With the financial crisis precipitated by the Wall Street crash biting deeper and the onset of the Great Depression, Hollywood was hurting; and the studio was in a much poorer position to mount an epic than it would have been earlier in the year, when Eisenstein was contracted. The team protested, demanded an interview with the costing department, and insisted that the film could be shot economically, but all their pleas were unavailing.[44]

They had to move on. But in the meantime there were appearances to keep up. Although they soon tired of the Hollywood social scene (and never personally encountered the 'orgy' side that others breathlessly described to them), there were certain obligations that couldn't be bypassed. Hell hosted a party for the Viertels and the Schulbergs. The press announced that she and Ivor, along with Eisenstein, were expected to attend a garden tea sponsored by the Progressive School of Los Angeles at the home of Colleen Moore – here they would mingle with 'some of the most famous educators in the West'. And Bessie and Jesse Lasky invited Hell and Ivor to a moonlight supper dance ('please bring your bathing suits') held on 9 August at their ocean-front home in Santa Monica; all Hollywood was there.[45]

Work continued, although Montagu remained pessimistic about the chances of creative self-fulfilment in the American industry. 'The machine is too big,' he wrote to H.G. Wells. 'Once in a lifetime one might get the opportunity to do a piece of work that was satisfying to oneself, or useful according to one's standards of usefulness. But this is a very rare and abstract prospect, so rare that it may even be a mirage.' Still, work paid the bills. Montagu found himself a lucrative sideline as expert consultant about English universities on *Charley's Aunt*. What matter that the producers failed to heed his advice that an Oxford undergraduate would not have a phone in his room, and wouldn't place a cricket bat beside a football on his sideboard? The $3,000 cheque he received came in very handy, especially since Eisenstein was spending a large chunk of the collective's income on books.[46]

At Paramount, the team had to find a new project. This time Lasky proposed a property the studio had acquired soon after its 1925 publication, Theodore Dreiser's highly regarded novel *An American Tragedy*. The story, based on fact, of a weak but ambitious young man who while pursuing a romance with a wealthy young society woman causes the death of his pregnant working-class girlfriend and is subsequently sentenced to the electric chair, was a challenging one for Hollywood. If Clyde Griffiths is guilty of murder when Roberta is drowned, he is a most unsympathetic protagonist; if, however, he is innocent, the narrative is an indictment of the American justice system. Moreover, the work as a whole was a biting critique of the values of capitalist society. It was not surprising that previous attempts at adaptation, including by D.W. Griffith and Ernst Lubitsch, had stumbled.

Montagu believed that to take the project on would be the kiss of death. 'It would never be permitted,' he was convinced, 'to foreigners, some even Russians, to make *An American Tragedy* in the way we were bound to make it, the only way that persons of integrity with respect for literature could possibly make it.' Writing to Robert Herring, he said: 'Certainly there is material there, but pessimistic material; if we agree to do it it will, I feel, be against our best judgement.' He discussed the situation with Eisenstein and Alexandrov, he says, 'far into the night'. It is possible that Eisenstein, who knew and liked Dreiser from meetings in Moscow and New York and admired his work, was less pessimistic: one account states, in fact, that he 'greeted the proposal with enthusiasm.' In any event, the decision was to take on the challenge: 'Our unanimous conclusion not to drop out at this stage ... was taken with eyes wide-open.'[47]

An American Tragedy was a massive novel and, Montagu felt, 'one of the stodgiest great books of literature. Stodgy ... because its virtues arise from the steady and concentrated accumulation of authentic detail.' The ambition of the writing team was to faithfully reproduce these qualities in their blueprint for the film, and they threw themselves into the task, Ivor records, 'with ferocious energy'. There was less background research this time round; it was a matter of working from the text, with the ideas springing, mostly, from Eisenstein's imagination. Then 'the conveyor belt process began to roll again', and after days and nights of furious toil a script emerged.[48]

This time, experimentation with sound took the form of internal monologue, appropriated by Eisenstein from the stream of consciousness being developed in literary fiction by Joyce and others. It was to be used as the film approached its climax, with Clyde debating with himself whether to carry out his murderous intentions:

As the boat glides into the darkness of the lake, so Clyde glides into the darkness of his thoughts. Two voices struggle with him – one: 'Kill – kill!' the echo of his dark resolve, the frantic cry of all his hopes of Sondra and society; the other: 'Don't – don't kill!' the expression of his weakness and his fears, of his sadness for Roberta and his shame before her. In the scenes that follow, these voices ripple in the waves that lap from the oars against the boat; they whisper in the beating of his heart; they comment, underscoring, upon the memories and alarums that pass through his mind; each ever struggling with the other for mastery, first one dominating, then weakening before the onset of its rival.

The goal, Eisenstein wrote, was to present 'the inner play, the conflict of doubts, the explosions of passion, the voice of reason, rapidly or in slow-motion, marking the differing rhythms of one and the other and, at the same time, contrasting with the almost complete absence of outer action: a feverish inner debate behind the stony mask of the face'.[49]

With some trepidation, no doubt, the team handed over their 'First Treatment' on 5 October, offering it up for the consideration of '1. The West Coast Magnates; 2. The East Coast Magnates; 3. Theodore Dreiser; 4. The Hays Organisation.' At a projected fourteen reels it was exceptionally long; very few Hollywood movies at the time were more than ten (the writers conceded it needed to be shrunk to twelve). Reactions were not slow in coming; 'The result,' says Montagu, 'was electrifying.'[50]

Schulberg told them it was 'the best scenario that Paramount had ever had', and all the other executives were in accord. At Lasky's bidding, Ivor and the Russians left immediately for the East Coast, to see at first hand the upstate New York locations where the action was set (and the real events had taken place). Then they were called into Lasky's office in New York city, and told their agreement was over.[51]

As with *Sutter's Gold*, it is likely that ideological concerns, internal studio politics, and financial considerations all played a part in the rejection of the script. As early as May, Montagu had become aware that however sympathetic Lasky may have been towards Eisenstein and his projects, his power at Paramount was waning. Lasky had hired the Soviet director, Ivor believed, because of the studio's tradition of making 'prestige' pictures that were not necessarily box-office bonanzas. 'But,' he wrote to Eisenstein, 'although they are still at the head, Zukor & Lasky no longer ARE Paramount, in the sense that they once were. Great financial interests (such as Kuhn, Loeb & Co) <u>are</u> the company. And a new tradition, with which Schulberg walks, holds that the only PRESTIGE picture, the only prestige worth having, is that the picture is good box office.'[52]

This analysis was borne out in a memo David O. Selznick, then executive assistant to Schulberg, wrote to his boss about the *American Tragedy* treatment. It was 'the most moving script I have ever read. It was so effective, that it was positively torturing. When I had finished it, I was so depressed that I wanted to reach for the bourbon bottle. As entertainment, I don't think it has one chance in a hundred.' It would be an 'inexcusable gamble', in

Selznick's view, 'to put into a subject as depressing as this one, anything like the cost that an Eisenstein production must necessarily entail.'

> If we want to make *An American Tragedy* as a glorious experiment, and purely for the advancement of the art (which I certainly do not think is the business of this organisation), then let's do it with [John] Cromwell directing, and chop three or four hundred thousand dollars off the loss ... Let's try new things, by all means. But let's keep these gambles within the bounds of those that would be indulged in by rational businessmen; and let's not put more money than we have into any one picture for years into a subject that will appeal to our vanity through the critical acclaim that must necessarily attach to its production, but that cannot possibly offer anything but a most miserable two hours to millions of happy-minded young Americans.[53]

A further consideration, if any more were needed, might well have been Eisenstein's heretical intention not to use professional actors. 'I think the art of acting ought to remain on the stage,' he argued, as he scoured gas stations and hotels in Los Angeles looking for a young man to play Clyde. But what really clinched the case was a successful redbaiting campaign.[54]

Back in June, Montagu's foe George A. Atkinson, the *Daily Express* film critic, had written to the City of New York Police Department denouncing Ivor as a 'cunning propagandist' in league with 'Moscow plotters' who had devoted 'the whole of his energies and not considerable [*sic*] intellect to the fomentation of industrial revolt', and urging the American authorities to deport him 'bag and baggage' without delay. 'We understand him here,' he added darkly, 'and know how to deal with him.' The letter had been referred to the Commissioner of Immigration at Ellis Island. Meanwhile, a certain Major Frank Pease had initiated a vicious public campaign against the 'Jewish Bolshevik' Eisenstein, a 'cut-throat red dog' who would 'turn the American cinema into a communist cesspool'. Eisenstein, with support from his admirers, was at first able to shrug off the attacks as the ravings of a crackpot (he was not in fact a member of the Communist Party). But Pease was persistent, and his virulence eventually led to the Fish Committee – an investigating committee of the US House of Representatives chaired by Congressman Hamilton Fish – being convened in Los Angeles on

8 October to look into 'communist activities' in California, and specifically those of Eisenstein. The resultant publicity undoubtedly convinced
Paramount executives that their brand was in danger of being tarnished, and
that Eisenstein and his collaborators needed to be let go forthwith.[55]

Lasky showed the team a pile of letters denouncing the studio for
treason, and thereupon the contract was cancelled. It was 23 October.
'Everything was discussed, arranged, with the utmost courtesy on either
side,' Montagu tells us. Writing to Hans Richter several months later, he
explained: 'In the end we were all thrown out, partly owing to external
politics (Welt Politik) and partly to internal (we were made, like everybody
else in Hollywood, pawns in the game for power between the various big
company executives).'[56]

According to one source, $30,000 was paid to Eisenstein as compen-
sation for the breaking of the contract. If that is the case, he apparently
did not see the money right away. Montagu reports that when the team
returned to Hollywood, their financial situation was 'near the border line.'
Anxious not to leave America empty-handed, Eisenstein put out feelers to
other studios. Among project ideas that were tossed about at this stage were
Lion Feuchtwanger's *Jud Süss*, Erich Maria Remarque's *Der Weg zurück*
(*The Road Back*), and Maurice Rostand's Great War drama *L'homme que j'ai
tué* (later filmed as *Broken Lullaby*), whose pacifist tone did not appeal. It
was at this time that Samuel Goldwyn made his notorious offer. 'Please tell
Mr Eisenstein,' he said to Ivor, 'that I have seen his film *Potemkin* and admire
it very much. What we should like would be for him to do something of the
same kind, but rather cheaper, for Ronald Colman.'[57]

Montagu was becoming impatient. He felt that in offering himself
around, Eisenstein was cheapening himself and becoming devalued. They
quarreled, and Ivor and Hell moved out of Coldwater Canyon to go and
stay with Chaplin (who entertained them, at Thanksgiving, by acting out
the whole story and all the gags of *City Lights* – 'the most dreadful experience of my life', Ivor says, since he kept dropping off to sleep). Chaplin
offered Montagu a job, but with his sights now set on heading home Ivor
did not take it. Eisenstein secured the backing of socialist novelist Upton
Sinclair for a film to be shot in Mexico, a project that Ivor tried to dis-
courage because of Sinclair's ignorance of film production, and there was a
Japanese offer that looked much more solid. Then Ivor and Hell made their

farewells and sailed back to England. They were accompanied by Sidney
Bernstein, who had been visiting Hollywood, with whom they played
bridge all the way across the Atlantic. They reached Southampton a few
days before Christmas.[58]

Ivor did not have enough left in the kitty to repay Uncle Lionel, but
Bernstein stepped in with a bridging loan. The falling out with Eisenstein
was quickly a thing of the past – 'It never disturbed the intimacy of our
friendship,' Montagu explains. 'The disagreement was ignored and forgotten.' One of his first acts on his return to London was to report in to
Comrade Bogomolov at the Soviet Embassy:

> By now you will surely have heard of our defeat – the defeat of Eisenstein
> and myself in our efforts to bring Red Revolution and Ruin to the U.S.!
> Alas, we did our best to make a film there but the forces of Law and Order
> were too clever for us. Will Hays and the Fish Committee discovered that
> behind our innocent exterior lay all sorts of machinations unsuspected by
> anybody else, least of all, of course, by ourselves.[59]

Montagu, now a man of 26, faced an uncertain future. He was through
with the cinema for the time being. Hollywood was barren of prospects,
and British filmmaking was dire: 'All the British film companies are
making quickies of well-known stage farce successes; practically sticking
the camera in the stalls and taking the whole six reels through in one shot.'
He declared to certain of his acquaintances that he had had enough of
films 'to last me for ten years' and that he was returning to zoology. But
more pressingly, his thoughts turned back to revolutionary politics. The
destiny of the international Communist movement had in fact never been
far from the back of his mind.[60]

9

TROTSKY

IN FEBRUARY 1929 Leon Trotsky was exiled from the Soviet Union and went to live, by agreement with the Turkish government, on the island of Prinkipo (Büyükada), in the Sea of Marmora near Constantinople (Istanbul). It was the latest phase in Stalin's repression of the Left Opposition, which had resulted in Trotskyists who did not renounce their views being arrested, banished to remote areas of the country, or incarcerated in isolated prisons for political offenders (where their conditions were much harsher than had been suffered by political prisoners under the tsars). Stalin's programme of accelerated industrialisation and forced collectivisation in the countryside undermined the oppositionists' objections to the party line, and broke their will to continue the fight. Prominent figures such as Radek and Preobrazhensky went over to Stalin's side; only Rakovsky held out. As Trotsky wrote that year in his autobiography, his closest friends were feeling the pressure: 'Some of them are vacillating, withdrawing, bowing before the enemy. Some are doing it because they are morally exhausted; others because they can find no other way out of the maze of circumstances; and still others because of the pressure of material reprisals.'[1]

But groups sympathetic to his views were forming in other parts of the world, and Trotsky was eager to shift his centre of operations to somewhere in Western Europe. He was also ill with malaria, and hoped to get better medical treatment than was available to him in Turkey. Germany rebuffed him. In May he was visited by the prominent British socialists Sidney and Beatrice Webb and discussed with them his wish to secure a refuge, and heartened by the election of a Labour government, he applied to Britain for a visa the following month (Sidney Webb, shortly to become Lord Passfield, was now a member of the Cabinet). To strengthen his case, Trotsky dispatched the French socialist Magdeleine Marx (Paz) to London to intercede with prime minister Ramsay MacDonald on his behalf. Marx stipulated the conditions Trotsky would submit to, including promising not to interfere in the affairs of Great Britain and to live incognito in a rural area, but her pleas were unavailing. On 12 July it was announced that the government would not admit the exiled revolutionary.[2]

At this time Montagu was still unsure what to make of the rift in the Soviet Communist Party between the dominant Stalinist faction and the Left Opposition. It was this, he says, which induced him to open a correspondence with Trotsky. On 1 July he wrote introducing himself. 'I am twenty-five years old,' he explained, 'a zoologist by profession, but have recently spent some time in literary work and in film production. I have taken part in the labour movement in England since 1918, and have visited Russia on three occasions since 1925, chiefly for purposes of zoological research.' If there was an opportunity, he would look forward to meeting a man 'for whose writings and activities I have so much respect.' Otherwise he would be happy to be of assistance in any way possible: 'For example, if you should require newspapers, books, news, any messages delivered, please instruct me.'[3]

Trotsky replied after he had learnt of the British government's refusal to grant him admission. Thanking Montagu for his 'kind letter', he asked if Ivor could give him any information about the circumstances of the decision, and pass on any commentary in papers such as the *Manchester Guardian*, which he could not access in Turkey. He also wondered if Montagu could send him the CPGB booklet *Where is Trotsky Going?*: 'I should like to know what sort of future was predicted to me by people who are not too clear-sighted in their own affairs.'[4]

Ivor quickly responded, enclosing *Where is Trotsky Going?* ('not very interesting; it appears to consist only of Opposition extracts, and Orthodox contradictions on the usual lines') and copies of the *Manchester Guardian* for 19 and 20 July. By now it had become clear that leading Liberals, who supported the minority Labour government but were not in the Cabinet, were strongly in favour of Trotsky's admission, citing the right of asylum; but that the key Labour ministers, especially Home Secretary J.R. Clynes, were vehemently opposed. In answer to questions in the House, Clynes stated: 'If Mr Trotsky were to come here, persons of mischievous intention would unquestionably seek to exploit his presence for their own ends, and if, in consequence, he became a source of grave embarrassment, the government could have no certainty of being able to secure his departure.' Clynes interpreted the right of asylum as the right of the government 'to grant asylum to any person whom it thinks fit to admit as a political refugee.' This interpretation was vigorously rebutted in a leader in the *Guardian*, which argued that 'the right of asylum has been recognised by judges and by leaders of all political parties in England. It has usually been supposed to refer to the rights of the individual, not to those of the supreme authority ...' The editorial went on to contend provocatively that 'to permit Mr Trotsky to enter England would be a source of strength to the Labour Government.'[5]

Montagu assured Trotsky there was no doubt 'that the last has not been heard of this question and that it will be vigorously reopened by the ILP (Fenner Brockway) and that at least a section of the Liberals will support him.' But ILP pressure alone would not be enough, since Clynes would be wary of 'discrediting himself by changing his mind' – this had been fatal for the first Labour government in the case of the dropped prosecution (for incitement to mutiny) of the Communist Johnny Campbell in 1924. Trotsky's best chances would be if Liberal pressure helped the ILP to force a vote in the House, or failing that, if he renewed his application in a few months' time, 'for English Ministers often use a passage of time to explain and justify any change of decision they desire to make, pretending that they remain consistent while only circumstances alter.'[6]

Brockway did reopen the question in the House of Commons on 24 July. He instanced Britain's proud record of giving asylum to political refugees, including Victor Hugo, Karl Marx, Garibaldi, and Mazzini, and appealed to the government to reverse its decision. His speech received a mixed reception from MPs, with Mr Thurtle (Lab. – Shoreditch) claiming that 'Trotsky despised and hated the Labour government, and would not scruple to destroy it by fair means or foul.' Clynes, in reply, reiterated his previous statements and added that 'the fact that endeavours were being made to establish better relations with Russia had been before the minds of the Government in reaching their decision.' The right of asylum, he averred, had not been impaired.[7]

On 26 July Montagu sent Trotsky a copy of the *Guardian* reporting this debate, along with issues of the *New Leader* (ILP) and *The Nation* (Maynard Keynes Liberal group) containing further commentary. He noted that the Liberals had not forced the issue, so the only option was to renew the application later – he suggested a delay of at least two months. Montagu singled out three points weighing with Clynes: the desire to establish better relations with the USSR, the absence of medical certificates from Trotsky, and the lack of certainty of being able to secure his deportation if the occasion arose (this being, in Ivor's view, the 'real crux', since there were many Russians resident in Britain who could not be deported because of their peculiar nationality status). Little could be done about the first, although it might have less weight when relations were actually resumed; but Trotsky could help his case if he secured relevant medical documentation and obtained assurances from the Turkish government that he would be readmitted if and when the time came.[8]

In the meantime, Montagu wrote, he had 'thought it well to consign to you a selected bundle of books.' The list, along with Ivor's annotations, makes for intriguing reading. There were three pamphlets: H.G. Wells's *Democracy Under Revision*, John Maynard Keynes's *The End of Laissez-Faire*, and *Shiva, or the Future of India* ('This is interesting because it was forbidden in India, for this queer reason. It repeated the criticisms and legitimate attacks on the lack of hygiene and the cruelty of Hinduism, <u>but urged the British Government to do something to reform them</u>.'). Two 'political philosophies' comprised Shaw's *Intelligent Woman's Guide to Socialism* and Wyndham Lewis's *Time and the Western Man* ('This shows immeasurable degree of confusion in thought, and some half-digested Keyserling, but is representative of a certain current of opinion influencing a proportion of the present feeling of extra-political intelligentsia'). There were five 'scientific papers' (including, strangely enough, I.A. Richards' *Principles of Literary Criticism*); *Possible Worlds*, by J.B.S. Haldane, was 'popular scientific speculation; interesting because the author has an exceedingly vigorous and able mind'. Finally, Montagu's choice of fiction suitable for the Russian revolutionary was: (a) *Martin Arrowsmith*, by Sinclair Lewis, for his 'pictures of modern American sociological types'; (b) *Clash*, Ellen Wilkinson's novel of the 1926 General Strike ('trivial rubbish', but 'interesting in its very naïveté and triviality as the serious production of a woman Labour MP, <u>once</u> an active militant left-winger'); (c) *Juno and the Paycock* ('O'Casey is certainly the greatest dramatist recently appearing in English'); (d) *The Plumed Serpent* – 'Lawrence is a fine writer, and represents a current of pagan retrogression in fiction corresponding to (not agreeing with) Wyndham Lewis in philosophy; (e) H.M. Tomlinson's *Gallion's Reach* ('just a good story well written'). Montagu hoped that 'some among them may be useful to you!'[9]

Somewhat overwhelmed by this bounty, Trotsky replied in French that he had not envisaged such significant consignments, and regretted that he could not reciprocate. Most of the material, he said, held great interest for him, and he would get on to reading it once he had finished writing his 'unhappy' (*malheureuse*) autobiography. But he begged Ivor not to send any more without consulting with him. Meanwhile, if he was not being indiscreet, could he enquire into Montagu's point of view on the different labour parties and organisations in England?[10]

Montagu replied at the end of August, after recovering from a bout of flu. He supplied Trotsky with a detailed autobiographical account of his activities in various fields to date. Explaining his decision not to become a member of the Communist Party on leaving Cambridge, he wrote that if he had joined he would have been 'without authority or income' but 'as a zoologist, in receipt of income, I was able in many ways to be useful to the party, to promote liaison between Russian and English zoologists, and USSR research workers and English libraries generally, and so forth.' Maintaining 'constant personal contact with members of the party', he was now a film producer, 'working hard to liberate the exhibition of Russian films in England.' What would Trotsky make of this? 'I am acutely aware,' Montagu conceded, 'that it might well be a record of the activity of one of the "dilettante petit-bourgeois" whom you so justly castigate.' But he was in a quandary: he could not devote himself fully to political activism, because 'I cannot clearly see a useful path in England of the present day.' At this time he was taking his cue from the 'brilliant biochemist' Haldane, 'who devotes himself wholly to research since he can see no point at which usefully to apply a lever of political energy.'[11]

As far as British politics was concerned, Ivor took issue with some of the views expressed by Trotsky in his *Where is Britain Going?* (1925). 'I am convinced,' he wrote, 'you have not grasped the peculiar effect upon revolutionary and working-class movements in England of national tradition and

local psychology.' English politics and social organisation were 'absolutely
empirical', devoid of theory. Marxism was the guiding principle of 'no party
or group in England today' – with the exception, no doubt, of the CP, but
'the influence of the CP upon the working class has been shattered for years
to come by the policies and tactics imposed upon it by a majority in the
Comintern quite out of touch with the real situation in England.' Ivor was
prepared to accept that Trotsky's analysis of the 'inevitable economic stresses'
that awaited England, and their 'inevitable effect in producing revolutionary results' was correct. But it would take a long time, and 'the progress in
influence on the working class that will be made meanwhile by a Marxian
party is infinitesimal.' The proletarian mind in England was entirely taken
up, Montagu argued, by sport and the cinema. But he would really welcome
an opportunity to discuss all this in person. On other matters, Ivor asked
for his correspondent's suggestions regarding recent Russian literature that
would be interesting to translate, and offered to be of help in translating or
placing for publication any of Trotsky's own writings in future.[12]

Meanwhile, he had not been idle on the question of Trotsky coming to
Britain. He had sounded out Brockway, who endorsed his plan of action, as
did his cousin Sir Herbert Samuel, a leading Liberal, who was in favour of
Trotsky's admission and offered to give Montagu advice at any time. In his
letter, Ivor reported that he had 'discreetly taken opinions in the ILP and
Liberal Party' and was convinced that the advice he had given was good.
An application supported by a Liberal, accompanied by medical certificates
and documentation from the Turkish government, would stand 'a very good
chance of success'.[13]

Trotsky – who by now had learnt that he had been secretly condemned
to death by the OGPU – responded to Ivor (in Russian) on 23 September.
He would get his youngest son, still in the USSR, to advise on new Russian
literature, as he himself was cut off. In terms of coming to England, the
medical certification was no problem, but he would not approach the
Turkish authorities for a guarantee unless his entry to England was assured
in advance – otherwise, if there were a refusal, he would be placed in 'a very
unfavourable and unpleasant situation'. To obtain a solid assurance, Trotsky
requested Ivor to carry out 'more serious and exact fieldwork', and suggested he enlist the help of ILP secretary John Paton, who had invited the
Russian to give a summer school presentation for the Party.[14]

Agreeing that personal conversation would be helpful, Trotsky issued an invitation for Montagu to be his guest 'should your business trips provide you with the opportunity of stopping en route in Constantinople'. He then went on to address, at length, the vexed issue of British empiricism. This was undoubtedly a national tradition, Trotsky granted, but Montagu was ignoring the economic factors. 'Empiricism, individualism, conservatism, the spirit of compromise – these are powerful forces, but they are defunct. English political empiricism is a fossilized product of those periods when Great Britain step by step won domination over the world ...' Ramsay MacDonald *could*, theoretically, put forward a bold programme of socialist reforms, 'but you understand that this is a fantastic prospect. MacDonald is incapable of any radical programme. His ministry will end in a pitiful and shameful fiasco and inevitably will become a source of not mitigating, but aggravating political contradictions.' Given this situation, there was no way that Trotsky could agree that there was nothing for a Marxist to do in present-day England. His suggestion for Montagu: set up a Marxist journal, completely independent of the current Communist Party ('goes without saying').[15]

Despite prompting from Trotsky in a letter dated 16 October, Montagu did not reply until 19 January 1930. His excuse was that he had been busy co-operating with Eisenstein 'in trying by every means to arrange the distribution in various parts of Europe of *The General Line* (*Staroye i novoye*), of which you must know, his film on the collectivisation of peasant farms'. It was 'most emphatically worth trying hard to get it shown', since 'it epitomises the whole of agricultural policy, must inevitably make it understood wherever it is shown, and also plays a part in the struggle against the kulaks.' However – a familiar story – 'All has in the end been fruitless, owing to the lack of appreciation of Western realities on the part of the Sovkino trading agents.' They would not put up the £3,000 necessary for sound synchronisation to make it marketable abroad.[16]

Ivor had continued to be active in the campaign to get Trotsky admitted to the UK. He reported that Paton had been unable to help, and they had agreed further action by the ILP was likely to be harmful, as there was now 'bitter hostility' between the government and the ILP leaders. Accordingly, he had been 'working through Liberals and Conservatives and through friends in the Government itself'. But no one would make an individual commitment. So he had no success to report, 'and the best I can say is that these manoeuvres are not yet at an end.' He remained on a quest for weighty signatures to sway Clynes ('a nervous person').[17]

By the end of the month Montagu was more optimistic. Writing on 30 January, he said that Shaw had agreed to sign a letter to Clynes that put the case for Trotsky's admission in terms of the right of asylum and his desire for specialist medical attention. It would contain a clause referring to assurances from the Turkish government that it would accept Trotsky's return. 'Please, on receipt of this letter,' he concluded, 'be so kind as to wire me at 80, Wardour Street whether you desire me to go ahead.'[18]

For Trotsky, the Turkish issue remained a sticking point. He predicted, in his reply on 5 February, that Clynes would not give a response without first consulting with the Soviet ambassador, Sokolnikov, who in turn would alert his counterpart in Ankara. The latter would apply pressure to the Turkish government to secure, not a refusal of the assurances sought, but an evasive, delaying answer that would serve everyone's purpose except Trotsky's. Accordingly, he felt it would be better to speak simply of a temporary stay in England, without any specific mention of Turkey.[19]

There the matter rested when Montagu departed for the United States, leaving the campaign in the hands of his friend Marjorie Wells, wife of H.G.'s son G.P. ('Gip'). Marjorie had been acting as H.G.'s secretary-manager since the death of his wife in 1927. Writing on 14 March, Trotsky did not refer to the visa issue. He discussed literary matters, enclosed a copy of his just-written article 'World Unemployment and the Five-Year Plan', and enquired as to Ivor's views on the current position of the Labour government and the Communist Party in Britain. Later that month there was a brief alarm on reports of Trotsky's worsening medical condition, but despite Ivor's urging nothing more eventuated in terms of the visa application.[20]

In fact, Ivor was concerned that Marjorie appeared to be doing very little to help the cause along. From Hollywood, he informed Trotsky that 'as far as I can judge from my wife's letters, her actions have been nil.' But, he went on, 'my wife is not entirely clear in this respect, and it is possible that Marjorie Wells has made endeavours and only that her success has been nil.' She was, he thought, 'even if lazy – completely to be trusted'.[21]

In this letter, dated 30 April, Montagu enlarged in great detail upon the efforts he had made to secure Trotsky's admission to the UK. Herbert

Samuel had been sympathetic, but he could not take a personal position outside that of the Liberal Party, and the young party member whom he recommended for the role proved non-committal. The senior Labour figure George Lansbury, whom Ivor knew slightly, was supportive but, as a Minister, bound by Cabinet responsibility. (Montagu thought Lansbury 'a darling' but 'woolly-minded'.) Lansbury recommended sending a deputation to Foreign Secretary Arthur Henderson, who might be induced to persuade Clynes to change his mind. However, Shaw told Ivor that he had spoken privately to Henderson, who refused to interfere in what was the province of his colleague the Home Secretary. The best option was therefore a formal letter to Clynes signed by a number of persons 'of weight and non-Left Wing standing'. H.G. Wells, contacted in the south of France, immediately agreed. C.P. Scott, editor of the *Manchester Guardian*, added his name 'as a Liberal of the old school'. The novelist John Galsworthy did not reply. J.L. Garvin, editor of the Conservative *Observer*, had published a leader critical of the government's decision in July 1929, but was not now inclined to reopen the question. Royden Buxton, brother of a Cabinet Minister, would think about it. Ivor remained hopeful that in the hands of Marjorie Wells the petition to Clynes 'will be so strongly signed that even if it does not secure your admission it will embarrass MacDonald so greatly to refuse it that at least the gaiety of nations may be increased.'[22]

In this lengthy letter, Montagu also traversed other matters. He was very enthusiastic about the 'World Unemployment' article, which argued for economic collaboration between social democratic governments and the USSR, to alleviate unemployment in the West and to further the cause of Soviet industrialisation under the Five-Year Plan. Ivor reported that he had had a dozen copies made and was circulating them among friends. He had also obtained and read Trotsky's autobiography (*My Life*), which had just appeared, and declared it 'full of splendid stuff'.[23]

Reflecting on his observations of American industrial efficiency, Montagu informed his Prinkipo comrade that he was now able to accept his prophecies respecting 'the inevitable collapse of the British system, to which prophecies I took, you will remember, marked exception before.' However, the Communist Party in Britain (and the American party seemed to be identical in this respect) was failing to take advantage of the economic crisis:

The closest contact is preserved between the Communist Party and the unemployed, but a largely blind contact, merely verbal, which brings no benefit to the unemployed, involves them in constant struggle, and makes them the shock troops of revolution when psychologically, of course, being underfed and in despair, they are the least able to endure such struggles with the prospect of supporting them to any sort of successful conclusion. Such instances as the march of the unemployed on London, organised a few months ago by the Communist Party, in which a number of the most starving enthusiasts were persuaded to march from their homes to London, enduring en route footsoreness and distress, some few survivors eventually holding a neglected Sunday meeting in London, and then being told – 'Goodbye. Thank you, you have done very well, but we can do no more for you,' and then advised to walk back home again, indicate the way in which what enthusiasm there is is often being wasted.

CP membership was decreasing. On the other hand, the number of Communist sympathisers in the trade unions was on the rise, but these workers 'fear to be open members of the Communist Party, because they can see no use in being so and would risk expulsion from their unions …' Communication was an issue. (In an earlier letter, Montagu had noted that, on Comintern instructions, the CP had launched a daily paper, the *Daily Worker*. It was 'incredibly bad', but 'those running it are extremely energetic, and may learn rapidly to improve it.')[24]

Ivor was not hopeful about the prospects for an independent Marxist journal in Britain. It would be difficult to make it financially viable, and there was 'no organisation or shadow of an organisation of the Left Wing, such as exists in France and in Germany' that could be made the nucleus of such an organ. However, he gave his commitment that if his Hollywood adventure 'should by any remote chance prove profitable', he would try to save something to put into the project.[25]

Discussing the Ramsay MacDonald administration, Trotsky had expressed the view that 'the poverty of this government by far surpasses the worst predictions'. He wondered how long it would last. Montagu gave as his opinion that it would 'certainly have a very long life', because the Liberals 'dare not face another election until a system of proportional representation,

which alone can save them their existence, has been introduced', while
the Conservatives could not force an election without the support of
the Liberals, and were in any case divided and 'anything but a prepared
fighting machine'.[26]

Montagu wrote again on 22 May, giving this time his views on
Hollywood. 'I will stay here and work until the undertaking is through,' he
told Trotsky. 'Then I hope, if I may, to pay a visit to you on my way home.'
His wife would shortly be arriving, and she would be able to inform him as
to what progress, if any, Marjorie Wells was making on the visa campaign.[27]

The truth was that the project had stalled. Marjorie confessed to Hell
on 13 May that she had 'done nothing at all so far!', explaining that she
had been 'terribly busy'. But she now intended writing ('on behalf of Ivor
Montagu') to A.G. Gardiner (a highly-regarded journalist and author),
Sir Martin Conway (art critic and Conservative politician), Dean William
Inge of St Paul's Cathedral, and newspaper magnate Lord Beaverbrook. If
their replies were favourable she would get back in touch with Shaw and
ask him to draft the letter.[28]

Montagu, while calling her letter 'shameful', told Marjorie that that he did
not like to think she was 'getting entangled in this business if it is going to
mean a volume of work that will cause inconvenience.' He had bequeathed
it to her because he felt 'that the inestimable critical judgment of political
personality which you share with me, would enable you to know what to
say to everyone' – and besides, she might help with getting H.G. on side.
If she could do with any assistance, his friend Bancroft Clark would do her
bidding. (Clark had just finished reading Trotsky's autobiography, had found
it 'enthralling', and was very willing to be enlisted in the campaign.)[29]

Marjorie made up for her former dawdling with a flurry of activity.
On 3 July she was able to report that she had sent out about thirty-three
letters in all, and had received promises of support from novelist Arnold
Bennett, astronomer Sir Richard Gregory, social psychologist Graham
Wallas and economist J.M. Keynes. Accordingly, she had asked Shaw to
draft the letter, though 'No one seems to think there is much chance of
Clynes' changing his mind.' Sir James Barrie's secretary had asked that he be
excused, while Galsworthy refused 'because he is not moved as a humanitarian in favour of a man, identified, with or without his will, with so much
bloodshed.' None of the politicians had replied as yet.[30]

The same day, the issue was again being aired in the House of Commons. Labour left-winger Ellen Wilkinson asked whether the Home Secretary 'was prepared to reconsider his refusal to grant a visa to visit this country for medical and personal reasons to Mr Leon Trotsky.' To cheers, Clynes replied that he regretted he was not prepared to reconsider the decision. Nonetheless, Marjorie pressed on. She communicated directly to Trotsky the results of the campaign to date, in a letter which the exile on Prinkipo found 'très amicale'.[31]

Bernard Shaw became a public advocate for Trotsky's cause in August, when his 'sparkling address' to the ILP Summer School was reported in the press:

> Was this wonderful man and extraordinary military genius kept out by a Socialist Government because he was a Socialist?' he asked. 'That was a very bad reason. If we assume he is a dangerous character, a 'caged lion', well, I should like us to have the key of the cage in case anyone else should let him out ... His welcome would be a becoming gesture, and I hope it will be made.[32]

Shaw, as agreed, proceeded to draft his letter to Clynes, as did H.G. Wells and, independently, the elderly Liberal statesman Augustine Birrell. The traditional rights of free speech and political asylum remained the dominant theme, with Shaw contending that 'as we do not persecute political opposition in this country we cannot make ourselves the instruments of such persecution by foreign governments', and Wells proclaiming that 'our national role has been to sustain the utmost liberty of thought and speech throughout the earth.' Shaw added a dig at the Labour government and other social democratic regimes of Western Europe, arguing that Trotsky, 'by using his ostracism as a proof of their bad faith he becomes the inspirer and the hero of all the militants of the extreme Left in every country.' After some delay, occasioned in part by the need to co-ordinate with Ellen Wilkinson, who was making her own moves, Marjorie Wells presented the letters, duly signed by a bevy of heavyweights, to Clynes on 5 November. As had been feared, the Home Secretary was unmoved. He had given the reasons for his decision (which had been made 'with the full approval of my colleagues') to the House on 18 July 1929; that decision had recently been reconfirmed in respect to an application made by Miss Wilkinson MP, and there was nothing in the representations now being made which would enable the government to reconsider its previous decision. That was that.[33]

As Montagu would discover, Ellen Wilkinson had also been active in the anti-censorship campaign. As secretary of the Parliamentary Films Committee she had organised a deputation to the Theatres & Music Halls Committee of the LCC in March 1930 that called on the council to change its policy regarding the exhibition of banned films (Soviet in particular) by private societies. The committee, after consulting with the BBFC, responded negatively, but the full council was more sympathetic, and subsequently the workers' film societies had fewer obstacles placed in their way.

On the national level Wilkinson, in line with Montagu's position, favoured circumventing or replacing the BBFC with a censorship body independent of the trade that would be subject to parliamentary scrutiny. At the very least an investigation was needed into the chaotic situation prevailing. But Home Secretary Clynes was not inclined to move on the matter, expressing his satisfaction with the present system. In July, Fenner Brockway reported to Ivor, the parliamentary committee arranged to meet Clynes with 'a really formidable deputation' demanding an inquiry; Brockway's impression was that 'he will establish a Departmental Commission to examine the situation, but not a Select Committee as we requested.' It was clear that there was little appetite within government for any substantive action, and though the issue dragged on into the following year and a short-lived Film Censorship Consultative Committee was eventually set up under the succeeding Home Secretary, Sir Herbert Samuel, no change in the legislation eventuated and things effectively continued as before.[34]

Several factors combined to take the steam out of the campaign. On the one hand there was little support across the parliamentary spectrum for direct government involvement, and a growing recognition by left-wing proponents of change that state censorship, rather than being liberating, could result in more rigid and irrevocable cuts and bans. The trade was satisfied with the existing arrangements, and there was a public perception that Montagu and his allies were seeking special privileges for a cultural elite and/or proponents of politically subversive views. Moreover, the Soviet films the activists were most concerned about were beginning to reach audiences through more liberal rulings by local authorities and distribution on non-inflammable (and thus non-censorable) 16mm film stock. The haphazard, patchwork system and lack of democratic accountability that Montagu railed against in *The Political Censorship of Films* would, in the best British pragmatic tradition, continue.

Meanwhile, Montagu's Hollywood venture was coming to an end. There was the standing invitation from Trotsky and his wife to visit them in Prinkipo. As it turned out, Ivor was not able to call in, as he had hoped, on his way back to Britain, and the plan was put on hold.[35]

On their return to London shortly before Christmas, Ivor and Hell settled back into the flat they had secured in February. Cheaper and roomier than the Leicester Square apartment, 19 New Park Court was in south London, on the second floor of a new block of flats above shops, 'just at the exact point,' Montagu was to observe, 'where Brixton Hill changes and goes all refined, becoming Streatham Hill.' It was 'a region of decaying and peeling ex-mansions with damp, desolate gardens between them and the road.' By this time Rowna had begun boarding at A.S. Neill's progressive school Summerhill in Leiston, Suffolk (where she soon distinguished herself by forging coins in the metal shop and passing them off in town for chocolates and cigarettes), but she joined them at Brixton when home on holiday. Hell's mother Kate ('an indomitable woman of a certain unobtrusive, common-sense stubbornness') became part of the household, and Hell's sister Amy (known as 'Do') came to stay at weekends. There was also, for a short while, a scruffy puppy called Betsy, who landed the Montagus with a hefty bill for car repairs when she ran out into heavy traffic, and shortly thereafter cost them more when the vet, determining that she was 'densely inhabited by worms', had her put down.[36]

Money was tight. The couple were in debt after their American travels – and Ivor turned down offers to write up his Hollywood experiences laced with personal gossip. Hell was working – it was probably around this time she found a job as private secretary to a minor film renter in Wardour Street, 'who used to pinch her bottom until she finally had railings built around her desk'. But Ivor was not in regular paid employment. He had toyed with the idea of returning to zoology, though did not, it seems, follow this up beyond some minor assignments. Trying to freelance in film and as a translator, he found the going tough. He remained scornful of the static, stagey pictures the British film industry was producing, and saw little scope for doing meaningful work. 'I have resolved firmly to leave the film business,' he wrote to his producer friend Bachmann in Hollywood. 'From several companies I have received a cast fishing line, from one a definite offer, but it seems preposterous to work at the small salaries which are all that the English film business can pay and the small opportunities it can afford to a director.' Not surprisingly, the agents he hoped would represent him did not find him a commercial proposition. 'I would talk about the rather esoteric writing projects I had to place, or my choosy attitude to the kind of film work I would be prepared to do, and the result was that they didn't want to know.'[37]

Contrary to his claim in the unpublished autobiography that 'I have never, at any time, had an agent,' Montagu was represented at this time by James B. Pinker & Sons, which had both London and New York branches. Still, the agency was not able to do much for him. Publication of the translation that he and Nolbandov had made of Isaac Babel's 'film-novel' *Benia Krik* had fallen through; his version of *Le Cocu magnifique* found neither publisher nor producer; while his proposal for a book on 'the technical and artistic development of motion pictures' intended for Benns Sixpenny Library was rejected. In response to a cheerful letter from Eisenstein in Mexico, he could only lament: 'Alas, am very sad here, & hard up ...'[38]

But he had the cushion, of course, of his family trust income, modest though it was. And his attention kept turning back more insistently to politics as the economic situation in Britain became ever more dire. 'The MacDonald government', as he recalled many years later, 'was completely incapable of facing up to the unemployment situation' while the 'orthodox economics' of Chancellor of the Exchequer Philip Snowden, 'no better than Churchill's had been, were the wrong recipe for reviving industry and only made matters worse.' In his quest for answers he took advantage of a trip to Budapest in February 1931 for the World Table Tennis Championships to fulfil his ambition of meeting Trotsky in person.[39]

He had proposed coming to stay for four or five days, to which Trotsky had replied: 'Your intention to visit Constantinople is splendid. We will be very glad to see you at our place.' It was not to be simply a private visit. Montagu had secured a commission from the *Manchester Guardian* for an interview setting forth Trotsky's views on the Five-Year Plan, plus 'anything on America from his point of view would be worth while.'[40]

There was a question of timing, as Trotsky was hoping to make a trip to Norway in February, but that did not eventuate. Accordingly, Montagu boarded a southbound train in Budapest after the championships were over, around the 18th. His journey was interrupted by flooding, which compelled the stranded passengers to trek on foot, with babies and hand luggage, across the Bulgarian hills above the inundated tracks. After a lengthy delay at the Turkish border and a torturous night on a crawling local train, Montagu finally reached Istanbul on a cold, wet and grey dawn.[41]

The 'puffing and leisurely Stamboul steamer', threading its way among 'the tiny islands of the Asiatic shore – holiday jewels that offer in summer the only accessible refuge from the heat of the town, but all at present deserted, shuttered, and gloomy', took him to the island of Prinkipo, home to a handful of fishermen and shepherds, and to the world's most promi-nent exiled revolutionary. The house was set, Montagu was to explain to *Guardian* readers, on the slope of a hill, 'with a couple of hundred yards of sparse shrubbery concealing it from idle sightseers.' It was, Trotsky's biogra-pher wrote, 'a spacious, dilapidated villa rented from a bankrupt pasha'; Ivor observed the 'decayed and peeling walls, odd fragments of brass peacocks, and some imperfect cherubs circling on the azure of a ceiling or two', betraying 'the grande seigneurie, now neglected in orthodox Turkish style.'[42]

Trotsky's wife Natalya, 'a short, motherly woman with an air of distress', made Ivor welcome. The man of the house was out fishing. In what the *Guardian* editor considered an 'admirable introduction to Trotsky', Montagu described what happened next:

> Down a steep path, tacking sideways, we descend to a stone jetty at the edge of the sea. Mrs Trotsky shades her eyes with her hand ... . Presently a boat is descried approaching us with oars. Within it are a young sailor, a boyish and enthusiastic policeman, and a third figure. The third figure rises and salutes us. He is Trotsky. He is short and broad, and his shortness is accentuated by a heavy leather jacket. He wears waterproof boots to his knees and a Sherlock Holmes cap, with the flaps meeting under his chin, to master the spray. It is now nearly two o'clock. He has been fish-ing since five this morning. He springs lightly ashore and leads us to the house. He is over fifty years old. I inquire after his health. His face is ruddy, and he assures us he is well, but it appears that he is subject to recurrent

attacks due to his old malaria. … After lunch Trotsky leads us upstairs, where already a working library is being established. No inch of space is visible beneath the serried ranks of magazines and papers that occupy the study. Now the principal and striking characteristic of Trotsky, even perhaps surprising to one who meets him personally for the first time, is his extraordinary charm, a charm that resides in a perfect frankness, an eager unaffectedness of manner.

Montagu and Trotsky sat down to talk. The terms of the interview agreed, questions planned, Trotsky set to work, 'dictating in a musical mixture of French and German'. They talked late into the night.[43]

Montagu was given a loaded revolver to put under his pillow, as a precaution against assassins. 'I did not know what precautions to take against the revolver,' he comments, 'and was terrified.' In the morning, insisting on his rights as an Englishman, he went fishing with Trotsky and the Turkish police who guarded him. Montagu tangled the lines, while Trotsky showed his proficiency in hooking mackerel and gurnards. Ivor later wrote:

> The memory I shall always retain of him is of our little boat, perilously poised on the very top of a wave raised by the wash of a passing steamer, ready to crash down on the top of a monstrous rock, looming up through the crystal clear depths of the water and reaching jaggedly near the surface – Trotsky himself perched aquiline in the stern and in a voice and with an authority that might have commanded armies, shouting the Turkish equivalent of 'In – out! In – out!' as the policemen rowed for dear life to get clear before the next wave-trough.[44]

It is unclear whether Montagu stayed as long as he originally intended enjoying the hospitality of the Trotsky household. In any event he was back in London by the beginning of March – just about the time that there was a fire at the Prinkipo house and much of Trotsky's library, including research notes for a book on current world affairs, lost. The veteran revolutionary took it in his stride; 'Life consists of ups and downs,' he observed philosophically in a letter to Montagu, who immediately offered to help with replacing the lost volumes. Ellen Wilkinson, he reported, was also keen to do what she could.[45]

The interview text was translated, checked by Trotsky, and published in the form of statements by the author in the *Manchester Guardian* of 27 and 28 March (Montagu was identified only as 'a Correspondent'). In the first, Trotsky declared that world opinion of the Soviet Five-Year Plan was characterised by two – contradictory – assertions, that it was Utopian and failing, and that it was such a success that it threatened capitalist economies by 'dumping'. Both were false. The Plan was certainly succeeding, to the extent that there was talk of bringing the time span down to four years; but there was no threat to Western economies because of the 'appalling backwardness' of the country the Soviets inherited: 'The Soviet Union will remain, even after the realisation of the Five-Year Plan, far behind the more advanced capitalist States.' He condemned calls in the West for an economic blockade of the USSR, stating that it could not be effective and would be but a 'prelude to war'. Asked by the interviewer what his differences on the policy were with the present Soviet government, Trotsky referred to the 'overspeeding zeal' with which the Plan was being pushed forward, without sufficient preparation, something that imperiled the whole industrialisation and collectivisation process. Returning to relations with the West, Trotsky floated a 'hypothesis' by which the British government sat at a round table with the USSR and, inspired by the methods by which the Plan was being implemented, worked out a scheme of economic co-operation.[46]

The second statement was devoted principally to the upcoming role of the United States in world affairs and the unprecedented growth of that nation's economic power. This would not be affected by the current Depression – 'in her time of crisis the hegemony of the United States will prove more complete, more brutal, more merciless than in her time of upward swing.' The potential preponderance of the USA in the world market was 'far greater than the actual preponderance of Great Britain in the most flourishing days of her world hegemony' and this strength would take a political form: 'The world will be witness of a great access of Yankee truculence in every sector of our planet.' Hence 'the next epoch will develop beneath the shadow of the powerful capitalist aggression of the United States.' Trotsky also commented on arms limitation agreements, then being negotiated in Geneva. The actual level of weapons held by the opposing powers at the outbreak of a war, he argued, was less significant than the capability of a country's industrial structure to manufacture armaments as hostilities continued. Moreover, it was 'entirely obvious', he contended, that 'a reduction of armaments prior to the conflict of two nations is much more favourable to the stronger than to the weaker.' An arms accord was no guarantee of peace, and indeed did not constitute even a lessening of war danger. 'If a pair of duellists or their seconds agree beforehand on the calibre of the revolvers, it in no way prevents one of them from being killed.'[47]

Undoubtedly the discussion between Montagu and Trotsky went beyond topics destined for the columns of a liberal newspaper. One thing is known: Trotsky still wanted to get to Norway, where he had been invited to give a series of lectures, and he enlisted Ivor's help in getting a transit visa for the UK. Montagu followed this up by making the case with George Lansbury, then First Commissioner of Works in the MacDonald government. Permission was granted on the basis of strict conditions, but Trotsky was not able to make the trip at this time.[48]

It seems clear that Trotsky also sought Montagu's help in getting material through to his collaborator Christian Rakovsky, then in internal exile in Siberia. Isaac Deutscher notes that at this time Trotsky's correspondence with his Russian followers 'was still fairly abundant, part of it being dispatched openly but part clandestinely, with coded signatures and addresses'. As the most prominent representative of the shrinking Left Opposition within the Soviet Union, Rakovsky's mail would have been particularly closely monitored by the OGPU. In his autobiographical manuscript, Montagu asserts that Trotsky 'spoke of friends still in Siberia, Rakovsky for example and asked if I could get a message through to him. I said I could not. Although I had liked Rakovsky when he was ambassador in London I think it would not have done, even if I could.' However, Montagu's correspondence from the time suggests that this account is not entirely candid. On 19 March he wrote to Trotsky: 'About the urgent matter of R. This is being pursued, and it is, I think, certain that success will be achieved with parcels ...' And on 9 April he informed Trotsky that 'the matter of our friend is progressing further. I will not mention it specifically in these letters unless you desire.'[49]

Correspondence with Ellen Wilkinson also suggests that Montagu sought her help, as a government MP, to make representations through official channels to ease Rakovsky's situation. She was eager to do what she could, but this was a difficult ask, complicated by the fact that trade negotiations with the Soviet Union (affecting her own constituency) were at a delicate stage. Bogomolov at the Embassy was approached, but evidently did not prove receptive to suggestions put to him ('really it is not sufficient for Bogomoloff to put his head in the sand and say nuffin,' Wilkinson complained to Ivor). It is not known if ultimately any pressure was effectively applied to the Soviet government, but it seems unlikely.[50]

Was Montagu acting throughout all his transactions with Trotsky as a clandestine agent of the Soviet secret police? Ben Macintyre suggests as much. 'He would frame his trip to Prinkipio [sic] as the innocent journey of a young idealist studying the splits in Russian communism. It seems more likely that he was sent by Moscow to gain Trotsky's confidence, and report back on his activities.' As with the claim of recruitment in 1927, certainty on this point cannot be gained until the OGPU and GRU archives are opened. Yet consideration of all the available evidence would indicate that Montagu was not in fact carrying out what would have been a considerable feat of dissimulation, that he was actually doing what he appeared to be doing: not acting under instructions from Stalin's government, but assisting Trotsky to oppose it.[51]

After his trip to Turkey, Montagu still felt himself at a loose end. 'Ivor is doing nothing, and has no plans,' Hell wrote to Iris Barry on 26 March, 'and so manages to keep every moment of the day occupied.' On 13 April he wrote to Bachmann outlining various possibilities he was considering for his immediate future: zoological research, returning to the USA for film work, becoming involved in politics, and finally 'retiring to Iceland or somewhere where my small regular income will be of reasonable power and where one can forget one's obligations to struggling humanity in the contemplation of sunsets by technicolor.' Given his psychological make-up one cannot imagine that the last was ever a serious option, and he revealed the direction he was likely to take in stating that 'economic conditions here are in such a state, decay so advanced, that political events of the near future will be profound and shocking. I have not the temperament to stand aside ...'[52]

There were certainly changes afoot, as he reported to Trotsky. Mosley's abandonment of Labour for his New Party, the 'pathetic spectacle' of the Conservatives split between Baldwin and Beaverbrook/Rothermere factions, Lloyd George presiding over a break-up of the Liberals, were leading to a reorientation 'in which the identity of the Social Democrats [i.e. Labour] with the other parties must, sooner or later, be realised by the working classes.' But Ivor remained unimpressed with the Communist Party's response to the crisis. There was no turnaround in the Party's diminishing influence, as reflected in the recent municipal election results. Exploring other avenues, he had met with several trade unionists who were not CP members and yet 'anxious to find grouping in a Marxist party', and he might have more news of this later.[53]

It turned out that no more was to be heard of this alternative Marxist cluster, and as the crisis deepened over the following months, Montagu began to feel he could no longer remain on the sidelines. Finally, in August, he decided to put aside his scruples and take the plunge. 'I received the pamphlets you sent me, and have obtained from the *Militant* all the others yet published,' he wrote to Trotsky.:

> After study, I find myself facing the conclusion that I must join the Party. The question in England is not: to join Party or Opposition. But: to join Party or refrain from joining anything or anyone … The Party tasks must contain certain lines on which work can be valuable; to wait outside of it because of incorrect lines it also contains is, I begin to feel, in England Utopianism.[54]

In later years Montagu was apt to couch his decision to join the CP as a considered rejection of Trotsky and Trotskyism. 'When I got home [from Prinkipo] I thought things out and made up my mind,' he wrote. Trotsky was 'all that I imagined *as a person*. But I felt that I understood now why he was impossible in a party, that his personality swamped his judgment and tactics as a serious politician.' Trotsky was a 'Big-Head' (*Bolshaya Golova*), as Grisha Alexandrov had called him, when Ivor questioned him in Hollywood. It was not that he was conceited, but that 'though he was able, even brilliant, he allowed this quality to divorce him from identity with what the masses were ready to accept or do.' Alexandrov's example was Trotsky's attempt to impose military discipline on workers in industrial reconstruction after the Civil War; Montagu now thought of Trotsky's speech at the 1927 central committee plenum at which he was expelled, a speech aimed, he concluded from reading the verbatim transcript Trotsky gave him, not at persuading and convincing, but 'toward display of the orator's brilliance and his ability to score off the dumb-witted'.[55]

That is how it may have seemed, in retrospect, but in Montagu's writings and actions of the time there is no trace of any repudiation of his mentor. In the same letter in which he announced his decision, he reported on the ideological orientation of the *Bharat*, an Indian student paper that Trotsky had asked him to find out about; informed his correspondent that the Congress paper *Liberty* was keen to publish an article with Trotsky's views on India; explained a minor change he had made in a letter of Trotsky's he had translated for publication in England; analysed recent developments in British politics (the Liberal Party leaderless, the New Party now only a Mosley fantasy, the ILP opposing the Unemployment Insurance Bill and threatened with disaffiliation from Labour, the government approaching the Conservatives to join in a 'national' Cabinet in view of the country's perilous financial condition); and asked for Trotsky's views on Stalin's new policy of greater rewards for technical experts. Montagu also enclosed newspaper clippings and Marjorie Wells's file of material on the visa application, and noted that he had earlier sent Leonov's novel *Sot*, which he was translating, and copies of *Liberty*, the Labour Research department circular, and *Labour Monthly*.[56]

Replying on 22 August, Trotsky wrote: 'As for your plans to join the Party, from my point of view I think it is the right step to take.'[57]

Two days later, Ramsay MacDonald resigned and agreed to form a National Government with Conservatives and Liberals. He, along with the Cabinet ministers who joined him, Philip Snowden and Jimmy Thomas, were expelled from their Party. The second Labour-led administration had ended, precisely as Trotsky had predicted back in September 1929, in a 'pitiful and shameful fiasco'. As for Montagu, he undoubtedly shared Trotsky's hope that the current state of England would in the next while 'lead to some more liveliness in the Communist ranks.'[58]

10

COMMITMENT

IN BRITAIN, RAPHAEL Samuel claimed that joining the Communist Party 'was experienced as a momentous event, equivalent in its intensity – to taking a decision for Christ.' If when opting finally to take out a Party card in or around August 1931, Ivor Montagu underwent such an existential watershed, he left no record of it.[1]

It is possible that because he did not join a local branch, the immediate effect on his lifestyle and psychology was not as great as for others. By this time the CPGB was granting greater leeway to its recruits from the intelligentsia, and the routine tasks inflicted on its proletarian members were not necessarily imposed on those who could contribute with brain rather than brawn. It had not always been so: just two years earlier the historian A.L. Morton had a 'hard time' joining up as an intellectual, and 'had to spend a long time chalking the streets.'[2]

Although he had moved to the fringes of the downmarket Brixton district, Montagu did not immerse himself in the local working-class culture in the way that other Communist intellectuals of the early 1930s did, including Christopher Caudwell, Clive and Noreen Branson, and Ivor's own cousin David Guest. The literary critic Alick West actually moved to Brixton because the Party's intellectual doyen Rajani Palme Dutt advised him to break with his middle-class surroundings. For Ivor, on the other hand, discovering at first hand how workers lived and thought was not a high priority. When filling out his Party questionnaire in 1942, he wrote: 'Weakest side is inner party work – practically no experience branch work & life ...'[3]

If for others becoming a Communist was almost equivalent to a religious conversion – Anthony Crosland speaks of 'the emotional need for a God, a religion … for something to believe in transcending the individual' – for Montagu it was simply a logical next step in his political evolution. He had been a socialist since his teenage years; the Labour Party was ideologically bankrupt, and the Communist Party, despite its minuscule size, was the only organisation on the Left actively combating the forces of capitalism at this time of severe economic crisis. Whatever reservations he may have had about the line it was pursuing paled into insignificance in comparison with the opportunities Party membership afforded him to devote his energies to the revolutionary cause.[4]

The Party that Montagu joined was a disappointment to the Communist International. Despite the abject failure of the Labour-led government to ameliorate the appalling economic conditions, the CP had not been able to pick up any significant support from disenchanted sectors of the working class. Its membership at the beginning of 1931, at slightly over 2,500, was the lowest in the Party's history. Since around 80 per cent of the membership were unemployed, organisation in workplaces was extremely difficult, and financially the Party remained heavily dependent on Comintern subsidies. Unsurprisingly, the CP came under heavy fire for its shortcomings from such heavyweights as Dmitri Manuilsky and Solomon Lozovsky at the 11th plenum of the Executive Committee of the Communist International (ECCI) in March–April.[5]

Undoubtedly a major factor in the Party's lack of appeal to the mass of workers was the 'Class Against Class' policy still being pursued at Comintern insistence. This sectarian line required the Labour Party to be vilified as 'social fascists'; social democracy was regarded as the main enemy, and social democratic parties were considered to be playing a leading role in preparing for war against the Soviet Union. Labour leaders in government were denounced as 'the betrayers of the working class, warmongers, colonial murderers, wage cutters and creators of unemployment'. The 'pseudo-Left' ILP was, if anything, worse; Harry Pollitt, who had now solidified his position as leader of the CP, regarded it as imperative to expose 'its programme of revolutionary phrases, trying by various illusions to draw the workers away from the daily struggle'. In the industrial field, Communists were expected to set up revolutionary trade unions in competition with the established unions affiliated to the TUC – a policy that in Britain was proving a complete failure.[6]

Yet by August, when Montagu made his commitment, there were some slight indications of a positive shift. A Workers' Charter campaign, emphasising immediate demands such as increased winter relief and higher unemployment benefits, had drawn 788 delegates to a convention in London in April. Party membership had crept above 3,000. Towards the end of the month the disintegration of the Labour-led government could not but enlarge the scope for alternative leadership on the Left.[7]

The person whom Montagu identified in his questionnaire as introducing him to the Party was Emile Burns. Some fifteen years older than his protégé, Burns was from a family of senior colonial administrators, and after study at Trinity College, Cambridge, had joined the CPGB with a left-wing group of the ILP in 1921. As an employee of the Labour Research Department he was noted for a series of anti-imperialist publications. Montagu had collaborated closely with Burns in the formation of the Federation of Workers' Film Societies, of which Burns was treasurer. By the time Montagu joined the Party, Burns had been elected to the central committee and was recognised as a leading Marxist theoretician.

One of Burns's roles within the movement had been national secretary of the Friends of Soviet Russia, and Montagu had had dealings with him in this connection regarding film distribution. It was to this organisation, now renamed the Friends of the Soviet Union (FSU), to which Montagu was at this point directed. Somewhat akin to the Society for Cultural Relations but aimed at a much wider membership, the FSU was the British affiliate of the International Association of Friends of the Soviet Union, founded at Comintern instigation in Moscow at the time of the tenth anniversary celebrations in November 1927. The international body set up its headquarters in Berlin, and held a congress at Essen in March 1930 at which Willi Münzenberg presided. It was around this time that Albert Inkpin, having been ousted from his role as general secretary of the CPGB as part of the 'Class Against Class' purge of perceived 'Rights', was appointed (following Comintern intervention) secretary-general of the International Association.[8]

Chief functions of the FSU in Britain, as in other countries, were to extend Communist influence and build support for the Soviet Union through publications, lectures and classes, film screenings, exhibitions,

congresses, and the organisation of trips to Russia by workers' delegations. Funded and directed by the Comintern, the FSU strove to maintain
a veneer of independence (by giving prominence, for example, to such
non-Communist supporters as George Bernard Shaw), but was treated by
the CPGB as an auxiliary agitprop arm of the Party. A central committee
resolution of November 1930, for instance, stated: 'The fight against the war
danger [and] the defence of the Soviet Union make the task of developing the Friends of Soviet Russia into a powerful mass organisation one of
the most important responsibilities of the Party. The mass sympathy for the
Workers Republic must be skilfully harnessed in this way.'[9]

In August 1931, presumably immediately upon joining the CP, Montagu
was appointed to a bookkeeping position in the FSU, and he soon became
national treasurer of the organisation. The man he was to work alongside
was the national organiser, Ernest (Ernie) Brown, who like Burns had been
part of the ILP intake to the CPGB in 1921. Brown had served as British
representative to ECCI in Moscow in 1924–25, and had been member of
the CP's central committee until dropped at the December 1929 Congress.
In 1930 he had been an organiser during the Bradford woollen mills strike,
following which he accompanied his activist wife Isabel to Moscow, where
she attended the Lenin School for foreign communists. Back in Britain, the
couple were both appointed to Comintern-linked positions, Ernie with the
FSU and Isabel with the Workers' International Relief (WIR), which she
was called upon to reactivate.[10]

Ivor's first task for the FSU was to receive contributions for a fund to send
a workers' delegation to Russia at the time of the fourteenth anniversary of
the revolution. It was decided that the delegation would take a tractor with
them 'as a gift to the Russian workers' Five-Year Plan'. It was believed that
'this will provide an excellent opportunity for showing the workers of the
Soviet Union that the mass of working-class people in Britain think on
contrary lines to those who are lying and plotting against them.' Initially
a party of forty was aimed at; eventually thirteen workers made the trip,
including seamen, engineers and miners. Although at the time of departure
all the money needed had yet to come in, it was confidently announced
that 'tractor will follow.'[11]

Montagu seems to have slotted into his new role as party functionary
with equanimity. 'The capitalist system has broken down here,' he reported

to Eisenstein on 6 October. 'MacDonald has become Conservative Prime Minister. There has been a mutiny in the Navy & the unemployed are daily rioting in the street. I am working with the CP.'[12]

They were stirring times indeed. There was a mood of militancy abroad, exemplified by the Invergordon mutiny in September, when around a thousand sailors took strike action against a proposed pay cut. With a general election looming, the CP 'maintained a ferocious attack on both the National government and the Labour opposition.' Montagu foresaw that he might end up in jail. 'We'll see,' he told Eisenstein. 'I am a great coward, & temperamentally do not like fighting (you can remember of course that in all our personal relations I was a man of peace); my temperament is suited to research or philosophy, but bugger it all, when your friends are going to jail & getting knocked on the conk by policemen what else can one do?'[13]

As a member he now looked on the Communist Party more favourably than he had in the past. 'My own impression,' he told Trotsky, 'is that most of its weaknesses are due to the temper of heresy hunting and sectarianism following on the attempted ideological purge of the Left and pretended purge of the Right in the past. But that the general line now given by the leadership tends to be a correct one and will improve its position.'[14]

With a Comintern subsidy of £5,250, the CP stood twenty-six candidates in the parliamentary election of 27 October. They received 75,000 votes in total; none won a seat. In comparison, MacDonald's National Government was returned with 14 million votes against 6.5 million for the Labour opposition. 'It was a harsh demonstration,' wrote historian E.H. Carr, 'of the inability of the CPGB to win the support of the worker, even in the face of a major crisis of capitalism.' Montagu, a realist, is unlikely to have been surprised by the dismal result. 'Of course things go very slowly in England,' he had written to Eisenstein. 'There will not be a big slide down but only gradually exacerbated small crises in succession.'[15]

The FSU celebrated the Soviet 14th anniversary in London with a 'mighty mobilisation' on 7 November, with contingents converging on Hyde Park, displaying 'red flags and other Communist emblems', from all points of the compass. 'When the procession was passing along the Victoria Embankment,' *The Times* reported, 'a number of men carrying staves were called on by the police to hand them over. This the men declined to do and the sticks were taken from them by force.' Several women were charged with assaulting the police. In the park, Montagu was one of a number of speakers who addressed the crowd from four platforms; others included Tom Mann, Harry Pollitt, Isabel Brown and John Strachey.[16]

Montagu's responsibilities were apparently extended several days later when, according to an MI5 informant, he was in charge of arrangements by the National Unemployed Workers' Movement (NUWM) to demonstrate at the opening of Parliament on 10 November. 'The arrangements miscarried,' MI5 noted, with Montagu being considered 'a very poor organiser'. If, in fact, a demonstration did take place, it made little impact; the fulsome report of the event in *The Times*, expatiating upon the 'pageantry and ceremony' featuring 'Indian Princes magnificently attired' and peeresses' jewels that 'sparkled and flashed', makes no mention of any protest.[17]

A few weeks earlier, in October, the translation by Ivor Montagu and Sergei Nolbandov of Leonid Leonov's novel *Sot* had been published. This was a contemporary drama of the Five-Year Plan, a narrative of the struggle to construct a paper mill on the boggy banks of the River Sot in northern Russia. The local populace – monks, peasants, intelligentsia – are moulded not without difficulty into the new proletariat, while the massive project is beset by confusion, inefficiency, and a flooding calamity. Layoffs and unrest follow, but eventually construction is resumed after a full-steam-ahead directive is received from Moscow.[18]

As Ivor noted in his introduction, Leonov's linguistic style was challenging: 'His language is never classical or smooth; he uses peasant dialect sometimes starkly colloquial, to gain naturalism in conversation, sometimes in an ornate pattern to gain a fairy-tale effect.' In fact, Leonov was 'continually altering his style to fit the character or mood described; this method risks preciosity and forcedness, but at its best it secures the peculiar vividness that has impressed Gorky [in a laudatory foreword to the novel], and which it has been the especial effort of the translators to preserve.'[19]

The decision to favour the literal over the graceful was not always a happy one. At times the reader is required to negotiate such thickets of tangled prose as: 'Toothed bands move out of the river, dragging to the shore their every-minute prey; wailingly sing the cranes, as they pile their wet captures into dark little alps; twice dear to Uvadiev are those steel, unfailing arms', or 'Occurred a final silence, more evil than any shouting; but ever in the intersecting breaths tossed the unsteady flame of the cresset.' *Sot* may have been about the Soviet nation rushing headlong into modernity, but its prose style, at least as rendered by Montagu and Nolbandov, was mired in antiquated syntax and obscurantist vocabulary. The *Sunday Times* reviewer gave credit to the translators 'who, I imagine, have made the mightiest efforts to preserve the author's own style,' but doubted that 'this gloomy and, to my mind, rather confused picture of a bit of the new Russia struggling to play its part in the much-advertised Five Years' Plan will prove to be to the taste of very many readers in this country.'[20]

Ivor was keen at this time to revisit the Soviet Union and see for himself what changes had been wrought. His idea was to set up a lecture tour through the good offices of Eisenstein's partner Pera Attasheva, who was well connected in cultural circles. The subject of his talks, he told Pera, would be Sergei Eisenstein – his translation of Eisenstein's seminal theoretical text, 'The Principles of Film Form' (also known as 'A Dialectic Approach to Film Form') had just appeared in *Close Up*. This was a miscalculation. Eisenstein, still in Mexico, was being talked of as a traitor for not returning to the USSR. Moreover, his work was beginning to be subjected to stinging criticism as the distance of his conceptions from those of the newly emerging aesthetic of socialist realism began to be apparent. A lengthy article in *International Literature* declared that 'despite their revolutionary tendency the cinematographic creations of Eisenstein still retain traces of the very bourgeois limitations denounced by him'; he was accused of 'technical fetishism' and of being 'unable to give a dialectical exposition of the mass or to understand the unity of the general and the particular.' *October* was 'a horde of dead objects covered with the dust of museums'; *The General Line*, 'the film dealing with the socialist reconstruction of the village is least of all interested in its social content!' It was possible that Eisenstein could be re-educated to overcome 'his traits of class limitation', but this could only be achieved through 'merciless exposure and criticism of his first films'.[21]

Unsurprisingly, Attasheva told Ivor that 'the idea of your coming here is very good, but the theme you choose for lecturing is not important enough,' while Eisenstein himself expressed his surprise at the lecturing topic 'being my person'. He did not think, he continued, 'that it is so far important subject of world wide interest.' Pera proposed instead that Ivor's focus be on the activities of the workers' film societies in Britain; an expenses-paid tour could very likely be arranged through the Association of Workers of Revolutionary Cinematography (usually referred to under its Russian acronym, ARRK), the international section of the Society for Proletarian Amateur Cinema and Photo, and VOKS in London (SCR) and Moscow. Unfortunately for this helpful suggestion, Montagu had to inform Attasheva that 'the fact of the matter is that the workers' film movement is dead. Killed suddenly just when it was beginning to be spreading, by the new line of Berlin film export refusing to send over any more films. It is back again at the old bad position of 1925.' As it turned out, Montagu found it impossible to arrange a visit at this time: on 24 December he told Pera that it might be necessary to postpone the trip 'because decaying capitalism decays so fast that it keeps me busy,' and on 21 January 1932 he wrote: 'Circumstances connected with important work here force me to postpone my plans for a visit. It is possible that they may be carried through in a more official manner with Party sponsorship round April.'[22]

Just what this 'important work' consisted is not altogether clear, but certainly his speaking engagements for the FSU now began to step up. On 13 December he spoke at the St Albans FSU conference on 'the organisation of branches of the FSU and the work of the FSU in general'. Discussion followed, 'and as a result three new branches were formed in Luton, Watford and Welwyn Garden City.' Three days later he showed 'pictures of Russia' at the Trades Hall, Walthamstow, for the Leyton and Walthamstow FSU. On 10 January, at the Poplar Town Hall, he was called on to support a member of the workers' delegation to the Soviet Union reporting to East London dockers on working conditions in the USSR. And on 15 January he lectured on Russian films, with illustrations, at an FSU event in the Southlands Library, Battersea.[23]

Then, on 18 January, Montagu addressed the Manchester branch of the FSU at the Cheetham Town Hall on the topic of 'Jewish Colonisation in the Soviet Union'. He told the audience, the *Manchester Guardian* reported, that 'the alleged oppression of Jews in Soviet Russia was an offensive lie.' The Soviet government had 'liberated all Jews from the disabilities imposed under the Czar's regime' and had established agricultural colonies 'in which Jews now worked and lived as a national entity.' When this scheme had developed sufficiently, Montagu explained, the government 'would encourage the forming of a Jewish National Soviet Republic.' Though there was no suppression of Jewish – or any other – religious activities, 'these activities had to help and not hinder the national life. Before a new synagogue could be built, for instance, the Soviet Union had to be satisfied that there was a sufficient population in the area to justify it.'[24]

Simultaneously, Montagu was collecting donations to cover the expenses of two new workers' delegations that would travel to the USSR in March. A women's group would participate in International Women's Day celebrations, while the general delegation would 'convey greetings to the All-Union Trades Union Congress.' It was a fundraising treadmill; in March Ivor began collecting for the 'biggest ever' solidarity delegation to visit the Soviet Union for May 1st celebrations, the cost for which was put at above £1,000.[25]

Although increasingly beholden to the Stalinist leadership of the CP and the Comintern, Montagu did not immediately give up his contacts with Trotsky. In a lengthy letter dated 9 October 1931, he systematically outlined the political situation in Britain as he saw it. Developments proved 'once again,' he told Trotsky, 'that my objections to your analysis of the English situation were at fault; that the speed of the recurrent crisis is accelerated to the point you forecast.' Analysing in turn the positions of the bourgeoisie and of the labour movement ('the lower ranks are already in a temper of extreme leftward feeling' with growing CP influence), he made several predictions: that Britain would have a 'Fascist', i.e. unconstitutional, government; that the Labour Party would suffer electoral defeat; and that the trade unions would embark on a series of strikes that would be defeated because of the lack of genuine leadership. The ILP, Montagu surmised, would be unable to sustain its hostility towards the CP: 'The rank and file of the Independent Labour Party in many districts is already collaborating with the Communist Party in the formation of campaign councils,' he wrote – a point that Trotsky noted with heavy marginal scoring.[26]

A friendly interchange continued. Trotsky sent Montagu some documents concerning the situation in England, and his theses regarding the international situation, particularly in Germany. He enquired about the possibility of a new edition of *Where is Britain Going?* For his part, Montagu sent Trotsky the CP election manifesto, arranged to have the *Daily Worker* forwarded to him, and passed around Trotsky's commentary on British questions ('I endorse it entirely'). He spoke with Unwin, the publisher of *Where is Britain Going?*, about the idea of a new edition; unfortunately 900 copies of the old edition remained unsold. Unwin proposed a new book that would renew interest in the work; Montagu suggested it might be possible to round up comrades to purchase and destroy the unsold copies.[27]

On 9 November Trotsky warmly recommended to Ivor an American comrade who was shortly to visit Britain. Max Shachtman was a leading figure in the Communist League of America, US section of the International Left Opposition and publisher of the *Militant*. 'In your usual friendliness I am sure you will help to pass his time in London with a maximum "comfort" and minimum expense,' Trotsky wrote. Simultaneously, he informed Shachtman that Montagu was 'a very good comrade, ready to assist as well as he can, and I am sure can facilitate your stay in London in every respect.' On the 28th Trotsky wrote again to Montagu, saying that Shachtman would be accompanied by 'a fine young comrade' in the same organisation, Albert Glotzer. He added: 'I trust that your official Party membership will not be an obstacle to meeting them and, if necessary, offering them friendly assistance one way or another.'[28]

Things did not work out as well as Trotsky hoped. 'Comrade Shachtman has not visited me,' Montagu informed him on 5 December. 'I have made enquiries but am disappointed to say I have not found him.' (This was undoubtedly because Shachtman had only just arrived after a twelve-hour storm-tossed crossing of the English Channel.) Glotzer travelled to England separately, and eventually contact was made. 'But our visit with Montague [*sic*] was surprisingly brief, especially in view of Trotsky's letter to Shachtman,' Glotzer was later to record:

> Montague was formally cordial, but we could not help feeling that he was unenthusiastic about our visit and our suggestions that he do something for the Opposition or for Trotsky personally. Trotsky had warned against compromising Montague, whose business organisation and interests were related to the Soviet Union. It was clear to us that Montague would never allow himself to be 'compromised' by the Russians, let alone by Trotsky.

Glotzer registered Montagu's attitude as 'unmistakably frigid', and on his return to New York, reporting to Trotsky on his visit, he made 'special note of the uneasiness I felt about Montague.'[29]

If it was true that at this time Ivor was beginning to distance himself from the revolutionary he had formerly held in such high regard, this was not

apparent in his correspondence. On 21 January 1932 he wrote with 'very
best greetings and wishes always and also to all the dwellers under your
roof', explaining what he had done to relieve Trotsky of some embarrassment caused by the actions of Shachtman. Without the author's knowledge
or approval, Shachtman had offered an essay by Trotsky on the international
situation to the *Manchester Guardian* – as Trotsky explained, 'one does not
offer theses which propagate a socialist revolution to a liberal newspaper!'
Unsurprisingly, it had been rejected. But what was worse, Shachtman had
then proceeded to offer the article to the *New Leader*, the organ of the ILP.
It was a serious matter, Trotsky told Montagu, if a piece dealing directly
with the question of the proletarian revolution were to appear in the left
social-democratic press, giving the impression that Labourites and communists were brothers in arms. Montagu was able to reassure Trotsky that
he had contacted both papers, that the *Guardian* had rejected the article for
reasons of length, and that the *New Leader* had received a cable from Trotsky
in time and would not publish the essay.[30]

Montagu also explained that Shachtman had agreed to take up the
question of purchasing the redundant copies of *Where is Britain Going?*,
but the American proved less than helpful in this connection also. Writing
to Trotsky on 31 July, Ivor reported that several letters on the subject to
Shachtman had produced 'only an indeterminate reply'.[31]

Montagu's relationship with Trotsky was inevitably being affected by
ongoing developments in the Communist movement. The Shachtman–
Glotzer visit had been aimed at promoting the formation of a Trotskyist
organisation in Britain; although nothing concrete had emerged from their
discussions with locals by the time the emissaries had returned to America,
a small revolt against the Comintern line in the CP was brewing in south
London, and by July the 'Balham group' was openly defiant of Pollitt and
had pledged its allegiance to the International Left Opposition. Its leader,
Reg Groves, was expelled from the CP in August, and other expulsions
from the Balham and Tooting branches followed.[32]

It is clear from Montagu's July letter that he was not moved to join the
Balham group of rebels. He told Trotsky:

I wish you to know that the activity of the CPGB is in a number of
respects undoubtedly upon much sounder lines than the activity of the

CP's of other countries, which I see described in the *Militant*. Certainly, there is the same temperamental bureaucratic weakness among the leaders. But this weakness does not appear to have an effect paralysing to the degree which reigns – for example – in America.

This statement would undoubtedly have confirmed Trotsky in his belief that Montagu was unlikely to become a disciple; already on 13 July he had told Groves that 'Ivor Montagu has, or had, some personal sympathy for me, but now he is even on that small scale paralysed by his adherence to the party.'[33]

For his part, Montagu seemed oblivious to the reservations his correspondent now held about him. In his lengthy letter, he complimented Trotsky on his recently published *History of the Russian Revolution* (and offered to send him reviews); urged Trotsky to contact him if he needed any material for his 'projected book of materialist-historical analysis of personalities'; enclosed various documents including 'a characteristic bravura piece by Shaw', a paper called *The China Forum*, a copy of the Indian student magazine *Bharat*, a published statement by Kerensky, and 'a memorandum on the political and economic situation of the ILP issued by one of the Left branches'; discussed at length the 'very intricate' position of the ILP now that it had decided to disaffiliate from the Labour Party; explained in detail how effectively the anti-war campaign was being conducted in Britain under CPGB auspices; and favourably reported on the work of the FSU in its organisation of factory-based delegations to Russia. He concluded with his customary warm good wishes.[34]

Trotsky, it seems, did not reply for many months; when he did write, in December, to his '*cher camarade*', he cited '*des raisons multiples*' for his long silence. His brief letter was chiefly concerned with asking Ivor if he could procure for him some high-quality fishing line, which he found impossible to obtain in Turkey. Montagu duly complied; Trotsky was very pleased with the tackle that arrived. It was now clear that the pair were on divergent political paths, but contacts continued into 1933. In March Ivor served as intermediary when the *Manchester Guardian* requested a response from Trotsky to the situation in Germany, and shortly thereafter he wrote introducing Sidney Bernstein, who hoped to pay a visit when in Turkey. Finally, in June, Trotsky sent Montagu an article asking him if he could place it in an

English newspaper. This was, it would seem, a step too far. Montagu apparently did not reply, and thereafter the correspondence ceased.[35]

As a CP member Montagu was gradually learning that his freedom of expression, if not yet his freedom of thought, was more curtailed than it had been in the past. Back in October 1931 his comrade Ralph Bond, preparing a periodical publication for the Federation of Workers' Film Societies, asked him for a short news story about Eisenstein in America. Ivor's piece, when he submitted it, was rejected. 'Personally,' Bond told him, 'it amused me very much, but the points against it are: - (1) It is too long and I cannot see how it can be cut very much. (2) It is all rather flippant and might get me into trouble with the big shots.' (The German writer Gustav Regler, reflecting on the experience of Communist intellectuals, was later to comment: 'I belonged to a political party resembling a religious order, in which acceptance and obedience, not speculation, were the first and last requirements ... To the Bolsheviks the Word was harshly indivisible: it was the minds of their intellectual adherents that they split in two, allowing no questions and treating laughter as a crime.') The following year Montagu was warned by Emile Burns against contributing to *The Plebs*, the Marxist journal associated with the labour college movement. 'It is in fact considered undesirable that any of us should write in the *Plebs*,' he was informed, 'because it creates the illusion of a united front which does not exist, and helps to give publicity to the journal particularly among our sympathisers.'[36]

The evidence would suggest that Montagu had found a comfortable home in the Party and did not chafe against such constrictions. He diligently continued his work at the FSU, repeatedly raising funds for the several workers' delegations to the Soviet Union that were sent each year. As he explained to Trotsky, he was proud of the way the trips were organised:

[W]e invariably and most strictly select a factory, run a campaign in that factory before, during and after the delegation period and obtain the delegate from a rank and file meeting of the workers in the factory after the campaign has raised interest among them. Thus not only bringing direct contact between a representative in whom those workers have confidence selected among themselves and the Soviet Union scene, but also obtaining organisational results from each factory. Whereas, it is pretty clear, that the American Friends of the Soviet Union still works by the old method of appointment, treating these delegations not as part of a wide campaign, but as holiday tours for hard-worked Party members.[37]

By early 1932 Montagu had become a member of the National Committee of the FSU, and in February he placed before the committee a draft constitution for the organisation. Around this time he also joined the editorial board of the FSU journal *Russia To-Day*. Alongside handling the organisation's finances and overseeing the delegate selection process, Montagu kept up a steady schedule of talks to FSU branches. Amongst other appearances, he lectured on art and culture in the USSR on 1 March 1932 in Islington, 29 March in Acton, and 24 April in Camden Town; on film and theatre in Soviet culture on 19 June in central London; and on the Five-Year Plan on 4 April in Bolton and during July in Chatham. Much of the FSU's propaganda focus was on countering 'lies about the real situation in Soviet Russia' purveyed by the capitalist press, and it was no doubt such an objective which motivated his talk 'How Religion is Persecuted in Russia!' given on 6 March in Fulham. In August Montagu was responsible for the third week of lectures at the 'Red' summer school at Bexhill-on-Sea. It was announced that, taking 'Soviet Economy' as his basis, he would 'bring in such questions as Soviet planned economy and capitalist chaos, the meaning and significance of the Five-Year Plan, the war danger and the Soviet Union.' There were also to be lectures, very likely Montagu's responsibility, on the role of the cinema in the class struggle.[38]

If Montagu was well satisfied with the work of the CPGB and the FSU, the organisations' parent body was not. Since the general strike of 1926, the Comintern operative Richard Krebs was later to write, the British party had become 'the most useless and expensive toy of the Communist International.' Representatives from the Comintern's West European Bureau (WEB) in Berlin were regularly sent undercover to audit and report back on the activities of the Party and its front organisations, and Krebs was dispatched in that capacity in the summer of 1932 by the head of the WEB, Georgi Dimitrov.[39]

He was not impressed. Moscow subsidies for the *Daily Worker*, he claimed, were being creamed off in the form of salaries and 'expenses' by 'a small clique of Central Committee members. "Expenses" included fairly luxurious apartments, maintenance of mistresses, vacation trips to the South Shore, and fur coats and automobiles for the wives of prominent British

Stalinists.' The pattern of corruption was replicated, according to Krebs, in other departments of the Communist movement:

> In the blazing summer heat of London, I investigated almost a score of communist offices bearing the name-plates of the many auxiliary organisations, and everywhere the picture was the same: well-groomed and voluble officials loafing behind a shiny desk, trim-looking secretaries, office hours from nine to four, heaps of paper plans and resolutions, portraits of Lenin and Stalin on the wall, and no contact worth mentioning with the labouring masses of Great Britain.[40]

One of Krebs' assignments was to inspect the London office of the Friends of the Soviet Union. Since the end of 1930, the FSU had received 'a special monthly allowance with which to combat the intensive British anti-Soviet campaign that centred around the employment of slave labour in the vast lumber camps of the GPU in the country around Archangelsk.' The organisation had been sent 'huge consignments of the handsome and expensive pictorial review, *USSR in Construction*, and money with which to finance a large-scale distribution of this publication among British teachers, college professors, and professional groups.' Investigating, Krebs found that 'the money had been spent to no good purpose while big stacks of *USSR in Construction* reposed in the cellars, thickly covered with dust.' Montagu makes no mention of this damaging review in his surviving correspondence.[41]

The Comintern was not the only body keeping an eye on him and his organisation. Krebs had one of his operations in England thwarted through police infiltration, and he developed a high regard for 'the proficiency of ... Scotland Yard in the art of sterilising in the gentlest manner any communist attempt at an offensive.' But he was probably unaware, as undoubtedly was Montagu, of the extent to which the movement had been penetrated. A part-time typist for the FSU, beginning in 1931 initially as an evening volunteer, was in fact MI5 agent Olga Gray, who had been instructed to make herself known in front organisations before joining the Party itself. It was possibly Gray who reported an overheard conversation between Ernie Brown and Montagu in December 1931.[42]

And Montagu continued to be monitored in his personal capacity. Under a Home Office Warrant (HOW) his mail was intercepted (it was through

reading his August 1931 letter to Trotsky that the authorities became aware
he was finally joining the CPGB), and local constables would send in
reports of his public lectures – occasionally with such additional snippets
as: 'During the week-end of the 17th-18th January, 1932, Dimitri MIRSKY
and Ivor MONTAGUE [sic] stayed at 8, Nelson Street, Chorlton-on-Medlock,
Manchester, the address of Comrade DRIBBON.' MI5 knew that he had been
suggested as a member of the Board of Contributors for a proposed Marxist
theoretical journal to be edited by Maurice Dobb, and took note of the
fact that in May 1932 Montagu acted as guarantor for a rental agreement
entered into by E.H. (Ernie) Brown. When applying for the renewal of his
HOW in June, the spies explained that he was 'now co-operating with the
Atlas Film Company in connection with the Association of Workers in the
Revolutionary Kino (A.R.R.K.) in Moscow.' In his Security Service file
he was described as 'about 27 years of age, broad-shouldered, over six foot,
has dark curly hair and is of distinctly Jewish appearance. His eyes are dark
brown and his complexion is pale. He is generally rather dirty and untidy.'[43]

MI5 could generally deduce fairly accurately what Montagu was up to.
But his correspondence in October 1932 with the champion Hungarian
table tennis player Zoltán Mechlovits had them stymied. Staffer Captain
Hugh Miller, a keen hunter of Bolshevik subversion, wrote to the head
of counter-intelligence at MI6, Major Valentine Vivian, on 8 November
expressing his frustration. Could a trace be taken out on Mechlovits and his
associate Bodanszky? 'The reason of our tentative interest in these people,'
Miller confessed, 'will appear to you rather quaint. They write intermina-
bly to Ivor MONTAGU about Table Tennis and the trying out of Table Tennis
balls. The exercise of this occupation over a period of many months has so
eaten into Zoltan MECHLOVITS' time that he has informed MONTAGU that he
cannot go on with it.' Montagu's enthusiasm for the sport was well known,
but 'even in England,' Miller continued, 'which is not noted for sanity in
this respect, we find it hard to believe that a gentleman can spend weeks
upon weeks testing Table Tennis balls.' Moreover – fuelling the suspicion
– 'we have on record a warning to MONTAGU from Berlin that a Doctor in
that city when writing to him, apparently on Table Tennis, will really be
furthering his divorce proceedings from his wife.' Miller and his colleagues
would be grateful, he told Vivian, 'if you could tell us whether the individuals in Budapest I have named to you are known to be queer in any other

way.' Vivian duly made enquiries of the Hungarian authorities, who could uncover nothing subversive about the persons in question.[44]

Politically, a feature of Montagu's activity over this period was his growing involvement in the anti-war movement. His interest had perhaps been piqued as early as February 1931 by a letter from his old Cambridge acquaintance Lella Florence, with whom he had kept in touch over the years. Now dwelling in 'a small castle in the Midlands' as the wife of a Birmingham University professor, she was initiating a disarmament campaign and thought that Chaplin, who was visiting Britain for the premiere of *City Lights*, could possibly be induced to endorse it. 'Ivor Darlint [*sic*]' she wrote:

Charlie Chaplin wants to come to Birmingham – it says so in the newspapers so it must be true, though it does seem difficult to account for this morbid desire … I've undertaken to organise a vast disarmament campaign during the last week in March – town hall meeting on the 20th. But it's so devastatingly disheartening – people won't think – or act – I've never tried a job so difficult. Now if Charlie were to appear for five minutes in favour of disarmament – immeasurable push to the whole campaign. But I expect the idea's quite fantastic – but is it?

It was a bold notion; it is not known if Montagu took it up with his tennis-playing companion, but in any event nothing seems to have come of it.[45]

Montagu's direct involvement in the peace movement did not come until the following year, when he attended the World Anti-War Congress held in Amsterdam on 27–29 August as a delegate of the National Committee of the FSU. Following the Japanese invasion of Manchuria in September 1931, which intensified concern about a possible attack on the Soviet Union, the Comintern had instructed the WEB to organise a conference of Communist parties in Berlin to plan a drive against imperialist war. This took place on 30–31 March. Willi Münzenberg, in his capacity as general secretary of the League Against Imperialism, and his offsider Louis Gibarti then proceeded to launch, probably on Münzenberg's initiative, a worldwide anti-war campaign. Capitalising on fears of the outbreak of a new major military conflict, this would draw in broad strata of the Left behind slogans approved by Moscow. The renowned French pacifist intellectuals

Henri Barbusse and Romain Rolland were recruited to head the campaign, and many other celebrities including Albert Einstein, Theodore Dreiser, Madame Sun Yat Sen, Bertrand Russell, Heinrich Mann, John Dos Passos and Maxim Gorky were persuaded to lend their names to the venture. The Congress was initially announced to take place in Geneva, but objections from the Swiss authorities led to it being relocated to the Netherlands.[46]

Montagu enthusiastically outlined developments in the campaign in Britain in his letter to Trotsky of 31 July. Anti-war councils were being set up in every locality, 'not merely to elect delegates – but to sit permanently and plan actively measures to adopt against war.' Within these councils, Party members 'emphasise and show that the war danger is particularly aimed against the Soviet Union, show that there is no method of avoiding the war danger except by destruction of the existing social system.' The movement, he contended, was 'awakening tremendous response'. Montagu knew from personal experience: he had in fact spoken at the Conference of Co-operators Against War held the previous Sunday, when more than 170 delegates had packed London's Essex Hall. Amidst condemnation of the League of Nations and international capitalism, participants called for 'the active participation of all co-operators in the fight against war', urged workers to refuse to handle war material for Japan, and elected two delegates to the upcoming World Congress.[47]

Enthusiasm for the movement was not shared by the leadership of the Labour Party and TUC and their affiliates in the Second International, which was quick to condemn the Congress as a Communist manoeuvre. However, the appeal of the Amsterdam event was such that in the end some 300 social democrats were reported to have defied their Party orders and attended. In all, the spectacular mass gathering attracted 2,196 delegates from twenty-seven countries, representing a broad range of trade unions and left-wing and pacifist organisations. The chief challenge for the Communist organisers was to retain the support of the pacifists, for whom they had scant regard, while promoting the major goal of the congress, mobilising international public opinion against any assault on the USSR. The unspoken sticking point was that the Russians might find themselves in a military alliance with one or more Western nations in any future conflict, and hence disarmament had to be downplayed and conscientious objection definitely not endorsed.[48]

Thus Münzenberg, in a speech hailed in the official British report as a highlight of the conference, attacked 'with terrific vigour' the Gandhian philosophy of an Indian National Congress Party delegate, who had said that he who receives a bullet is braver than he who fires it. 'May be,' said Münzenberg, 'but it's a fact that he who fires the bullet stays upright, while he who receives it falls to the ground. And we, we workers ... do not wish to die. We wish to defeat the White Army, to triumph with the Red Army. We will the death of Capitalism and the triumph of Socialism.' The remark 'brought the whole Congress cheering to its feet.'[49]

The manifesto issuing from the Congress condemned the Japanese invasion of China; war propaganda; the 'huge and ever-growing armaments' of nations preparing for war, and in particular poison gases and disease germs; imperialist rivalries, and protectionist measures that 'merely deepen the crisis'; the destruction of foodstuffs that had resulted from the current capitalist breakdown; and attacks on the Soviet Union, including 'attempts at destruction by sabotage'. It praised Japanese workers for showing 'how the fight against imperialist war must be carried on' by holding up war production and munition convoys. It blasted the Treaty of Versailles for ascribing the sole responsibility for the Great War to Germany, which had contributed to the growth of 'Fascist reaction'. It contended that 'every imperialist power, whether it be the United States, or England, or France, or Japan, or Italy, is working for war' – Germany presumably could not be included in this category because of its defeat – and drew attention to 'the leading role played by French imperialism'. According to the manifesto, the drive to war could only be resisted by 'the concerted action of workers, peasants and all who are exploited, and oppressed'; pacifist gestures by individuals were futile, and plebiscites would be ineffectual. 'Above all', the manifesto stated, 'the Congress warns the public against governmental institutions, and especially the League of Nations, which functions at Geneva as the immediate mouthpiece of the imperialist powers.' The Second International was criticised for its hostile attitude to the Congress, with activists being reminded of the betrayal of the anti-war cause by the socialist parties in August 1914; while finally the manifesto called for mass action from the world's proletariat who, 'though holding divergent political opinions', could yet enter upon 'the tragic disorder of our times ... in closed and disciplined ranks and so raise their powerful voice.'[50]

Despite the show of unity, tensions were immediately apparent. Rolland was not able to attend the Congress because of ill health, but his Declaration had been read. Following the event he stated that he would not be able to sign the manifesto because of its dismissal of conscientious objectors. This could clearly have led to a damaging split in the movement, and the international bureau of the World Committee Against Imperialist War moved to shore up its position, issuing a statement in December 1932. The document, authorised by the Communist parties of France, Germany and the Soviet Union and 'probably written by Willi Münzenberg', asserted that 'conscientious objectors have their place in our ranks ... and that unconditionally.' Whether the message got through to the militant Communist rank-and-file was another matter.[51]

Montagu returned from Amsterdam on 30 August in the company of a German cabinetmaker and journalist, Karl Schabrod, editor of the Düsseldorf Communist paper *Freiheit*. Schabrod had recently trained at the Lenin School in Moscow, which is perhaps why he gave his occupation at the border as 'student'. Montagu vouched for Schabrod's leaving the country after his permitted stay of one month, although it turned out he remained longer than that. MI5 were under few illusions about Schabrod, noting that he stayed with Ernest and Isabel Brown, and was 'almost certainly in this country as an agent of the WIR, sent to build up a strike organisation in an area where there was then a strike.' Whether Ivor collaborated with him on this mission, if in fact this is what Schabrod was up to, is not known, though MI5 did ascertain that he took his German comrade to the dog races.[52]

Montagu's commitment to the anti-war campaign stepped up after the Congress. MI5 noted on his file in September that he had been elected to the movement's permanent international committee, and in speeches in connection with the FSU delegation to be sent to the USSR in November he stressed the war danger. Thus at a meeting in Springburn, Scotland, on 9 October, attended by nearly a thousand workers, Montagu spoke, according to the police report that reached MI5, 'mainly re preparations that are being made for war against Russia in this country'.[53]

This was also the theme of the National Anti-War Conference held in Bermondsey Town Hall on Sunday, 13 November. Jointly organised by the FSU and the National Committee of the Anti-War Movement, into which the British section of the League Against Imperialism had morphed, the conference was strongly focused on the Soviet Union: the agenda, it was announced, would 'provide for reports and resolutions on the gains of the Russian Revolution, and the next steps to fight the danger of imperialist war'. Chairing the afternoon session, Montagu took the opportunity to critique the pacifist position, saying that what the Peace Army (an organisation whose members would, it was mooted, stand in nonviolent resistance between enemy forces) was opposed to was 'all use of arms under any circumstances'. A resolution carried 'with cheers' called for a vigorous campaign against war, 'strengthening and extending by every possible means of existing local anti-war committees by visitation to trade union branches, Co-operative Guilds, organisations of women, ex-Service men's organisations, branches of the No More War movement, and similar bodies.' Concentration on war industries was called for, 'with a view to the establishment of anti-war organisations in all factories of war material'.[54]

Although he was by then heavily engaged elsewhere, Montagu kept up his commitment to the cause into 1933. On 7 January he was in Manchester, and after having addressed apprentices outside the Metropolitan-Vickers works on the Soviet Five-Year Plan at midday, he represented the British Anti-War Council at a public meeting in the evening, warning that despite the League of Nations and the Kellogg Pact, 'we were faced today with a situation more alarming than existed in 1914.' On 9 January he chaired a public meeting of the Anti-War Council in the Memorial Hall, Farringdon Street, London EC4, attended by more than a thousand people. Speakers included Harry Pollitt, who declared: 'We must not only unmask the League of Nations, but we must unmask the support of the Second International, of Henderson & Co., for the League of Nations.' Dorothy Woodman of the Union of Democratic Control (UDC) focused on the arms industry, asserting that 'you could not throw a stone in the House of Lords without hitting someone who stands to gain in the event of war.' Other speakers warned against underestimating the danger of war on the USSR and attacked 'insincere pacifists who wanted peace yet supported the League of Nations and therefore capitalism'.[55]

At a meeting of the Walthamstow branch of the FSU on 21 February, Montagu spoke for an hour to an audience of about fifty. The local police sergeant prepared a detailed report, which was forwarded via Special Branch to MI5. Montagu's topic was worldwide war preparations: he had recently learnt, for example, that 'an officer of the British Army had visited Latvia to find out strategic military positions – an indication that preparations are being made in the case of a clash with Russia.' There was no prospect of war being averted by actions of the League of Nations (the disarmament proposals were so full of provisos they meant nothing), the British Empire (which allowed slavery to exist), or the Peace Army (which had declared that the war between China and Japan had been settled). The only way to prevent war, he argued, was 'by the masses organising and refusing to support any government which embarks on war'. Montagu no doubt expanded on these arguments in speaking on 'The Present Threatening Danger of War' to the Society for International Studies in Holborn on 24 February, and on 'War and Oppressed Nationalities' for the FSU at the Cypriot Club in Soho on 26 February.[56]

Then the main themes of the Amsterdam conference were reiterated at the National Congress Against War on 4–5 March, again held at the Bermondsey Town Hall. Amidst the usual vituperation against pacifists, the League of Nations and the imperialist powers, the 1,500 delegates heard pleas from a diverse range of speakers and came together in agreeing on a resolution that the most pressing task was the stopping of the transport of munitions. In seconding the resolution, Montagu urged comrades to realise the urgency of the situation, pointed out that the Soviet government's proposal in 1927 for the total suppression of all armed forces and all armaments had been dismissed as utopian, and declared that the working class was fighting to prohibit the use of armies in imperialist oppression. 'Are we going to allow ammunition to go to Hong Kong?' he asked. 'Are we to support the law in South Africa which allows a native who does not keep his contract to be flogged; are we to allow bombs to be dropped on Indian villages?'[57]

An Australian reporter who was far from sympathetic to what he perceived as the aggressive, anti-capitalist tenor of the Congress as a whole ('Many of the speakers made it clear that they were prepared to use all the engines of war against the capitalists') was impressed by Montagu, an 'arresting orator' whom he placed among the 'extremely interesting personalities' of the gathering:

> Born into the privileged classes, he showed his sympathy with the workers by a certain grubbiness of hands and a distinct negligence of attire.

He took up a fighting stance, put up his clenched fists, and looked as though he was prepared to engage in immediate and personal conflict with anyone who opposed him. He urged attack on anyone who prepared for war.[58]

Perhaps Ivor had become affected by the actors he was mixing with. For now, against all the expectations he had had after returning disillusioned from Hollywood, he was back firmly ensconced in the British film industry.

11

GAUMONT-BRITISH

FOR ALL MONTAGU'S engagement in radical politics, the cinema always retained a fascination for him. Even in early 1931, when his pronounced disgust with the commercial industry was at its height, he was elaborating a concept for a one-reel film that would incorporate his ideas about image and sound montage. *Cup Tie Special* was pitched to Mick Balcon at Gainsborough, and with the producer's encouragement Ivor went ahead and developed a full scenario. The notion had occurred to him when with a high-spirited football crowd on a train to Birmingham. 'By scripting into a musical pattern the actual sequence of sounds that occurs on such an excursion,' he suggested, 'it might be possible to recreate in an audience that mood of crowd enthusiasm.' His thoughts on audio-visual integration were evident in sequences such as:

> Zzz – zzz – zzz …
> Rattles come whirling against the background of the sky.
> Pff-pff-pff …
> Steam rising and puffing from the smokestack of an engine …
> Wheeee-oo,
> The Whistle shrieks a piercing, decisive signal … [1]

It was to be no avant-garde experiment for film society audiences alone. Release could be timed to coincide with the fourth round of the FA Cup competition, 'when public interest in such matters' – as he stressed to potential investors – 'is at its height throughout the country.' Gainsborough costed the film at £600–£700, which was unfortunately considered too much for a one-off short. Montagu then offered the project around, receiving an encouraging response from the Western Electric Company (which was presumably interested in showcasing its sound recording apparatus), and Balcon kept *Cup Tie Special* on the books at the studio through 1932. But nothing finally eventuated.[2]

In August 1931 a 19-year-old Oxford University dropout wrote to Montagu seeking his advice on how to get into the film industry. Ivor's reply was succinct: 'If your idea in going into the cinema in England would be to do good and intelligent work – I reply, whatever your qualities, impossible – out of the question.' His correspondent might wish to find congenial employment 'irrespective as to whether the product is worth while or no', but in that case he should be warned that 'if you enter the service of a British company to learn the business, they will pay you nothing as long as they can and as little as they can afterwards.'[3]

Clearly Montagu's opinion of the industry had not changed for the better, and for the time being he was content to remain a spectator. The Film Society, of which he was still a Council member, continued to offer audiences a challenging selection of the type of product that was not being manufactured in the British studios. In the years 1931–32 it showed, for example, Dziga Vertov's stunningly avant-garde documentary *Chelovek s Kino-Apparatom*/*Man with a Movie Camera* (USSR, 1929), Georg Wilhelm Pabst's adaptation of the Brecht-Weill *Die 3 Groschen Oper*/*The 3 Penny Opera* (Germany, 1931), Leontine Sagan's groundbreaking drama of lesbian attraction, *Mädchen in Uniform* (Germany, 1931), and Slatan Dudow's experimental political drama of unemployment and the Communist youth movement in Germany, co-scripted by Brecht, *Kuhle Wampe* (1932). Ilya Trauberg's innovative take on the revolutionary movement in China, *Goluboy Ekspress*/*China Express*/*The Blue Express* (USSR, 1929), with music by Edmund Meisel, was screened in April 1931 at Sidney Bernstein's theatre the Phoenix, since the usual Tivoli venue was unavailable; Bernstein's biographer Caroline Moorehead tells us that 'he was not put off when an anonymous letter threatened that the theatre would be blown up if he allowed such pernicious Russian propaganda to be shown.'[4]

In November that year, Dziga Vertov came to London in person with his new sound film, *Entuziazm/Enthusiasm* (USSR, 1931), an experimental documentary about the implementation of the Five-Year Plan in the Don Basin. For the Film Society screening, 'he sat in the back row of the Dress Circle clutching the sound box, with its red and black buttons for controlling the volume. During the second half of the last reel, when the film was showing the triumphs of Russian nationwide industrialisation, with howling wirelesses, blaring sirens, clattering of Bessemers and clanging of heavy machinery, Vertov seemed to go berserk.' According to Moorehead, 'He started pressing the red buttons over and over again until the building trembled and members of the audience, half-demented by the hoots and roars and jangles, fled the cinema' – or at least, as Society stalwart Sidney Cole recalled, pulled coats over their heads to minimise the impact. In Montagu's account of the incident, Vertov insisted on 'bending the bar of the projector that fixed a maximum volume for sound reproduction'. There was a struggle, Moorehead writes, to wrest control of the box from Vertov, who 'hung on grimly'. Thorold Dickinson, who had helped set up the screening, tried to hit him. 'Only when the reel finished in a cacophony of industrial sound,' she concludes, 'did Vertov, evidently well pleased with his sound effects, and uttering a loud grunt of satisfaction, yield up the box.'[5]

Montagu gave a retrospective report on the Film Society in an article he wrote for a new journal, *Cinema Quarterly*, in late 1932. Reflecting on the spread of repertory (arthouse) cinemas and more adventurous commercial exhibition practices, which meant that 'you can see films like *Hauptmann von Köpenick* in the West End, and like *M* and *Turksib* and *Le Million* all over the place,' he suggested 'it really is worth asking ourselves whether we have any excuse for being.' His conclusion was that the Society still had a role to play, firstly in mitigating the impact of the erratic censorship system, especially for societies outside London, and secondly in campaigning for relief from an inelastic interpretation of the Quota Act, which was making life difficult for the exhibitors of non-mainstream films.[6]

Publication of the article became an occasion for the resumption of hostilities between Montagu and his old foe George A. Atkinson of the *Express*. Recalling the early days of the Film Society, Ivor wrote: 'Atkinson – for reasons no one else has ever known and which he has possibly by now forgotten himself – thought it wiser suddenly to attack the Society for trying

to get Russian films he himself had recommended to it …' Atkinson immediately hit back in print, declaring:

> I withdrew, as many people know, because I had reached the absolute
> conviction that Ivor was far more interested in Soviet propaganda than he
> was in showing Russian films as a cultural device, and the full story of his
> connection with the work of the federated film societies in this country
> would show that I was right. I do not think that there would be any dif-
> ficulty in proving that the federated film societies in this country were,
> possibly still are, closely connected with the subversive activities of the
> Third International, and I do not think that Ivor, to do him justice, would
> dispute the fact.

Montagu's assailant was fudging a point here; the Federation of Workers'
Film Societies, by now virtually in abeyance, certainly had ties with the
Comintern, but the network associated with the Film Society in London,
with which the *Cinema Quarterly* article was concerned, just as certainly had
none. Ivor had ammunition to fight back; it would appear, though, that he
was unwilling to drag out the mud-slinging.[7]

The provincial societies basing themselves on the London model had
in fact only just come together in a Federation of British Film Societies,
formed in September 1932. Ivor, having attended the founding conference
and put forward the draft constitution, was in a good position to report on
the development in the *Week-End Review*. He stressed that the purpose of
the new body as a pressure group would be to campaign for uniform interpretation of censorship regulations and standard application of the 'privilege
for private performance' throughout the country, together with action in
parallel on the Quota Act issue. The Federation would promote the establishment of a 'permanent Commission to deal with all the special problems
of the non-commercial cinema' whose functions would include 'certifying
films for special duty and quota treatment' and 'certifying societies built on
certain model rules for uniform privileges'.[8]

It was at this time that Montagu became involved in the escalating dispute between Eisenstein and Upton Sinclair over their Mexican project,
Que viva México!. Sinclair, who had financed the film, had called a halt to
shooting in January 1932 after it had gone well over the initial budget.

Although the material was incomplete, Eisenstein was confident it could be restructured and looked forward to editing it in Moscow. However, negotiations between the various parties involved, both American and Soviet, to allow this to happen had broken down. On 29 September, having heard from Eisenstein that he was having a lot of 'bureaucratic troubles' over the shipment of the film, Montagu wrote to Sinclair. Film historians Harry M. Geduld and Ronald Gottesman record that he offered 'to use his influence with Eisenstein and the Russian authorities to see whether the differences could be settled amicably by the parties concerned and Eisenstein be enabled to cut and edit his picture.' Sinclair's reply was non-committal (Montagu thought it 'incredibly smug'); on 28 November Ivor wrote again ('softly', he told Eisenstein). After observing that the Russian director 'was a difficult person to deal with in matters of business,' he suggested 'a way in which Eisenstein might be able to cut the film in Russia without having to export the negative to the Soviet Union. A positive print could be made of all the available footage; Eisenstein could cut and edit the positive print and return the film to Hollywood to be matched there with the negative by a person in whom Eisenstein had confidence.' Regretfully, this eminently sensible suggestion was not taken up.[9]

A very public war of words erupted between Sinclair and Eisenstein supporters when a Hollywood-cut version of some of the material was released as *Thunder Over Mexico* in May 1933. Montagu fired off an early salvo in a letter published in the *New Clarion* 'condemning Sinclair for his "destructive impatience" in having the film cut by a hack editor.' He followed this up with an article in July in the same paper, asserting that 'Sinclair had impatiently ignored all offers to find a solution for *Que viva México!*, including an offer made by himself to "to help expedite matters".' As accusations and counter-accusations flew, Montagu came back one more time in January 1934 in an article in *The New Statesman and Nation*. 'What a storm over *Storm Over Mexico!*' he wrote. 'The plot is no new one. The work of art massacred by the insensitive Hollywood cutter is a legend as old as Stroheim, and the incorruptible artist shaking the dust of money-grubbing off his pants is a publicity story as ancient as Reinhardt.' He proceeded to take apart Sinclair's claims, entirely refuting the charge that Eisenstein was extravagant and impractical, though admitting that in saying he could make the film for $25,000 he was 'a perfectly sincere optimist and utterly irresponsible'. His conclusion was that 'the real tragedy of the Mexican film is not the loss of a doubtful masterpiece, nor even the issue of imperialist propaganda under a Soviet citizen's name. Too many sadder things are happening in the world for us to waste many a tear on these. The tragedy lies in the self-exposure of a man who for so many years has been in the forefront of the struggle for liberal ideas.'[10]

The article was published as one of the periodical columns Montagu had been writing since October 1932, when he was appointed the *Week-End Review*'s resident film critic. He contributed a review article on a fairly regular basis to the weekly magazine until the end of 1933, when it was incorporated in *The New Statesman and Nation*. His services were retained after the amalgamation, and he continued writing film reviews until May 1934.

Montagu remained as alert as he had been in his earlier stints as a critic to the aesthetic qualities of cinema, to the delights of comedy, the pleasure of immersion in a well-developed drama, and the beguiling appeal of stars. Though writing for an educated readership, he adopted a populist approach and avoided any taint of the highbrow, even giving Jean Cocteau's remarkable avant-garde tour de force *Le Sang d'un poète / The Blood of a Poet* (France, 1932) a negative notice. But what particularly distinguishes the new body of work from his earlier criticism is an enhanced emphasis – perhaps stemming in part from the critique of censorship he had been involved in – on two crucial dimensions of cinematic representation, the erotic and the ideological.

Ivor was smitten by Greta Garbo's appearance in *Grand Hotel* (October 1932). 'The Garbo has never been so young, so happy,' he wrote. 'Now, for the first time in an age, her eyes light up without afterthought as her lover approaches her ...' The all-star cast was the film's strength, 'for we make stars, like gods, in our own image. And whereas the God of our church is stern, good, wise, a sort of Freudian supercensor, the stars in their beauty, personality, fecklessness, represent for each of us an apotheosis of the libido.' He developed the thought later in the month:

Films are attacked for waking sexual curiosity in the young, for giving sexual pleasure to the old ... I challenge the whole basis of the attack. What is wrong with sexual curiosity or sexual pleasure? Has it ever done anyone any harm? There is not a shred of evidence that sexual indulgence (as opposed to over-indulgence, or self-indulgence – but the propaganda of that in films is another story) ever hurt a flea, or an infant for that matter ... '[11]

These columns may very well have caught the eye of his friend Dr Norman Haire, who was editing a series of books on sexology and psychology, and who now suggested to the publisher Allen Lane that Ivor be invited to contribute to the series a book on 'Sex and the Film'. Lane duly passed on the invitation, but Montagu, though 'very interested' in the proposition, was too busy on production work to take it up.[12]

In March 1933 Gustav Machaty's groundbreaking *Ekstase/Ecstasy* (Czechoslovakia/Austria, 1933) starring Hedy Kiesler (Lamarr) was shown at the Film Society. It was possibly the first film, outside pornography, to depict sexual intercourse and female orgasm. Montagu reviewed it in the *Week-End Review*, lamenting the fact that 'the public will never see this film until it is castrated. I am unsophisticated enough,' he continued, 'to find nakedness charming, in some people. I recognise, but am undismayed by, the erotic source of my pleasure in the lyric scenes in this film of the stallion's courtship. Unfortunately the censors are sure to recognise it also, and, pandering to repression, they will prevent, dear reader, these scenes from also delighting you.'[13]

The reviewer's prognostication proved correct, and *Ekstase* was banned; the public were, however, permitted to feast upon the sight of scantily clad beauties in Hollywood musicals such as the Eddie Cantor vehicles *The Kid from Spain* (1933) and *Roman Scandals* (1934). Of the former, Montagu wrote: 'The dances, accomplished by well-constructed women wearing over their primary and secondary sexual characteristics that minimum of veiling the vanishing of which would shatter the foundations of the British Empire, are often beautifully and symmetrically photographed from above.' The latter, in similar vein, placed on exhibition 'a collection of mammary glands so rich and varied that it must be of considerable value in the anthropological study of the American peoples.' Frankly, viewers (predominantly male) were deriving sexual satisfaction from the display of (near) nudity in film, and in Montagu's opinion the fact should be acknowledged and welcomed, without hypocrisy. In March 1934 he commented on *Search for Beauty* (USA, 1934), 'an exposure of the foul wens and dirty-minded publishers

Ivor's father Louis Montagu, 2nd Baron Swaythling: a prominent banker, he was active in Jewish causes, a keen shot, excellent golfer, and collector of japonaiserie. (By permission of the Labour History Archive, Manchester)

Ivor's sister Joyce and mother Gladys, Lady Swaythling, photograph by E.O. Hoppé: Montagu described his mother as 'very pretty, gay, charming, vivacious … constantly ready to laugh and pleased by jokes'. (Labour History Archive, Manchester / © 2017 Curatorial Assistance, Inc./E.O. Hoppé Estate Collection)

Ivor as a toddler: the family was newly minted aristocracy and one of the wealthiest in Britain. (By permission of the Labour History Archive, Manchester)

Ivor as a young boy: 'I was a spoiled brat.' (By permission of the Labour History Archive, Manchester)

Number 28 Kensington Court, London, Ivor's family home: its resplendent furnishings included lacquered cabinets, art nouveau fireplaces, and chairs upholstered in scarlet silk. (Russell Campbell)

Townhill Park House, near Southampton, the Swaythling country estate: the 1790s villa was restored and enlarged in 1911–12. (Russell Campbell)

Rat drawing by Ivor as a pupil at Westminster: he was given leeway to follow his zoological bent rather than drawing cylinders and pyramids in art class, but rebelled against the school's authoritarianism. (By permission of the Labour History Archive, Manchester)

Ivor Montagu as a young man: 'I think now that the reason for my lack of success in romance at this time was the fact that I had no social graces whatever.' (By permission of the Labour History Archive, Manchester)

Waxworks (frame): the Film Society champions experiment in the cinema with its first feature presentation, 1925. (Private collection)

Sverdlov Place and Bolshoi Theatre, Moscow, 1925, photograph by Montagu: at the Bolshoi he saw theatre, opera, ballet, and brachydactyl dwarf tumblers from England. (By permission of the Labour History Archive, Manchester)

Number 20 Old Buildings, Lincoln's Inn, Montagu's residence, *c.* 1925–27: his flat had an extremely narrow, winding staircase' and poky, low-ceilinged rooms. (Russell Campbell)

Montagu in Tiflis (Tbilisi), summer 1925: the city was scorching, as he set about procuring poison gas to smoke out the elusive *Prometheomys*. (By permission of the Labour History Archive, Manchester)

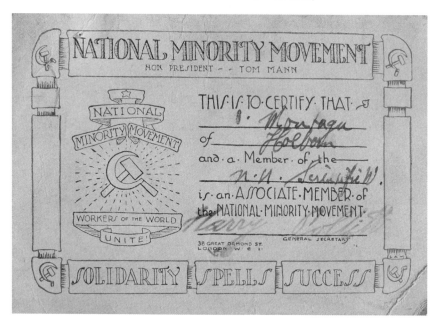

Montagu's National Minority Movement membership card, 1925: he was an activist in the National Union of Scientific Workers. (By permission of the Labour History Archive, Manchester)

General Strike, London, May 1926: Montagu was a cycling courier, delivering the *British Worker*. (By permission of the People's History Museum)

Above: Ivor and Eileen Montagu at the time of their wedding, 1927, photograph by Sasha: 'at least he managed to give her a satisfying languishing and romantic look.' (Getty Images/Hulton Archive)

Left: Number 6 Dansey Yard (now Place), Soho, premises of Brunel & Montagu Ltd: it featured a tiny office, a claustrophobic projection theatre, and minuscule cutting rooms. (Russell Campbell)

On the *Day-Dreams* set, 1928, a prize examplar of 'the aesthetics of play': (left to right)
Charles Laughton, Eileen Hellstern (continuity), Ivor Montagu, Renee de Vaux, Freddie
Young (camera), Elsa Lanchester, Lionel Rich (producer), Frank Wells (art director), Walter
Wichelow (make-up). (Courtesy of the BFI National Archive)

Elsa Lanchester in *Blue Bottles* (1929): firing satirical jabs at capitalist society's law
enforcement. (Courtesy of the BFI National Archive)

Blue Bottles (frame): 'in his employment of trick photography, unusual camera angles and symbolism, we observe a criticism of contemporary technique which blends very happily with its subject.' (Private collection)

Left: Montagu in a lighter moment: he had a 'warm and certainly idiosyncratic charisma'. (By permission of the People's History Museum)

Below: With George Bernard Shaw in *Melodie der Welt*, 1929 (frame): Montagu seated on a handy pile of bricks, concealing the fact that 'my old grey flannel trousers had a big hole in the seat through which my shirt projected.' (Private collection)

Leon Trotsky in his study, Prinkipo, Turkey, 1931: the exiled revolutionary had set up his headquarters in 'a spacious, dilapidated villa rented from a bankrupt pasha.' (Getty Images/ Hulton Archive)

The Man Who Knew Too Much (1934): Frank Vosper, Leslie Banks, Edna Best, Peter Lorre. Montagu was instrumental in the casting of Lorre, a political emigré from Germany. (Courtesy of Patrick McGilligan)

Hitchcock shooting *The 39 Steps* (1935), with Madeleine Carroll and Robert Donat:
'It had long been my conviction ... sustained by working with Hitchcock, that a good
director must have something of the sadist in him.' (Courtesy of Patrick McGilligan)

Secret Agent, 1936 (frame): Madeleine Carroll, John Gielgud, Peter Lorre. Montagu protested
that a switch in the ending to appease the censors 'destroys and makes nugatory the whole
carefully balanced thematic expression of the film.' (Private collection)

Sabotage, 1936 (frame): Sylvia Sidney. The American star was disturbed to the point of weeping by Hitchcock's fragmented manner of shooting, and Montagu, as associate producer, was called upon 'to embrace and comfort her as best he can.' (Private collection)

NEAL LAWSON

"SAK"

IVOR MONTAGU

"HARRY"

KINGSLEY MARTIN

ISOBEL BROWN CHARMED OUR BUS FARES HOME FROM OUR POCKETS!

SOME OF THE AUDIENCE

PROF. H. LASKI

MARO

"MARO" ATTENDS THE KINGSWAY HALL MEETING

Montagu features in a *Daily Worker* cartoon, 25 September 1933. At the meeting, attended by a crowd of 4,000, he presented the findings of the Commission of Enquiry into the burning of the Reichstag. (Private collection)

Hunger march demonstration, early 1930s: Montagu was one of several cameramen filming the February 1934 hunger march at Hyde Park for the Kino production unit. (By permission of the People's History Museum)

Ranelagh Gardens, Stamford Brook, London, the Montagu residence 1934–39: there was almost certainly no Communist Party branch in this comfortable middle-class suburb. (Russell Campbell)

Caricature of Montagu by Sergei Eisenstein, Moscow, 1936: Ivor paid a flying visit to the Soviet filmmaker to discuss the staging of battle scenes in *King Solomon's Mines*, which he was to direct. (By permission of the Labour History Archive, Manchester)

Behind the Spanish Lines, 1938 (frame): the filmmakers shot amidst the still-smoking rubble following Mussolini's aerial bombardment of Barcelona. (Private collection)

Left: Portrait of Montagu, *c.* 1930s: 'one of the first real intellectual artists of the cinema.' (By permission of the People's History Museum)

Below: The 15th CPGB Congress, Birmingham, 1938: Montagu spoke on the role of art and artists in the working-class movement, and shot coverage of the event with a Progressive Film Institute crew. (By permission of the People's History Museum)

Peace and Plenty (1939): the satirical puppet figure of Prime Minister Neville Chamberlain was crafted by Elsa Lanchester's mother. (Courtesy of the BFI National Archive)

Montagu's *Daily Worker* press pass, 1939: when the Soviet Union invaded Finland the paper asked him to go to Russia as a war correspondent, but he was refused an exit permit. (By permission of the Labour History Archive, Manchester)

'Knowle', Bucks Hill, Hertfordshire, Montagu's home 1939–54: in mid-1940, noticing suspicious goings-on, the local constabulary were keen to search the premises, but were advised by MI5 that 'such action would be a little premature at the present time.' Shortly afterwards, Montagu was recruited as an agent of Soviet military intelligence. (Russell Campbell)

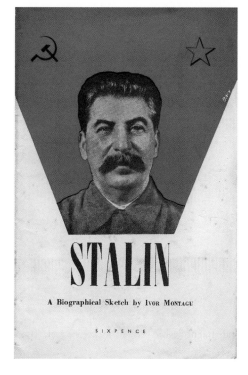

Montagu's pamphlet *Stalin: A Biographical Sketch* (1942): 'Who is not fortified in his own effort by the knowledge that Stalin's courage, Stalin's sagacity, Stalin's inflexible will are applied at the decisive point?' (Private collection)

Montagu, *c.* 1940s. His MI5 file noted that he 'has dark curly hair and is of distinctly Jewish appearance. His eyes are dark brown and his complexion is pale. He is generally rather dirty and untidy.' (Courtesy of the BFI National Archive)

Montagu receiving the Lenin Peace Prize, Moscow, 1959: 'the life of this man is a vivid example of a progressive representative of the Western intelligentsia finding his real calling in joint struggle with the people.' (By permission of the People's History Museum)

Montagu as elder statesman of radical film, *c.* 1980. (By permission of the People's History Museum)

who blot our civilisation by pretending to praise health and beauty, while at the same time exploiting the sensual pleasure of gazing at comely stripped bodies. As the film itself' – he pointedly remarked – 'pretends to praise health and beauty, while all the time exploiting the sensual pleasure of gazing at comely stripped bodies, I suppose there is a joke somewhere. Perhaps it lies in the fact that said sensual pleasure is altogether harmless and social, being one of the few we can enjoy without doing injury to our fellows.'[14]

Montagu kept up his critique of the censorship regime. '[S]pare a tear of sentiment for the Board of Film Censors,' he implored the public, 'a snowdrop of innocence growing on the dungheap of this evil world. The members of the Board were born very, very many years ago, gentle reader, before even Krafft-Ebbing was thought of and while the Marquis de Sade was still one of the Bright Young People of Paris society.' While the guardians of public morality censored sex and nudity, they had few qualms about violence, whether of the horror-movie type, as in *The Hounds of Zaroff* (*The Most Dangerous Game*, USA, 1932), or in a war film – the Board was prepared to approve for showing '*to little children!*' a 'piece of fiendish propaganda for war', *The Flag Lieutenant* (UK, 1932).[15]

Given his activism in the anti-war cause, Montagu was especially on the lookout for the ways in which military action was portrayed on screen. *The Flag Lieutenant* was:

the more diabolical because its propaganda is probably quite unconscious. Swathed in a veil of comedy and the decent story of an English naval officer whose admirable, if conventional, reticence and modesty lead to misunderstanding, lies a kernel of poison. For behind it is a calm taken-for-grantedness of the nobility of war, of the propriety of leading a life pledged, if need be, to kill obediently those with whom one has no quarrel, of the possibility of being a sportsman and yet pitting against the soft bodies of natives the hard might of armour-piercing shells. Tally-ho!

Similarly, the German nationalist epic *The Rebel* (*Der Rebell*, 1932), released in its English-language version in August 1933, was an inducement for war, 'a tocsin cry to the Germanic peoples to take revenge upon the French in 19— for the revenge taken by the French in 1919 for the revenge taken by the Germans in 1871 for what the French did about 1870.' Significantly, the

picture with its 'barbarous vendetta-theme' had been hailed by Propaganda
Minister Goebbels; it had 'as little merit as a film as a speech by Hitler has
as an essay in reasoned persuasion or the theory of the Aryan race has as a
serious contribution to anthropology.'[16]

The occasional film might carry a covert anti-militarist message. Thus
Smilin' Through (USA, 1932), a story of wartime love, 'for all its saccharine
and superficiality ... helps us to hate their guns and long to destroy them
from the face of the earth.' But this was an exception. Reviewing *I Was a
Spy* (UK, 1933), Montagu noted an alarming trend. Gone was the 'engulfing
of humanity by horror' which was the way warfare was depicted in *The Big
Parade, All Quiet on the Western Front, Westfront 1918*, and others of a few years
past. In the new picture:

> the sole dramatic contradiction is between a lauded desire to dish the
> enemy and a fright at the natural danger it puts one in, the consumma-
> tion of the conflict is the enemy's defeat ... What attraction can this film
> have, save the rousing of chauvinistic passion? ... One cannot escape the
> conclusion that, when the war-drums roll again and once more the shat-
> tered bodies begin to trickle back into the hospitals, the producers of this
> film will be able to comfort themselves with the reflection that they have
> helped to prepare each citizen to do his bit.[17]

The filming of Noël Coward's play *Cavalcade* (USA, 1933) enabled Ivor
to skewer the class (to which he himself of course belonged) responsible
for war:

> a class that arrogates to itself the name of England. A class that throughout
> thirty-odd years is shown never once doing a scrap of productive work,
> and whose only contact with its servants is to ridicule them. A class whose
> only message of hope for the future is that courage and sacrifice and loy-
> alty have produced murder and misery and waste for thirty years, so let us
> go on being courageous and self-sacrificing and loyal ...

Meanwhile, the British working class was being represented 'as consisting
solely of jovial, half-witted clowns ... No one ever saw the like, except with
Negroes or farmers, in an American film.'[18]

Documentary, of course, was the exception; but Montagu seldom commented on the productions of Grierson's GPO Film Unit or other nonfiction filmmakers. Over one important film, however, he did engage in the critical debate. This was Robert Flaherty's *Man of Aran*, released in April 1934. In a lengthy *New Statesman* review, he attacked the reverence accorded documentary film – by Dziga Vertov, for example – 'as though it constituted a particle of Absolute Truth'. *Man of Aran*, he argued, was 'rare, austere, and moving … But still a document that presents only one side.' Man's struggle with nature was 'incomplete unless it embraces the struggle of man with man', and Flaherty's film omitted the impact on his protagonists' lives of ruthless landlords, steep tariffs on cattle, and the economic crisis. Then in the *Daily Worker* he returned to the fray with a more overt political slant, criticising regular critic Dave Bennett's laudatory review of the film. Flaherty, he wrote, was 'not just going to "remote, primitive corners of the earth where the class struggle doesn't exist." There are no such places. What Flaherty is really doing is something much worse. Pretending that the class struggle can be ignored or doesn't reach to "romantic" places a long way away.' *Man of Aran* was a lying fairy tale. Exploitation and oppression 'exists on Aran as elsewhere, and the harm of Flaherty's work lies in its being so cleverly made that it blinds us to the fact that, from the social point of view, it is just as much fake as any other capitalist film.'[19]

British pictures seldom alluded to the Depression, but American movies, Montagu observed, were not so reticent. The problem was the solutions they came up with. *Working Wives* (*Week-End Marriage*, 1932) was 'presumably designed to cure America's 12,000,000 unemployment problem by inducing all the wives to quit their jobs.' *He Learned About Women* (1933) offered 'the old soup-kitchen method' of the rich giving their surplus to the poor. *Mr. Robinson Crusoe* (1932) suggested 'abolishing civilisation and returning to the spinning-wheel'. The proposal of *Invisible Power* (*Washington Merry-Go-Round*, 1932) was 'thorough-going Nazi … kill off all the naughty people, and then only the nice ones will be left'; while the remedy proffered by *Gabriel Over the White House* (1933) was actually 'naked Hitler-Fascism' with 'the incorporation of the unemployed into military camps at cut-wages'. *Prosperity* (1932) put forward 'nothing less than the latest scheme of our friend Professor Miles Walker. Put all the people lying idle on to helping themselves with the material lying idle.' The difficulty was how to persuade the people who owned the material to let it be employed for free, 'without using a gun on them' – a problem the movie conveniently sidestepped.[20]

Whatever their ideological shortcomings, American films continued to rate more highly than the British in entertainment value. Montagu compared *Working Wives* with *Men of To-morrow* (1932), a UK production directed by Leontine Sagan, a 'beautiful piece of work' which nonetheless lacked pace and energy. 'Hollywood's supremacy is not just a question of technical experience or wider markets. It is the result of a faster rate of social living ... Everybody who made *Working Wives*, from scenarist to cutter, was infected with that liveliness; no audience that sees the two films together can fail to realise the kernel of the British problem.'[21]

Montagu's pessimism about the local film industry was thus, it would seem, confirmed. And yet there were glimmers of hope. *Rome Express* (1932) was 'a British film that invites comparisons with the outstanding American productions of the day ... From scenarist to scissors, a fine team has combined to make a much smoother unity than *Grand Hotel*, a story in which the intricacies of the plot are much more deftly blended, and its development never dragging.' *The Good Companions* (1933), a musical based on a J.B. Priestley novel, admirably evoked sympathy for its characters and was 'an example of a film job effectively and feelingly done'. Finally, there was *Orders is Orders* (1933), which 'starts well, goes on better, and finishes best. It has form, it has a riotous pace beside which the languorous pallidities of crisis-stricken Hollywood are snail-like and insipid, it has character and is magnificently funny. Believe it or not, this is a British film.'[22]

In the case of these positive reviews, however, there was a certain undeclared conflict of interest, for all three of the films he praised were productions of the Gaumont-British Picture Corporation, the firm for which Montagu had been working since October 1932. In that month, to make a bit of money, but possibly also with the belief that some good work might be done, Ivor heeded a call from Michael Balcon and re-entered the industry.

It was a crisis situation, and 'Mick must have remembered his troubleshooter.' A musical directed by the itinerant Italian veteran Carmine Gallone was about to go into production at the British Lion studios at Beaconsfield, Buckinghamshire, as a joint venture with Gaumont-British. *King of the Ritz* was to be an English-language adaptation of the Henry Kistemaekers play *Le Roi des palaces*, which Gallone had already filmed under that title in France;

Betty Stockfeld was being retained from that production, to star alongside Stanley Lupino. The problem was, according to Montagu's later recollection, that it had 'a script so flatulent it needed at least £10,000 taken out of it before shooting started' – and it was 'due to go on the floor in exactly three days' time.' The fact that it was a musical and he was, as he confessed, tone-deaf did not deter him. Ivor pleaded for and received a week's postponement of the shoot, duly revised the script, and oversaw the production as filming commenced. Though his engagement was to have been a one-off appointment, 'just a few weeks', Balcon was obviously pleased enough with Montagu's performance to offer him a permanent job, and he was placed under contract at £25 a week as an associate producer. (Modestly, Montagu explains: 'It may seem odd that I was to be entrusted with so responsible a task, but in those days the aura of Hollywood was so elevated that any Britisher who had visited the place and came back alive found some of it rub off on him.')[23]

Gaumont-British at the time Montagu joined it was the largest film company in the world outside the USA, with more than 14,000 employees. The Ostrer brothers, merchant bankers, had bought out Léon Gaumont's interests when he had withdrawn from Britain, and had proceeded to create a powerful vertically-integrated combine by strategic acquisition of production companies, distributors and cinema chains. Among the companies now fully integrated into the Ostrer empire was Gainsborough, with its studio at Islington, and Balcon had become Head of Production both there and at G-B's main studio at Lime Grove, Shepherd's Bush, supervising an output of twenty or more films a year. Above him in the company hierarchy were managing directors Mark Ostrer and C.M. Woolf, to whom the president, Isidore Ostrer, delegated most responsibility in the film production side of the business.[24]

Balcon recalled that 'none of us, in those days, so far as I know, had any particular sympathy with Ivor's political outlook but we all admired him, not only for his high intellectual attainments (he was a biologist of some stature) but for his warm and generous nature.' The producer noted, as MI5 informants had done, that Montagu was not a classy dresser: 'Perhaps as part of his "rebellion", he was completely indifferent to conventional clothes and I rarely if ever saw him in anything other than a tweed coat and slacks, with a woollen sweater as an alternative.'[25]

The associate producer (AP), Montagu explains, was 'someone who deputises for the producer-in-chief [Balcon] and exercises his authority in relation to a fraction of the projects undertaken by the chief.' At G–B two or three pictures a year would be allotted to each AP, who was 'charged with acting as parent substitute at every stage from conception to delivery.' Montagu took his place alongside a handful of other APs, who included his old friend Angus MacPhail (who also headed the scenario department), Chandos Balcon (Mick's brother), and Edward Black, formerly the proprietor of a theatre chain that G–B had bought out.[26]

'My theory has always been that the ideal associate producer puts his feet up on his desk or reads a book because he's organised everybody so well he doesn't have to say anything after the picture's started,' Montagu was later to recount. Certainly, progress on *King of the Ritz* was sufficiently in hand by the end of January 1933 to enable him take a week off to attend the World Table Tennis Championships at Baden bei Wien in Austria (the England men's team won a bronze). Back at Beaconsfield he oversaw the final phase of post-production, and the picture was released in March. Montagu left no record of how well he got on with Gallone, nominally the producer as well as director of the film, but he retained fond memories of the experience: 'Production was smooth enough,' he asserted, 'to get an Academy Award nomination in that year.' It was an apocryphal claim. *King of the Ritz* met with a fairly cool critical reception: it was 'by no means without the faults that ruin so many photographed plays,' opined *The Times* reviewer. 'It makes a desperate attempt to be bright and frivolous, but there is something wooden and over self-conscious about it, and it never achieves either ingenuity or freshness.' It did not feature among the top fifty box-office releases in Britain in 1933.[27]

Montagu next got involved, it would seem, in researching and scripting *Northbound*, an adventure story based on the ill-fated flight of Umberto Nobile's airship *Italia* in the Arctic in 1928. Survivors were rescued by the Soviet icebreaker *Krassin*. 'It is disconcerting,' observes Geoff Brown, 'to find the bastion of the Film Society and promoter of Soviet film art bashing out rabid clichés at the typewriter in a hunt for commercial success.' The treatment featured a romantic encounter between the second wireless operator and a young Spitzbergen woman 'taken erotically as far as we wish' and 'a scene of broths and warm fires and wrapping and puppy dog sentiment on board the icebreaker'. Ivor was clearly in a cynical mood. The film was not made.[28]

The writer/director/producer carried over this somewhat equivocal attitude to his subsequent project, again an adventure story, though this time a documentary. The *Manchester Guardian* on 4 April announced that the Houston Everest expedition had met with 'complete success … the world's highest mountain has surrendered to the all-conquering aeroplane.' Saluting the 'splendid achievement', it asked: 'What strange account will the adventurers have brought back of Everest and its great south face as no living eye has seen it? What strange photographs and film record may they have obtained for the rest of us to share – of the unknown Himalayas, looked at from a height higher than bird has ever gone?'[29]

The expedition had indeed been filmed, by a small crew of cameramen directed by Geoffrey Barkas. *Wings Over Everest* was to be a major G-B featurette production, and Montagu was put in charge of integrating the footage into an extended narrative that would tell the whole tale of the enterprise, including reconstructed sequences of the preparations made for the aerial assault on the peak. Since this offered an opportunity for the British upper crust who had funded and mounted the venture to satirise themselves without realising it, it appealed to the mischievous side of Montagu's nature.[30]

He was most pleased ('a gem of a scene') with a sequence in which the immensely wealthy Lady Houston, who put up the money for the expedition, discusses the project with its leader, Lord Clydesdale. The benefactress was not feeling well, so she was filmed sitting up royally in bed in her Scottish mansion, sporting a fur wrap and a turban 'with the largest emerald in the world'. The 76-year-old was insistent that she be made up to look young. 'However, when we went to film her,' Montagu was to recall with relish, 'it was very very sad, the sagging elderly flesh had been made up and made up and made up and it still sagged. The more it was made up the more tired it got.'[31]

'But isn't it most terribly dangerous?' the patriotic philanthropist enquires of the intrepid young pilot. 'No more than walking across Hampstead Heath on a foggy night,' he offhandedly replies. As a determined defender of the Empire, Lady Houston was keen to do anything that might help thwart the drive for Indian independence. Hence, as she explains on camera, 'What appeals to me is that the people of India, if this is a success, and it's going to be a success, will then know that we are not the decadents that their leaders are trying to make us out to be.' (Montagu remembered 'trying to deflect her from fierce references to Gandhi, currently fasting and in danger of dying. 'He has high blood pressure,' she countered. 'It does him good to fast.')[32]

Interviewed for television late in life, Montagu related that 'when Woolf and his cronies came out from seeing it they were clutching each other in hysterics of laughter.' It really was, he contended, 'the most absurd thing ever made – but truthful, not of the upper class but of the way they would see themselves.'[33]

The four-reel *Wings Over Everest* was eventually released in June 1934, on a bill with another Gallone musical remake, *Two Hearts in Waltz Time*. Montagu shared the directing credit with Barkas. Critics praised the sequences detailing the careful construction of the aircraft ('a few pounds too much, and the plane might fail to cross the summit,' the narrator explains), the spectacular aerial photography, and the unobtrusive commentary. They were, on the whole, less enthusiastic about the dramatised dialogue scenes. The *Observer* critic, clearly attuned to Montagu's point of view, declared that the film, 'as a study in the engaging nonchalance of the Englishman in face of danger … is successful in the highest degree.' Paul Rotha, however, writing in *Sight and Sound*, felt that:

> the English sequence of preparation … lacks the planned construction of good documentary, its style too chatty for conviction. This is accentuated by the 'Play up, you chaps!' attitude adopted throughout by most of the persons appearing in the film and stamps the whole picture with that false sincerity associated with the fifth form.

Similarly, the *Bookman* reviewer felt that the dramatisation, though ingenious and lively, 'seems to me to suffer from an air of too elaborate contrivance … all this popularisation, though it is deftly done and keeps wholly free from false heroics, is at the expense of the film's documentary character.'[34]

In 1936, *Wings Over Everest* won an Academy Award for Best Short Subject (Novelty). Its American running time, twenty-two minutes, was just over half that of its length on British release (forty-two minutes). Perhaps the contentious dramatised scenes had been cut.

Work at Gaumont-British did not preclude anti-fascist campaigning (see Chapter 12) or other forms of activity. In February 1934 Montagu lectured at Marx House, Clerkenwell Green, on 'Art and Propaganda' and 'The Films', and led a Distinguished Guests debate at the University of London Union, proposing the motion: 'That the Film is now Pre-eminent in the World of Dramatic Art.' On 18 February he sent his agent J. Ralph Pinker, in response to a publisher's request for a book on the modern film, 'the long delayed film synopsis'. The material, he explained, 'will take chiefly the form of anecdotes and generalisations from them. It will endeavour to be polemical and suggestive, rather than exhaustive, and will not at any point be usable as a technical manual.' There was no reason why, he confidently asserted, 'in the event of a contract, the work should not proceed steadily.' Whether the anecdotal approach did not appeal, or for some other reason, the project did not proceed.[35]

Meanwhile Montagu began what was to be his priority at the studio, supervising all the pictures Alfred Hitchcock was to make for the corporation. Hitch had been at a loose end following *Waltzes from Vienna* (1933), made independently, and Balcon was pleased to sign him up. His first project was an espionage thriller, *The Man Who Knew Too Much*, that he had begun developing with the writer Charles Bennett. Montagu became involved in the scripting workshops for the film, which established a pattern for all of Hitchcock's projects at G-B. They were generally held in the sitting room at Hitchcock's home, with the director holding court in black silk pyjamas. Sometimes Alma Hitchcock, Alfred's wife and collaborator, would be there; sometimes, too, Angus MacPhail. 'The unfolding story,' Montagu relates, 'was elaborated with suggestions from all of us; everything was welcome, if not always agreed.' The story conferences were 'a feast of fancy and of dialectic, a mixture of composing crosswords and solving them, both laced with humour.' The notes from these sessions would be consolidated into a screenplay by Bennett. Other writers might be called upon too, especially to work on the dialogue, but the final sign-off was Hitchcock's; neither Montagu nor Balcon overruled him.[36]

In later years Montagu was to assert, 'I knew that I couldn't make political statements in films that would reach the general public because of all the barriers that there were.' Certainly the films he produced at G-B are devoid of any specific left-wing content. But he slipped a little class caricature into *Wings Over Everest*, and the Hitchcock thrillers he supervised were to allude, unmistakably even if obliquely, to the growing menace of war and fascism. In *The Man Who Knew Too Much* there is a particularly pointed piece of dialogue. The official from the Foreign Office asks the parents of the kidnapped child: 'Tell me, in June 1914, had you ever heard of a place called Sarajevo? Course you hadn't. I doubt if you'd even heard of the Archduke Ferdinand. But in a month's time, because a man you'd never heard of killed another man you'd never heard of in a place you'd never heard of, this country was at war.'[37]

The plot was given chilling substance with the casting of Peter Lorre to play the principal villain opposite Leslie Banks and Edna Best. Montagu had heard from Willi Münzenberg's offsider Otto Katz that Lorre, celebrated for his portrayal of the child murderer in Fritz Lang's *M*, was penniless and living in a Paris boarding house with other anti-Nazi refugees. Excited, Ivor arranged with Balcon for Lorre to come to London, and he was signed up for the production, despite his limited command of English. Initially cast in a smaller role, Lorre was switched to playing the criminal mastermind at Hitchcock's insistence.[38]

Shooting, at the Shepherd's Bush studio, took place between 29 May and 2 August – a generous schedule. Recently rebuilt and enlarged, the spacious studio complex boasted five production stages (four sound-proofed), a rooftop equipped for outdoor filming, a heated water tank for maritime scenes, an orchestration theatre, a laboratory, and all the ancillary facilities required. But it had its drawbacks. There was no backlot – and since location filming was difficult, costly and therefore rare, outdoor scenes frequently had an artificial look to them. There was inadequate dressing room accommodation and no storage space, so sets had to be broken down after each production. And none of the stages was on the ground floor, with the result that scenery had to be carried up piecemeal in massive lifts.[39]

Hitchcock made the most of the advantages and the drawbacks. He was, says Montagu, 'a joy to work with', infinitely patient and popular with cast and crew. From the AP's perspective, his great virtue was that he was 'a superb visual director and he never built an inch of a set that wasn't needed for the shot, which he'd worked out beforehand. Many of the British producers in those days used to build a four-walled set, stand in the middle of it and make up their minds what the action was to be, and then move away the wall that got in the way. And that of course was very expensive ...'[40]

After negotiation with the censors over the climactic scene based on the 1911 Siege of Sidney Street, *The Man Who Knew Too Much* was completed and screened for the studio's top brass. At this point a crisis arose, of which there are numerous, conflicting, accounts, including from Montagu. What seems to have happened is that the Ostrer brothers were uncertain about the film's appeal and referred the matter to Woolf, who was standing in as production chief while Balcon was away in the United States. Woolf summoned Hitchcock, told him the film was appallingly rubbish, and ordered Maurice Elvey to shoot some new scenes to be inserted. Hitch, according to one account, was 'practically suicidal'; Montagu, however, was able to obtain a delay until Balcon could determine the issue.[41]

In the interim Woolf demanded to see the new script the team were working on – *The 39 Steps*, an adaptation of the John Buchan thriller – decided that it too was worthless, and gave Hitchcock and Montagu a month's notice, during which time they were to develop a screenplay based on the life of Leslie Stuart, composer of the hit turn-of-the-century musical *Florodora*. 'Fortunately Mick came back in time,' Montagu relates, 'to save both us and the studio.' *The Man Who Knew Too Much* was released as originally filmed in December 1934 and proved both a critical and a popular success. Development of *The 39 Steps* was allowed to proceed. And several months later Woolf quit Gaumont-British.[42]

Meanwhile, Montagu had other productions on his hands. *My Old Dutch*, released in October 1934, was a sentimental warhorse based on a popular 1890s music hall song by Albert Chevalier. First filmed as a US short in 1911, the tale of a cockney couple's life was expanded to feature length in England in 1915 and remade in Hollywood in 1926. The sound version, shot at the Gainsborough studio in Islington under the direction of Sinclair Hill, starred Betty Balfour and Michael Hogan. This retelling offered a panorama of the tribulations of the pair and their family over several generations, focusing particularly on the war years, and ingeniously incorporated footage from the 1915 version featuring Chevalier himself. The theme, 'the struggles of a typical workman and his wife to make a career for their son', could well have appealed to Montagu, the film becoming a working-class counterpart, replete with scenes set during the General Strike, to the upper-class *Cavalcade*. The middle-class reviewers of the *Manchester Guardian* and the *Observer* were tellingly condescending: 'Not without merit in its class, which is heavily sentimental'; 'It would be idle to pretend that it will not be an unqualified success all up and down our simple and very sentimental country.' But the trade papers praised Hill's direction, said to 'leave little or nothing to be desired', and commented that 'unusual care was taken with regard to detail for a relatively unpretentious picture.'[43]

My Heart is Calling, released in January 1935, would have been less to Montagu's taste. Another joint-production musical comedy under the direction of Carmine Gallone, it had already been filmed as *Mein Herz ruft nach dir* in Germany and *Mon coeur t'appelle* in France. Jan Kiepura starred in all three versions as the tenor in a touring opera company challenging the incumbent ensemble at the opera house in Monte Carlo, with the assistance of a female stowaway played (in this and in the German original) by Martha Eggerth. *My Heart is Calling* broke no box-office records but seems to have been reasonably well received: the *Times* reviewer complained that the presentation of a 'mutilated' *Tosca* was heavy-handed, but that frivolity was the film's strength, and at its best it was 'amusing, occasionally witty, and always fast-moving'.[44]

The US release of *The Man Who Knew Too Much* was hampered through its stars being unknown that side of the Atlantic. Balcon was making a determined bid for G-B to break into the American market, and hence for *The 39 Steps* the leading roles went to actors who had had some exposure in the US, Robert Donat and Madeleine Carroll. 'When we cast Madeleine Carroll,' Montagu recalls, ' ... we chose her for her beauty, which Hitch, with his precise sarcasm, designated as "glossy".' Her part, which did not exist in the Buchan original, was expanded to cater for certain Hitchcockian predilections. 'We deliberately wrote the script,' Montagu continues, 'to include her undignified handcuff scene on the bed, and being led out from under the waterfall looking like a drowned rat.' Hitchcock biographers have detailed the rough treatment the director inflicted on his star during the shoot, leading to accusations of sadism. Montagu refutes the charge: 'Madeleine was a trouper,' he claims, 'and turned the tables on us by appreciating this treatment and asking for more ... This quality in her was what enabled her to play perfectly both the spiteful resentment and, credibly, the build-up to final reconciliation with the hero.' As to sadism:

It had long been my conviction … sustained by working with Hitchcock, that a good director must have something of the sadist in him. I do not necessarily mean to a pathological degree, but that his looking at things and telling characters to do this, undergo that, is necessarily akin to dominating them, ordering them about.[45]

As with *The Man Who Knew Too Much*, this espionage thriller carried anti-fascist overtones. Raymond Durgnat mentions the Gestapo-like leather coats of the villain's henchmen and the depiction of the villain himself (played by Godfrey Tearle), 'a squirearchical character almost as charming and gracious as Sir Oswald Mosley', leader of the British Union of Fascists. The man is traitor rather than foreigner, with an alarmingly extensive network of collaborators, and as Mark Glancy has argued, the story 'portrays Britain as a country threatened as much by its own disunity and lethargy as it is by any foreign power.'[46]

Filmed January–March 1935 and released in June, *The 39 Steps* was given much more extensive publicity and studio backing than its predecessor, and reaped the rewards. Well received critically (though Alistair Cooke and Graham Greene were lukewarm), it became one of the top British box-office hits of the year, boasting a record run of five continuous months' business in the West End of London. It also achieved impressive results in the United States, particularly New York. G-B Chairman Mark Ostrer singled the film out in his annual address to shareholders, describing it as 'a milestone in the history of our industry'.[47]

While raising Hitchcock's profile, its success undoubtedly consolidated Montagu's position at G-B, which had again been in doubt. A disagreement in February had led to his giving notice of his intention to resign once he had completed his current assignments, from which he was only dissuaded by earnest intervention on the part of Mick Balcon. The production chief put in writing his appreciation of Ivor's work and his attempts to resolve the dispute ('I for one am more than grateful for the way in which you are trying to help in the present emergency over certain matters'). Ivor was only partially mollified, since in March he reaffirmed that he was 'planning to discontinue my present employment'. Polite wrangling with management, including argument over an overdue holiday, continued in Balcon's absence.[48]

The dispute Balcon refers to was apparently an issue of industrial relations at the studio, since he goes on to say that 'any small changes which are
being made now are made with a desire to make better working conditions
all the way round.' And thus it may be the occasion on which Montagu
was instrumental in thwarting an attempt by G-B management to organise
its employees in a company union. It was at G-B, back in 1933, that agitation among studio workers had led to the formation of the Association
of Cinematographic Technicians (ACT). The union – whose membership
included directors, cameramen, sound technicians, editors, and art department and laboratory workers – met with stiff opposition from the employers,
and made little headway until George Elvin, formerly an organiser for the
British Workers' Sports Association, was appointed General Secretary in
January 1934. Montagu was involved, although he described the atmosphere
at that time as being 'very snobbish' – people 'didn't want to degrade themselves by being associated with the idea of a trade union'; a Conservative MP
(Sir Reginald Mitchell Banks) was recruited to serve as president.[49]

But with effective organisation at grassroots level, pressure on the studios
to improve the low wages and often dismal working conditions endured by
technicians gradually built up. Montagu was elected vice-president of the
union in May 1935, and at the AGM in May 1936 he took the chair. 'We all
knew Ivor Montagu was made for the job,' the ACT journal reported, 'but
the way he steered through this super-production at the speed of a "quickie"
without, however, refusing anybody a hearing or rushing past essential business, brought forth paeans of praise.'[50]

The organisation at that time was on a high note, membership having
grown from 88 to 900 in the course of a year. Nevertheless, resistance from
the employers remained strong. Julius Hagen at Twickenham gave union
members 'one hour in which to decide whether to leave the ACT or the
studio', while G-B 'dithered between taking the same action as Hagen
or forming a company union of their own.' According to Montagu's
account, 'Some tried to organise a company union and sell the idea to
Mick. Now Mick is a man of very decent instincts and very fine to work
with but he doesn't always see things that are new to him clearly right
away.' Management called a mass meeting, but evidently fearful of a hostile
reception, or thinking better of the idea, Balcon did not show up. Montagu
took the chair, 'Mick didn't come up, the meeting was adjourned, it was

dispersed and the manager, Boxall, was authorised to recognise the union.' It was a breakthrough, which led to other studios following suit and eventually, in December 1936, to ACT's negotiation of a collective agreement with G-B at Shepherd's Bush, its first studio contract.[51]

Meanwhile, back on the job, an indication of the difficulties Montagu faced in performing his supervisory duties is given by a letter he wrote in April 1935 to Chandos Balcon, who was the first port of call for APs with problems and stood in for his brother during Mick's frequent absences overseas. The film was *The Passing of the Third Floor Back*; the director, the Austrian Berthold Viertel. Montagu was being instructed to put pressure on Viertel to be more economical in his shooting, forgoing shots that were not necessary; he informed management that with this director it was not possible ['owing to the nature of his limitations (and qualities) he is unable to visualise their unnecessaryness before he sees them on the screen, and there is therefore no common ground for discussion']. Montagu was over-ruled; he applied the pressure; Viertel went over his head to the corporation executives, who thereupon supported the director and thus undermined Montagu's position. Ivor protested that this eroded his authority, not only with Viertel, but also with other directors ('How can it be expected that Hitchcock, for instance, will continue, to the reasonably disciplined extent he has hitherto observed, to discuss with me and persuade me to any extra scene and expenses, if another director is not obliged to'). If the protest had any effect, it was clearly not enough to satisfy him: several weeks later he wrote again to Chandos, asking if he might to quit his employment before the picture was finished.[52]

His wish was not granted; and things had clearly changed by the latter half of the year (and, perhaps significantly, after Woolf's departure). In October Montagu received a new contract as Associate Producer, backdated to 1 May, at a salary of £80 per week, more than three times what he received when first employed in the job.[53]

In the second half of May, Montagu took his long-delayed holiday, journeying with Hell to France and Switzerland. In the resort town of Kandersteg, Hitchcock and Charles Bennett joined them and the party drove on to the Lauterbrunnen Valley. Here they spent days roaming round its woodlands and waterfalls with an eye to possible locations for Hitch's next project, *Secret Agent*, and 'talking the story over day and night'.

Back in England, Montagu entered the London tennis championships at Queen's Club, West Kensington, and was pitted against a young American newcomer, Don Budge (who sported 'possibly the reddest hair that has ever been seen on a lawn tennis court'). It was a brief match: Budge 'disposed of the Hon. Ivor Montagu by 6-0, 6-0 in what must be nearly record time.'[54]

Ivor returned to work. *The Passing of the Third Floor Back* was in post-production. Starring Conrad Veidt in the role of a mysterious Christ-like stranger who transforms the miserable lives of the inhabitants of a run-down boarding house, it was based on a pre-war story and play by Jerome K. Jerome that had been previously filmed in 1918. There were obvious religious connotations, but Viertel was 'a Marxist of sorts', and the story also had, in this version, a 'rigour of class analysis' which Sue Harper contends 'should probably be attributed to him' – but might also have been abetted by Montagu. Released in October, the film received mixed reviews – a typical middlebrow critic again having problems with sentimentality and 'the inscrutable mysteries of taste' – but it was enjoyed (to his surprise, he confessed) by Graham Greene: 'The pious note has been toned down, the milk of human kindness in the original play has been agreeably watered, and the types in the small London "private hotel" are observed with malicious realism.'[55]

Outside work Montagu remained active in the Film Society, which continued to treat its members to rich cinematic experiences not otherwise available. Highlights in the years 1933–35 included Pudovkin's *Prostoy sluchay/A Simple Case* (1932) and *Dezertir/Deserter* (1933), Fritz Lang's *Das Testament von Dr. Mabuse/The Testament of Dr. Mabuse* (1933), Jean Vigo's *Zéro de conduite* (1933) and *L'Atalante* (1934), and in avant-garde territory, Jean Cocteau's *Le Sang d'un poète/Blood of a Poet* (1932), Berthold Bartosch's *L'Idée/The Idea* (1932), and experimental shorts by Oskar Fischinger and László Moholy-Nagy.

A heroic achievement was the exhibition of Eisenstein's *Oktyabr/October* (1928), never before seen in Britain, in March 1934. 'Gigantic 13-reeler, lasted 2½ hours,' reported the *Daily Express*, 'punctuated by bursts of applause from well-fed Red intelligentsia.' The Edmund Meisel score had been composed for the much shorter German version of the film, and the conductor (Ernest Irving from Ealing studios), had only a day to rehearse with the orchestra in an attempt to make it fit. As Montagu explained, since 'Meisel arranged every note to correspond to a movement on the screen this was not just not easy, it was bloody impossible. Ernest performed miracles, but as the picture approached its finish the end of the score was racing the end title and it was a problem of which would reach the winning post first.' The orchestra, it seems, was made to repeat the last chords of the score 'eleven times, very slowly'. By such means the conductor made sound and image 'arrive within a few bars of each other', and when the end title came up, he 'hurled his baton high into the air'; the house, Montagu recalls, 'was ecstatic.'[56]

Seated behind Ivor, it was reported, was H. G. Wells, 'who clapped loudly when Lenin appeared on the screen.' The 'Red intelligentsia' were given a further opportunity to salute their hero in October 1935, when the Film Society showed Vertov's *Tri pesni o Lenine / Three Songs of Lenin* (1934). In preparation for the screening, the titles giving the words of the 'songs' were literally translated from the Russian by Montagu, and then passed to W. H. Auden, at the time working at the G.P.O. Film Unit, to be rendered into verse. Thus 'My face was in a dark prison/Blind was my life/without light or learning/I was a slave though unchained/but into this dark came a light-ray/The ray of truth of Lenin' became the more mellifluous, and rhyming, 'My face in a dark prison lay/And blind my life remained/No learning mine nor light of day,/A slave although unchained/Till through my darkness shone a ray/And Lenin's truth I gained.' At the screening the poetic paean to the dead dictator was received, as it had been in the Soviet Union, with strong emotion; Wells had declared: 'It is one of the greatest and most beautiful films I have ever seen.' (Two years later Stalin, determined that the cult of personality not be restricted to Lenin, arranged for a number of shots linking the two leaders to be inserted, and an additional section showing how he was carrying on Lenin's work to be added.)[57]

At Gaumont-British, Montagu was busy on a crime drama, *The First Offence*, a remake of Billy Wilder's first feature, *La Mauvaise Graine* (France, 1934). A low-budget 'quota quickie', it told the story of the spoilt son of a wealthy family joining a gang of car thieves. As with the Gallone films, some of the original cast were retained, but the French leads were replaced by John Mills and Lilli Palmer. Direction was in the hands of former theatre impresario Herbert Mason. Released as a second feature in March 1936, it created little stir, although Gill Plain observes that it was one of two films that 'worked to construct Mills as a prototypical English action hero'.[58]

Studio memos that have survived from this period indicate that, apart from the films he personally supervised, Montagu was involved in a broad range of pre-production decisions from scripting to casting. Thus, in February 1936 he suggested to MacPhail that he might like to have the scenarios for 'The Kingdom of Loquacia' and 'Deep Waters' looked at and returned: 'The Ruritania one, like all Ruritanian things, looks worthless, but the other might be a wild possibility for George Arliss in the style of *Old English*.' The following month he protested to MacPhail that a love story implicitly criticising England's divorce legislation had been turned into its opposite, 'an entirely different story about two nice persons in love with one another who, having an infatuation for two other persons, are prevented by the wise and intelligent divorce laws from following their respective infatuations, and instead are happily reunited.' On casting, cables between Michael Balcon and Mark Ostrer reveal that Montagu's opinion was often sought and highly valued. He was asked, for example, whether Erich von Stroheim would be right for the part of Ogarev in a planned production of *Michael Strogoff* ('IVOR STATES LIKES NAME SUGGESTED OGAREV BUT HEARD RUMOUR NOT STABLE PSYCHOLOGICALLY'), and he advised that, for another production, Una Merkel should be preferred to Alice Brady, 'WHOM HE STILL DEEPLY MISTRUSTS AUDIENCE THIS SIDE'.[59]

Montagu's main preoccupation at this time was the third Hitchcock G-B film, *Secret Agent*. Based on the Ashenden stories of W. Somerset Maugham, who had himself been a wartime SIS agent, and on an unperformed play by Campbell Dixon, the film was set in 1916 and centred on the activities of British counter-espionage. 'Ashenden' (John Gielgud), his 'wife' (Madeleine Carroll) and a preposterous 'General' (Peter Lorre) are dispatched to Switzerland on a mission to eliminate an enemy agent who is endangering the success of the Allies' campaign in the Middle East. The wrong man is killed (by the General), but finally the real spy, Marvin (Robert Young) — who has been flirting with Mrs Ashenden, and is deliberately made to look an appealing character — meets his death.

An indication of the seriousness with which Montagu took the writing of *Secret Agent* and its moral implications is given by two lengthy memos he sent to Michael Balcon shortly before the film's release in May 1936.

At the insistence of the BBFC, the ending had been changed: whereas originally the climax was the General killing Marvin, now Marvin killed the General shortly before dying himself as the result of an accident. The switch, Montagu protested, 'destroys and makes nugatory the whole carefully balanced thematic expression of the film', making the story 'ridiculous and null'; if the General is killed, 'then the vile thing the hero and heroine feared' – the cold-blooded murder of a sympathetic human being – 'never happens, they are wrong, and become instead merely a couple of irresolute cissies whose shilly-shallying results in the death of their unwaveringly dutiful colleague.' Montagu conceded that it was possible that 'the ending altered as for release will not materially lessen the enjoyment of the spectator. It is certain, however, that it must lessen the significance of his after impression.' His case was argued in considerable detail, centring on the film's depiction of the ethical conflict between duty and humane feelings (and in the context, it was a theme 'which is not insignificant, one that implies a criticism of war'). But the changes had been made, and Montagu confessed that, even if Balcon were to be persuaded to his point of view, 'I am at a loss to see what now can be done about it.'[60]

Marvin's death occurs in the wreck of a train that has been bombed. To accentuate the shock impact, Hitchcock and Montagu, inspired by Eisenstein, asked experimental filmmaker Len Lye to handpaint on the film red and yellow flames, an idea that Lye extrapolated 'by adding the impression that the film itself had caught fire in the projector'. At a preview screening, Montagu recalled, this so incensed the projectionist that he stormed out of the box 'threatening to punch us on the nose'. The experience 'left no doubt at all about the power of the dialectical change,' but G-B executives feared disturbances at cinemas around the country, 'cold feet prevailed', and the effect was removed.[61]

Secret Agent received mixed notices. *The Times* reviewer, for example, felt that humour and the macabre were out of balance, but in spite of that, 'Mr Hitchcock has given us, not the film we expected from him, but one which, judged by any standard other than the highest, would seem full of merit, discernment, and entertainment.' Hitchcock later came to view it as a failure, for the reason that the Gielgud character lacked a positive purpose and the audience could not root for him: he has an assignment, 'but the job is distasteful and he is reluctant to do it.' The film nonetheless proved reasonably popular with the public.[62]

Montagu and Hitch had already begun work on their next thriller, *Sabotage*, an adaptation of Joseph Conrad's sombre novel of terrorist intrigue in London, *The Secret Agent*. Ivor's keenest memory of this production was the role he played in calming the nerves of the film's American star, Sylvia Sidney. Theatre-trained, she was disturbed by Hitchcock's method of shooting a scene in pre-determined fragments, sometimes without any dialogue to key the mood. 'Many were the times I was called up from my office,' relates Montagu, with perhaps a little of the raconteur's licence, 'to find her weeping, in which emergency of course it is the AP's duty to embrace and comfort her as best he can. She was not to be consoled. She wanted to go home.' He was able to persuade her, he says, to go through with the filming of her big scene in which, half by accident, she stabs her bomb-plotting husband (Oscar Homolka) to death. 'A real Hitch scene, made up of close-ups and inserts, eyes, expressions, forks, potatoes, cabbages.' Sidney played it as directed, then broke down 'in total unhappiness'. But when she saw the edited rough-cut projected, 'our star was dazed ... "Hollywood must hear of this," she said.' In a mostly cool review in *The Times*, the instant when the gaze of Verloc meets that of his wife across a table on which there lies a carving knife is singled out as the film's 'one brilliant moment'.[63]

Berthold Viertel's next film after *The Passing of the Third Floor Back* was *Rhodes of Africa*, released in March 1936. This inaugurated a trilogy of G-B British Empire epics, the second and third of which involved Montagu. *The Great Barrier*, directed by Milton Rosmer, was an historical drama of the building of the Canadian Pacific Railway through the Rockies. As AP, Ivor would have overseen the development of the script, which did not impress the *Times* reviewer when the picture was released in February 1937: 'The film halts and gets somewhat dismally lost between the personal element, the document, and adventure so fantastic that there is no attempt to explain it.' Montagu was on firmer ground with *King Solomon's Mines*, based on the celebrated African adventure novel (1885) by H. Rider Haggard. Studio records document Montagu's week-by-week commitment to the development of this project from June 1935 right through to the summer of 1936, shortly before shooting was scheduled to commence. In November Ivor was allotted an assistant with this work, Derek Twist, an editor whose credits included *The 39 Steps*, *The Passing of the Third Floor Back* and *Rhodes of Africa*.

The time and resources devoted to the film were understandable, given that the designated director was Montagu himself.[64]

Several writers worked on the script. Charles Bennett was involved at the beginning, though he objected (so he claims) to the addition of a leading female role ('a damn silly idea') and took himself off the project. (Later he was to say that as the film was 'crammed with writers' it became 'over-written and tedious', but nevertheless he was 'pleased with the suspense delivered in its final scenes.') By May 1936, Montagu had three versions to work with, one by Bennett and Twist, and two by the G-B staff writer Michael Hogan. Apart from the creation of a part for Anna Lee, the major departure from the novel in the screenplay that eventually emerged – and it is this that very likely most excited Ivor – was an enlargement of the role of the African tribal chief Umbopa, to be played by Paul Robeson. As Jeffrey Richards explains:

> Not only is he mentor, protector, adviser and guide of the English adventurers, he also uses them to further his own restoration to the throne of the Kukuana. Once he reaches Kukuanaland, Umbopa effectively takes charge of the expedition. He rescues the whites when they are trapped in the mines by the evil witchdoctor Gagool. The film closes with Umbopa, now ruler of an independent Kukuanaland, shaking hands with Allan Quatermain and seeing the whites off with a rendition of the most popular of three Spoliansky songs, 'Mighty Mountain'.[65]

Much consideration was given to the casting of the central role of Allan Quartermain (as it was actually spelt in the film). In Hollywood, Mick Balcon pushed for the popular US supporting actor Charles Butterworth, but Montagu had doubts and preferred the alternative, Roland Young. A crunch point was reached at the end of November 1935, when Harold Boxall cabled Balcon:

IVOR HAS REALLY HAD LENGTHY DISCUSSION WRITERS AND ALL CONCERNED REGARDING BUTTERWORTH ASSUME YOUR PREFERENCE HIM DUE ADDITIONAL STAR VALUE AMERICA OVER YOUNG STOP IN THIS CONNECTION IVOR WISHES REMIND YOU ROBESONS PROMISE PLAY FILM IF FREE ULTIMATE PRODUCTION DATE STOP APART FROM QUESTION COST IVOR WRITERS ALSO CONCERNED

BUTTERWORTHS MANNERISMS STOP YOUNG CERTAIN ABLE FIT PART STOP
BUTTERWORTH WOULD ONLY BE POSSIBLE IF HE THOUGHT HIMSELF CAPA-
BLE PLAYING STRAIGHT IN VIEW THESE COMMENTS THEY THINK VERY MUCH
SAFER YOUNG.

Montagu had his way; Balcon replied: 'IN VIEW IVORS COMMENT AM DEFI-
NITELY ENGAGING ROLAND YOUNG GLAD YOU REMINDED ME PAUL ROBSON [sic] AS
HAVE QUITE OVERLOOKED THIS POINT'. Young was in fact to appear in the film,
though not as Quartermain – this role fell to Cedric Hardwicke instead.[66]

By July 1936, things were all set for production on Montagu's first
feature as director. The African exteriors were being shot by Geoffrey
Barkas, Ivor's co-director on *Wings Over Everest*. Robeson's availability
was confirmed, and songs had been written for him. The studio stages
were booked. But at the last moment, Montagu had qualms. The script
called for lively battle scenes between rival factions of the Kukuana, and
Montagu 'felt very uncomfortable about them.' Seizing a window of
opportunity, he made a flying visit to Moscow to discuss their staging
with Eisenstein. When there, as he later recounted, 'there was a terrible
drought. I got ill. I came back with this illness, so I got taken off the subject and another director was put on it.'[67]

Robert Stevenson, up-and-coming G-B director, replaced him. On
recovering from his illness, Montagu went back to his AP work at the studio.
But the Spanish Civil War had broken out, and he was dead set on getting
involved. On 1 September, Ivor sent Mick Balcon two months' notice of his
termination of contract.[68]

He promised that in serving out his time, 'I shall of course do my best to
help Bob through "King Sol" to the best advantage, see "Sabotage" through,
and get Hitch going with his next.' *Sabotage* was in the midst of shooting,
and it was now that Montagu (according to his own account) had a critical
disagreement with Hitchcock. For the suspense scene in which the boy
carries a time bomb across London on public transport, Hitch wanted a
tram: it would convey 'London' to American audiences. Montagu baulked.
The shots involved – it was just the beginning of the sequence – 'would
last about thirty seconds. To make them, we would have to build a concrete
base to carry the lines that would carry the tram from the nearest point in
the street where it normally passed to the nearest point on the lot where it

would have to be filmed. Cost – £3,000. For thirty seconds! I did not think it worth it.' Hitch disagreed. Montagu would not quarrel, instead asking to be relieved of his responsibilities for the production. (In the event, prudence prevailed and Hitchcock had to make do with a bus.)[69]

Montagu had one more crisis to contend with. *King Solomon's Mines* was in danger of going over budget. And since G-B was in dire financial straits, this was serious. 'I am informed by the costing department,' he told MacPhail, 'that the new ending for *King Solomon's Mines* worked out by Mr Pertwee from our suggestions represents a savings in costs of only £1,400. The saving required on this ending by the Corporation is £5,000. It is clear therefore that we shall have to think of another ending quickly. I should be grateful for your suggestions.' What transpired is not known (and the spectacular eruption that ends the film as released does not suggest scrimping). But in any event, his contract was coming to a close. The financial situation of the Gaumont-British Picture Corporation – which was about to lead to a major restructuring, with the Shepherd's Bush studios being closed down – would no longer concern him. On 1 November, he was a free man.[70]

12

FIGHTING FASCISM

ON 30 JANUARY 1933, Adolf Hitler was appointed Chancellor of Germany. Italians had already endured a decade of fascism, but under the Nazis the ideology was to take a particularly virulent form. For an activist like Montagu, who was both a Communist and a Jew, events that winter in Germany precipitated a significant shift in his own political focus and in that of the movement to which he belonged.

The pivotal moment was the burning of the Reichstag on the night of 27 February. Caught redhanded and admitting to the arson was a young Dutchman, Marinus van der Lubbe, who had once belonged to the Communist Party in the Netherlands. The Nazi leadership claimed that the fire signalled the start of a planned Communist insurrection, and the following day secured the passage of an emergency decree suspending civil liberties. Police and SA stormtroopers now had virtually unlimited powers, which were exercised swiftly and ruthlessly, to raid offices of the *Kommunistische Partei Deutschlands* (KPD) and arrest Party members, including Reichstag deputies.

Tens of thousands of Communists, followed soon after by socialists, were rounded up and incarcerated in hastily constructed concentration camps, and scores murdered. After the elections on 5 March, in which participation by the parties of the Left was severely constrained, the KPD was declared illegal and its property seized.

The response of the Comintern to the Nazi reign of terror was to issue a manifesto that marked the beginning of the end of the 'Class Against

Class' policy. While continuing to berate the social-democratic parties for collaboration with the bourgeoisie, the ECCI, 'in view of fascism's offensive against the German working class, unleashing all the forces of world reaction,' called on all communist parties 'to make a further attempt to establish a united fighting front with the social-democratic working masses through the social-democratic parties.' In Britain, Pollitt recognised that this would entail making approaches not only to the members, but also to the leadership, of the Labour Party and the ILP — a stark turnaround from the existing attitude of outright hostility. In moving a resolution on Germany at the Anti-War Congress in March, he declared: 'We want a fighting united front against War and Fascism, no matter what our views are, so long as we are united in this.'[1]

Meanwhile Willi Münzenberg, having eluded the Nazi crackdown by escaping across the border, settled in Paris. He immediately received instructions from Moscow, brought to him by Comintern functionary Otto Katz, to organise a committee to aid those affected by Nazi persecution. Accordingly, he committed the IAH to founding a 'World Committee for the Relief of the Victims of German Fascism'. He charged Katz with establishing international headquarters in Amsterdam and sections in Switzerland, Belgium, Czechoslovakia, and Great Britain.[2]

In London the WIR responded by organising a mass meeting on 24 March, at which, it was reported, 'fifty-eight volunteers came forward to form a campaign committee for German relief.' Montagu was involved very much from the start, if not at this point then shortly thereafter. Concrete arrangements were put in place at the following meeting, held on 29 March, which was addressed by 'a representative of the International Relief Committee from Amsterdam' — Otto Katz, travelling under the alias of Rudolph Katz. (His biographer records that 'he cut a dapper figure in his suit, fawn spats and dark blue bow tie.') Fifty pounds were collected for relief purposes — the WIR had already been sending food parcels to distressed working-class families in Germany — and the British section (known for short as the 'German Relief Committee') was established, with Isabel Brown of the WIR and Dorothy Woodman, of the Union of Democratic Control, acting as joint secretaries. Fellow-travelling Labour peer Lord Marley, already enlisted as chairman of the international organisation (Albert Einstein was nominally the 'president'), became head of the local section as well. Ellen Wilkinson, who had lost her parliamentary seat in the 1931 general election, came forward as one of the treasurers. Such well-known public figures as Tom Mann, Kingsley Martin, Victor Gollancz, James Maxton, Sidney Bernstein and J.B.S. Haldane were soon announced as being attached to the campaign.[3]

Montagu's involvement took a personal turn with the arrival in England of Elfriede Stoecker, wife of a prominent German Communist, and her two children. Walter Stoecker, who had been a Reichstag deputy until July 1932, was arrested on the night of the fire, and was now in indefinite detention. Montagu knew Walter Stoecker – they had probably met at the Amsterdam Anti-War Congress the previous August, at which Ivor represented the British FSU and Stoecker the German *Bund der Freunde der Sowjetunion*. Elfriede asked if a home could be found for the children, so that she could return to Germany and, as the WIR pamphlet *Germany To-Day – Britain To-Morrow?* put it, 'go freely into the conflict for liberty.' In conjunction with the Relief Committee, Ivor and Hell offered to take on the responsibility, and they found themselves acting *in loco parentis* for Helmuth, aged 12, and Helga, 8. In May, MI5 intercepted a touching letter from Stoecker, imprisoned in the Sonnenburg concentration camp, to his son and daughter, concerned about their wellbeing, wondering how they were doing at school and whether they had made friends, and urging them to learn English but not to forget to practise their German. The school Helmuth and Helga were enrolled in was A.S. Neill's Summerhill, which Hell's daughter Rowna, now 11, was still attending. (Later the children were given a foster home by a Captain Lamont in Yorkshire.)[4]

Among those lucky to escape the Nazi crackdown was Ernst Toller, who wrote to Montagu on 8 March: 'A happy accident caused that I am free. I was just in Zurich, when they wanted to arrest me in Berlin.' Ivor proposed an anti-fascist speaking tour in Britain for Toller, but in the event the writer's other international engagements precluded this from taking place. Montagu's own political lecturing, mostly under the auspices of the FSU, did not immediately target fascism, perhaps because throughout 1933 Stalin remained indecisive about the stance his country should adopt to the aggressive new regime in Germany. Instead Ivor was impelled to step up his flag-waving for the Soviet Union in the face of renewed public attacks over the Metro-Vickers affair.[5]

On 11 March, six British electrical engineers employed by Metropolitan-Vickers in the USSR, along with a number of Russians, were arrested on charges of espionage and sabotage. The following month they were put on trial, with five of the British workers being convicted. Three were deported, and two sentenced to imprisonment. At the time it was widely believed that the charges were fabricated, and the confessions made by some of the defendants extorted by OGPU pressure. The British government suspended negotiations on a trade agreement with the Soviet Union, and then imposed an embargo that would remain in place until the imprisoned engineers were released. Montagu proclaimed the integrity of the trial and the guilt of the accused at public meetings held by the FSU in Wandsworth on 21 April ('Dispel Anti-Soviet Lies'), Deptford on 24 April ('Freedom and Justice in the Soviet Union'), Hampstead on 11 May ('Position of Englishmen, Jews and Nationals in USSR'), and Greenwich on 22 May ('The Embargo – its Effect on Unemployment'). The Greenwich meeting, according to a Special Branch report, was 'attended by about 200 people, the majority of whom appeared to be local unemployed.' In his address Ivor 'gave a description of the trial of the Metropolitan-Vickers engineers in Moscow, asserting that the government knew that these men were guilty of the crimes with which they were charged, but had made the trial an excuse for breaking off trade relations with Soviet Russia.' On 28 May he spoke in Finsbury Park at one of a number of rallies staged by the FSU to protest against the embargo, and at a Trafalgar Square Solidarity Day demonstration on 11 June organised by the WIR he claimed that the government was preparing for war on the Soviet Union – a far-fetched accusation – and it was for this reason that the USSR had to hold the trial.[6]

As it happened there was a kernel of truth in the prosecution's accusations of espionage. In 1930 the major companies supplying electrical equipment to the Soviet Union, including Metro-Vickers, had reached an agreement with British and other Western intelligence services to pass on information gathered in the USSR on Soviet industrial and defence capabilities, and one of the key figures involved – as the OGPU had discovered – was C.S. Richards, London manager of Metro-Vickers and a former military intelligence agent in Russia. The vehement denials of the foreign secretary, Sir John Simon, that any of the defendants were employed by British Intelligence may have been technically correct, but his claim that the

Metro-Vickers Company 'has not, and never has had, any connexion whatever with our Intelligence Service' was undoubtedly untrue. However, the
credibility of the Moscow trial proceedings was eroded by the extravagant
detail in the spying charges and the absurdity of the claims of wrecking, as
well as the retraction in the courtroom, in some cases, of previously given
confessions. On 1 July, after some weeks of negotiations, the prison sentences were commuted, the men released and the embargo lifted. It was
probably with some relief that Montagu could turn his attention to more
substantial political campaigning.[7]

The Labour Party had rejected united front overtures from the CPGB,
but talks with the now-disaffiliated ILP were proceeding. A joint CPGB-
ILP anti-fascist demonstration in Hyde Park on 7 May attracted a crowd
of 100,000. Then, in early June, Montagu, on behalf of the FSU, was one of
more than 3,000 delegates thronging the European Workers' Anti-Fascist
Congress at the Salle Pleyel in Paris. The gathering, organised behind the
scenes by Münzenberg, was a continuation of the Amsterdam anti-war
movement and sponsored, although with some misgivings, by ECCI ('More
openly than at Amsterdam,' says Babette Gross, 'the meeting at Paris was
run by the Communists,' although Richard Krebs claims that the attend-
ees included many 'guileless pilgrims' belonging to the liberal camp, few
of whom 'had the faintest notion that the force which had organised and
financed the World Congress [sic], written all the resolutions and made all
the decisions in advance of its formal opening, was the Comintern'). The
focus was mainly on Germany, but an International Labour Defence (ILD)
pamphlet produced for the congress claimed that 'fascist reaction is increasing in every capitalist country' and documented the repression of dissent
and the imprisonment, torture and murder of workers and activists in many
states including Poland, Italy, Yugoslavia, Romania, Finland and Japan. It is
noteworthy that the manifesto issued by the congress made few concessions
to the social democrats: it declared that the menace of fascism even in the
'so-called democratic countries' could not be combatted 'without breaking
completely with workers' co-operation with the bourgeoisie, without an
implacable revolutionary struggle'. As for ongoing action, it was agreed to
establish the European Workers' Anti-Fascist Union, which merged with
the World Committee Against Imperialist War in August to form what
became the World Committee Against War and Fascism.[8]

Meanwhile, the propaganda work in Paris of the World Committee for the Relief of the Victims of German Fascism continued (it does not seem that the mooted Amsterdam headquarters eventuated). Four Communists had been arrested and accused of complicity, along with van der Lubbe, in the burning of the Reichstag: Ernst Torgler, chairman of the KPD parliamentary caucus, and three Bulgarians employed in the Comintern's West European Bureau – Georgi Dimitrov, its head, Vasili Tanev and Blagoi Popov. The Committee took on the task of, on the one hand, demonstrating their innocence, and on the other, making a persuasive case that the fire had been set by the Nazis in order to provide a pretext for outlawing the parties of the Left. To this end, Otto Katz had put together (anonymously) an exposé of German fascism, *The Brown Book of the Hitler Terror and the Burning of the Reichstag*, which was shortly to be published in multiple language editions. He had also set about organising an ingenious publicity stunt for which Münzenberg had obtained Comintern approval in early June: a 'legal commission of enquiry' into the Reichstag fire, to be held in London immediately prior to the trial in Germany, at which evidence pointing to a lack of Communist involvement and Nazi culpability could be presented.[9]

On 30 June Katz returned to London and attended an informal cocktail party held for him by Ellen Wilkinson, to which she had invited Montagu along with 'a mixed selection of bourgeois celebrities'. The group then went on to the Kingsway Hall for a public meeting sponsored by the German Relief Committee, at which the featured speaker was journalist Egon Erwin Kisch. Kisch had been arrested and imprisoned the day after the Reichstag fire, but as a Czechoslovak citizen was released and deported. 'We had a wonderful meeting with a big attendance and great enthusiasm,' Montagu was to tell Toller. In the following days Katz discussed with members of the committee the forthcoming release of *The Brown Book*, whose English edition was to be published by Victor Gollancz, in a translation by Emile Burns. He also created a press sensation by releasing evidence pointing to Goering's complicity in the burning of the Reichstag, and excited the militants with his proposal for a 'counter-trial'.[10]

MI5 was taking a keen interest in Katz's activities. It also remained suspicious of Montagu, but here his family connections were proving helpful in throwing a spanner in the works. Aggrieved that his personal correspondence was being intercepted, he had complained to his cousin Sir Herbert Samuel, then Home Secretary, in September 1932. Samuel replied that he was passing on the letter to the Home Office 'in order that the points which you mention may be borne in mind'. By June 1933, when Montagu's Home Office warrant came up for renewal, Samuel was no longer in office, but remained influential. Despite MI5's anxiety to maintain the HOW, Home Office resistance proved telling and the warrant was cancelled, to be 'brought up again for consideration in three months' time.' The reconsideration did not occur.[11]

Montagu and his associates in the German Relief Committee became heavily involved in the planning process for the counter-trial. Münzenberg's collaborators assembled an international team of distinguished jurists to take part in what was to be called the Commission of Enquiry, under the chairmanship of English lawyer Denis Nowell Pritt, KC. Though described by Montagu as 'largely non-political' at that time, Pritt was a Labour Party member who had become strongly pro-Soviet after a visit to the USSR as a member of a New Fabian Research Bureau delegation in 1932. Prominent amongst other members of the panel was the French parliamentarian Gaston Bergery, who had been instrumental in securing legal residence in France for Münzenberg. Katz collected evidence and organised witnesses to appear at the hearing, while the London committee secured the use of the Law Society's courtroom as a venue that would lend appropriate gravity to the proceedings. The Foreign Office, anxious not to upset Germany, tried to intervene. Katz, carrying crucial documents, was detained at Croydon airport and an order made prohibiting his entry to the UK, but Ellen Wilkinson, procuring the support of Arthur Henderson in parliament, was able to have the order overturned; while the government's attempt to have the Law Society room booking revoked was unsuccessful.[12]

Montagu, asked in 1965 for a contribution to a Bulgarian collection of memoirs of Dimitrov, recalled with pleasure the organising meetings held in Wilkinson's small Bloomsbury flat. He had a higher opinion of the diminutive redhead's abilities as a politician and activist than as a novelist. 'Her emotional sympathy made her appreciate the character of Nazism before nearly all her colleagues,' he wrote. 'Her restless energy and a conscience that would not be still made her impossible for the right-wing to cage by any bans or discouragement.' Complementing her was Isabel Brown, 'comfortable but never placid, a rock, fine organiser and the greatest fund-raising orator I have ever known'. Others, Ivor noted, 'came and went.'

They included Lord Marley; Harry Pollitt; Dorothy Woodman; Frederick Voigt, formerly *Manchester Guardian* Berlin correspondent; John Jagger, the trade-unionist MP; and barrister Neil Lawson, 'whose study of the case and scrupulous care not only provided the technical foundation for the commission but avoided innumerable pitfalls.' There was also the 'donkey-work at telephone and typewriter' admirably performed by Olive Budden (wife of prominent Communist Robin Page Arnot; she doubled as a translator at the Enquiry) and Ivor's wife Hell.[13]

Montagu was called on to assist with fundraising. It was a dispiriting task. 'I remember many office doors closed in my face,' he wrote, '– the banker who replied to me that it was the duty of Jews not to oppose Hitler or give him any provocation or excuse, a young man of religious family who declared that no harm could befall anyone at the hands of fascism so long as he prayed faithfully and led a humble and upright life.' But if the bankers were not forthcoming, contributions came from 'tailors in the East End of London, miners in West Wales and unemployed in Lancashire and on Clydeside'.

Montagu's particular responsibility, however, was press and publicity work. He knew it was vital that the Enquiry come across 'as a research in the dispassionate discovery of the facts' – otherwise the Nazis could discredit it as a propaganda exercise. 'The organisers of the Commission would be denounced as Reds financed by Jews, its members as dupes or partisans, men whose minds were made up in advance.' To advise him on the approach to take he had help from several journalists: Voigt, Kingsley Martin (editor of the *New Statesman*), and Frederick Kuh (European correspondent of several American newspapers).[14]

On 13 September, the eve of the opening of the Commission of Enquiry, a reception and press conference hosted by Lady Marley and Sidney Bernstein was held at the Hotel Washington in Mayfair. Montagu would have been pleased by Pritt's statement: the Commission had been established 'by various people who were interested in the cause of justice and who were gravely anxious lest the trial at Leipzig should proceed without any real defence being put forward on behalf of the prisoners'; it was 'composed of a number of eminent jurists of various Continental countries', and was meeting with a view to receiving and considering evidence 'as fairly and impartially and quietly as it possibly could'.[15]

Further lustre accrued to the proceedings the following day when the opening address was given by Sir Stafford Cripps, who had been Solicitor General in the MacDonald Labour-led government. Watching from the gallery of the packed courtroom was Montagu, amidst a bevy of celebrities including H.G. Wells, Labour leader George Lansbury, ILP activist and former MP Jennie Lee, and political scientist Harold Laski. The parade of witnesses then commenced.[16]

The Commission heard evidence on the political situation in Germany at the time, and who stood to gain from the conflagration. It enquired into the layout and guarding of the Reichstag building, and the nature of the fire itself. And it received testimony on the character of van der Lubbe (negative), and on that of Torgler and Dimitrov (positive), together with evidence of their whereabouts on the night of the fire. The witnesses included Dr Rudolf Breitscheid, Chairman of the Parliamentary Social Democratic Party in the Reichstag; Dr Albert Grzesinski, former president of police in Berlin (a Social Democrat who had ordered the shooting of Communist demonstrators in 1929); Professor Georg Bernhard, editor of the *Vossische Zeitung*; Frau Elise Schütz, whose husband Walter, a Communist Reichstag deputy, had been murdered by the SA; Ernst Toller; and prominent KPD parliamentarians Wilhelm Koenen and Otto Kühne. In addition, Kurt Torgler, aged 14, gave evidence about his father, and Elena Dimitrova about her brother.

In his 'Memories of the Counter-Trial', Montagu relates 'a story against myself' ('I am not a very good conspirator'). Koenen, he maintains, had fled Germany without a passport and was in England illegally. It was necessary to implement a procedure to prevent him being tailed by a Nazi agent or police spy when he left the courtroom. Accordingly the doors were locked when he gave his evidence, and remained locked until he had time to get away. Montagu's role was to abet this process. The Law Society building had exits into two different streets:

> I had several men of differing ages, dress and appearance, with and without umbrellas, bowler hats, etc. to wait in the corridors inside each of these doors, and two or three taxis to wait outside each one. When Koenen was ready to go all these men would emerge with him at about the same time from both doors. Some would walk away down the street and some

would go in taxis. Thus any waiting spy would have no idea whom to
follow and Koenen could get away to a pre-arranged address and lie low
until he could leave the country.

All went well until Koenen got into a taxi: Montagu had forgotten to give
him the address. (While there is no reason to doubt the essential facts of
this entertaining anecdote, it is probable that Montagu misremembers the
witness in question. Both *The Times* and the *Manchester Guardian* record the
doors being locked for Otto Kühne, rather than Koenen.)[17]

Despite Montagu's claims that the Enquiry could only operate persuasively 'if it were run, rigorously and exactly, as a research in the dispassionate
discovery of the facts' and that 'Pritt made it a strict principle that no one
should be called to give evidence whom he had not carefully examined
beforehand to ensure that what he or she had to say would be proper and
relevant', the Commission received some dubious testimony – along the
same lines as provocative assertions made in its Comintern predecessor, the
Brown Book, which had been published in England just a few weeks earlier. A certain 'Herr W.S.' testified that a list of names of homosexuals he
had seen linked van der Lubbe to SA commander Ernst Röhm. And only
slightly more convincingly, a deposition from a Parisian secretary claimed to
explain the origins of the highly contentious 'Oberfohren Memorandum'
– which was entered into evidence, and purported to give the now-dead
leader of the Nationalist Party's explanation of how the Nazis had burnt
the Reichstag. Though the Commission treated this evidence with a certain
scepticism, the press coverage would undoubtedly have been pleasing to the
Enquiry organisers.[18]

After four days of hearings the Commissioners retreated to a hotel room,
where during a marathon thirty-eight-hour session (fortified by sandwiches
provided by Hell), with Bergery preparing a draft in French and Pritt pound-
ing out an English translation on his typewriter ('in the adjacent bathroom,
seated for the purpose on the only possible furniture which such rooms dispose,' Montagu recalls), they prepared their twenty-seven-page *Official Findings*.
The conclusions were straightforward: that van der Lubbe was not a member,
but an opponent of the Communist Party, that no connection could be traced
between the Communist Party and the burning of the Reichstag, that the other
defendants were not concerned in any way with the fire, that van der Lubbe

cannot have acted alone, and that 'grave grounds exist for suspecting that the Reichstag was set on fire by, or on behalf of, leading personalities of the National Socialist Party.' The findings were read out at a public meeting at Caxton Hall on 20 September; the following day the trial of van der Lubbe, Torgler, Dimitrov, Tanev and Popov for high treason opened in Leipzig.[19]

The conclusions of the Commission were widely publicised internationally (including in Germany), and generated intense public interest. In London, the German Relief Committee and sister organisations seized the moment, while condemning the 'frame-up', to call for a united front against fascism. A round of mass meetings and demonstrations began with an impressive event on 22 September, when a crowd of 4,000 packed the Kingsway Hall and a nearby overflow venue. Under the chairmanship of Ellen Wilkinson, Montagu reported on the work of the Commission, emphasised the tributes paid to Torgler by his political opponents, and predicted that the question of 'Who fired the Reichstag?' would not be answered at Leipzig. 'Let us remember Sacco and Vanzetti, let us remember Tom Mooney, rotting in jail,' he told the audience, 'and in remembering these, let us build up united action to save Torgler and his comrades.' Other speakers included Neil Lawson, Kingsley Martin, Isabel Brown, Dorothy Woodman, Harry Pollitt, and Harold Laski; when Frau Schütz described the murder of her husband, 'The audience rose as one man, shouts of "Red Front!" rang through the building and the International was sung with great vigour.' Montagu spoke again at the Whitechapel Art Gallery on 26 September, and once more at the Kingsway Hall on 13 October, when he described developments at the Leipzig trial in detail.[20]

All this time Ivor remained busy at his day job at Gaumont-British, but at the end of October he took several weeks' leave to make his long-desired return visit to the Soviet Union. As he left no record of this trip, one can only speculate how much was devoted to his official duties (he was part of an FSU delegation), how much to Comintern networking, how much to film business, and how much to holidaying (zoology and table tennis were probably off the agenda this time). He was a speaker at a delegation farewell meeting at Blackfriars on 27 October, and thanks to vigilant policemen, we know that he sailed from London for Leningrad on 28 October on the m.v. *Alexei Rykoff*, accompanied by Hell, and that he arrived back from Leningrad at Hay's Wharf at 8 a.m. on 24 November on the m.v. *Smolny*.[21]

The one thing that is known for certain is that he caught up with Eisenstein, who was licking his wounds over the *Que viva México!* disaster, teaching at the film school and writing a book. It was the books that struck Montagu in the one-room apartment the filmmaker had in the run-down building at Chysti Prudi 23 in downtown Moscow, with its peeling paint and cracked stone stairs. (The flat belonged to Sergei's old friend Maxim Straukh, who had the adjoining room.) Eisenstein's lair was 'everywhere knee-deep in books. He could, of course, never find a wanted one and, if something had to be looked up, he had each time to buy another copy.' Marie Seton confirms that the 'piles of magazines, newspapers and books' left but a minimum space for movement, but she mentions also the large bed covered in a multi-coloured Mexican blanket, the 'rickety little table with a reading lamp', and the 'collection of beautiful miniature Japanese theatre masks, several gigantic, highly ornamented Mexican sombreros, some peasant pottery and an array of plaster figures of the Virgin and saints.' It was here, on 13 November, that Eisenstein threw a party; Jay Leyda records that the guests comprised himself and 'Pera, the Moussinacs, the Montagus, Tisse, Shub, Louis Fischer, [and] Alexandrov, newly returned with oranges …' (Earlier in the day it had been the young film student's duty to take Ivor and Hell to the Museum of Modern Western Art.)[22]

In a letter to Alexandrov several weeks before his trip, Montagu had joked about conditions in the Soviet Union. 'Alas, with all this work [on *Wings Over Everest*],' he wrote, 'I have had little time for exercise – a few weeks tennis before I damaged my elbow, and that is all, consequently I have got very fat. I imagine that in "starving U.S.S.R." you will have yourself resumed the beautiful figure which you were on the point of losing through Hollywood luxury!' Around the same time he had heard from a Soviet agrarian official, Vasil Kolarov, that the 1933 harvest was '*märchenhaft*' (like a fairy tale). 'We all knew,' Ivor recalled later, 'of the hardships, struggle and even starvation being endured in USSR in the course of fulfilling Lenin's behest to collectivise agriculture in order to secure the base for Socialism and this one word brought first news of the great breakthrough that meant the issue was decided.' These are perhaps the only, oblique, references in Montagu's writing to the terror-famine in the Ukraine and southern Russia, resulting from forced collectivisation, which had cost six to seven million lives. If he looked into this and other unsavoury aspects of Stalin's regime during this visit – 25,000 slave labourers had died in constructing the recently opened Baltic-White Sea Canal, for example – Montagu made no mention of it in any of his available correspondence. It is certain that he would have expressed no doubts when speaking at 'London's Welcome to Delegates Just Back from the Soviet Union' at the Grand Palais on 18 December.[23]

Meanwhile the Leipzig trial had proceeded, with much of the court's time being devoted to attempts to counter the allegations made in the *Brown Book* and the findings of the counter-trial. Van der Lubbe, apparently drugged, remained slumped and incommunicative through most of the proceedings, while Dimitrov seized the opportunity to make defiant anti-Nazi speeches, at one stage provoking Hermann Goering, who was giving evidence, into such a rage that the President of the Reichstag threatened to deal with his Communist antagonist outside the courtroom. As the trial neared its end it became increasingly clear that the prosecution had failed to make a convincing case against the four Communists and it was likely that they would be acquitted. Katz returned to London, meeting up again with Montagu and other members of the organising committee, and on 18–20 December the Legal Commission reassembled. The members examined reports of the evidence presented in Leipzig, coming to conclusions that simply reinforced the findings of the original enquiry.[24]

But at this stage alarming rumours reached London through Voigt's German contacts that there was a plot to stage a lynch-mob assassination of Dimitrov if and when he was released. Voigt argued that the likelihood of this taking place would be lessened if British observers were on the spot. The organising committee canvassed the idea of sending a large party including 'two Socialist peers, MPs and others', but according to the *Daily Express*, 'the peers thought again and the project fell through.' The task was left to Montagu and Dorothy Woodman, who travelled forthwith to Leipzig and were present ('somewhat nervous', Ivor admits) when the chief judge delivered the verdict on 23 December. The court did in fact pronounce van der Lubbe guilty and acquit the others – while nevertheless declaring 'that the allegations against leading German Ministers and others had been disproved … that the fire was the work of Communists, and that the German people had early in 1933 stood in peril of delivery to Communism.' The defendants were retained in 'protective' custody, and no *attentat* took place.[25]

According to press reports, the mission of Montagu and Woodman, who were accompanied by an English barrister, Douglas Benabu, and a Czechoslovakian lawyer, was to gain permission to travel with the Bulgarians to the frontier – it was understood that Czechoslovakia had agreed to admit the trio – and to secure an armed guard for them. Montagu stated that 'we were prepared to provide the necessary documents to enable the men to go to another country if they were released, but no one would listen to the offer.' Enquiries with Leipzig police and the Ministry of the Interior in Berlin proving fruitless, he and Woodman returned to London. Supporters of the acquitted defendants then organised a relay of female writers to go to Leipzig, accompany Dimitrov's mother on her visits to the prison, and keep a close watch on the authorities. 'By this means my office in the film studio where I was then working,' Montagu relates, 'was in touch with Leipzig almost every hour.' He too went back, this time 'with accreditation from Lord Marley in his capacity of Leader of the official Opposition in the Lords to demand the release of Dimitrov and his comrades.'[26]

Organisation in London was sustained. Two days after the guillotining of van der Lubbe on 10 January 1934, Ivor reported on his Leipzig experiences at a conference held in the Essex Hall to plan new steps in the campaign to free Dimitrov. It was felt that the scope of activity needed to be widened, and a resolution moved by Montagu was passed 'agreeing to the dissolution of the existing Reichstag Prisoners' Defence Committee and approving the formation of a committee for the liberation and defence of all political prisoners in Hitler-Germany without distinction of race, religions, or politics'. Although the four Reichstag defendants would remain the main focus, Montagu noted that 'many persons have been executed by axe of whose opportunities for defence we know nothing,' and the tasks of the new committee could include sending persons to look at the concentration camps, and finding lawyers to attend and report on political trials. Those elected to the committee, 'with power to add to their number', were a familiar lot: along with Montagu, there were Lord and Lady Marley, Ellen Wilkinson, Isabel Brown, John Jagger, and Kingsley Martin.[27]

This conference was followed by a mass meeting of more than 2,000 at the Kingsway Hall on 22 January with Lord Marley in the chair, when Woodman and Montagu detailed the responses they had received from interviewing the German authorities. Other speakers included left-wing

journalists John Strachey and Hannen Swaffer. The campaign was instrumental in swinging English public opinion firmly against the German
government – *The Times*, for example, published two leaders protesting the
delay in releasing the Bulgarians. Whether in response to international pressure or for other reasons, Dimitrov, Popov and Tanev, having been granted
Soviet citizenship, were released and flown to Moscow on 27 February.[28]

Several writers have contended that the counter-trial and the trial itself
may not have been altogether what they appeared on the surface, an epic
battle between the forces of Communism and Fascism. Both Richard Krebs
and Ruth Fischer, drawing on insider information they were privy to at
the time, relate that there was a secret agreement – which Dimitrov knew
of – between the OGPU and the Gestapo by which the Bulgarians would
be freed. Negotiations were undertaken, allegedly, whereby the trio would
be exchanged for three German officers imprisoned as spies in the USSR.
Jonathan Miles concludes that the counter-trial was 'part of an elaborate
sleight-of-hand, concealing Stalin's discreet overtures to Hitler'; Stephen
Koch that 'the show was almost certainly a covertly controlled collaboration between the two dictators.' Be that as it may, it is indisputable that the
Legal Commission of Enquiry and the campaign around it were highly
efficacious in alerting the world to the murderous nature of the regime that
had seized power in Germany. As Montagu later asserted, 'all possibilities of
an open alliance between the Western governments and the Nazis were put
to flight' by the growing anti-fascist sentiment which had been generated;
and for this he, as the member of the organising committee most responsible for press liaison and publicity, can take some credit.[29]

Another regular function of the Relief Committee, following the success
of the *Brown Book*, was arranging publication of English editions of books
put out by Münzenberg's publishing house, Éditions du Carrefour, in Paris.
Montagu told Bert Hogenkamp: 'I was accustomed to receive copies of
underground literature, still photographs, manuscripts and books (these last
from Carrefour in Paris) for use by the committee and finding publishers
of the consequent English versions.' A January 1934 letter from Montagu
to Katz mentions 'the Barbusse book' (probably the author's Stalin biography), the second *Brown Book* (*The Reichstag Fire Trial: The Second Brown
Book of the Hitler Terror*), 'the Kisch book' (very likely *Secret China* by Egon
Erwin Kisch), and 'Nazi Führer', that is undoubtedly what became *Heil!*,

an anonymous publication which appeared in December 1934 comprising unflattering potted biographies, rewritten by Montagu, of the Nazi leaders. Two other works in progress, 'The Brown Book III' and 'the Schönstadt novel' do not appear to have seen the light of day.[30]

Meanwhile, Montagu was active behind the scenes in supporting a new initiative in the field of working-class cinema. Atlas Films and the Federation of Workers' Film Societies had foundered, starved of Soviet product and battered by quota requirements and censorship constraints. In their place Kino, initially a co-operative association, evolved towards the end of 1933 from the film section of the Workers' Theatre Movement (WTM). Prime movers were Charles Mann (son of Tom Mann), a member of the agitprop group the Rebel Players and editor of the WTM's journal, and Ivan Seruya, an activist in the FSU and the Young Communist League. Mann had taken part in the International Workers' Theatre Olympiad held in Moscow in May 1933, and been enthused by what he heard at a cinema conference mounted alongside by the International Union of Revolutionary Theatre. A conclusion of the conference was that 'the theatre section of the IURT in each country was to be held responsible for the building up of a revolutionary film movement', if such a movement did not already exist. Kino was launched with ambitious plans, including taking on the 'struggle against all war, characteristic [sic], pacifist, and other reactionary films by organising criticisms and exposures in the Press, mass protests, demonstrations, and rallying of audiences in protest of various films', but in the event its main fields of activity were, firstly, to distribute and exhibit Soviet films on 16mm (which being on non-inflammable film stock was theoretically exempt from censorship) and, secondly, to set up a production unit for making workers' films.[31]

Rachael Low contends that Kino was founded by 'Ivor Montagu and others', but his actual involvement was less prominent than this. Other historians have asserted that the formation of the organisation was 'backed by Ivor Montagu' and that 'Montagu's involvement was only indirect', which would appear to be closer to the mark. Such assistance as he was able to offer was no doubt facilitated by the fact that Kino's headquarters was at the same address – 33 Ormond Yard, London WC1 – as the Friends of the Soviet Union, for which he remained treasurer. As Kino developed, Ivor became chiefly helpful to the organisation in two capacities, in securing Soviet films for distribution, and as an advisor on censorship.[32]

Trying to import films from the USSR remained a struggle. 'We never could get the damned things,' Montagu was later to complain. 'It was a very thankless task.' Initially he was able to pass on to Kino Eisenstein's *Battleship Potemkin* and *The General Line*, both of which had screened at the Film Society. In November 1934 Nikolai Lebedev's *Soldatskii syn/Son of a Soldier* (1928) became available, followed by *Novyi Vavilon/The New Babylon* (Grigori Kozintsev and Leonid Trauberg, 1929) in January 1935. But the real breakthrough did not come until February that year, when Montagu negotiated an agreement with Soyuzintorgkino (formerly Sovkino) giving Kino 16mm distribution rights in Britain for all Soviet films it wished to acquire, without any upfront charge. (At the same time Montagu established the Progressive Film Institute [PFI], a small company to handle distribution of Soviet and other political films in 35mm.) By the end of the year, Kino was able to add to its catalogue four further Russian features – *Mother* (Pudovkin, 1926), *Storm Over Asia* (Pudovkin, 1928), *October/Ten Days That Shook the World* (Eisenstein, 1928) and *Privideniye, kotoroye ne vozvrashchayetsya/The Ghost That Never Returns* (Abram Room, 1930) – as well as a number of shorts and documentaries.[33]

Although 16mm film was exempt from licensing put in place under the 1909 Cinematograph Films Act and was not subject to the Quota Act, local councils, the police and the Home Office still pulled out all that stops to suppress the exhibition of Soviet pictures. As Montagu explained in an article for *Kino News* in 1935, when the working-class movement tried to exploit loopholes in the law, 'every method is used to prevent it, even to illegal threats and intimidation by the Special Department of Scotland Yard.' By putting pressure on the owners of premises, the LCC was able to block advertised screenings of *Potemkin* by the St Pancras branch of the FSU on 11 December 1933, the Jubilee Street branch of the CPGB on 5 January 1934, and the FSU in Plumstead on 15 February 1934. But as Montagu was able to advise Kino, council bans of this nature were unenforceable. Kino fought back, and before long Soviet films were being shown widely to working-class audiences up and down the country. The authorities now tried two further tactics. One was to claim that the safety stock used for 16mm film was, in fact, inflammable. This move was seen off in a test case at Jarrow, when Kino and a miners' lodge were prosecuted for screening *Potemkin*. 'Kino's defending lawyer,' Montagu wrote, 'had no difficulty in showing that, by the definition claimed by the Home Office "expert", all sorts of material like toughened woods would be inflammable ...' The prosecution failed. The other move was an initiative by the Home Office to amend the law on exhibition so that 16mm film would be subject to the same censorship constraints as 35mm film. After astute lobbying by Kino and its allies – 'substandard' film was now being widely used by educational institutions – this tactic was also unavailing, and the idea was dropped. Whereas Montagu had been frustrated in his previous battles against political censorship, in the arena of noncommercial exhibition he could claim a victory.[34]

One of the first projects of Kino's production unit was to collaborate with the National Unemployed Workers' Movement to make 'an official workers' record' of the 1934 national hunger march. This was all the more important in that the newsreel companies were complying with a London Metropolitan Police request to refrain from covering the event. Kino appealed to *Daily Worker* readers with access to a movie camera of any gauge to take footage of the march, and one of those who complied was Montagu. Contingents from various parts of the country and their supporters converged for a mass demonstration in Hyde Park on Sunday 25 February, and a police informant reported that Montagu was acting as a marshal of the SW London contingent. Moreover, 'It was noticed that MONTAGU and Ivan SERUYA were each using a portable cinema camera. They appears [*sic*] to be taking photographs of groups [of] Police Officers in uniform and of S.B. officers taking shorthand notes.' Montagu left no record of whether any of his footage made it into the final film, the ten-minute silent documentary *National Hunger March 1934*, which was completed and released the following month.[35]

The aims of the march, a united-front initiative of the CP and the ILP, were to demand the abolition of the means test, restore benefit cuts, and to defeat the government's Unemployment Bill, which would compel the unemployed to work at benefit rates. On the weekend of the demonstration, a Congress of Action was held at the Bermondsey Town Hall, to which Montagu brought a message of solidarity from Dimitrov, still in prison. In the following days there was intense lobbying of Parliament, but Prime Minister Ramsay MacDonald refused to meet a deputation from the marchers.[36]

Kino's activities were not always seriously political. On 21 July Montagu was one of the announced speakers (the other was Herbert Marshall, just back from studying with Eisenstein in Moscow) at Kino's Film Festival and Fun Fair held in the King Alfred School Gardens in Golders Green, north London. Promised attractions, along with the talks and film show, included a performance by the Rebel Players, side shows, competitions, and 'have your film taken'. A footslogging Special Branch detective dutifully attended in case something subversive might be going on, and thanks to his detailed account we know that sadly there were not many takers for the 'fun and interest for young and old!'. 'Only 25–30 persons' attended during the afternoon (engaging in sports and games 'with little or no enthusiasm'), although about twenty more showed up for the open-air film show in the evening, when Ivan Seruya projected 'scenes from various parts of the world, including Russian life, all of which had some bearing on the conditions of either peasants or industrial manner of living.' Montagu's talk on cinema was clearly devoid of sedition, since 'no speeches came under notice', and the no doubt disappointed officer was compelled to report that 'the people who patronised the festival did not appear to devote their attention to any act of a revolutionary nature.'[37]

By this time Ivor and Hell had moved (in May, shortly after his 30th birthday) to a comfortable middle-class suburb in west London. The couple became the paying guests of Mrs Silverthorne at Flat 29, Ranelagh Gardens, Stamford Brook Avenue, Stamford Brook, W6. It was a stylish five-storey red-brick mansion block with peppermint stripes above the entrance. Here, amidst sylvan surroundings, there was almost certainly no local branch of the Communist Party to join, even if Ivor had felt so inclined.[38]

Despite his film industry employment, Montagu was unflaggingly fulfilling his propaganda duties for the Soviet Union. On 12 March he shared a platform with Lord Marley, William Rust, Isabel Brown and others at an FSU All-London Rally at the Shoreditch Town Hall, reporting on – so it was advertised – 'the great gains already achieved and the gigantic Socialist plans for the next period of four years'. About 400 attended. Then in April he spoke at several meetings in support of Ted Bramley, Communist candidate in the Hammersmith North by-election, taking the opportunity to discuss conditions for Russian workers. (The constituents were not much impressed: Bramley received 614 votes, fewer than the 697 he got in 1931.)[39]

On 30 June the FSU held its national conference (at which Montagu presented the balance sheet, evidently not too healthy), and the following day it staged a large-scale Conference of Friendship with the Soviet Union in the Bermondsey Town Hall. Andrew Rothstein's opening speech on 'the struggle for Socialist construction' was followed by Montagu's on 'proposals for strengthening support of the Soviet Union'. In his 'detailed analysis of the imperialist moves towards war against the Soviet Union', Ivor noted that the Disarmament Conference had collapsed and the capitalist powers were arming 'on a bigger scale than ever'. In the van of the armaments race, he contended, was 'Britain, and its allies on the Eastern and Western frontiers of Soviet Russia – Japan and Germany'. His speech, 'warmly applauded', clearly reflected Soviet fears of an aggressive Anglo-German alliance – which the National Government's friendly overtures towards Hitler would have done nothing to dispel, though to speak of the countries as 'allies' at this time was palpably inaccurate.[40]

Defence of the Soviet Union continued to be the FSU's main preoccupation in the following months. In September a campaign was launched in conjunction with the British Anti-War Movement to protest against Japanese aggression in the Far East, with concern that it might turn against the USSR clearly evident. On 7 September Montagu chaired a mass meeting (about 400 attended) in support of the campaign at the Memorial Hall in Farringdon Street, with speakers including Harry Pollitt and Ernie Brown; a deputation was to be elected to take the resolution of the meeting to the Japanese Embassy.[41]

A prominent member of the FSU and valued ally of Montagu in his anti-fascist campaigning was the left-leaning Anglo-Irish aristocrat, the Earl of Listowel. Hence when Judith, Countess of Listowel, discovered an awkward item of information about the Soviet Union it was, as Montagu wrote to Andrew Rothstein in August, 'exceedingly important to humour her'. The point in question was 'an alleged decree, alleged to have been issued in the last few weeks by the Soviet government, expressly laying it down as a law that families of persons who leave the Soviet Union without permission, whether they aided them or perhaps had not seen them for several years, are liable to punishment'. The Countess – who was the daughter of a Hungarian diplomat, and a foreign correspondent educated at the London School of Economics – did actually have her facts straight, though the provision applied only to the families of military personnel. As Robert Conquest notes, a decree of 9 June, later incorporated into the Criminal Code, provided that 'members of the family aware of the intended offence were subject to up to ten years' imprisonment, while … those who knew nothing whatever about it – "the remaining adult members of the traitor's family, and those living with him or dependent on him at the time" – were made liable to a five-year exile.' Whether Montagu's request to be elucidated on the matter by Rothstein was fulfilled is not known, but it is somewhat telling that he appears less concerned about a flagrant breach of human rights than about placating the woman he describes as 'a general nuisance'.[42]

The main focus of Montagu's political activity during 1934 remained the ongoing fight against fascism. Münzenberg's lieutenant, Louis Gibarti, was keen to institute an enquiry in England into Nazi atrocities and approached Ivor on the subject, but nothing eventuated at this juncture. By the time the German Relief Committee held its national conference on 2 June fascism had spread to Austria, where the Dollfuss regime, having crushed the February uprising, had now promulgated a corporatist constitution allowing a renewed crackdown on socialists: implying that the committee needed to broaden its focus of attention, Montagu called for efforts to relieve the distress of Austrian victims of fascism. Another keynote of the conference was Neil Lawson's report on a new Nazi decree on the 'People's Courts', which would deprive political prisoners of the right of defence; everything had to be done, he stressed, 'to mobilise wide mass opinion in support of Thaelmann'.[43]

Ernst Thaelmann, KPD leader, had been imprisoned without trial and held in solitary confinement since March 1933. Kurt Thomas, a Social Democrat miner from the Saar who had managed to interview him in prison, was to have attended the conference; he had arrived at Newhaven carrying a letter of introduction to Montagu, but been denied entry. In moving a resolution of protest, Ivor explained:

> When he went to see Thaelmann he planned a series of questions which were censored by the police. One of the questions they cut out was, 'Are you being ill-treated?' but in the course of the interview Thaelmann suddenly said, 'I have been tortured and I am being tortured,' whereupon the police dragged him away and threw out Kurt Thomas and his companion.[44]

Shortly afterwards attention turned back sharply to homegrown fascism. Sir Oswald Mosley's British Union of Fascists (BUF), with support from newspaper magnate Lord Rothermere, was becoming a force to be reckoned with. On 7 June, Mosley's Blackshirts held a rally at Olympia in West London, which large numbers of opponents, urged on by the Communist Party, did their utmost to disrupt. An effective counter-demonstration was held outside, while inside the hall interjectors heckled Mosley's speech until being forcibly ejected and then severely beaten up, as police stood by. Montagu does not appear to have been personally present, but in a pamphlet, *Blackshirt Brutality: The Story of Olympia* published in August, he collated a large number of eyewitness accounts of the extreme violence inflicted on hecklers and other protesters by the BUF stewards.[45]

In analysing the event, he described the fascist dictatorships that had seized power in Europe, arguing that fascism:

> in order for it to keep up its pretence to be 'something new' and not just the strengthening of the grip of the existing ruling class ... invariably organises an army of private thugs and beaters-up of its own to impose ... [its] dictatorship, enabling the regular army and police to stand constitutionally and 'impartially' by, keeping the ring as it were, until the working-class movement is crushed.

Fascism everywhere was imposed with 'bestial and sadistic methods', and the brutality was 'not even apologised for, but proclaimed as something "good" and "manly"'. Blackshirt violence was 'an integral part of the Mosley movement', and the evidence showed that 'Mosley planned for what was to happen at Olympia, dictated it while it happened, and endorsed it after it had taken place.' How was the growth of fascism to be countered? Those who opposed Communist tactics upheld 'freedom of speech' – but this was 'the Freedom of Speech that the German Social Democrats gave to Hitler till he smashed their own Party and the Trade Unions and Co-operatives', 'the Freedom of Speech that the Austrian Social Democrats gave to Dollfuss till he slew their wives and children and took away their homes', and here in Britain, 'the Freedom of Speech that gives Mosley a paper of millions circulation and the pick of any hall in the country, but denies, through private ownership, the Communists access to any hall large enough to hold a rally'.

Attacking the Labour Party leadership for its opposition to a united-front policy, Montagu concluded that resistance to fascism required 'an active union of all those prepared to work to that end, of whatever party they may be members ... an *active* union of the *whole* working class, together with all individuals of the so-called middle class who sincerely wish to fight Fascism.' With the Communist Party now reaching out beyond its constituency of militant workers, it was clear that 'Class Against Class' was now well and truly a thing of the past. *Blackshirt Brutality*, a thirty-page pamphlet for a penny, went through at least three printings in quick order.[46]

The Relief Committee's public campaigning continued in July. At a meeting at the Essex Hall on the 20th, with about 300 in attendance, Montagu detailed recent events in Germany – no doubt Hitler's bloody purge of Röhm and the SA leadership. Other speakers included notable non-Communists such as the Labour MP Aneurin Bevan. On 30 July Montagu chaired another meeting, at the Conway Hall, at which Ellen Wilkinson and John Strachey reported on their recent visit to Germany aimed at securing the release of Thaelmann and Torgler. Both speakers commented on the increasing success of underground revolutionary activity and paid tribute to the effectiveness of the committee's relief efforts. Montagu surveyed events in Germany under Hitler and discussed the assassination of Dollfuss (who was murdered by Nazi agents as part of a failed coup attempt on 25 July). In closing the meeting – which was packed to overflowing, with 400 in attendance – he noted the number of new faces and declared that it showed 'what could be achieved by correct united front work, obtaining constantly increasing support among ever wider sections of the people.'[47]

Public anti-fascist sentiment was, in fact, rapidly spreading. The vicious brutality at Olympia had alienated many members of the middle class previously inclined to look favourably on Mosley's movement, and Rothermere had withdrawn his support. Then, on 9 September, a BUF rally in Hyde Park drew only 2,500 Blackshirts, against the massive crowd of 100,000 or more who turned out in peaceful counter-demonstrations called by the CPGB – despite the fact that the Labour Party had cautioned its followers not to attend.[48]

The Relief Committee capitalised on the popular mood at meetings held at the Essex Hall on 26 September (when Montagu was one of many speakers calling for more support for the victims of fascism during the coming winter) and at the Kingsway Hall on 12 October (when there was a crowd of 1,500, and Montagu berated government attitudes towards the Communists). Although many of those attending these events would undoubtedly have been Labour Party supporters, the socialist leadership remained aloof, continuing to rebuff united-front calls from the CPGB. At its annual conference in October, rejecting claims by Professor Harold Laski and Lord Marley that the Relief Committee was a non-party phil-anthropic body, the LP placed the committee on its list of proscribed organisations associated with the Communist International.[49]

At this stage, although saving Thaelmann remained a core objective – there were reports that he was to be put on trial, but this did not occur – the committee found itself expanding its horizons in the light of inter-national developments. In Spain, a miners' strike in Asturias that developed into a revolutionary uprising was put down with extreme brutality by troops under the command of General Francisco Franco. Casualties were high and tens of thousands were imprisoned. The Relief Committee (now tending to drop the 'German' from its name) sent a fact-finding mission consisting of Ellen Wilkinson, the Earl of Listowel and Otto Katz, and organised a Food Ship for Spain; Montagu spoke to an audience of 1,000 in support of this new anti-fascist campaign at the City Hall, Glasgow, on 18 November, though his particular topic was the Nazi concentration camps. Meanwhile, the committee became involved in agitation in the Saar against reunification with Germany, to be voted on in a forthcom-ing plebiscite. Montagu obtained a memorandum on the plebiscite from Professor J.L. Brierly, an international lawyer based in Oxford, and it was proposed (from Paris), that Ivor should approach the writer W.R. Titterton about supporting or joining a Catholic delegation to the territory. (In the event Communist initiatives proved unavailing, with more than 90 per cent voting in January 1935 for reunification.)[50]

Back in July, Willi Münzenberg had made a successful speaking tour of the United States in support of the worldwide campaign to free Thaelmann. A Thaelmann Liberation Committee was formed, and it commissioned the production of a compilation documentary, *Ernst Thaelmann: Fighter Against Fascism*, which was released in September. In due course the film made its way via Paris to the Relief Committee in London, where Montagu re-edited it for British audiences, shortening it (it was 'far too long' in his opinion) and removing American-oriented sequences.[51]

Free Thaelmann!, as Montagu's version was titled, is a silent film, twenty-five minutes in length. Composed principally of footage from the archives of the IAH companies Weltfilm and Prometheus as well as some Soviet material, it recounts Thaelmann's life as Communist leader in the Weimar Republic, with footage of Red Front Fighter assemblies and marches, May Day rallies, sports festivals, and the 1932 presidential election campaign in which he was the KPD candidate ('Five million votes for Thaelmann!'). It then covers Hitler's rise to power ('with the aid of Thyssen, Krupp, Hugenberg and all the forces of finance capital' – the standard Communist line that exaggerated big business support for the Nazis), the Reichstag fire and trial (including Dimitrov speaking in court, and after his release in the Soviet Union), book-burning, the Nazi terror and torture, and underground opposition (particularly the distribution of 'over a hundred daily and weekly anti-fascist publications'). In a concluding montage, an image of Thaelmann behind bars ('Two years in jail – WITHOUT TRIAL') is intercut with scenes of protest demonstrations around the world – the English shots feature Lord Marley – and police repression. According to Montagu's recollection, *Free Thaelmann!* was less focused than the American original on Thaelmann as an individual, in keeping with the more general remit of the sponsoring body.[52]

The re-editing was completed by March 1935. Montagu hoped to be able to distribute the film on 35mm through the PFI. But when he submitted it to the BBFC, it was rejected on the grounds that it violated the code veto on notorious criminals. 'When I hotly disputed its applicability to the case,' Montagu related, 'the censor replied, "But he's in prison isn't he?" and plainly disbelieved my information to him that thousands were detained in concentration camps without either trial or charge.' In correspondence over the issue, BBFC secretary J. Brooke Wilkinson wrote:

> I have to inform you that we are still of the opinion that this film is unsuitable for public exhibition in this country ... Mr Shortt is definitely of the opinion that the film, as shewn, is a deliberate insult to the ruling regime of a country with whom we are in friendly relations. Moreover, he considers that if any German happened to be in the audience when

the film was being exhibited, it would very likely lead to a serious breach
of the peace.

Free Thaelmann! was also banned by the LCC, and accordingly it was
reduced to 16mm and distributed by Kino, beginning in July, to worker and
community organisations.[53]

Free Thaelmann! was not the only film giving Montagu censorship has-
sles in 1935. He was in repeated contact with the BBFC and the LCC over
Soviet features he wished to release, first on behalf of Brunel & Montagu
Ltd, and then for the PFI. He was willing to make alterations if required:
thus he consented to the removal of the red colouring of the mutineers'
flag in *Battleship Potemkin*, and to the addition of a title at the beginning of
Storm Over Asia stating that 'the military forces shown are not intended to
be representative of any particular nation.' Though a small number of features thus became available for commercial distribution, the PFI was unable
to make strong inroads into the theatrical market. Reflecting many years
later, Montagu wrote:

> Rarely did we breach the barriers into the public cinemas of the com-
> mercial world ... But living hand-to-mouth, with the aid of one or two
> art cinemas in London and Glasgow, a few owned by miners' lodges in
> South Wales, and shows to trade union branches and to political and 'film
> art' societies in cooperative society halls and the like, we fought on for
> several years.[54]

Montagu's Communist activism while employed as an executive at
Gaumont-British was becoming a matter of public comment, but he
retained the support of Mick Balcon. During 1935 he seems to have cut
back a little on his public speaking engagements, while remaining as busy
as ever as an organiser behind the scenes. There were certainly a sprinkling
of talks: for the Relief Committee in Kingsway Hall on 5 March, on the
banning of *Free Thaelmann!*; for the FSU (Paddington), on 16 April; at a
Relief Committee rally in Trafalgar Square on International Solidarity
Day, 23 June; for the Workers' Film and Photo League's one-day school in
Hampstead on 7 July, on 'The Film in Relation to Modern Society'; and for
the London Film Institute Society on 3 November, on Soviet films. But his

main political activity appears to have involved organising an enquiry into
Nazi atrocities, protesting against Italian aggression in Abyssinia (and the
British government's response), and helping mount a Congress of Peace and
Friendship with the USSR.[55]

The Relief Committee's Commission of Enquiry into the Nazi Terror
was an initiative of Otto Katz, who first proposed the idea to Isabel Brown
on 25 April. Springing probably from Gibarti's 1934 proposal, and aimed
at exposing terrorist attacks against German refugees now living abroad,
this 'conference or a legal commission or a trial or however you would
call it' was intended to be run along the lines of the 1933 counter-trial.
Initial organising was hampered by the fact that in May, Montagu was travelling in Europe; 'We miss Ivor very much for this work,' Brown told Katz.
But he was back in London in June, and things proceeded. On the 7th
he sent a letter to the writer Princess Bibesco (Anthony Asquith's sister
Elizabeth) in Paris, asking if she would become a member of the commission, and urging her to see Katz about it. German witnesses were lined
up to appear, Denis Pritt's participation was secured, and other prominent
persons, including Lord Listowel, Vyvyan Adams MP, and Seymour Cocks
MP, were approached about taking part. A planning meeting organised by
Montagu was held at the Caxton Hall, Westminster, on 10–11 July, with
about thirty present. But at this point things stalled. Colonel Sir Vernon
Kell of MI5 reported, no doubt with some relief, that 'our latest information is to the effect that the idea is falling rather flat. It seems that upon
examination of the material regarding individual cases those responsible for
the Commission are of the opinion that concrete proof of governmental
implication is impossible …'. The project was abandoned.[56]

During 1935 a crisis arose in Abyssinia (Ethiopia), with Italian aggression against Haile Selassie's nation gradually building up. In July the World
Committee Against War and Fascism (headquartered in Paris) suggested that
Montagu should be the English delegate in their mission to that country,
but nothing came of the idea. The following month Montagu was moved to
write a letter to his boss, Mark Ostrer, concerning the company's newsreel
coverage of the crisis:

Gaumont-British has a newsreel out this week which takes up a very
sharp political position in respect to the impending war of aggression by

Italy against Abyssinia. ... I have always been informed and understood that the Corporation, as such, had no politics and have been content to work for it in that belief. You will understand therefore that I am rather worried by this newsreel, which appears to indicate a departure from the political impartiality I understood to be characteristic of the Corporation's activities.

No doubt the item took a line favouring the Italian position; there is no response from Ostrer in the files. In October, as Montagu had anticipated, there was a full-scale invasion; on the 20th, he spoke at a conference and rally in the Middlesbrough Town Hall devoted to the question, 'How can we assist in bringing to a speedy termination the deplorable slaughter now taking place in Abyssinia, and thus preserve the peace of the world?', and a week later, when various organisations in London mounted a public discussion of 'What can we do about Abyssinia?', he took part (so the ubiquitous police spies tell us) from the body of the hall. No doubt he spoke against the government's policy of appeasement; in December he was spotted in Parliament, described by MI5 as one of the 'extremists' lobbying MPs to protest against the action of the government in supporting the Italo-Abyssinian peace plan.[57]

The Congress of Peace and Friendship with the USSR was first mooted in June, according to MI5, by FSU stalwarts Lord Listowel and Mrs Cecil Chesterton (a writer and Fabian socialist) at 'one of a series of non-diplomatic receptions held at the Soviet Embassy in London'. The context in which this congress was to take place was now very different from that of earlier similar events. The Soviet Union had joined the League of Nations and, in May, concluded a Treaty of Mutual Assistance with France. It was symptomatic of the shift in orientation that at the planning meeting held on 26 September Britain was no longer accused of being an imperialist power preparing aggression against the USSR; Listowel argued that 'Germany, Italy and Japan are the three principal countries responsible for the war danger.' It was essential, he contended, that for the maintenance of world peace there be closer collaboration between the USSR and Great Britain. At this meeting, held in the Conway Hall, Montagu was appointed to the provisional committee.[58]

All branches of the FSU were instructed to further the project. After securing the endorsement of prominent celebrities including Paul Robeson,

Bernard Shaw and the Bishop of Birmingham, the Congress duly took place in London on 7–8 December, with 800 delegates representing, so it was said, more than a million British citizens. Montagu spoke on 'Film, with reference to conditions in Russia', but he was probably more concerned with the political dimensions of the event. It represented a triumph for the Comintern's new Popular Front strategy (recently announced by Dimitrov at the Seventh World Congress), with key speeches being delivered by, among others, Conservative MP Robert Boothby, leading ILP member Lord Allen of Hurtwood, and Labour MP Seymour Cocks. Commmunists and crypto-Communists (Montagu excluded) were very much in the background. The unanimously carried resolution commended the Soviet Union's efforts to promote world peace, urged the Government to promote trade and friendly intercourse between Britain and the USSR, and declared the Congress's conviction that 'the interests of international peace and the welfare of mankind require the closest possible cooperation in international affairs between the Governments of Great Britain and the USSR.'[59]

What probably pleased Montagu the most was the endorsement given before the Congress by new Labour leader Clement Attlee, who had taken over from George Lansbury in October, and had led the Party to a gratifying result in the November general election (though the National Government under Stanley Baldwin was returned to office, Labour increased the number of seats it held from 52 to 154). Attlee welcomed the opportunity afforded by the Congress for Britain and the USSR to get together, declaring:

> I feel that these two great world states, although widely different, both realise the urgent need for preserving peace and have a common inter-est in promoting it. In particular, the British Labour Party, like the USSR, have a vision of a World Co-operative Commonwealth based on Socialism and lasting peace which, in my view, can be ensured only by the application of Socialist principles to world affairs.

Here at last, in the struggle against fascism, was a united front of socialists and Communists (even if unofficially) in action.[60]

13

MOSCOW AND MADRID

IT WAS BUSINESS as usual when Montagu addressed the FSU conference on the Soviet Union and Peace at the Besant Hall in London on Saturday, 23 May 1936. Chairing the afternoon session, he was to speak on 'Prosperity in the USSR Today' – though as real wages, towards the end of the second Five-Year Plan, were now half what they had been in 1929, this was something of a tall order. Perhaps he switched his topic to the old rallying cry of defence of the socialist fatherland; MI5's police spy reported merely that he urged all workers 'to band together and be ever on the alert to resist any attempt by their capitalist masters to attack that country.' The plea undoubtedly reflected Soviet paranoia rather than any realistic assessment of the war plans of the Western democracies, and was slightly out of step with the tenor of the conference as a whole, which supported Moscow's drive for collective security and urged the British government to join the Franco-Soviet Pact that had come into effect in March.[1]

Tensions in the Soviet Union had slowly built up following the assassination of Leningrad party chief Sergei Kirov in December 1934, and what a subsequent historian would term 'the quiet terror' – with a party purge, deportations, imprisonment and executions – was underway. Whatever news of this reached the West presented a challenge for Soviet apologists, one that Montagu was happy to accept. 'USSR has always been a land of the free,' he blithely declared in the July issue of *Left Book News*, monthly organ of the highly successful new popular-front initiative, the Left Book Club (LBC). Praising the merits of the liberal Soviet constitution that had recently been promulgated (which 'simply concretises and organises that liberty which ... has constantly been part of the Soviet citizens' daily rights'), he was keen to defuse any scepticism that might arise. The Labour-aligned paper the *Daily Herald* had the temerity to suggest that whatever the law, the USSR government would not keep to it; events following the Kirov murder were evidence enough of that. (Within two weeks of the killing some ninety 'White Guardists' were secretly tried in military tribunals, found guilty of preparing to organise terrorist acts, and summarily executed.) Ivor riposted that it was not true that the legal procedure was not followed: 'Secret trial in case of danger to the state is provided for in Soviet law,' he asserted – and 'the *in camera* trials at the time of Kirov can only be attacked by someone who is ready to take the attitude: that the Soviet government are liars ...' He was certainly not to be numbered amongst such patent enemies of progress.[2]

Montagu, it was clear, was determined to downplay any suspicion that the new constitution was mere window-dressing. 'If anyone has the rubber stamp idea of Soviet democracy,' he wrote, 'the present discussion going on around the proposed new family and abortion laws must be a revelation to him.' Indeed, as he attested, the draft legislation outlawing abortion had been met at 'meeting after meeting' with 'the sharpest, and reasoned, criticism of the proposals, criticism and opposition fill the columns of the papers.' The measure was, in fact, almost universally condemned – and then on 27 June, unfortunately for democracy, it was enacted by decree without significant amendment (a development which probably missed Ivor's deadline).[3]

As Montagu was hailing the liberties of the Soviet citizen, works by oppositionists (including Trotsky, Zinoviev, Kamenev and Preobrazhensky) were being taken off library shelves by order of Moscow. The purge extended to London, where suspect items in the library of the Society for Cultural Relations were removed by a member of the Soviet Embassy staff (possibly press attaché Serge Vinogradoff, who was VOKS representative on the committee) and incinerated. It was perhaps this act that lay behind the turmoil that erupted at a special general meeting of the society on 2 July, although it was financial concerns that came to the forefront in the heated debate. It was reported that 'as many as seven or eight members were endeavouring to shout one another down, and there were cries of "Leave the Chair," "If you call me a liar, I'll resign" (from Mr D.N. Pritt, KC), and a variety of votes of censure.' Treasurer Lord Marley survived cries of 'sloppy non-sense' and repeated demands for circulation of a financial statement. The role of defending the executive fell to long-serving member the Hon. Ivor Montagu, sporting for the occasion a bright red waistcoat, who explained that 'economies were necessary, hence the proposal to take smaller premises and "release" the secretaries.'[4]

In his first contribution on Soviet affairs to *Left Book News*, in June, Ivor had addressed the question of 'Culture'. Here he had been on compara-tively firm ground. He extolled the fact that the Soviet Union had three times as many university students per head of population as Great Britain, while 'the paramountly important aspect is that the pupils qualifying for the advantages of this education are drawn with equal facility from the *whole* population, the *mass*.' It was '*mass culture*', in fact, which was, of all developments in the USSR, 'perhaps the one most pregnant with majestic possibilities for the human species.' The article heralded the million organ-ised chess players in the country, but revealingly did not touch on the arts, whose majestic possibilities were not at this time readily apparent. There was no mention of the fact, for example, that in January Shostakovich's highly popular opera *Lady Macbeth of Mtensk District* had incurred the dis-pleasure of Stalin, leading to vehement denunciations of the composer and the initiation of an official campaign against 'formalism' in the arts, which would shortly trip up Ivor's close friend and colleague Eisenstein.[5]

After a period in the wilderness, Eisenstein was now working on a new film, *Bezhin lug/Bezhin Meadow*, based on the true story of a peasant boy who denounced his father to the authorities. Production had begun in 1935, and writing to Montagu in May 1936, he was confident that he would be 'through with it in autumn if everything continues to be all right.' He was delighted that Ivor and Hell would be coming to stay, and that he would be able to put them up in the new four-room apartment he had acquired. Eisenstein also had a car; he was clearly benefitting from the differential pay now accruing to professionals and technical experts. But there were certain items unobtainable in Moscow. 'If you want to be so lovely and bring me something from London,' he suggested, they might procure him a horn for his Ford, or electrical double-adaptor plugs, or 'a good big sporting cap ("hairy")', or possibly a dozen Van Heusen Egyptian cotton collars, Style No. 1, size 16.[6]

It is not known if Ivor and Hell were able to gratify their host's desires. They flew to Moscow via Berlin (accompanied by Harry Pollitt) on 19 July, and returned via the same route on the 26th. On this brief visit Montagu's preoccupation was presumably with film matters, since he had come to seek Eisenstein's advice on the directing of *King Solomon's Mines*; as for Eisenstein, he had been instructed by film industry head Boris Shumyatsky to rewrite the *Bezhin Meadow* script and reshoot a large part of it, since it failed to comply with socialist-realist tenets in its depiction of the rural class struggle. (On the rewrite Eisenstein was collaborating with Isaac Babel, whose *Benia Krik* Montagu had finally succeeded in finding a publisher for in Britain.)[7]

Three weeks after Montagu had returned to London, on 19 August, a political trial opened in Moscow. The sixteen defendants comprised two groups: the majority, including Zinoviev, Kamenev, and other prominent figures, were Bolsheviks who had participated in the Opposition led by Trotsky in 1926–27, while the remainder were obscure figures, several of them secret agents of the OGPU and its successor, the NKVD, whose role as fictitious defendants was effectively to serve as state's witnesses. Trotsky and Lev Sedov, his son, were also accused, *in absentia*. The main charge was that the miscreants had engaged, under Trotsky's instructions, in a terrorist conspiracy aimed at the murder of Stalin and other Soviet leaders. The hearing, by the Supreme Court's Military Collegium, took place in the small October Hall of the House of Unions, before a handpicked audience. Over the next few days the accused, with one partial exception (I.N. Smirnov), ignominiously confessed to all the charges laid against them other than collaboration with the Gestapo. On 24 June they were found guilty and sentenced to death, and by the next morning (following prosecutor Vyshinsky's exhortation, headlined in *Pravda*, 'The Mad Dogs Must Be Shot!') they had been executed.

The Comintern was aware that press coverage of the trial internationally would need to be carefully handled. Apart from the inherent unlikelihood of Marxist politicians such as Zinoviev and Kamenev, who had long since recanted their opposition to Stalin's leadership, becoming terrorists and traitors to the Soviet Union, the case presented against them was weak and flawed. The defendants, supposedly at their own request, were not represented by defence counsel. Not a single piece of material evidence to corroborate the terror plot was presented in court, the stories told were contradictory and at one or two crucial points demonstrably untrue, and the convictions, as Vadim Z. Rogovin has noted, 'were constructed exclusively on the slander and self-slander of the accused and the witnesses.' Pains were therefore taken to enlist observers sympathetic to Stalin's regime to present a favourable view of the proceedings in the West. One of the key figures in this process was Montagu's friend and collaborator D.N. Pritt, KC.[8]

Pritt attended the trial (later somewhat ingenuously claiming that he did so reluctantly and only after the urging of his wife). He wrote articles for the *News Chronicle* upholding the probity of the proceedings ('The Moscow Trial was a Fair Trial'), authored a pamphlet, *The Zinoviev Trial* (published by Gollancz) that went to some lengths to answer criticisms that had been raised, and provided a preface for the edited transcript of the trial published by the Anglo-Russian Parliamentary Committee. In doing so, the evidence strongly suggests that he was acting as a witting agent of the NKVD. A clandestine radio transmission on 23 October from the Comintern to the CPGB, intercepted by MI5, instructed Harry Pollitt and Douglas Parsons (manager at the Communist publishers Lawrence & Wishart) to 'arrange with PRITT and GOLLANCZ for publication of pamphlet ZINOVIEV trial in French, German (?) Czech, Spanish, Dutch, Scandinavian languages. All our publishers are informed. Arrange for suitable honorarium.' The message also suggested that publication in the USA should be organised, if that had not already been done (the pamphlet appeared in an American edition as *At the Moscow Trial* in 1937). Pritt's status as an agent of the OGPU/NKVD was later affirmed by Soviet defector Walter Krivitsky, who informed MI5 in 1940 that Pritt was 'bound to the Soviets. Even if at a later stage Pritt should desire to change his views and cease to work for Stalin, he will not be permitted to do so.'[9]

Montagu's role in the affair seems to have been as a junior understudy to Pritt. He could not speak first-hand of the events in Moscow, but in 'The U.S.S.R. Month By Month: The Trial', his contribution to the October *Left Book News*, he ignored weaknesses in the case mounted against the defendants and ridiculed explanations that had been proffered for the confessions. It was not credible, he contended, that the veteran Bolsheviks had been drugged, or tortured, or swindled by an offer of pardon, nor that they were sacrificing themselves for the party, or had a 'Russian' desire to confess. More likely, he suggested, was 'the daring, the audacious theory that the prisoners confessed because, perhaps, after all, they really had done what they confessed to.' As for his erstwhile friend Trotsky, Montagu was constrained to admit that he had been taken in by the 'glamour' of the man who had devoted all his life, '*in his belief*, to revolution and to socialism', but who was now rightly called counter-revolutionary and Fascist. Ivor cited the prosecution's (dubious) evidence that Trotsky had directly ordered acts of terror, and repeated the (specious) argument that in his 1932 advice to members of the USSR Central Executive Committee (in an Open Letter!) to 'remove Stalin' (actually quoting Lenin), he was advocating assassination. 'Behind Trotsky, whatsoever his motive,' Montagu warned, finally, 'stands the Gestapo.'[10]

Ivor returned to the fray at the beginning of the new year, in a letter to *The New Statesman and Nation*. 'It is amazing what a mess people get themselves into when they try to explain the "Moscow confessions" by any cause other than the guilt of the accused,' he pronounced, and proceeded to heap heavy sarcasm on an opinion piece by Leonard Woolf: 'Just as drooling old ladies imagined themselves to have had intercourse with Satan at the Sabbath, when it was popular to believe this possible, so again the current "popular delusion" is now "so powerful" that these veteran revolutionaries had "induced" in them "the hallucination of guilt".' While Woolf's particular speculation may have been wide of the mark, the fact was, as Montagu was undoubtedly aware and was trying hard to deny, the 'Trial of the Sixteen' as it came to be called bore a significant resemblance to the witch trials and proceedings of the Inquisition of earlier centuries. This was a case that had been made with great cogency in a recently published pamphlet by Friedrich Adler, the Austrian social democrat who was Secretary of the Labour and Socialist International. As Adler pointed out, the Zinoviev case was the latest in a series of political trials in the Soviet Union notable for the absence of documentary evidence and the drilling of defendants by the secret police during the preliminary investigation, and 'just as in the case of all the earlier trials of this kind a "collective confession" was organised which is grotesque as a whole, and in its details rests upon false self-accusations.' This was a powerful argument, and it is unsurprising that Montagu felt impelled to discredit it.[11]

In the last week of January 1937, Stalin and the NKVD staged a second show trial. This time the defendants included a man with whom Montagu was almost certainly personally acquainted. This was Grigori Sokolnikov, a member of Lenin's first Politburo, who had served as Soviet Ambassador in London from 1929 to 1932. Sokolnikov was in the dock along with such other prominent Bolsheviks as the journalist Karl Radek and the industrial administrator Georgy Pyatakov. The crimes they were accused of were even more fanciful than those alleged in the Zinoviev trial. The veteran revolutionaries and their accomplices had supposedly conspired with Trotsky to overthrow the Soviet government by force, aiming to secure the military defeat of the USSR, the dismemberment of the country to the advantage of foreign aggressors, and the restoration of capitalism. They had engaged in espionage on behalf of Germany and Japan, organised widespread terrorist and sabotage groups, and attempted to assassinate leaders of the government. No material evidence was presented to substantiate any of these manifold claims. The accused all readily admitted their guilt, and all were convicted; on 30 January, thirteen were sentenced to death, while four (including Sokolnikov and Radek) received prison sentences.[12]

Montagu had by this time become a journalist on the Communist *Daily Worker*, and it is intriguing to find comments on the staff discussion of the trial in an MI5 file. 'M/7' reported that he was 'very much impressed by the obvious belief of those present in the truth of the accusations against the accused. 'Even such a hardened campaigner as Walter HOLMES appeared to be quite certain that there was good foundation for the charges.' The informant went on to state 'that it was a revelation to him that such wild charges, such unorthodox procedure and such flimsy evidence could be accepted by several comparatively intelligent men and he instanced this as a striking example of how the propaganda of Communism has become a part of these [people's] make-up.'[13]

It fell to Montagu's lot to counter the negative coverage the trial had been receiving in some sections of the press. (It was, of course, *de rigueur* that the paper follow the line laid down by Moscow. When the line didn't arrive soon enough, this could be frustrating. On 17 November 1936, for example, Pollitt sent a coded radio message to the CPGB Comintern rep Robin Page Arnot saying: 'Draw your attention very bad news service your end on such questions as arrest Nazi Saboteurs. Our paper will not print anything about USSR that does not come from you but we are placed in an impossible position as a daily paper.')[14]

In this case instructions had been sent out by the ECCI Secretariat to party leaders internationally at the beginning of the trial. They were to organise a campaign 'to refute the arguments of the bourgeois and social democratic press, who will attempt to discredit the trial. You are to start immediately, in the press and among the masses, a campaign against Trotsky and Trotskyism, [depicting] them as terrorist agents, gangs of wreckers, saboteurs, spies and accomplices of the Gestapo.'[15]

The message was no doubt passed on by Pollitt to Montagu, who complied. In 'How Press Flung a Smokescreen Over Moscow Trial' (2 February), Ivor asserted that the reason the trial was described by some as incredible was 'the necessity to conceal its reality as the defeat of one more, and the latest, of the never-ceasing endeavours of aggressive capitalism to destroy the Soviet Union by intervention.' From the first days of the Revolution the White Guards were supported by the Lloyd Georges and the Churchills, and ever since, 'remnants of the old Russian intellectuals, like the "Industrial Party", adventurist-putschists like the Social-Revolutionary Group, and now at last the opportunist elements of Left and Right, have each proved soil favourable for the development of such plots.' The *Daily Herald* had asked for 'better evidence than confessions' to establish guilt, but, 'actually, of course, confessions or rather admissions of the type at these trials, dovetailing and confirmed by spirited debate with fellow defendants, are the very best possible evidence.' However, 'the most noteworthy feature of the whole British Press reaction on the trial' was, according to Montagu, 'the universal concealment of the Nazi and imperialist part in the plot' – abetted, of course, by the Trotsky group, whose 'final degeneration … collaboration with Fascism, waits at the end of the path, not of working-class unity, but of collaboration and compromise with capitalism.'[16]

Montagu redoubled his offensive against the doubters in his April contribution to *Left News*, as the LBC publication was now called. 'The U.S.S.R. Month By Month: The Guilty' was an extended assault on Trotsky mounted by means of a hotchpotch of highly selective quotations. It is chiefly interesting as Ivor's personal *mea culpa* for his former attachment to his erstwhile idol:

> To what young intellectual was Trotsky not then a hero! Not only the
> brilliance of his irony, but that particular Utopianism and reckless polemi-
> cal disregard of mundane fact which is the seed of his menace, made him
> an especially attractive idol for those whose impulse to the revolution

was romantic rather than based on working-class experience. How much easier to read Trotsky, than the writings of someone more meticulous, and thereby the more pedestrian!

The non-Marxist innocent, Montagu now proclaimed, 'and I was one once, perhaps we all are until we roll up our sleeves,' thought not of 'a Party, but a tea-party'. It is true that in execrating Trotsky, Montagu did not directly charge him with terrorism, sabotage and espionage, as Soviet apologists were enjoined to do – perhaps he had difficulty believing this of the man he had gone fishing with. Nor did he descend to the level of verbal abuse that the minor defendants in the second trial were wont to employ – 'his venomous fangs have not yet been extracted' (Boguslavsky), 'the stuffy, stinking, foul, evil-smelling Trotskyite underworld' (Drobnis) – the Honourable Ivor was an English gentleman, after all. But the substance of his accusation was nevertheless damning: 'The man to whom lie open the columns of Hearst, the propaganda machine of Goebbels, the man who aims at a common target side by side with Hitler and Japan, this is the man who today is marching with the big battalions.'[17]

It was a classic smear attack, and recognised as such by the English Trotskyists. In 'Ivor Montagu – The Hireling', published in the cyclostyled *Information Bulletin of the British Committee for the Defence of Leon Trotsky*, Charles Sumner tore apart Montagu's allegations. 'Distortion and misquotation are the last resort of those venal persons who, having long since lost or sold all personal dignity, are reduced to substitute for political argument, lies and slander,' he wrote. Sumner went on to show convincingly that Montagu could make his case that Trotsky was fomenting war between Germany and the USSR, calling for the assassination of Stalin, and contributing to the right-wing Hearst press only by twisting of the facts and significant textual omissions in quotation. Moreover, in summarising Trotsky's refutation of the charges against him Montagu had selected 'isolated words and phrases from no less than six sources and jumble[d] them together in such a way that Trotsky's explanation seems fragmentary and confused,' when 'as Montagu knows well, a perfectly convincing and consistent explanation is to be found either in Trotsky's Hippodrome speech, *I Stake My Life!*, or in an article published in the *Red Flag* for March, 1937.' With some justification, Sumner could conclude that 'in the long and dishonourable history of political slander and falsification it would be difficult to find a baser or more vicious specimen of this poisonous art than Ivor Montagu's article.'[18]

'The Guilty' had been distributed in *Left News* to the Left Book Club membership, which by now totalled more than 40,000. Trotskyists countered by sending the *Information Bulletin* to the conveners of the many LBC groups that had sprung up. This aroused some consternation. A Mrs Jensen wrote to LBC publisher Victor Gollancz saying that the *Bulletin* was 'causing some confusion in the groups' and wondering if the section dealing with Montagu's article could be answered by him. In turn, Gollancz wrote on 31 May to Ivor, then in Geneva, relaying the request. He hoped that Ivor might find the time to write a detailed reply, which Gollancz would circulate to the conveners. 'In spite of the disadvantages of this,' he wrote, '– for of course what the Trotskyists want to do is precisely to make us debate with them – nevertheless I think the advantages outweigh the disadvantages.' It would seem that Montagu did not take up the challenge. What he himself felt about being called a venal liar can only be a matter of conjecture.[19]

★

Back in April 1936, at the Kino AGM, Montagu had argued forcefully that the workers' film movement should concentrate on making documentaries. Producing features for commercial distribution would be prohibitively expensive. He was shortly to seize the opportunity to put this belief into practice, personally. In July a military uprising against the democratic government of Republican Spain led to the outbreak of a fierce civil war, and the spontaneous resistance of workers' militias to the fascist insurgents ignited strong support on the Left in Britain. Montagu was present (along with Isabel and Ernest Brown) at Victoria Station on 23 August when a British Medical Unit left for Spain, and now that he had been relieved of his directorial duties on *King Solomon's Mines* he conceived the idea of going himself to document the conflict.[20]

Giving Gaumont-British two months' notice, after which he would be free to travel, Ivor flung himself in the interim into support work for the Republic. The rebel forces led by General Francisco Franco were receiving military aid from Germany and Italy, in spite of the Non-Intervention

Agreement (sponsored by France and Britain) to which they were signatories. Montagu helped organise a Committee of Enquiry into Breaches of International Law in Spain, and attended the hearing held on 24 September under the chairmanship of Eleanor Rathbone, MP. Evidence was heard from members of an English delegation that had been in Spain, and the Committee's report, published in October, detailed a 'large amount of evidence showing German assistance both before and after August 8 1936, the date upon which the German government informed the French Government that no war material had been sent or would be sent to the Spanish rebels'.[21]

In November Ivor prepared for filming in Spain. It was to be a PFI production, and Hell, the company secretary, purchased for the expedition two 16mm silent Kodak cassette cameras. As cameraman Montagu recruited Norman McLaren. The young filmmaker, fresh out of art school in Glasgow, had recently co-directed the lively polemic *Hell UnLtd*, which accused armaments manufacturers of fomenting war. Though Montagu claims not to have known his political views, McLaren was, in fact, a member of the Communist Party and was keen to volunteer for the job. He had just begun work at the GPO Film Unit, but its head John Grierson was happy to give him a temporary leave of absence.[22]

On 17 November Montagu and McLaren set off, armed with a letter of accreditation from the Spanish Ambassador. Leaving Folkestone on the Boulogne ferry, they were spotted by the ever-vigilant border police, 'dressed as for cross-country hiking, each carrying a well-laden rucksack'. In Paris they would undoubtedly have checked in with Otto Katz, now running the news agency Agence Espagne for the Republican government. A Münzenberg creation, the Agence had large funds at its disposal, partly from Madrid and partly from the Comintern, to disseminate propaganda for the Republican cause. Montagu was to assert that expenses for the film production came out of his own pocket – 'The costs were light and came easily out of my savings'– but Katz could certainly have offered logistic, if not financial support; and Ivor notes that he supplied introductions. Another port of call would have been the office run by the filmmaker (and Spanish Communist Party member) Luis Buñuel, whom Ivor had met in Hollywood. Buñuel was charged by the Spanish Embassy with coordinating and promoting international motion-picture coverage of the conflict from the Loyalist side, and his biographer records that he issued permits for Montagu and McLaren.[23]

From Paris they flew over the Pyrenees to Barcelona, reached Albacete (training base of the newly formed International Brigade) and from there made their way, perching on a lorry loaded with shells, to Madrid. The capital city was being bombed by German planes and Franco's troops were closing in fast; the filmmakers were determined to record the damage and the popular resistance.[24]

They shot for five days, McLaren filming under Montagu's direction and Montagu working the second camera. (Despite the fact that Ivor was self-confessedly 'utterly incompetent with any kind of filming or taking photographs', the Kodak was so simple to operate that 'any dumb cluck could use it'.) Taking the advice of Soviet documentarian Roman Karmen, they started at the morgue. Montagu records:

> I had never seen death before. I am inclined to be hesitant and physical courage is not at all natural to me, yet the sight of these neat inanimate rows of children and grownups whose feelings and hopes, akin to my own and suddenly cut short, I could so easily imagine, hardened me and made me impersonal.

There were two corpses in militia uniform that he never forgot:

> A man of sixty with domed bald head, and clean-shaven features set in a scowl of yellow wax, and a young girl, handsome, fiery yet peaceful, as though abruptly turned off, like a tap.[25]

They filmed heavy Junker bombers indiscriminately dropping their deadly loads, and tiny Soviet Mosca fighters chasing them away. 'The destruction was terrific,' McLaren was to tell his parents:

> Hundreds of men immediately get to work clearing the debris in order to try and rescue the men, women and children who are trapped underneath the colossal mountain of twisted ironwork, fallen walls, and smashed up furniture, some of whom may be alive, others squashed and wounded, and others dead.

The wrecked buildings the filmmakers documented included the offices of the Socialist newspaper *Libertad* and the church of San Sebastian.[26]

They came under fire – Montagu remembered 'the puffs of dust in the road and the "pit" of bullets on sandbags' as they injudiciously turned a corner. They documented an assault by the fascists on University City, visited Loyalist troops on the front line, and filmed the Palace of the Dukes of Alba ablaze from incendiary bombs (this was shot in colour, but they were to discover they had no means of making colour prints). Montagu was clutching an unexploded bomb so McLaren could film the German markings on it when a shell came low overhead. 'At the whine,' he relates, 'I flung myself down, idiotically clutching the unexploded incendiary firmly under my stomach as I hit the pavement. This was perhaps one of my luckier, as it was certainly one of my more foolish, moments.'[27]

Other material they gathered included street scenes of everyday life under the siege, the civilian population being evacuated, the wounded being treated in hospital, and the militia parading, building barricades, and relaxing with music. They were also able to film scenes with the International Brigade, including shots of Ludwig Renn, commandant of the Thaelmann Battalion, and Hans Beimler, political commissar of the battalion and former Reichstag deputy, who was to lose his life four days later.

Part of Buñuel's job in Paris was to secure copies of newsreel and documentary material shot in Spain for further distribution as stock footage, and this applied particularly to the items being filmed regularly for the USSR by Karmen and his assistant. It is likely that Montagu obtained some of this footage – showing, for example, food supplies being unloaded from a Soviet ship – on the film unit's return journey.[28]

Back in England, Montagu and his editor Bill Megarry cut the material at breakneck speed ('in a few hours', Montagu says, with perhaps a little exaggeration) at the Kodak premises in Harrow. Copious intertitles, as well as animated maps were prepared. *The Defence of Madrid*, a silent 16mm film 45 minutes in length, was ready for a preview screening at the Besant Hall on 22 December, when Montagu introduced it to a selected audience including, according to MI5, 'practically all the well-known leaders of the various extremist and peace groups in London'.[29]

Being on 16mm, the film could not be shown in commercial cinemas, but it did not have to run the censorship gauntlet. It was handed to Kino for distribution, and twice-nightly public screenings commenced at the Memorial Hall, Farringdon Street, on 28 December. Speakers accompanying the initial presentations included Montagu, Pritt, Isabel Brown, and former Labour MP Leah Manning, who was secretary of the Spanish Medical Aid Committee.[30]

Introducing his documentary to the public, Montagu 'emphasised that it was made in five days and was, he knew, far from perfect,' and it certainly bears the hallmarks of being slapped together in a hurry. One implication of the haste with which it was produced was that it was released anachronistically as a silent film, lacking a music and commentary soundtrack. Yet it provided for many Britons their first chance of seeing close-range images of the impact of aerial bombardment on a civilian population, and for this reason alone it was of major importance.[31]

Stalin had by this time swung Soviet support in behind the embattled Republican government, although somewhat surreptitiously in view of the arms embargo that was in place. Unsurprisingly given its genesis, *The Defence of Madrid* follows the Comintern line in downplaying the class conflict and revolutionary aspects of the Civil War, portraying the struggle as one of democratic against predominantly foreign fascist forces (Soviet military aid to the Republic is unacknowledged). Thus there are graphics showing the flow of money, propaganda and munitions to Spain from Nazi Germany and Fascist Italy, and shots of Eleanor Rathbone intercut with titles indicating the findings of the Committee of Enquiry: 'Moorish levies', 'Nazi bombers', 'Fascist tanks'. The role of the Soviet Union is depicted as one of offering humanitarian aid, and Montagu no doubt enjoyed editing a little propaganda montage in which the title 'Shall we send food to the people of Spain?' is followed by a shot of a large crowd raising their hands, and then a medium shot of Stalin also signalling his assent.

The immediate political function of *The Defence of Madrid* was to bolster the medical aid to Spain campaign, and in this it was highly effective. Thus at the first screening:

> Miss Isabel Brown, who described the film as 'the most authentic picture the British public has yet succeeded in getting', appealed for funds for medical supplies and clothing. She stated that an ambulance, a doctor, and two dressers had today left from Victoria, and next week the first anti-gas ambulance would be delivered. Over £45 was quickly collected ...'

The film proved enormously popular, and within a month Kino was able to report that eleven prints had been struck, about 15,000 people had attended more than fifty screenings all over Britain, and copies had been sent to the USA, France, Sweden and Switzerland. A CP organiser in north Wales bought his own print and recalled that he 'saw that film twice daily for four months and made as many speeches and appeals.' Reporting to the 14th National Congress of the CPGB in May 1937, the Central Committee asserted that *The Defence of Madrid* 'has been shown in over 400 centres, in most cases by our Party organisations or through their initiative.' Kino was ultimately to claim that the film had raised more than £8,000 for the National Joint Committee for Spanish Relief.[32]

Meanwhile, the Civil War's potential for screen entertainment was being assessed in Hollywood. In January, Montagu made what may have been a telling intervention in the motion picture industry's coverage of events in Spain. Twentieth-Century Fox had announced the forthcoming production of a film on the Siege of the Alcazar, a celebrated incident of the early stages of the war in which several hundred Nationalist Civil Guard, cadets and civilians holed up in the Toledo fortress withstood a Republican siege for two months, until relieved by Franco's Army. In an open letter to Darryl F. Zanuck, published in *World Film News* and reprinted in the US, Montagu invited the producer to reflect on just who the real heroes were. 'The tale of traitors, armed to the teeth and with ample stores, cowering behind walls fourteen feet thick. While the man-in-the-street, a peaceable bloke like you and me, took off his coat and, in shirt sleeves and armed with a fowling piece, set about their punishment.' The defenders of the Alcazar had women with them – '*but it was not only their own womenfolk they took.*' Some were snatched, on a holiday afternoon: 'Shall we call them "hostages"?' Montagu challenged Zanuck, finally, to show the actual origins of the siege: 'That afternoon when it started the good people of Toledo didn't suddenly get excited and drive the cadets into the fortress. The cadets, *knowing that what they were about to do would meet the unanimous indignation of the people*, withdrew into their barracks. And they withdrew into it, *knowing they would be cut off for a long time.*' The following month, the *Daily Worker* was able to claim that 'the letter received great publicity and was largely responsible for the proposed film being abandoned.'[33]

The PFI followed the success of *The Defence of Madrid* with a series of short reportage documentaries on the Civil War compiled and re-edited from their own footage as well as Spanish and Soviet newsreel material, probably procured through Buñuel's Paris office. The company now had the time and resources to add soundtracks, and in some cases to release on 35mm. The films, which appeared progressively during 1937, included *News from Spain*, directed by Herbert Marshall, with a ('non-political') commentary spoken by Isabel Brown; *Crime Against Madrid*, a re-edited version of an early film made by the Spanish CNT trade union organisation; *Madrid Today*, a short film excerpted from *Crime Against Madrid* showing the bombing of the city, narrated by Marshall; and *Mr Attlee in Spain*, a newsreel record of the Labour leader's visit to the Republic, accompanied by Ellen Wilkinson MP and Philip Noel-Baker MP, in December. Public screenings of these pictures were monitored by Special Branch plainclothesmen, who reported, for example, that *Madrid Today* was a 'significant piece of propaganda', the tempo of the film being 'very skilfully ... increased as women are shown assisting men in the trenches near Madrid'.[34]

Earlier, Montagu had become involved in a subtle intrigue to secure support for Soviet foreign policy at the League of Nations. In August 1936 he met with Otto Katz, who was in London lobbying MPs for a shift away from the current British attitude of placating the fascist powers in Europe, towards adherence to the principle, advanced by the USSR, of collective security against aggression. Katz no doubt also consulted with Geoffrey Bing, a Labour Party activist and covert Communist who was to set up the British branch of Katz's *Agence Espagne*, the Spanish News Agency. Very possibly at Katz's instigation, Montagu and Bing made contact with the left-wing New Zealand-born lawyer John Platts-Mills. In New Zealand a Labour government had recently come to power, and showed signs of pursuing a foreign policy independent of Britain. As Platts-Mills tells it, Bing ('a splendid conspirator') proposed that the New Zealand representative at the League of Nations, High Commissioner William Jordan, be persuaded to second a motion on collective security to be moved by the Soviet Union's Maxim Litvinov. It would be a chance 'to unite Europe against the Fascists and head off a world war.'[35]

Through Platts-Mills, Bing and Montagu met with Jordan, supplying him with a copy of Litvinov's speech. Jordan was attracted to the idea, according to Platts-Mills, and secured government approval for it. Montagu and Platts-Mills then prepared a speech for him. Jordan 'co-operated fully and prepared thoroughly', rehearsing it several times 'with appropriate gestures ... in front of a full-sized mirror'. Then, at Geneva, 'he did his job in a manful fashion and put New Zealand on the map at the League of Nations.'[36]

Platts-Mills's account is vague and inconsistent as to the dates when this supposedly occurred, and has not been independently verified. But, in fact, New Zealand did take a strong line on sanctions and collective security at League sessions in the autumn of 1936, distancing itself from positions taken by UK Foreign Secretary Anthony Eden. The anecdote may possibly refer to Jordan's address on 29 September, which was, according to the *Manchester Guardian*, 'the most interesting speech of the day'. Emphasising the war danger arising from the growth of national armaments, Jordan said that 'the peril was imminent and the League was drifting.' Alluding to the League's failure over Abyssinia, he called for a return to the principles of the Covenant and warned that sanctions would be no more effective in future unless they were made immediate and automatic, took the form of a complete boycott, and had behind them 'the certainty that the Powers applying the sanctions are able, and, if necessary, prepared to enforce them'. The speech does not appear to have been in support of a Soviet resolution, but the *Guardian* commented that it was 'nearer to that of Mr Litvinoff than to that of Mr Eden'.[37]

When Jordan addressed the League of Nations Council in Geneva on 28 May the following year, Montagu was present as Special Correspondent for the *Daily Worker*. The topic was Spain; the question what to do about flagrant violations of the Non-Intervention Agreement – now very much to the fore following the German bombing of Guernica in April. The New Zealand representative again had a speech drafted for him, this time, it seems, by W.B. Sutch, a member of the New Zealand delegation and in all likelihood a crypto-Communist. Montagu was probably put in contact with Sutch by Andrew Rothstein, who was also in Geneva as TASS correspondent; in any event, a copy of the draft speech was leaked to him. This called for tough action by the League, supervening the ineffective Non-Intervention Committee. But when the speech was delivered it was considerably softer, with Jordan stating that he had been assured that the job of restoring peace and good order in Spain could be entrusted to the Committee.[38]

The clear inference was that the High Commissioner had been subjected to British pressure; Montagu made this claim explicitly in a sensational news story for the *Daily Worker*. 'Eden Slashes Dominion Delegate's Speech', ran the headline. 'At the very last moment, actually in the public Council session,' Ivor reported, 'during the translation of a preceding speech, Eden strolled over to Jordan, the New Zealand delegate, and blue-pencilled his draft like a schoolmaster correcting a boy's homework.' This had a devastating impact, he went on to claim:

> Jordan, who is an old man [he was 58], was left in the air. When the time came for him to speak, he rose, animated by the moral purpose that had inspired his draft, but with shattered material in which he could only flounder. ... [E]very time he came near a conclusion, he had to gasp, sweat, re-arrange his papers, and look for some other point to continue his speech without too big a gap.[39]

What had actually occurred was hotly disputed at the time, with both Eden and Jordan denying that any 'blue-pencilling' took place. But when asked by Ellen Wilkinson in the House of Commons as to whether it was a fact 'that the right hon. Gentleman made no representations to the representative of the New Zealand government which caused him to modify the speech he had originally decided to make?', Eden sidestepped the question. And a furious Jordan was to give contradictory accounts of the incident. It is hard to escape the conclusion that the *Daily Worker* story, recapitulated in its essentials in the *New Statesman and Nation*, was a piece of Comintern mischief-making that, however inaccurate in detail, dramatically highlighted real differences within the Commonwealth on foreign policy towards the Fascist states. As such it was undoubtedly a source of embarrassment to the National Government and its new Prime Minister, Neville Chamberlain. 'What took place at the Council meeting at Geneva has been pretty widely spread here,' Montagu wrote conspiratorially from London to Rothstein. 'I believe BUP [the fascist British Union Party] has been talking, though how on earth they think they know anything I can't imagine.'[40]

Ivor referred again to the position taken on Spain at the League by the UK in an article published in the July 1937 *Labour Monthly*. In a scathing critique of Eden's foreign policy, he accused the National Government of

being 'as contemptuous of League obligations as Fascist powers', of 'acqui-
escing in their aggression upon Spain by land, sea and air and presenting
them with the authority to impose a blockade', of 'yielding Nazi Germany
a free hand in the East', and of 'advancing Nazi plans of dismemberment in
the centre'. It was a policy, he contended, 'which makes war inevitable'.[41]

Having left Gaumont-British and completed *The Defence of Madrid*,
Montagu was free to undertake a number of speaking engagements. During
1937, in addition to introducing film screenings, he spoke around the country on 'Fascism or Democracy?' (2 February), the Workers' Sports Movement
(9 February), 'Dialectical Materialism' (14 February), Jewish settlement
in the USSR (2 May), the Palestine situation (15 July), 'The Allies of the
Working Class' (7 November), the rise of the Soviet Union (11 November),
the 20th anniversary of the USSR (12 November), the capitalist system
(14 November, 3 p.m.), the theory of communism (14 November, 8 p.m.),
'The Imperialist Stage of Capitalism' (c. 17 November), 'The Last Stage of
Capitalism' (24 November), 'The Fascist Press and Propaganda Machine'
(6 December), and the growth of monopoly capitalism (c.10 December).
Sponsoring bodies were generally CPGB or FSU branches, but included
other organisations such as the Holborn and St Pancras People's Front
Propaganda Committee, the London Labour Sports Association, the
Organisation for the Jewish Colonisation in the USSR, the Relief
Committee for the Victims of Fascism, and the Hammersmith Workers'
Social Club. Audience numbers, insofar as they were recorded by undercover police, ranged from 'about 30' to the extraordinary 1,000 who
thronged Glasgow City Hall to hear about the last stage of capitalism and
the crisis of imperialism.[42]

But during this period Ivor devoted most of his time to journalism. He was
on the regular staff of the *Daily Worker*, which operated out of a converted
tea warehouse in Cayton Street, in the East End. Though the editor at the
time was the ideologically rigid Rajani Palme Dutt, there was 'a rather free-
and-easy atmosphere and even a certain amount of heterodoxy' – which
did not, of course, make its way into the paper, but rather into a short-
lived satirical house magazine, *Black Marx*. A close colleague of Montagu's
was Claud Cockburn, who wrote under the name of 'Frank Pitcairn' and
who had to struggle to keep his copy free of the irreverence he deployed in
his influential political newsletter, *The Week*. During 1937 Montagu made

frequent contributions to the *Daily Worker*, including a regular feature, 'The World This Week', whose focus was generally international and invariably polemical. He also wrote for *Left News*, as well as *Labour Monthly*.[43]

Firing broadsides at the British ruling elite and its sympathy for the European dictators, he repeatedly excoriated the National Government for its failure to embrace the idea of collective security and its lack of support for sanctions at the League of Nations. The Fascists' continual aggression could be arrested, he maintained, by 'declaring resolutely that, beyond this point, aggressors will be stopped, by any means.' But this meant: 'with the Soviet Union, against the Fascist powers. The ruling classes of Britain prefer "isolation", i.e., reliance on the changing tight-rope-balance of power, and what amounts, despite all these make-believe defence games, to leaving the population vulnerable.' Favourably reviewing *The Road to War*, a publication of the New Fabian Research Department, he declared the book 'an indictment, comprehensive, damning and incontrovertible of the National Government's foreign policy,' and concluded that 'the replacement of the National Government is, as the authors show, a task more urgent than any other in the whole world today.'[44]

But the Labour Party and the TUC, too, came in for their share of criticism, particularly for their inaction over Spain. 'What has the National Council of Labour done since September to oppose "non-intervention"?' Montagu asked in February. 'Come on! Tell us, Mr Attlee! Tell us, Sir Walter!' Come June, nothing had changed: 'Today British Labour remains silent as Non-Intervention is discarded and the British Government decides the fate of Spain alone with the aggressor nations.'[45]

With respect to the British mandate of Palestine, site of prolonged clashes between Jews and Arabs, Montagu opposed the partition plan put forward in July 1937 by the Peel Commission, calling it a 'naked imperial document' embodying 'a classic example of "divide and rule"'. 'All the trouble in Palestine has been made by British Imperialism,' he argued. 'The British Government proposes two national States – perpetually in conflict, because States founded on a basis of mutual national exclusiveness and with large minorities of their national neighbours inside them are, under capitalist conditions, bound to be in bitter conflict.' Zionists claiming Palestine, he contended in a later column, 'speak with the accents of Mussolini, claiming an Empire, or Hitler, or Japan in China'; their 'sanctimonious talk about the Old Testament' is a 'perversion of Judaism'. Hence 'Jews who were not Jewish Nazis would know their only "right" in Palestine is such as they can negotiate with liberated Arabs and share in equal and non-exclusive citizenship there with all inhabitants, not discriminating.'[46]

Montagu was scathing about British rule in the colonies. In January he denounced the new, undemocratic Indian Constitution as a manoeuvre to perpetuate imperial control, and commended the opposition to it by the Indian National Congress's Jawaharlal Nehru. In May, on the occasion of George VI's Coronation, he penned a fierce exposé of oppression in the Empire, instancing the slave trade (on which the prosperity of Manchester was built), the destruction of colonial peoples' traditional ways of life, massacres in Tasmania and India, labourers forced to work for a pittance, and the theft of fertile lands in Africa, with the inhabitants being herded into barren moorlands, jailed if they protested, and killed if they continued to resist. In August, he alerted readers to the nearly 150 Indian prisoners on hunger strike in the Andaman Islands, starving slowly to death: 'Didn't know that, perhaps, did you? Didn't know that our Government keeps hundreds of our fellow citizens in jail indefinitely without trial, just like Hitler. Didn't know that our Government transports convicts (politicals included) to a filthy, fever-ridden island (not my description, that of a Government Commission), just like Devil's Island, or Botany Bay hundreds of years ago.'[47]

Of course, Ivor also wrote about the Soviet Union. The two show trials had been the trigger for a mass purge that would go down in history as the Great Terror. As hundreds of thousands of Soviet citizens were being arrested by the NKVD and then either shot or dispatched to the slave labour camps known as the gulag, Montagu wrote: 'Soviet society has, as a matter of fact, done rather well so far. People in the Soviet Union are, as a matter of fact, in general rather pleased about it.' When, in June, Marshal of the Soviet Union Mikhail Tukhachevsky and eight other generals were tried before a secret military tribunal, found guilty of treason, and executed, Montagu called it 'a staggering blow to Fascist aspirations'. (Here he was again taking a lead from the Comintern, whose suggested formulation was 'a Bolshevik blow against Fascist war-mongers'.) Within nine days of the trial a further 980 officers were arrested, decapitating the army, which was, in Ivor's words, 'one with its people' in a 'society where people are united'. In July, Montagu declared that the USSR had 'the most democratic elections in the world', omitting to mention, for example, that the 139 members and candidates of the CPSU's central committee elected at the 17th congress in 1934 were being progressively liquidated; eventually 98 would be arrested and shot. When the Moscow–Volga Canal was completed, Montagu rejoiced that the 'late enemies of the people' who built it were being released 'not to the rubbish heap like ex-prisoners in the glutted capitalist labour market, but to assured jobs, free travel home, bonuses, certificates ... full rights of citizenship'; of the appalling conditions they endured while working on the project he said not a word, while many of the remaining prisoners were not, in fact, released, but executed on Stalin's orders.[48]

The terror was by now claiming many of Montagu's former associates and acquaintances. Mikhail Tomsky, the trade union leader who assisted him on his first visit to the Soviet Union, committed suicide on 22 August 1936, the day before an investigation ordered by Vyshinsky into his alleged crimes was to begin. Olga Kameneva, the former head of VOKS, who helped facilitate Ivor's translation projects, was arrested and imprisoned the same month. Dmitry Bogomolov, Montagu's former contact in the Soviet Embassy and a supporter of his film distribution schemes, was recalled to Moscow from China in November 1936, and in 1937 arrested, sentenced to death, and shot. Christian Rakovsky, Soviet Ambassador to the UK 1923–25 and the Trotsky associate whom Montagu arranged to send parcels to when he was in internal exile, was arrested on 27 January 1937. Shortly afterwards, Ivor's Moscow comrades, Max Petrovsky and Rose Cohen, fell victim to the purge. Petrovsky was arrested on 11 March, and Cohen, after several anguished months, on 13 August. British Communist leaders, who had been on close terms of friendship with the couple for many years, made strong representations on their behalf behind the scenes, but no public protest. Their interventions were unavailing. Petrovsky was executed in September, and on 28 November, Cohen was found guilty by the Military Collegium of the USSR Supreme Court of being a resident agent of British Intelligence. She was secretly shot the same day.[49]

Not all of the details of the repression were known at the time, nor its scale. Montagu's role as a Soviet apologist was to denounce those who attempted to bring the facts before the public. He had been tolerant, in April, of André Gide's criticisms in his book *Back from the USSR*, putting them down to the French author's 'lack of real knowledge of his own world as much as of the Soviet Union'. But Gide's *Afterthoughts on the USSR*, published in October, were a different matter. 'From month to month the state of the U.S.S.R. gets worse,' Gide wrote. 'From head to foot of the re-formed social ladder, the most favoured are the most servile, the most cowardly, the most cringing, the basest. All who refuse to stoop are mowed down or deported one after the other.' Stalin, he observed, 'will bear nothing but approval; all who do not applaud him he considers his enemies.' In an appendix, Gide included a letter from the former communist activist and Soviet official A. Rudolf, who spoke frankly of the 'mass executions of the thousands of "counter-revolutionaries" in the concentration camps of the White Sea, of Siberia and of Turkestan'. Montagu dismissed the book as anti-Soviet slander. 'The present reviewer predicted that it was, alas, inevitable, that with a man of Gide's conceit, the endeavour to justify his first reaction would eventually take him far from all trace of conscientiousness and into a mood of unscrupulous hatred.' His book was 'a heavy enough tombstone to bury M. Gide till the day of doom'.[50]

That month *The Return of the Scarlet Pimpernel* was released. It depicted Robespierre as the paranoid dictator of a post-revolutionary regime, presiding over a reign of terror and purging his political opponents, including fellow radicals, by accusing them of treason and having them condemned to death. The film's contemporary parallels, however, ceased at the climax, which showed one member of the Convention with the courage to speak up against the tyrant, precipitating a popular uprising and Robespierre's overthrow. One of the writers on the film, and its associate producer, was Montagu's old friend and business partner, Adrian Brunel. Playing Robespierre's secretary, secretly a member of the anti-dictatorship Pimpernel League, was Ivor's Film Society co-conspirator, Hugh Miller.

14

AGITPROP

MONTAGU GOT OUT of the commercial film industry at the right time. At the end of 1936 a speculative bubble burst, finance dried up, production plummeted and unemployment surged. A well-researched analysis of the studio system, *Money Behind the Screen* by F.D. Klingender and Stuart Legg, demonstrated just how shaky film investment had become. First published in summary form in *World Film News*, it was later released as a book. Reviewing it in the *Daily Worker* in March 1937, Ivor wrote: 'So criminally reckless is the bulk of financial investment that the facts of this report came largely as a surprise to the City, and produced an instant drawing in of horns.' Profit-hungry investors were now likely to place their money elsewhere: 'The present armaments boom, with its multitude of investment alternatives, is likely to produce a lean period for films, which this book may well accelerate.'[1]

His prognostications proved accurate. Production was still stagnating at the end of May, when Montagu's address as acting president of the technicians' union ACT was read at the organisation's AGM. (He was unfortunately 'unavoidably prevented from being present', being in Geneva at the time.) The livelihood of hundreds of technicians was being affected, through no fault of their own. They were prepared to make temporary sacrifices in an emergency situation, Ivor argued, but the union was 'sternly resolved that the present position of the industry shall not be made a pretext to depress conditions, particularly among the lowest paid of our members, under excuse of an economy which is infinitesimal and leaves in every way untouched the abuses which are the cause of the present production plight.' Any scheme for restructuring of the industry, he contended, must involve consultation with technicians and their representatives. It was, therefore, 'our duty and intention to participate, as we have begun to do in the past year, in any enquiries and consultations undertaken as a preliminary to new legislation.'[2]

The 1927 Quota Act was due to expire, and in 1936 the Board of Trade had set up a departmental committee to make recommendations as to what should replace it. The Moyne Committee's report was, in Montagu's view, 'unexpectedly good'. It supported a continuation of the quota system, but came down hard on the 'quota quickie', since the generally poor standard of the mini-budget film was universally acknowledged. Ivor noted that though the quickie provided employment, 'it is regarded as by no means a blessing even by the technicians, since its general cheapness brings down wages all round, and its general perfunctoriness prevents them from acquiring the skill and experience of their American colleagues.' To avert the problem, the Committee proposed a quality test (which Montagu found problematic) and a Films Commission as an oversight body, which did not find favour with the industry.[3]

ACT made submissions both to the Moyne Committee and, later, on the government's White Paper. The union called for an increased quota, for a minimum cost test (rather than a quality judging panel), a separate quota for short films, a fair wages clause, and restrictions on the number of foreign technicians allowed on a production. An intensive campaign, in conjunction with other film industry unions, was organised. On one occasion members made their views known at Westminster, 'pouring into the committee room in the Commons, and cramming the stairs leading to it, so that the committee members were unable to get in', before marching up Whitehall to the Strand.[4]

ACT's lobbying proved effective. When finally passed on 30 March 1938, the Cinematograph Films Act incorporated much of what the union had demanded. There was a small quota increase for features. To deal with the quota quickie issue, minimum labour costs were set at £7,500, with provision for double and triple quota for higher-budget productions (something to which the union was opposed). There was a quota for shorts (against strong opposition from both renters and exhibitors), and a provision that wages and conditions of employment of studio workers be not inferior to those in government departments. The question of foreign technicians was addressed by a clause stating that to qualify as a British film for quota purposes, 'not less than the requisite amount of labour costs represents payments paid or payable in respect of the labour or services of British subjects or persons domiciled in some part of His Majesty's dominions.' Montagu and his fellow ACT office-holders (he had been re-elected as vice-president) must have been well pleased; indeed, in his assessment George Elvin concluded that 'we can, therefore, justifiably congratulate ourselves.'[5]

Montagu could also feel some satisfaction with other provisions of the new legislation. Back in June 1936 he had pointed out in an article for *World Film News* that the Quota Act had had the unintended consequence of handicapping imported 'high-brow' or 'artistic' films. The very limited box-office returns to be expected from such productions could not compensate a renter for the costs of the British quota films he would have to produce or acquire in return. Ivor's proposal was for an exemption for films 'of educational or cultural effect', with a limit on the extent of exhibition. He gave evidence on behalf of the Film Society, no doubt along these lines, to the Moyne Committee. The legislators heeded the call. Section 4 of the new Act granted 'exemption in respect of films for which demand is limited', while Section 35 provided that the Act did not apply, along with newsreels and advertising films, to imported films 'of an educational character' that had been certified by the Board of Education.[6]

It was not that, as a realist and a Marxist, Montagu set any great store by the legislation. The reason, in his opinion, why the studios were in the doldrums and 35 per cent of technicians were unemployed was that American firms dominated the industry, making British production unprofitable, and no amount of juggling with the quota was going to change that. What was more, he argued in a piece for the ACT journal *Cine-Technician*, there was scarcely a producer who cared about pictures and was committed to building a viable filmmaking business; many were simply speculators. 'US competition makes film production a poor man with a hard life, but speculation makes him a rotten one, his heart and lungs festering pasture for maggots, his movements a jerky galvanism, subsiding whenever the artificial current is removed.' The British industry needed protection, and quotas helped a little. But the major problem was the monopoly booking power of the large companies, and to expect legislation against that 'from a government in our society here today is the same as if the grocer round the corner expected it to save him from the chain stores.'[7]

Montagu expanded on these thoughts in 'Profit-sharks Kill British Films', a December 1937 article for the *Daily Worker*. Adequate protection for the domestic industry would never be given, he argued, because the US exporters would not like it. 'They would strike. They would send no films to British cinemas. British cinema owners would be ruined, because without American films they could not find enough films to keep their cinemas open all the year round.' The government did not dream of provoking such a crisis in Anglo-American trade. Instead it was offering, Montagu claimed:

> quite cynically and hypocritically, to introduce a sort of sham protection. This sham is not designed to make British film production profitable, but to appear to do so, and thus delude incautious investors into putting up a certain amount of money for film production, and so result in a certain number of films being made, before the investors find out their mistake.

Some producers had attracted finance for higher-budget films designed for export to America, but this purpose had never been more than 'a swindle at the worst, a pipe-dream at the best', since the US market, highly developed towards monopoly capitalism, was tightly ruled by eight vertical trusts, in their turn controlled by 'no more than a couple of banking groups', and not open to competition.[8]

What was to be done? 'The only solution, if there is to be a film production industry,' Ivor concluded, 'since profit will never call it into being, is to run it like the education system, as a charge on the State for the State's benefit.' Something along the lines, perhaps, of the way it was done in the Soviet Union ... In both articles he held out the Soviet system as a preferable alternative to capitalist boom and bust, with better conditions and more secure employment for the workers. (It was perhaps not an altogether happy comparison. The Soviet film industry was scarcely a model of efficiency and productivity, and in 1937 had seen a marked curtailment in output. And stringent ideological requirements were making life difficult for filmmakers: Eisenstein's reworked version of *Bezhin Meadow*, for example, had been banned and the director subjected to a storm of abuse for his alleged formalism.)[9]

Nonetheless it was a Soviet film that Montagu, turning his attention for once to aesthetics, held out as an example of the correct use of colour in the cinema. In 'Ivor Montagu Sees Red' (*Cine-Technician*, March–April 1938), he acknowledged that the Soviet colour system was 'frightful, lousy and untruthful beyond compare with a dozen other systems' (films were the one aspect of life in the USSR he was prepared to be critical about), but that in *Grunya Kornakova/Nightingale – My Nightingale* (Nikolai Ekk, 1936, the first Soviet colour film), the makers had achieved something that 'people who invented colour dream of'. The scene involved a heroine with Gretchen-blonde hair, and a hero who, shot through the breast, waved his handkerchief stained with his heart's blood. 'I assure you,' Ivor told his readers, 'believe it or not, the simple hokum of that flaxen hair lifts up the seduction scene to the 'nth degree above black and white, as does that waving red-stained kerchief.' The problem in the capitalist film industry was that the experts packed their films with 'funny-colour monstrosities … "Come and see the blue skies, or the green pinewoods, or the yellow deserts, or the gay scarlet uniforms, or the Max Factor complexions." What the public wants to see is the story, and all these colours, beautiful as they may be, get in the way.' Colour had to be subtle, and subordinated to the demands of the narrative. 'Before you can tell a story in colour,' he argued, 'you must learn how to tone down and subdue colour so you don't notice it where it is not wanted.' It is doubtful if the colour film experts, intent on marketing their rival systems, were convinced.[10]

It was around this time that Montagu participated in staging what he termed a 'gem of mischief'. The Film Society had obtained two documentaries of the conquest of Abyssinia, one Soviet (*Abissiniya/Abyssinia*, 1935) and the other Italian (*Il cammino degli eroi/The Path of the Heroes*, 1936), borrowed from the Italian Embassy. They showed the conflict from the two opposed sides, and to emphasise the contrast in stylistic and ideological approach, the Society for its programme on 5 December 1937 intercut sequences, clearly labelling which was which. The programme notes alerted audiences to the 'exceedingly striking' comparison:

The first film concerns itself as thoroughly as its sparse material allows with people, and their social relations, and what is happening to them. The second concentrates with a high degree of effectiveness upon impersonal processes, such as organisation and the like.

An example, according to Montagu, was 'the Italian boasting of their bombing attacks and the beauty of the falling and exploding bombs intercut with the suffering and slaughter among the recipients.' He maintained that 'the resulting impression was staggering,' while Thorold Dickinson reported that it was 'too much for the audience. After two hours of relentless demonstration, they left the theatre, shocked and shamed into uneasy silence.' The Italian Embassy was not pleased, while the Luce Institute, producer of *The Path of the Heroes*, put its lawyers on the case, demanding that the Film Society issue a public statement to make it known that 'the two films in question are quite distinct and that it was by mere coincidence that you projected the two cinematographic documents with an unauthorised interpolation.'[11]

At the end of 1937 Montagu curtailed his regular reporting duties for the *Daily Worker*, although he became chairman of the editorial board (in which capacity, as MI5 were informed by their undercover agent, 'he does not seem very pleased with the manner in which the affairs of the paper are conducted'). The reason for cutting back on his journalism was undoubtedly because he was getting back into political filmmaking. This came at the instigation of Otto Katz, who had left the Münzenberg fold and was now working, as Ivor describes it, 'as a sort of private public-relations officer' for Spanish Republican Prime Minister Juan Negrín. Sometime in 1937 Katz approached Montagu with a proposition. 'He came to me and said the Spanish Government would be prepared to put up the money to make some more films, and I was authorised by the British CP to go ahead. The Spanish Government realised that films made by outsiders could be more effective than their own films.' The sponsorship would enable him, this time, to work in the professional theatrical gauge of 35mm and incorporate sound. Undoubtedly embroidering the tale a little, Montagu states that the sum he received was £3,000, which he carried in cash in his pocket, in trepidation lest he lose it.[12]

This time Montagu acted solely as producer, securing the services of fellow ACT vice-presidents Thorold Dickinson and Sidney Cole as directors. The remainder of the unit comprised cameramen Alan Lawson and Arthur Graham, and editors/assistants Philip Leacock and Raymond Pitt. With left-wing convictions, the crew members volunteered for the job, working only, as Ivor recalled, for expenses. There was an initial snag.

Permits were required for travel to Spain, as part of the non-intervention policy, and the Foreign Office refused to issue them. 'It was the Christmas recess and, as is their habit, the incumbent civil servants played it that their superiors – to whom appeal might have lain – were hard to get.' Ivor called on Clement Attlee, Leader of the Opposition, who had just returned from visiting the British Battalion of the International Brigade and lending his support. In Hampstead, Ivor 'stood beside him in the vestibule of his villa, while first he forced Eden's telephone number out of the officials and then caught Eden in Scotland to extract the permits.'[13]

With this documentation Montagu immediately travelled to Barcelona, where the capital had now been relocated because of Franco's advances. The prime minister was fully occupied with the battle for Teruel, and Ivor was not able to see him personally, but as he reported to Attlee on his return, 'the arrangements for the films have gone perfectly satisfactorily through his office.' Back in London Montagu made further preparations, including procuring accreditation from the Spanish Ambassador and from Harry Pollitt of the CPGB. Then he and Pitt left for Spain, as an advance party. It was 13 January 1938.[14]

In Barcelona, Montagu finalised terms of agreement for the production with the Cinema Department of the Subsecretariat of Propaganda. It was proposed that the PFI make three or four short films, 'dealing especially with: the Cortes and the democratic parties and personalities, education, refugees, defence organisations'. The Subsecretariat would take care of hotel and living expenses for the unit while they were in Spain, and provide interpreters and cars. It would also be responsible for providing lights and sound recording equipment, developing and printing the film, making available cutting rooms, and shooting titles. The British filmmakers (whose salaries were to be the responsibility of the PFI) would bring their own cameras (two Newman Sinclairs and two Eyemos) and supply the film stock. The PFI would arrange the exploitation of the films in Britain and later in other territories, with total profits going to the Spanish government. In the letter of contract dated 15 January in which these terms are outlined, there is no mention of any cash payment to the PFI. (There is some suggestion that the Subsecretariat was making its support conditional on Montagu securing international distribution outlets. He contacted Louis Fischer in Paris seeking his opinion on whether there might be a market in the United States for the education film, saying, according to Fischer, 'If yes, the Spaniards will help me finance the enterprise.')[15]

While Ivor was making these arrangements, Hell in London was organising (not without difficulty) financial guarantees for the rented cameras and travel for the remaining crew members. The letter in which she gives the business details is intriguing from another angle, since it hints strongly at tension in the marital relationship. 'Ivor darling,' it begins, 'I've written six letters to you and destroyed every one, so I'll try to keep to practical things' and it ends: 'Darling your letter made me very unhappy and I cry every time nobody is looking which is nearly all the time so I shant write any more.'[16]

The rest of the crew arrived just in time to experience the bombing by Italian planes of Barcelona. At three-hourly intervals between 16 and 18 January, Mussolini's aircraft (with Spanish markings) indiscriminately bombarded the city, leaving around 1,000 dead and 2,000 wounded. Montagu related that 'anti-aircraft defence was meagre, and our unit lodged uncomfortably in an hotel next to the post and telecommunications building, one of the chief targets.' Both Sidney Cole and Thorold Dickinson later published their impressions. Cole (who managed to sleep through the night raids) wrote of damage in the Calle de Cortes, 'seven solidly built eight-storey houses' being 'completely shattered', while 'two or three of them had vanished completely.' Dickinson observed twenty bombs being dropped at 11.30 at night down by the port: 'Watching from our bedroom window it was a fascinating sight, but daylight revealed scenes of devastation which increased with appalling frequency during our ten weeks in the country.' The raids had a paralysing effect on one member of the unit, probably Ray Pitt, who found he could no longer digest food, and had to be sent back to England.[17]

The filmmakers shot amidst the still-smoking rubble the morning after the raids, and dispatched the footage post-haste to London for incorporation in newsreels. But as Cole was to explain, 'our main object was not to stress such horrors as these, but rather the everyday life of a country fighting a war on its own soil, an angle that gets rather overlooked when people have become accustomed to journalistic exaggeration.' The crew remained in Spain gathering footage in and around Barcelona, Valencia and Madrid until March, while Montagu went to and fro, at one point dashing back to London to attend the celebrations marking the Film Society's 100th performance. The documentary assignment was a challenging one. The planned army film made little progress, since they had difficulty getting facilities. Dickinson, chiefly responsible for the education film, stated that they were not able to prepare a script and on their visits to children's colonies, schools, factories and mines they 'only had a couple of hours in any given spot – just time to look around, concoct a plan of action in a couple of minutes and then shoot.'[18]

On 14 March Montagu gave a talk over Station EAR, Madrid, broadcasting to America. He stressed the 'fortitude and friendliness, serenity and optimism' of the former capital's citizens, and spoke of equitable distribution of food, full cinemas, research work continuing 'within range of the enemy's guns', new schools going up, women 'warming their bones as they sew' and children 'skipping among the ruins'. But outside the city the war situation had deteriorated, and Franco's army was threatening to advance to the coast, cutting off Madrid. The films the unit had come to make were not completed, and Montagu faced the decision of whether to stay on in Spain to finish the work, with the possibility that none of what they shot would be of use in the end to the Republican cause, or to leave and hope to get what they had into circulation as quickly as possible. He chose the latter, revising the arrangement with the Spanish government so that the films would now be edited in Britain.[19]

As Cole and Dickinson began working on the material in London, Montagu returned to Spain. One cameraman had stayed behind to film news items, and Ivor still hoped he would be able to obtain some footage of the army in action, which despite having authorisation from high command he had not been able to do up to that point. It was at this time, if Louis Fischer is to be believed, that Ivor made a direct contribution to the Republican government's international public relations offensive. As Fischer tells the story:

> Throughout my stay in Barcelona, I visited the Foreign Office every day, and every day I saw Ivor Montagu sitting in [foreign minister Julio Álvarez] del Vayo's antechamber still waiting for permission from the War Department to take moving pictures at the front ... Once he said to me, 'You know, it seems to me that the Loyalist government ought

to enunciate its war aims, a sort of Fourteen Points programme like Woodrow Wilson's.'

Fischer says he enthusiastically passed the idea on to del Vayo, who in turn talked to Negrín; together the two drafted thirteen war aims, which received the backing of Cabinet and the influential Spanish Communist Party (PCE) and were issued by the government on 30 April.[20]

Designed to appeal to the Western democracies, especially Britain and France, the manifesto proclaimed a nation that would be free of foreign interference, with free elections, freedom of religion, and respect for civil rights and property rights. Negrín warmly promoted the document, and it was widely disseminated; Western leaders, however, were unmoved. As Fernando Claudín commented: 'The "Western governments" might be sympathetic to the chimerical image of Spanish Republican reality that the PCE and Negrín endeavoured to present, but they were organically incapable of accepting the reality that was hidden behind this image, that of a revolutionary proletariat ready to raise its head again at the first opportunity.' They were certainly also wary of granting Stalin a foothold in Western Europe.[21]

Finally, Montagu was able to get close to the front, although battle coverage still eluded him. In mid-April he filmed a visit by Harry Pollitt to the British Battalion of the International Brigade, then stationed just behind the front line after the retreat from Teruel. It was probably at this time that he encountered his cousin David Guest, who was serving with the battalion and was to be killed several months later. The short film that resulted from this shoot, titled *International Brigade*, does not appear to have survived; Montagu refers to it as 'a companion piece to the wonderful torchlight scene at Victoria Station in London filmed by the enterprise of our entire trade union when Attlee welcomed the battalion on the withdrawal of its surviving remnant some months later.'[22]

Back in London, Montagu supervised the post-production of the two major documentaries that were to emerge from the PFI expedition. The more successful was the education reportage, *Spanish ABC*. Relying heavily on graphs and statistics, the film demonstrated how the Republic, even in wartime conditions, was striving imaginatively to overcome national backwardness (a 52 per cent illiteracy rate at the end of the monarchy in 1931). Thousands of schools were being opened, while 'militiamen of culture' were teaching workers in their factories and soldiers on the front line. (As Dickinson reported: 'At the front, 300 yards from the insurgent lines, we entered a little shell-pocked cottage and found twenty to thirty soldiers learning trigonometry.') Meanwhile research continued – a Jesuit meteorologist is seen at work in his observatory – and cultural treasures, like artworks in the Prado, were being protected from the ravages of battle. The film also included shots of evacuation and refugee children in their new homes, no doubt vestiges of the original intention to devote a whole documentary to the topic. With a restrained commentary written by Montagu and spoken by the Communist C.G.T. Giles, *Spanish A.B.C.*, nineteen minutes in length, was released in June 1938. It was favourably received, *Sight and Sound* commenting: 'All these activities are amply documented by the film and presented simply and efficiently. It is an extraordinary and moving picture of conviction and determination unshaken by the horrors and dangers of war.'[23]

The second film was, as Montagu admitted, more of a hodgepodge. *Behind the Spanish Lines* was intent on persuading its audience that, contrary to pro-Nationalist propaganda, Republican Spain was a constitutional working democracy under the guidance of politicians of various persuasions. Amongst those depicted are President Manuel Azaña, President of Catalonia Lluís Companys ('a liberal'), foreign minister del Vayo, former prime minister José Giral, and minister of justice Ramón Gonzalez Peña. (Montagu was to lament: 'Alas, only, we could not by any means get a short interview with Negrín – he spoke perfect English and it would have been just the clincher for Britain and the US but, although as I mentioned he formally was sponsoring our enterprise he would never appear for us – he swore he was too shy and I am sure this was true!')[24]

The film shows the bombed ruins of the Cortes building in Madrid, and explains that because of the heavy bombardment of Barcelona the parliament now meets in the mountainside monastery of Montserrat. The documentary then turns to illustrating the thesis that, as Montagu's commentary maintains, 'despite the air raids, life goes on much as ever in republican Spain.' There are sequences depicting an open prisoner-of-war camp, the free press, a maternity home, army cadets in training, an anti-fascist open-air theatre performance, a mine run co-operatively by the workers, a band playing and villagers dancing. The war returns with a vengeance in the final segment of the film, with graphic shots of bombed ships off the coast (many of them British) and salvage work amidst the ruins in Barcelona. Two captured airmen, an Italian and a German, are interrogated, admitting that they are officers in their countries' regular forces. The Spanish people's determination to resist is then portrayed in scenes of mass rallies (with La Pasionaria speaking), soldiers in the front line, munitions being manufactured, youthful volunteer airmen in the Republic's chaser squadron, and militia on the march. About the same length as *Spanish A.B.C.*, and released at the same time, *Behind the Spanish Lines* was not as well received, the *Sight and Sound* reviewer considering it 'more propagandist' and less well made. But it was widely used in support of the Republican cause in Britain, and was exported, as Ivor recalled, to India, New Zealand, Canada and the USA.[25]

Footage of the interrogation of captured servicemen (which had been shot in sync-sound, with a concealed microphone) was also separately edited into two film documents designed to demonstrate conclusively that Germany and Italy were violating the Non-Intervention Agreement. *Prisoners Prove Intervention in Spain* was a five-minute item, edited by Montagu, depicting the questioning of Gino Poggi, an Italian airman, and Rudolf Ruecker, a German Air Force officer whose plane had been shot down after taking part in the March 1938 bombing raid on the British steamer *Stanwell* in Tarragona harbour. Intercut shots of massively damaged Barcelona buildings and of the wrecked ship gave chilling evidence of the effectiveness of the air raids, while close-ups of German inscriptions on the downed plane proved its origin. The film was shown on 23 April to a large crowd in Queen's Hall, London, at a National Emergency Conference on Spain organised by the Relief Committee for the Victims of Fascism. The following month it was exhibited in cinemas of the Granada circuit owned by Montagu's friend Sidney Bernstein. *Testimony on Non-Intervention*, thirty-one minutes in length, was not made for general release, being intended for the Non-Intervention Committee. It showed the interrogation in some detail of two Italian Army sergeant-majors, an Italian Air Force lieutenant and a German Air Force corporal, whose testimony made it clear that regular Italian troops were on the ground in Spain, and that Italian and German air force personnel were stationed there. *Testimony* was screened in May to an invited audience in Geneva in conjunction with resumed League of Nations debate on foreign intervention in Spain. Montagu was later to comment: 'In contrast to the International Brigade, idealistic youngsters ready for self-sacrifice, tough trade-unionists, heroic anti-fascists, all civilians, these German and Italian officers and Italian soldiers comprised detachments of their respective regular armed forces,' who had come to Spain under orders.[26]

Another variant on this theme was *Non-Intervention*, a nine-minute PFI film produced by Montagu in 1938 based on material photographed by Spanish government troops after their defeat of Italian forces in the Battle of Guadalajara (March 1937). It was reported as showing 'field guns, shells, tanks, tractors, cartridges, gas masks, uniforms, telephones, and lorries with regimental particulars, manufacturers' trade marks and other printed matter stamped on them in the Italian language,' while filmed documents demonstrated that the troops involved in the offensive were conscript units of the regular Italian Army.[27]

The final PFI production devoted to aspects of the Civil War was *Britain Expects*. This was a short film, shot on 35mm, devoted to documenting attacks on British merchant ships attempting to run the blockade imposed by the Non-Intervention Committee forces and bring supplies to Republican Spain. Among them was the *Marie Llewellyn*, skippered by David 'Potato' Jones, which had been bombed by Franco's planes off the Basque coast. 'The incident provided one more proof,' Montagu later argued:

> that such 'insults to the flag' are not reasons for governmental protest, but only pretexts for such, so used when the government concerned finds it in its favour to pick a quarrel (as with the pretext for the first world war). But that when its policy is to encourage aggressors – as Chamberlain's was with Hitler and Mussolini – it will stand any injury or violence from them without turning a hair.

With sponsorship from the National Union of Seamen and the Officers (Merchant Navy) Federation, Montagu assembled footage from Spain and interviewed survivors of the attacks, producing what the *Daily Herald* was to term 'a tremendous indictment' of Chamberlain's foreign policy.[28]

Such pointed political commentary did not find favour with the British Board of Film Censors. The Board threatened to ban the film, taking exception, without giving any reason, to such statements in the narration as 'Mussolini's own newspaper boasts of the successes of Italian aviation in bombing the shipping in Spanish ports. His purpose and that of Germany is plain.' Particularly unacceptable was the comment: 'The Prime Minister, in stating in the House of Commons that nothing could be done, became the first in British history to fail to give protection to British shipping.' Discussing the objection with Montagu, BBFC secretary Brooke Wilkinson asserted: 'We could not allow this. It has not been approved by the Prime Minister.' Ivor asked if this meant that anything said about the Prime Minister in a film had to be submitted for his approval. 'Naturally,' was the reply.[29]

While the arguing continued, Ivor had the film reduced to 16mm and handed over to Kino for non-commercial exhibition, where the BBFC could not touch it. This loophole was an irritant to the political establishment, and there were renewed moves afoot to make substandard film subject to censorship. However, the initiative was again sternly resisted by educational and community organisations. Kino and the PFI made a joint submission to the Cinematograph Advisory Committee, probably authored by Montagu, on the subject, and in the end no restrictive legislation eventuated. *Britain Expects* was eagerly exhibited by the usual Kino clientele of left-leaning organisations.[30]

But Montagu was still keen to have it shown in regular cinemas. He secured an admission from the BBFC that the points at issue were being submitted to the Foreign Office. Since this could compromise the supposed independence of the Board if it were made public, and the Foreign Office 'was certainly not ready to take on its shoulders the hornets' nest that would have been raised had they [be]come evidently responsible for any prohibition,' Ivor's bargaining power was enhanced, and after intercession by the pro-Loyalist politician the Duchess of Atholl, *Britain Expects* was passed with cuts. The Duchess was also instrumental in prevailing upon the ABC circuit to give it an experimental commercial release in six theatres. Montagu records that it was 'excellently received by the public but within a few days the circuit had collected enough reports from sycophantic cinema managers in their employ ("not the sort of film suitable for our theatres") to provide excuse for them to bring the experiment to an end.' Trevor Ryan notes that by this time (March 1939), 'the entire Spanish coast was under the control of Franco's forces and only Madrid remained in Republican hands – that is, ... attacks on British shipping had ceased.'[31]

In 1974, several of Montagu's Spanish Civil War films were revived, along with others including Joris Ivens's *Spanish Earth*, in screenings at the National Film Theatre. Reviewing the event for the anarchist newspaper *Freedom*, Julius Hogben praised *Spanish A.B.C.* ('as visual and constructive and satisfying as Ivor Montagu's other work leads [us] to expect – the best film shown') but faulted all the productions included in the retrospective for omitting the anarchist contribution to the struggle. Shown Hogben's article, Montagu replied privately to him at some length. The lack of coverage of anarchist effort or policy in Spain, he argued, was not due to any 'studied or deliberate neglect on the part of those who made the films'. They were Popular Front productions, stressing unity in the struggle against Franco. There were genuine differences of opinion, it was true, 'about how far to go with social change, to maintain the spirit and exaltation of the masses, and how to reconcile this with the necessary unity that had to be maintained not to throw the liberal middle classes into the hands of the fascists and to alienate the sympathy necessary to thwart the fascists abroad.' But these differences were overcome and unity achieved, Montagu maintained, in the three areas covered by the major PFI productions – the army, the education programmes, and the government. 'No one told us to "omit" anarchists or anyone else, and anarchists as well as anyone else co-operated with us in Spain, for these three things were at that time three outstanding things of the policy of all.'[32]

Failing to pay attention to all the currents of resistance prevailing on the Republican side (or even to mention revolution or socialism) was to be a recurrent criticism in reassessments of the PFI films. Paul Marris, for example, contended that they 'remained silent on the political situation behind the lines, and continued to disseminate, implicitly and uncritically, a version of the struggle that accorded with the Comintern's.' This was hardly surprising, given the circumstances of their production. But the films were also faulted for failing to document the true horror of internecine warfare. As Rachael Low was to write:

> It is very noticeable that they emphasise the normality of life and the valuable social policies of the Spanish Government, but show

comparatively little action, whether ground fighting or air raids, few refugees, little of the bitterness and suffering endured by a country split by civil war. Nor is there much effort to examine or explain the nature and reasons for the tragedy, or the real issue of democracy and fascism. They form a curiously antiseptic, and presumably ineffective, exercise in the art of persuasion.[33]

Montagu's other filmmaking activity at this time arose out of his involvement in CPGB activities, which included assisting in the Propaganda Department at the Party's headquarters in 16 King Street. As a delegate to the 15th CPGB Congress held at the Birmingham Town Hall on 16–19 September 1938, he chose to speak on the role of art and artists, broadly defined, in the working-class movement. The Party's work in the field, he argued, 'has to regenerate British art in much the same way as it has to regenerate British life in any other field.' Art could be brought 'into our whole lives and our daily work', while artists could work with 'the actual things that people are worried about' – he instanced the films about Spain and China that Kino was distributing. Practitioners who were 'dissatisfied with the barrenness of their work in the existing period' would be attracted to the movement, but everything should not be left to the professionals. There was no reason why Party meetings should be drab, for example: their stage management should not be neglected, and groups should learn to bring into their work 'a factor by which they can show that the message that they give is not a dry thing but a … human thing … that restores some of the colour of life that capitalism is driving out of it.'[34]

Montagu brought along a PFI crew and they filmed selected highlights of the conference in 16mm, though without the capacity for sync-sound, a decided handicap. 'A film of a congress – how could that be exciting?' asked the *Daily Worker* columnist six weeks later, when the *XVth Congress Film* (also known as *C.P. Congress – Birmingham 1938*) was one of two pictures that reportedly 'delighted and enthused the hundreds who formed the longest queue ever seen outside St Pancras Town Hall, two films that encouraged scores among the audience to put their names down as recruits for the Party.' (The other was the Soviet picture *Esli zavtra voyna/ If War Should Come*, portraying the Red Army beating back an attack from Nazi Germany.) The source of the appeal, the columnist asserted – it was none other than Ivor Montagu – was that 'we see personalities who are an epitome of contemporary working-class history: Tom Mann, the leader of the fight against non-unionism in the Notts coalfields; trade unionists like Arthur Horner and Claude Berridge; Hannington, militant fighter for the unemployed; Copeman and the boys of the British Battalion of the International Brigade.' The ten-minute film also depicted Harry Pollitt delivering his report (beneath gigantic banner portraits of Marx, Engels, Lenin and Stalin), the Party's sole MP Willie Gallacher, delegates in discussion, Unity Theatre performing their play *Plant in the Sun*, the Unity Male Voice Choir, the newly-elected Central Committee coming up on the platform, and the whole assembly engaged in community singing. 'All combine', Montagu claimed, 'in a picture of a party whose keynote is life and activity.'[35]

The extant print is silent, and it is hard to imagine it generating much enthusiasm. But when released it had a soundtrack of 'accompanied music, drums, singing' and was warmly received by Party activists. One writer described it as 'an exciting and inspiring film' that 'brings out the vitality of the Congress' and 'will bring audiences to their feet in admiration.' It was released by Kino, which described it as 'a stirring record' that would 'greatly help you to recruit to the Party and get a mass sale of the Congress Reports.'[36]

As the Congress was meeting, the Sudetenland crisis was coming to a head. At the end of the month, signing the Munich Agreement, Britain and France acceded to Hitler's demands over Czechoslavakia, and Neville Chamberlain triumphantly proclaimed 'peace for our time' to a relieved nation. Somewhat more perspicaciously, Montagu analysed developments in an article for *Labour Monthly*. The Nazi intent of world empire, he argued in 'Hitler's Europe', had taken 'the stride forward that has transformed dream to a menace of reality.' With a defensive line in the Sudeten mountains, a powerful army, an air force within flying distance of German industrial centres, and defence agreements with many other nations, Czechoslovakia was in a position to repulse any German attack; the use of military force against it was 'unthinkable'. And 'with Czechoslovakia in existence, the roads to the Nazi aims of expansion and conquest were firmly barred and blocked.' Now, however, the mountain defences were gone; Germany had acquired control in its new territories over lead, zinc, coal and timber resources, as well as motor works and metal factories; and what was left of Czechoslovakia was 'already a German vassal', in economic and political subjection to the Nazis. The Munich Agreement made manifest the refusal of the Chamberlain and Daladier governments to co-operate with the Soviet Union against Fascism, and 'with this reinforcement, the Nazi Empire is today in a position to carry forward its offensive throughout Europe.' Montagu's conclusion, in hindsight, has a prophetic ring. 'We cannot defeat Hitler,' he suggested, 'until we remove from the power to betray the Chamberlains and Daladiers who betray for Hitler.' However, there was one element in the equation about which Ivor was somewhat less prescient. There was a well-armed country, he averred, 'that will ever be found on the side of democracy and freedom'. He was, one could maintain, as blind about the Soviet Union as Chamberlain was about Nazi Germany.[37]

For the Soviet Union in 1938 would not have scored highly in the democracy and freedom stakes. At the third show trial in March, Nikolai Bukharin, former head of the Comintern, and twenty others belonging to the 'Bloc of Rightists and Trotskyites' were accused of murder, espionage, terrorist conspiracy, wrecking and expediting preparations for foreign intervention. Among those found guilty and sentenced to death, on as flimsy grounds as the previous two trials, were Bukharin, former Soviet premier Alexei Rykov, and former head of the NKVD Genrikh Yagoda; also condemned were Montagu's acquaintances, the former chargé d'affaires Arkady Rosengolts, who was shot, and ambassador Christian Rakovsky, who was sentenced to twenty years in prison. On this occasion Ivor does not seem to have been called upon to defend the legitimacy of proceedings, perhaps because Comintern headquarters, being subjected to severe purges, was in disarray. He nonetheless remained active in the FSU, which was experiencing its own form of disorganisation; in January, as MI5 noted, it had 'recently lost a great deal of money through bad management, dishonesty etc., and Ivor Montagu has taken up the matter and made several changes described as drastic.' In the USSR the Great Terror advanced during the year to the point at which nearly 766,000 individuals had been arrested, of whom 385,000 were sentenced to be shot.[38]

Back in Britain, Harry Pollitt, in his report to the 15th Congress, had declared that the meeting was a challenge to the Chamberlain government, which was 'betraying the national interests of the British people, no less

than it is betraying the interests of world peace.' Its pro-Fascist policy was
dictated by a 'small clique of monopoly capitalists' who wished to 'create a
state of affairs similar to that in Germany because they see in the Labour
movement a hindrance to the free development of their class interests.' The
Congress therefore had 'one supreme aim – to formulate a policy that will
help the Labour Movement, and all progressive people who realise the serious consequences of the economic crisis, the threat of war and the peril
that faces democracy, to combine in one common effort to overthrow the
National Government.'[39]

It was this People's Front line that the CP wished to push in the run-up
to the next general election, due at the latest in 1940, and to promote it
the Party commissioned from Montagu the production of an agitprop
film. Whether the idea was initially his, or whether he was approached, it is
unclear – Ivor gives both versions. But it is certain that the project appealed.
He may even, as he claimed, have put up the requisite £900 budget from
his personal savings.[40]

Montagu scripted the half-hour film, as he later explained:

... in the style of how I'd write an article, a literary article, and then
translated it into visual terms. The logic of it would be the logic of if
I'd sat down to write a pamphlet or a leading article on the necessity of
overthrowing the Chamberlain Government for the harm it was doing
England and internationally.

With scant resources at his disposal, Ivor drew on the talent of friends:
Elsa Lanchester's mother, for example, supplied a Chamberlain marionette
whose jerking was to provide some entertaining comic moments. The
film was shot with a crew of PFI and ACT technicians over the winter of
1938/39, and released in April as *Peace and Plenty* (the ironic title was taken
from the 15th Congress published report, entitled *For Peace and Plenty*).[41]

Cutting together library footage, stills, graphics, animation, puppetry and
live action, with a scathing narration and a percussive musical score, Montagu
constructed a damning indictment of the Tory government's record. On
the home front, the members of Chamberlain's Cabinet – identified as
wealthy landowners and stockholders – are shown presiding over a society
in which a quarter of the population have incomes below the subsistence

level, living in atrocious slum conditions, in poor health, unemployed or with low wages, with no opportunity for advancement. Internationally, the Tories have been in power when Japan seized Manchuria, Mussolini seized Abyssinia, and Hitler seized Austria and Czechoslovakia; the aggressive dictators are Chamberlain's friends, and the nation is scandalously ill-prepared to defend against attack. To clinch the argument, Harry Pollitt (unidentified) delivers a speech to camera, calling for an anti-fascist alliance with France, the Soviet Union, and the United States, and calling on all opponents of Chamberlain to make common cause and sweep the National Government out of office. The popular front policies so permeate the film that in this piece of electioneering propaganda, the name of the sponsoring party is not mentioned once.

Rejecting the sober documentary style he had employed for the Spanish films, Montagu aimed in *Peace and Plenty* for 'violent caricature and violent political contrast'. He deliberately used a great number of stills, particularly those of politicians 'in some utterly ludicrous position'. The technique worked: a report in *The Times*, for example, noted that 'for the most part it gains its effect by contrast: illustrations of the evils of our time, bad housing, under-nourishment, ill-health, unemployment, or, in foreign affairs, war and oppression, are followed by grotesque photographs of politicians engaged in inappropriate or painfully appropriate pursuits. The film contains many harrowing scenes ...'[42]

Released on 16mm, *Peace and Plenty* was handled by Kino and was enthusiastically exhibited by left-wing activists to politically-engaged audiences throughout England, Wales and Scotland. In the House of Commons, Willie Gallacher arranged a screening on 14 June chaired – in the spirit of anti-Chamberlain unity – by Liberal leader Sir Archibald Sinclair. Montagu recalled:

The place was absolutely packed. The debating chamber must have been deserted. Afterwards, it was very entertaining to hear the MPs as they went away, saying to one another: 'Now that's the thing we ought to have for our party!' They didn't seem to realise that the content had something to do with the force of the film and not every party could make such a bitter, acid film.

The Times reported that 'many supporters of the government were there out of curiosity, and Mr Gallacher seemed much impressed by the sporting instinct of his political opponents.' The reception it received would have reassured Montagu that his investment in the project was worthwhile, even if financially he had taken a hit; in May he reported to Eisenstein that he was now working on a commercial script 'in order to pay for the loss incurred on the production of our Party picture.'[43]

A final filmmaking project Montagu was involved in at this time was an adaptation of Ellen Wilkinson's *The Town That Was Murdered*, a history of the north-eastern industrial town of Jarrow, and in particular the recent destruction of the shipbuilding industry with its devastating impact on the workers. Conceived of as a fiction film on life in the Distressed Areas, it was to be a production of the newly-formed Left Book Club Film Group, financed through advance subscriptions. The idea was developed by a team comprising Montagu, Thorold Dickinson, Sidney Cole, Christopher Brunel and Max Anderson (all of whom had been associated with the PFI). As Trevor Ryan recounts, an exploratory visit was made to Jarrow and stills taken, but the film did not materialise through lack of finance, and the LBC Film Group dissolved on the outbreak of war in September.[44]

Over this period there was a marked falling off in Montagu's public speaking engagements. In 1938, no doubt among other things, he spoke on the Chinese Eighth Route Army, formerly the Red Army (24 or 25 January, accompanying a screening of the documentary *China Strikes Back*), the Palestine situation (21 July), the International Brigade (11 September), aid for Spain (20 November), and Fascism and the war crisis (29 November). The following year he addressed audiences on the topics of 'Films in Crisis' (19 February) and 'The Fifth Column versus the People of Britain' (1 August). He also introduced Soviet film screenings on 25 and 26 March. Whenever the occasion arose, he continued to hold out the USSR as a model society. Thus he contended that the Palestine problem could only be solved by an immediate conference of representatives of both sides; 'the country could then be governed in the same manner as Soviet Russia where 500 races and creeds live together in enviable peace.' (In a similar vein, Montagu argued in a July 1939 article that in the fields of women's emancipation from domestic drudgery, limitations on hours of work, availability of education, and guaranteed full employment, 'our British measure of liberty is already outstripped, not in Utopia, but in the real, actual world, in the USSR.')[45]

At the *Daily Worker*, Montagu was acting as foreign editor, contributing after 1937 only the occasional bylined article. In July 1938, for example, he expressed his opinion on an exhibition of contemporary German art labelled 'degenerate' by the Nazis. Though acknowledging the 'extraordinarily rich variety' of the work on show, he maintained that 'it is not here, in this style, that the future for Germany lies. It lies in a more active realism that can come only from sharing in life instead of exalting egoistic and sensual individualism.' Then in May 1939 be contributed an article based on an interview with Jacques Duclos, Communist Vice-President of the French Chamber of Deputies ('You should not believe abroad the lies that are told of French military and defence weakness,' Duclos asserted). As Montagu was possibly aware, Duclos had formerly worked for the Comintern West European Bureau in Berlin, was a longstanding OGPU/NKVD espionage agent, and was responsible for liaison between the French Communist Party (PCF) and the Soviet apparat.[46]

Over the summer, Montagu's articles in the *Daily Worker* became more frequent. He proffered a satirical dig at the upper-class sport of grouse-shooting (12 August), and a critical review of H.G. Wells's *The Fate of Homo Sapiens* (16 August), which granted the 'salutary and stimulating shrewdness of many of its observations', but attacked the pessimistic conclusion reached because 'his approach to sociology is completely unscientific' and because 'H.G. hates the working class and has done throughout his life.' But Ivor's major contribution for the month appeared two days after the bombshell signing, on 23 August, of the Nazi-Soviet Pact. The treaty of non-aggression derailed the negotiations that had been proceeding for a three-way mutual assistance agreement between Britain, France and the Soviet Union. Montagu's article made no attempt to analyse the implications of the Pact, not surprisingly perhaps as the anti-fascist collective-security line Communist parties had pushed for the past four years had suddenly to be abandoned. Instead, 'Strongest Country in the World' simply gloated about the military and industrial might of the Soviet Union: 'the Soviet Army is the most perfectly mechanised in the world', 'the USSR possesses at the present time the most powerful submarine fleet in the world', 'today there is no agriculture more mechanically advanced than that of the USSR', etc.

In short, 'the backward, unequipped Russia of the Tsars has been transformed under the leadership of the Communist Party of the Soviet Union, under the wise guidance of Lenin and Stalin, to a Socialist state covering one-sixth of the world, the strongest people with the greatest resources on earth.' Comment on the Pact was left to an introductory box, in which the paper stated that 'by a master-stroke of foreign policy, the Soviet Union has struck a mighty blow for peace and Socialism against the Fascist war plans.'[47]

Five days later, assured that the move would meet no resistance from the USSR, Hitler invaded Poland. In response, Britain and France declared war on Germany. Then, on 17 September, Soviet troops overran Polish defences in the east, advancing to the demarcation line secretly agreed between the two powers of the non-aggression pact. Soviet military prowess was amply on display; convincing sceptics that the land of socialism had not departed from its oft-proclaimed peace-loving policy would be Ivor's next duty. And no doubt, in the general confusion of the 'phoney war', with no outright hostilities between Britain and Germany, and with little he could do in film production or distribution, he was putting his mind to how else he might deploy his energies.

15

ESPIONAGE

WITH THE OUTBREAK of war, Britain instituted a massive evacuation campaign, relocating millions of civilians, particularly children, from cities vulnerable to aerial bombardment. Montagu, too, was taking no chances. In October 1939 he moved with his family from London to rural Hertfordshire, renting (for £2 a week) 'Knowle', a two-storey semi-detached stone cottage in Bucks Hill, near King's Langley. Across the road was a pub, the Rose & Crown, where Rowna, now 17 years old, could sometimes be spotted having a drink with soldiers. Hell, who had joined the CP in March, worked at home assisting Ivor in a secretarial capacity. Also forming part of the household, helping with the domestic chores as well as carrying out any necessary translation from German, was Elfriede Stoecker, known as 'Friedel'; her struggle to obtain her husband's release from Nazi detention had been in vain, and Walter Stoecker had died of typhus in Buchenwald on 10 March 1939.[1]

Montagu commuted into London each day to his desk at the *Daily Worker*, where he had now resumed, it would seem, something approaching full-time employment. Here, amidst the tensions and confusions of the Comintern *volte-face* occasioned by the non-aggression pact, and the uncertainties of Communist policy toward the war, personal relations were taking on a new intensity. As one staffer at the time put it:

Living and working under conditions of considerable strain, with the popular tide flowing against them and recognising no moral restraints of any sort in their personal lives, it was not unnatural that what was, apparently, normally a very loose, amoral atmosphere had become one which was supercharged with sex.

But if Ivor was affected – and there had been the time in the not so distant past when his marriage had gone through a rocky patch – there is nothing in the archives to confirm it.[2]

The editor of the paper at this time was J.R. (Johnny) Campbell, who had been in the Soviet Union during the Great Terror, knew what had been going on, and said nothing about it in his anti-Trotsky polemic *Soviet Policy and Its Critics*, published in February 1939. His rationale (as he later expressed it) was that war was coming and nothing should detract from the defence of the USSR against fascist aggression. When Germany invaded Poland, Campbell stood staunchly alongside Pollitt and the rest of the CPGB's Central Committee in calling for a war 'on two fronts', against the Nazis, and against the Chamberlain government. The line of this 2 September manifesto was backed up in Pollitt's pamphlet *How to Win the War*, issued on 14 September. But such a policy was not to Stalin's liking. He declared that the distinction between democratic and fascist states no longer applied: the war was an imperialist one that Communists should not support. Comintern head Dimitrov was ordered to ensure that member parties got the message, and in the case of the CPGB it was delivered by D.F. ('Dave') Springhall returning from Moscow on 25 September. After vigorous debate the Central Committee accepted the change of line, with only Pollitt, Campbell and Gallacher opposed. Pollitt and Campbell were forced to recant; Pollitt was removed from the post of General Secretary, his position taken over by a secretariat headed by Rajani Palme Dutt, while Campbell was replaced as *Daily Worker* editor by Bill Rust. To have the party's only MP opposing the new line would have been too much of an embarrassment, so Gallacher's vote was recorded as being in favour. The CPGB's manifesto 'Stop the War!', issued on 7 October, superseded the position paper of 2 September and raised the demand for an immediate peace conference – something that Hitler, with the support of the Soviet government, was at this time in fact proposing.[3]

Montagu tiptoed nimbly around these convulsions. Writing for the *Daily Worker*, he advanced the 'war on two fronts' line while it remained in force. In a series of dispatches from around the country in late September and early October, he noted how committed workers were to the war effort. 'How to Get Munitions' (25 September), for example, began with quoting a resolution of Sheffield shop stewards: 'We declare our full support for the struggle against Nazi aggression and call upon the membership of the Amalgamated Engineering Union in the Sheffield district to take their full part in bringing about the speediest possible defeat of German Fascism.' But everywhere efforts to reorganise industry to meet wartime needs and to provide adequate civil defence protection were being hampered by employers riding roughshod over trade unions and by the hidebound ruling-class mentality of the Chamberlain administration. Even implementation of the black-out was being botched, with a surge in road casualties; while the clampdown on entertainment was a stupid mistake: 'Quite disastrously, the authorities ever since the war began have tried to put over a feeling that recreation is an unpatriotic sin, instead of a vital necessity.' In sum, 'We can't trust the bosses to win this war,' Montagu quotes one engineer as saying.[4]

The tone changes radically in Montagu's two articles on Poland, published on 14 and 17 October. There is now no trumpeting of resistance to Nazi aggression. The ECCI Secretariat, in a 'short thesis' received by the CPGB Central Committee on 2 October, had declared that 'the international working class may under no conditions defend fascist Poland which has refused the aid of the Soviet Union and repressed other nationalities.' Montagu took the cue. The country that had been invaded and occupied by Germany and the Soviet Union merited no sympathy, let alone active support: it had been, 'for the vast bulk of its people, a gigantic jail'; it was 'the nearest thing in modern Europe to the corruption and repression of the former Tsarist Empire.' Noblemen enjoyed immense wealth while the bulk of the peasant population lived in abject penury; moreover, 'the Nazis had nothing on the Polish gentry', since 'the persecution of the Jews in Poland long ante-dated that in Germany.' Thus the Soviet military conquest was an act of liberation. The Polish government officials and generals had fled; the Red Army 'entered to save all the thus deserted country not yet overrun.'[5]

It was now pointless, according to Montagu, to try to use military force to crush fascism, as he argued in November:

To get rid of an ideology you must analyse its cause to know what you should be fighting to produce the desired result and 'Hitlerism' won't go unless we get rid of British and French imperialism, that built up Hitler, encouraged him in his aggressions, and would if successful, guided by the same principles, build up and encourage once more successors to him in the same or other quarters of the globe.

In the Winter issue of *Fabian Quarterly*, answering a socialist proponent of all-out struggle against Germany, he denied that the CPGB's decision to repudiate the 'war on two fronts' policy was taken 'in tame obedience to directions from Moscow'. Not at all: the Communist ear was 'close ... to the British working class, to factories and to homes, and it did not take many days' practical experience of this policy to teach us that it just wouldn't work.' To back the war was simply to strengthen the Chamberlain government and the ruling class; 'the aims with which the peoples are being deluded into supporting it can never be attained, but only made more distant, by the victory of either warring group.' Though Montagu (and other CP writers) did not use the term, the position being advanced by the party at this time was close to the idea of 'revolutionary defeatism' propounded by Lenin during the First World War; and indeed in a later article Ivor lumped Chamberlain and French premier Daladier in with Hitler, Mussolini and Franco as reactionary imperialists, contending that *any* victory 'inflicts suffering and massacre on the masses and rivets their chains more firmly upon them.'[6]

Throughout the CP's policy and leadership crisis Ivor remained on close friendly terms with Pollitt, inviting him out to his new home ('I had a grand time at your house today,' the deposed General Secretary reported) and lending him £15 in his hour of need. Then at the end of November the two joined forces in canvassing for the CP candidate in the by-election in Stretford, greater Manchester. As Labour was not contesting the seat in accordance with the electoral truce negotiated by the major parties, the field was wide open for an attack on the Chamberlain government. In the event the CP's stop-the-war plea failed to make a strong impression, the Conservative candidate being returned with an overwhelming majority.[7]

The Communists' task was made tougher at this time by the Soviet invasion of Finland. Begun on 30 November, it had come about after the failure of negotiations aimed at shifting the border further away from Leningrad. The military action was presented as a pre-emptive strike aimed at shoring up the USSR's defences, but as there was never the slightest chance that tiny Finland would attack its giant neighbour, and the prospect of assault by other powers using this route was remote, some further justifications were needed to dispel the suspicion that it was an act of imperialist aggression. Montagu accordingly resorted to a similar rhetorical strategy to that he had used in the case of Poland. Democracy in Finland was but a façade, he argued in a lengthy article for the January 1940 *Labour Monthly*. Since the victory of the Whites in the Civil War, the ranks of workers and small peasants had been decimated and 'unremitting rule over them maintained by the Finno-Swedish bankers, business men and big agrarians by alternating waves of Fascist terror or "Social Democrat" co-operation (backed by veiled fascist forces in the state apparatus) according to the degree of resistance of the working class.' Hence, as in Poland, the entry of Soviet armed forces would result in the liberation of the working people. The USSR had 'concluded a treaty of mutual alliance with a revolutionary Finnish people's government [i.e. the 'Finnish Democratic Republic' headed by Comintern official Otto Kuusinen] and set about helping it to clear those who had seized and controlled Finland, with the help of imperial backers, out from their country.' And thus 'the Red Army, side by side with the Finnish workers, forges onward through the blizzard. The boundaries of Socialism are being extended.'[8]

This was a line Ivor pushed repeatedly, in talks on Finland on 8 December (Stepney Russia To-Day Society), 13 January (Conway Hall), 28 January (Labour Hall, Barking), 2 February (Stepney Russia To-Day Society), and 26 February (Hendon Branch, CPGB). At the Conway Hall, according to the police informant, 'Montagu alluded to the scandalous tirades led by the British Press against the conduct of Russia against Finland, and went on to justify her actions and explain that the legitimate Government of Finland did not represent the majority.' Expanding on the theme with the Stepney *Russia To-Day* Readers Group, Montagu argued that Finland had been 'controlled by the Fascist White Guard, with the aid of Germany, financed by Great Britain and the United States. Britain in particular considered Finland as a useful base for future attacks on the USSR. The Capitalists' plan had been to drive Russia into war with Germany; when this failed, the solution had been to make Finland provoke Russia into hostilities.' Ivor also helped define the Communist position on the conflict in articles for the CPGB's journal *World News and Views* in December ('Soviet Union and Finland')

and January ('Finland – Two Worlds Meet'), and in a *Daily Worker* review of *Russia, Finland and the Baltic* by W.P. and Zelda Coates.[9]

TUC General Secretary Sir Walter Citrine presented a rather different picture from that promulgated by Montagu when he visited Finland on a National Council of Labour fact-finding mission in January, accompanied by Philip Noel-Baker, Labour MP, and John Downie, of the Co-operative Union. According to Citrine, far from being side by side with the invaders, Finnish workers were united with all other sectors of the community in their determination to repulse them. In statements to the press and in his book *My Finnish Diary*, published as a Penguin Special in March, Citrine reported on Soviet air raids: the destruction of working-class neighbourhoods by means of incendiary bombs, the devastation wrought by high explosives, and the machine-gunning of civilians by Soviet aviators. On the ground, Soviet soldiers were brave but poorly led and trained; in bitter winter weather they were only lightly clad, received poor rations, and were kept in the front line with NKVD rifles at their backs. Citrine was told that the ratio of Soviet military casualties to that of the Finnish army was fifty to one; though sceptical, he was given enough evidence to be convinced it was true. As for the idea of Finnish workers welcoming their liberation, this was a joke: they were well aware that their housing and general conditions of life were far in advance of those prevailing in Russia, Citrine maintained, and hence they had not the slightest desire to fall under Soviet hegemony. On his return to Britain, Citrine made an urgent appeal for artillery and aircraft to be sent to bolster Finnish defences.[10]

Clearly this challenge to the Communist account of the conflict, with the real danger that British munitions would be used against the USSR, demanded a response. 'ANSWER TO CITRINE, DOWNIE & NOEL-BAKER!' announced the *Daily Worker*. 'Hear what W.J.R. Squance, Ivor Montagu and Mrs. Henrotte have to say. Friday next, February 16, 7.30, Holborn Hall'. Thanks to the ever-vigilant MI5 spies, we know that on this occasion Montagu decided on *ad hominem* attack, confining his speech 'to the life histories of the three men who had recently returned from Finland … traitors to the cause of true socialism.'[11]

Citrine hit back in the Introduction to his *Diary*. Here he wrote of 'the sycophants who extol everything Russian, and who seek to justify cruelty, terrorism and barbarism, not to mention wicked perversion of the truth and wilful lying, when committed on behalf of the Soviet Union.' Such people were quick to condemn the bombing of Chinese cities by the Japanese, and of Guernica by the Germans, as atrocities; but 'the merciless bombing by Russian 'planes of defenceless Finnish people passes without comment, or is palliated by hypocritical phrases, such as "liberating the people of Finland".' Montagu retaliated in his review of the book, published in the *Daily Worker* of 23 March. The device of the diary, he alleged, was a means by which Citrine could set down 'the most outrageous slanders on the U.S.S.R., and whitewashing lies about Finnish conditions'. Citrine 'does not appear to have asked to see any of the Finnish workers, not yet executed but confined in the White Guard government's jails and camps for their opposition to the war.' Regarding the machine-gunning of civilians, 'the evidence has a way of petering out into insinuations and assumptions.' Montagu does not mention the bombing raids, nor the claim that Soviet troops on the ground were poorly equipped and led. But there was no need for a substantial reply, for 'history has already given a sufficient answer to this sort of drivel.'[12]

There was a reason that Montagu was not able to respond more directly to some of Citrine's claims. In January the *Daily Worker* had asked Ivor to go to the Soviet Union, and Frank Pitcairn (Claud Cockburn) to go to Finland, to act as war correspondents for the paper. Their applications for exit permits were refused. MI5 reports were critical to this decision. On 26 January, Oswald 'Jasper' Harker wrote to S.A. Newsam of the Home Office on the subject of Montagu's application, declaring:

In our opinion a Communist Party member of his standing should not be allowed to leave the country at present, nor is there any good journalistic reason for his visit, as the *Daily Worker* can already get all the material it needs from the Soviet Union. It does not seem desirable to allow the Communist Party to have a courier travelling from this country to Moscow. There can be no doubt that the Party would use MONTAGU for this purpose.

In turn, Newsam informed Stafford of the Passport Office that after consultation with the Foreign Office the applications by Montagu and Cockburn had been refused. Newsam wrote:

In our view it is one thing to allow the *Daily Worker* to conduct its war propaganda in this country; it is another thing to give to such a newspaper special facilities for sending correspondents abroad for the purpose of facilitating propaganda. Moreover, in the case of Ivor Montagu it would be inconsistent with our friendly attitude towards the Finns to give facilities to a well-known Communist to go to Moscow for the purpose of sending pro-Soviet and anti-Finn dispatches.[13]

A storm of protest arose when the decision was made public on 5 February. The *Daily Worker* pointed out that British newspapers that had correspondents in Finland and the Soviet Union included *The Times*, the *Daily Telegraph*, the *Daily Express*, the *Evening Standard*, the *Daily Herald*, the *News Chronicle*, and the *Sunday Times*. 'The millionaire Press can get permits,' it tartly commented, 'The working-class Press – No.' It was understandable, the article went on, 'that at a moment when the capitalist newspapers are full of lies about the Red Army, the Chamberlain government is not anxious to have Ivor Montagu as an eyewitness.' In following days messages condemning the government's action flooded in from journalists, trade unionists, and others concerned about infringement of civil liberties.[14]

In a contribution to the *Daily Worker* on 10 February, Montagu wrote about what he would look for in the Soviet Union if he were permitted to go. He was puzzled, he said, by reports he had read lately that the Red Army 'piles up its dead in reckless heaps' and 'loses whole divisions, cut off through starvation', since 'quite an influential person in USSR – it was Stalin – said not long ago that human beings, people, were the most precious capital of the country.' He was puzzled, too, that the Soviet aeroplanes operating in the conflict were said to be old types outflown by the Finnish fighters, since he had seen with his own eyes, 'Soviet-built chasers streaking across the skies of Spain and the pride of the German and Italian air forces in panic flight before them.' He would like, he concluded, 'to see with my own eyes again', and to talk to the Finns 'who are fighting to liberate their country'.[15]

The following day a mass rally to protest the ban was held in Holborn Hall and the adjacent small hall, with 1,500 (so the *Daily Worker* claimed) in attendance. Labour MP Colonel Josiah Wedgwood was in the chair. Montagu 'made a devastating exposure of previous lie campaigns against the USSR and was received with immense enthusiasm.' Pitcairn/Cockburn maintained that the ban was 'an attempt to turn out the lights over Finland', while *Daily Worker* editor Bill Rust asserted that the British government, with the aid of the Labour leaders, was 'preparing direct intervention against the Soviet Union … That is the real reason for the Pitcairn-Montagu blackout.'[16]

On 14 February Wedgwood raised the issue in Parliament, to be told that the Home Secretary would not reconsider the matter. 'Labour members,' the *Manchester Guardian* reported, 'were loudest in the almost universal chorus of approval' for the refusal. 'My right hon. and gallant Friend must understand,' Under-Secretary Osbert Peake declaimed, 'that restrictions are placed upon foreign travel in time of war. Generally speaking the onus is on the applicant to show that his proposed journey is in the public interest. In this case my right hon. Friend cannot see that that burden of proof has been discharged.' Gallacher interjected. 'Does the Minister mean,' he asked, 'that it is not in the public interest that people in this country should get information other than that which they get from the Goebbelised Press?' There was no reply.[17]

In a letter to Labour leader Clement Attlee, Montagu pertinently questioned the 'public interest' criterion cited by Peake, pointing out, 'I know of many cases where wealthy persons have been allowed to take their usual holidays in Switzerland, France and elsewhere this winter' and that 'if the principle is correct, it gives a precious poor chance to anyone in strong disagreement with the Government to get an exit visa at all.' He informed Attlee that he had been given a chance, following Wedgwood's intervention, to explain to the private secretary of Home Secretary Sir John Anderson that he had an assurance from the Soviet authorities that he would receive a visa and would be able to take photographic and cinematographic apparatus – 'I did look on it as a great opportunity to do something particularly useful that possibly no one else could have got the opportunity to do, get historical records both by camera and eyewitness that perhaps now will never be obtained.' Attlee promised to discuss the matter with Wedgwood.[18]

Meanwhile, MI5 was on the alert since the agency had received information – how accurate is difficult to say – that Montagu and Cockburn were intending to leave the country and proceed to their destinations without a permit. A possible route, it was believed, was through Northern Ireland and Eire, so ports were alerted and the Defence Ministry in Dublin issued with full particulars. Arrests would follow should either of the individuals slip through the cordon. In the event, either the authorities were acting on false information or Montagu and Cockburn thought better of the idea – perhaps because, by March, hostilities in Finland were drawing to a close.

In an intriguing postscript to the whole exit permit saga, MI5 recorded on 13 March that 'it is interesting to note with regard to Ivor MONTAGU there was a conflict of opinion at the Soviet Embassy over the question of MONTAGU going to the Finnish war front. It was realised that if the Russians allowed him to go, they would have to allow other newspaper correspondents to go, and they were in the past unwilling to do this.'[19]

On the same day the signing of the Moscow Peace Treaty put an end to the Winter War. The USSR took over 11 per cent of Finnish territory including a buffer zone for Leningrad, while Finland retained its sovereignty. Nothing more was heard of the 'Finnish Democratic Republic'. Meanwhile, a Politburo meeting on 5 March determined the fate of 22,000 members of the Polish Officer Corps – many of them reservists, and factory owners, landlords, professionals or government officials in civilian life – captured during the invasion and occupation of eastern Poland. During April and May they were systematically shot, some – notoriously – to be buried in the Katyn forest. (When the bodies were discovered by the Germans in 1943, Montagu poured scorn on the claim that the Soviets were responsible.) The NKVD then seized and deported a further 109,000 Poles, including a large number of Jews; a typical sentence was eight years in the Siberian gulag. Such was the liberation of eastern Poland Montagu had celebrated back in October; the facts were, of course, kept secret at the time.[20]

As the wider war ground on, the notion of 'federal union' was attracting an upsurge of interest. Hostilities between nations could be averted, so it was argued, by ceding certain sovereign powers to a higher, supra-national authority, in a kind of United States of Europe or Atlantic Union. The idea was promulgated by the American Clarence K. Streit (*Union Now*, 1939) and the British author W.B. Curry (*The Case for Federal Union*, 1939), had been seized on enthusiastically by a number of politicians and academics, and in speeches by Chamberlain and Daladier had begun to be looked on as a war aim. To Communists, the objective seemed suspiciously like a capitalist power bloc directed against the growing strength of the Soviet Union. In an astute polemic published as a pamphlet, *The Federal Union Myth*, by the CPGB in February, Montagu questioned the claims made by federal union advocates. Applying a Marxist analysis (and leaning heavily on Lenin), he pointed out that any pooling of resources that would take place would be transacted by the existing owners, 'operating through existing governments, in existing (capitalist) systems of society'. As promoted, for example, by Churchill, the idea simply meant the hegemony of Anglo-French imperialism; the union would not ensure peace, but would constitute 'the organisation of reaction to fight internally against progress and externally against the states and combinations outside'. Since it did not challenge the state control wielded by capitalists, Montagu concluded, federal union promised only 'an extension of all-power to those who have faced us with disaster. A vista of wars of counter-revolution, wars of secession, wars of repression, wars with other combinations, war to restore capitalism to the USSR.' The argument found an admirer in D.N. Pritt: 'It is brilliant,' he wrote to the printers.[21]

Montagu compensated for his inability to serve the Party cause as a reporter on the Red Army front lines by redoubling his efforts as a public speaker. In the month of April alone he spoke on at least eight occasions at rallies for the Daily Worker Readers' League, from Nottingham to Stepney, Walthamstow to Huddersfield. His recurrent theme was that the British government was attempting to switch the war into one between Germany and the Soviet Union, but failing. He also continued to address meetings for the Russia To-Day Society, as the FSU was now called.[22]

Ivor had at this time little involvement in the film industry. Brunel & Montagu Ltd had long been inactive, and Kino was in the process of being wound up. The PFI remained in existence, but there was not much it could do in the wartime situation. He had not looked for employment again with Mick Balcon, now at Ealing Studios, but he remained active in the technicians' union, and at the ACT AGM on 14 April he moved a resolution instructing the General Council to explore the advisability, 'in view of the failure hitherto of private enterprise to produce an adequate supply of satisfactory films', of pushing for the nationalisation of part or the whole of the film industry. 'It is time,' he said, 'that when we urge the necessity of Government assistance to the industry we should begin to consider whether it is always necessary to start by paying a share of that subsidy to the promoters.' The motion passed with six dissentients.[23]

As a CP propagandist Montagu continued putting heat on the incumbent leadership of the Labour Party and the TUC. At a *Labour Monthly* conference in February, he argued that the capitalists' attack on wartime working conditions had been allowed to take place precisely because of the support given by the leadership of the working-class organisations to the war. In an article for that journal in May, he denounced the National Executive of the Labour Party as 'Chamberlain's Yes-Men', basking in the 'gentle plaudits from the press of the millionaires they serve'. The LP, he contended, had followed a policy of class collaboration, 'the unity of the household above and below stairs'; the Social Democracy it stood for could today 'find no better programme than to stand in the *forefront* of these urging the expansion of slaughter and the placing of burdens and restrictions on the working class!'.[24]

Montagu must have felt that subsequent developments only confirmed this analysis. On 10 May, following the resignation of Chamberlain, Winston Churchill formed a new administration, which the LP National Executive unanimously agreed to participate in. The decision was overwhelmingly endorsed at the party's conference in Bournemouth three days later. Montagu was at the conference, and could have been in no doubt about the unpopularity of the CP position to which he was committed. Clement Attlee may even have had him in mind when he declared:

> The Labour Party took their stand because they knew that should the Nazis win there would be an end of freedom of thought and conscience, an end of the rights of workers to combine and an end or crushing down of spiritual forces built up over thousands of years. He had sympathy with genuine pacifists, although he could not agree with them; but he had little patience with those who today, in face of tremendous events, talked claptrap about imperialist wars. (Cheers.)

When Ivor himself got a chance to speak, it was to put in a plea for an agreement between Britain and the Soviet Union, maintaining that negotiations the previous year had broken down because the USSR found out that it was being used to further the end of imperialists. MI5's informant did not record what sort of reception he received.[25]

Since 1931, after abandoning his flirtation with Oswald Mosley and the New Party, former Labour MP Evelyn John St Loe Strachey had been a staunch supporter of the Communist cause. As a populariser of Marxist theory with a string of publications under his belt (his tract *Why You Should Be a Socialist*, issued at a price of 2*d* by Gollancz in 1938, sold 250,000 copies), John Strachey was of great value to the Party. Hence there was consternation in 1940 when, first, his book *A Programme for Progress* put forward a reform-ist rather than revolutionary position, and then, more alarmingly, he openly criticised the CPGB line in print. In a letter to the *New Statesman and Nation* published on 27 April, Strachey argued that the tenor of *Daily Worker* coverage of the German invasion of Denmark and Norway was to lay the blame on Britain and France. He was driven to the conclusion that 'those controlling the *Daily Worker* are prepared, for the sake of what they consider to be the interests of the Soviet Union, to give way to Hitler to any extent, and that they are utterly irresponsible as to the consequences to the British people of such unlimited giving away.' As long as that remained the case he, 'and, it seems, almost everybody else in the country, can have nothing to do with them ...'[26]

Montagu knew Strachey well. They had worked together in the British Anti-War Movement, the German Relief Committee, and the CPGB's Agitprop Department, as well as on the *Daily Worker*, to which Strachey had been a regular contributor between 1935 and 1939. Now, reading the letter at King's Langley where he was laid up with sinus trouble, Ivor worriedly put in a phone call to Emile Burns. Strachey, he explained, had quoted 'one or two inconsistencies' from the *Daily Worker* and made it look as though the CP was supporting Hitler. Evidently distressed (so the MI5 officer who intercepted the call reported), Montagu continued, 'It is quite incredible after all his caution, that he should come out like this.' Burns tried to laugh it off, but agreed that an answer must be made. Montagu would draft a reply, and Burns would go over it for him.[27]

Four days later Montagu reported to Burns that he had written a reply. He had been wondering whether he ought to go and see Strachey, but later thought it a waste of time. As it turned out, the reply that was published was by *Daily Worker* editor Bill Rust. Montagu did, however, speak to Strachey, since MI5 learnt (through *New Statesman* editor Kingsley Martin) that he had asked his friend to 'shut up squabbling in print'. Strachey was not about to do so.[28]

At this point the war situation, and the CPGB's response to it, changed dramatically. At the end of May British forces began to be evacuated at Dunkirk, and in June France was crushed under Hitler's blitzkrieg. The Communist catchcry was no longer 'Stop the war!'; instead the Party agitated for the formation of a 'People's Government' that could wage a 'People's War' and win a 'People's Peace'. In an article for *Left News* in July, Strachey supported the demand that the 'Men of Munich' be excluded from the government, but insisted there be a recognition that 'the line taken by the *Daily Worker* this spring was by far the most terrible mistake which the British Communist Party has ever made.' If the workers have been taught that it is an unjust imperialist war, he argued, 'what objection will they have if anyone seeks to save them from bombing by doing what Pétain did in France?' It was necessary to face the fact, he continued, that 'this immense tragedy could never have taken place if the will of the French people to resist Hitler's fascism had not been weakened by nine months of revolutionary defeatist propaganda.' In Britain, if the CP had stuck to Pollitt's original war-on-two-fronts line 'it would now have a dominating position in the Labour movement: it would be in a position to secure the removal of the friends of Fascism and the formation of a People's Government.'[29]

Strachey was now clearly distancing himself from the Party. The parting of the ways of two old comrades became apparent in the extensive exchange of letters between him and Montagu that now took place. It was a correspondence that was peppered with cheerfully traded insults. Montagu told Strachey that he was 'completely crackers', that his letter to the *New Statesman* was a 'drivelling piece', and that his paragraph about France in the *Left News* article was 'idiotically and blindly malicious and untrue'. Strachey retorted that Montagu was behaving 'childishly', 'hysterically' leaping to conclusions, and was going to 'extraordinary lengths of casuistry'. Through the thicket of accusations and counter-accusations, the two made their positions clear. Ivor claimed that Strachey's published criticisms were directed to discredit the CPGB; in Strachey's view, however, they were 'a desperate attempt to prevent the CP ruinously discrediting itself'. For Strachey, the primary goal in the current situation was to strengthen the will of the British working class to resist Nazi aggression, a task for which the CP, having advanced its 'revolutionary defeatist' line, was hopelessly compromised. For Montagu, on the other hand, the overthrow of capitalism remained the key objective: 'I do not in the least agree "at last" that Nazi imperialism (your word "aggression") is the chief world danger.' It was a curious turnaround; having fought ferociously against fascism on the propaganda field for the last seven years, now, with Nazi bombers blitzing London, Ivor (and the Comintern) were placing a higher priority on the class struggle. It came down, as Strachey commented, to 'a differing estimate of the importance of fascism'.[30]

At the heart of their disagreements was their thinking about the role of intellectuals in the Communist movement. For Strachey, it was their duty to publicly protest if in their opinion the Party was making a disastrous mistake. (He explained to Ivor that before going public, he had taken the matter up 'in several long and detailed conversations with leading Party figures during the winter'.) Montagu, however, was convinced that the CP had to be supported, whatever the mistakes of the leadership, because it was no ordinary party but

> the organ of organisation of the struggle of the W.C. [working class]; it is a part of the international organisation of the W.C., closely linked to the advanced and conscious sections of the W.C., revolutionary and leading the struggle of the W.C. in which alone the latter can acquire experience to learn the necessity for fighting for its independent interests against those of the capitalists and big bourgeoisie, etc.

They were poles apart; Montagu would remain in the movement, Strachey would not. But the break was effected without personal bitterness. 'When's your sciatica going to sanction squash again?' Ivor asked. 'The sciatica is steadily approaching the squash point,' Strachey replied. 'I played tennis the other day for the first time. I will try and get hold of you, say, next month; but squash is, to my mind, a definite stage further in strenuousness than tennis.'[31]

All this while the British authorities were keeping a discreet eye on the Honourable Ivor. They had been aware since September the previous year that he and Andrew Rothstein were the principal contacts between the CPGB and the Soviet Embassy. They also knew that he had been carrying out liaison work between CP HQ and the Midlands, facilitated by his frequent lecture tours. And, of course, his propaganda activities were well known. But in February 1940 suspicions arose that he might be doing a little more to advance the cause of Soviet Communism. On the 20th, a senior official of the Pathe Gazette newsreel company telephoned the Metropolitan Police to report that Montagu had been observed watching Pathe cameramen outside the GPO at Watford as they prepared to go to a secret station to film the work of the Observer Corps. He was unable to say if Montagu followed the party to the secret station, but thought police should know the coincidence of Montagu being present at the spot where the meeting had been arranged. Receiving the report, Roger Hollis at MI5 noted that he had spoken to D3, 'who did not think Montagu could gather anything secret unless he got into the station'.[32]

Then in May the local constabulary began to notice suspicious goings-on around Montagu's Hertfordshire home. 'He is in possession of a car,' Constable Cyril Kemp reported, 'and appears to have plenty of money … His wife told a local resident they were motoring to Bournemouth and when asked how they got the petrol [which was strictly rationed], replied that her husband could get plenty.' Just after he took possession of the premises 'he had a large office built about 50 yards from the house, which is believed to have cost him £100. He stated that he required the office to store about 3,000 books. There is a telephone and a wireless at this office and he can be seen on the 'phone for very long periods'. Before he had the phone he used the one at the Rose & Crown, 'and the landlord informed me that when he received the telephone account some of Montague's [sic] trunk calls amounted to as much as 7/–.' Constable Kemp was also informed that there was another wireless set in the house and the 'German woman' (Elfriede Stoecker) 'can be heard translating German broadcasts.' Rowna, who was now employed at Sellicks Motors in Watford, was 'heard to say that her mother did not get much sleep as her father got up at all hours of the night.' (Indeed, on 25 April Montagu told Dutt that he had listened to the 2 a.m. news from New York.) Kemp's report was forwarded to Sir Vernon Kell of MI5 by the Hertfordshire Chief Constable, Captain S.M.E. Fairman, who wrote: 'Before deciding upon the desirability of searching his premises under regulation 88a of the Defence Regulations 1939, I should be glad to have any information you may have about him.'[33]

It was two weeks before Jasper Harker replied on behalf of MI5. Filling Fairman in briefly on Montagu's Communist activities, he advised in respect of the proposal to search the 'Knowle' premises that 'my own feeling is that such action would be a little premature at the present time.' The agency was aware that Ivor spent a large amount of his time listening to radio broadcasts, especially Soviet and American, and frequently reported information he had gleaned to Emile Burns, who edited the Party weekly World News and Views. On 18 June, for example, Burns was particularly interested to learn of a proposed economic unification of the western hemisphere, and of the sending of the US Navy to French possessions in America. Harker said he would be interested to have any further information that might come the way of the Hertfordshire Police, but all they could immediately report was that Montagu was not particularly known to members of the movement locally, and that he was away from home almost daily, 'believed to visit London in connection with his business as a Journalist and Film Critic.' In passing this on, Fairman told Harker that in view of the latter's remarks, 'no direct contact has been made with the household at "Knowle", Bucks Hill, King's Langley and the premises will of course not be searched until the time is more opportune.'[34]

It was at this time, under the nose of the security service, that Montagu was in fact recruited as an agent of Soviet military intelligence, the GRU. On 25 July, Simon Davidovich Kremer, Secretary to the Soviet Military Attaché in London, informed Moscow in a coded cable that Montagu, 'brother of Lord Montagu, the well-known local Communist, journalist and lecturer' had reported to him that he had been 'detailed to organise work with me, but that he had not yet obtained a single contact.' It was not that he was a prime candidate for espionage himself: the only secret information he was privy to came from Communist sources, and he was not in the public service, the armed forces, or munitions manufacturing. It was true that with a press pass as a *Daily Worker* journalist he had access to sites from which the general public were excluded. But the new asset, given the codename INTELLIGENTSIA and identified as 'a representative of the X GROUP', was probably signed up for his potential as a networker and talent spotter: as Kremer noted, he had 'contacts through his influential relations'. The GRU officer 'came to an agreement with him about his work and pointed out the importance of speed.' The cable was one of a number that the security services intercepted, but were not able to decrypt (as part of a joint US–UK programme named *Venona*) until the 1960s.[35]

At this first meeting, Montagu had no information of military value to impart, but gave Kremer his analysis of recent political developments, which the Russian duly passed on to Moscow. Hitler had made a speech to the Reichstag on 19 July in which he appealed to the British 'warmongers' to capitulate; it would not, Ivor said, 'make a great impression here'. The 'SAU-SAGE-DEALERS' – as the Germans were codenamed – had been given their answer earlier by Churchill, who found their terms unacceptable. The speech in reply by Halifax was notable, Montagu thought, for its appeal to

Christianity, which would impress Pétain, Franco and the Pope, as well as having an anti-fascist edge to it. There was an anti-German mood in the army that was so strong that 'the Conservative Party is afraid of risking talking about peace.' They might do so if Britain were to suffer some serious defeat or the Germans started effective bombing. Churchill, according to Ivor, was 'supporting Chamberlain's group so as to give the ANTI-SAUSAGE-DEALER mood no chance of developing into a movement of the left.' As to the recent removal of Generals Ironside and Gort from their commands, it was undoubtedly related to the defeat of the British Expeditionary Force in Flanders.[36]

INTELLIGENTSIA is next mentioned in an intercepted cable dated 16 August. In this, GRU headquarters are informed that their agent has not located anyone in the military finance department, and has 'been given the address of one officer but he has not found him yet.' He had promised to deliver some documentary material from Professor Haldane (his old friend from Cambridge), who was working on an Admiralty assignment concerned with submarines, but this had yet to arrive. Clearly unimpressed, his controller added, 'I have taken the opportunity of pointing out to the X GROUP that we need a man of a different calibre and one who is bolder than INTELLIGENTSIA.'[37]

By 6 September, Montagu had delivered Haldane's report, which was on the human impact of long-time submersion in submarines. (Haldane was at this time working at the Royal Navy's secret underwater research station at Gosport, and was later identified by MI5 as an X Group member.) Kremer remarked:

> However, he does not deny the main point that for a month he has not been in touch with the British Army colonel picked out for work with us although the latter does come to London. I have told the X GROUP via NOBILITY to give us someone else because of this. INTELLIGENTSIA lives in the provinces and it is difficult to contact him.

The identity of NOBILITY, mentioned a number of times in the *Venona* intercepts, remains unknown. He was a journalist; candidates could include Claud Cockburn; Andrew Rothstein, now TASS correspondent in London; and George Bilainkin, a diplomatic reporter – all of whom had their phones tapped by MI5 in 1940 because they were suspected of leaking confidential information received from embassies and legations. Another possibility is Montagu's *Daily Worker* colleague Walter Holmes, who was also being closely watched by MI5. Holmes had been a member of W.N. Ewer's spy ring in the 1920s, was since suspected of undertaking undercover missions for the Comintern, and was known to be in touch with Soviet officials.[38]

On 7 September Kremer received a hurry-up from DIRECTOR in Moscow. 'By 20th September,' he was instructed, 'complete the formalities on the X GROUP comprising three military sources and start to obtain documentary material.' But by the 26th, the hapless GRU officer could only report that 'execution of the points in your order on the organisation, armament and numerical strength of divisions and corps is being held up because of bad work by the X GROUP.'[39]

INTELLIGENTSIA finally came up with some important information on 2 October, though it was probably gleaned by chance rather than as a result of diligent digging. He informed his handler that:

the X GROUP has reported to him that a girl working in a government establishment noticed in one document that the British had broken some Soviet code or other and apparently she noticed in a/the document the following [words]: 'Soviet Embassy in Germany'. I stated that this was a matter of exceptional importance and he should put to the group the question of developing this report [further].[40]

By 11 October Colonel I.A. Sklyarov had returned from New York to his post as Soviet Air and Military Attaché in London, and Montagu now reported to him. In Sklyarov's dispatch of that date there is no mention of the code-breaking, but INTELLIGENTSIA was able to pass on the presumably valuable information that 'the British really do render delayed-action bombs safe by freezing the bombs' exploder mechanism.' Several days later, Ivor told the colonel what he had learnt from an officer of the Air Ministry:

The shortage of trained night navigators is confirmed by the fact that the SAUSAGE-DEALERS have not used strong forces of aircraft in night air-raids on Britain. He stated that the British pilots who fly by night over Germany have an extra four months' training in addition to the usual six months' training. Apparently when there has been no [anti-aircraft] fire the SAUSAGE-DEALERS have been bombing from a height of up to

5,000 metres and at a speed of 290 kph, and from 6,000–7,000 metres at
a speed of 400 kph when there has been no firing [*sic*]. He considers that
the SAUSAGE-DEALERS proceed towards the target along a radio beam.[41]

The last sentence was a reference to the German Knickebein radio
navigation system, for which the RAF was actively developing counter-
measures. One commentator observes that Montagu was here betraying
'a highly classified secret, known only to a handful of intelligence chiefs,
senior RAF officers and government scientists' and – since it is probable that at this time intelligence gathered by the Soviets that would be
useful to the Nazis was being passed on to them – 'if caught, he would
certainly have been arrested and prosecuted under the Treason Act.' In
point of fact, however, Knickebein was a fairly open secret. THERAPEUTIST,
another (unidentified) informant, had already reported that 'when he visited a sound-ranging post the soldiers told him that the SAUSAGE-DEALERS
find their way to Birmingham and other Midland towns by means of a
directional radio beam originating in France,' and on 16 October NOBIL-
ITY passed on further information about the use of the system in dropping
bombs on the Filton aircraft factory in Bristol.[42]

More treasonable, one would think, was the divulging of data by the
artillery colonel, now codenamed RESERVIST, whom Montagu had finally
contacted and recruited into the X Group. On 18 October RESERVIST
reported in detail to Sklyarov on the organisational structure of the Home
Forces, the production of tanks and deployment of tank divisions, the
arming of troops with anti-tank guns, artillery and anti-aircraft guns in use
by the British, and the country's coastal defences ('He considers that the
War Office is not making the slightest use of the experience of the French
and the coastal defence is based on a network of blockhouses that are weak
in design with no allowance made for the manoeuvrability or strong artillery and tank equipment of the SAUSAGE-DEALERS'). RESERVIST promised to
bring to his next meeting with the GRU 'his notes on the campaign in
France and information on the way the British Army is organised'.[43]

INTELLIGENTSIA is last mentioned in the *Venona* GRU texts on 4 November.
Most of this cable is unintelligible, but it records that Montagu has received
some material from a serviceman friend in a Liverpool regiment stationed in
North Wales. The X Group is last heard of on 20 December, when NOBILITY

passes on documents the group has received from a CPGB member engaged in technical work in intelligence departments. Thereafter, though the intercepted cables continue through 1941, Montagu disappears from the record. It could well be that the Soviets decided he was more use to them as a propagandist than as a spy. It might also be that there was concern for the reputation of the Party should he be caught: Bob Stewart, long responsible for CPGB undercover work, was known to hold the view that no prominent Party member should be used for espionage. But the decrypted cables are only a small sample of the total, and there are a few other tantalising hints about the extent of Ivor's clandestine activity at this time.[44]

On 19 October, for example, Montagu invited Constantine Zinchenko, 2nd secretary at the Soviet Embassy, to lunch with him and someone whose name sounded like Dr Wiebers. His secretary would let Zinchenko know the place of the meeting in a letter, not over the telephone. Then on 9 November Ivor received a call from Dave Springhall, CPGB National Organiser and later revealed to have been engaged in Soviet espionage. MI5's account of the conversation reveals a certain deficiency in conspiratorial tradecraft on Ivor's part:

> SPRINGHALL ... gave him the following address. A. MORGAN, 316, Avery Hill Road, S.E.9 (Tel. ELTHAM 2585). He did not do this openly but asked IVOR to look at a certain page of that book and at the name three from the top. When IVOR said 'Is it Avery Hill?', SPRINGHALL stopped him quickly and said 'Yes, that's it' ... [45]

A further hint of surreptitious behaviour came the way of MI5 on 3 March 1941. On that date Montagu was at CPGB headquarters at 16 King Street and 'rang up a Mr Lewis DARLEY (phonetic) whose secretary replied, "it is not ready yet but will be ready this afternoon." IVOR said, "I'm speaking from London. I'll call for it this afternoon. Will you ask him to leave it outside – locked. I have a set of keys and I can open it."' A handwritten inscription on the file reads: 'This may not be as sinister as it sounds, but you will like to note for Montagu.' Finally, there was the occasion on 16 April when, in the course of casual observation on 11 Highgate West Hill, N.6, the residence of Albert Lancaster Lloyd, Ivor Montagu was seen by police sergeant F. Jordan:

to arrive in motor car, Index No. AUR.853, at 3 pm … After a brief visit to the house he left, travelling as a passenger in the car, the registered owner of which is John GIFFEN of 'Driftwood', Watford Rd, St. Albans, who has not previously come under the notice of Special Branch. At the same time two men of decided foreign appearance, possibly Russian, left on foot, and another man left on a bicycle and he is believed to have entered the grounds of the U.S.S.R. Trade Delegation which is nearby.

Observation would continue to be kept on the house, the police reported, 'as this address appears to be a meeting place of Communists or those who at one time were engaged in the production of the *Daily Worker*, and any useful information will be submitted.'[46]

Meanwhile, Montagu remained heavily engaged in the propaganda effort for the Communist cause. His short book *The Traitor Class*, published in September 1940, was a damning indictment of the Chamberlain clique, and of ruling elites in other times and places who sacrificed their fellow countrymen to protect their own class privileges. It was to prove both highly popular with the public and highly controversial within leading circles of the Party.

There are strong continuities between the arguments of the book and those Montagu had advanced before the war in published articles and the film *Peace and Plenty*. In 1938 he had contended that 'we cannot defeat Hitler until we remove from the power to betray the Chamberlains and Daladiers who betray for Hitler.' Now, in 1940, he continued his attack on 'those whose class background determines assistance to German imperialism', excoriating the Cabinet ministers whose policy of appeasement had resulted in the war, not because of individual shortcomings (as had been the argument of another popular polemic of the time, *Guilty Men* by 'Cato'), but because 'the ruling class was bound to reject collective security for class reasons'. In the present situation, Montagu asserted:

The path to a successful issue for the people, the path to freedom, peace and safety can be pursued only by a new government, by the transfer of power to the people, and away from the class rulers whose class interests make it impossible for them to pursue the necessary measures and make treachery their inevitable course.[47]

The difficulty was that for Party hard-liners like Dutt and Rust, now in the ascendancy, this line of reasoning sounded suspiciously like the anti-fascist rhetoric of the pre-war era. Montagu had failed to grasp the imperialist nature of the war – or, as they more judiciously phrased it, his words were open to misinterpretation. 'The present line,' Rajani Palme Dutt told him, when he submitted the manuscript for his appraisal, 'has a very strong character of national defencism, i.e. support of the existing imperialist war and demand for its more effect [*sic*] prosecution, in the name of "national defence", war for democracy against fascism.' This could certainly not be tolerated. The very title, Dutt said, 'raises dangers of creating real misunderstanding', while referring to the ruling class as the 'Fifth Column' promoted the idea that it was sabotaging a war for national independence.[48]

Montagu took heed. The revised manuscript took a stronger anti-imperialist line and was shorn of references to victory over Hitler. Yet Dutt was only partially appeased:

With regard to the inset denouncing the conception of friendship with a Germany which has done this, that and the other, it is a very dangerous line of argument, because it appears to imply that a Government we approve of would go to war with every Fascist state. On the contrary, we approve of the Soviet Union's policy of peaceful relations with the German state, although it is a Nazi state, and would wish our Government to pursue a similar policy.

The offending passage went, and *The Traitor Class* (without the clarifying subtitle Dutt had asked for) was released.[49]

Pritt received it warmly. Montagu, he asserted, 'carries the reader down to the root causes of all the various activities of the ruling classes of Britain and France throughout this tragic period, activities which to the superficial observer seemed to be no more than criminal folly, and exposes the whole class-war basis and motivation of their conduct.' (In a private letter to his friend, Pritt wrote: 'Do you know you are probably the only political writer in this country who is better than I am?') Pollitt was also complimentary, though perhaps guilty of falling into the same doctrinal traps as Montagu was accused of doing: 'As you read this section,' he wrote, 'it will be borne in on the reader, that the Mosley group are only the small fry, the really powerful men and forces are still at large, preparing now, to make a deal with Hitler at the first opportunity.' (It is not clear if his review was published.)[50]

But Bill Rust was by no means willing simply to add to the accolades. His critique, published in the November *Labour Monthly* with the full force of the CPGB Secretariat behind it, paid the obligatory compliments to his comrade in journalism ('Ivor Montagu has exposed the rottenness and treachery of the ruling class with great vigour and he deals many shrewd blows'), but was otherwise intent on castigating the author for his failure to make his political conclusions clear. The parallel drawn between France and Britain was inexact, and it was 'fundamentally incorrect' to contend that the pre-war appeasement policy of the British ruling class was continuing; on the contrary, there was a 'desperate and bloody struggle now developing throughout the world between the rival imperialist blocs.' It was necessary 'to imbue the people with the conviction that they can bring the bloodshed and horror to an end by taking power into their own hands'; this, Rust implied, *The Traitor Class* failed to do.[51]

Montagu, apprised of the criticisms in advance of publication, was willing to grant that the book did not provide 'a full guide to the present situation'. But he bristled at the suggestion that his mode of analysis, discrediting the ruling class and the Labour leaders collaborating with it, did not constitute a valuable contribution to the current struggle. 'Bugger it all,' he wrote back to Rust, 'I don't write for my own satisfaction but to turn out something useful' – and indeed, if there was fundamental problem with the book, 'R.P.D. should have sat on it at the first draft.' Reading between the lines, it is hard to escape the conclusion that, committed as he was to toeing the party line, Montagu just could not bring himself to believe that whether Churchill or Hitler won the war was a matter of indifference to British workers.[52]

Yet his writing increasingly gave this impression. In 'Victory for What?' (*Labour Monthly*, January 1941) he asserted that 'the 'New Order' that the Anglo-American coalition proposes to establish by force of arms is, in fact and already, taking shape as simply and as concretely as that of Adolf Hitler.' And in 'The Partners' (*Daily Worker*, 9 January 1941) he argued that 'the various members of the ruling class international, whatever the conflicts of interest that from time to time divide them, can always find time to lend each other a helping hand when it is a question of dealing blows against the vanguard of the working-class movement' – as an instance he cited 'the recent partnership of Hitler, Mussolini, Halifax, Eden, Daladier, Roosevelt in strangling and bludgeoning Republican Spain'. On the home front, Ernest Bevin's Ministry of Labour, in a similar alignment of class interests, 'does not scruple gladly to make use of the slanders and lies of Hitler, designed to discredit militants and provoke the working class, when it is a question of trying to blacken the repute of Communists.' (In what Montagu undoubtedly viewed as a vindication of this line of argument, the *Daily Worker* was shortly shut down by Home Secretary Herbert Morrison, a Labour minister.)[53]

In other journalism, Ivor did not slacken in his encomiums for the Soviet Union. The building of the Ferghana Canal at breakneck speed by voluntary labour was 'the third great stage in the development of Socialist man'. The addition in ten or eleven months of five new republics (Estonia, Karelo Finland, Latvia, Lithuania and Moldavia) to the 'family of peoples linked together' by their 'free choice' in the Socialist Union was 'not bad going' and in strongest contrast with the 'enslavements and conquests of imperialist war'. (There was no hint, of course, of the Stalinist repressions taking place in these occupied territories.) Capitalist Britain, with its 'ten-bob-a-week pittance' for pensioners, had restored old age to 'grinding poverty', but in the USSR 'all working people ... have the right to maintenance in old age, irrespective of their capacity to work, the earnings of their relatives, or anything else.' And on New Year's Day 1941, radio listeners around the world, Ivor reported, were able to join in the festivities celebrating 'the wonderful record of the Soviet peoples for the year that was passed; increased output, new housing, new peoples joining the Soviet family, new talents, the rejoicing of the Soviet people in writing, in sports, and in the theatre ...' (It was the year, too, in which the author Isaac Babel, whose work Ivor had translated, was arrested and executed; in which Vsevelod Meyerhold, the experimental theatre director whom Ivor had been disappointed not to meet when visiting Moscow in 1925, was put to death after torture; in which his Comintern collaborator Willi Münzenberg met a grisly death in a French forest; and in which Trotsky was struck down in Mexico by an NKVD assassin on Stalin's orders. These things Montagu did not report.)[54]

During this period Ivor did on the odd occasion return to film criticism, but only to make a political point. Ernst Lubitsch's *Ninotchka* (1939), a satire on all things Soviet, left him unamused. The film had its good jokes, he was prepared to admit, and its star Greta Garbo her 'immense charm', but it was 'deadly poison masquerading as a joke, hoping to insinuate itself into the system on a plea of "tolerance" for humour, oh so innocent "humour".' Contrary to what *Ninotchka* suggested, the USSR was awash with champagne and cosmetics and had such an abundance of bread they were thinking of giving it away for free. Montagu was convinced it was no accident that the film was issued at a time 'when the discrediting of the Soviet Union in the eyes of the masses is vital to the ruling class, and by the company [MGM] whose chief in America is the principal enemy of trade unionism in the industry.'[55]

In contrast, Montagu championed *The Great Dictator* (1940), Chaplin's politically-charged lampoon of Hitler. Ivor claimed personal involvement in the genesis of the movie, since he had sent Chaplin a copy of the anti-semitic book *Juden sehen Dich an* (*The Jews are Watching You*) back in 1933. In this Nazi propaganda tract Chaplin is included as a Jew, although to his knowledge the comedian had no Jewish ancestry. He is described as 'a marionette, as ugly as he is puerile ... a Jew-tumbler, as boring as he is repulsive.' *The Great Dictator* was, in Montagu's opinion, Chaplin's long-delayed riposte – yet the filmmaker had resisted the temptation to turn his revenge into war propaganda. Some might find the film's content naive, Montagu granted, since 'Charlie is by every instinct an anarchist who has never grasped the means to win the under-dog's battle, the class struggle and the independent action and party of the working class.' Yet he had defiantly taken on the role of Jew, and his final anti-war speech:

> ... vibrates with a sincerity, a deep love of humanity, and above all, in the circumstances of today, a courage that would have brought a twinkle of approval to the eyes of Vanzetti, the old fish-peddler ... Chaplin triumphs over the scorn of the Nazis and those who then befriended them, and who still rule over us.

The reception of the film in Great Britain and the United States, Montagu later wrote, 'has provided an exposure at once of the time-serving venality of the critics of the capitalist press, and of the gulf of envy which separates them from an artist fortunate or courageous enough to dare express an independent mind.'[56]

In January 1941, Ivor and Hell took in Willie Gallacher after the MP's London landlord was killed by a mine. It was at this time that Montagu was called up with his age group, and he registered at St Albans for military service. Now aged 36, he passed his medical and stated that he would prefer to serve in the Air Force. Special Branch observed that he seemed anxious to join the military; indeed, he later told those attending a meeting of the Russia To-Day Society in Horsham:

> I hope if I get in I shall make a ruddy good soldier. What I want to do is influence the others. I don't believe in the least, in this business of individual action, which does not advance your cause. An individual who says 'I will not fight', is not in any way advancing the remedy. That is why I say 'Don't refuse military service.'[57]

This speech was cited by MI5 when it intervened to prevent any such subversion of the troops taking place. Montagu received his calling-up papers for 9 May. But the security authorities took swift action. Consulted by T.M. Harmer, Esq., at the Ministry of Labour and National Service, MI5 advised: 'We have considerable information about this man, dating back to 1926, and it appears most undesirable that he should be allowed to serve in H.M. Forces.' The Ministry took heed.[58]

At the last moment Ivor received a telegram notifying him that his enlistment notice had been cancelled. When he explained this to Emile Burns over the phone, there was, the MI5 eavesdropper reported, 'much laughter'. More laughter ensued when Burns remarked, 'I expect they checked up on you.' Montagu commented that he had rung Harry Pollitt, 'and he seemed to have no doubt about it at all.' Burns didn't expect Ivor was sorry. 'Well it leaves one in a state of uncertainty,' Montagu replied. 'I do not know whether to resume my professional life for the time being. Anyhow that means I shall be in circulation again for the time being.' This was certainly the case. On 24 May, Harmer confirmed to MI5 that 'the enlistment notice directing him to report to the R.A.F. was withdrawn and … the necessary steps have been taken to ensure that he will not be called up for service in any branch of the Armed Forces.'[59]

Ironically this proscription did not count against Montagu in his role as referee for other Communists attempting to enlist, if John Platts-Mills is to be believed. 'We used to advise the would-be servicemen to get testimonials of honesty, decency and loyalty from such people as D.N. Pritt or Ivor

Montagu,' he writes. 'Here were two people whom the armed forces would not have tolerated in their ranks, but a letter from either was enough to get someone else in.'[60]

Meanwhile, Ivor kept his hand in as a lecturer. On 4 May he 'spoke rapidly and without notes' from 2.30 p.m. to 5.30 p.m. at the Conway Hall under the auspices of Unity Theatre and the Russia To-Day Society, his subject being 'The Cinema in the USSR'. The police spy was able to report that he 'gave a commentary on photographs of scenes etc., which owing to the inability to use his machine was spasmodic and during which the majority of the audience left the hall.'[61]

A few days later the conflict with Germany took a dramatic turn. On 10 May Deputy Führer Rudolf Hess flew solo to Scotland, parachuted to earth and demanded to speak with the Duke of Hamilton, whom he believed would be sympathetic to his proposals for a negotiated peace between the adversaries. Montagu took it as further evidence of his long-reiterated claim that certain of the British ruling class had aspirations to share the world with Hitler, and published an article to that effect in *World News and Views*. In 'Hess and His Friends' Hamilton is described as 'not a believer in the "anti-Fascist" war', an ex-member of Anglo-German Fellowship and by implication a member of that capitulationist section of the aristocracy that would dearly like to turn the war against the Soviet Union.[62]

The Duke, whose aeronautical exploits (as Lord Clydesdale) Montagu had extolled in *Wings Over Everest*, took umbrage at the insinuation that he was a friend of Hess, a Nazi-lover and traitor to his country. He denied he knew the man, and sued Montagu and his publisher and printer for libel. At the same time he took out a writ against Harry Pollitt and Ted Bramley, as members of the London District Committee of the CPGB, for an anonymous leaflet it had published, *Why is Hess Here?*, in which claims against Hamilton were made slightly more explicitly.[63]

The action was to cause Ivor some anxiety over the coming months. His mother, Lady Swaythling, prevailed upon aviation pioneer Lord Sempill to intercede with Hamilton, but the Duke was not to be swayed. In February 1942, however, it was announced in the High Court that both actions had been settled. The defendants issued an apology, declaring:

(1) That the statements complained of were directed solely against Hess and the political tendency to welcome Hess and against any proposals which Hess may have brought which were bound to be contrary to the best interests of this country. (2) That they had no intention whatever of impugning the character or loyalty of the plaintiff, and unreservedly accept the plaintiff's assurance that he had no sympathy with the Nazis or the Government in Germany; that he had never met Hess; and that he has never received any letter from Hess at any time.[64]

Back in June 1941, when Hamilton was initiating the legal action, Montagu was preoccupied with another propaganda project. This was a somewhat delayed response to John Strachey's 'exceptionally stupid' article in *Left News*, September 1940, which welcomed growing American assistance to the British war effort. For Montagu, as for the CPGB in general, this simply meant buttressing the ruling class at home while strengthening the position of the US capitalists in the global arena. Ivor's pamphlet *'Roll on, Mississippi!'*, published by *Labour Monthly* in the latter half of June, chose to argue this case by means of a hodgepodge assembly of quotations and statistics, snippets of invective and tidbits of scandal. Attempts by the US to thwart the economic independence of Latin American nations are exposed and assailed; profiteering by defence contractors documented and denounced; racism and suppression of trade union militancy revealed and condemned. The millions in America, Montagu wrote, 'who sympathise with the British people and with the peoples over-run by Hitler see their sympathy made use of by capitalist interests to profit from British armaments, to establish a dictatorship and drag their country into war.' But nothing had altered 'the resolute opposition of the people to participation in the war', and they would continue to resist.[65]

Unfortunately for this line of argument, Germany's invasion of the Soviet Union on 22 June, occurring within a week of the pamphlet's publication, rendered it instantly obsolete. The CPGB, in lockstep with Communist parties internationally, made another U-turn, becoming overnight gung-ho supporters of the war against Hitler. Any and all assistance in the struggle was to be accepted, even if it came from profiteering US imperialists. *'Roll on, Mississippi!'* was withdrawn. For Montagu, 37 years old, the interwar period had now come to a decisive end.[66]

16

EPILOGUE

TOWARDS THE END of 1942, at a time when Anglo-Russian Committees studded with Tories and Liberals as well as Communists were proliferating, Ivor Montagu's brother Stuart – the 3rd Baron Swaythling, member of the House of Lords – circulated a verse that poked a little gentle fun at the Stalin fan club:

> Let's have less nonsense from the Friends of Joe,
> We laud, we love him; but the nonsense – no.
> In 1940, when we bore the brunt
> We could have done, boys, with a Second Front.
> A continent went down a cataract,
> But Russia did not think it right to act.
> Not ready? No. And who shall call her wrong?
> Far better not to strike till you are strong.
> Better, perhaps, though this was not our fate,
> To make new treaties with a man you hate.
> Alas, these shy manoeuvres had to end,
> When Hitler leaped upon his largest friend
> (And if he'd not, I wonder, by the way,
> If Russia would be in the war today).
> But who rushed out to aid the giant then –
> A giant rich in corn, and oil, and men,
> Long, long prepared, and having, so they say,

The most enlightened ruler of the day?
<u>This</u> tiny island, antiquated, tired,
Effete, capitalist, and uninspired!
<u>This</u> tiny island, wounded in the war
Through taking tyrants on two years before! ... [1]

'Less Nonsense' by A.P.H. (A.P. Herbert) had been published in *Truth*, a journal that was in all probability – as Ivor was quick to point out in rebuking his brother for disseminating the ditty – 'owned and controlled by a narrow but extremely powerful caucus of influential Conservatives' whose policy over long periods of time had 'run parallel to that of fascist publications.' In short, Ivor was not amused by this satirical dig at the USSR and its supporters, which was immediately rendered suspect by the context in which it appeared. The purpose of praising the Soviet war effort, he told Stuart, was to inspire emulation, which it was effectively doing. The poem could only undermine morale; and 'politically i.e. practically, what matters in circulating something is not whether it is true, but what will be the effect of circulating it at the given particular time.'[2]

Montagu was at times a witty writer and could be jovial in person (he was dubbed, in the TV interview programme he recorded in 1982, 'An Impish Figure'), but he had none of his colleague Claud Cockburn's sense of irreverent humour when it came to politics. For Ivor, Communism and the defence of the Soviet Union were deadly serious causes, and would remain so for the rest of his life, jostling at times for his attention with film and table tennis, but never abandoned.

When Nazi troops invaded the USSR in 1941, Stalin's catastrophic blundering arguably led to the loss of millions of lives and brought his country to the brink of defeat. Montagu would have none of this. In a series of pamphlets produced in quick succession – *The Red Army* (July 1941), *Ruby Star* (November 1941, with R. Palme Dutt), and *Stalin: A Biographical Sketch* (March 1942) – he lauded the strength and tenacity of the Soviet armed forces, the agricultural and industrial might of the USSR's planned economy, and the wisdom and fortitude of the commander in chief. 'What British man or woman, what man or woman throughout the world, does not sleep more easily, labour and fight with new confidence, because Stalin is at the helm,' he asked, '– who would not

feel the perils encompassing himself and his dearest increased ten thousand fold were that great guidance gone?' The gushing panegyrics flow,
drowning out the miserable plaints of the doubters. 'How much the lie
has been given to these slanderers by the courage, endurance, decision and
strategic skill with which he has guided and inspired the colossal military
operations of the present day'; 'Who is not fortified in his own effort
by the knowledge that Stalin's courage, Stalin's sagacity, Stalin's inflexible
will are applied at the decisive point?' It was not a time, Montagu would
undoubtedly have argued, for the truth.[3]

Throughout 1942 the pamphlets continued: *Sevastopol* (with Ilya
Ehrenburg), a series on Soviet leaders Kalinin, Timoshenko, Voroshilov and
Molotov, and *Zero Hour − Second Front*. Meanwhile, Montagu slaked the
sudden British thirst for Russian films by the preparation of English versions of Soviet material and organising their distribution and exhibition;
among major successes with the public was the documentary *The Defeat
of the German Armies Near Moscow* (1942). With Herbert Marshall, Ivor also
began editing a series of books of 'Life and Literature in the Soviet Union':
titles, sometimes featuring his own translations, included *Soviet Heroes*,
Mayakovsky and His Poetry, *Soviet Musicians*, *The Crocodile Album of Soviet
Humour*, and several volumes of *Soviet Short Stories*.[4]

When the ban on the *Daily Worker* was lifted in September 1942, Montagu
rejoined the staff as leader and special feature writer, and member of the
editorial board. (Bernard Shaw reproached him for his 'preoccupation with
the D.W.', urging him instead to foster the production of films 'devoted
entirely to lectures, political, scientific, religious, and aesthetic,' but his faithful fan D.N. Pritt was impressed, telling him in 1943 that 'the quality of your
leaders gets better and better.')[5]

Ivor got his lecture film opportunity in 1944, when he was approached
by Sidney Bernstein, then head of the Films Division of the Ministry of
Information, to script a documentary exposing the scientific fallacies of
Nazi racial theories. In the end Montagu not only scripted the film, but
directed it (at Ealing Studios), using J.B.S. Haldane and Julian Huxley as
advisors. *Man − One Family*, sixteen minutes in length, mashed together
newsreel footage, animation, straight documentary and dramatised
sequences in order to debunk the doctrine of the master race. Handled by
the Ministry of Information, the film was shown after the war in the UK

and the liberated countries of Europe (a title claims that it has been translated into sixteen languages), and was critically well received.[6]

At its 17th Congress, held at the Shoreditch Town Hall in October 1944,
the CPGB jettisoned the system by which members of the central committee were selected by a panel, subject only to endorsement by conference
delegates. Now the executive committee, as it was renamed, was elected by
direct ballot. In the vote that was taken, in recognition no doubt of his high
profile in the party – he had been serving as secretary of the International
Affairs Committee, in addition to his work as a journalist – Montagu was a
successful candidate. He was re-elected in November the following year, but
at the 19th Congress, held in February 1947, the panel system was revived
and he lost his position. He seems to have left no record of his experience in
the guiding councils of the party to whose cause he was devoted.[7]

The July 1945 UK general election resulted in a landslide victory for the
Labour Party. Ivor and Hell supported the campaign of D.N. Pritt, who had
been expelled from the LP for his pro-Soviet views in 1940, but continued
to hold the seat of Hammersmith North as an Independent Labour MP.
The 1945 result was a triumph for the team, with Pritt being returned
with a massive majority over his Conservative rival, and the official Labour
candidate badly beaten.[8]

During the hostilities a ban had been in place on Ivor's accreditation as a
war correspondent for the *Daily Worker*. His plea to Clement Attlee to have
it lifted had been unavailing. The end of the war had not eased restrictions
on the movement of civilian journalists, but now with the Labour leader
in power, Montagu's accreditation was finally granted. He immediately
arranged to travel to Germany to cover the dramatic unfolding of events.[9]

His first assignment took him to Lüneburg, where he reported on the
Belsen trial, the arraignment of forty-five former SS officers and *kapos* in
the Bergen-Belsen and Auschwitz concentration camps before a British
military tribunal. His dispatches relayed the horrific testimony of eyewit-
nesses to the mass murder. Learning of film taken by the Red Army on
entering Auschwitz, Montagu procured it from the Soviet authorities in
Berlin, and it was screened in court for the prosecution. After a stint reporting from Berlin, Ivor proceeded to Nuremberg for the war crimes trial of
prominent Nazis, which he hailed as 'a decisive step forward in civilised
history': for the first time, 'leaders of a State are being made as responsible

to the world for the harm they have done as petty, private gangsters are responsible to the ordinary police and courts of their own countries.'[10]

In 1946 Montagu travelled extensively in Eastern Europe, reporting back to the *Daily Worker* and the Communist Party from behind what was now being dubbed the Iron Curtain. On 26 November, Kim Philby of MI6 informed MI5 that according to their Public Relations staff in Vienna, Montagu's was the first case in memory 'in which no help was asked of Public Relations in getting him the necessary clearances, transport, etc., and that it is, therefore, a fair assumption that he had good contacts with the Soviet authorities.' MI5 confirmed this speculation, advising Philby that 'we have ascertained that the Soviet authorities had approved Ivor Montagu's visit to Berlin, Vienna, Budapest and Bucharest and had informed their representatives accordingly.' In Sofia, Ivor interviewed Dimitrov, who had just assumed office as Bulgarian premier.[11]

In November, Montagu witnessed the general election in Romania, with the country still occupied by Soviet troops. Victory was achieved by a bloc including the Communist Party through, commentators claimed, widespread intimidation, violence, and electoral fraud. In his report in the *Daily Worker*, Ivor wrote: 'Voting took place in perfect order at all the stations I saw.' There was violence outside Bucharest, but it had been carried out by the Opposition in a failed attempt to discredit the election. He admitted that 'wild rumours' were circulating about omissions in the electoral lists and voting papers for sale on the black market, but such 'defects' affected the Communist Party as well as other parties. Back in London, Ivor told the Hampstead Anglo-Soviet Friendship Society a slightly different story. Discussing the elections in Bulgaria as well as Romania, he agreed, according to the Special Branch informant, that:

> a certain amount of force and restraint had been used by the governments of these countries, but said that it was inevitable owing to the chaotic and peculiar circumstances. The opposition parties were mere relics of former fascist and pro-German movements, who were committing sabotage and assassination whenever they could.

Perhaps uneasy in his conscience, Montagu then made an unusual admission. MI5 learnt that he had:

confessed to members of the Romanian Legation that he did not want
to sign the declaration which was handed to him in Bucharest about the
election, and had suggested that they should alter the text slightly before
he signed it. The Romanians refused, so Montagu 'because he represented
a Communist paper' had no alternative but to sign. He admitted to the
Legation that what he had signed was entirely untrue; he had heard, seen
and known of incidents and disorders before and during the election.[12]

Switching back, perhaps with some relief, from politics to film in 1947,
Montagu accepted an invitation from Mick Balcon to join the staff at Ealing
Studios. The particular occasion was the development of a film on a topic
that had fascinated Ivor since childhood. *Scott of the Antarctic* was to star John
Mills under the direction of Charles Frend; Montagu wrote the script, in
collaboration with Walter Meade. The associate producer was Ivor's Spanish
documentary collaborator and fellow Communist, Sidney Cole. On release
in 1948 it received a Royal Command performance and positive reviews,
with Dilys Powell in the *Sunday Times* describing it as 'a record of tragedy which makes no concessions to sentimentality: no fanfares, no angel
choirs, no it-was-all-for-the-best; no love, indeed, in the cinema sense, for
the emotion honourably touched on deserves a word less profaned; nothing
but the record of solitude, struggle and death.' In retrospect, Montagu considered his major contribution to the film was the implied criticism of the
British ruling class in Scott's fatal preference for ponies over dogs.[13]

Montagu's other major project at Ealing was *Another Shore*, a gentle
comedy set in Dublin. For this he acted as associate producer, with Charles
Crichton directing and Robert Beatty and Moira Lister in the leading
roles. This production took him frequently to Ireland during 1948, and
he seized the opportunity to establish contacts with Irish comrades. The
film was well received on its release in November, with *The Times* hailing
its 'unhackneyed' plot (it was scripted by Walter Meade from the novel
by Kenneth Reddin) and declaring: 'To some it will seem an intolerable
hotch-potch of bogus Irish whimsicalities; for others it will have charm,
naivety, and freshness … If a casting vote is demanded it goes unhesitat-
ingly to those in favour of the film.'[14]

In late 1949 Montagu's contract at Ealing was not renewed: he was the
victim, he later claimed, of blacklisting. It was at this stage that he moved

into full-time work for the Soviet-sponsored peace movement, which would be his principal employment for the next thirteen years.[15]

Stalin had dissolved the Comintern in 1943 in a gesture aimed at appeasing his wartime allies, the UK and the USA. In the post-war period, coordination of Communist parties, particularly in Eastern Europe, under Soviet direction was undertaken by the Cominform (Communist Information Bureau), established in September 1947. It was at the founding conference that the Soviet representative, Andrei Zhdanov, propounded the 'two camp' thesis of a world sharply divided between the 'peace-loving' nations, at the vanguard of which stood the Soviet Union, and the 'warmongering' capitalist countries, spearheaded by the United States. Communist parties internationally were thenceforth enjoined to promulgate the 'struggle for peace' as the pivot of their activities.[16]

Along with his longtime left-wing ally Kingsley Martin, Montagu attended the Congress of Intellectuals in Defence of Peace held in Wroclaw, Poland, in August 1948. Here, amidst the rubble of a city in ruins, he rubbed shoulders with such luminaries as Pablo Picasso, Louis Aragon, Bertolt Brecht, György Lukács, and Ilya Ehrenburg. Montagu proposed that the film people should mount their own appeal for peace to their colleagues internationally, and he and Vsevolod Pudovkin drafted the text. After the Congress, a British Cultural Committee for Peace was formed; Montagu became active in it, but Martin declined to become involved, claiming that the Communists now wanted 'stooges' rather than allies.[17]

In April 1949 Ivor was a delegate at the first World Peace Congress, held in Paris (and also Prague, after disruption by the French authorities). It was at this conference (supported by a subvention of $100,000 ordered by the Soviet Politburo) that an international body, the World Committee of Partisans for Peace, was established. It was placed under the administration of a Communist-dominated Executive Bureau chaired by French scientist Frédéric Joliot-Curie, with Jean Lafitte, a leading member of the PCF, as general secretary. In accordance with a recommendation that national committees be established, the British Cultural Committee for Peace became the British Peace Committee in May; Montagu was elected a member of the executive.[18]

Montagu next lent his support to the movement by attending the All-Union Peace Conference held in Moscow in August 1949. This was principally a domestic Soviet affair, convened by the Soviet National Peace Committee with support from trade unions and writers' and women's organisations. His travelling companion on the trip – his first to the USSR since 1936 – and fellow guest was J.D. Bernal, one of the Spillikins whom he had consorted with in Cambridge, and now a member of the Executive Bureau of the World Committee of Partisans for Peace.[19]

It was a time of considerable tension in the Communist movement, with the breakaway of Tito's Yugoslavia from the Soviet bloc. (Montagu obligingly contributed to the denigration of the erstwhile partisan hero, labelling him 'Wall Street glamour boy' and a 'tawdry pawn' of the Pentagon.) Stalin's show trials were resumed, this time by remote control. In Hungary, foreign minister László Rajk was accused of being a 'Titoist spy' and an agent of western imperialism, found guilty and executed. Montagu had not the slightest doubt about the legitimacy of the trial. 'There is something terribly old-world and rather pitiful about the attempts to discredit the proceedings by comparing them with those in Moscow,' he wrote. 'As if today any serious, honest person in the slightest doubted the reality of the terrible treasons from which Soviet justice saved the Union, and the world, before the war by its vigilance.' In December, on the occasion of Stalin's 70th birthday, Ivor and Hell sent the great leader a cable: 'FROM A VILLAGE NEAR LONDON WE SEND WARM LOVE AND WISHES FOR MANY MORE HAPPY YEARS OF INSPIRATION TO MANKIND'.[20]

In February 1950, Montagu was one of twelve delegates from the World Committee of Partisans for Peace who applied to enter the United States as part of a 'peace mission' to the US Congress. Others included Picasso, Dr Hewlett Johnson (the 'Red' Dean of Canterbury), and Dr Max Cosyns, Belgium's leading atomic scientist. They intended 'to demand that Congress end the arms race by the reduction of war budgets and standing armies, ban the atomic bomb, end the Indonesian, Malayan and Indo-Chinese wars, end the "oppression of peace fighters of all countries", and end the war of nerves by signing a peace pact among the great powers.' Not surprisingly, the party were denied visas.[21]

The Cold War was intensifying – becoming hot with the invasion of South Korea by North Korean forces in June – and Montagu was to encounter a great deal more obstructiveness from the authorities on his next assignment. This was to act as chairman of the organising committee for the second World Peace Congress. Initially slated for Genoa, until the Italian government made it known it would refuse delegates' visas, this was rescheduled for England in November. A large enough venue in London not being made available, Montagu settled on the Sheffield City Hall. Immensely complex arrangements were put in place to host the expected 2,500 delegates, including, for example, the installation of 2,845 pairs of earphones for simultaneous translation into six languages by a team of thirty-seven interpreters – all for naught. The Attlee government denounced the congress as 'bogus' and deliberately sabotaged the event by refusing admission at the last minute to the great majority of foreign delegates, including leaders of the movement, and cancelling charter flights. The congress was shifted to Warsaw.[22]

It was in Warsaw, at this second World Congress, that the organisation was consolidated as the World Peace Council (WPC). As the Communist delegates (very likely the vast majority) would have guessed, the Council was ultimately under the control of the Communist Party of the Soviet Union, being funded and directed by the International Department of the CPSU Central Committee. As such its purpose was to advance the interests of Soviet foreign policy; in its call for peace, for example, it denounced the US as the aggressor in the Korean War. (At the congress, 5,000 delegates cheered for fifteen minutes when Joliot-Curie declared that 'the American conception of civilisation' was leading to war.) Montagu was elected to the world presidium of the Council, and his position as a member of the secretariat confirmed.[23]

The congress was filmed under the direction of Joris Ivens and Jerzy Szelubski (Jerzy Bossak), and the documentary *Pokój zdobedzie swiat/Peace Will Win* released in 1951. An introductory newsreel montage depicting the global situation from a Communist perspective was followed by 'speeches, committee meetings and cheerful delegates greeting each other'. A tendentious section intercut footage of the US military dropping napalm bombs with a North Korean woman explaining that 'good people lived in her country and villains in America,' to the strains of Beethoven's Fifth. Up to his old editing tricks, Montagu cut the film down from its original ninety minutes to, as he recalled, half an hour.[24]

Initially headquartered in Paris, the WPC moved subsequently to Prague and then, in 1954, to Vienna. At the start, Montagu was involved in promulgating the Stockholm Appeal. Launched in March 1950, it called for the

outlawing of atomic weapons, and eventually garnered a claimed 500 million signatures. (In 'The Bomb-Mongers', an article in *Labour Monthly*,
Montagu wrote: 'If you are against the atomic bomb, you CANNOT oppose
the Peace Petition. It's as simple as that.') Subsequently, his duties for the
organisation were undoubtedly connected with the running of the frequent congresses, held in Stockholm (1951), Vienna (1952), Budapest (1953),
Helsinki (1955), Stockholm (1958) and Moscow (1962). Joliot-Curie served
as WPC president until 1958, when he was succeeded by J.D. Bernal.[25]

In the February 1950 general election, in an indication of how far
public opinion had swung against the crypto-Communists in parliament,
D.N. Pritt lost his seat. (Another casualty was John Platts-Mills, who like
Pritt had been expelled from the Labour Party.) When Attlee went to the
polls again in October 1951 in an attempt to shore up his slender majority,
Montagu was selected to stand as a Communist candidate in Pritt's former
constituency of Hammersmith North. In an election pamphlet, he set forth
his credentials: 'I have been active in the Labour Movement since I was
fourteen, and a trade unionist for twenty-five years. I have always fought for
the present and future interests of the working people. I pledge myself to
remain true to that struggle.' Regretfully, he did not get to test the mood of
the electorate, as the CP decided to withdraw the great majority of its candidates, including Montagu, in order not to split the left-wing vote. (The
gesture bore some fruit, as the Labour Party increased its overall vote; but
the Conservatives won more seats and Churchill returned to power.)[26]

In February 1952, the governments of North Korea and China alleged
that the US had carried our air drops of infected insects bearing plague,
cholera and other diseases over North Korean territory. The charges were
immediately denied by the United States. Refusing to accept the denial,
Montagu told the CPGB congress in April that US planes had dropped
more than 2,000 bacterial bombs on Korea and China, containing 'the germs
of plague, typhus, anthrax, typhoid, dysentery and encephalitis'. He personally travelled to the affected areas, and produced a film on the subject,
shown at the WPC Council meeting in East Berlin in July. In his capacity
as WPC secretary Montagu was undoubtedly also involved in organising a
scientific commission to travel to the areas in question and investigate (the
International Red Cross had offered its services, which had been rejected
by the Chinese). The commission, headed by the distinguished biochemist

Dr Joseph Needham, a sinologist closely aligned with the Communist Party, issued a report in September validating the charges. As was apparent at the time, the commission made no field investigations of its own, relying on 'evidence' submitted by Chinese scientists, and the 'confessions' of captured US airmen (which were retracted once the men returned to the US). In his book *Plot against Peace* published late in 1952, Montagu upheld the integrity of the data presented to the scientific commission, and claimed that 'the "rebutting" data emanating from US and British official circles and published in the press are not only false but often deliberately so.' Subsequent research has determined that, although the US was in fact developing a bacteriological warfare capability, all the allegations of it being deployed in Korea were contrived and fraudulent, and the 'evidence' fabricated.[27]

In October, Montagu passed through Prague and, as was his habit, rang up Otto Katz to arrange for them to lunch together. Since returning to Czechoslovakia after the war, Katz had become foreign editor of the Communist daily *Rude Pravo* and an official of the intelligence service of the Ministry of Information. Otto's wife told Ivor that he was away for ten days; the following day, however, a government employee informed Montagu at the WPC office that Katz had been arrested. Ivor's conversation at CPGB headquarters when he discussed this with Bob (Stewart?) was bugged by MI5. Montagu was 'a bit worried', the spies reported, in case Katz was 'scrubbed'. Katz had 'many times been near people who have turned out bad ones, e.g. Willi Münzenberg.' Ivor asked Bob what he should do about it; 'should he keep his mouth shut and say nothing or if that is the wrong thing to do.' Bob didn't think it was easy to say. 'A joke was made,' the transcriber recorded, 'of what they called the English disease, that it was a trial for comrades and a test of character because those who hadn't made a good job of this didn't realise the inevitability of it – on the other hand those who were real comrades understood the necessity of it and took it very well.' If Montagu did decide to plead for his friend and comrade, it was in vain. Katz, with Rudolf Slánsky, General Secretary of the Czechoslovak Communist Party, and twelve other leading Communists were put on trial, on orders of Moscow, and convicted of participating in a Troskyite–Titoite–Zionist conspiracy. Eleven of the defendants were Jews. All confessed, under duress or after torture. Katz, along with ten others, was executed.[28]

Montagu's book *Plot against Peace* was a counterblast to the Cold War anti-Communist rhetoric issuing from the news media of the West, often with covert government subsidies. An extended, rambling polemic, it excoriates the United States as a hotbed of militarism, racism, corruption, surveillance of citizens, drug addiction, juvenile crime, and gruesome television. It denounces big business and its manipulation of the American political process, and accuses the US of dominating the United Nations. In contrast, its rhapsodic vision of the USSR features 'the towering shapes of the crane-mounted dwellings building swiftly on the Moscow streets, the neat warm cottages in the countryside, the lovely trees and gardens, the shops bursting not just with goods but with people buying them at prices that have fallen five times within a tiny space.' The youth are 'smiling and confident, calm and earnest', the children 'happy and sure as members of one family with no barriers to betterment'. (It is no surprise that there is no mention of the 2.5 million Soviet citizens in the slave labour camps of the gulag.) Occasionally Montagu makes acute observations – such as pointing out that only in the case of Korea did the UN order intervention and expansion of the war, as opposed to mediation and conciliation – but within the overall Manichaean framework, they tend to lose traction. So oblivious does the writer seem to the lack of credibility that his blatant partisanship induces, that he can contend that an accusation that the World Peace Council is 'Communist' or 'under Communist influence' is 'childish and irrelevant'.[29]

On 13 January 1953, the Soviet press announced that nine Kremlin doctors had been arrested. Predominantly Jewish, they were accused of causing the deaths, by deliberate ill-treatment, of Politburo members Andrei Zhdanov and Alexander Shcherbakov, and of plotting to kill a number of military leaders. All, it was claimed, were 'paid agents' of American and British intelligence organisations, and most had connections with 'Joint', the international Jewish charitable organisation that was alleged to be under the control of US intelligence and to carry out 'broad-scale espionage, terroristic, and other subversive activities'. The arrests followed a number of repressive measures that had been taken since 1948 against Jews in the USSR, and the Slánsky trial in Czechoslovakia. It was feared in the West that the 'Doctors' Plot' heralded a new wave of anti-Semitism in the Soviet Union and Eastern Europe.[30]

The president of the Anglo-Jewish Association was Ivor's brother, Ewen Montagu. On 15 January Ewen issued a statement expressing the association's horror at the 'virulent anti-Semitic trends which were becoming daily more pronounced in Iron Curtain countries, and the news from Moscow underlined the fact that the Kremlin was leading the hunt.' Although Communists might argue that the accusations were anti-Zionist rather than anti-Semitic, it was undeniable 'that this new wave of persecution will give freer expression to the latent anti-Semitism which is endemic in Eastern Europe.' Ivor could not let this go unchallenged, even if it meant publicly attacking his brother, from whom he was now estranged. He wrote to the *Jewish Chronicle*:

> Since my return to this country a few days ago, I have been able to check details of a series of reckless statements, wicked in their falsity, by leading figures in the Jewish community – the Chief Rabbi, the President of the Anglo-Jewish Association, officers of the Jewish Board of Deputies and others – pretending that anti-Semitism is being promoted in the countries of Eastern Europe. I testify to the truth … The allegation that anti-Semitism is officially encouraged, or growing among the public, or felt with apprehension among Jewish people in these regions is a monstrous falsehood.[31]

As these words were being written, hundreds more Jewish medical practitioners were being arrested, imprisoned and shot; in Czechoslovakia, large-scale arrests of Communists and socialists with an 'international' background were taking place. The Doctors' Plot trial and subsequent executions were to be the trigger, historians speculate, for an intensified wave of repression, perhaps including the mass deportation of Jews to Siberia. But on 5 March, before the trial could be staged, Stalin died. Within a month, the charges against the Kremlin doctors were dismissed and all the accused released and exonerated.[32]

The sudden turnaround placed Soviet apologists abroad in an embarrassing situation. Beverley Baxter, the former *Daily Express* editor and an old friend of the Montagu family, could not resist the temptation to have a dig. Now a Conservative MP, Baxter penned a profile of Montagu published in a Dutch newspaper. He had confronted Ivor when news of the arrests became public. How did he judge this medieval persecution of Jews?

'I pointed out to him,' Baxter relates, 'that these Jewish doctors would first be tortured before they appeared in court, that they would confess everything and would even demand capital punishment.' 'There are good Jews and bad Jews,' Ivor had replied. 'Of course they are guilty.' When the Kremlin announced that they had been falsely accused and were entirely innocent, Baxter visited Montagu, convinced that he could force him into a corner. 'What do you think now about the flawless Russian judicial system?' Montagu replied without a moment's hesitation. 'There has never been a clearer indication that under the Communists nobody will be treated unjustly. The Soviet parliament agreed that errors had been made and alerted the whole world to the truth.'[33]

In September 1954, Ivor and Hell went on holiday to the Mongolian People's Republic. He had met Mongolian delegates at peace conferences, and received an invitation to visit. The country's extraordinary isolation was such that no one from Britain had visited in thirty years. He had no intention, he says, of writing a book, but as it turned out he could not forgo the opportunity. *Land of Blue Sky* duly appeared in 1956. Modestly presenting his credentials ('I am no specialist, and no expert: I have a wide, but superficial smattering of a lot of subjects'), Montagu here paints a vivid portrait of Mongolia in language that is a refreshing change from the lacklustre propaganda of *Plot against Peace*. Covering geography, climate, history, economics, education, health services, cultural life and sport in between colourful personal travel anecdotes, *Land of Blue Sky* gives a warmly positive, though not extravagant, account of an emerging socialist nation that had been in the Soviet bloc since 1924. It skates very lightly, of course, over the purges that occurred in the drive to collectivisation in 1928–32, and the brutal Stalinist repression of 1937–39.[34]

Shortly after midnight on 25 February 1956, Soviet leader Nikita Khrushchev dropped a bombshell. His 'Secret Speech' made to delegates at the CPSU's 20th Congress lambasted Stalin for the 'extraordinary mass terror' implemented under his rule 'directed not at the remnants of the defeated exploiting classes but against the honest workers of the party and of the Soviet State; against them were made lying, slanderous and absurd accusations.' Other charges were that he had ordered the use of torture, disastrously mishandled the defence of the Soviet Union against Germany, deported whole nationalities to remote regions of the country, and encouraged the growth of a cult of personality around himself. News of the speech trickled out to Communist parties in the West; finally, in June, the text was made public by the US State Department. The shock it induced was compounded in October–November when a popular uprising in Hungary was crushed by invading Soviet forces.[35]

These events precipitated a crisis in the CPGB. A cyclostyled journal, *The Reasoner*, began to appear in July, highly critical of the functioning of 'democratic centralism' in the party. In November, a number of prominent Communist intellectuals composed a letter to the *Daily Worker* expressing their concerns. Refused publication, it subsequently appeared in the *Tribune* and the *New Statesman*. 'We feel that the uncritical support given by the Executive Committee of the Communist Party to the Soviet action in Hungary is the undesirable culmination of years of distortion of fact, and failure by British Communists to think out political problems for themselves,' wrote the group, which included the historians Eric Hobsbawm and Christopher Hill, the mathematician Hyman Levy, the economist Ronald Meek, the novelist Doris Lessing, the poet Hugh MacDiarmid, and others. The letter continued:

> We had hoped that the revelations made at the Twentieth Congress of the Communist Party of the Soviet Union would have made our leadership and press realise that Marxist ideas will only be acceptable in the British labour movement if they arise from the truth about the world we live in. The exposure of grave crimes and abuses in the USSR, and the recent revolt of workers and intellectuals against the pseudo-Communist bureaucracies and police systems of Poland and Hungary, have shown that for the past twelve years we have based our political analyses on a false presentation of the facts – not on an out-of-date theory, for we still consider the Marxist method to be correct.[36]

Montagu was not amongst the signatories of this statement. His allegiance to the Communist cause as interpreted by the Soviet and British party leaderships was unshakeable – and after all, he was still a paid agent of the Kremlin. In this he was not alone. Other leading CP intellectuals – men such as Rajani Palme Dutt, Robin Page Arnot, Emile Burns, James Klugmann and Andrew Rothstein – also remained staunch, whatever the unpalatable news from Moscow or Budapest. It was not that Montagu was unprepared to grant the critics any ground. In 'Hungary – Cold War Heritage', published in the December *Labour Monthly*, he referred to the 'crimes and errors of the leadership of the Communist Party of Hungary' and 'the grave mistakes and blunders of the Communist Party of the Soviet Union in relation to Hungary, stemming from the state of affairs a corner of which was revealed at the 20th Congress.' But the tragic truth was that, whatever the circumstances of their arrival in the first place, Soviet troops had to remain in Hungary to prevent the resurgence of fascism, which, he reminded his readers, 'had a deeper, solider mass basis even than in Germany or Italy.' By November, the armed populace had broken up into 'a thousand trigger-happy gangs' and the White Terror had begun; the 'honest protest of youth and workers' was being exploited by Washington's 'Freedom Fighters', anxious for a pretext to intervene. 'The true, practical path to advance the freedom and democratic development of Hungary,' Ivor concluded, 'as of all other countries, is by way of the liquidation of the two confronting cold-war blocs ...'[37]

The revolt in the ranks of the CPGB led to the creation of a Commission on Inner Party Democracy, which reported in December, and then to the convening of a special Congress in April 1957. Debate centred on the applicability of Leninist democratic centralism to the party in current British conditions. In this the CPGB leadership, strongly committed to existing procedures, had the firm backing of Montagu. In the event the rebels demanding greater democracy were heavily outnumbered, unsurprisingly as many of the disaffected had by now left the party. Ivor reflected on the situation in a letter to John Gollan, who had taken over from Pollitt as general secretary, later in the year. 'The demand of oppositional elements for a right of continued opposition or "contracting-out" (standing aside) from decisions they disagreed with took very few tricks,' he wrote. 'At least that was my experience. It was too obviously an expression of a lack of faith and too obviously any concession to it would have disrupted and even destroyed the party as an organised and coordinated force.' And the following year, writing to a party comrade, Montagu was fiercely defensive of the actions the executive committee had taken:

On the general question of the party leadership having funked the issue of the 20th Congress revelations, I completely and entirely disagree. Indeed,

I think this is one of the most monstrously untrue allegations that has ever been made about the party, and it is a tragedy (but I suppose inevitable) that good comrades within the ranks of the party should have been shaken by its endless repetition by the party's enemies.[38]

The Soviet crackdown in Hungary had an impact on the work of the World Peace Council. In July 1958, Bertrand Russell, president of the Campaign for Nuclear Disarmament, withdrew his support for the upcoming World Congress on Disarmament and International Co-operation in Stockholm in protest against the secret trial and execution of toppled premier Imre Nagy, and the WPC's failure to condemn the USSR's actions. Montagu carried on regardless, and his loyalty was recognised the following year. On 1 May 1959 he was awarded – along with Nikita Khrushchev, American civil rights activist W.E.B. Du Bois, Greek poet Kostas Varnalis, and East German politician Otto Buchwitz – the Lenin Peace Prize. The citation declared that he was one of the world's 'outstanding fighters for peace' and noted that although he had been born into an aristocratic family, 'the life of this man is a vivid example of a progressive representative of the Western intelligentsia finding his real calling in joint struggle with the people.' Later in the year he travelled to Moscow to receive the prize, which came with a cash award of £12,500, in person. He assured his Kremlin audience that 'the forces of war had been shaken and weakened' but 'peace will not be handed out on a plate' – it had to be won.[39]

One arena in which Montagu had actively striven to transcend Cold War barriers was that of sport. He claimed to have hectored Stalin after the war about the need for the Soviet Union to join the Olympic movement, a plea that the politburo acceded to in 1951. (It is unlikely that this was in person; as far as is known, Montagu never met Stalin.) As president of the International Table Tennis Federation he ensured that world championships were staged in Budapest and Bucharest as well as Western Europe, India and Japan, and Prague and Ljubljana would follow in the 1960s. Perhaps the high point of his 'ping-pong diplomacy' was convincing China to hold the championships in Beijing in 1961. Although the movement of foreign team members was strictly controlled to prevent their seeing evidence of the man-made famine then ravaging the country, the event proved a triumph for China and a step out of its international isolation, and Montagu was feted by Zhou Enlai.[40]

In 1962 the World Conference for General Disarmament and Peace, a WPC event, was held in Moscow. Bertrand Russell, now president of the anti-war Committee of 100, was back on board, submitting to the conference specific proposals for disarmament and arms control. Controversy erupted when a group of delegates announced they were planning to stage a protest march demanding an end to all nuclear tests, including Soviet. Leading figures in the British delegation, including Kingsley Martin and Sydney Silverman MP, opposed the march, and Montagu relayed information he had received from the Moscow city authorities that they considered such a demonstration a 'breach of hospitality', and marchers would be liable to deportation. A small demonstration nevertheless took place in Red Square before the protesters' banners were seized; no other action against the delegates was apparently taken. The closing resolution of the Conference was that it was 'firmly opposed to all testing of nuclear bombs and similar devices'.[41]

The following year the Limited Test Ban Treaty was signed; and Montagu welcomed it for its halting of nuclear pollution and because it marked '*the first concrete agreement in this field*'. It was by no means universal: France and China refused to sign, and underground tests were still permitted. Peace supporters also had cause for concern about US pressure on Cuba, the 'undeclared war' in Vietnam, military build-up in West Germany, white racist regimes in Africa, and the continued ostracism of China, all of which called for a united programme of action. But the opportunity to fight for such a programme, Montagu declared, was 'greater now that the *first step* has brought the movement confidence and undermined the obstructions of the cold war warriors who declared *any* step not only undesirable but impossible.' On such an optimistic note, he retired from the WPC secretariat.[42]

Ivor now concentrated on his writing. While maintaining his prolific output of journal articles, principally for *Labour Monthly* and *Marxism Today*, he devoted himself to four substantial book projects. The first fulfilled an aspiration he had entertained in the 1920s and revived several times since, a general survey of the cinema. It was followed by an exposé of the resurgence of Nazism in Germany, and two colourful volumes of autobiography.

Film World (Penguin, 1964) reflects Montagu's manifold engagements with the cinema as enthusiast, practitioner, critic and battler against censorship. Divided into sections on Film as Science, Film as Art, Film as Commodity, and Film as Vehicle, it is a potpourri of industrial history,

artistic theory, technical explication, personal anecdote, statistical documentation and political critique such as only he could have written. Although
there is, curiously, considerable discussion of contemporary television technique, much of the book is stuck in the past of silent film and the transition
to sound, with the aesthetic arguments advanced at that time. The *Sight and
Sound* reviewer, Peter Harcourt, found it a sad book; and indeed it is disconcerting to find the founder of the Film Society dismissing modern cinema
out of hand. 'The meaning of Antonioni's objects becomes indecipherable,'
Montagu claims, '… Alain Resnais has developed a technique of the por-
tentous so obscure that no one can tell what anything portends'; while, as
Harcourt comments, 'Godard's name (like Fellini's earlier) is relegated to a
footnote, Truffaut's to just one item in a list; Bergman's to a parenthesis (and
even then, it is mis-spelled).' What Harcourt does find compelling is the
book's analysis of the domination of the industry by business interests: here,
Montagu's 'old Soviet allegiances make him a sharp yet sober critic of our
relentlessly commercial ways.'[43]

Ivor next accepted a commission from Panther Books to report on the
resurgence of the far right in West German politics. His paperback *Germany's
New Nazis* (1967), hailed by the *Economist* as 'informative, up-to-date, and
briskly presented', focused particularly on the *Nationaldemokratische Partei
Deutschlands* (NDP), then beginning to achieve success in local and state
elections. Montagu assessed its programme, its leaders, and the sources of its
electoral support, while criticising the Cold War policy of the West, the fruit
of which had been 'the growth of an atmosphere in which neo-Nazism
could not help but fester.' The book was particularly chilling in detailing the
extent to which ex-Nazis and State functionaries under Hitler continued to
hold prominent roles in the Federal Republic – including the serving president and chancellor. Reviewers welcomed Montagu's 'well-documented'
analysis, stressing that the neo-Nazis were a small force, but willing to grant,
as one wrote, that 'an economic recession big enough to hit the average West
German's living standards might sweep the NDP into the Bonn Parliament
– and this is the secret nightmare of every West German politician.'[44]

Montagu's two exercises in autobiography followed. The first, *With
Eisenstein in Hollywood* (1968), covered his involvement in the film industry
in 1929–30, particularly the American adventure. The second, *The Youngest
Son* (1970), recounted his life up to the age of 23 – 1927 was the year in

which he married and in which his father died. Liberated from all propagandist imperatives, Ivor's writing here comes alive, with a verve and sense of humour seldom to be found in the bulk of his voluminous journalistic output. Laced with evocative reminiscence, often self-deprecating, the memoirs found an appreciative audience: Dilys Powell wrote of *With Eisenstein in Hollywood* that 'it is history and it is the best, the very best, gossip; anyhow irresistible,' while *The Youngest Son* was described as being 'unusually rich in anecdote, witty observation and footnotes for the historian.'[45]

The books established Montagu as a congenial elder statesman of left-wing film, a man whom television interviewers and documentary makers were happy to feature as he entered the quiet years of his retirement. In 1968 his service to the union movement had been recognised when, along with John Grierson, he was made an honorary member of what was now ACTT (the Association of Cinematograph Television and Allied Technicians). Shortly after *The Youngest Son* appeared, Ivor and Hell moved from Hertfordshire to remote Rousay, in the Orkney Islands off the north coast of Scotland, 'having retired there not to be, like Greta Garbo, alone, but far enough away to get work done.' His writing now tended to focus on warm recollections of his early years in the film world.[46]

But he was not done with politics, Communism and the Soviet Union. The publication of Alexander Solzhenitsyn's *The Gulag Archipelago* in 1974 ignited renewed Cold War attacks on the socialist homeland, and Montagu again leapt to its defence. In 'Solzhenitsyn, Gulag and the Solzhenitsyn Industry' (*Marxism Today*, December 1974), he is careful to acknowledge the 'horrors and injustices' to which the Soviet people have been subject. But he skirts lightly over the mass murders, and the trumped-up charges, the imprisonment in squalor, the torture, sleep deprivation, starvation and slave labour that millions had experienced, and which Solzhenitsyn describes in brutal detail. Montagu discounts the book – and the criticism of the Soviet system to which it has given rise – on the grounds that it is literary fiction, not history (but he does not refute any of its historical claims), that it contains no new revelations (the faults in penal administration were 'declared at the time of the 20th Congress – and largely corrected thereafter'), that it leaves out the historical context (White Terror, the German build-up under Hitler, etc.) in which the camps operated, and that the text is vitiated by the author's snobbery, hatred, and blinkered vision.[47]

As a schoolboy, Ivor had written, 'Russia sends her prisoners to Siberia, where they work, and there is hardly any colder and more horrible place than Siberia.' As an adult, Montagu's empathy for the inmates of the Soviet gulag is tempered by his steadfast belief that capitalism is capable of worse: in Solzhenitsyn's world, 'there is no Indonesia, no South Vietnam, no Chile, no Greece, no Turkey, no South Korea, no South Africa, Israel or Brazil, no Northern Ireland.' Some five years later, asked to assess the development of the Soviet Union, he replied: 'On the scale of world history, as well as so far as the achievements, welfare and happiness of the vast majority of the people are concerned – overwhelmingly positive.'[48]

In March 1983, Montagu returned to Barcelona after forty-five years to screen and discuss, under British Council auspices, his films of the Civil War. It was a busy programme. 'Exhausting? Quite the contrary, inspiring, invigorating … I have never had a more lively and relaxing time.' The following year, he was inducted into the International Jewish Sports Hall of Fame. Then, on 4 October, Hell died at the age of 80. Five weeks later, at the same age, Ivor followed. It was 5 November – Guy Fawkes' Day, appropriately enough for a lifelong anti-establishment rebel. His wealth at the time of his death was a modest £137,138.[49]

After his death, Montagu slipped out of the public eye, remembered only occasionally for his contribution to the sport of table tennis. But in 1999 he suddenly hit the headlines. 'Revealed: the greatest secret of the Cold War' screamed the *Daily Express* headline: 'A controversial new book exposes two traitors at the heart of the British establishment' – Ivor and his old comrade and X Group conspirator J.B.S. Haldane. The preview of Nigel West's *Venona* was mired by error (the muddling of the espionage identities of Montagu and Haldane, the reiteration of the myth that Ivor was 'very rich'), but it ensured that from then on the name of the youngest son of the 2nd Baron Swaythling would forever be linked with intrigue and scandal. The question remained as to why the pair were never prosecuted, for which West had an answer: without physical evidence, they would have to have confessed – but 'both were sophisticated, hardened Marxists and they could easily decline to be interviewed by MI5.'[50]

★

During two crucial decades, the 1920s and 1930s, Ivor Montagu was a leading standard-bearer in Britain for film as art. In the Film Society, and as importer and distributor of Soviet productions, he worked assiduously to place alternative cinematic practices before the public. In his reviewing he championed directors who had learnt how to use the new medium imaginatively, with serious themes and stylistic grace.

He was equivocal about the avant-garde. The Film Society screened an impressive array of experimental work, and Montagu personally encouraged and supported the pioneering celluloid artist Len Lye. He happily took part in a congress for independent cinema with the likes of Hans Richter, Walter Ruttmann, and Alberto Cavalcanti. Yet he was cool towards work such as Cocteau's *Blood of a Poet*. The avant-garde was 'in advance,' he was to say, 'but of course very often you advance up a blind alley.' He had no wish to be part of an elitist coterie like the *Close Up* group. (It was true, as Caroline Lejeune charged, that there was an exclusivity to the Film Society because of the high subscription rates; but its screenings paved the way for the arthouse cinemas that soon sprang up, open to the general public.)[51]

For Montagu, what counted most was the application of artistry and intelligence to mainstream cinema. In his own practice within the industry, commissioning modernist intertitles for *The Lodger*; imparting an edge of social criticism to the scripts he worked on, with Brunel, Eisenstein and Hitchcock; pushing for inspired pieces of casting (one thinks of Nadia Sibirskaia and Peter Lorre); editing for pace and clarity; arguing for the retention of a film's integrity against the demands of the censor (*Secret Agent*) – these were the sorts of contributions Montagu felt able to make, within the accepted confines of a commercial system.

As a director, similar considerations applied. The Wells comedies incorporated experimental techniques of camera angle and montage within a popular genre of satirical comedy. As the critic Seb Manley was to argue, 'Montagu's innovation as a filmmaker was to move confidently between the populist forms of a successful national industry, and the unorthodox transformations of cinematic language that were developing on the continent.'[52]

Ivor often despaired of the fate of film under capitalism, and was wont to suggest that only within a nationalised industry could filmmakers be freely creative. But as a staunch union man and a hard-headed lobbyist, he fought hard for the betterment of conditions within the existing studio system.

Provisions incorporated in the 1938 Cinematograph Films Act at the urging of ACT were a significant achievement.

Montagu battled, too, against the draconian censorship regime. As he lucidly pointed out, the BBFC operated under a quirk of the law without any democratic accountability. The publicity his anti-censorship campaign generated undoubtedly pressured both the Board and local authorities to be more liberal in their rulings than would otherwise have been the case. Yet, for all his rebellion against it, Montagu was a member of Britain's ruling elite, and his arguments were compromised by the paternalistic assumption that while censorship might be requisite for the hoi polloi, it should not apply to responsible citizens who could be relied upon not to riot in the aisles.

Montagu was no brilliantly subversive *auteur*, like Jean Vigo in France. He was not an entrepreneurial producer of sensitivity and flair, like his boss Mick Balcon, nor an astute businessman establishing a chain of cinemas, like his friend Sidney Bernstein. As a writer, he did not build up a body of penetrating Marxist criticism, like his American contemporary Harry Alan Potamkin. What he excelled at, in the film world, was organising, collaborating, liaising, networking. He thus fulfilled the classic role of the intellectual as go-between, bringing into contact European cinema and British audiences, La Sarraz and Hollywood, Soviet and Western filmmakers, art and industry, sparking the release of new creative energies. It is sadly ironic that when the cinema finally unleashed its full potential as the art form of the twentieth century, with the New Wave breakthroughs of the 1960s, Montagu was no longer responsive.

The workers' film societies, which Montagu assisted in getting off the ground, were not about film as art. Their role was as an outlet for left-wing propaganda, principally Soviet films that could not be screened commercially. Montagu's connections and his skill at moving lithely between the equally labyrinthine worlds of Soviet motion-picture importation and British censorship enforcement made him an invaluable behind-the-scenes operator for both the Federation of Workers' Film Societies and its successors, Kino and the Progressive Film Institute.

It was the task of the intelligentsia, Mannheim wrote, to provide an interpretation of the world for their society. The oppositional, progressive viewpoint could, of course, not be expected from those whom Koestler described as being 'snugly tucked into the social hierarchy' – like Ivor's brothers Stuart and Ewen. It was those rebels who, like Montagu, formed an 'unanchored, *relatively* classless stratum' who could provide a critical perspective on the British Establishment and the other capitalist regimes which ruled vast swathes of the world. This, Montagu did in spades, as organiser, journalist, filmmaker, author.[53]

Psychologically, the origins of Montagu's radicalism can undoubtedly be ascribed to conflict with a father whose liberal views in politics were accompanied by the traditionally domineering behaviour of a patriarch in the home. 'The father is more or less forced into the role of representing "Society" to his son,' Mannheim observed, and Ivor's rejection of Louis Montagu's authoritarian stance from a young age soon fused into rebellion against the political system he stood for (and indeed, helped prop up financially). The embrace of the socialist alternative followed naturally from the decline of liberalism and the cataclysm of the Great War.[54]

As it turned out, Montagu's most trenchant criticism was not aimed at the Liberal politicians in his father's circle, to several of whom he was related. In fact, he collaborated closely with some of them (as he did with Labour MPs) both in his anti-censorship campaign and (though he was to downplay it in later years) in his lobbying to have Trotsky admitted to the UK. His devastatingly scathing attacks were directed at the aristocratic Tory elite who dominated Britain in the 1930s and who clustered around Chamberlain in the shameful years of appeasement. In numerous articles, in the film *Peace and Plenty* and his book *The Traitor Class*, he denounced the members of the National Government for enriching themselves while presiding over a nation mired in misery and conniving at imperialist aggression in Asia, Africa and Europe. Equally relevantly and astutely, he consistently drew attention to state-sanctioned oppression in the colonies of the British Empire.

Just as telling, in the interwar years, was his anti-fascist activity. With the Reichstag Fire counter-trial and the manifold variety of his work for the Relief Committee for the Victims of German Fascism – including taking in political refugees himself – Montagu made a vital contribution in exposing to the world the terrorist nature of Hitler's regime. In semi-clandestine manoeuvring he strove to swing support at the League of Nations in behind the policy of collective security for checking Nazi belligerence. And the documentaries he made in Spain during the Civil War brought home to the

British public (and audiences in other territories to which the films were exported) the true nature of the conflict as a desperate fight for survival by a popularly-elected government under attack from an insubordinate military massively abetted by the armed forces of Fascist Italy and Germany. He later continued the theme in analysing Nazi racial ideology in *Man – One Family*, and warning of a far right resurgence in *Germany's New Nazis*.

But there was also the Soviet Union. The conundrum at the centre of Ivor Montagu's biography is how a highly intelligent fighter for social justice could become a cheerleader for one of the most brutal tyrannies the world has ever known. It is an issue that many another chronicler of the Communist movement has wrestled with. As Michael David-Fox recently wrote: 'Explaining the blindness of Western intellectuals when they looked at Stalinism has proven one of the most durable riddles in the history of twentieth-century politics and intellectual life.'[55]

From the start, Ivor was an enthusiastic partisan of the Bolshevik transformation of Russian society. For a Marxist, the symbolism of a state in which the working class had (supposedly) seized power was enormously compelling. Yet for a number of years, exercising his independence of thought, he did not join up with the local advocates of the Soviet revolutionary road, the CPGB. He kept a promise to his father, until he turned 21. But even then he kept aloof, uncertain, he tells us, how to evaluate the conflict between Trotsky and Stalin. When he began corresponding with Trotsky, he displayed a lively critical awareness in assessing the prospects for a Communist future in the UK and how it might best be advanced. At this time, he was unimpressed both by the CP, in its Class Against Class phase, and by its newly launched organ, the *Daily Worker*.

The turning point came in 1931. No longer content to sit on the sidelines while the British people were being pummeled by the economic crisis, Montagu swallowed his misgivings and joined the Party, becoming a paid official in one of its satellite bodies, and later a journalist on its newspaper. The result was the loss of his intellectual independence. As Mannheim has argued, political parties are forced into a dogmatic direction through the very fact of their being public fighting organisations. In the interwar period, 'the more intellectuals became party functionaries, the more they lost the virtue of receptivity and elasticity which they had brought with them from their previous labile situation.'[56]

This was especially the case for Montagu in that the CPGB was a Leninist party organised on the basis of 'democratic centralism', forbidding the criticism of any aspect of the party line once it had been adopted. Furthermore, the party line was not one that the members were free to decide upon for themselves. The CPGB, as a section of the Communist International (and heavily dependent on Moscow subsidies), was bound to follow ECCI dictates, while the ECCI itself was dominated by the CPSU and ultimately Stalin. As Koestler, like Montagu a party functionary at this time, has contended, the revolutionary movement during the period of the Comintern's existence was governed by a 'semi-Asiatic dictatorship' whose European extension 'needed not intellectuals, but a ruthless and uncritically obedient bureaucracy. The few members of the Western intelligentsia who were accepted into its ranks lost first the right, and soon even the desire, for "independent thought"; they became fanatic sectarians and Party-hacks, while the best among them met a tragic end.'[57]

Montagu's commitment to the CP and the international Communist movement evolved from a logical calculation as to how best he might help the cause of socialism to a faith that was as deeply-rooted as that of any religious believer. Like a newlywed pledging his allegiance 'for better or for worse', like a volunteer soldier signing up for military discipline, like an obedient employee happy to accept his boss's orders because he approves of what the firm is doing, Montagu gave up his right to make personal judgments and act upon them, for the sake of what he perceived to be the greater good. From that point on, nothing he was told about the Soviet Union could disturb his conviction that it represented the future for humanity. As his Comintern comrade Louis Fischer was later to write:

> One's general alignment with a cause is more compelling than all but the most shocking facts about it. Just as religious conviction is impervious to logical argument and, indeed, does not result from logical processes, just as nationalist devotion or personal affection defies a mountain of evidence, so my pro-Soviet attitude attained complete independence from day-to-day events.

Fischer's experience was similar to that of Koestler, who explained: 'A faith that is held "in spite of" is always more resilient and less open to disillusion than one that is based on a "because".' Montagu himself attested: 'Flaws in socialist argument could not shake me, just as disappointments in socialist experience recognised in after life have not been able to.'[58]

Communists who, like Montagu, stuck with the Party despite disillusioning moments could validate their attitude as service to the cause through thick and thin; those who left, or criticised, were traitors and enemies. The Party faithful were bound together in what Edward Shils terms an 'ideological primary group', separated by sharply defined boundaries from the outside world. 'Stringent discipline over conduct and belief' was a feature of such groups; 'intense solidarity and unwavering loyalty' were demanded.[59]

It is instructive to compare Montagu's correspondence with Trotsky, 1929–31, with his dialogue with Strachey in 1940. In the former, he is exchanging ideas; in the latter, he is scoring debating points. It is the difference between an open mind and a closed mind. Koestler's concept of the 'magic aura' is applicable to the obstinacy with which Montagu resisted any attempt to undermine, by the submission of empirical evidence, his faith in the USSR:

> The inner defences are unconscious. They consist in a kind of magic aura which the mind builds around its cherished belief. Arguments which penetrate into the magic aura are not dealt with rationally but by a specific type of pseudo-reasoning. Absurdities and contradictions which outside the magic aura would be rejected at once are made acceptable by specious rationalisations ... Under these circumstances almost every discussion with myth-addicts, whether public or private, is doomed to failure. The debate is from the beginning removed from the level of objectivity; arguments are not considered on their merit, but according to whether they fit into the system, and if not, how they can be made to fit.[60]

It is no surprise that Montagu consistently gave glowing accounts of life in the Soviet Union. That was his job, as an executive of the FSU. Moreover, it accorded with the pattern observed by Paul Hollander in which intellectuals alienated from their own society found their values realised in another. For they had to be in a position, he argued, 'to point, at least tentatively, to the actualisation of their ideals in some existing society in order to lend strength to their social criticism at home'. Moreover, 'for those looking for alternatives to their decrepit and uninspiring society it was not possible to admit to flaws in the counter-model. Either the Soviet Union was wholly or overwhelmingly admirable and exhilarating, or else it ceased to be of interest altogether.' And there was also another mechanism at work. Montagu's thinking was to take the form of what Mannheim terms the utopian mentality, through which 'the collective unconscious, guided by wishful representation and the will to action, hides certain aspects of reality. It turns its back on everything which would shake its belief or paralyse its desire to change things.' The white-and-black vision of a world divided into opposed socialist and capitalist domains – 'the disposition to distinguish sharply between good and evil and to refuse to admit the permissibility of any admixture', as Shils expresses it – was ever present in Montagu's imagination, but came to its full flowering in the Cold War tract *Plot against Peace.*[61]

As early as 1924, Montagu had expressed the view that democracy was only another form of dictatorship, and that to usher in a new world order, it was necessary to be 'violently and inflexibly tyrannical and disciplined' – as in Russia. Such opinions were likely dismissed at the time as undergraduate extravagance, but it is noticeable that in the prolific commentaries on the Soviet Union that followed, there is a disturbing lack of concern for, or blindness towards the absence of, civil liberties and the rule of law, together with a lack of empathy towards the victims of repression and injustice. Whether it is making light of the horrific Ukrainian famine, regarding someone who draws attention to a Soviet decree infringing human rights as a 'general nuisance', maintaining that secret trials and summary executions are in accord with Soviet law, referring to wrongful arrest, imprisonment and torture with euphemisms such as 'administrative measures', or skating over the suffering of gulag inmates by speaking of faults in penal administration that have long since been 'largely corrected', Montagu's writing betrays the mindset of a doctrinaire Marxist-Leninist oblivious to the human cost at which revolutionary advances – if such they are – have been bought.[62]

Heavily invested as he was in an ideological politics ascribing overriding significance to the proletariat and viewing the bourgeoisie as the source of all evil, Montagu joined those whom Shils describes as believing 'that they are in possession [of] and in contact with what is ultimately right and true'. Fortified by this conviction, Ivor, like other Communists, had scant compunction about playing fast and loose with the facts when it suited a propaganda purpose. Paul Johnson writes of intellectuals that, 'anxious as they are to promote the redeeming, transcending Truth, the establishment of which they see as their mission on behalf of humanity, they have not much patience with the mundane, everyday truths represented by objective facts which get in the way of their arguments.' Always, after 1931, Montagu's writing about the USSR is marked by evasion and denial; repeatedly he permitted himself to be the vehicle through which the Kremlin version of events, however distorted or untrue, was disseminated to the public. When defending the Moscow Trials, justifying the Soviet invasions of Poland and Finland, falsely attributing the Katyn massacre to the Germans, denying the violence and fraud that accompanied the Romanian elections, accusing the US forces in Korea of germ warfare, and discounting reports of anti-Semitic persecutions in the Soviet Union and Eastern Europe, Montagu was an active and willing participant in Communist disinformation campaigns.[63]

As a corollary of this, Montagu shamelessly attacked and belittled anyone who tried to expose the truth: Leonard Woolf, speculating on why the defendants in the Zinoviev trial had confessed; Trotsky, revealing the falsified evidence on which the convictions had been procured; André Gide, alerting the world to the Great Terror; his own brother Ewen Montagu, disclosing the increasingly perilous position of Jews in territories under Stalin's sway. It is difficult not to concur with Charles Sumner's characterisation of Ivor as one of 'those venal persons who, having long since lost or sold all personal dignity, are reduced to substitute for political argument, lies and slander.'[64]

Montagu's willingness to serve the Soviet Union extended to wartime espionage. Placing allegiance to his adopted class ahead of allegiance to the bourgeois-governed nation, and viewing the USSR as the home of socialism and the ally of the working class in Britain, Montagu, like numbers of other Communists, was prepared to engage in activities that patriots, and perhaps the law, would regard as treasonable. Had, in fact, the information that it is known the X Group passed on to the GRU in 1940 remained in the Soviet Union, it is unlikely that British security would have been compromised – and indeed the UK was to give the USSR incomparably more help in the years ahead. But if, as the security services strongly suspected, intelligence in this period was being shared between the Soviets and the

Nazis, the information could conceivably have aided the Luftwaffe in its targeting of British cities. This, needless to say, would not have helped the cause of British workers, let alone any other citizens subject to the Blitz; but if such a thought ever crossed Montagu's mind, he left no trace of it.

Ultimately it must be acknowledged that Montagu's admirable commitment to progressive causes – anti-imperialism, anti-fascism, peace, socialism – was severely compromised by his advocacy work for a repressive dictatorship. Whether gullible or culpable, whether grossly deluded or knowingly colluding in the murderous criminality of the Stalinist regime, Montagu in always pushing the Soviet line undermined the credibility of the campaigns he was involved in. Thus the fascist menace suddenly evaporated at the very moment Hitler's troops were storming through Poland; fake atrocity stories (germ warfare) threw doubt on accounts of actual atrocities (the South Korean massacre of political prisoners); while the word 'peace', as John Jenks argues, emerged from its treatment at the hands of the World Peace Council 'battered, bruised, and debased'.[65]

The Honourable Ivor Montagu was indeed a man of his time, a member of the British intelligentsia who broke away from his privileged background to fight for the working class. He devoted his energies to the new art of cinema and the revolutionary transformation of society; his life was one of creative achievement and generosity of spirit. But in joining the Communist Party and becoming a propagandist for the Soviet Union he surrendered his intellectual and moral integrity. His cultural thinking became ossified; his political thinking warped. It is a tale of corruption, but it is not his alone. *Codename Intelligentsia* is the melancholy story of the havoc wreaked by Soviet Communism on the progressive causes of the twentieth century, and the individuals who espoused them.

BIBLIOGRAPHY

Archive Files

BFISC	British Film Institute Special Collections, London
CP/CENT	Communist Party of Great Britain Archive
CP/IND/MONT	Communist Party of Great Britain Archive, Ivor Montagu Papers
CP/IND/POLL	Communist Party of Great Britain Archive, Harry Pollitt Papers
CP/IORG	Communist Party of Great Britain Archive, International Organisation Papers
CP/ORG	Communist Party of Great Britain Archive, Organisation Papers
IM	Ivor Montagu Collection
MEB	Michael Balcon Collection
LHASC	Labour History Archive and Study Centre, People's History Museum, Manchester
MS Russ 13.1	Leon Trotsky exile papers, Houghton Library, Harvard College Library, Cambridge MA, USA

Security Service Files, National Archives, Kew

KV2/598-600	Ivor Goldsmid Samuel Montagu
KV2/786	Evelyn John St. Loe Strachey

KV2/1001	Walter Milton Holmes
KV2/1382–84	Otto Katz
KV2/1552–53	Francis Claud Cockburn, alias Frank Pitcairn
KV2/1596	Douglas Frank Springhall, aliases 'Springy', 'Peter', 'Zenoff/Zanoff', usually known as 'Dave'
KV2/3197	Ernest Henry Brown
KV2/3221	Sidney Lewis Bernstein
KV5/71	Russian Oil Products Ltd

National Security Agency Files, USA

| *Venona* | Intercepted Soviet intelligence communications, deciphered in the *Venona* programme. Online at the Internet Archive website: https://archive.org/details/nsia-venona |

Newspapers and Journals

CM	*Cambridge Mercury*
CT	*Cine-Technician*
DE	*Daily Express*
DH	*Daily Herald*
DMa	*Daily Mail*
DMi	*Daily Mirror*
DW	*Daily Worker*
EN	*Evening News*
ES	*Evening Standard*
FT	*Financial Times*
GH	*Glasgow Herald*
JACT	*Journal of the Association of Cine-Technicians*
KW	*Kinematograph (Kine) Weekly*
LAT	*Los Angeles Times*
Lis	*Listener*
LM	*Labour Monthly*
MG	*Manchester Guardian*
NSN	*New Statesman and Nation*

NYT	*New York Times*
Obs	*Observer*
SE	*Sunday Express*
SG	*Sunday Graphic*
SS	*Sight and Sound*
ST	*Sunday Times*
WER	*Week-End Review*
WNV	*World News and Views*
WP	*Washington Post*
YP	*Yorkshire Post*

By Ivor Montagu [IM]

Books

TTT	*Table Tennis To-Day* (Heffer, 1924)
TC	*The Traitor Class* (Lawrence & Wishart, 1940)
PP	*Plot against Peace* (Lawrence & Wishart, 1952)
LBS	*Land of Blue Sky: A Portrait of Modern Mongolia* (Dennis Dobson, 1956)
FW	*Film World: A Guide to Cinema* (Penguin, 1964)
GNN	*Germany's New Nazis* (Panther, 1967)
WEH	*With Eisenstein in Hollywood: A Chapter of Autobiography* (Seven Seas, 1968)
YS	*The Youngest Son: Autobiographical Sketches* (Lawrence & Wishart, 1970)

Pamphlets

PCF	*The Political Censorship of Films* (Victor Gollancz, 1929)
BB	*Blackshirt Brutality: The Story of Olympia* (Workers' Bookshop, 1934)
FUM	*The Federal Union Myth* (Communist Party of Great Britain, 1940)
ROM	*'Roll on, Mississippi!'* (Labour Monthly, 1941)
RA	*The Red Army: Fifty Questions Answered* (Russia Today Society, n.d. [1941])
RS	*Ruby Star* (Labour Monthly, n.d. [1941]) [with R. Palme Dutt]
Sta	*Stalin: A Biographial Sketch* (Communist Party of Great Britain, 1942)

Sev   *Sevastopol* (Communist Party of Great Britain, 1942) [with
           Ilya Ehrenburg]
SLK   *Soviet Leaders: Kalinin* (Communist Party of Great Britain, 1942)
SLT   *Soviet Leaders: Timoshenko* (Communist Party of Great Britain,
           1942)
SLV   *Soviet Leaders: Voroshilov* (Communist Party of Great Britain,
           1942)
SLM   *Soviet Leaders: Molotov* (Communist Party of Great Britain, 1942)
ZH   *Zero Hour – Second Front* (Labour Monthly, n.d. [1942])

Articles and Book Contributions

IM (1922). *On a Further Collection of Mammals from the Inner Hebrides*
    (Proceedings of the Zoological Society of London)
_____ (1923a). 'By the Way', *Cambridge Mercury* 7 Nov., 119–20
_____ (1923b). 'By the Way (Concluded)', *Cambridge Mercury* 21 Nov., 140–1
_____ (1924). 'How Many Times', *Cambridge Mercury* 30 Apr., 75–6
_____ (1925a). 'Spalax: a Little-known European Mammal', *Discovery* 6:61
    (Jan.), 15–7
_____ (1925b). ' "Not Highbrows": A Defence of the Film Society',
    Kinematograph Weekly 15 Oct., 69
_____ (1925c). 'Present Day Russia and the Film: An Analysis Based on
    Observations on the Spot', *Kinematograph Weekly* 29 Oct., 36
_____ (1925d). 'Present Day Russia and the Film II: The Trend of
    Production', *Kinematograph Weekly* 12 Nov., 52
_____ (1925e). 'Present-Day Russia and the Film - III', *Kinematograph
    Weekly* 10 Dec., 28
_____ (1927). 'Social Ideology in the Cinema', *Plebs* (Aug.), 263–66
_____ (1928). 'Film Society: Notes on the 17th Programme', *Close Up* 2:1
    (Jan.), 80–82
_____ (1930). 'The Censorship of Sex in Films' in Norman Haire, ed.,
    W.L.S.R. World League for Sexual Reform: Proceedings of the Third Congress
    (Kegan Paul, Trench, Trubner & Co.), 323–32
_____ (1932). 'The Film Society, London', *Cinema Quarterly* 1:1 (Winter
    1932/33), reprinted in Macpherson ed. 1980, 105–07
_____ (1935). 'Film Censorship', *Kino News* (Winter), reprinted in
    Macpherson ed. 1980, 113–15

_____ (1936a). 'Ivor Montagu States Case for Specialised Showings', *World Film News* 1:3 (Jun.), 27

_____ (1936b). 'The U.S.S.R. Month By Month: Culture', *Left Book News* No. 2 (Jun.), 28–30

_____ (1936c). 'The U.S.S.R. Month By Month: The Land of the Free', *Left Book News* No. 3 (Jul.), 46–48

_____ (1936d). 'The U.S.S.R. Month By Month: The Trial', *Left Book News* No. 6 (Oct.), 123–28

_____ (1937a). 'The Siege of the Alcazar', *World Film News* 1:10 (Jan.), 10–11

_____ (1937b). 'The U.S.S.R. Month by Month: Half Way Back', *Left News* No. 11 (Mar.), 279–84

_____ (1937c). 'The U.S.S.R. Month By Month: The Guilty', *Left News* No. 12 (Apr.), 326–32

_____ (1937d). 'The Eden-Hitler Axis', *Labour Monthly* 19:7 (Jul.), 402–10

_____ (1937e). 'A Christmas Call from the Workhouse', *Cine-Technician* 3:13 (Dec.–Jan. 1937/38), 171–72

_____ (1937f). 'The Moyne Report', *Sight and Sound* 5:20 (Winter), 120–22

_____ (1938a). 'Ivor Montagu Sees Red', *Cine-Technician* 3:14 (Mar.–Apr.), 205

_____ (1938b). 'Hitler's Europe', *Labour Monthly* 20:11 (Nov.), 674–85

_____ (1939a). 'Leysin' in Haden Guest ed. 1939, 42–50

_____ (1939b). 'Communist Policy: A Reply to Arnold-Forster', *Fabian Quarterly* 24 (Winter 1939/40), 30–32

_____ (1940a). 'The Truth about Finland', *Labour Monthly* 22:1 (Jan.), 15–28

_____ (1940b). 'Bournemouth Inquest', *Labour Monthly* 22:5 (May), 279–87

_____ (1941). 'Victory for What?', *Labour Monthly* 23:1 (Jan.), 31–38

_____ (1948). 'A Biographical Note' in *Eisenstein 1898–1948* (Film Section of the Society for Cultural Relations with the U.S.S.R.), 5–14

_____ (1949). 'Wall Street Glamour Boy', *Labour Monthly* 31:12 (Dec.), 374–78

_____ (1950). 'The Bomb-Mongers', *Labour Monthly* 32:8 (Aug.), 366–70

_____ (1956). 'Hungary – Cold War Heritage', *Labour Monthly* 38:12 (Dec.), 551–59

_____ (1958). 'Adrian Brunel, 1892–1958', *Film & TV Technician* 24:159 (Apr.), 230–31

_____ (1960). 'Personal Memoir' in Pudovkin 1960, 11–18

_____ (1963). 'A New Climate?', *Labour Monthly* 45:11 (Nov.), 498–503

_____ (1969). 'Foreword' in Nizhny 1969, ix–xiv

_____ (1970). 'Birmingham Sparrow: In Memoriam, Iris Barry, 1896–1969', *Sight and Sound* 39:2 (Spring), 106–08

_____ (1972). 'The Impact of Soviet Culture, 1922–1972', *Anglo-Soviet Journal* (Dec.), 6–21

_____ (1974). 'Solzhenitsyn, Gulag and the Solzhenitsyn Industry', *Marxism Today* (Dec.), 367–76

_____ (1975). 'Old Man's Mumble: Reflections on a Semi-centenary', *Sight and Sound* 44:4 (Autumn), 220–24, 247

_____ (1977). 'Michael Balcon, 1896–1977: Islington and the Bush', *Sight and Sound* 47:1 (Winter), 9–11

_____ (1980a). 'The Origin of *Free Thaelmann!*', *Sight and Sound* 49:2 (Spring), 130–31

_____ (1980b). 'Working with Hitchcock', *Sight and Sound* 49:3 (Summer), 189–93

_____ (1999). 'The Peacemonger' in Swann and Aprahamian eds, 1999, 12–34

Manuscripts

'Anti-Fascist Films'	'Anti-Fascist Films of the Thirties and Forties', typescript, n.d., CP/IND/MONT/2/5
Autobio II	The unpublished draft second volume of Ivor Montagu's autobiography, dated 1970-71, CP/IND/MONT/2/3 (sometimes referred to as *Like It Was*, a title Montagu was toying with)

Interviews

Hogenkamp iv	Bert Hogenkamp, interview with Ivor Montagu, 6 Sep 1974, published in Dutch translation as 'Interview met Ivor Montagu' in *Skrien* No. 51 (Jul-Aug 1975), 25-33
Screen iv	Lovell, Alan, Sam Rohdie, and Peter Wollen. 'Interview with Ivor Montagu', *Screen* 13:3 (Autumn 1972), 71-113

Visions iv   'Ivor Montagu:'An Impish Figure'', *Visions*, broadcast
                           24 Nov 1982, copy (including rushes) in BFI National
                           Archive, London

Other

Abel, Richard (1988). *French Film Theory and Criticism: A History/Anthology,*
     1907–1939 (Princeton University)

Andow, John, et al., ed. (1983). *Action! Fifty Years in the Life of a Union*
     (ACTT/PEAR Publications)

Andrew, Christopher (1986). *Secret Service: The Making of the British*
     Intelligence Community (Hodder & Stoughton)

_____ (2010). *The Defence of the Realm: The Authorized History of MI5*
     (Penguin)

Andrews, Geoff, Nina Fishman and Kevin Morgan, eds, (1995). *Opening the*
     Books: Essays on the Social and Cultural History of British Communism (Pluto)

Anon. (1972). *The Film Society Programmes, 1925–1939* (Arno)

Applebaum, Anne (2004). *Gulag: A History of the Soviet Camps* (Penguin)

Armes, Roy (1978). *A Critical History of British Cinema* (Oxford University)

Avrich, Paul (1967). *The Russian Anarchists* (Princeton University)

_____ (1995). *Anarchist Voices: An Oral History of Anarchism in America*
     (Princeton University)

Balcon, Michael (1969). *Michael Balcon Presents ... A Lifetime of Films*
     (Hutchinson)

_____ (1971a). Review of Rachael Low, *History of the British Film 1918–*
     1929, Sight and Sound 40:3 (Summer), 169–70

_____ (1971b). 'One of the Pack', *Film and Television Technician* 37:317 (Nov)

Bamford, Kenton (1999). *Distorted Images: British National Identity and Film*
     in the 1920s (I.B. Tauris)

Barna, Yon (1973). *Eisenstein* (Little, Brown)

Barr, Charles (1999). *English Hitchcock* (Cameron & Hollis)

_____, ed. (1986). *All Our Yesterdays: 90 Years of British Cinema* (BFI)

Baxter, John (1994). *Buñuel* (Fourth Estate)

Beasley, Rebecca, and Philip Ross Bullock, eds, (2013). *Russia in Britain,*
     1880-1940 (Oxford University)

Beckett, Francis (1998). *Enemy Within: The Rise and Fall of the British*
     Communist Party (Merlin; first published 1995)

_____ (2004). *Stalin's British Victims* (Sutton)

Behlmer, Rudy, ed. (1972). *Memo from David O. Selznick* (Viking)

Bennett, Bruce S. (1988). *New Zealand's Moral Foreign Policy 1935–1939: The Promotion of Collective Security through the League of Nations* (New Zealand Institute of International Affairs)

Bennett, Charles (2014). *Hitchcock's Partner in Suspense: The Life of Screenwriter Charles Bennett*, ed. John Charles Bennett (University Press of Kentucky)

Bergan, Ronald (1999). *Eisenstein: A Life in Conflict* (Overlook)

Bermant, Chaim (1971). *The Cousinhood* (Macmillan)

Bernstein, Sidney (Lord) (1975). 'The Fans Who Made Film History', *Times* 23 Oct, 11

Boyle, Andrew (1980). *The Climate of Treason* (Hodder & Stoughton)

Brackman, Roman (2001). *The Secret File of Joseph Stalin: A Hidden Life* (Frank Cass)

Branson, Noreen (1985). *History of the Communist Party of Great Britain, 1927–1941* (Lawrence & Wishart)

Brentford, Viscount (1929). *Do We Need a Censor?* (Faber & Faber)

Brown, Geoff (1984). 'Table Tennis over Everest', *Sight and Sound* 53:2 (Spring), 98–99

_____ (2008). 'Life Among the Rats: The *Cinéaste*-Writer in British Film Studios, 1926–36,' *Journal of Cinema and Television* Vol. 5 (2008), 242–61

_____, and Laurence Kardish (1984). *Michael Balcon: The Pursuit of British Cinema* (Museum of Modern Art, New York)

Brown, Julie, and Annette Davison, eds, (2013). *The Sounds of the Silents in Britain* (Oxford University)

Brunel, Adrian (1949). *Nice Work: The Story of Thirty Years in British Film Production* (Forbes Robertson)

Bryher [Annie Winifred Ellerman] (1929). *Film Problems of Soviet Russia* (Territet)

Burke, David (2008). *The Spy Who Came in from the Co-op: Melita Norwood and the Ending of Cold War Espionage* (Boydell)

_____ (2010). 'Theodore Rothstein and the Genesis of British Marxism,' Praxis: The Bulletin of the Marx Memorial Library No. 152 (Winter), 9–18

_____ (2011). 'Andrew Rothstein and the Crucible of British Communism,' Praxis: The Bulletin of the Marx Memorial Library No. 153 (Autumn), 12–18

Butterworth, Alex (2010). *The World That Never Was: A True Story of Dreamers, Schemers, Anarchists and Secret Agents* (The Bodley Head)

Campbell, J.R. (1939). *Soviet Policy and Its Critics* (Victor Gollancz)

Campbell, Russell (1982). *Cinema Strikes Back: Radical Filmmaking in the United States, 1930–1942* (UMI Research)

Carr, E.H. (1982). *The Twilight of the Comintern, 1930–1935* (Macmillan)

Chase, William J. (2001). *Enemies Within the Gates? The Comintern and Stalinist Repression, 1934–1939* (Yale University)

Chaudron, Gerald (1989). *New Zealand and the League of Nations* (PhD thesis, History, University of Canterbury)

Citrine, Sir Walter (1938). *I Search for Truth in Russia* (George Routledge & Sons)

———— (1940). *My Finnish Diary* (Penguin)

Claudín, Fernando (1975). *The Communist Movement from Comintern to Cominform, Part One: The Crisis of the Communist International* (Monthly Review)

Coates, W.P., and Zelda K. Coates, eds, (1937). *The Moscow Trial (January, 1937) and Two Speeches by J. Stalin* (Anglo-Russian Parliamentary Committee)

Clews, John C. (1964). *Communist Propaganda Techniques* (Praeger)

Cockburn, Claud (1967). *I, Claud ... The Autobiography of Claud Cockburn* (Penguin)

Cole, Sidney (1938). 'Shooting in Spain', *Cine-Technician* 4:15 (May–Jun), 1–2.

Conquest, Robert (1990). *The Great Terror: A Reassessment* (Oxford University)

Cook, Pam, ed. (1997). *Gainsborough Pictures* (Cassell)

Costello, John (1989). *Mask of Treachery* (Pan)

Craik, William W. (1964). *The Central Labour College, 1909–29: A Chapter in the History of Adult Working-Class Education* (Lawrence & Wishart)

Croall, Jonathan (1983). *Neill of Summerhill: The Permanent Rebel* (Pantheon)

Crossman, Richard, ed. (1965). *The God That Failed* (Bantam; first published 1950)

Curran, James, and Vincent Porter, eds, (1983). *British Cinema History* (Weidenfeld & Nicolson)

Dallin, David J. (1955). *Soviet Espionage* (Yale University)

David-Fox, Michael (2012). *Showcasing the Great Experiment: Cultural Diplomacy and Western Visitors to the Soviet Union, 1921–1941* (Oxford University)

Deacon, Richard [Donald McCormick] (1979). *The British Connection: Russia's Manipulation of British Individuals and Institutions* (Hamish Hamilton)

Deery, Phillip (2002). 'The Dove Flies East: Whitehall, Warsaw and the 1950 World Peace Congress', *Australian Journal of Politics and History* 48:2, 449–68

Deutscher, Isaac (1970a). *The Prophet Unarmed: Trotsky: 1921–1929* (Oxford University; first published 1959)

_____ (1970b). *The Prophet Outcast: Trotsky: 1929–1940* (Oxford University; first published 1963)

Dewar, Hugo (1976). *Communist Politics in Britain: The CPGB from its Origins to the Second World War* (Pluto)

Dickinson, Thorold (1938). 'Spanish A.B.C.', *Sight and Sound* 7:25 (Spring), 30

Dobson, Terence (2006). *The Film Work of Norman McLaren* (John Libbey)

Donald, James, Anne Friedberg and Laura Marcus, eds, (1998). *Close Up 1927–1933: Cinema and Modernism* (Princeton University)

Durgnat, Raymond (1974). *The Strange Case of Alfred Hitchcock, or The Plain Man's Hitchcock* (Faber & Faber)

Eisenstein, Sergei (1957). *Film Form: Essays in Film Theory and The Film Sense*, ed. Jay Leyda (World; first published in separate volumes 1949, 1942)

_____ (1983). *Immoral Memories: An Autobiography*, trans. Herbert Marshall (Houghton Mifflin)

_____ (1995). *Selected Works, Volume IV: Beyond the Stars: The Memoirs of Sergei Eisenstein*, ed. Richard Taylor (BFI/Seagull)

van der Esch, P.A.M. (1951). *Prelude to War: The International Repercussions of the Spanish Civil War, 1936–1939* (Martinus Nijhoff)

Farr, William (1938). 'Two Topical Films', *Sight and Sound* 7:26 (Summer), 90

Firsov, Fridrikh I. (2004). 'Dimitrov, the Comintern and Stalinist Repression' in McLoughlin and McDermott eds, 2004, 56–81

Fischer, Louis (1986). *Men and Politics: Europe Between the Two World Wars* (Harper & Row; first published 1941)

Fischer, Ruth (1948). *Stalin and German Communism: A Study in the Origins of the State Party* (Harvard University)

Fisher, David James (1988). *Romain Rolland and the Politics of Intellectual Engagement* (University of California)

Gallacher, William (1966). *The Last Memoirs* (Lawrence & Wishart)

Geduld, Harry M., and Ronald Gottesman, eds, (1970). *Sergei Eisenstein and Upton Sinclair: The Making & Unmaking of Que Viva Mexico!* (Thames & Hudson)

Gide, André (1938). *Afterthoughts on the U.S.S.R.* (Dial Press; first published 1937)

Gitlow, Benjamin (1948). *The Whole of Their Lives: Communism in America – A Personal History and Intimate Portrayal of its Leaders* (Charles Scribner's Sons)

Glancy, Mark (2003). *The 39 Steps* (I.B. Tauris)

Gledhill, Christine (2003). *Reframing British Cinema, 1918–1928: Between Restraint and Passion* (BFI)

Glotzer, Albert (1989). *Trotsky: Memoir & Critique* (Prometheus)

Gollancz, Victor, ed. (1941). *The Betrayal of the Left* (Victor Gollancz)

Grant, Ted (2002). *History of British Trotskyism* (Wellred)

Griffin, Nicholas (2014). *Ping-Pong Diplomacy: Ivor Montagu and the Astonishing Story Behind the Game That Changed the World* (Simon & Schuster)

Gross, Babette (1974). *Willi Münzenberg: A Political Biography* (Michigan State University)

Gruber, Helmut (1974). *Soviet Russia Masters the Comintern: International Communism in the Era of Stalin's Ascendancy* (Anchor/Doubleday)

Gubern, Román, and Paul Hammond (2012). *Luis Buñuel: The Red Years, 1929–1939* (University of Wisconsin)

Haden Guest, Carmel, ed. (1939). *David Guest: A Scientist Fights for Freedom (1911-1938)* (Lawrence & Wishart)

Haggith, Toby, and Joanna Newman, eds, (2005). *Holocaust and the Moving Image: Representations in Film and Television Since 1933* (Wallflower)

Hallas, Duncan (2008). *The Comintern* (Haymarket; first published 1985)

Hankins, Leslie Kathleen (2004). 'Iris Barry, Writer and *Cinéaste*, Forming Film Culture in London 1924–1926: The *Adelphi*, the *Spectator*, the Film Society, and the British *Vogue*', *Modernism/Modernity* 11:3, 488–515

Hannington, Wal (1979). *Unemployed Struggles, 1919–1936: My Life and Struggles Amongst the Unemployed* (Lawrence & Wishart; first published 1936)

Hardy, Sylvia (2002). 'H.G. Wells and British Silent Cinema: The War of the Worlds' in Higson ed. 2002, 242–55

Haslam, Jonathan (1984). *The Soviet Union and the Struggle for Collective Security in Europe, 1933–39* (Macmillan)

Hays, Arthur Garfield (1942). *City Lawyer: The Autobiography of a Law Practice* (Simon & Schuster)

Higson, Andrew, ed. (2002). *Young and Innocent? The Cinema in Britain, 1896-1930* (University of Exeter)

Hill, May (1982). *Red Roses for Isabel* (May Hill)

[Hogben], Julius (1974). 'Spanish Civil War Films – National Film Theatre', *Freedom*, 23 Mar., 6

Hogenkamp, Bert (1979). 'Making Films with a Purpose': Film-making and the Working Class' in Clark et al. eds, 1979, 257–70

———— (1986). *Deadly Parallels: Film and the Left in Britain 1929–1939* (Lawrence & Wishart)

Hollander, Paul (1981). *Political Pilgrims: Travels of Western Intellectuals in the Soviet Union, China and Cuba 1928-1978* (Oxford University)

Holmes, Colin (1979). 'Trotsky and Britain: The 'Closed File'', *Bulletin – Society for the Study of Labour History* Issue 39 (Autumn), 33–38

Hornstein, David P. (1993). *Arthur Ewert: A Life for the Comintern* (University Press of America)

Horrocks, Roger (2001). *Len Lye: A Biography* (Auckland University)

Howarth, T.E.B. (1978). *Cambridge Between Two Wars* (Collins)

Hyde, Douglas (1952). *I Believed: The Autobiography of a Former British Communist* (Reprint Society; first published 1950)

Jenks, John (2006). *British Propaganda and News Media in the Cold War* (Edinburgh University)

Johnson, Paul (1990). *Intellectuals* (HarperCollins)

Johnstone, Monty (1997). 'The CPGB, the Comintern and the War, 1939–1941: Filling in the Blank Spots', *Science & Society* 61:1 (Spring), 27–45.

Jones, Stephen G. (1987). *The British Labour Movement and Film, 1918–1939* (Routledge & Kegan Paul)

Jupp, James (1982). *The Radical Left in Britain, 1931–1941* (Frank Cass)

Kadish, Sharman (1992). *Bolsheviks and British Jews: The Anglo-Jewish Community, Britain and the Russian Revolution* (Frank Cass)

Kemp, Philip (1997). 'Not for Peckham: Michael Balcon and Gainsborough's International Trajectory in the 1920s' in Cook 1997, 13–30

Kenez, Peter (1992). *Cinema and Soviet Society, 1917–1953* (Cambridge University)

Kitrinos, Robert W. (1986). 'The CPSU Central Committee's International Department' in Robbin F. Laird and Eric P. Hoffmann, eds, *Soviet Foreign Policy in a Changing World* (Aldine, 1986), 180–206

Klugmann, James (1968). *History of the Communist Party of Great Britain, Volume One: Formation and Early Years, 1919–1924* (Lawrence & Wishart)

_____ (1969). *History of the Communist Party of Great Britain, Volume Two: 1925–1927: The General Strike* (Lawrence & Wishart)

Koch, Stephen (1996). *Double Lives: Stalin, Willi Münzenberg and the Seduction of the Intellectuals* (HarperCollins)

Koestler, Arthur (1965). *The Yogi and the Commissar and Other Essays* (Macmillan; first published 1945)

_____ (2005). *The Invisible Writing: The Second Volume of an Autobiography: 1932–40* (Vintage; first published 1954)

Laybourn, Keith (2006). *Marxism in Britain: Dissent, Decline and Re-emergence 1945–c. 2000* (Routledge)

Lazitch, Branco, in collaboration with Milorad M. Drachkovitch (1986). *Biographical Dictionary of the Comintern* (Hoover Institution, Stanford University)

Lenauer, Jean (1929). 'The Independent Cinema Congress', *Close Up* 5:4 (Oct), reprinted in Macpherson ed. 1980, 168–69, and Donald et al. 1998, 274–77

Lenin, V.I. (1950a). *The State and Revolution, Selected Works in Two Volumes, II* (Lawrence & Wishart; first published 1917), 141–225

_____ (1950b). *'Left-Wing' Communism, an Infantile Disorder, Selected Works in Two Volumes, II* (Lawrence & Wishart; first published 1920), 571–644

Leonov, Leonid (1931). *Sot*, trans. Ivor Montagu & Sergei Nolbandov (Putnam)

Levine, Naomi B. (1991). *Politics, Religion and Love: The Story of H.H. Asquith, Venetia Stanley and Edwin Montagu, Based on the Life and Letters of Edwin Samuel Montagu* (New York University)

Leyda, Jay (1973). *Kino: A History of the Russian and Soviet Film* (George Allen & Unwin; first published 1960)

_____, and Zina Voynow (1982). *Eisenstein at Work* (Random House)

Liebknecht, Karl (1973). *Militarism and Anti-Militarism* (Rivers; first published 1907), online version Karl Liebknecht Internet Archive, www.marxists.org/archive/liebknecht-k/works/1907/militarism-antimilitarism/ (accessed 9 Feb. 2014)

Litvinoff, Barnet (1969). *A Peculiar People: Inside World Jewry Today* (Weidenfeld and Nicolson)

Low, Rachael (1971). *The History of the British Film 1918–1929* (George Allen & Unwin)

_____ (1979). *The History of the British Film 1929–1939: Films of Comment and Persuasion of the 1930s* (George Allen & Unwin)

_____ (1985). *The History of the British Film 1929–1939: Film Making in 1930s Britain* (George Allen & Unwin)

Lygo, Emily (2013). 'Promoting Soviet Culture in Britain: The History of the Society for Cultural Relations Between the Peoples of the British Commonwealth and the USSR, 1924–1945', *Modern Language Review* 108:2, (Apr), 571–96

Macfarlane, L.J. (1966). *The British Communist Party: Its Origin and Development until 1929* (MacGibbon & Kee)

Macintyre, Ben (2010). *Operation Mincemeat: The True Spy Story That Changed the Course of World War II* (Bloomsbury)

Macintyre, Stuart (1980). *A Proletarian Science: Marxism in Britain 1917–1933* (Cambridge University)

Macleod, Alison (1997). *The Death of Uncle Joe* (Merlin)

Macpherson, Don, ed. (1980). *Traditions of Independence: British Cinema in the Thirties* (BFI)

Mahon, John (1976). *Harry Pollitt: A Biography* (Lawrence & Wishart)

Manley, Seb (2008). 'Comedy and Experimentation in British Alternative Film: The Funny Peculiar Case of Ivor Montagu's *Bluebottles*', *Scope* Issue 10 (Feb.)

Mannheim, Karl (1936). *Ideology and Utopia: An Introduction to the Sociology of Knowledge* (Harcourt, Brace & World)

_____ (1952). *Essays on the Sociology of Knowlege*, ed. Paul Kecskemeti (Routledge & Kegan Paul)

Marcus, Laura (2007). *The Tenth Muse: Writing About Cinema in the Modernist Period* (Oxford University)

Marris, Paul (1980). 'Politics and "Independent" Film in the Decade of Defeat' in Macpherson ed. 1980, 70–95

Marshall, Herbert (1983). *Masters of the Soviet Cinema: Crippled Creative Biographies* (Routledge & Kegan Paul)

Masters, Anthony (1986). *The Man Who Was M: The Life of Maxwell Knight* (Collins)

McCarthy, Margaret (1953). *Generation in Revolt* (William Heinemann)

McDermott, Kevin, and Jeremy Agnew (1996). *The Comintern: A History of International Communism from Lenin to Stalin* (Macmillan)

McGilligan, Patrick (2003). *Alfred Hitchcock: A Life in Darkness and Light* (Wiley)

McIntyre, W. David, and W.J. Gardner, eds, (1971). *Speeches and Documents on New Zealand History* (Oxford University)

McLoughlin, Barry, and Kevin McDermott, eds, (2004). *Stalin's Terror: High Politics and Mass Repression in the Soviet Union* (Palgrave Macmillan)

McMeekin, Sean (2003). *The Red Millionaire: A Political Biography of Willi Münzenberg, Moscow's Secret Propaganda Tsar in the West* (Yale University)

Medvedev, Roy (1989). *Let History Judge: The Origins and Consequences of Stalinism* (Columbia University)

Miles, Jonathan (2011). *The Nine Lives of Otto Katz: The Remarkable Story of a Communist Super-Spy* (Bantam)

Millar, J.P.M. (1979). *The Labour College Movement* (NCLC Publishing Society)

Miller, Henry K. (2012). 'From *Battleship Potemkin* to *Drifters,*' in booklet accompanying BFI DVD release *The Soviet Influence: Battleship Potemkin/ Drifters*

———— (2013). *Where We Came In: Minority Film Culture in Britain, 1917–1940* (PhD thesis, Birkbeck, University of London)

Montefiore, Simon Sebag (2004). *Stalin: The Court of the Red Tsar* (Orion)

Moorehead, Caroline (1984). *Sidney Bernstein: A Biography* (Jonathan Cape)

Morgan, Kevin (1993). *Harry Pollitt* (Manchester University)

———— (1998). 'Harry Pollitt, the British Communist Party and International Communism' in Tauno Saarela and Kimmo Rentola, eds, *Communism National & International* (SHS), 183–206

————, and Gidon Cohen (2003). 'Cohen, Rose (1894–1937)' in Keith Gildart, David Howell and Neville Kirk, eds, *Dictionary of Labour Biography, Vol. XI* (Palgrave Macmillan), 31–39

————, Gidon Cohen and Andrew Flinn, eds, (2007). *Communists and British Society, 1920–1991* (Rivers Oram)

Moussinac, Léon (1970). *Sergei Eisenstein* (Crown)

Murphy, Robert (1986). 'Under the Shadow of Hollywood' in Barr ed. 1986, 47–71

Mycroft, Walter C. (2006). *Walter C. Mycroft: The Time of My Life: The Memoirs of a British Film Producer*, ed. Vincent Porter (Scarecrow)

Newton, Kenneth (1969). *The Sociology of British Communism* (Allen Lane)

Nizhny, Vladimir (1969). *Lessons with Eisenstein* (Hill and Wang; first published 1962)

Ostrer, Nigel (2010). *The Ostrers & Gaumont British* (www.gaumontbritish.com)

Parkinson, David, ed. (1995). *The Graham Greene Film Reader: Reviews, Essays, Interviews & Film Stories* (Applause)

Pearson, George (1957). *Flashback: The Autobiography of a British Film-maker* (George Allen & Unwin)

Pelling, Henry (1963). *A History of British Trade Unionism* (Penguin)

_____ (1975). *The British Communist Party: A Historical Profile* (Adam & Charles Black; first published 1958)

Petersson, Fredrik (2013). *'We are Neither Visionaries Nor Utopian Dreamers': Willi Münzenberg, the League Against Imperialism, and the Comintern, 1925–1933* (PhD thesis, History, Åbo Akademi, Sweden)

Phelps, Guy (1975). *Film Censorship* (Victor Gollancz)

Platts-Mills, John (2002). *Muck, Silk and Socialism: Recollections of a Left-wing Queen's Counsel* (Paper Publishing)

Pollitt, Harry (1941). *Serving My Time: An Apprenticeship to Politics* (Lawrence & Wishart)

Porter, Vincent (2013). 'Council of the Film Society (*act.* 1925–1939)', *Oxford Dictionary of National Biography*, Oxford University (www. oxforddnb.com/view/theme/101220, accessed 5 Aug 2013)

Pritt, D.N. (1965). *The Autobiography of D.N. Pritt, Part One: From Right to Left* (Lawrence & Wishart)

Pronay, Nicholas (1982). 'The Political Censorship of Film in Britain between the Wars' in Pronay and Spring eds, 1982, 98–125

_____, and D.W. Spring, eds, (1982). *Propaganda, Politics and Film, 1918–45* (Macmillan)

Pudovkin, V.I. (1960). *Film Technique and Film Acting*, ed. Ivor Montagu (Grove)

Regler, Gustav (1959). *The Owl of Minerva: The Autobiography of Gustav Regler* (Rupert Hart-Davis)

Richards, Jeffrey, ed. (2000). *The Unknown 1930s: An Alternative History of the British Cinema, 1929–39* (I. B. Tauris)

Riley, John (2013). 'Sound at the Film Society' in Brown and Davison 2013, 263–82

Riordan, Jim (2008). 'The Hon. Ivor Montagu (1904–1984): Founding Father of Table Tennis,' *Sport in History* 28:3, 512–530

_____ (2009). *Comrade Jim: The Spy Who Played for Spartak* (HarperCollins)

Rogovin, Vadim Z. (1998). *1937: Stalin's Year of Terror* (Mehring)

Rolph, C.H. (1973). *Kingsley: The Life, Letters and Diaries of Kingsley Martin* (Victor Gollancz)

Rotha, Paul, and Richard Griffith (1967). *The Film Till Now: A Survey of World Cinema* (Hamlyn; first published 1930)

Rust, William (1940). 'Imperialism and Counter-Revolution' (review of *The Traitor Class* by Ivor Montagu), *Labour Monthly* 22:11 (Nov), 607–08

———— (1949). *The Story of the Daily Worker* (People's Press)

Ryall, Tom (1986). *Alfred Hitchcock & the British Cinema* (University of Illinois)

Ryan, Trevor (1980). 'Film and Political Organisations in Britain 1929–39' in Macpherson 1980, 51–69

———— (1986). *Labour and the Media in Britain 1929–1939: A Study of the Attitudes of the Labour Movement towards the New Media, Film and Radio, and of its Attempts to Use them for Political Purposes* (PhD thesis, History, University of Leeds), 2 vols

Samson, Jen (1986). 'The Film Society, 1925–1939' in Barr ed. 1986, 306–13

Schatz, Thomas (1988). *The Genius of the System: Hollywood Filmmaking in the Studio Era* (Pantheon)

Schoots, Hans (2000). *Living Dangerously: A Biography of Joris Ivens* (Amsterdam University)

Schulberg, Budd (1981). *Moving Pictures: Memoirs of a Hollywood Prince* (Stein and Day)

Sedgwick, John (1996). 'Michael Balcon's Close Encounter with the American Market, 1934–1936', *Historical Journal of Film, Radio and Television* 16:3, 333–48

Seton, Marie (1960). *Sergei M. Eisenstein: A Biography* (Grove; first published 1952)

Sexton, Jamie (2002). 'The Film Society and the Creation of an Alternative Film Culture in Britain in the 1920s' in Higson ed. 2002, 291–305

———— (2008). *Alternative Film Culture in Inter-war Britain* (University of Exeter)

Shaw, Bernard (1997). *Bernard Shaw on Cinema*, ed. Bernard F. Dukore (Southern Illinois University)

Shearer, David (2004). 'Social Disorder, Mass Repression and the NKVD during the 1930s' in McLoughlin and McDermott eds,, 2004, 85–117

Shenk, Timothy (2013). *Maurice Dobb: Political Economist* (Palgrave Macmillan)

Shils, Edward (1972). *The Intellectuals and the Powers and Other Essays* (University of Chicago)

Simone, André [Otto Katz] (1941). *Men of Europe* (Modern Age)

Sitton, Robert (2014). *Lady in the Dark: Iris Barry and the Art of Film*

(Columbia University)

Skudder, Susan Mary (1986). *'Bringing It Home': New Zealand Responses to the Spanish Civil War, 1936–1939* (PhD thesis, History, University of Waikato)

Smith, James (2013a). *British Writers and MI5 Surveillance, 1930–1960* (Cambridge University)

——— (2013b). 'Soviet Films and British Intelligence in the 1930s: The Case of Kino Films and MI5' in Beasley and Bullock eds, 2013, 241–57

Snyder, Timothy (2011). *Bloodlands: Europe Between Hitler and Stalin* (Vintage)

Solzhenitsyn, Alexander (1974). *The Gulag Archipelago, 1918–1956* (Collins/Fontana)

Souvarine, Boris ([1939]). *Stalin: A Critical Survey of Bolshevism* (Secker and Warburg, n.d.)

Spoto, Donald (1983). *The Life of Alfred Hitchcock: The Dark Side of Genius* (Collins)

Spratt, Philip (1955). *Blowing up India: Reminiscences and Reflections of a Former Comintern Emissary* (Prachi Prakashan)

Stern, Ludmila (2007). *Western Intellectuals and the Soviet Union, 1920–40: From Red Square to the Left Bank* (Routledge)

Steward, Fred (1999). 'Political Formation' in Swann and Aprahamian eds, 1999, 37–77

Stollery, Martin (2009). 'Technicians of the Unknown Cinema: British Critical Discourse and the Analysis of Collaboration in Film Production', *Film History* 21:4 (Dec), 373–93

Strachey, John (1940). 'The C.P. Line – Now', *Left News* No. 50 (Jul), 1498–99

Swallow, Norman (1976). *Eisenstein: A Documentary Portrait* (George Allen & Unwin)

Swann, Brenda, and Francis Aprahamian, eds, (1999). *J.D. Bernal: A Life in Science and Politics* (Verso)

Taylor, A.J.P. (1975). *English History 1914–1945* (Penguin; first published 1965)

Taylor, John Russell (1978). *Hitch: The Life and Work of Alfred Hitchcock* (Faber & Faber)

Taylor, Richard (2002). *October* (BFI)

Thorpe, Andrew (2000). *The British Communist Party and Moscow, 1920–43*

(Manchester University)

Trotsky, Leon (1920). *Dictatorship vs. Democracy [Terrorism and Communism]* (Workers Party of America), www.marxists.org/archive/trotsky/1920/terrcomm/ (accessed 27 Mar. 2014)

―――― (1970). *My Life: An Attempt at an Autobiography* (Pathfinder; first published 1930)

―――― (1979). *Writings of Leon Trotsky: Supplement (1929–33)*, ed. George Breitman (Pathfinder)

Truffaut, François (1967). *Hitchcock* (Simon & Schuster)

Tucker, Robert C. (1990). *Stalin in Power: The Revolution from Above, 1928–1941* (W.W. Norton)

Turvey, Gerry (2000). '"That Insatiable Body": Ivor Montagu's Confrontation with British Film Censorship', *Journal of Popular British Cinema: Forbidden British Cinema 3*, 31–44

Valtin, Jan [Richard Krebs] (1941). *Out of the Night* (Alliance)

Vernon, Betty D. (1982). *Ellen Wilkinson, 1891–1947* (Croom Helm)

Vest, James M. (2004). 'Metamorphoses of *Downhill*: From Stage Play to Cinematic Treatment and Film', *Hitchcock Annual* 13 (2004/2005), 64–91

―――― (2005). 'The Making of *Downhill* and Its Impact on Hitchcock's Reputation', *Hitchcock Annual* 14 (2005/2006), 50–94

Wells, Herbert George (1908). *This Misery of Boots* (BiblioLife, n.d.)

West, Alick (1969). *One Man in His Time: An Autobiography* (George Allen & Unwin)

West, Nigel [Rupert Allason] (2005). *MASK: MI5's Penetration of the Communist Party of Great Britain* (Routledge)

Wilkinson, Rosaleen (2004). *Townhill Park: The Life and Times of a Gertrude Jekyll Garden* (Rosaleen Wilkinson)

Willcox, Temple (1990). 'Soviet Films, Censorship and the British Government: A Matter of the Public Interest', *Historical Journal of Film, Radio and Television* 10:3, 275–92

Wood, Neal (1959). *Communism and British Intellectuals* (Columbia University)

Worley, Matthew (2002). *Class Against Class: The Communist Party in Britain Between the Wars* (I.B. Tauris)

Young, Freddie (1999). *Seventy Light Years: An Autobiography* (Faber & Faber)

NOTES

For additional footnote material, please see:
https://victoria.academia.edu/RussellCampbell

1. Prologue

1   Mannheim 1936, 10.
2   Mannheim 1952, 291.
3   Koestler 1965, 75.
4   CP/IND/MONT/1/3, LHASC.
5   CP/IND/MONT/1/3, LHASC.
6   Balcon 1969, 26–7, 83; Low 1979b, 196; Brown 2008, 249; Riordan 2009, 55; Macintyre 2010, 90.
7   Levine 1991, 13–6; *YS* 20.
8   Levine 1991, 20–1; Bermant 1971, 200–9.
9   *YS* 20. In *The Youngest Son*, Ivor gives this version of the verse: 'Lord Swaythling, whom the people knew,/And loved, as Samuel Montagu,/Is known unto the fiends of hell,/As Mr. Moses Samuel.' *YS* 18. However, in the Corrigenda with the unpublished second volume of the autobiography, he writes: 'My middle brother sends me a different version of the poem about my grandfather … This sounds very much more like authentic Belloc than the doggerel which had stuck in my memory.' CP/IND/MONT/02/03, LHASC.
10 *Times* 26 Jul. 1911, 6; *YS* 12, 15, 42, 51.
11 *YS* 16, 82, 162; *ST* 12 Jun. 1927, 17.
12 Kadish 1992, 55; Levine 1991, 7; Bermant 1971, *passim*.
13 *YS* 87.
14 *YS* 11–4.
15 *YS* 52; http://en.wikipedia.org/wiki/Townhill_Park_House (accessed 28 Aug. 2017); Wilkinson 2004, 24–6, 48–9.
16 *YS* 47–50.

17   *YS* 60, 66, 70, 75, 93, 116, 119.

18   *YS* 83; *FW* 8,18.

19   *YS* 49.

20   *YS* 68, 81, 84–5.

21   *YS* 78, 107–11, 114; Croall 1983, 170.

22   *YS* 93, 96–7; Wilkinson 2004, 59–61; 'The New Naval War Game', ms, CP/IND/MONT/1/2, LHASC.

23   Young 1999, 21–2.

24   *YS* 121–2; Liebknecht 1973, Sections I–1.2, II–3; Wells 1908, 26, 33–4, 49.

25   *YS* 122, 145.

26   Wells 1908, 52–3; *YS* 126; Klugmann 1968, 16; Macintyre 1980, 20; Macfarlane 1966, 22.

27   *YS* 127; Lenin 1950a, 159; Macintyre 1980, 23.

28   *YS* 127–9; IM, quoted in Croall 1983, 170.

29   *YS* 124–5; http://en.wikipedia.org/wiki/Leslie_Haden-Guest,_1st_Baron_Haden-Guest (accessed 28 Aug. 2017).

30   *YS* 125; Edward R. Pease, Hon. Sec., the Fabian Society, to IM, 12 Feb. 1919, CP/IND/MONT/8/11, LHASC; League of Free Nations Association Member's Card, year ending August 4, 1919, CP/IND/MONT/1/4, LHASC; *Times* 27 Feb. 1919, 10.

31   Kadish 1992, 6, 121–3.

32   J.T. Lyne for T.E. Quelch, Secretary, Central London Branch, British Socialist Party, to IM, 24 Nov. 1919, CP/IND/MONT/4/6, LHASC.

33   Klugmann 1968, 16; H. Alexander and E.C. Fairchild to Members of the British Socialist Party, 9 June 1919, CP/IND/MONT/4/6, LHASC.

34   Lyne to IM, 24 Nov 1919; IM's British Socialist Party membership card, Central London branch, monthly subscriptions paid January–June 1919, CP/IND/MONT/4/11, LHASC.

35   Burke 2010, 17–8; Klugmann 1968, 17; Andrew 1986, 352; *YS* 338.

36   *YS* 113, 130.

37   *YS* 130, 135–8, 166; IM to Leon Trotsky, 29 Aug. 1929, Item 3382, MS Russ 13.1.

2. Cambridge

1   *YS* 183, 188.

2   *YS* 181–2, 185, 187, 221; Howarth 1978, 58, 143; Basil Willey, quoted in Howarth, 70.

3   *YS* 188, 229–32.

4   *YS* 206–8; IM 1922, copy in CP/IND/MONT/1/2; British Museum (Natural History), note dated 31 Aug. 1923, CP/IND/MONT/2/6, LHASC.

5   *YS* 209–13; IM 1923a; IM 1923b; British Museum (Natural History), note dated 6 Mar. 1924, CP/IND/MONT/2/6, LHASC.

6   *YS* 243–9; IM 1925a, copy in CP/IND/MONT/12/6, LHASC.

7   *YS* 215–6; Letter to the editor from Ivor G.S. Montagu, *Lawn Tennis and Badminton* 1 Apr. 1922, in CP/IND/MONT/3/4, LHASC.

8   *YS* 217–8; 'A Table Tennis Club', *The Granta* 1 Dec. 1922, 173; 'Table Tennis', *The Granta* 20 Apr. 1923, 370.

9   *YS* 218–9; Riordan 2008, 520–3; Griffin 2014, 12–3; 'Hit and Miss Start to Sport of Ping Pong', *DMa* 20 Jun. 2001, 52.

10 *YS* 220.

11 *TTT*; 'Table Tennis To-Day,' *DMi* 16 Jun. 1924; T.L.-E., 'The Montagu Method,' *The Granta* 30 May 1924, 454, in CP/IND/MONT/12/10, LHASC; unsigned review of *Table Tennis To-Day*, clipping identified as 'OC May 17 24,' (possibly *The Old Cambridge*) in CP/IND/MONT/3/4, LHASC; unidentified Cambridge publication clipping, 17 May 1924, CP/IND/MONT/12/6, LHASC.

12 Howarth 1978, 22; *YS* 199–200; Levine 1991, 52–3.

13 R.A. Butler, card, to IM, 10 Mar. 1924, CP/IND/MONT/7/2, LHASC; Cambridge Union debate programme, 29 Apr. 1924, CP/IND/MONT/1/2, LHASC; 'Union Notes,' *The Gownsman* 3 May 1924, 9, in CP/IND/MONT/1/2, LHASC.

14 *YS* 224; programmes for *Hamlet* (Feb. 1924) and *The Birds* (Feb.–Mar. 1924) in CP/IND/MONT/13/2, LHASC; programmes for *Man and the Masses* (May 1924), *Saint Joan* (May 1924), *The Old Batchelour* (Jun. 1924) and *The Pleasure Garden* (Jun. 1924) in CP/IND/MONT/13/1, LHASC; George Bernard Shaw to IM, 3 Apr. 1924, licence to perform *The Shewing-up of Blanco Posnet* at the People's Theatre in Cambridge, receipt for author's fees of 8s. 3d, in CP/IND/MONT/6/11, LHASC; People's Theatre poster for week of 21 Apr. 1924, in CP/IND/MONT/13/1, LHASC.

15 *YS* 225, 228; William A. Harris to IM, 28 Mar. 1923, 8 Aug. 1923, and 26 Aug. 1923, in CP/IND/MONT/7/7, LHASC; *The Gownsman* 3 May 1924, in CP/IND/MONT/1/2, LHASC; D.S. Hunt to IM, n.d. [ca May 1924], CP/IND/MONT/7/7, LHASC; *WEH* 47.

16 IM, 'London Art Exhibitions', *CM* 27 Apr. 1923, 20; IM, 'The Drama', *CM* 21 Nov. 1923, 150–1; IM, 'Six Unities and a Multiplicity', *CM* 6 Feb. 1924, 25–6; IM, 'The Drama', *CM* 20 Feb. 1924, 33; IM, 'The O.U.D.S. Hamlet', *CM* 20 Feb. 1924, 43–4; [IM], 'Masse-Mensch', *CM* 2 Jun. 1924, 99–100. The *Masse-Mensch* piece is uncredited but is almost certainly by Montagu.

17 IM 1924.

18 *YS* 195, 233; Low 1971, 34n; Brown 2008, 243; Sexton 2008, 173 n16; *Screen* iv, 72; Pearson 1957, 122–3; 'Two New Clubs', *CM* 7 Nov. 1923, 120; 'Editorial Notes', *CM* 5 Mar. 1924, 47–8.

19 Wood 1959, 104; Howarth 1978, 142; Kingsley Martin, quoted in Rolph 1973, 81.

20 *YS* 197, 199, 241; Howarth 1978, 145–6; Rolph 1973, 69; letter from Geoffrey Lloyd, Cambridge University Conservative Association, to IM, 30 Oct. 1923, CP/IND/MONT/7/9, LHASC.

21 *YS* 198; Spratt 1955, 17; letters and meeting notices concerning Cambridge Trades Council and Labour Party in CP/IND/MONT/4/4, LHASC; IM to Leon Trotsky, 29 Aug. 1929, Item 3382, MS Russ 13.1.

22 *YS* 202–3.

23 *YS* 196–7; IM 1999, 213; Rolph 1973, 69; Howarth 1978, 146; Newton 1969, 21; IM to Leon Trotsky, 29 Aug. 1929, Item 3382, MS Russ 13.1; Costello 1989, 185.

24 *YS* 196–7; IM 1999, 213; Shenk 2013, 33; Macintyre 1980, 169; Boyle 1980, 41.

25 *YS* 196; Howarth 1978, 144, 146–4; Shenk 2013, 25.

26 Deacon [McCormick] 1979, 119–20; Costello 1989, 153–4; *YS* 283–4.

27 Dr Lancelot Hogben, Society for Experimental Biology, to IM, 3 Jul. 1924, CP/IND/MONT/7/7, LHASC; Alfred L. Bacharach, National Union of Scientific Workers, to IM, 11 Jul. 1924, CP/IND/MONT/4/4, LHASC.

28 Lenin 1950b, 617–8; Gruber 1974, 114.

29 *YS* 200–1.

30 *YS* 200–1; Levine 1991, 665–7; Bermant 1971, 266.

31 *YS* 230; Aubrey Clark to IM, 2 Dec. 1923, CP/IND/MONT/7/3, LHASC; Autobio II, 78.

32 *YS* 222–3; Howarth 1978, 50–3.

33 *YS* 225–8; Newmarket Official Race Card, first spring meeting, 9 May 1924, in CP/IND/MONT/16, LHASC.

34 *YS* 186, 240–1; www.swarthmore.edu/library/peace/DG100-150/ DG126LFlorence.html (accessed 28 Aug. 2017); Howarth 1978, 52.

35 'Psychological note on a poem written 22.2.24', IM Item 47b, BFISC.

36 *YS* 242–3.

37 *YS* 224, 250, 281; Fred Steward, 'Political Formation' in Swann and Aprahamian 1999, 52; Membership card, South Kensington Labour Party, 1924, in CP/IND/MONT/1/4, LHASC; A.M. Griffiths, Secretary, 1917 Club to IM, 8 Feb. 1924, informing him that he has been elected a member of the Club, CP/IND/MONT/4/8, LHASC; London County Council – Marylebone Institute, Student's Admission Card – Session 1924–5, entitling IM to admission to Russian classes on Wednesday evenings (and French on Friday), IM Item 47b, BFISC.

38 *YS* 250–8.

39 *YS* 250–60; IM 1939a, 47–8; theatre programmes in CP/IND/MONT/14/6 and CP/IND/MONT/14/7, LHASC; IM to Prof. Samuel Weiss, 10 Feb. 1974, CP/IND/MONT/6/14, LHASC.

40 *YS* 261–3.

41 *YS* 120, 261.

42 *YS* 262.

3. Film Culture

1 *YS* 264–5.

2 *YS* 265–6.

3 *YS* 266–7.

4 *YS* 265, 267.

5 *YS* 268; Moorehead 1984, 21. There are many accounts of the genesis of the Film Society and its subsequent history. Those drawn on in this chapter include: *YS* 268–81, 322–6, 332–5; IM 1932; IM 1975; *Screen* iv, 72–6, 84; Bernstein 1975; Macpherson 1980, 103–5; Marcus 2007, 259–77; Miller 2013, 90–6, 100–4, 107–13; Porter 2013; Samson 1986; Sexton 2002: Sexton 2008, 12–37.

6 Symon Gould, Director, Film Arts Guild, New York, to IM, 22 Nov. 1928, IM Item 43, BFISC; Spoto 1983, 71; Low 1985, 33; Walter Mycroft, *ES* 18 Nov. 1924, 12, and 2 Dec. 1924, 12, cited in Mycroft 2006, xiii.

7   Macpherson 1980, 103; Abel 1988, 324; Marcus 2007, 260; *YS* 274.

8   *YS* 274; IM 1932, 105; Brunel 1949, 112; Heinrich Fraenkel to IM, 14 Mar. and 1 Apr. 1925, IM Item 42, BFISC.

9   Hankins 2004, 500; Iris Barry, quoted in Hankins, 492.

10 *YS* 277; Mycroft 2006, 119, 122.

11 *YS* 275–7; Moorehead 1984, 21–2.

12 *YS* 279; card from IM, 28 Kensington Court, pencil draft, IM Item 7, BFISC.

13 *YS* 279–80; Film Society promotional leaflet [1925], IM Item 6, BFISC.

14 'Society to Show Uncensored Cinema Films', *DE* 7 May 1925, 1.

15 *YS* 280–1; Caroline A. Lejeune to IM, 7 Apr. 1925, and 4 May 1925, IM Item 46, BFISC; IM 1932, 106; C.A.L., 'The Week on the Screen', *MG* 12 Sep. 1925, 9.

16 *YS* 276–9; Samson 1986, 307; *Screen* iv 109; Hardy 2002, 255n.

17 Iris Barry to IM, n.d. [ca May–June 1925], IM Item 311, BFISC.

18 *YS* 278; Walter Hart, Gilbert Samuel & Co., Solicitors, to IM, 25 Sep. 1925, IM Item 7, BFISC.

19 Pearson 1957, 132–3; IM 1932, 106; *Screen* iv, 73–4.

20 Anon. 1972, 4; Moorehead 1984, 23.

21 *YS* 272–3, 275; IM 1975, 222; Sexton 2002, 293.

22 IM 1932, 106; *YS* 273–4; Sexton 2008, 19; Anon. 1972, 32.

23 Bernstein 1975, 'Raising Film Taste', *ST* 25 Oct. 1925, 16; Hankins 2004, 494; IM 1925b.

24 Brunel 1949, 114.

25 G.A. Atkinson, 'Gossip from the Cinema', *SE* 11 Oct. 1925, 6.

26 *YS* 324–6; G.A. Atkinson, 'Gossip from the Cinema', *SE* 25 Oct. 1925, 4.

27 *YS* 319–24; IM 1932, 106; IM 1975, 221; IM 1970, 107; Moorehead 1984, 23–4; 'Raising Film Taste', *ST* 25 Oct. 1925, 16; 'L.C.C. and the Army Reserve', *Times* 28 Oct. 1925, 16; 'Sunday Kinema Shows:', *MG* 28 Oct. 1925, 10.

28 Iris Barry, quoted in Sitton 2014, 117; IM 1970, 107; Brunel 1949, 113; Moorehead 1984, 23, 25; Mycroft 2006, 122.

29 Anon. 1972, 2–3. The programme notes are unsigned, but Montagu later explained that he wrote the notes for the first four seasons. Sexton 2008, 33.

30 Anon. 1972, 32.

31 IM 1932, 107; IM 1975, 224; Mycroft 2006, 123; Anon. 1972, 14.

32 *YS* 333–4; Riley 2013, 274; Mycroft 2006, 123–4.

33 *YS* 274; Mado to IM, 11 May 1926, intercepted letter, KV2/598.

34 *YS* 319, 327–8, 358–9, 362. Rowna Ely was the daughter of William Ernest Ely.

35 *YS* 327–9; Mycroft 2006, 120; Brunel 1949, 133.

36 *YS* 270–2.

37 *YS* 336; programmes in CP/IND/MONT, LHASC, for *Much Ado About Nothing* (9–21 Feb. 1925), *A Winter's Tale* (23 Feb. – 7 Mar. 1925), *Macbeth* (16 Mar. – 4 Apr. 1925), *The Taming of the Shrew* (26 Oct. – 7 Nov. 1925), *Antony and Cleopatra* (30 Nov. – 18 Dec. 1925), *As You Like It* (1–19 Mar. 1926), all at The Old Vic, mont/14/2; *The Assignation* by Dryden (25–26 Jan. 1925) at The Aldwych Theatre, mont/13/1; *Rule a Wife and Have a Wife* by Beaumont & Fletcher (28 Jun. 1925), The Renaissance Theatre at The Scala Theatre,

mont/14/3; *Tragical History of Dr Faustus* by Marlowe (25–26 Jan. 1926), The Phoenix, New Oxford Theatre, mont/13/2,; *The Bright Island* by Arnold Bennett (15–16 Feb. 1925), The Aldwych Theatre, mont/13/1; *A Comedy of Good and Evil* by Richard Hughes (30 Mar. 1925), Ambassadors Theatre, mont/14/2; *The Colonnade* by Stark Young (5–6 Apr. 1925), Aldwych Theatre, mont/13/1; *The Plough and the Stars* by Sean O'Casey (first performance 12 May, 1926), The Fortune Theatre, mont/14/2; *Les Sylphides*, Diaghileff's Russian Ballet (5–12 Jan. 1925), London Coliseum, mont/13/2; variety performance (18 Jan. 1925), Royal Court Theatre, mont/14/2.

38 Programme, variety performance (18 Jan. 1925), Royal Court Theatre, CP/IND/MONT/14/2, LHASC; *YS* 336; Elsa Lanchester to IM, Mar. 1925, sub renewal reminder notice for Select Evenings, IM Item 46, BFISC; 'London's "Cave of Harmony"', *ST* 25 Sep. 1927, 21.

39 *YS* 251, 272; 'Plays and Players', *ST* 27 Sep. 1925, 6; Autobio II, 88; George Bernard Shaw to IM, 6 Jun. 1926, CP/IND/MONT/6/12, LHASC.

40 Ernst Toller to IM, 14 Dec. 1925, IM Item 462, BFISC.

41 *YS* 345; H.H., 'Two American Films: From Bagdad to Bunker's Hill', *Obs* 28 Sep. 1924, 11; Robert Bell, *The Observer,* to IM, 26 Nov. 1925 and 10 Dec. 1925, IM Item 84 (1), BFISC.

42 *Obs* 29 Nov. 1925, 9B; H.H., ''Peter Pan' on the Film: Some New Ideas', *Obs* 18 Jan. 1925, 9; I.M., 'Peter Pan', *Obs* 3 Jan. 1926, 15; Robert Bell to IM, 28 Jan. 1926, IM Item 84 (1), BFISC.

43 *Obs* 29 Nov. 1925, 9B; 14 Mar. 1926, 23.

44 *Obs* 14 Feb. 1926, 16.

45 *Obs* 31 Jan. 1926, 17; 18 Apr. 1926, 5; 17 Jan. 1926, 14; 20 Dec. 1925, 19.

46 *Obs* 28 Feb. 1926, 17

47 *Obs* 7 Feb. 1926, 18; Marcus 2007, 307.

48 *Obs* 3 Jan. 1926, 15.

49 IM, corrected proof, *The Volga Boatman* review; Robert Bell, *The Observer,* to IM, 24 Apr. 1926; in IM Item 84(1), BFISC.

50 *YS* 345–6; *Obs* 30 May 1926, 22; IM, draft *Big Parade* review, IM Item 84(1), BFISC; R.M. Barrington Ward, *The Observer,* to IM, 28 May and 1 Jun. 1926, IM Item 84(1), BFISC.

4. *The Proletarian Cause*

1 Spratt 1955, 18.

2 *YS* 132.

3 Trotsky 1920, Introduction, Chap 1, Chap 2.

4 IM, 'Prophecies', unidentified journal, 173, 176, CP/IND/MONT/12/10, LHASC.

5 *YS* 203, 283; Peter Kapitza to IM, 24 Mar. and 4 May 1925, CP/IND/MONT/7/8, LHASC; KV2/598.

6 *YS* 291; Andrew 1986, 305–7; Avrich 1967, 136; Butterworth 2010, 404; Avrich 1995, 16–7; *Longines Chronoscope with Princess Alexandra Kropotkin*, 1951-09-03, www.youtube.com/watch?v=2kEqYAlliwI (accessed 28 Aug. 2017).

7 Sasha Kropotkin to IM, 7 May 1925, CP/IND/MONT/7/8, LHASC.

8 *YS* 281–2.

9   *YS* 286–7.

10 *YS* 285–90; IM 1925e, 28, in CP/IND/MONT/9/8, LHASC.

11 *YS* 290–1; http://en.wikipedia.org/wiki/Solomon_Lozovsky (accessed 28 Aug. 2017); http://en.wikipedia.org/wiki/Yakov_Peters (accessed 28 Aug. 2017).

12 *YS* 295; programmes for *Petrushka* and *Les Sylphides* (24 May 1925), *Don Quixote* (27 May 1925), and *The Mandate* (no date), CP/IND/MONT/14/4, LHASC.

13 *YS* 293–9.

14 [IM], untitled paper, with sections 'A. Prospects of Russian Films in England' and 'B. History of Relations with Russian Film Industry', in IM Item 7A, BFISC.

15 *YS* 301; [IM], untitled paper, IM Item 7A, BFISC; Leyda 1973, 197.

16 *YS* 301–3; IM, 'The Odyssey of Masha the Bear', *EN* 18 Nov. 1925, in CP/IND/MONT/12/10, LHASC.

17 Peter Kapitza to IM, 23 Jun. 1925, CP/IND/MONT/7/8, LHASC.

18 Maurice Dobb to IM, 6 Jul. 1925, CP/IND/MONT/5/8, LHASC; Craik 1964, 130–5; Millar 1979, 44, 80–1, 87; Macintyre 1980, 78–9; Worley 2002, 200–1.

19 *YS* 305–9.

20 *YS* 309–10.

21 *YS* 310–1.

22 *YS* 316–7; John Maynard Keynes, quoted in Howarth 1978, 146; programme for *Rusian and Ludmila* (7 Sep. 1925), CP/IND/MONT/14/4, LHASC.

23 Leyda 1973, 145–7, 186.

24 Campbell 1982, 29–31.

25 *YS* 301; [IM], untitled paper, IM Item 7A, BFISC; IM 1925d, 52, in CP/IND/MONT/9/8, LHASC.

26 [IM], untitled paper, IM Item 7A, BFISC.

27 *YS* 304; IM, 'Lawn Tennis in Soviet Russia', *Lawn Tennis and Badminton* 17 Oct. 1925, 718, in CP/IND/MONT/3/4, LHASC; IM, 'Football in Soviet Russia', *Football Echo* 26 Sep. 1925, 1, in CP/IND/MONT/12/10, LHASC.

28 IM 1925c, 36; IM 1925d, 52; IM 1925e, 28, in CP/IND/MONT/9/8.

29 Trotsky 1970, 328.

30 *YS* 295–6, 298, 339.

31 IM, untitled pencil ms, IM Item 199, BFISC. It was probably written in 1927.

32 Harry Pollitt, General Secretary, National Minority Movement, to IM, 16 Sep. and 21 Sep. 1925, CP/IND/MONT/8/10, LHASC.

33 Pollitt 1941, 205; Gruber 1974, 117; 'Socialists Resent Luxury of Soviet Delegates', *DE* 12 Sep. 1925, 9.

34 *YS* 339–40.

35 Bow Street Police Court, *Rex v. Inkpin and Others*, 28 Oct. 1925, transcript, CP/IND/POLL/15/07, LHASC; Klugmann 1969, 36, 66, 89.

36 A. Meakins, Secretary, Holborn Labour Party and Trades Council, to IM, 22 Dec. 1925, informing him that his application for membership has been accepted, CP/IND/MONT/4/4, LHASC: Steward 1999, 52; Kingsley Martin to IM, 12 Dec. 1925, CP/IND/MONT/7/9, LHASC.

37 [IM], 'Memorandum on Working-Class Police Body' (typescript, n.d. [1925]), CP/IND/MONT/7/3, LHASC.

38 [IM], 'Memorandum on Working-Class Police Body', 6.

39 Maurice Dobb to IM, 28 Dec. 1925 and 12 Jan. 1926, CP/IND/
    MONT/5/8, LHASC.

40 Klugmann 1969, 101–3.

41 IM to Walter Citrine, 7 May 1926, and [IM], 'Memorandum on Labour
    Patrol Body', CP/IND/MONT/7/3, LHASC.

42 YS 343; Taylor 1975, 308–10.

43 Moorehead 1984, 32; Klugmann 1969, 153, 155.

44 YS 340–2; Steward 1999, 52; Howarth 1978, 148–9.

45 IM to Walter Citrine, 7 May 1926, and Citrine to IM, 8 May 1926, CP/
    IND/MONT/7/3, LHASC.

46 YS 341; KV2/1598.

47 YS 343; Gruber 1974, 121; Pelling 1963, 176–7; Bermant 1971, 347.

48 Hornstein 1993, 66; Fischer 1948, 561; Deutscher 1970a, 267; Souvarine
    [1939], 428.

49 Klugmann 1969, 163–6; Olive N. Franklin to IM, n.d. [ca Jun. 1926], CP/
    IND/MONT/7/5, LHASC; Holborn Labour Party and Trades Council to
    IM, 22 Jun. 1926, CP/IND/MONT/4/4, LHASC.

50 YS 344; Steward 1999, 53; Holborn Labour Party and Trades Council to
    'Comrade', 15 Jun. 1926, KV2/1598; J.D. Bernal et al. to 'Comrade', 27 Sep.
    1926, KV2/1598; Dewar 1976, 39–41; Macfarlane 1966, 189.

51 YS 344.

5. The Film Industry

1   Low 1971, 156; Ryall 1986, 39; Murphy 1986, 51; 'The British Film Industry',
    ST 19 Apr. 1925, 14.

2   Ryall 1986, 38; 'The British Film Industry', ST 19 Apr. 1925, 14; 'British
    Films for British Cinemas', ST 13 Dec. 1925, 23; 'British Films', ST 4 Oct.
    1925, 14; 'British Film Industry', ST 21 Jun. 1925, 14.

3   Flyer, The Guildhouse, 'Seventh Course of Addresses', IM Item 43, BFISC;
    'The British Film Industry', Times 25 Jan. 1926, 18.

4   Low 1971, 134–5, 166–7; Kemp 1997, 13; Balcon 1969, 15, 51.

5   Low 1971, 171; Balcon, Gainsborough, to IM (c/- A. Brunel), 10 Feb. 1926,
    IM Item 43A, BFISC.

6   YS 330–1; IM 1980b, 189.

7   YS 346–7; IM 1958, 230; Low 1971, 149.

8   YS 336; Balcon 1971a, 170.

9   YS 275, 347; IM 1958, 230; IM 1975, 223; IM 1977, 9–10; Brunel 1949,
    123; card, IVOR MONTAGU, 20 Old Buildings, Lincoln's Inn – also at 6
    Dansey Yard, Wardour St, IM Item 7, BFISC.

10 Lady Swaythling to IM, 25 Jun. 1926, intercepted letter, KV2/598.

11 YS 348; IM 1980b, 189.

12 YS 349–50; IM 1977, 10; IM 1980b, 189–90.

13 YS 348–50; IM 1980b, 190, Taylor 1978, 81–2.

14 YS 356; Programme of the Congrès International du Cinématographe, Paris
    1926, IM Item 26A, BFISC; 'International Film Congress – Inaugural Meeting

in Paris', *Times* 28 Sep. 1926, 12; Low 1971, 36; 'International Educational Cinematographic Institute (IECI)', http://atom.archives.unesco.org/international-educational-cinematographic-institute-ieci (accessed 28 Aug. 2017).

15   Sexton 2008, 26; Anon. 1972, 35.

16   Lord Beaverbrook to IM, 29 Oct. 1926, CP/IND/MONT/7/2, LHASC.

17   *YS* 350–1; Brunel 1949, 126–7; George Hopton, Piccadilly Pictures, to IM, 25 Nov. 1926, IM Item 20, BFISC.

18   *YS* 352–3; Brunel 1949, 128; Low 1971, 276; Nadia Sibirskaia to IM, 1 Oct. 1926, intercepted letter, KV2/598; Gledhill 2003, 76.

19   Brunel 1949, 126–7; Armes 1978, 71–2.

20   *YS* 353–4; George Hopton, Piccadilly Pictures, to IM, 25 Nov. 1926, and Balcon to IM, 1 Sep. 1926, Item 43A, BFISC; KV2/598.

21   *YS* 369; Balcon 1969, 26–7, 83; Balcon to IM, 2 Dec. 1926, 8 Dec. 1926, 7 Jan. 1927, and 16 Feb. 1927, IM Item 43A, BFISC.

22   Vest 2005, 55; Vest 2004, 70.

23   *YS* 359; IM 1977, 9–10; Balcon to IM, 24 Feb. 1927, IM Item 43A, BFISC.

24   'The Film in Schools', *Times* 6 Jan. 1927, 15; 'Education of Youth', *GH* 6 Jan. 1927, 10.

25   *YS* 355–8; Riordan 2008, 524–6; Griffin 2014, 2.

26   *YS* 359–60; 'Peer's Son Weds A Typist', *DE* 24 Feb. 1924; 'Typist Bride of Peer's Son', *DMi* 24 Feb. 1927, 3.

27   *YS* 361–4.

28   *YS* 364.

29   *YS* 365–8; Mycroft 2006, 120–1; 'Bride in a Wig and Mask', *DE* 26 Feb. 1927; 'Hon. Ivor Montagu Marries a Typist', *NYT* 24 Feb. 1927, 18; 'Titled Banker's Son Takes Typist Bride', *WP* 24 Feb. 1927; 'Son of England's Richest Man Weds Stenographer', *Chicago Daily Tribune* 24 Feb. 1927, 25.

30   *YS* 335–6, 369–73; 'British Lords Collect Fleas and Do Knitting', *WP* 5 Mar. 1927, 12; 'Lord Picks Out Own Fleas', *LAT* 5 Mar. 1927, 4.

31   *YS* 365, 368, 374–5; 'British Queen Sets Example in Democracy', *Berkeley Daily Gazette* 21 Mar. 1927, 7.

32   Brunel to IM, 24 Mar. 1927; Autobio II, 14–5.

33   *FW* 141. See also Autobio II, 18–9; *Screen* iv, 80; IM 1980b, 191.

34   Autobio II, 19; IM to Balcon, 14 Apr. 1927, IM Item 43A, BFISC.

35   Balcon to IM, 22 Apr. 1927, IM Item 43A, BFISC.

36   Autobio II, 7–8; Eisenstein 1995, 357. Montagu's numbering of pages on his manuscript is erratic; there are two pages '7' and '8'.

37   Autobio II, 8–11 (there are two pages '8', '9', and '10'); Brunel 1949, 133.

38   'Bishop Who Has Never Entered Kinema', *MG* 8 Jun. 1927, 8; Moorehead 1984, 50; Low 1971, 33.

39   *YS* 376–8.

40   Autobio II, 4–10; IM, autobiographical notes, CP/IND/MONT/2/2, LHASC; 'Death of Lord Swaythling', *ST* 12 Jun. 1927, 17; Death notice, *Times* 13 Jun. 1927, 1; 'Wills and Bequests', *Times* 26 Jul. 1927, 17.

41   Autobio II, 4–5.

42   Brunel 1949, 118; Autobio II, 36.

43   Stollery 2009, 3–4; IM Item 35, BFISC; Brunel 1949, 119; *YS* 330.
44   Autobio II, 33–4; *YS* 331; Brunel 1949, 119.
45   Brunel 1949, 118; Low 1971, 179, 362.
46   *YS* 332; Anon. 1972, 67; Autobio II, 36.
47   Anon. 1972, 78–9, 82–3, 90–1, 126; Brunel & Montagu Ltd. List of Films
     Edited, 1 May 1928, IM Item 35, BFISC; Low 1971, 471; Autobio II, 36.
48   Ian Dalrymple to Anne Simor, 4 Oct. 1975, IM Item 16, BFISC.
49   IM 1927, 263–6.

6. Cultural Relations

1   Eric Walter White, *Parnassus to Let: An Essay About Rhythm in the Films*
     (Hogarth Press, 1928), 42, quoted in Marcus 2007, xiii.
2   Catherine Rabinovitch, SCR, to IM, 16 Sep. 1925, CP/IND/
     MONT/8/12, LHASC.
3   David-Fox 2012, 34–5.
4   David-Fox 2012, 81–2; Lygo 2013, 572–6; Stern 2007, 132–3; 'The Intellectual
     Bond with Russia', *MG* 11 Jul. 1924, 10; Appendix, Special Branch report,
     *The Activities of Russian Soviet Organizations in Great Britain and Ireland Since
     the A.R.C.O.S. Raid, May 1927–April 1929*, 3, 4, in KV5/71.
5   *First Annual Report of the S.C.R. ... 1924–5*, in CP/IND/MONT/8/12,
     LHASC; Burke 2011, 12.
6   Maurice Dobb to IM, 12 Jan. 1926, CP/IND/MONT/5/8, LHASC; *A
     Private Exhibition of Russian Posters, Books & Peasant Handicraft* (leaflet), CP/
     IND/MONT/8/12, LHASC; *Second Annual Report of the S.C.R. ... 1925–6*,
     6–8, in CP/IND/MONT/8/12, LHASC; 'The Theatre under Bolshevism',
     MG 23 Jun. 1926, 12.
7   [IM], untitled paper, IM Item 7A, BFISC; Ryan 1986, Vol. 1, 144.
8   [IM], untitled paper, IM Item 7A, BFISC; Gibarti to IM, 9 Jan. 1925 [*sic*, but
     must be 1926] and 22 Mar. 1926, IM Item 7A, BFISC.
9   Francesco Misiano, Mezhrabpom-Russ, Moscow, to IM, 23 Mar. 1926 [in
     German], IM Item 462, BFISC.
10   [IM] to Comrade Messiano [Misiano], n.d. [ca Mar–Apr 1926], IM Item 7A, BFISC.
11   J. Sternberg [?], Asst Manager, Kniga (England) Ltd to IM, 10 July 1926; D.
     Bogomolov to The Sovkino Company, 21 Sep. 1926; D. Bogomoloff [*sic*] to
     IM, 5 Oct. 1926; intercepted letters, KV2/598.
12   Photokino Abteilung, USSR Handelsvertretung in Deutschland, to IM, Film
     Society, 6 Jan. 1927, IM Item 7A, BFISC; Anon. 1972, 58.
13   Lygo 2013, 584; David-Fox 2012, 83; SCR Financial Appeal, 21 Jun. 1927,
     CP/IND/MONT/8/12, LHASC.
14   Scorecard Middlesex vs Hampshire match, May 1927, CP/IND/MONT/15,
     LHASC; theatre programme, *Convicts*, Holborn Empire, week commencing 16
     May 1927, CP/IND/MONT/14/2, LHASC; theatre programme, variety, Victoria
     Palace, week commencing 16 May 1927, CP/IND/MONT/14/[3], LHASC;
     race card, Epsom Races second day, 1 Jun. 1927, CP/IND/MONT/17, LHASC.
15   Autobio II, 28–31; Beckett 1998, 69–70; Beckett 2004, 21; Morgan and Cohen
     2003, 31–9; Mahon 1976, 96; Morgan 1993, 26; file note, 25 Apr. 1938, KV2/1396.

16 Rose Cohen to IM, 11 Jul. 1927, CP/IND/MONT/7/3, LHASC.

17 IM to Cohen, 9 Aug. 1927, CP/IND/MONT/7/3, LHASC.

18 IM, Film Society, to Direktor, Photokino Abteilung, USSR
    Handelsvertetung in Deutschland, 2 Sep. 1927, IM Item 7A, BFISC.

19 IM to Direktor, Photokino Abteilung, 2 Sep. 1927; Photokino Abteilung,
    USSR Handelsvertretung in Deutschland, to Film Society, 8 Sep. 1927, IM
    Item 7A, BFISC; theatre programmes, Das Vornehme Cabaret, München,
    1–30 Sep. 1927, and *Hoppla, wir leben!*, Piscatorbühne, Berlin, Sep. 1927, CP/
    IND/MONT/14/6, LHASC; Sidney Bernstein to A. Berman, First National
    Pictures Ltd, Berlin, 5 Sep. 1927, IM Item 40 (3), BFISC.

20 IM to 'Genosse' Tuscherer, Kino Abteilung, USSR Handelsvertretung, Berlin,
    30 Sep. 1927, IM Item 49b, BFISC.

21 Home Office Warrant, 30 Sep. 1927, KV2/598; Memo to G.P.O. (I.B.), 24
    Oct. 1927, KV2/598.

22 Cohen to IM, 10 Oct. 1927, IM Item 199, BFISC.

23 IM to Yarotsky, 19 Oct. 1927, intercepted cable, KV2/598; G. Gilliat, *Evening
    Standard*, to IM, 19 Oct. 1927, CP/IND/MONT/3/8, LHASC.

24 Autobio II, 22.

25 Andrew 2010, 147; Beckett 1998, 17; Pollitt 1941, 191; Autobio II, 23.

26 Autobio II, 23–6; theatre programme, *Dorothea Angermann*, Deutsches
    Theater, Berlin, week 18–24 Oct. 1927, CP/IND/MONT/14/6, LHASC;
    IM, note sheet, USSR visit 1927, CP/IND/MONT/2/7, LHASC.

27 'Trial in Moscow of "British Spies"', *Times* 24 Oct. 1927, 12.

28 Secretariat Leicester Square to Murphy, Moscow, 24 Oct. 1927, intercepted
    cable, KV2/598; IM, diary notes, USSR visit 1927, IM Item 199, BFISC.

29 Autobio II, 26–7.

30 Autobio II, 29–30; IM to 'Comrade', undated note, CP/IND/MONT/8/3,
    LHASC; Gitlow 1948, 173; IM to Ernst Toller, 15 Nov. 1927, IM Item 462, BFISC.

31 IM, diary notes, USSR visit 1927; Autobio II, 29–32; '"British Spies" in
    Russia', *Times* 31 Oct. 1927, 14; theatre programmes, *La Périchole* and
    Lysistrata, Moscow Art Theatre, n.d., and Revolution 10th Anniversary
    Concert, Bolshoi Theatre, 6 & 8 Nov. 1927, CP/IND/MONT/14/4,
    LHASC; IM to 'Comrade', undated note; IM to Catherine Rabinovitch,
    SCR, 23 Dec. 1927, CP/IND/MONT/8/12, LHASC.

32 'Soviet Frees 20,000 Convicts', *ES* 5 Nov. 1927, 3; 'Bolshevist Envoy Kills
    Himself', *ES* 18 Nov. 1927, 10.

33 IM, diary notes, USSR visit 1927; Autobio II, 31; IM to Petrovsky, 18 Jan.
    [1928], CP/IND/MONT/7/10, LHASC; David-Fox 2012, 43.

34 Autobio II, 30–1; IM, untitled typescript, IM Item 55, BFISC; Leyda 1973,
    235n, 238–9; Taylor 2002, 15–6, 82n.

35 Deutscher 1970a, 296, 357–8, 366–7; Morgan 1998, 187–8.

36 Autobio II, 30; Gallacher 1966, 226–7.

37 Gross 1974, 178; McCarthy 1953, 110.

38 IM, diary notes, USSR visit 1927; IM, 'A Soviet Hollywood' (typescript), IM
    Item 55, BFISC.

39   IM, diary notes, USSR visit 1927; Invitation Card to the International Congress of the Friends of the USSR, Moscow, 10 Nov. 1927, CP/IND/MONT/1/4, LHASC; David-Fox 2012, 124–5.

40   Macintyre 2010, 83–4.

41   IM to Ernst Toller, 15 Nov. 1927, IM Item 462, BFISC.

42   Costello 1989, 154; S. Turov to IM, 18 Nov. 1927 [in German], intercepted letter, KV2/598.

43   IM to Secretary of State for Home Affairs, 30 Nov. 1927; C.D. Robinson, Home Office, to IM, 29 Dec. 1927, CP/IND/MONT/6/11, LHASC; IM to Stuart Montagu, 2 Jan. 1928; Stuart Montagu to IM, 4 Jan. 1928, CP/IND/MONT/8/3, LHASC; IM to Stuart Montagu, 6 Jan. 1928, CP/IND/MONT/7/11, LHASC.

44   Notice & Agenda, 3rd AGM of SCR, 21 Nov. 1927; *Fourth Annual Report of the S.C.R. … 1927–1928*, 3–5; SCR, Circular, Dec. 1927; Invitation to SCR At Home, 16 Dec. [1927]; all in CP/IND/MONT/8/12, LHASC.

45   IM to Catherine Rabinovitch, Hon. Secretary, SCR, 8 Dec. 1927; Rabinovitch to IM, 13 Dec. 1927; IM to Rabinovitch, 14 Dec. 1927; IM to Rabinovitch, 23 Dec. 1927; all in CP/IND/MONT/8/12, LHASC.

46   Invitation to IM & Mrs Montagu from Mrs Victor Gollancz, At Home, 15 Dec. [1927]; IM to Victor Gollancz, 28 Dec. 1927; Gollancz to IM, 10 Jan. 1928; all in IM Item 43, BFISC.

47   Programmes for *The Admirable Bashville* and *Happy Families*, Chelsea Palace Theatre, 12 Dec. 1927; Variety, The Alhambra, week commencing 12 Dec. 1927; Concert Demonstration, Prof Leo Theremin, Royal Albert Hall, 12 Dec. [1927], all in CP/IND/MONT/14/2; Haynes et al. 2009, 362–3.

48   IM to George Bernard Shaw, 29 Dec. 1927; Shaw to IM, 1 Jan. 1928, CP/IND/MONT/6/12, LHASC; IM 1928; Anon. 1972, 65–7; IM to Kenneth Macpherson, *Close Up*, 7 Feb. 1928, IM Item 41, BFISC.

49   Autobio II, 87; IM, 'A Study in Film Pot-Boilers', *SG* 8 Jan. 1928, 9; IM, 'Features of the Films', *SG* 15 Jan. 1928, 11; IM, 'Features of the Films', *SG* 22 Jan. 1928, 11.

50   W. Thomson Hill, *Sunday Graphic*, to IM, 21 Jan. 1927 [*sic*, 1928]; IM to Hill, 7 Feb. 1928, IM Item 43, BFISC.

51   'England Bids for a Record', *DE* 10 Jan. 1928, 9; The Dragoman, 'Talk of the Town', *DE* 10 Jan. 1928.

52   IM, Brunel & Montagu Ltd, to 'Genosse' Zehrer, Kino Abteilung, USSR Handelsvertretung in Deutschland, 2 Dec. and 22 Dec. 1927, and IM to P. Simunek, 2 Dec. 1927, IM Item 49b, BFISC.

53   IM to 'Genosse' Zehrer, 31 Dec. 1927, IM Item 49b, BFISC; IM to Petrovsky, 18 Jan. [1928].

54   Rabinovitch to IM, 2 Feb. 1928; SCR notice, *Polikouschka* [*sic*] screening, 8 Feb. [1928]; Rabinovitch to IM, 9 Feb. 1928; *Fourth Annual Report*, 7; all in CP/IND/MONT/8/12, LHASC.

7. Subversive Cinema

1   *Hansard* (Commons) 7 Apr. 1927, vol. 204 col. 2240, cited in Jones 1987, 104.

2   Pronay 1982, 116.

3   Phelps 1975, 145; Pronay 1982, 111; Smith 2013a, 12.

4   Willcox 1990, 275–7.

5   *WEH* 18–9.

6   IM to Stuart Montagu, 4 May 1928; Stuart Montagu to IM, 10 May 1928; IM to Stuart Montagu, 11 May 1928; Stuart Montagu to IM, 16 May 1928; IM to Stuart Montagu, 20 May 1928; all in IM Item 47b, BFISC; IM to Adrian Brunel, 4 May 1928, IM Item 40A, BFISC; IM to Simon Rowson, 20 May 1928, IM Item 84(2), BFISC.

7   *WEH* 19; Hardy 2002, 252.

8   *WEH* 19–20; Gledhill 2008.

9   *WEH* 21–2; Young 1999, 21.

10 Sexton 2008, 63; Brunel 1949, 141.

11 R.H., 'H.G. Wells on the Screen', *MG* 12 Sep. 1929, 6; 'New Film Comedies', *Times* 12 Sep. 1929, 10.

12 Autobio II, 82; *WEH* 23.

13 IM to Michael Balcon, 3 Jul. 1928, IM Item 43A, BFISC; '*Table Tennis To-Day*', *Table Tennis Collector* 48 (Spring 2008), 8–9; Cedric Belfrage to IM, 24 Apr. 1929, IM Item 40–3, BFISC.

14 *YS* 146–7; telegrams and letters re Ruttmann's visit to London, IM Items 40A and 49b, BFISC; *Melodie der Welt* (Ruttmann, Germany, 1929).

15 IM to George Bernard Shaw, 28 Apr. and 15 May 1928, CP/IND/MONT/6/12, LHASC; *YS* 147; IM to Rowson, 24 Nov. 1928.

16 IM to Rowson, 24 Nov. 1928; IM to Lord Beaverbrook, 10 Jul. 1929, IM Item 40–3, BFISC; IM to Leslie Haden Guest, 21 Aug. and 23 Dec. 1929, IM Item 36, BFISC.

17 Brunel 1949, 122.

18 [IM], 'Film Portraits Ltd. Proposed Private Company' (typescript), IM Item 35, BFISC; 'Enclosure: Proposal by Brunel & Montagu Ltd., May 7th, 1929', IM Item 35, BFISC.

19 Programme, Southampton F.C. Supporters Club Second Annual Dinner, Bungalow Cafe, Southampton, 25 Apr. 1928, CP/IND/MONT/16, LHASC; W.S. Kennedy to IM, 16 May 1928, CP/IND/MONT/4/8, LHASC; Agnes Turner to IM, 11 Jun. 1928, CP/IND/MONT/8/1, LHASC; Victor Gollancz to IM, 1 Oct. 1928, IM to Gollancz, 5 Oct. 1928, and Gollancz to IM, 8 Oct. 1928, IM Item 43, BFISC; flier, Lectures on Education at Leigh Holt Street, Autumn 1928, IM Item 46, BFISC; National Council of Labour Colleges, Southend Branch, to IM, 9 Sep. 1928, CP/IND/MONT/4/4, LHASC; Catherine Rabinovitch to IM, 16 Oct. 1928, CP/IND/MONT/8/12, LHASC.

20 IM to Herr Oesterheld, Oesterheld & Co. Verlag, 28 Nov. 1927, IM Item 462, BFISC.

21 Autobio II, 48; Miller 2013, 164.

22 Anon. 1972, 96–8; Hay Chowl, 'Propaganda,' *Close Up* Vol. 4 No. 1 (Jan. 1929), 27, quoted in Marcus 2013, 229; Marshall 1983, 12; The Dragoman,

'Talk of London', *DE* 22 Oct. 1928, 19; '*Mother*', *ST* 28 Oct. 1928, 13.

23 L.S. Oswald to IM, 19 Nov. 1928, IM Item 7, BFISC.

24 Anon. 1972, 98; IM, *FW* 261; Secretary, BBFC, to IM, 4 Dec. 1928, IM Item 89, BFISC; T.P. O'Connor to IM, 14 Dec. 1928, IM Item 84 (1), BFISC.

25 Rotha and Griffith 1967, 388; IM 1932, 107; *Hansard* (Commons), 7 Feb. 1929, vol. 224 col. 1926–27; Montagu H. Cox, Clerk of the Council, London County Council, to the Secretary, the Film Society, 25 Feb. 1929, IM Item 7, BFISC.

26 Writ, 27 Feb. 1929, between Sidney Lewis Bernstein and others, plaintiffs, and Sunday Pictorial Newspapers (1920) Ltd and Walter Alexander Mutch, defendants, IM Item 3, BFISC; Moorehead 1984, 25–6.

27 Autobio II, 52; IM 1960, 14; 'Types Instead of Actors' in Pudovkin 1960, 165–73.

28 Autobio II, 50–52; Brunel 1949, 116; Manageress, St James's Palace Chambers, to J.M. Harvey, Film Society, 19 Feb. 1929, IM Item 7, BFISC.

29 IM to Petrovsky, 7 Feb. 1929, IM Item 84 (1), BFISC.

30 IM to Petrovsky, 9 Apr. 1929, IM Item 84 (1), BFISC.

31 Manager, Lloyds Bank Ltd, to IM, 14 May 1929, intercepted letter, KV2/598; IM to Pudovkin, 24 May 1929, IM Item 89, BFISC; IM, 'Outline of Sound Film by Proposed New Method', IM Item 32, BFISC; Boyd, British International Pictures, to IM, 10 Apr. 1929, IM Item 29, BFISC.

32 IM to W.J. [Pope?], 10 Apr. 1929, CP/IND/MONT/8/3, LHASC; IM to C.L. Lewis, 17 Apr. 1929, CP/IND/MONT/7/9, LHASC.

33 Macfarlane 1966, 229; IM to Trotsky, 1 Jul. 1929, CP/IND/MONT/4/10, LHASC.

34 Pudovkin 1960, 210, 23, 24–5; Brown 2008, 245.

35 Autobio II, 88–9; IM to Bennett, 30 Sep. 1929, Bennett to IM, 1 Oct. 1929, IM Item 40–3, BFISC.

36 *WEH* 13–6; IM to Robert Aron, 21 May 1929, IM Item 30, BFISC; Moussinac 1970, 35–6; Lenauer 1929.

37 Eisenstein 1983, 134; Miller 2012, 6; IM to Robert Aron, 21 May 1929; IM 1948, 7; Proceedings of the Congress, 1st session [in French], IM Item 30, BFISC; IM, 'A Great Russian Film Director', *Lis* Issue 1035 (25 Nov. 1948), 809.

38 *WEH* 13–6; Moussinac 1970, 36; Seton 1960, 128–9; Barna 1973, 139–40; Swallow 1976, 74; Bergan 1999, 158–9; Eisenstein 1983, 134–7; www.cinematheque.ch/i/documents-de-cinema/complement-de-programme/tempete-sur-la-sarraz-1929/ (accessed 28 Aug. 2017).

39 Eisenstein 1983, 135–6.

40 Programme, 3rd International Congress of the World League for Sexual Reform, CP/IND/MONT/4/9, LHASC.

41 IM 1930, 323, 324–5.

42 IM 1930, 327–9, 331–2; Autobio II, 13.

43 *PCF* 11, 14.

44 *PCF* 3.

45 George Bernard Shaw, 'Views on the Censorship', *British Film Journal*, Apr.– May 1928, reprinted in Shaw 1997, 54–5; Bryher 1929, 55.

46 *PCF* 4, 14; Turvey 2000, 36; IM to Major H.L. Nathan, MP, 21 Sep. 1929, IM

Item 47b, BFISC; IM to Comrade Marianov, Berlin, 13 Sep. 1929, IM Item 44, BFISC.

47 *PCF* 43–4; Ryan 1986, Vol. 1, 150, 165; Worley 2002, 213.

48 Federation of Workers' Film Societies Political Statement, IM Item 75, BFISC; Ryan 1986, Vol. 1, 163; Worley 2002, 214; Jones 1987, 170.

49 Minutes of meeting of the Provisional Council of the National Association of Workers' Film Societies, 28 Oct. 1929, IM Item 75, BFISC; IM to J.M. Harvey, 29 Nov. 1929, IM Item 7, BFISC.

50 IM to Monica Ewer, *Daily Herald*, 18 Jan. 1930, IM Item 42, BFISC; Hogenkamp 1986, 39.

51 Minutes of FWFS executive committee meetings, Nov. 1929 – Feb. 1930, IM Item 75, BFISC; Jones 1987, 167; Ryan 1980, 54.

52 Brentford 1929, 9, 21.

53 Memorandum sent by IM to John Strachey, 27 Sep. 1929, IM Item 66, BFISC; Turvey 2000, 36; Willcox 1990, 284, 286; Low 1979b, 168; Sir William Jowitt to Strachey, 27 Nov. 1929, IM Item 66, BFISC; Ellen Wilkinson and IM, circular letter inviting attendance at a meeting on 24 Feb. to discuss film censorship, 20 Feb. 1930, IM Item 65, BFISC; IM to Robert Herring, 17 Feb. 1930, IM Item 44, BFISC.

54 Boyd, British International Pictures, to IM, 30 Oct. 1929, and IM to Walter Mycroft, 25 Feb. 1930, IM Item 29, BFISC; Autobio II, 11; IM to George Bernard Shaw, 2 Apr. 1929, CP/IND/MONT/6/12, LHASC; IM to A.S. Neill, 2 Oct. 1929, IM Item 47b, BFISC.

8. Hollywood

1   IM, untitled ms (pencil) on the future of the sound film, ca 1929, IM Item 34, BFISC; IM, 'Outline of Sound Film by Proposed New Method', IM Item 32, BFISC; Boyd, British International Pictures, to IM, 10 Apr. 1929, IM Item 29, BFISC.

2   IM to Walter Mycroft, British International Pictures, 22 Jun. 1929, IM Item 29, BFISC; The Dragoman, 'The Talk of London', *DE* 29 Aug. 1929.

3   The Dragoman, 'The Talk of London', *DE* 29 Aug. 1929; IM, typescript memo on sound apparatus, ca 1929, IM Item 33, BFISC; Arthur Levey to William Fox, New York, 4 Mar. 1930, IM Item 46, BFISC.

4   Autobio II, 94–5.

5   Anon. 1972, 128–30.

6   Anon. 1972, 131.

7   Miller 2012, 7; Balcon 1969, 51; *WEH* 31–2; Eisenstein 1983, 88.

8   Brunel 1949, 115; IM to Aliens Dept, attn Mr Grant, 9 Nov. 1929, IM Item 108, BFISC; Seton 1960, 142–5; Basil Wright, précis notes, 'Eisenstein's London Lectures in Film Theory', in Seton 1960, 482–5; Swallow 1976, 79–80; Bergan 1999, 167–8; *WEH* 30; IM 1969, xiv; IM to Richter, 18 Oct. 1929, IM Item 84(2), BFISC; Richter to IM, 28 Oct. 1929, IM Item 84(2), BFISC; Richter to IM, 6 Nov. 1929, IM Item 84(2), BFISC.

9   Moorehead 1984, 28; Seton 1960, 146; Lord Bernstein and IM, 'Professor J. Isaacs', *Times* 19 May 1973, 16.

10   *WEH* 32; IM, *FW* 7; Richard Braithwaite to IM, 7 Dec. 1929, IM Item
     40(6), BFISC; Seton 1960, 147; Eisenstein 1983, 165, 271; Barna 1973, 146.
11   *WEH* 29.
12   Autobio II, 97; *WEH* 34–6; Levey to William Fox, 4 Mar. 1930, Levey to IM,
     4 Mar. 1930, IM Item 46, BFISC; IM to Iris Barry, 14 Feb. 1930, IM Item
     311, BFISC.
13   R.M. Anthony, manager, Wayfarers Travel Agency, to IM, 1 Mar. 1930, IM
     Item 28A, BFISC; Levey to IM, cable, 5 Mar. 1930, IM Item 46, BFISC;
     'Talks from Majestic in Harbor to London', *NYT* 12 Mar. 1930, 22.
14   Geoffrey M.E. Franklin, Wayfarers Travel Agency, to IM, 24 Feb. 1930, IM
     Item 28A, BFISC; WEH 37, 40; Autobio II, 98–9; NYT 3 Jan. 1933, cited
     in http://en.wikipedia.org/wiki/Belle_Moskowitz (accessed 28 Aug. 2017);
     http://en.wikipedia.org/wiki/Henry_Moskowitz_%28civil_rights_leader%29
     (accessed 28 Aug. 2017).
15   Autobio II, 99–100; *WEH* 41–2; programmes for *Aristocrats*, Artef at the
     American Laboratory Theatre, n.d.; Mei Lang-Fang's company at the
     National Theatre, week beginning 17 Mar. 1930; and *The Green Pastures*,
     Mansfield Theatre, week beginning 31 Mar. 1930; all in CP/IND/
     MONT/14/[5], LHASC.
16   *WEH* 42, 124–5.
17   *WEH* 40–1; Autobio II, 99–100; Eleanor Roosevelt to IM, 24 Mar. 1930, IM
     Item 84(2), BFISC.
18   *WEH* 41; IM to Eisenstein [re Lasky proposal], n.d. [ca Mar.–Apr. 1930],
     IM Item 104, BFISC; IM to Eisenstein and Eisenstein to IM, cables, 31 Mar.
     1930, 2 Apr. 1930, 3 Apr. 1930, 9 Apr. 1930, IM Item 105, BFISC.
19   *WEH* 43–4, 46; Autobio II, 101.
20   *WEH* 48–9; IM to Mr [D.A.] Doran, New York, 30 Apr. 1930, IM Item 41,
     BFISC.
21   IM to Eisenstein, cable, 18 Apr. 1930, IM Item 105, BFISC; IM [?] to
     unidentified recipient, Paris, cable [in French], 19 Apr. 1930; IM Item 105,
     BFISC; IM to Eisenstein, cables, Apr. 1930, IM Item 41, BFISC.
22   *WEH* 70–1; IM to Eisenstein, 9 May 1930, IM Item 104, BFISC.
23   *WEH* 77–8; Leyda and Voynow 1982, 41; Bergan 1999, 188–9; Seton 1960,
     157; pay slip, 'Compensation Payable to Serge Michailovitch Eisenstein under
     Agreement of 5-3-30', IM Item 48(1), BFISC.
24   Hollywood Correspondent [Cedric Belfrage], 'Crashing Hollywood's Gates',
     Film Weekly 17 May 1930, 5.
25   IM to Doran, 30 Apr. 1930; *WEH* 50–62; 'English Film Producer Goes to
     Paramount', *LAT* 18 May 1930, B12.
26   IM to Eisenstein, 9 May 1930; IM to Leon Trotsky, 22 May 1930, Item 3387,
     MS Russ 13.1.
27   IM to Lionel Montagu, 6 May 1930; IM to Galantière, 30 Apr. 1930; IM to
     Gilbert Seldes, 14 Jul. 1930, IM Item 49(1), BFISC.
28   IM to Lionel Montagu, 6 May 1930; IM to Eisenstein, 9 May 1930.
29   IM to Eisenstein, 9 May 1930; IM to Eisenstein, n.d. [ca Jun. 1930], IM Item
     104, BFISC.

30 IM to Eisenstein, n.d. [ca Jun. 1930]; Eisenstein to IM, telegram, 24 May 1930, IM Item 105, BFISC; *WEH* 64–5, 67, 68–70.

31 Ponting to IM, 30 Apr. 1930, and IM to Ponting, 11 Jun. 1930, IM Item 48(1), BFISC.

32 *WEH* 73–5; IM to Gilbert Seldes, 14 Jul. 1930, IM Item 49 (1), BFISC.

33 *WEH* 75–9; Seton 1960, 165–6: Autobio II, 102.

34 *YS* 105.

35 *WEH* 82–5.

36 *WEH* 87, 91; Bergan 1999, 200; Autobio II, 89–90; IM 1948, 14.

37 *WEH* 79–80, 85.

38 *WEH* 33, 101; Barna 1973, 152; Bergan 1999, 203; Leyda and Voynow 1982, 43, 59; Eisenstein 1983, 126; Geduld and Gottesman 1970, 13.

39 *WEH* 102–5, 345; Bordwell 1993, 17; Leyda and Voynow 1982, 43–5; Bergan 1999, 203–5; Seton 1960, 171.

40 Eisenstein 1983, 253.

41 *WEH* 105–6, 342; Eisenstein 1983, 168; Seton 1960, 171–2.

42 *WEH* 106–7; Seton 1960, 172.

43 IM to Robert Herring, 27 Aug. 1930, IM Item 44, BFISC; *WEH* 107–8, 158, 181.

44 *WEH* 108–13; Seton 1960, 172; Schulberg 1981, 369.

45 *WEH* 118; Leyda and Voynow 1982, 71; 'Educators of Note to Attend Tea Tomorrow', *LAT* 28 Jul. 1930, A9; Bessie & Jesse Lasky to IM & Hell, telegram, 4 Aug. 1930, IM Item 46, BFISC; 'Society of Cinemaland', *LAT* 10 Aug. 1930, B13.

46 *WEH* 125–6; IM to H. G. Wells, 27 Aug. 1930, IM Item 49b, BFISC; IM 1969, xiii.

47 *WEH* 113–6; IM to Herring, 27 Aug. 1930; Geduld and Gottesman 1970, 13.

48 *WEH* 114–20.

49 *WEH* 293; Eisenstein 1957, 105.

50 *WEH* 120; Seton 1960, 183.

51 *WEH* 120.

52 IM to Eisenstein, 9 May 1930.

53 David O. Selznick, memo to B.P. Schulberg, 8 Oct. 1930, in Behlmer 1972, 26–7.

54 Seton 1960, 174, 185.

55 John O'Brien, Chief Inspector, Police Dept, City of New York, to Commissioner of Immigration, Ellis Island, N.Y., 7 Jul. 1930, CP/IND/ MONT/1/1, LHASC; *WEH* 121; Seton 1960, 167–8, 174–6, 184–6.

56 *WEH* 121; Seton 1960, 185–6; IM to Hans Richter, 20 Mar. 1931, IM Item 84(2).

57 Schatz 1988, 78; Eisenstein 1983, 126; Seton 1960, 185; *WEH* 122–3.

58 *WEH* 89, 123, 127–8; Autobio II, 103.

59 *WEH* 128, 139; IM to Lionel Montagu, 20 Dec. 1930, IM Item 47c, BFISC; IM to D. Bogomolov, 20 Dec. 1930, IM Item 40–5, BFISC.

60 IM to Gilbert Seldes, 31 Dec. 1930, IM Item 49(1), BFISC; IM to Nadia Sibirskaia, 31 Dec. 1930, IM Item 49(2), BFISC.

9. Trotsky

1   Trotsky 1970, xxxv.
2   Holmes 1979, 33–6; 'Trotsky Applies to Mr. Ramsay MacDonald', *MG* 10 Jun. 1929, 15; 'Our London Correspondence', *MG* 12 Jul. 1929, 10.
3   Autobio II, 114; IM to Trotsky, 1 Jul. 1929, Item 3379, MS Russ 13.1, also CP/IND/MONT/4/10, LHASC.
4   Trotsky to IM, 14 Jul. 1929, Item 9263, MS Russ 13.1. The date is incorrectly catalogued as 29 Jul.
5   IM to Trotsky, 20 Jul. 1929, Item 3380, MS Russ 13.1, also CP/IND/ MONT/4/10, LHASC; *Hansard* (Commons) 18 Jul. 1929, vol. 230 col. 603; 'Our London Correspondence', *MG* 19 Jul. 1929, 12; 'Questions in the Commons', *MG* 19 Jul. 1929, 16; 'The Right of Asylum', *MG* 20 Jul. 1929, 12.
6   IM to Trotsky, 20 Jul. 1929.
7   'Government Cuts Naval Programme', *MG* 25 Jul. 1929, 15.
8   IM to Trotsky, 26 Jul. 1929, Item 3381, MS Russ 13.1.
9   IM to Trotsky, 26 Jul. 1929.
10 Trotsky to IM [in French], 30 Jul. 1929, Item 9264, MS Russ 13.1, also CP/ IND/MONT/4/10, LHASC.
11 IM to Trotsky, 29 Aug. 1929, Item 3382, MS Russ 13.1.
12 IM to Trotsky, 29 Aug. 1929.
13 IM to Trotsky, 30 Apr. 1930; IM to Trotsky, 29 Aug. 1929.
14 'Trotsky's Peril', *MG*, 17 Aug. 1929, 15; Trotsky to IM [in Russian], 23 Sep. 1929, Item 9266, MS Russ 13.1 [translation by Steve Marder].
15 Trotsky to IM [in Russian], 23 Sep. 1929 [translation by Steve Marder].
16 Trotsky to IM [in French], 16 Oct. 1929, Item 9267, MS Russ 13.1; IM to Trotsky, 19 Jan. 1930, Item 3383, MS Russ 13.1.
17 IM to Trotsky, 19 Jan. 1930.
18 IM to Trotsky, 30 Jan. 1930, Item 3384, MS Russ 13.1.
19 Trotsky to IM [in French], 5 Feb. 1930, Item 9268, MS Russ 13.1.
20 Trotsky to IM, 14 Mar. 1930, Item 9269; IM to Trotsky (cable), 22 Mar. 1930, Item 3385; Trotsky to IM (cable), 23 Mar. 1930, Item 9270; IM to Trotsky, 30 Apr. 1930, all in MS Russ 13.1.
21 IM to Trotsky, 30 Apr. 1930.
22 IM to Trotsky, 30 Apr. 1930.
23 IM to Trotsky, 30 Apr. 1930; Leon Trotsky, 'World Unemployment and the Five-Year Plan' [14 Mar. 1930], www.marxists.org/archive/trotsky/1930/ unemployment/02.htm (accessed 28 Aug. 2017).
24 IM to Trotsky, 30 Apr. 1930; IM to Trotsky, 19 Jan. 1930.
25 IM to Trotsky, 30 Apr. 1930
26 Trotsky to IM, 14 Mar. 1930; IM to Trotsky, 30 Apr. 1930.
27 IM to Trotsky, 22 May 1930.
28 Marjorie Wells to Eileen Montagu, 13 May 1930, CP/IND/MONT/4/10, LHASC.
29 IM to Marjorie Wells, 11 Jun. 1930, CP/IND/MONT/4/10, LHASC; Bancroft Clark to IM, 25 May 1930, CP/IND/MONT/5/6, LHASC.
30 Marjorie Wells to IM, 3 Jul. 1930, CP/IND/MONT/4/10.
31 'No Passport for Mr Trotsky', *MG* 4 Jul. 1930, 16; Trotsky to IM [in French],

16 Jul. 1930, Item 9271, MS Russ 13.1.

32 'Mr Bernard Shaw at ILP School', *MG* 4 Aug. 1930, 14.

33 Shaw to Clynes, draft, n.d.; H.G. Wells to J.R. Clynes, draft, n.d.; Augustine Birrell to J.R. Clynes, draft, n.d.; G.P. Wells to IM, n.d. [c Aug. 1930]; Clynes to Marjorie Wells, 15 Nov. 1930 [copy]; Marjorie Wells to IM, 19 Nov. 1930; all in CP/IND/MONT/4/10, LHASC.

34 Brockway to IM, 11 Sep. 1930, IM Item 65, BFISC. See also J.M. Harvey to IM, IM Item 7, BFISC.

35 Trotsky to IM [in French], 16 Jul. 1930, Item 9271, MS Russ 13.1.

36 Autobio II, 97, 107–10; IM to Iris Barry, 14 Feb. 1930, IM Item 311, BFISC; IM to A.S. Neill, 23 Jul. 1929, Neill to IM, 26 Jul. 1929, IM to Neill, 2 Oct. 1929, IM Item 47b, BFISC; Croall 1983, 170, 188.

37 Autobio II, 110–2; IM to J.G. Bachmann, 7 Feb. 1931, IM Item 40–2, BFISC.

38 Autobio II, 112; IM to Eric Pinker, New York, 5 Jun. 1930; Sergei Nolbandov [?] to R. [J. Ralph?] Pinker, London, 29 Oct. 1930; J. Ralph Pinker to Nolbandov, 30 Oct. 1930; IM to Eric Pinker, 31 Dec. 1930; J. Ralph Pinker to IM, 14 Jan. 1931, all in Item 48(1), BFISC; IM to Babel, Moscow, 31 Dec. 1930, IM Item 40–2, BFISC; Eisenstein to IM, n.d. [ca Jan. 1931], and IM to Eisenstein, 2 Feb. 1931, IM Item 104, BFISC.

39 Autobio II, 112, 118.

40 IM to Trotsky, 7 Jan. 1931, Item 3388, MS Russ 13.1; Trotsky to IM [in Russian], 16 Jan. 1931, Item 9272, MS Russ 13.1 [translation by Steve Marder]; Autobio II, 119–20; James Bone, London Office, *Manchester Guardian*, to IM, 29 Jan. 1931, CP/IND/MONT/4/10, LHASC.

41 Trotsky to IM, 16 Jan. 1931; Trotsky to IM [in Russian], 6 Feb. 1931, Item 9273, MS Russ 13.1; IM to Trotsky, cable [in French], 18 Feb. 1931, Item 3391, MS Russ 13.1; Autobio II, 120–1.

42 [IM], 'An Interview with Trotsky', *MG* 27 Mar. 1931, 9; [IM], 'Trotsky's House at Prinkipo', *MG* 3 Mar. 1931, 8; Deutscher 1970b, 14.

43 Autobio II, 121–2; James Bone to IM, 5 Mar. 1931, CP/IND/MONT/4/10, LHASC; [IM], 'An Interview with Trotsky'.

44 Autobio II, 122–3; 'Trotsky's House at Prinkipo'.

45 'Trotsky's House Burnt Down', *MG* 2 Mar. 1931, 12; Trotsky to IM [in German], 3 Mar. 1931, Item 9275, MS Russ 13.1; IM to Trotsky, 19 Mar. 1931, Item 3392, MS Russ 13.1; Deutscher 1970b, 148–9.

46 [IM], 'An Interview with Trotsky', 9–10.

47 [IM], 'Interviews with Trotsky II', *MG* 28 Mar. 1931, 11–2.

48 IM to Trotsky, 19 Mar. 1931, Item 3392; IM to Trotsky, 9 Apr. 1931, Item 3393; IM to Trotsky, 12 Aug. 1931, Item 3395; Trotsky to IM [in German], 22 Aug. 1931, Item 9278, all in MS Russ 13.1; Autobio II, 121–2; George Lansbury to IM, 2 Apr. 1931, CP/IND/MONT/4/10, LHASC.

49 Autobio II, 121; Deutscher 1970b, 150; IM to Trotsky, 19 Mar. 1931; IM to Trotsky, 9 Apr. 1931.

50 Ellen Wilkinson to IM, 25 Mar. 1931, 2 Jun. 1931, and 8 Jun. 1931, all in CP/IND/MONT/4/10, LHASC.

51 Macintyre 2010, 84.

52   Hell Montagu to Iris Barry, 26 Mar. 1931, IM Item 311, BFISC; IM to J.G.
     Bachmann, 13 Apr. 1931, IM Item 40–2, BFISC.
53   IM to Trotsky, 19 Mar. 1931.
54   IM to Trotsky, 12 Aug. 1931.
55   Autobio II, 124–5, 114–5.
56   IM to Trotsky, 12 Aug. 1931.
57   Trotsky to IM [in German], 22 Aug. 1931 [translation by Gerd Pohlmann].
58   Trotsky to IM, 23 Sep. 1929; Trotsky to IM, 22 Aug. 1931.

10. Commitment

1   Raphael Samuel, quoted in Morgan, Cohen and Flinn eds, 2007, 2.
2   Morgan, Cohen and Flinn eds, 2007, 79.
3   Morgan, Cohen and Flinn eds, 2007, 81; West 1969, 167; IM, Party
     Registration Form, CPGB, 10 Nov. 1942, CP/CENT/pers/5/05, LHASC.
4   Anthony Crosland, quoted in Morgan, Cohen and Flinn eds, 2007, 49.
5   See e.g. Carr 1982, 210–4; Thorpe 2000, 174–7, 284; Jupp 1982, 31–3.
6   Jupp 1982, 31; Carr 1982, 213, 217.
7   Carr 1982, 212; Jupp 1982, 32.
8   Burns to IM, 6 Sep. 1928, intercepted letter, KV2/598; Thorpe 2000, 158;
     Carr 1982, 385; Lazitch and Drachkovitch 1986, 192.
9   'Resolution on the New Political Situation in Great Britain and the Tasks
     of the Party', 19 Nov. 1930 (cyclostyled), 14, CPGB Statements 1930s, CP/
     CENT/stat/1/2, LHASC.
10   'To Take a Tractor With Them', *DW* 27 Aug. 1931, 2; 'Banker-Peer's Son
     Acts as Communist Cashier', *DE* 29 Aug. 1931; Hill 1982, 10, 12–3, 17, 62;
     Branson 1985, 339–40.
11   'To Take a Tractor With Them'; 'Factories, Pits and Ships to Send to U.S.S.R.',
     DW 7 Sep. 1931, 2; 'British Delegation Leaves', *DW* 31 Oct. 1931, 5.
12   IM to Eisenstein, 6 Oct. 1931, IM Item 104, BFISC.
13   Thorpe 2000, 180; IM to Eisenstein, 6 Oct. 1931.
14   IM to Trotsky, 9 Oct. 1931, Item 3396, MS Russ 13.1.
15   Thorpe 2000, 181; Carr 1982, 214; IM to Eisenstein, 6 Oct. 1931.
16   'Plans for a Mighty Mobilisation To-Morrow', *DW* 6 Nov. 1931, 5; 'Police
     and Communist Procession', *Times* 9 Nov. 1931, 14.
17   KV2/1599; 'The Opening of Parliament', *Times* 11 Nov. 1931, 9.
18   Leonov 1931.
19   IM, 'Note', Leonov 1931, viii.
20   Leonov 1931, 6, 32; Ralph Straus, 'The Russian Scene', *ST* 3 Jan. 1932, 9.
21   Pera Attasheva to IM, n.d. [ca Oct. 1931], IM Item 108, BFISC; Eisenstein,
     Mexico City, to IM, 25 Nov. 1931, IM Item 104, BFISC; Sergei Eisenstein,
     'The Principles of Film Form', trans. IM, *Close Up* 8:3 (Sep 1931); Ivan
     Anisimov, 'The Films of Eisenstein', *International Literature* No. 3 (1931), in
     Seton 1960, 494–503.
22   Attasheva to IM, n.d. [ca Oct. 1931], IM Item 108, BFISC; Eisenstein to IM, 25
     Nov. 1931, IM Item 104, BFISC; IM to Attasheva, 8 Oct. 1931; IM to Attasheva,
     24 Dec. 1931; IM to Attasheva, 21 Jan. 1932; all IM Item 108, BFISC.

23 *DW* 5 Dec. 1931, 6; 'Friends of the Soviet Union', *DW* 17 Dec. 1931, 5; *DW* 15 Dec. 1931, 4; 'Delegates' Reports', *DW* 9 Jan. 1932, 5; *DW* 14 Jan. 1932, 4.

24 *DW* 16 Jan. 1932, 6; 'Soviet and the Jews', *MG* 18 Jan. 1932, 11.

25 'The Delegations in March', *DW* 7 Jan. 1932, 5; 'Solidarity Delegation for May 1', *DW* 21 Mar. 1932, 5; 'May 1 Delegation to Soviet Union', *DW* 22 Mar. 1932, 5; 'Campaign for a Monster Delegation', *DW* 24 Mar. 1932, 5; 'Lancashire Keen on Delegation' *DW* 28 Mar. 1932, 5.

26 IM to Trotsky, 9 Oct. 1931.

27 Trotsky to IM, 9 Nov. 1931, Item 9279, MS Russ 13.1; Trotsky to IM [in Russian], 28 Nov. 1931, Item 9280, MS Russ 13.1 [translation by Steve Marder]; IM to Trotsky, 5 Dec. 1931, Item 3397, MS Russ 13.1.

28 Trotsky to IM, 9 Nov. 1931; Trotsky to Max Shachtman, 9 Nov. 1931, Trotsky 1979, 99; Trotsky to IM, 28 Nov. 1931.

29 IM to Trotsky, 5 Dec. 1931; Glotzer 1989, 81–2.

30 IM to Trotsky, 21 Jan. 1932, Item 3398, MS Russ 13.1; Trotsky to IM [in German], 31 Dec. 1931, Item 9281, MS Russ 13.1 [translation by Gerd Pohlmann].

31 IM to Trotsky, 21 Jan. 1932; IM to Trotsky, 31 Jul. 1932, Item 3399, MS Russ 13.1. See also IM to Max Shachtman, 21 Jan. 1932, IM Item 49 (1), BFISC.

32 Trotsky 1979, 375; Carr 1982, 216–7; Grant 2002, 27–9.

33 IM to Trotsky, 31 Jul. 1932; Trotsky to Reg Groves, 13 Jul. 1932 [intercepted letter, excerpt], KV2/598.

34 IM to Trotsky, 31 Jul. 1932.

35 Trotsky to IM [in French], 18 Dec. 1932, Item 9282; IM to Trotsky, 1 Mar. 1933, Item 3400; Trotsky to IM, 11 Mar. 1933, Item 9283; IM to Trotsky, 22 Mar. 1933, Item 3401; Trotsky to IM [in French], 29 Mar. 1933, Item 9284; IM to Trotsky [in German], n.d. [ca Mar. 1933], Item 3402 [translation by Gerd Pohlmann]; Trotsky to IM [in French], 5 May 1933, Item 9285; Trotsky to IM, 7 Jun. 1933, Item 9286; all MS Russ 13.1.

36 Bond to IM, 10 Oct. 1931 and 14 Jan. 1932, IM Item 75, BFISC; Regler 1959, 168; Emile Burns to IM, 6 Nov. 1932, IM Item 40–6, BFISC.

37 IM to Trotsky, 31 Jul. 1932.

38 KV2/598; DW 1 Mar. 1932, 4; *DW* 29 Mar. 1932, 6; *DW* 22 Apr. 1932, 4; *DW* 13 Jun. 1932, 4; *DW* 4 Apr. 1932, 4; *DW* 30 Jul. 1932, 4; *DW* 5 Mar. 1932, 6; '"Red" Summer School Sure of Success', *DW* 26 Jul. 1932, 6.

39 Valtin [Krebs] 1941, 321–4.

40 Valtin [Krebs] 1941, 325–6.

41 Valtin [Krebs] 1941, 326.

42 Valtin [Krebs] 1941, 324; Andrew 2010, 179; Andrew 1986, 520–1; Masters 1986, 48–9; Burke 2008, 87; Report by M/12, 11 Dec. [1931], KV2/3197.

43 KV2/598.

44 KV2/598, including Mechlovits to IM [in German], 15 Oct. 1932 [intercepted letter] and H.M.M. [Hugh M. Miller] to V. Vivian, 8 Nov. 1932.

45 Lella Florence to IM, 16 Dec. [1929?] and 'Feb something' [1931], IM Item 49 (2), BFISC.

46 Carr 1982, 387–9; Gross 1974, 222–7; Petersson 2013, 463–6; *World Anti-War Congress*, flyer, League Against Imperialism, London, Jun. 1932, and *United*

Front Against War: Report and Manifesto of the World Anti-War Congress at Amsterdam, August 27th–29th, 1932, both in CP/IORG/misc/04/03, LHASC.

47   IM to Trotsky, 31 Jul. 1932; 'Co-operators and War Menace', *DW* 26 Jul. 1932, 5.

48   'The "Anti-War Congress"', *MG* 29 Jul. 1932, 7; *United Front Against War*, Fisher 1988, 158–66.

49   *United Front Against War*, 4.

50   *United Front Against War*, 6–11.

51   Fisher 1988, 167–8.

52   KV2/598; Karl Schabrod Wikipedia entry, http://de.wikipedia.org/wiki/Karl_Schabrod (accessed 28 Aug. 2017).

53   KV2/598; KV2/599; 'Campaign Growing for November Delegation', *DW* 12 Oct. 1932, 6.

54   'British Delegation to the Soviet Union', *DW* 13 Oct. 1932, 6; 'National Anti-War Conference', *DW* 14 Nov. 1932, 1.

55   Report on 'Communist Activities' by County Police Office, Trafford Park, 6 Jan. 1933, KV2/598; 'Education or Armaments' *MG* 7 Jan. 1933, 17; 'Great Anti-War Meeting in London', *DW* 12 Jan. 1933, 2.

56   Report of Walthamstow police, 21 Feb. 1933, KV2/598; *DW* 24 Feb. 1933, 2;

57   'Great Anti-War Congress Prepares for Action', *DW* 6 Mar. 1933, 6; *War: Monthly Bulletin of the British Anti-War Council* No. 4, 15 Mar. 1933 [Montagu p 5], in CP/IORG/misc/04/03, LHASC; *National Congress Against War, Bermondsey Town Hall, March 4th and 5th 1933, War, Declaration of Council* (cyclostyled), in CP/IORG/misc/04/03, LHASC; John Strachey, *The British Anti-War Movement* (pamphlet, British Anti-War Movement, May 1933), 9–10, KV2/786.

58   Owen Morton Spencer, 'Bellicose Pacifists', *Sydney Morning Herald*, 13 May 1933, 5.

11. Gaumont-British

1   IM, *Scenario for One Reel Film cup tie special*, Aug. 1931, and *Notes on the One-reel Film Proposition cup tie special*, Aug. 1932, IM Item 27, BFISC.

2   *Notes on the One-reel Film Proposition cup tie special*; G. Skilbeck, Western Electric Company Ltd., to IM, 27 Apr. 1932, IM Item 49b, BFISC.

3   Frank Sainsbury to IM, 31 Aug. 1931; IM to Sainsbury, 10 Oct. 1931; both IM Item 49 (2), BFISC.

4   Anon. 1972, 172–241; Moorehead 1984, 66.

5   Anon. 172, 194–6; Moorehead 1984, 27; Sidney Cole to Anne Simor, 4 Oct. 1975, IM Item 16, BFISC; IM 1975, 224.

6   IM 1932, 107.

7   IM 1932, 106; G.A. Atkinson, 'Ivor Montagu, the B.B.C., James Fairlie, and Myself', unidentified newspaper clipping [probably early Oct. 1932], IM Item 7, BFISC.

8   'Film Societies', *MG* 6 Sep. 1932, 6; IM, 'A Federation of Film Societies', *WER* 17 Sep. 1932, 309–10.

9   Eisenstein to IM, date unclear, 1932, and IM to Eisenstein, 28 Nov. 1932, IM Item 104, BFISC; Geduld and Gottesman eds, 1970, 357, 368–9.

10   Geduld and Gottesman eds, 1970, 372 (*New Clarion* 8 May 1933); Seton 1960, 273 (*New Clarion* 29 Jul. 1933); IM, 'The Sinclair Tragedy', *NSN* 20 Jan. 1934, 85–6.

11 *WER* 1 Oct. 1932, 374, and 22 Oct. 1932, 483.

12 Allen Lane, John Lane the Bodley Head Ltd., to IM, 31 Oct. 1932; IM to Lane, 2 Nov. 1932; both in IM Item 46, BFISC.

13 *WER* 18 Mar. 1933, 305.

14 *WER* 25 Mar. 1933, 330; *NSN* 21 Apr. 1934, 597; *NSN* 25 Mar. 1934, 451.

15 *WER* 10 Dec. 1932, 702; *WER* 22 Oct. 1932, 483.

16 *WER* 22 Oct. 1932, 483; *WER* 12 Aug. 1933, 163.

17 *WER* 19 Nov. 1932, 614; *WER* 9 Sep. 1933, 247.

18 *WER* 25 Feb. 1933, 203; *WER* 22 Oct. 1932, 483.

19 *NSN* 28 Apr. 1934, 638; *DW* 8 May 1934, 4.

20 *WER* 8 Oct. 1932, 408; *WER* 7 Jan. 1933, 13–4; *WER* 17 Jun. 1933, 686.

21 *WER* 8 Oct. 1932, 408.

22 *WER* 26 Nov. 1932, 639; *WER* 4 Mar. 1933, 247; *WER* 15 Jul. 1933, 59.

23 IM 1977, 10; IM 1980b, 191; Studio accountant, Gaumont-British Picture Corporation Ltd., to IM, 21 Jan. 1933, intercepted letter, KV2/598.

24 'Company Meeting', *Times* 19 Sep. 1933, 18; Ostrer 2010, 146; Sedgwick 1996, 333–4; Curran and Porter eds, 1983, 57, 66.

25 Balcon 1969, 83.

26 IM 1980b, 191; Sedgwick 1996, 334.

27 *Visions* iv; IM 1980b, 191; 'New Films in London', *Times* 3 Apr. 1933, 12; Richards ed. 2000, 26–7.

28 Brown 2008, 254, 260 n14; IM Item 38, BFISC.

29 'Wings Over Everest', *MG* 4 Apr. 1933, 8.

30 *Visions* iv.

31 *Visions* iv.

32 Brown 1984, 98.

33 Rushes for *Visions* programme, 24 Nov. 1982, BFI National Archive.

34 'Some New Films of the Week', *Obs* 3 Jun. 1934, 3; P.R. [Paul Rotha], 'Wings Over Everest', *SS* 3:10 (Summer 1934), 73–4; Charles Davy, 'Wings Over Everest and Secrets of Nature', *The Bookman*, Jul. 1934, 196.

35 *DW* 2 Feb. 1934, 4; *DW* 24 Feb. 1934, 4; "Film is Now Pre-Eminent", *ST* 4 Feb. 1934, 22; J. Ralph Pinker, James B. Pinker & Son, to IM, 8 Nov. 1933; IM to Pinker, 18 Feb. 1934; both IM Item 48 (1), BFISC.

36 IM 1980b, 191–2; Spoto 1983, 141; McGilligan 2003, 157; Barr 1999, 162.

37 *Screen* iv, 89.

38 Miles 2011, 188; McGilligan 2003, 161; Truffaut 1967, 61.

39 Ostrer 2010, 186–97; Low 1985, 131; Sedgwick 1996, 343.

40 IM 1980b, 191–2; *Screen* iv, 88.

41 *Screen* iv 77–8; IM 1980b, 192–3; McGilligan 2003, 167–8; Taylor 1978, 130; Ryall 1986, 104; Spoto 1983, 143; Brown and Kardish 1984, 25; Bennett 2014, 53–4.

42 IM 1980b, 193; *FW* 239n.

43 *KW* 13 Sep. 1934, 20 Sep. 1934, and 4 Oct. 1934, quoted in Bamford 1999, 154; *MG* 30 Oct. 1934, 13; *Obs* 14 Oct. 1934, 18.

44 *Times* 18 Feb. 1935, 10.

45 IM 1980b, 193; IM, *WEH* 90, quoted in Spoto 1983, 149.

46 Durgnat 1974, 126; Glancy 2003, 7.

47   Ryall 1986, 105; Glancy 2003, 85–90; Jones 1987, 14. 'Company Meetings',
     Times 29 Sep. 1935, 18.
48   IM to Harold Boxall, 4 Feb. 1935; M.E. Balcon to IM, 6 Feb. 1935; IM to
     Boxall, 4 Mar. 1935; IM to S.C. Balcon, 25 Apr. 1935; Boxall to IM, 25 Apr.
     1935; IM to Boxall, 25 Apr. 1935; all in IM Item 43, BFISC.
49   M.E. Balcon to IM, 6 Feb. 1935; Andow et al. ed. 1983, 9–13; *Screen* iv, 97;
     'Film Society Personalities', *World Film News* 1:6 (Sep. 1936), 41.
50   *JACT* 1:2 (Aug 1935), 44; 'Technicians' Day of Reckoning', *JACT* 2:6 (Aug.–
     Oct. 1936), 62.
51   'Pioneers', 50; *Screen* iv, 97–8; Low 1985, 29.
52   'Recommendations of Committee of Production Procedure', 9 Nov. 1934,
     MEB-1086, BFISC; IM to S.C. Balcon, 5 Apr. and 25 Apr. 1935, IM Item 43, BFISC.
53   Mark Ostrer [?] to IM, 29 Oct. 1935, IM Item 43, BFISC.
54   KV2/599; McGilligan 2003, 180; Taylor 1978, 135; 'Lawn Tennis', *YP* 18 Jun. 1935, 4.
55   Sue Harper, '"Thinking Forward and Up": The British Films of Conrad Veidt',
     Richards ed. 2000, 131; R.K., '*Passing of the Third Floor Back*', *MG* 4 Feb. 1936,
     11; Graham Greene, in *The Spectator*, 1 Nov. 1935, Parkinson ed. 1995, 43.
56   William Hickey, 'These Names Make News', *DE* 12 Mar. 1934, 6; IM 1975,
     224, 247; Moorehead 1984, 27.
57   Hickey, 'These Names Make News'; Anon. 1972, 329–34; IM Items 181 and
     182, BFISC; David Collard, 'Comrade Auden', *Times Literary Supplement*, 20
     May 2009, 14; *DW* 21 Aug. 1934, 4; Marshall 1983, 86.
58   Gill Plain, *John Mills and British Cinema: Masculinity, Identity and Nation*
     (Oxford University, 2006), 31.
59   IM to Angus MacPhail, 17 Feb. 1936 and 24 Mar. 1936, IM Item 60, BFISC;
     cables between M.E. Balcon and Mark Ostrer, IM Item 61, BFISC.
60   IM, 'Note on Adaptation of *Secret Agent*', undated, and IM to M.E. Balcon, 4
     May 1936, IM Item 57, BFISC.
61   *FW* 124; Horrocks 2001, 153; Taylor 1978, 137.
62   'New Films in London', *Times* 11 May 1936, 10; Truffaut 1967, 73.
63   IM 1980b, 193; 'New Films in London', *Times* 7 Dec. 1936, 12.
64   'Gaumont Cinema', *Times* 5 Feb. 1937, 12; IM, Weekly Reports, G-B
     Shepherd's Bush, 1935–6, IM Item 60, BFISC; Mark Ostrer to M.E. Balcon,
     cable, 15 Nov. 1935, IM Item 61, BFISC.
65   '*King Solomon's Mines* (1937 film)', https://en.wikipedia.org/wiki/King_
     Solomon%27s_Mines_%281937_film%29 (accessed 28 Aug. 2017); Bennett
     2014, 50; IM Weekly Report, 15 May 1936, IM Item 60, BFISC; Richards,
     'Paul Robeson: The Black Man as Film Hero' in Barr ed. 1986, 337–8.
66   Balcon to Mark Ostrer [?], cable, 23 Nov. 1935; Balcon to Ostrer, cable, 26 Nov.
     1935; Ostrer [?] to Balcon, cable, 26 Nov. 1935; Ostrer [?] to Balcon, cable (2), 26
     Nov. 1935; Balcon to Ostrer, cable, 27 Nov. 1935; Boxall to Balcon, cable, 28 Nov.
     1935; Balcon to Boxall [?]. cable, 30 Nov. 1935; all in IM Item 61, BFISC.
67   IM, interview with Bert Hogenkamp, 6 Sep. 1974, in Hogenkamp 1986, 173 n41.
68   IM to Balcon, 1 Sep. 1936, IM Item 43, BFISC.
69   IM to Balcon, 1 Sep. 1936; IM 1980b, 193.
70   IM to Angus MacPhail, 14 Oct. 1936, IM Item 60, BFISC.

12. Fighting Fascism

1   'ECCI Statement on the German Situation and on the United Front',
     5 Mar. 1933, in Jane Degras, ed., *The Communist International, 1919–1943:
     Documents, Volume III, 1929–1943* (F. Cass, 1971), 253; 'Hitler, Fascism and the
     Workers!', *War* No. 4 (Mar. 1933), 10, in CP/IORG/misc/04/03, LHASC.

2   Gross 1974, 241–2; Koch 1996, 65–6; Miles 2011, 111; 'Note on Otto Katz', 4
     Aug. 1944, MI5, KV2/3221.

3   *DW* 24 Mar. 1933, 3; 'Fine London Meeting Against Fascist Terror', *DW* 28
     Mar. 1933, 5; 'New Committee for German Relief', *DW* 31 Mar. 1933, 5;
     'Note on Otto Katz', KV2/3221; Miles 2011, 115; Rolph 1973, 181; *Germany
     To-Day – Britain To-Morrow?* (pamphlet, 2nd edition, WIR, n.d. [ca Apr.
     1933]), in CP/ORG/misc/10/12, LHASC.

4   *Germany To-Day – Britain To-Morrow?*, 10–1; 'Biographische Datenbanken:
     Stoecker, Walter', www.bundesstiftung-aufarbeitung.de/wer-war-wer-in-
     der-ddr-%2363%3B-1424.html?ID=5250 (accessed 28 Aug. 2017); Elfriede
     Stoecker, Berlin, to Ivor and Eileen Montagu, 29 Apr. 1933, intercepted letter,
     KV2/598; Walter Stoecker to Helmuth and Helga Stoecker, 31 May 1933,
     intercepted letter [in German], KV2/598; Eileen Montagu to Registration
     Department, Friends Committee for Refugees & Aliens, 7 Nov. 1944, CP/
     IND/MONT/6/16, LHASC.

5   Toller to IM, 8 Mar. 1933; IM to Toller, 28 Mar. 1933; IM to Toller, 23 Apr. 1933;
     Toller to IM, 9 Jul. 1933; IM to Toller, 28 Jul. 1933; all in IM Item 462, BFISC.

6   *DW* 20 Apr. 1933, 4; *DW* 24 Apr. 1933, 4; *DW* 10 May 1933, 6; *DW* 20 May 1933,
     4; *DW* 24 May 1933, 3; 'Strike Chairman for the Square', *DW* 2 Jun. 1933, 3;
     'Thousands Attend London's Solidarity Day Meet', *DW* 12 Jun. 1933, 1; KV2/598.

7   Haslam 1984, 16–9; 'Sir John Simon's Statement', *Times* 15 Apr. 1933, 10.

8   Carr 1982, 226, 392–4; Gross 1974, 260; Valtin [Krebs] 1941, 471; 'On fascist
     reaction and increasing white terorr [*sic*]' (pamphlet) (ILD [1933]), delegates' folder,
     European Workers' Anti-Fascist Congress, CP/IND/MONT/4/11, LHASC.

9   Gross 1974, 251; McMeekin 2003, 267.

10   Miles 2011, 139–41; Wilkinson to IM, 26 Jun. 1933, intercepted letter,
     KV2/1382; Wilkinson to Katz, 27 Jun. 1933, intercepted letter, KV2/1382;
     G.M.L., SB report, 30 Jun. 1933, KV2/598; IM to Toller, 28 Jul. 1933, IM
     Item 462, BFISC; 'Reichstag Fire Sensation', *DH* 5 Jul. 1933; 'Revelations
     About the Reichstag Fire', *DW* 3 Jul. 1933.

11   KV2/598: Herbert Samuel to IM, 3 Oct. 1932; authorisation for mail
     intercept, 22 Jun. 1933; internal memos 6 Jul. 1933 and 7 Jul. 1933; notice of
     suspension of HOW, 8 Jul. 1933; KV2/599: minute sheet, 20 Apr. 1937.

12   IM, 'Memories of the Counter-Trial' (typescript, 1965), 6, 8–11, CP/IND/
     MONT/2/4, LHASC; Pritt 1965, 36–9, 56; Miles 2011, 151–2.

13   'Memories of the Counter-Trial', 3–4; Prof R. Abramov, Director, Institute
     of the History of the Bulgarian Communist Party, to IM, 2 Jul. 1965 and 24
     Jul. 1965, CP/IND/MONT/2/4, LHASC; Vernon 1982, 162.

14   'Memories of the Counter-Trial', 4, 7–8; Hill 1982, 53.

15   'Reichstag Fire', *Times* 14 Sep. 1933, 12.

16   'The Reichstag Fire Inquiry', *MG* 15 Sep. 1933, 4.

17 'Memories of the Counter-Trial', 11–2; *Times* 19 Sep. 1933, 5; *MG* 19 Sep. 1933, 12.

18 'Memories of the Counter-Trial', 4, 7.

19 'Memories of the Counter-Trial', 14; Pritt 1965, 63–4; Hays 1942, 349–50; *Official Findings*, 26.

20 'Reichstag Inquiry Report Endorsed at Great London Meetings', *DW* 25 Sep. 1933, 4; *DW* 23 Sep. 1933, 3; 'Helping Victims of Fascist Terror', *DW* 16 Oct. 1933, 3; KV2/599.

21 *DW* 26 Oct. 1933, 4; KV2/599.

22 IM 1969a, xiii; Seton 1960, 251–2; Leyda 1973, 304.

23 IM to Alexandrov, 4 Oct. 1933; 'Memories of the Counter-Trial', 14; Conquest 1990, 20; Applebaum 2004, 519; Montefiore 2004, 123; *DW* 15 Dec. 1933, 4.

24 KV2/599; Pritt 1965, 72–3.

25 Rolph 1973, 181–2; '"By Air to Save the Reds"', *DE* 23 Dec. 1933, 9; 'Memories of the Counter-Trial', 15; 'Reichstag Fire Trial', *Times* 23 Dec. 1933, 10; 'Reichstag Fire Trial', *Times* 27 Dec. 1933, 10.

26 'Red Cap of Death', *ST* 24 Dec. 1933, 9; 'A New Treason Trial?', *MG* 27 Dec. 1933, 9; Dorothy Woodman, 'Dimitrova and Her Son', *MG* 26 Jan. 1934, 9; 'Memories of the Counter-Trial', 15–6.

27 'Fight to Free Dimitrov', *DW* 9 Jan. 1934, 1; 'Victims of the Nazis', *MG* 13 Jan. 1934, 15; KV2/599.

28 'Dimitrov Must Be Released!', *DW* 17 Jan. 1934, 1; meeting notices, *DW* 17 Jan. 1934, 1, and *DW* 22 Jan. 1934, 1; KV2/599; 'Dimitroff', *Times* 18 Jan. 1934, 13; 'Dimitroff', *Times* 21 Feb. 1934, 15; 'The Release of Dimitroff', *Times* 28 Feb. 1934, 14: Pritt 1965, 74–7.

29 Valtin [Krebs] 1941, 492–3; Fischer 1948, 308n–09n; Miles 2011, 162; Koch 1996, 57; 'Memories of the Counter-Trial', 15.

30 IM to Hogenkamp, 2 Apr. 1979, IM Item 401, BFISC; IM to Katz, intercepted letter, 12 Jan. 1934, KV2/1382.

31 Hogenkamp 1986, 79–80; Charles Mann, 'Film Section of the W.T.M.', *DW* 7 Nov. 1933, 6. See also Ryan 1986 vol. 1, 206–8.

32 Low 1979b, 179; Smith 2013b, 243; Ryan 1986 vol. 1, 204.

33 Hogenkamp 1986, 171 (quoting Montagu in a 1974 interview); Ryan 1986 vol. 1, 208–10; Hogenkamp 1979, 260; 'Our Complete List', *Kino News* (Winter 1935), 4.

34 IM 1935; *FW* 266–7; Hogenkamp 1986, 83–7; Turvey 2000, 40.

35 Ryan 1986 vol. 1, 286–8; Hogenkamp 1986, 111, 222; KV2/599.

36 Hannington 1979, 285.

37 *DW* 21 Jul. 1934, 5; Smith 2013b, 252–3.

38 IM and Mrs Montagu to Isabel Brown, 24 May 1934, intercepted change of address postcard, KV2/599; SB report, 22 Jan. 1935, KV2/599.

39 *DW* 9 Mar. 1934, 3; *DW* 18 Apr. 1934, 4; KV2/599.

40 'Big Support for Soviet Friends Conference', *DW* 28 Jun. 1934, 2; *DW* 29 Jun. 1934, 4; 'Britain Leads in To-Day's War Race', *DW* 2 Jul. 1934, 1; KV2/599.

41 'Youth Anti-War Parade To-Day', *DW* 1 Sep. 1934, 1; *DW* 6 Sep. 1934, 4; KV2/599.

42 IM to Andrew Rothstein, 14 Aug. 1934, intercepted letter, KV2/599; Conquest 1990, 75.

43 File note, letter of Louis Gibarti to IM, ca Apr. 1934, KV2/599; '279 Delegates at German Relief Conference', *DW* 4 Jun. 1934, 3; KV2/599.

44 'Ban on Saar Delegate', *ST* 3 Jun. 1934, 18; 'An Interview with Thaelmann', *MG* 4 Jun. 1934, 11.

45 'London's Counter-Challenge to Mosley Fascists', *DW* 7 Jun. 1934, 1; 'London Workers Storm Olympia', *DW* 8 Jun. 1934, 1; *BB*.

46 *BB* 5, 6, 7, 22, 27, 28, 30.

47 *DW* 19 Jul. 1934, 3; *DW* 25 Jul. 1934, 4; 'Fight to Save Victims of Fascism', *DW* 1 Aug. 1934, 2; 'Immediate Aid for Thaelmann', *DW* 14 Jul. 1934, 1; KV2/599.

48 Branson 1985, 122–4.

49 *DW* 22 Sep. 1934, 1; KV2/599; 'Labour Party Conference', *Times* 2 Oct. 1934, 7.

50 Simone [Katz] 1941, 147–3; 'Glasgow's Drive for Food Ship', *DW* 20 Nov. 1934, 1; file note, Nov. 1934, KV2/599; letters from German Relief Committee, Paris, to Isabel Brown, Nov. 1934, KV2/599.

51 Gross 1974, 270–1; Campbell 1982, 84–5; Bert Hogenkamp, '*Free Thaelmann*: Thaelmann's trail', *Jump Cut* 21 (Nov. 1979), 27; IM 1980a, 130–1; KV2/599; *Visions* iv rushes.

52 IM to Bert Hogenkamp, 10 Mar. 1978 and 2 Apr. 1979, IM Item 401, BFISC.

53 'Film Ban at Kingsway Hall Meeting', *DW* 7 Mar. 1935, 1; *FW* 264–5; J. Brooke Wilkinson, BBFC, to IM, 14 Jun. 1935, IM Item 70, BFISC; *DW* 22 Jul. 1935, 4; *Kino News* (Winter 1935), 4.

54 Clerk of the Council, LCC, to Secretary, Brunel & Montagu Ltd, 8 Apr. 1935 and 11 May 1935, and other correspondence, IM Item 70, BFISC; 'Anti-Fascist Films', 2.

55 *DW* 7 Mar. 1935, 1; KV2/599; Peter Porcupine, 'Film Notes', *DW* 25 Jun. 1935, 4; *DW* 3 Jul. 1935, 4; Peter Porcupine, 'Film Notes', *DW* 9 Jul. 1935, 4; Olwen Vaughan, London Film Institute Society, to IM, 4 Nov. 1935, IM Item 7, BFISC.

56 Katz to Brown, 25 Apr. 1935 and 22 May 1938, intercepted letters, KV2/1383; col. Sir Vernon Kell to Sir Ernest Holderness, Home Office, cc C.J. Norton, Foreign Office, 2 May 1935, KV2/1383; Brown to Katz, 24 May 1935, intercepted letter, KV2/1383; Kell to Holderness, 1 Jun. 1935, KV2/1383; IM to Princess Bibesco, 7 Jun. 1935, intercepted letter, KV2/1383; Kell to Norton, 4 Jul. 1935, KV2/1383; file note, 10 Jul. 1935, KV2/599; Kell to Norton, 17 Sep. 1935, KV2/1383.

57 KV2/599; IM to Mark Ostrer, managing director and chairman, Gaumont-British Picture Corporation, 27 Aug. 1935, IM Item 43, BFISC; 'Peace Rally for Tees-Side', *DW* 16 Oct. 1935, 2.

58 KV2/599, including Sir Vernon Kell, MI5, to J.J. Norton, Foreign Office, 12 Oct. 1935.

59 KV2/599; 'British Public Men's Greetings to U.S.S.R.', *DW* 3 Dec. 1935, 1; 'Great Congress Opens To-Day in London', *DW* 7 Dec. 1935, 3; 'Anglo-Russian Relations', *Times* 9 Dec. 1935, 8.

60 'Great Congress Opens To-Day in London'.

13. *Moscow and Madrid*

1   'Soviet Union and Peace', *DW* 21 May 1936, 5; KV2/599.

2   Tucker 1990, 303; IM 1936c, 46, 48.

3   IM 1936c, 47; Fischer 1986, 347–8; Tucker 1990, 357–8.

4   IM 1936b, 47; Conquest 1990, 74; David-Fox 2012, 300; *SCR Annual Report 1936*, 6, in CP/IND/MONT/8/9, LHASC; 'Uproar in Anglo-Soviet Society', *Blackshirt* 11 Jul. 1936, quoting *DMa* 3 Jul. 1936.
5   IM 1936b; Fischer 1986, 343–4; Tucker 1990, 554–5.
6   Eisenstein to IM, 12 May 1936 and 11 Jun. [?] 1936, IM Item 107, BFISC.
7   KV2/599; Seton 1960, 361; Kenez 1992, 150; Isaac Babel, *Benia Krik: a film-novel*, translated by Ivor Montagu and S.S. Nolbandov (Collet's, 1935).
8   Rogovin 1998, 17.
9   Pritt 1965, 109; Tucker 1990, 372–3; D.N. Pritt, The Zinoviev Trial (Victor Gollancz, 1936); The Moscow Trial (Anglo-Russian Parliamentary Committee, 1936); West [Allason] 2005, 198, 311; D.N. Pritt, At the Moscow Trial (International Publishers, 1937).
10 IM 1936d, 123–4, 126, 127–8.
11 IM, letter to editor, *NSN* 2 Jan. 1937, 11; Friedrich Adler, *The Witchcraft Trial in Moscow* (Labour Publications, 1936), www.marxists.org/archive/adler-friedrich/1936/trials.htm (accessed 28 Aug. 2017).
12 See e.g. Conquest 1990, 147–67.
13 File note, ca Jan.–Feb. 1937, KV2/1001.
14 West [Allason] 2005, 117.
15 Firsov 2004, 60.
16 IM, 'How Press Flung a Smokescreen Over Moscow Trial', *DW* 2 Feb. 1937, 4.
17 IM 1937c, 326, 330, 332; Coates and Coates eds, 1937, 330, 332.
18 Charles Sumner, 'Ivor Montagu – The Hireling', *Information Bulletin of the British Committee for the Defence of Leon Trotsky* No. 1 (May 1937), 3–8, CP/IND/MONT/4/10, LHASC.
19 Kathleen P. Jensen to Victor Gollancz, n.d. (ca May 1937); Gollancz to IM, 31 May 1937; both CP/IND/MONT/7/6, LHASC.
20 *Kino News*, Spring 1936, in Macpherson ed. 1980, 151; KV2/599.
21 IM to Balcon, 1 Sep. 1936, IM Item 43, BFISC; Koestler 2005, 394–5; Ryan 1986 vol. 1, 228–9; 'Supply of Arms to Spain', *Times* 25 Sep. 1936, 8; KV2/599; *Report, Committee of Inquiry into Breaches of International Law in Spain* (King & Son, Oct. 1936), quoted in Esch 1951, 38. See also 'Report of Committee of Inquiry', *DW* 7 Oct. 1936, 3.
22 'Anti-Fascist Films', 3; Hogenkamp iv; Dobson 2006, 16, 57.
23 KV2/599; 'Anti-Fascist Films', 3; Baxter 1994, 163.
24 Norman McLaren, letter to his parents, 2 Dec. 1936, Grierson Archive, University of Stirling; 'Anti-Fascist Films', 3.
25 Hogenkamp iv; 'Anti-Fascist Films', 3.
26 McLaren, letter to his parents.
27 'Anti-Fascist Films', 4.
28 Gubern and Hammond 2012, 270–2.
29 'Anti-Fascist Films', 4; KV2/599.
30 '"The Defence of Madrid"', *MG* 29 Dec. 1936, 10.
31 '"The Defence of Madrid"'.
32 '"The Defence of Madrid"'; *Kino News* information sheet, 25 Jan. 1937, CP/IND/MONT/9/8, LHASC; Hyde 1952, 58; Jones 1987, 181; Ryan 1986 vol. 1, 255n.

33 IM 1937a; 'Read This Again at 7:30 Tonight', *DW* 18 Feb. 1937, 2.

34 Hogenkamp 1986, 157, 174, 224; *Kino Films Price List* and film flyers, CP/IORG/misc/04/04, LHASC; *DW* 3 Apr. 1937, 5; Gubern and Hammond 2012, 274; Smith 2013b, 254.

35 Miles 2011, 235; Koestler 2005, 409; Platts-Mills 2002, 92–3.

36 Platts-Mills 2002, 93–4.

37 'Future Use of Sanctions', *MG* 30 Sep. 1936, 12.

38 Bennett 1988, 49–52; Chaudron 1989, 269–74; McIntyre and Gardner, eds, 1971, 361–4.

39 IM, 'Eden Slashes Dominion Delegate's Speech', *DW* 1 Jun. 1937, 3; IM 1937d; Skudder 1986, 35–46; Chaudron 1989, 274–5.

40 *Hansard* (Commons) 9 Jun. 1937, vol. 324 col. 1738; 'Critic', 'A London Diary', *NSN* 5 Jun. 1937, 914; Robert Dell, 'The Garden of Eden', *NSN* 12 Jun. 1937, 953–4; Robert Dell, letter to editor, *NSN* 19 Jun. 1937, 999; IM to Andrew Rothstein, [?] Jun. 1937, excerpted KV2/599.

41 IM 1937d, 409.

42 *DW* 2 Feb. 1937, 2; 'Labour Sport on Threshold of New Life', *DW* 12 Feb. 1937, 6; *DW* 13 Feb. 1937, 6; *DW* 17 Apr. 1937, 6; *DW* 6 Nov. 1937, 6; *DW* 8 Nov. 1937, 6; *DW* 13 Nov. 1937, 6; *DW* 13 Nov. 1937, 6; MI5 file notes, 2 Feb. 1937, 2 May 1937, 15 Jul. 1937, 11 Nov. 1937, 12 Nov. 1937, 18 Nov. 1937, 24 Nov. 1937, 6 Dec. 1937, ca 10 Dec. 1937, KV2/599.

43 Kevin Morgan, 'The Communist Party and the *Daily Worker* 1930–56' in Andrews et al. ed. 1995, 148; Cockburn 1967, 170.

44 IM, 'The World This Week', *DW* 16 Jan. 1937, 4; IM, 'The World This Week', *DW* 14 Aug. 1937, 4; IM, '*The Road to War*: Review', *DW* 26 Apr. 1937, 4.

45 IM, 'Bloody Carnival in Malaga', *DW* 11 Feb. 1937, 4; IM, 'The World This Week', *DW* 12 Jun. 1937, 4.

46 IM, 'The World This Week', *DW* 10 Jul. 1937, 4; 'The World This Week', *DW* 14 Aug. 1937, 4.

47 IM, 'India Goes to the Polls', *DW* 19 Jan. 1937, 3; IM, 'This Pride of Empire', *DW* 13 May 1937, 4; IM, 'Round the World with Ivor Montagu', *DW* 21 Aug. 1937, 4.

48 IM 1937b, 282; IM, 'A Blow at Fascism', *DW* 19 Jun. 1937, 4; Firsov 2004, 67; Conquest 1990, 205; IM, 'The World This Week', *DW* 10 Jul. 1937, 4; Hallas 2008, 145; IM, 'Round the World with Ivor Montagu', *DW* 24 Jul. 1937, 4; John Martens, 'The J.V. Stalin Moscow-Volga Canal', http://john-martens.com/stalin_moscow_volga_canal.html (accessed 28 Aug. 2017).

49 Tucker 1990, 374; Medvedev 1989, 356–7; Citrine 1938, 364; http://persona.rin.ru/eng/view/f/0/32997/dmitry-v-bogomolov (accessed 28 Aug. 2017); Stern 2007, 207; Chase 2001, 492; Beckett 2004, 54, 58–62; Thorpe 2000, 237–41; Morgan and Cohen 2003, 35–6; ECCI papers, CP/CENT/ci/01/09, LHASC; http://spartacus-educational.com/TUcohenR.htm (accessed 28 Aug. 2017).

50 IM 1937b, 283; Gide 1938, 6, 34, 67, 138; IM, 'Light – But Heavy Enough for a Tombstone', *DW* 27 Oct. 1937, 7.

14. Agitprop

1   F.D. Klingender and Stuart Legg, *Money Behind the Screen: A Report Prepared on Behalf of the Film Council* (Film Council, 1937); IM, 'Money Behind the Films', *DW* 3 Mar. 1937, 7.

2   'Technicians Review the Past and Discuss the Future', *CT* 3:11 (Aug.–Sep. 1937), 119.

3   IM 1937f, 122, 120, 121.

4   Jones 1987, 100–1; Andow et al. ed. 1983, 17; Sidney Cole, 'Quota and Quality', *JACT* 2:6 (Aug.–Oct. 1936), 46–8; George H. Elvin, 'Ten Years – of What?', *CT* 4:15 (May–Jun. 1938), 15–8.

5   Low 1985, 50; Low 1979, 6; Cinematograph Films Act 1938, Sections 25, 26, 34; Elvin, 'Ten Years – of What?', 17.

6   IM 1936a; SB report, 7 Jan. 1937, KV2/599; Cinematograph Films Act 1938, Sections 4, 35.

7   IM 1937e.

8   IM, 'Profit-sharks Kill British Films', *DW* 3 Dec. 1937, 4.

9   IM, 'Profit-sharks Kill British Films', *DW* 3 Dec. 1937, 4; IM 1937e.

10 IM 1938a.

11 IM 1975, 224; Anon. 1972, 400–1; 'Anti-Fascist Films', 2–3; Thorold Dickinson, '£10,000,000 for £18', *CT* 4:15 (May–Jun. 1938), 19; Barbara Frey, Secretary, Film Society, to IM, 8 Dec. 1937, enclosing letter from F. Del Giudice representing Luce Institute, IM Item 7, BFISC.

12 MI5 file note, 17 Dec. 1937, KV2/599; Hogenkamp iv; 'Anti-Fascist Films', 5.

13 'Anti-Fascist Films', 5; Hogenkamp iv.

14 IM to Clement Attlee, 7 Jan. 1937 [*sic*, but must be 1938], CP/IND/MONT/7/1, LHASC; Embajador de la Republica Española en Londres, letter of accreditation for IM, 10 Jan. 1938, IM Item 84, BFISC; Harry Pollitt, CPGB Central Committee, To Whom It May Concern, 12 Jan. 1938, IM Item 84, BFISC; MI5 file note, 13 Jan. 1938, KV2/599.

15 IM, Producer, PFI, to Chief of Cinema Dept, Subsecretariat of Propaganda, 15 Jan. 1938, IM Item 84, BFISC; Fischer 1986, 475.

16 Hell to IM, 17 Jan. 1938, IM Item 84, BFISC.

17 'Anti-Fascist Films', 5; Cole 1938, 1; Dickinson 1938, 30; Hogenkamp iv.

18 IM to Bert Hogenkamp, 9 Sep. 1974, IM Item 401, BFISC; Cole 1938, 1; Montagu UK departure and arrival dates, KV2/599; Sidney Cole to Anne Simor, 4 Oct. 1975, IM Item 16, BFISC; Hogenkamp iv; Dickinson 1938, 30.

19 IM, American Broadcast, Station EAR, Madrid, 14 Mar. 1938, IM Item 84, BFISC; 'Anti-Fascist Films', 6; Hogenkamp iv; IM to Monsieur Gay, 19 Mar. 1938, IM Item 84, BFISC.

20 Fischer 1986, 491–2; Ejército del Centro de España, letter of authorisation to Ivor Montagu to film at the front lines, 11 Mar. 1938, IM Item 84, BFISC.

21 Claudín 1975, 236.

22 Ryan 1986 vol. 1, 234; 'Anti-Fascist Films', 6.

23 Dickinson 1938, 30; *DW* 25 Jun. 1938, 4; Farr 1938, 90.

24 Hogenkamp iv; IM to Bert Hogenkamp, 9 Sep. 1974, IM Item 401, BFISC.

25 Farr 1938, 90; Ryan 1986 vol. 1, 220.

26 Ryan 1986 vol. 1, 222; 'Anti-Fascist Films', 6; Jane Morgan, 'Prisoners Talk in This Newsreel', *DW* 26 Apr. 1938, 3.

27 Low 1979, 229; 'Intervention in Spain', *MG* 28 Oct. 1938, 3.

28 Ryan 1986 vol. 1, 74, 222, 234–5; 'Anti-Fascist Films', 7.

29 Montagu's notes, Discussion of Exceptions, 9 Dec. 1938 and 12 Dec. 1938, IM Item 71, BFISC.

30 'Memorandum of evidence to be submitted to the Cinematograph Advisory Committee to the Home Office on the subject of sub-standard films by Messrs Kino Films (1935) Ltd and Progressive Film Institute Ltd', n.d. (ca Jan. 1939), CP/IND/MONT/9/8, LHASC, also IM Item 263, BFISC.

31 IM to Geoffrey Mander MP, 2 Jan. 1939, IM Item 71, BFISC; *Screen* iv, 90; 'Anti-Fascist Films', 7; Ryan 1986 vol. 1, 75.

32 Hogben 1974; IM to Julius Hogben, 15 May 1974, IM Item 279, BFISC.

33 Marris 1980, 86; Low 1979, 190.

34 MI5 file note, 19 Sep. 1938, KV2/599; CPGB 15th Congress Proceedings, 18 Sep. 1938, CP/CENT/cong/04/07, LHASC.

35 I.M., 'Two Good Films', *DW* 5 Dec. 1938, 2; Ryan 1986 vol. 1, 236.

36 Kino ad, *DW* 29 Oct. 1935, 5; Jane Morgan, 'New Film Shows Big Congress', *DW* 5 Oct. 1938, 5.

37 IM 1938b.

38 MI5 file note, 17 Jan. 1938, KV2/599; Shearer 2004, 103.

39 Harry Pollitt, 'Economic Security, Peace and Democracy', Report to 15th Congress of the CPGB, *For Peace and Plenty: Report of the Fifteenth Congress of the C.P.G.B.* (CPGB, 1938), 26–7.

40 Hogenkamp iv ('I put the idea to the Party'); *Screen* iv, 96 ('The Party man who was running the campaign against Chamberlain wanted *Peace and Plenty*'); Ryan 1986 vol. 1, 236.

41 *Screen* iv, 92; Ryan 1986 vol. 1, 236.

42 *Screen* iv, 91, 92; 'A Communist Film', *Times* 20 Apr. 1939, 12.

43 Ryan 1986 vol. 1, 238–9; Hogenkamp iv; Hogenkamp 1986, 202–3; 'Political Notes', *Times* 15 Jun. 1939, 8; IM to Eisenstein, 1 May 1939, IM Item 104, BFISC.

44 Ellen Wilkinson, *The Town That Was Murdered: The Life-Story of Jarrow* (Victor Gollancz, 1939); *CT* 4:20 (Mar.–Apr. 1939), 182; Ryan 1986 vol. 1, 251–2.

45 *DW* 15 Jan. 1938, 6; 'Biggest March of Memory', *DW* 13 Sep. 1938, 5; 'A Worker's Notebook', *DW* 24 Nov. 1938, 2; *DW* 26 Nov. 1938, 6; *DW* 18 Feb. 1939, 6; *DW* 1 Aug. 1939, 8; *DW* 22 Mar. 1939, 6; *DW* 23 Mar. 1939, 23; MI5 file notes, 21 Jul. 1938, 11 Sep. 1938, 20 Nov. 1938, 29 Nov. 1938, 1 Aug. 1939; IM, 'What is Freedom? – 7', *News Chronicle* 11 Jul. 1939, CP/IND/MONT/12/10, typescript in CP/IND/MONT/3/8, LHASC.

46 IM, 'Museum' of German Artists', *DW* 12 Jul. 1938, 5; IM, 'Five Point Plan for France Today', *DW* 9 May 1939, 2; Lazitch and Drachkovitch 1986, 103; Dallin 1955, 47–9, 87.

47 IM, 'Something to Grouse About', *DW* 12 Aug. 1939, 7; IM, 'Fate of H.G. Wells', *DW* 16 Aug. 1939, 7; IM, 'Strongest Country in the World', *DW* 25 Aug. 1939, 2.

15. Espionage

1   Cyril Kemp, report to Supt. 'C' Division, Watford, 25 May 1940, KV2/599;
     Eileen Montagu, [Communist] Party Registration Form, 17 Nov. 1942, CP/
     CENT/pers/5/03, LHASC.

2   Hyde 1952, 79.

3   Macleod 1997, 101; Campbell 1939; Johnstone 1997, 28–30.

4   IM, 'ARP 'Fourth Army' Weakened by Wage Attack', *DW* 19 Sep. 1939,
     2; IM, 'How Not to Get Munitions', *DW* 23 Sep. 1939, 3; IM, 'How to
     Get Munitions', *DW* 25 Sep. 1939, 3; IM, 'Ivor Montagu Tours the Great
     Black-Out', *DW* 29 Sep. 1939, 3; IM, 'Some New Trenches and Some Tory
     "Dugouts"', *DW* 3 Oct. 1939, 3.

5   McDermott and Agnew 1996, 247; IM, 'Poland and Freedom', *DW* 14 Oct.
     1939, 4; IM, 'Poland and Freedom', *DW* 17 Oct. 1939, 3.

6   IM, 'Ideologies and Force', *DW* 25 Nov. 1939, 4; IM 1939b; IM, 'We Want
     Peace', *DW* 18 Jan. 1940, 3.

7   Pollitt to IM, 1 Nov. 1939, 21 Nov. 1939 and 23 Nov. 1939, CP/IND/MONT/8/6,
     LHASC; 'More Helpers Wanted', *DW* 4 Dec. 1939, 1; Mahon 1976, 257.

8   IM 1940a.

9   *DW* 2 Dec. 1939, 5; *DW* 6 Jan. 1940, 5; *DW* 27 Jan. 1940, 5; *DW* 23 Feb. 1940,
     4; file notes, 13 Jan. 1940, 2 Feb. 1940, 2 Dec. 1939, 20 Jan. 1940, KV2/599; IM,
     'New Book Blows Up Anti-Soviet Pretensions', *DW* 22 Feb. 1940, 4.

10   Citrine 1940, 53, 73–4, 77, 93–4, 105, 133, 138, 140, 155, 162–3, 178; 'Need of
     Help to Finland', *Times* 10 Feb. 1940, 6.

11   *DW* 13 Feb. 1940, 2; file note, 16 Feb. 1940, KV2/599.

12   Citrine 1940, 10–11; IM, 'When Two Knights of the Empire Shake Hands',
     DW 23 Mar. 1940, 4.

13   IM, application for exit permit, 26 Jan. 1940, KV2/599; O.A.H. [Oswald
     Harker], MI5, to S.A. Newsam, Home Office, 26 Jan. 1940, KV2/599;
     Newsam to Stafford, Passport Office, 2 Feb. 1940, KV2/599.

14   'Government Ban Our Reporters from Finland', *DW* 5 Feb. 1940, 1.

15   IM, 'The Things I Would Look For in U.S.S.R.', *DW* 10 Feb. 1940, 4.

16   *DW* 10 Feb. 1940, 1; 'Banned Reporters', *DW* 12 Feb. 1940, 1; file note, 11
     Feb. 1940, KV2/599.

17   *Hansard* (Commons) 14 Feb. 1940, vol. 357 col. 754–5; 'Our London
     Correspondence', *MG* 15 Feb. 1940, 6.

18   IM to Attlee, 16 Feb. 1940, and Attlee to IM, 20 Feb. 1940, CP/IND/
     MONT/8/4, LHASC.

19   File note, 6 Feb. 1940; Hollis, memo to D.4b., 10 Feb. 1940; Hollis, memo to B.9,
     10 Feb. 1940; G.H. Ferguson (for Lt. Col. J.H. Adam) to S.C.O.s Perth, Newcastle,
     London, Folkestone, Newhaven, Southampton, Shoreham, Heston, Hull, 12 Feb.
     1940; [?] to Col. Liam Archer, Defence Ministry, Dublin, 14 Feb. 1940; E. Gilfillan,
     Royal Ulster Constabulary, Belfast, to Capt. C.M. Liddell, 23 Feb. 1940; Liddell [?]
     to Gilfillan, 1 Mar. 1940; file note, 13 Mar. 1940; all KV2/599.

20   Snyder 2011, 125–6, 135–8; Montefiore 2004, 340–1; IM, 'The Polish Plot',
     DW 4 May 1943, 2.

21   *FUM*, 4, 5, 10, 21–2; D.N. Pritt to Marston Printing Co., 29 Feb. 1940, CP/

IND/MONT/6/7, LHASC.

22 *DW* 30 Mar. 1940, 6; *DW* 2 Apr. 1940, 4; *DW* 5 Apr. 1940, 4; *DW* 11 Apr. 1940, 4; *DW* 20 Apr. 1940, 4; *DW* 29 Apr. 1940, 1; file note, 4 Apr. 1940, KV2/599. See also IM, 'Planning the New War on Russia', *Russia To-Day*, March 1940, summary in KV2/599.

23 'War is No Excuse for Low Wages', *DW* 16 Apr. 1940, 4.

24 'Labour & the War: Our Conference', *LM* 22:3 (Mar. 1940), 143; IM 1940b, 279, 280, 281.

25 'Labour and New Government', *Times* 14 May 1940, 10; file note, 14 May 1940, KV2/599.

26 Emile Burns, 'Strachey Progresses Backwards', *DW* 2 Mar. 1940, 4; John Strachey, letter, *NSN* 27 Apr. 1940, 559.

27 File note, 26 Apr. 1940, KV2/599; file note, 26 Apr. 1940, KV2/786.

28 File note, 30 Apr. 1940, KV2/599; William Rust, letter, *NSN* 4 May 1940, 588–9; file note, 22 May 1940, KV2/786.

29 Strachey 1940.

30 IM to Strachey, 19 Jul. 1940; Strachey to IM, 22 Jul. 1940; IM to Strachey, 28 Jul. 1940; Strachey to IM, 2 Aug. 1940; IM to Strachey, 9 Aug. 1940; Strachey to IM, 16 Aug. 1940; IM to Strachey, 21 Aug. 1940; Strachey to IM, 26 Aug. 1940; all in CP/IND/MONT/6/13, LHASC.

31 Strachey to IM, 16 Aug. 1940; IM to Strachey, 28 Jul. 1940; IM to Strachey, 21 Aug. 1940; Strachey to IM, 26 Aug. 1940; all in CP/IND/MONT/6/13, LHASC.

32 File note, 21 Sep. 1939, KV2/599; SB report, 20 Feb. 1940, KV2/599.

33 Cyril Kemp, report to Supt. 'C' Division, Watford, 25 May 1940, KV2/599; file note, 25 Apr. 1940, KV2/599; Capt. S.M.E. Fairman to Sir Vernon Kell, 30 May 1940, KV2/599.

34 Lt. Col. O.A. Harker to Capt. Fairman, 15 Jun. 1940, KV2/599; file note, 18 Jun. 1940, KV2/599; Sgt. Murphy to Supt. 'C' Division, Watford, 1 Jul. 1940, KV2/599; Fairman to Harker, 2 Jul. 1940, KV2/599.

35 *Venona*, London to Moscow, No. 812, 25 Jul. 1940; Andrew 2010, 378–9.

36 *Venona*, London to Moscow, No. 812, 25 Jul. 1940.

37 *Venona*, London to Moscow, No. 895, 16 Aug. 1940; Andrew 2010, 379.

38 *Venona*, London to Moscow, No. 987, 6 Sep. 1940; Andrew 2010, 379; Macintyre 2010, 89; Sir Vernon Kell, MI5, to Sir Alexander Maxwell, Home Office, 15 May 1940, KV2/1553.

39 *Venona*, Moscow to London, No. 450, 7 Sep. 1940; *Venona*, London to Moscow, No. 1071, 26 Sep. 1940.

40 *Venona*, London to Moscow, No. 1099, 2 Oct. 1940. Words in square brackets were inserted by the translator.

41 *Venona*, London to Moscow, No. 1149, 11 Oct. 1940; *Venona*, London to Moscow, No. 1165, 15 Oct. 1940.

42 Macintyre 2010, 90–1; *Venona*, London to Moscow, No. 990, 7 Sep. 1940; *Venona*, London to Moscow, No. 1170, 16 Oct. 1940.

43 *Venona*, London to Moscow, No. 1188, 18 Oct. 1940.

44 *Venona*, London to Moscow, No. 1255, 4 Nov. 1940; *Venona*, London to Moscow, No. 1424, 20 Dec. 1940; F.2.a., 'The Case of D.F. Springhall', 25

Aug. 1943, KV2/1596.

45   Extract from Special Material from SIS (MI6), 4 Sep.–19 Oct. 1940, KV2/599; file note, 9 Nov. 1940, KV2/599.

46   Extract from Tel. Check Temple Bar 4277, 3 Mar. 1941, KV2/599; SB report, 17 Apr. 1941, KV2/599.

47   IM 1938b, 685; *TC*, 34, 49, 134.

48   R.P. Dutt to IM, 29 Jul. 1940, CP/IND/MONT/5/9, LHASC.

49   R.P. Dutt to IM, 10 Aug. 1940, CP/IND/MONT/5/9, LHASC.

50   D.N. Pritt, 'The Traitor Class', *DW* 25 Sep. 1940, 4; Pritt to IM, 24 Sep. 1940, CP/IND/MONT/2/9, LHASC; Harry Pollitt, review of *The Traitor Class*, typescript, CP/IND/MONT/6/6, LHASC.

51   Rust 1940; William Rust to IM, 15 Oct. 1940, CP/IND/POLL/03/05, LHASC.

52   IM to William Rust, n.d. [ca Oct. 1940], CP/IND/POLL/03/05.

53   IM 1941, 31; IM, 'The Partners', *DW* 9 Jan. 1941, 5.

54   IM, 'Rassulayevites …', *DW* 25 Oct. 1939, 4; IM, 'Socialist Union', *DW* 1 Aug. 1940, 6; IM, 'Pensioners of Socialism', *DW* 14 Sep. 1940, 6; IM, 'Heard Soviet Festivities', *DW* 2 Jan. 1941, 7.

55   IM, 'Garbo in Plot No. 2', *DW* 19 Feb. 1940, 4.

56   IM, 'Charlie Hits Back', *DW* 16 Dec. 1940, 6; IM, 'Chaplin and His Critics', *WNV* 21:5 (1 Feb. 1941), 78.

57   File note, 28 Jan. 1941, KV2/599; file note, 18 Jan. 1941, KV2/599; file note, 21 Apr. 1941, KV2/599.

58   File note, 28 Apr. 1941, KV2/599; Gallacher 1966, 277.

59   Tel. check, 9 May 1941, KV2/599; T.M. Harmer, Ministry of Labour and National Service, to Major W.A. Alexander, MI5, 24 May 1941, KV2/599. See also M. Johnstone for Major Alexander to Harmer, 8 May 1941, KV2/599; Alexander to Harmer, 21 May 1941, KV2/599; file note, M. Johnstone, 1 Jun. 1941, KV2/599; file note, 25 Jun. 1941, KV2/600

60   Platts-Mills 2002, 134.

61   SB report, 4 May 1941, KV2/599.

62   IM, 'Hess and His Friends', *WNV* 21:21 (24 May 1941), 321–33.

63   Writ, 6 Jun. 1941, between the Duke of Hamilton, plaintiff, and H. Goodman and others, defendants; Writ, 6 Jun. 1941, between the Duke of Hamilton, plaintiff, and Harry Pollitt and others, defendants; both in CP/IND/POLL/15/07.

64   Lady Swaythling–Lord Sempill conversation, Tel. Check Sloane 1838, 2 Sep. 1941, KV2/600; 'High Court of Justice – King's Bench Division – Duke of Hamilton's Libel Actions Settled', *Times* 19 Feb. 1942, 8.

65   *ROM*, esp. 1, 22, 11. Strachey's 'The American Question' is reprinted in Gollancz ed. 1941, 83–106.

66   SB report, 19 Jul. 1941, KV2/600.

16. Epilogue

1   IM to Stuart Montagu, 30 Nov. 1942, CP/IND/MONT/10/1, LHASC.

2   'Less Nonsense' was published in *Truth*, 31 Oct. 1942.

3   *RA*; *RS* 15; *Sta* 15, 31.

4   Pamphlets: *Sev, SLK, SLT, SLV, SLM, ZH. The Defeat of the German Armies Near Moscow* was the British version, prepared by Montagu, of *Razgrom nemetzkikh voisk pod Moskvoi*, directed by Leonid Varlamov and Ilya Kopalin. The American version, retitled *Moscow Strikes Back*, won an Academy Award.

5   Rust 1949, 98; George Bernard Shaw to IM, 28 Oct. 1942, CP/IND/ MONT/6/12, LHASC; D.N. Pritt to IM, 7 Aug. 1943, CP/IND/ MONT/6/7, LHASC.

6   File note, 19 May 1944, KV2/3221; Haggith and Newman eds, 2005, 112–3.

7   Laybourn 2006, 35; SB report, 28 Nov. 1945, KV2/600.

8   Pritt to IM, 14 Jul. 1945, CP/IND/MONT/6/7, LHASC.

9   IM to Attlee, 12 Jun. 1944; Attlee to IM, 15 Jun. 1944; IM to Attlee, 21 Jun. 1944; all in CP/IND/MONT/7/1.

10   'On the Spot', *DW* 15 Sep. 1945, 1; Walter Holmes, 'A Worker's Notebook', *DW* 16 Oct. 1945, 2; IM to William Rust, ca 7 Oct. 1945, intercepted letter, KV2/600; IM, 'The Courtroom at Nuremberg', *DW* 1 Dec. 1945, 2.

11   H.A.R. (Kim) Philby to MI5, 26 Nov. 1946, KV2/600; MI5 to Philby, 3 Dec. 1946, KV2/600; IM, 'Our Future is Bright, Says Dimitrov', DW 28 Nov. 1946.

12   IM, 'Eager Crowds Flock to Polling Booths in Rumania', *DW* 21 Nov. 1946; SB report, 21 Jan. 1947, KV2/600; file note, 4 Feb. 1947, KV2/600.

13   Dilys Powell, 'Films of the Week', *ST* 5 Dec. 1948, 2; rushes, *Visions* iv.

14   'New Films in London', *Times* 29 Nov. 1948, 7.

15   *Screen* iv, 25.

16   Deery 2002, 450; Clews 1964, 42–5.

17   SB report, 29 Aug. 1948, KV2/601; IM 1960, 17–8; Jenks 2006, 116.

18   Deery 2002, 450; Jenks 2006, 116. See also IM 1999, 219.

19   Boris Grekov, Chairman, Organisational Committee, to IM, cable, 10 Aug. 1949, KV2/601; SB report, 21 Aug. 1949, KV2/601; SB report, 9 Sep. 1949, KV2/601; Deery 2002, 451; IM 1999, 220.

20   IM 1949, 375, 377; Ivor and Hell Montagu, cable to Stalin (draft), Dec. 1949, CP/IND/MONT/12/4, LHASC.

21   'Picasso "Peace Mission"', *NYT* 21 Feb. 1950, 11; 'Partisans of Peace', *Times* 4 Mar. 1950, 6.

22   Deery 2002, esp 453; IM 1999, 221–2; '"Bogus" Peace Congress", *Times* 2 Nov. 1950, 2; '"Peace" Air-Lift Halts', *DE* 10 Nov. 1950; 'Visits to "Peace" Congress', *Times* 10 Nov. 1950, 6; 'Warsaw 'Peace' Congress', *Times* 13 Nov. 1950, 4.

23   Kitrinos 1986, 181, 189, 190; 'Prof. Joliot-Curie's Attack on U.S.', *Times* 18 Nov. 1950, 6; Committee on Un-American Activities, U.S. House of Representatives (1951), 165.

24   Rushes, *Visions* iv; Schoots 2000, 234.

25   *PP* 110; IM 1950; IM 1999, 221, 224–5.

26   Ivor Montagu election pamphlet, ca Sep. 1951, CP/IND/MONT/5/4, LHASC.

27   Milton Leitenberg, 'New Russian Evidence on the Korean War Biological Warfare Allegations: Background and Analysis', *Cold War International History Project Bulletin* 11 (1998), 185–7; 'Mr. Acheson on Reported Epidemics', *Times* 5 Mar. 1952, 3; 'Reds Ignore Denial, Ask Germ War Ban', *Miami Daily News* 15 Apr. 1952, 15; 'Primate Says Red Dean is Thorn in Flesh of Church', *Canberra*

Times 17 Jul. 1952, 1; rushes, *Visions* iv; 'Dr. Needham on Germ Warfare Charges', *Times* 16 Oct. 1952, 3; Clews 1964, 206, 219–20; PP 71. See also Tom Buchanan, 'The Courage of Galileo: Joseph Needham and the 'Germ Warfare' Allegations in the Korean War', *History* 86, Issue 284, (Oct. 2001), 503–22.

28   File note, 24 Oct. 1952, KV2/1384.

29   *PP* 25–32, 56, 67, 103; Applebaum 2004, 516.

30   'Doctors Arrested in Russia', *Times* 13 Jan. 1953, 6; 'Jews Accused of Plot to Kill Soviet Leaders', *Times* 14 Jan. 1953, 6; 'Moscow Takes Over', *Times* 14 Jan. 1953, 7.

31   'British Jews' Horror at Anti-Semitic Trends', *MG* 15 Jan. 1953, 10; 'Spur to E. European Anti-Semitism', *Times* 15 Jan. 1953, 5; IM to Editor, *Jewish Chronicle*, 26 Jan. 1953, CP/IND/MONT/3/8, LHASC.

32   Litvinoff 1969, 89; Applebaum 2004, 427; Montefiore 2004, 637; Brackman 2001, 388–9, 400.

33   Beverley Baxter, 'Troonsafstand in het rijk van de geest', *Elseviers Weekblad* 18 Apr. 1953 [translation by Bert Hogenkamp].

34   *LBS*, esp 13.

35   'Mr. Khrushchev Details Crimes of Stalin', *Times* 5 Jun. 1956, 8; '"Unmasking" of Stalin', *Times* 5 Jun. 1956, 10; 'Indictment of Stalin', *Times* 11 Jun. 1956, 8; www.theguardian.com/theguardian/2007/apr/26/greatspeeches1 (accessed 28 Aug. 2017).

36   Pelling 1975, 173–5; Donald Sassoon, 'Eric Hobsbawm, 1917–2012', *New Left Review* 77 (Sep.–Oct.° 2012), 36; Chimen Abransky et al. to Editor, *NSN* 1 Dec. 1956, 701.

37   IM 1956, 551, 557–9.

38   Pelling 1975, 175–81; IM to 'Johnny' [Gollan], 16 Dec. 1957, CP/IND/MONT/4/5, LHASC; IM to Comrade Orna, 30 Apr. 1958, CP/IND/MONT/4/5, LHASC.

39   'Russell Scores Reds', *NYT* 10 Jul. 1958, 12, cited in John Ballantyne, 'Australia's Dr Jim Cairns and the Soviet KGB', *National Observer* 64 (Autumn 2005), n6; 'Peace Prize Award to Mr. Khrushchev', *Times* 1 May 1959, 12; 'Lenin Peace Prize to Khrushchev', *Age* (Melbourne) 2 May 1959, 1; Griffin 2014, 92–4; https://en.wikipedia.org/wiki/Lenin_Peace_Prize (accessed 28 Aug. 2017).

40   Riordan 2009, 55; Griffin 2014, 85, 102–3, 117–25.

41   'Protest by Moscow Peace Delegation', *Times* 10 Jul. 1962, 9; 'Anti-Nuclear Demonstrators Threatened', *Times* 13 Jul. 1962, 12; 'March Row', *DE* 13 Jul. 1962; 'Banners Seized in Red Square Protest', *Times* 14 Jul. 1962, 8; 'Moscow Anti-Bomb Congress Ends', *Times* 16 Jul. 1962, 8.

42   IM 1963, esp 498, 499, 503.

43   *FW* 290; Peter Harcourt, review of *Film World*, *SS* 34:2 (Spring 1965), 100–1.

44   *GNN*, esp 119; Panther ad, *Times* 13 Jul. 1967, 7; 'Dismal Minority', *Economist* 18 Nov. 1967, 751; Antony Terry, 'A Secret Nightmare', *ST* 16 Jul. 1967, 43.

45   *WEH*; *YS*; Dilys Powell, 'League of Vandals', *ST* 16 Feb. 1969, 54; E.S. Turner, 'Rallying the Bedmakers', *Lis* 27 Aug. 1970, 282.

46   Andow et al. ed. 1983, 175; IM 1972, 8.

47   IM 1974, esp 374; Solzhenitsyn 1974.

48 CP/IND/MONT/1/3, LHASC; IM 1974, 375–6; 'Montagu', typescript, ca 1979, CP/IND/MONT/1/1, LHASC.

49 IM, 'Return to Spain', unidentified clipping, CP/IND/MONT/9/8, LHASC; www.jewishsports.net/BioPages/Tables/LastNameSearch.htm (accessed 19 Apr. 2016); probate, 12 Apr. 1985, CGPLA Eng & Wales. See also Ossia Trilling, 'Leisure: George Orwell Slept Here', *FT* 9 Apr. 1983, 9.

50 Jay Iliff, 'Revealed: The Greatest Secret of the Cold War', *DE* 22 Apr. 1999, 33.

51 *Visions* iv rushes.

52 Manley 2008, 1.

53 Mannheim 1936, 10, 155; Koestler 1965, 75.

54 Mannheim 1952, 301n.

55 David-Fox 2012, 244.

56 Mannheim 1936, 37–8.

57 Koestler 1965, 80.

58 Louis Fischer, in Crossman ed. 1965, 183; Koestler 2005, 189; *YS* 190.

59 Shils 1972, 29.

60 Koestler 1965, 119.

61 Hollander 1981, 8, 167; Mannheim 1936, 40; Shils 1972, 19–20.

62 IM, 'Prophecies', unidentified journal, 176, CP/IND/MONT/12/10, LHASC.

63 Shils 1972, 30, 42; Johnson 1990, 269.

64 Charles Sumner, 'Ivor Montagu – The Hireling', *Information Bulletin of the British Committee for the Defence of Leon Trotsky* No. 1 (May 1937), 3, CP/IND/MONT/4/10, LHASC.

65 Jenks 2006, 55, 115.

INDEX